Citizenship in Diverse Societies

Citizenship in Diverse Societies

Edited by

WILL KYMLICKA

and

WAYNE NORMAN

OXFORD
UNIVERSITY PRESS

OXFORD
UNIVERSITY PRESS

Great Clarendon Street, Oxford OX2 6DP
Oxford University Press is a department of the University of Oxford.
It furthers the University's objective of excellence in research, scholarship,
and education by publishing worldwide in

Oxford New York

Athens Auckland Bangkok Bogotá Buenos Aires Calcutta
Cape Town Chennai Dar es Salaam Delhi Florence Hong Kong Istanbul
Karachi Kuala Lumpur Madrid Melbourne Mexico City Mumbai
Nairobi Paris São Paulo Singapore Taipei Tokyo Toronto Warsaw
and associated companies in Berlin Ibadan

Oxford is a registered trade mark of Oxford University Press
in the UK and in certain other countries

Published in the United States
by Oxford University Press Inc., New York

British Library Cataloguing in Publication Data

Data available

Library of Congress Cataloging-in-Publication Data

Citizenship in diverse societies / edited by Will Kymlicka and Wayne Norman.
Includes bibliographical references and index.
1. Minorities—Civil rights. 2. Ethnic groups—Civil rights. 3. Representative
government and representation. 4. Citizenship. 5. Multiculturalism. I. Kymlicka, Will.
II. Norman, Wayne, Dr.
JF1061 .C57 2000 305.8—dc21 99–049336

ISBN 0–19–829644–4
ISBN 0–19–829770–X (pbk.)

10 9 8 7 6 5 4 3 2 1

Typeset by BookMan Services
Printed in Great Britain
on acid-free paper by
Biddles Ltd
Guildford and King's Lynn

To
Sue and Chantale

Acknowledgements

This volume grew out of a multidisciplinary research network on democracy and ethnic diversity that was generously funded by the Social Sciences and Humanities Research Council of Canada. Our colleagues in this network included Janet Hiebert, Robert Howse, Diane Lamoureux, Dominique Leydet, Joseph Carens, Lesley Jacobs, Lukas Sosöe, Daniel Weinstock, and Denise Réaume. We would like to thank them for their advice and assistance in planning for this volume and the conference that provided a dry run for many of its chapters. The conference itself succeeded not only on the strength of the papers and the discussions, but also because of the generosity of the University of Toronto Law School, and the tireless efforts of Diana Reynolds, Susan Donaldson, Michael Kocsis, Lise Charlebois, and Neus Torbisco.

From the beginning we conceived of this project not as a collection of essays, but as a book being collectively written by a diverse group of scholars. To the extent that we have realized this goal, we are indebted first and foremost to our co-authors who were all willing to make substantial revisions to their texts in response to our own comments, as well as those of conference commentators, and anonymous readers from Oxford University Press. We must also thank Dominic Byatt and Amanda Watkins of the Press for their enthusiastic support throughout; and Bryn Williams-Jones for harmonizing the citation styles of authors from six countries and seven academic disciplines while cheerfully and efficiently compiling the bibliography.

Finally we must express our sadness over the sudden and untimely death of one of our authors, Graham Smith, in April 1999, as the manuscript was being prepared for copy-editing. Graham was only forty-six, and with his death we have lost one of the foremost scholars of citizenship and diversity in the post-soviet world.

WK
WJN

Queen's University, Kingston, Canada
University of British Columbia, Vancouver, Canada
August 1999

Contents

IV: GENDER AND ETHNIC DIVERSITY

V: LANGUAGE RIGHTS

VI: THE RIGHTS OF INDIGENOUS PEOPLES

VII: FEDERALISM AND NATIONALISM

List of Contributors

WILL KYMLICKA is Professor of Philosophy at Queen's University, Kingston, Ontario, Canada.

WAYNE NORMAN holds the Chair in Business Ethics in the Centre for Applied Ethics at the University of British Columbia, Vancouver, Canada.

EAMONN CALLAN is Professor of Education at Stanford University. When he wrote this chapter he was Professor of Education at the University of Alberta.

JEFF SPINNER-HALEV is Schlesinger Associate Professor of Social Justice at the University of Nebraska, Lincoln, Nebraska.

JANE MANSBRIDGE is a Professor of Public Policy at the Kennedy School of Government at Harvard University.

MELISSA S. WILLIAMS is Associate Professor of Political Science at the University of Toronto, Toronto, Canada.

JEREMY WALDRON is the Maurice and Hilda Friedman Professor of Law, and Director of the Center for Law and Philosophy, at Columbia University, New York.

DR. TARIQ MODOOD is Professor of Sociology, Politics and Public Policy, and Director of the Centre for the Study of Ethnicity and Citizenship, at the University of Bristol, Bristol, UK.

AYELET SHACHAR is Assistant Professor of Law at the University of Toronto. When she wrote this chapter she was a postdoctoral fellow at Yale University.

SAWITRI SAHARSO teaches on gender and ethnicity at the Faculty of Social and Cultural Sciences, Free University of Amsterdam.

DENISE RÉAUME is Professor of Law at the University of Toronto.

PIERRE COULOMBE was Assistant Professor of Political Science at the University of Ottawa when he wrote this chapter.

JACOB T. LEVY is Assistant Professor of Political Science at the University of Chicago.

JOHN BORROWS is Associate Professor of Law at the University of Toronto. When he wrote the present chapter he was Director of First Nations Legal Studies at the University of British Columbia.

GRAHAM SMITH was Director of Post-Soviet States Research Programme, Fellow of Sidney Sussex College, and Lecturer in the Department of Geography, University of Cambridge.

RAINER BAUBÖCK is a Research Fellow in the Politics Department at the Institute for Advanced Studies in Vienna, and Research Associate at the European Centre for Social Welfare Policy and Research.

1

Citizenship in Culturally Diverse Societies: Issues, Contexts, Concepts

WILL KYMLICKA AND WAYNE NORMAN

> There is no more dynamic social figure in modern history than The Citizen
>
> > (Ralf Dahrendorf, *Citizenship and Beyond*)
>
> 'Citizen' and 'Citizenship' are powerful words. They speak of respect, of rights, of dignity . . . We find no pejorative uses. It is a weighty, monumental, humanist word.
>
> > (Nancy Fraser and Linda Gordon, 'Civil Citizenship against Social Citizenship?', in Bart Van Steenburgen (ed.), *The Condition of Citizenship*)

The last ten years have witnessed a remarkable upsurge of interest in two topics amongst political philosophers: the rights and status of ethnocultural minorities in multi-ethnic societies (the 'minority rights–multiculturalism' debate), and the virtues, practices, and responsibilities of democratic citizenship (the 'citizenship–civic virtue' debate). To a surprising extent, these two debates have developed independently of one another, with only a few isolated discussions of their interconnection. The aim of this volume is to connect these two topics in a more systematic way. We want to explore how emerging theories of minority rights and multiculturalism affect the virtues and practices of democratic citizenship, and to see how emerging theories of citizenship and civic virtue affect the rights and status of ethnocultural minorities.

There are potential tensions between these two concerns. In fact, defenders of minority rights have often been suspicious of appeals to some ideal of 'good citizenship', which they see as reflecting a demand that minorities should quietly learn to play by the majority's rules. (See e.g. Samson 1999.) Conversely, those who wish to promote a more robust conception of civic virtue and democratic citizenship have often been suspicious of appeals to minority rights, which they see as reflecting the sort of politics of narrow self-interest that they seek to overcome. (See e.g. Ward 1991.)

Despite these long-standing mutual suspicions, it is increasingly recognized that any plausible or attractive political theory must attend to both the claims of ethnocultural minorities and the promotion of responsible democratic citizenship. In this Introduction we will explore how these two debates have developed, why they have gradually come into closer contact, and what some of the potential tensions are between them. We hope this will help situate the more specific analyses of citizenship and diversity in the following chapters.

1. The New Debate on Minority Rights

Let us start with the new debate amongst political philosophers concerning the rights of ethnocultural groups within Western democracies. We use the term 'the rights of ethnocultural minorities' (or, for brevity's sake, 'minority rights') in a loose way, to refer to a wide range of public policies, legal rights, and constitutional provisions sought by ethnic groups for the accommodation of their cultural differences. Groups claiming minority rights include immigrant groups, indigenous peoples, national minorities, racial groups, and ethnoreligious sects; and their claims range from multicultural policies to language rights to respecting treaties with indigenous peoples. Other theorists use different terms to describe these sorts of claims—e.g. 'multiculturalism', 'group rights', or 'differentiated citizenship'. Each term has its drawbacks, but for the purposes of this Introduction we will use 'minority rights' as the umbrella term.

'Minority rights' is a heterogeneous category, and we will explore some of the different types of minority rights in Section 6. Nevertheless, all minority rights we discuss here share two important features: (a) they go beyond the familiar set of common civil and political rights of individual citizenship which are protected in all liberal democracies; and (b) they are adopted with the intention of recognizing and accommodating the distinctive identities and needs of ethnocultural groups.

In recent years political philosophers have shown a great deal of interested in the normative issues raised by such minority rights. What are the moral arguments for or against such rights? In particular, how do minority rights relate to the underlying principles of liberal democracy, such as individual freedom, social equality, and democracy? Are they consistent with these principles? Do they promote these values? Or do they conflict with them?

The philosophical debate on these questions has evolved dramatically over the past two decades. In the mid-1980s there were very few political philosophers or political theorists working in the area.[1] Indeed, for most of this cestury issues of ethnicity have been seen as marginal by political philosophers. (Much the same can be said about many other academic disciplines, from sociology to geography and history.) Today, however, after decades of relative

---

[1] The most important of these was Vernon Van Dyke, who published a handful of essays on this topic in the 1970s and early 1980s (e.g. Van Dyke 1977, 1982, 1985). There were also a few legal theorists who discussed the role of minority rights in international law, and their connection to human rights principles of non-discrimination.

neglect, the question of minority rights has moved to the forefront of political theory. There are a number of reasons for this. Most obviously, the collapse of communism in 1989 sent waves of ethnic nationalism ripping through Eastern Europe, with dramatic consequences for the process of democratization. Optimistic assumptions that liberal democracy would emerge smoothly from the ashes of communism were challenged by issues of ethnicity and nationalism. But there were many factors within long-established Western democracies that also pointed to the salience of ethnicity: the nativist backlash against immigrants and refugees in many Western countries (especially France, Britain, Germany, and the United States); the resurgence and political mobilization of indigenous peoples, resulting in the draft Declaration of the Rights of Indigenous Peoples at the United Nations; and the ongoing, even growing, threat of secession within some of the most flourishing Western democracies, from Quebec to Scotland, Flanders, and Catalonia.

All of these factors, which came to a head at the beginning of the 1990s, made it clear that Western liberal democracies had not in fact met or overcome the challenges posed by ethnocultural diversity. It is not surprising, therefore, that political theorists have increasingly turned their attention to this issue. For example, in the last few years we have seen the first philosophical books in English on the normative issues involved in secession, nationalism, immigration, multiculturalism, and indigenous rights.[2]

But not only has this debate attracted more attention and participation; its very terms have also changed dramatically. The first wave of writings on minority rights was primarily focused on assessing the *justice* of claims by ethnic groups for the accommodation of their cultural differences. This reflected the fact that opposition to such claims has traditionally been stated in the language of justice. Critics of minority rights had long argued that justice required state institutions to be 'colour-blind'. To ascribe rights or benefits on the basis of membership in ascriptive groups was seen as morally arbitrary and inherently discriminatory, necessarily creating first- and second-class citizens.

The first task confronting any defender of minority rights, therefore, was to try to overcome this presumption, and to show that deviations from 'difference-blind' rules that are adopted in order to accommodate ethnocultural differences are not inherently unjust. Several authors took up this task, attempting to defend the justice of certain kinds of multicultural

---

[2] Baubock (1994a); Buchanan (1991); Kymlicka (1995a); Miller (1995); Spinner (1994); Tamir (1993); Taylor (1992); Tully (1995); Young (1990); Phillips (1995); Canovan (1996); Gilbert (1998). With the exception of Plamenatz (1960), we are not aware of any full-length books written by philosophers in English on any of these topics predating 1990. For collections of recent philosophical articles on these issues, see Kymlicka (1995b); J. Baker (1994); Shapiro and Kymlicka (1997); Beiner (1999); Couture *et al.* (1998); Lehning (1998); Moore (1998); McKim and McMahan (1997).

accommodations or group-specific rights.[3] These authors used a variety of arguments to make their case, most of which can be seen as resting on a common strategy. They all claim that while difference-blind institutions purport to be neutral amongst different ethnocultural groups, they are in fact implicitly tilted towards the needs, interests, and identities of the majority group; and this creates a range of burdens, barriers, stigmatizations, and exclusions for members of minority groups. The adoption of certain minority rights, it is argued, helps to remedy the disadvantages that minorities suffer within difference-blind institutions, and in doing so promotes fairness. Minority rights do not constitute unfair privileges or invidious forms of discrimination, but rather compensate for unfair disadvantages, and so are consistent with, and may indeed be required by, justice.

In our view, this first stage in the debate is coming to a close, with the defenders of minority rights having effectively made their case. We do not mean, of course, that ethnic groups have always been successful in getting their claims accepted and implemented, although there is a clear trend throughout the Western democracies towards greater recognition of minority rights. Rather, we are claiming that defenders of minority rights have successfully redefined the terms of public debate in two profound ways: (*a*) few thoughtful people continue to think that justice can simply be *defined* in terms of difference-blind rules or institutions. Instead, it is now widely recognized that difference-blind rules and institutions can cause disadvantages for particular groups. Whether justice requires common rules for all, or differential rules for diverse groups, is something to be assessed case-by-case in particular contexts, not assumed in advance; (*b*) as a result, the burden of proof has shifted. The burden of proof no longer falls solely on defenders of multiculturalism to show that their proposed reforms would not create injustices; it is now shared with defenders of difference-blind institutions, who must try to show that the status quo does not create injustices for minority groups and their members.

The first wave of minority rights theorists have, in other words, unsettled the complacency with which liberals used to dismiss claims for minority rights, and have successfully levelled the playing field when debating the merits of the claims by particular ethnic groups. It is an interesting question why minority rights theorists have been so successful in changing the public debate so quickly.[4] In part, this success is built on a growing acknowledgement of the many ways that mainstream institutions implicitly favour the majority—e.g. by using the majority's language, calendar, and symbols. Moreover, it is difficult to see how all of these biases could be overcome. The

---

[3] See Young (1990); Minow (1990); Parekh (1990); Phillips (1992); Taylor (1992); Spinner (1994); Tully (1995).

[4] For some speculation on this question, see Kymlicka (1998*b*).

idea that public institutions could genuinely be neutral amongst languages or religious calendars seems increasingly implausible.

But there is also a growing awareness of the importance of certain interests that had typically been ignored by liberal theories of justice; e.g. interests in recognition, identity, language, and cultural membership. If these interests are ignored or trivialized by the state, then people will feel harmed—and indeed will be harmed—even if their civil, political, and welfare rights are respected. If state institutions fail to recognize and respect people's culture and identity, the result can be serious damage to people's self-respect and sense of agency.[5]

So the original justice-based grounds for blanket opposition to minority rights have faded. This has not meant that philosophical and political opposition to minority rights has disappeared, or even significantly diminished. But it now takes a new form. Or rather it takes two forms: the first questions the justice of specific minority rights claims in particular contexts, focusing on the way particular policies may entail an unjust distribution of the benefits and burdens associated with identity and culture; the second shifts the focus away from justice towards issues of *citizenship*, focusing not on the justice or injustice of particular policies, but rather on the way that the general trend towards minority rights threatens to erode the sorts of civic virtues and citizenship practices that sustain a healthy democracy.

2. The New Debate over Citizenship

It is at this point that the debate over minority rights merges with the debate over the virtues and practices of democratic citizenship—a debate that has been developing independently over the last decade. Indeed, there has been an explosion of interest in the concept of citizenship amongst political theorists. In 1978 it could be confidently stated that 'the concept of citizenship has gone out of fashion among political thinkers' (Van Gunsteren 1978: 9). By 1990 Derek Heater claimed that citizenship had become the 'buzzword' amongst thinkers on all points of the political spectrum (Heater 1990: 293).

There are a number of reasons for this growing interest in citizenship throughout the 1990s. One reason is related to the rise of minority rights. Debates over multiculturalism have often been fractious, and have put a considerable strain on the norms of civility and good citizenship. Some people fear that the tyranny of 'political correctness' and 'culture wars' has made it difficult for people to participate as citizens; others fear the inevitable backlash that has accompanied the increased presence or visibility of

---

[5] Taylor (1992); Margalit and Raz (1990); Tamir (1993).

minority groups. But there are several other recent political events and trends throughout the world that point to the importance of citizenship practices. These include increased voter apathy and long-term welfare dependency in the United States, the erosion of the welfare state, and the failure of environmental policies that rely on voluntary citizen co-operation.

These events made it clear that the health and stability of a modern democracy depends, not only on the justice of its institutions, but also on the qualities and attitudes of its citizens: e.g. their sense of identity, and how they view potentially competing forms of national, regional, ethnic, or religious identities; their ability to tolerate and work together with others who are different from themselves; their desire to participate in the political process in order to promote the public good and hold political authorities accountable; their willingness to show self-restraint and exercise personal responsibility in their economic demands, and in personal choices that affect their health and the environment; and their sense of justice and commitment to a fair distribution of resources. Without citizens who possess these qualities, 'the ability of liberal societies to function successfully progressively diminishes' (Galston 1991: 220).[6]

It is not surprising, therefore, that there should be increasing calls for 'a theory of citizenship'. Political theorists in the 1970s and 1980s focused primarily on what Rawls called the 'basic structure' of society: constitutional rights, political decision-making procedures, social institutions.[7] Today, however, it is widely accepted that political theorists must also pay attention to the qualities and dispositions of the citizens who operate within these institutions and procedures. Hence political theorists in the 1990s focused on the identity and conduct of individual citizens, including their responsibilities, loyalties, and roles.

The need for such a theory of citizenship received dramatic support from Robert Putnam's influential study of the performance of regional governments in Italy (Putnam 1993). He showed that these regional governments, set up in the post-war period, performed very differently, despite having more or less identical institutions. And it appears that the best explanation for the variation in performance was not differences in the income or education of the citizens, but rather differences in their civic virtue, what Putnam calls their 'social capital'—their ability to trust, their willingness to participate, their sense of justice.

---

6 This may account for the recent interest in citizenship promotion amongst governments (e.g. Britain's Commission on Citizenship, *Encouraging Citizenship*, 1990; Senate of Australia, *Active Citizenship Revisited*, 1991; Senate of Canada, *Canadian Citizenship: Sharing the Responsibility*, 1993). For a more detailed discussion of this renewed focus on citizenship within contemporary political philosophy, see Kymlicka and Norman (1994).

7 Rawls says that the 'basic structure' of society is the primary subject of a theory of justice (Rawls 1971: 7–11).

While Putnam's particular study has been disputed,[8] the general point that the virtues and identities of citizens are important and independent factors in democratic governance is now widely accepted. And this has led to a veritable flood of writings on issues of civic virtues and practices, civic identities, and citizenship education.[9]

The first task for theorists of citizenship was to specify more concretely the sorts of civic virtues required for a flourishing democracy. According to William Galston's prominent account, responsible citizenship requires four types of civic virtues: (i) *general* virtues: courage; law-abidingness; loyalty; (ii) *social* virtues: independence; open-mindedness; (iii) *economic* virtues: work ethic; capacity to delay self-gratification; adaptability to economic and technological change; and (iv) *political* virtues: capacity to discern and respect the rights of others; willingness to demand only what can be paid for; ability to evaluate the performance of those in office; willingness to engage in public discourse (Galston 1991: 221–4).

Other authors offer a slightly different list, but Galston's account captures a core set of concerns in the citizenship literature. Indeed, it is difficult to imagine anyone really disagreeing with the desirability of these sorts of qualities. The hard questions arise when we ask what exactly governments can or should do to promote these virtues. How should governments ensure that citizens are active rather than passive; critical rather than deferential or apathetic in the face of injustice; responsible rather than greedy or short-sighted; tolerant rather than prejudiced or xenophobic? How should governments ensure that citizens feel a sense of membership in and belonging to their political community, rather than alienation and disaffection? How should governments ensure that citizens identify and feel solidarity with co-citizens, rather than indifference or hatred towards others?

This is where the real disputes arise. Perhaps just for that reason, many writers on citizenship have avoided taking a clear stand on the public policy implications of their theories. They focus more on describing desirable qualities of citizens, and less on what policies should be adopted to encourage or compel citizens to adopt these desirable virtues and practices. As a result, a cynic might argue that many works on citizenship reduce to a platitude: namely, society would be better if the people in it were nicer and more thoughtful.[10]

Fortunately, this timidity is slowly disappearing, and we are now seeing more discussions of the policy implications of theories of citizenship. And

---

[8] For a review, see Sabetti (1996).

[9] For the pre-1994 literature, see the bibliography in Kymlicka and Norman (1994) and the collected essays in Beiner (1995). For more recent writings, see Janoski (1998); Dagger (1997); Callan (1997); Van Gunsteren (1998a); Shafir (1998); Hutchings and Dannreuther (1998); Lister (1998).

[10] This was our own uncharitable conclusion in Kymlicka and Norman (1994: 369).

some important differences have emerged in how political theorists would approach citizenship promotion. In particular, political theorists disagree about the role of ethnic and religious groups in promoting citizenship. Some theorists say that the best 'schools of citizenship' are the voluntary associations and organizations of civil society, including ethnic and religious groups, and that the best thing the state can do is simply to let these organizations alone (see e.g. Glendon 1995; Walzer 1995). Others argue that the sort of socialization provided by ethnic and religious groups can inhibit, as well as promote, responsible citizenship, and that mandatory citizenship education in the schools is needed to supplement and correct the lessons learned in civil society (see e.g. Callan 1997; Arneson and Shapiro 1996). Some go even further and argue that the state must actively intervene in certain ethnic and religious groups, to prevent them from passing on illiberal or undemocratic attitudes and practices (see e.g. Okin 1997). As the essays in this volume show, these differing accounts of how best to promote democratic citizenship have profound repercussions for minority rights.

This disagreement about how best to promote responsible citizenship reflects another emerging trend in the literature—namely, the need to adapt theories of citizenship to the realities of modern pluralistic societies. Much of Galston's list recalls discussions of civic virtue in the city-states of ancient Greece or Renaissance Italy. And indeed several authors explicitly describe themselves as trying to recover and retrieve the classical republican tradition of political thought, drawing on thinkers such as Aristotle, Rousseau, and Machiavelli (Oldfield 1990; Skinner 1992; Pocock 1992). But it is increasingly recognized that the sorts of civic virtues required for a large pluralistic modern society, and the appropriate means to promote them, may differ from those required for a small, homogeneous city-state. The goals of citizenship, and the means of promoting it, must take into account the levels and forms of ethnic and religious pluralism.

This idea helps explain the growing attention paid to one particular virtue on Galston's list: the need to engage in public discourse. The decisions of government in a democracy should be made publicly, through free and open discussion. This is as necessary now as it was in the democracies of the ancient world. But in a modern pluralistic society the virtue of public discourse is not just the willingness to participate in politics, or to make one's views known. It also

includes the willingness to listen seriously to a range of views which, given the diversity of liberal societies, will include ideas the listener is bound to find strange and even obnoxious. The virtue of political discourse also includes the willingness to set forth one's own views intelligibly and candidly as the basis for a politics of persuasion rather than manipulation or coercion. (Galston 1991: 227)

Stephen Macedo (1990) calls this the virtue of 'public reasonableness'.

Liberal citizens must give *reasons* for their political demands, not just state preferences or make threats. Moreover, these reasons must be *public* reasons; for example, reasons capable of persuading people of different ethnic or religious groups. In ancient Greece or in seventeenth-century New England towns it might have been enough to invoke tradition or Scripture. But in a modern pluralistic society liberal citizens must justify their political demands in terms that fellow citizens can understand and accept as consistent with their status as free and equal citizens. This requires a conscientious effort to distinguish those beliefs that are matters of private faith from those that are capable of public defence, and to see how issues look from the point of view of those with differing religious commitments and cultural backgrounds.

This particular conception of public reasonableness—one that seeks to separate public reasons, on the one hand, from religious beliefs and cultural traditions, on the other—is distinctly modern. Its prominence in the recent literature on citizenship is partly related to the recognition that modern societies are ethnically and religiously diverse. But it also reflects another important shift in contemporary democratic theory: the shift from 'vote-centric' to 'talk-centric' democratic theory.[11] Vote-centric theories see democracy as an area in which fixed, pre-existing preferences and interests compete through fair decision procedures or aggregation mechanisms (such as majority vote). But it is now widely recognized that such a conception cannot fulfil norms of democratic legitimacy, since the outcomes can only represent winners and not a common will; and ethnocultural or other marginalized minorities may be permanently excluded from real power within the system.

To overcome the shortcomings of the vote-centric approach, democratic theorists increasingly focus on the processes of deliberation and opinion formation that precede voting. Theorists have shifted their focus from what goes on in the voting booth to what goes in the public deliberations of civil society. If minorities are to have any real influence in a majoritarian system, it will be through participating in the formation of public opinion, rather than through winning a majority vote. As Simone Chambers puts it, 'voice rather than votes is the vehicle of empowerment' (Chambers 1998: 17). As a result, a wide range of theorists—political liberals, civic republicans, deliberative democrats—have identified public reasonableness as one of the key issues for citizenship in modern societies.

But here again, in diverse societies voice will be effective only if there is a conception of public reasonableness that does not simply reflect the majority's cultural traditions, language, and religion, but is, rather, accessible to and inclusive of the various ethnic and religious groups within society. In this way, amongst others, the new concern with citizenship virtues and practices,

---

[11] For more details, see Ch. 4 by Mansbridge and Ch. 5 by Williams.

despite its classical heritage, springs from distinctly modern realities and problems.

3. The Need for an Integrated Theory of Diverse Citizenship

So far, we have sketched the development of two debates. In one debate it is increasingly accepted that minority rights claims cannot be dismissed as inherently unjust, and instead are sometimes consistent with, if not required by, principles of justice. In the other debate most theorists now accept that the functioning of society depends not only on the justice of its institutions or constitution, but also on the virtues, identities, and practices of its citizens, including their ability to co-operate, deliberate, and feel solidarity with those who belong to different ethnic and religious groups.

The obvious question then becomes: how are these two issues related? In particular, how do minority rights affect the virtues and practices of democratic citizenship? As we noted earlier, it is often supposed that minority rights will have a negative impact on citizenship practices, or will inhibit the state's ability to promote citizenship effectively. Many critics worry that minority rights involve the 'politicization of ethnicity', and that any measures that heighten the salience of ethnicity in public life are divisive (see e.g. Glazer 1983: 227). Over time they create a spiral of competition, mistrust, and antagonism between ethnic groups. Policies that increase the salience of ethnic identities are said to act 'like a corrosive on metal, eating away at the ties of connectedness that bind us together as a nation' (Ward 1991: 598). On this view, liberal democracies must prevent ethnic identities from becoming politicized by rejecting any minority rights or multiculturalism policies that involve the explicit public recognition of ethnic groups.

The strong version of this critique treats minority rights as the first step on the road to Yugoslavia-style civil war. A more moderate (and more plausible) version states that while minority rights may not lead to civil war, they will erode the ability of citizens to fulfil their responsibilities as democratic citizens—e.g. by weakening citizens' ability to communicate, trust, and feel solidarity across group differences. And so even if a particular minority rights policy is not itself unjust, examined in isolation, the trend towards the increased salience of ethnicity will erode the norms and practices of responsible citizenship, and so reduce the overall functioning of the state.

How valid is this fear? To what extent does it justify denying or limiting what would otherwise be legitimate claims to minority rights? Until recently, many defenders of minority rights have simply dismissed this worry, and expressed scepticism about appeals to citizenship. This is understandable since in many multi-ethnic and multinational states the rhetoric of citizenship has been used historically as a way of advancing the interests of the dominant national group. The discourse of citizenship has rarely provided a neutral framework for resolving disputes between the majority and minority groups; more often it has served as a cover by which the majority nation extends its language, institutions, mobility rights, and political power at the expense of the minority, all in the name of turning supposedly 'disloyal' or 'troublesome' minorities into 'good citizens'.

Several of the essays in this volume provide evidence of this historical (mis)use of citizenship talk to justify the assimilation or oppression of minorities. It is not surprising that many minority groups are sceptical when members of a majority oppose minority rights on the grounds that they erode our sense of 'citizenship'. Yet we believe that concerns about the impact of minority rights on citizenship cannot be ignored. There are legitimate interests that are tied up with the promotion of a sense of common citizenship in multi-ethnic countries. Multi-ethnic countries are as much in need of the virtues, practices, and institutions of democratic citizenship as mono-ethnic countries. If anything, multi-ethnic countries are *more* in need of such things as public reasonableness, mutual respect, critical attitudes towards government, tolerance, willingness to participate in politics, forums for shared political deliberation, and solidarity.

And there are legitimate concerns that some minority groups, perhaps in response to the rigid conception of citizenship advanced by the majority, have appealed to notions of identity and difference that leave little room for the promotion or nurturing of these aspects of democratic citizenship and social unity. Some groups may indeed seek to reject their citizenship in the larger society altogether, through secession. But even groups that accept that their members are citizens of a larger state sometimes retreat to a notion of citizenship that is little more than passive obedience to the law, and reluctant acceptance of the status quo.[12] And there is a fear that various forms of minority rights could encourage and entrench these passive, inward-looking, and resentful forms of group identity that inhibit wider political co-operation, dialogue, and solidarity.

These sorts of concerns are legitimate, and deserve serious consideration. However, we believe that this worry cannot be evaluated in the abstract, or through armchair speculation, as if it were a purely conceptual issue. Rather, we need to evaluate these potential conflicts between citizenship and diversity through careful examination of specific contexts and case-studies, and in light of a deeper understanding of the various patterns of ethnic relations.

[12] Defenders of the Amish and other isolationist religious groups often say that they are good citizens because they are law-abiding, even though they show no interest in the affairs of the larger society, and take no interest in their status as citizens. For a critique of this view that passive obedience to the law is a sufficient conception of democratic citizenship, see Arneson and Shapiro (1996); Spinner (1994).

4. Diverse Citizenship in the Wider Context of Ethnic-Conflict Management

One natural place to look for answers to our questions about citizenship in diverse societies is in the ethnic-conflict literature. Although the potential tensions between minority rights and citizenship have not yet attracted adequate attention from political philosophers, this problem has been the focus of a very active debate among social scientists engaged in ethnic-conflict studies.[13] These studies have been largely historical and descriptive in nature: looking at actual ways governments—both democratic and non-democratic —have tried to 'manage' ethnic conflicts, and attempting to give explanations for successes and failures. It may, therefore, be instructive to begin with a survey of the broad range of policy options open to states with inter-ethnic tensions, as viewed through the lens of ethnic-conflict theory. The following is adapted from John McGarry and Brendan O'Leary's 'taxonomy of the macro-political forms of ethnic conflict regulation' (McGarry and O'Leary 1993: 4–38):

1. *Methods for eliminating differences*
   (*a*) genocide
   (*b*) forced mass-population transfers
   (*c*) partition and/or secession
   (*d*) assimilation.
2. *Methods for managing differences*
   (*a*) hegemonic control
   (*b*) territorial autonomy (cantonization and/or federalization)
   (*c*) non-territorial autonomy (consociationalism or power-sharing)
   (*d*) multicultural integration.[14] (McGarry and O'Leary 1993: 4)

This typology provides a healthy reminder that there are many 'methods' of ethnic-conflict resolution, widely used around the world, that fall outside the bounds of contemporary theorizing about minority rights and democratic citizenship. It goes without saying, for example, that the first two methods for eliminating differences—genocide and forced mass-population transfers (or

---

[13] See Horowitz (1985) for the *locus classicus* of these debates, as well as the journal *Ethnic and Racial Studies*, which was launched in 1978.

[14] For our own purposes of showing what we take to be a full range of policy options, we have modified McGarry and O'Leary's scheme by removing the word 'integration' from their category 1(*d*), and using it to form an additional category, 2(*d*). In effect, they would call many of the policies we include within this final category 'micropolitical forms of ethnic conflict regulation' (1993: 38 n. 2). We have also omitted one of their 'methods for managing differences', namely, 'arbitration (third-party intervention)', in part because this looks more like a process for arriving at one or more of the other sorts of concrete methods.

'ethnic cleansing')—are without defenders amongst contemporary Western political theorists. (It is worth recalling, however, that Western democracies have in the past used forced population transfers: for example, in dealing with indigenous peoples, in order to gain access to their lands and resources; and in brokered solutions following wars in the Balkans, Central Europe, the Indian subcontinent, and elsewhere.)

The first system for managing (as opposed to *eliminating*) differences, namely, hegemonic control, also has few defenders. With hegemonic control the ruling class does not attempt to eliminate or merge the identities of minority groups, but is merely content to make any 'overtly violent ethnic contest for state power either "unthinkable" or "unworkable" on the part of the subordinated communities' (McGarry and O'Leary 1993: 23). Hegemonic control is possible even in formal conditions of democracy and equal citizenship. Citing the case of Northern Ireland, McGarry and O'Leary note that 'where there are two or more deeply established ethnic communities, and where the members of these communities do not agree on the basic institutions and policies the regime should pursue, or where the relevant ethnic communities are not internally fragmented on key policy preferences in ways which cross-cut each other, then "majority rule" can become an instrument of hegemonic control' (McGarry and O'Leary 1993: 25). Indeed, many ethnic-conflict theorists consider this to be the most commonly used method for achieving stability in multi-ethnic societies, democratic and non-democratic (Lustick 1979; McGarry and O'Leary 1993: 23).

These methods of regulating ethnic conflict fall outside the bounds of political theorizing, not, alas, because they are uncommon or unfeasible, but because amongst Western political theorists no one disputes that these are unjust and illegitimate.

The legitimacy of the remaining forms of ethnic-conflict regulation is, however, a matter of considerable debate. For example, the third option for eliminating differences, secession, has been the subject of growing debate in recent years, and has been vigorously defended by several theorists with impeccable liberal credentials.[15] However, even defenders of a right to secession rarely claim that it will eliminate ethnic conflict. It is generally recognized that secession merely relocates issues of ethnic conflict and minority rights to the successor states, often with brutal consequences (see Horowitz 1997; Norman 1998). With some 5,000 to 8,000 ethnocultural groups in the world, and only around 200 states, simple arithmetic dictates that most states (at the moment over 90 per cent) are inevitably going to be shared by more than one ethnic group, and often by dozens. This means, in effect, that whatever the legitimacy of secession, it does not eliminate the need for the other methods for managing ethnic conflict. Even if secession is allowed, the successor states

---

[15] See e.g. Beran (1984); Nielsen (1993); Wellman (1995); Gauthier (1994); Philpott (1995).

will usually have to adopt some other technique for managing their ethnic differences (such as assimilation, federalism, or multiculturalism).

There has also been a major dispute about the legitimacy of assimilation, the last method for eliminating difference. By 'assimilation as a method for eliminating difference', McGarry and O'Leary have in mind 'the idea of trying to eliminate difference within the state by seeking to integrate or assimilate the relevant ethnic communities into a new transcendent identity' (McGarry and O'Leary 1993: 17). This can be done more or less coercively: at the more coercive end the assimilationist state can ban associations and publications that seek to foster or reproduce a minority identity, or compel all citizens to stop using surnames that reflect a minority background; at the less coercive end the assimilationist state can respect the individual civil rights of citizens, but refuse to accord any recognition or support to minority languages and cultures, and insist that all public schools, government institutions, street signs, and public holidays reflect the dominant language and culture. In either case, the goal over time is to compel or pressure all citizens to see themselves as members of a single, common national culture that merges all pre-existing ethnic differences.

It is important to distinguish assimilation from what we might call 'multicultural integration'. Both involve fashioning a new transcendent identity—the identity of citizenship, or full, equal membership in the state. And both seek to integrate people from various ethnic backgrounds into common social and political institutions. However, multicultural integration does not have the intent or expectation of eliminating other cultural differences between subgroups in the state. Rather, it accepts that ethnocultural identities matter to citizens, will endure over time, and must be recognized and accommodated within these common institutions. The hope is that citizens from different backgrounds can all recognize themselves, and feel at home, within such institutions.

The relative merits of assimilation and multicultural integration are still a matter of some debate. To be sure, there is near-universal rejection of the more coercive forms of assimilation that have been pursued by unsavoury dictators and ruling classes throughout the modern era as they banned minority languages and religions and rewrote history in the attempt to assimilate minority groups into the larger nation. But assimilation has also been the preferred method of some of the most enlightened regimes in modern history. As McGarry and O'Leary note, it 'has been the official aspiration of civil rights leaders in the USA, the African National Congress in South Africa, unionist integrationists in Northern Ireland, and the democratic left in those European countries striving to cope with immigrant influxes' (1993: 17). Similarly, this option was surely the orthodoxy among political philosophers in the UK and the USA until the emergence of multiculturalist critics in the last decade. (In France, where republican traditions are well entrenched in political philosophy, it is probably still the default position.)

But as we noted earlier, these days most political theorists, at least in the English-speaking world, believe that some forms of recognition and accommodation of minority groups are justifiable in at least some circumstances. As a result, assimilation has gone out of favour amongst Western theorists.[16] Hence, most political theorists working on these issues, including all the authors in this volume, focus on one or more of the last three methods for managing differences from the above taxonomy; namely, territorial autonomy (e.g. federalism), non-territorial power-sharing (e.g. consociationalism), or multicultural integration.

This points to an important feature of the contemporary debate. Most democracies, historically, have adopted strategies to manage ethnic conflict that we now view as morally indefensible—from the forced movement of indigenous peoples to hegemonic control to assimilation. As these approaches have gradually been rejected as either unworkable or morally indefensible, people have been looking round for other models or paradigms of ethnic relations. And the three best-known alternatives—federalism, consociationalism, and multicultural integration—all involve significant elements of minority rights.

Many scholars in the ethnic-conflict field advocate one or more of these three options as having proven success in managing ethnic conflict. And indeed it is important to note that several democratic countries have decades, even centuries, of experience with these forms of managing diversity. But it is not clear how much comfort defenders of minority rights can draw from the ethnic-conflict literature.

For one thing, normative political philosophers are likely to have somewhat different criteria for evaluating the success of these approaches. In the context of ethnic-conflict studies, the focus is on explaining how state governments can control ethnocultural conflicts and maintain political stability. The aim is to avoid violence and instability. Political philosophers, by contrast, are likely to care not only about the absence of violence, but also about the extent to which society meets norms of justice, individual freedom, and deliberative democracy.[17] A multi-ethnic society could be relatively

---

[16] Of course, most theorists would agree that individuals should be free to assimilate, if they so choose. But few people think that the government's goal should be to encourage everyone to make that choice, and fewer still think that the government should adopt policies that pressure individuals to do so.

[17] This difference is partly reflected in the terminology used. In the context of ethnic-conflict studies, it is natural to refer to methods of *managing* differences, as if diversity is always a regrettable problem threatening the stability or integrity of the state. Political philosophers are more likely to speak in terms of minority rights and of policies for *respecting* diversity and difference, and to treat it as an open question whether such policies pose a threat to common

stable, and yet score very poorly in terms of the virtues and practices of democratic citizenship. Political philosophers will want to know if and when apparently 'successful' forms of managing diversity involve the erosion of cherished values of democratic citizenship; and this sort of information is not always available in the ethnic-conflict literature which is primarily concerned with descriptive, not normative, issues.

Moreover, many of the minority claims being advanced today go beyond traditional forms of federalism, consociationalism, or multicultural integration. These forms of managing diversity are all undergoing transformations as a result of such factors as new migration flows, global communications, and the influence of human rights and post-colonial ideologies. Indeed, ethnic relations in most Western democracies are in a state of flux, as old assumptions and expectations are being questioned and challenged. Nineteenth-century policies aimed at hegemonic control or assimilation may be out of date, but so too are nineteenth-century forms of federalism or consociationalism. The demands of indigenous peoples, transnational migrants, African Americans, and other groups cannot easily be satisfied by these traditional mechanisms.

Much of the debate in political theory concerns these new, and untested, claims for minority rights. Precisely because many demands are untested, and given that ethnic relations are in a general state of flux, they raise fears that cannot be placated by pointing to the historic success of more traditional forms of minority rights. It is not clear, for example, that traditional safeguards and limitations will apply to new forms of minority rights. This fear is exacerbated by the widespread perception that these claims are grounded in a more absolutist, exclusive, and non-negotiable conception of identity than earlier forms of minority claims. The underlying logic of modern identity claims, it is said, make compromise, tolerance, and deliberation particularly difficult to achieve.

As a result, there is a concern that the sorts of minority rights being claimed today may put us on a particularly steep and slippery slope. If we accept one group's claims for a particular minority right, we will be pushed by the logic of their claim to grant them more and more rights; and then we will be compelled to grant the same rights to all other groups that might request them. And so we will be trapped in an endless spiral of ever-greater claims by an ever-greater number of groups.

Whether this is an accurate perception of the logic of identity claims is, of course, controversial (this is one of the central topics in Waldron's chapter: Chapter 6). But one can only assuage this fear by providing some alternative account of the moral basis and logic of minority rights claims.

citizenship and the goals of justice and stability in the larger political community. This, of course, is the guiding question of this volume.

This suggests that there is still a key role for political philosophers to play in assessing the relationship between minority rights and citizenship. First, in so far as it is important to look at the impact of minority rights—not only on stability, but also on norms of democratic citizenship—then philosophical work needs to be done to clarify the relevant normative standards of citizenship. Secondly, in so far as many minority rights claims are relatively new and untested, philosophical work is required to clarify the underlying logic of these new claims, and to identify the extent to which they entail or engender an undesirable absolutist or non-negotiable conception of culture and identity. And thirdly, if there is some conflict between respecting the legitimate claims of minorities and promoting desirable citizenship virtues and practices, what sorts of trade-offs between these values are appropriate and morally defensible?

We take these concerns seriously, and our aim in this volume is to assess them as systematically as possible. However, we believe that this worry cannot be evaluated in the abstract, as if all forms of minority rights have the same impact on citizenship. Rather, as we have argued, these potential conflicts must be addressed through careful examination of specific contexts. We need to examine how specific forms of minority rights for specific groups affect specific practices and virtues of citizenship.

For this reason, we have invited the authors in this volume to embed their theoretical and normative discussions of citizenship in diverse societies within specific policy debates. These policy contexts range widely, from religious schooling in Canada to indigenous land rights in Australia to federal reforms in post-communist Russia. But they are all focused on a very similar challenge: how to show respect for diversity in a pluralistic society without at the same time damaging or eroding the bonds and virtues of citizenship. By examining and comparing these debates in various contexts, we hope to learn whether there is a notion of citizenship for multi-ethnic states that fairly accommodates ethnocultural differences, while still maintaining and promoting the sorts of virtues, practices, institutions, and solidarity needed for a flourishing democracy.

We will not attempt to summarize the findings of the authors in this volume. Given the complexities of the issues, and the disparate policies being studied, their findings cannot be summarized in the form of simple generalizations or conclusions. What we will do instead, in the remainder of our Introduction, is to fill in the broader context within which these more specific debates occur. The chapters in this volume analyse several important examples of the potential conflict between citizenship and diversity, but obviously there are many other such examples involving different sorts of groups, in different countries, making different sorts of minority rights claims. It will be helpful, therefore, to give at least a rough indication of the fuller range of issues that fall under the heading of citizenship and diversity.

We will do this by introducing a series of typologies and distinctions regarding types of minority groups (Section 5); types of minority rights claims (Section 6); and aspects of citizenship that might be threatened by minority rights (Section 7). These typologies will make clear that the examples discussed in this volume are in reality just a small fraction of the cases where citizenship and diversity can conflict. However, these typologies will also show, we hope, that while this volume is not a comprehensive examination of all such cases, it does provide a representative sample of the major debates about citizenship and diversity.

5. A Note on Different Kinds of Minority Groups

In order to identify the underlying logic and social implications of minority rights claims, we need first to consider what sorts of groups exist within the state. Different kinds of groups face very different kinds of challenges finding their place within the larger state, and therefore demand different kinds of special accommodations. A persistent source of confusion in both academic and popular discussions of multiculturalism is to assume that all kinds of cultural minorities are demanding the same kinds of rights for the same reasons. For example, many critics fail to notice that while national minority groups (like the Scottish) typically seek autonomy from the central government to govern their own affairs, immigrant groups tend to ask for measures that will make it easier for them to participate in the central institutions of the state. And even when different kinds of groups do demand similar kinds of minority rights (say, for representation or recognition) they may be doing it for very different purposes. For this reason, we cannot discuss the implications of different cultural rights for citizenship until we have a clearer idea of the variety of ethnocultural groups in modern states.

There is no single definitive typology of forms of ethnocultural diversity. However, there are some significant ways of distinguishing kinds of groups that clarify our understanding of the political stakes in a great number of culturally diverse states. The following list provides a rough and preliminary typology of minority groups, focusing on the sorts of ethnocultural communities discussed by the authors of this volume:

A. National minorities
    (a) stateless nations
    (b) indigenous peoples
B. Immigrant minorities
    (c) with citizenship or rights to become citizens
    (d) without rights to become citizens ('metics')

    (*e*) refugees
C. Religious groups
    (*f*) isolationist
    (*g*) non-isolationist
D. *Sui generis* groups
    (*h*) African Americans
    (*i*) Roma (gypsies)
    (*j*) Russians in former Soviet states, etc, etc.

A. *National minorities*. Although the word 'nation' is often used to refer to states, we follow all contemporary scholars of nationalism in using it to refer to a specific type of community or society that may or may not have its own state. For more than a century political philosophers and social scientists have debated the question 'What is a nation?', but we do not have to settle this debate here.[18] It is often noted that for any list of the defining features of nationhood, there are indisputable examples of nations that do not meet all of the conditions. For example, nations typically have a common language that distinguishes them from their neighbours, though Germany and Austria are certainly distinct nations with the same language, and the Swiss share a common national identity despite speaking four different 'national' languages. Partly for this reason, many scholars follow Max Weber in thinking of nations as 'communities of sentiment' (Weber 1948). In effect, communities qualify as nations when they think of themselves as nations. And as it turns out, these groups tend to be historical communities, more or less institutionally complete, occupying a given territory or homeland, and sharing a distinct language and mass culture. The important point for our purposes here is that on any of the standard answers to the question 'What is a nation?', it becomes clear that there are many times more nations than there are states, and in fact relatively few states that do not contain more than one national community. National minorities are national communities that share a state with one or more larger (or more dominant) nations.[19] The authors in this volume discuss two different kinds of national minorities which we might call stateless nations and indigenous peoples.

(*a*) *Stateless nations*, or nations without a state in which they are the majority—a state literally to call their own—exist in all parts of the world. They find themselves sharing states with other nations for a variety of reasons. They may have been conquered and annexed by a larger state or empire in the past; ceded from one empire to another; or united with another

---

[18] See Renan (1939); Miller (1995); Norman (1999).

[19] In a few cases, such as apartheid-era South Africa and present-day Syria, minority communities have ruled over the majority. Most of what is said about minority nations or minority rights would apply equally to oppressed majorities in situations like these.

kingdom through royal marriage. In a few cases, multination states have arisen from a more or less voluntary agreement between two or more national communities to form a mutually beneficial federation or union. However they were incorporated, national minorities have typically sought to maintain or enhance their political autonomy, either through outright secession or, more commonly, through some form of regional autonomy. And they typically mobilize along nationalist lines, using the language of 'nationhood' to describe and justify these demands for self-government. While the ideology of nationalism has typically seen full-fledged independence as the 'normal' or 'natural' end-point, economic or demographic reasons make this unfeasible for many national minorities. Moreover, the historical ideal of a fully sovereign state is increasingly obsolete in today's world of transnational institutions and economies. Hence there is a growing interest in exploring other forms of self-government, such as federalism. In one way or another, the accommodation of stateless nations is the primary focus of Chapters 10, 11, 14, and 15, by Réaume, Coulombe, Smith, and Bauböck.

(b) *Indigenous peoples* also meet the criteria of minority nationhood and exist on all (the inhabited) continents. Typically their traditional lands were overrun by settlers and then forcibly, or through treaties, incorporated into states run by outsiders. While other minority nations dream of a status like nation-states—with similar economic, social, and cultural achievements— indigenous peoples usually seek something rather different: the ability to maintain certain traditional ways of life and beliefs while nevertheless participating on their own terms in the modern world. In addition to the autonomy needed to work out that sort of project, indigenous peoples also typically require of the larger society long-overdue expressions of respect and recognition to begin to make amends for indignities they suffered for decades or centuries as second-class citizens (or even non-citizens and slaves). With examples drawn from Australia, New Zealand, North America, South Africa, and elsewhere, Chapters 12 and 13, by Levy and Borrows, explore issues about the best way to balance structures of self-government for indigenous peoples with their need to participate effectively in the institutions of the larger state.

B. *Immigrant minorities.* A second source of ethnocultural diversity is immigration, that is, the decision of individuals and families to leave their original homeland and emigrate to another society, often leaving their friends and relatives behind. This decision is typically made for economic reasons, although sometimes also for political reasons: to move to a freer or more democratic country. It is essential to distinguish two categories of immigrants—those who have the right to become citizens and those who do not. We add refugees as a third category with special needs and motivations, even though in practice they will fall into one or the other of these categories in different states.

(c) *Immigrants with rights of citizenship.* These are people who arrive under an immigration policy that gives them the right to become citizens after a relatively short period of time (say, three to five years) subject only to minimal conditions (e.g. learning the official language, and knowing something about the country's history and political institutions). This has been the traditional policy governing immigration in the three major 'countries of immigration', namely, the United States, Canada, and Australia—and also, to varying degrees, in former colonial powers like Britain, France, and the Netherlands, which allowed large numbers of former colonial subjects access to citizenship. Most of the discussions of immigrant groups in this volume concern people who have citizenship or access to citizenship, and who sometimes ask for special accommodations in their new countries for their religious, linguistic, or cultural differences. These issues are the primary focus of Chapters 6 and 7, by Waldron and Modood, and are discussed in different contexts in a number of other chapters.

(d) *Immigrants without rights of citizenship*. Some migrants are never given the opportunity to become citizens, either because they entered the country illegally (e.g. many North Africans in Italy), or because they entered as students or 'guest-workers' but have overstayed their initial visas (e.g. many Turks in Germany). When they entered the country, these people were not conceived of as future citizens, or even as long-term residents, and indeed in most cases they would not have been allowed to enter in the first place if they had asked to be permanent residents and future citizens. However, despite the official rules, they have settled more or less permanently. In principle, and to some extent in practice, many face the threat of deportation if they are detected by the authorities or if they are convicted of a crime. But they none the less form sizeable communities in certain countries, engage in some form of employment, legal or illegal, and may have married and formed families. Borrowing a term from ancient Greece, Michael Walzer calls these groups 'metics'—that is, long-term residents who are none the less excluded from the polis (Walzer 1983). Metics raise different challenges from those of immigrant citizens. They face enormous obstacles to integration—legal, political, economic, social, and psychological—and so tend to exist at the margins of the larger society. Where such marginalized communities exist, the danger arises of the creation of a permanently disfranchised, alienated, and racially defined underclass.

(e) *Refugees*. In many parts of the world, including Eastern Europe, Africa, and Central Asia, most of the migrants today are refugees seeking asylum, rather than voluntary immigrants admitted under an immigration policy. This raises important questions about the aim of multicultural integration. Since none of the chapters of this volume deals explicitly with the special problems of refugees, we will make a few observations here in the Introduction.

Of course, Western democracies accept many refugees in addition to other immigrants.[20] But in the West it has been possible to treat refugees, for all intents and purposes, as if they were immigrants. Governments (and the general public) expect that refugees, like immigrants, will settle permanently and take out citizenship in their new country; and this expectation has been borne out in practice. One reason why this has been possible is that refugees in Western democracies tend to arrive in small numbers from distant lands, usually as individuals or families rather than in large groups. It is, therefore, easier for them to integrate, and more difficult for them to return to their country of origin. However, in Eastern Europe, Central Africa, Central Asia, and elsewhere, refugees often come in great numbers from short distances, which makes integration more difficult and the prospect of return more likely. Under these conditions, it is not clear whether it is appropriate to expect or to encourage migrants to integrate, rather than simply providing safe asylum until things improve in their country of origin.

In most cases, if refugees stay in their new country for many years, it will become their new home. They may cling to the hope of returning to their country of origin. But if they have stayed long enough to get a job and to start raising a family in their new country, they are very unlikely to leave. When they do decide to stay, most commentators now accept that the only viable and just long-term solution is to allow and encourage their integration into the mainstream society. This is the only way to avoid the injustices and conflicts associated with the marginalization of metics. Adopting such a policy not only avoids the dangers of marginalization, but also allows a country to take maximal advantage of the skills and education of the refugees, so that they become a benefit to their new country, not a drain. As with other ethnocultural minorities, it is an open question—the one debated throughout this volume—when the provision of various cultural rights will help or hinder integration of minorities into a common citizenship.

C. *Religious groups*. There are many ways one could distinguish religious groups for the sake of clarifying questions about special rights. Given the discussions in this volume it makes sense to distinguish what we call isolationist and non-isolationist religious communities.

(ƒ) *Isolationist religious groups*. Whereas most immigrants wish to participate in the larger society, there are some small immigrant groups that voluntarily isolate themselves from the larger society and avoid participating in politics or civil society. This option of voluntary marginalization is only likely to be attractive to religious sects whose theology requires them to avoid most contact with the modern world—such as the Hutterites in Canada, or the Amish in the United States, both of whom came to North America from Europe to avoid persecution for their pacifist religious beliefs. The Hutterites

[20] Canada, for example, accepts a number of immigrants each year equivalent to about 1 per cent of its total population, and about one-tenth of these are refugees.

and Amish are unconcerned about their marginalization within the larger society and polity, since they view its 'worldly' institutions as corrupt, and seek to maintain the same traditional way of life they had in their original homeland. Indeed, they have demanded the right to take their children out of school before the legal age of 16, in order to protect them from such corrupting influences.

Spinner-Halev calls the members of such groups 'partial citizens', because they voluntarily waive both the rights and responsibilities of democratic citizenship. They waive the right to vote and to hold office (as well as their right to welfare benefits), but by the same token they also evade their civic responsibility to help tackle the country's problems. Moreover, they are often organized internally in illiberal ways. For this reason, many people have thought that the state should intervene in such groups, at least to ensure that children are adequately informed about their opportunities in the outside world. However, in practice, most democratic states do tolerate these groups, so long as they do not harm people inside or outside the group, and so long as members are legally free to leave.

(g) *Non-isolationist religious groups*. Isolationist religious groups are quite rare in the Western world. Much more common are religious communities whose faith differs from either the religion of the majority, or the secular beliefs of the larger society and state institutions. Members of these communities may share the same ethnocultural background or citizenship identity as the majority—as is typical of many fundamentalist Protestants and devout Catholics in North America (Chapters 2 and 3, by Callan and Spinner-Halev, focus mainly on these groups). Or their religion may actually be part of their ethnocultural heritage, as is the case, say, of most Muslim communities in Western Europe (these groups, particularly in Britain, are the focus of Modood's chapter). By and large, these groups are seeking not to remove themselves from mainstream society, but rather to shield themselves (or their children) from very specific aspects of mainstream culture that are at odds with their faith, and to exempt themselves from certain general rules that seem to discriminate against them. A classic example now is the case of Sikhs, who seek exemptions from certain military and police dress codes concerning appropriate head gear, not because they wish to withdraw from mainstream society, but because they wish to participate in these central institutions like everyone else without having to compromise their beliefs for the sake of an arbitrary regulation.

D. Sui generis *groups*. As any reference book on ethnic conflict makes clear, there are a number of ethnocultural groups in the world that do not fit comfortably within any of the categories we have just discussed. We listed the Roma, who, unlike national minorities, have a homeland that is everywhere and nowhere; as well as Russian settlers in countries that seceded from the Soviet Union, and who, unlike typical immigrants, never voluntarily left what they saw as their homeland to begin a new life in another nation.[21] The only *sui generis* group discussed at length in this volume, however, is African Americans (see in particular the chapters by Williams and Mansbridge).

(*h*) *African Americans*.[22] African Americans do not fit the voluntary immigrant pattern, not only because they were brought to America involuntarily as slaves, but also because they were prevented (rather than encouraged) from integrating into the institutions of the majority culture (e.g. through racial segregation, laws against miscegenation, and the teaching of literacy). Nor do they fit the national minority pattern, since they do not have a traditional homeland in America in which they are a majority, or a common language that distinguishes them from the majority. They came from a variety of African cultures, with different languages, and no attempt was made to keep together those with a common ethnic background. On the contrary, people from the same culture (even from the same family) were typically split up once in America. Moreover, before emancipation they were legally prohibited from trying to re-create their own cultural structure (e.g. all forms of black association, except Christian churches, were illegal). The situation of African Americans, therefore, is virtually unique, although the use of 'race' to define subordinate groups is certainly more common. Given their distinctive situation, it is widely accepted that they will also have distinctive demands which cannot be captured by either the immigrant model of integration or the national minority model of self-government, although they may draw elements from both.

6. Classifying Ways of Respecting Diversity

As we have seen, different sorts of groups have different histories, needs, aspirations, and identities; and these differences influence the sorts of claims that they tend to make on the state. Of course, at one level we can say that all of these groups are engaged in 'identity politics', 'the politics of difference', or 'the politics of recognition'. However, if our aim is to see how minority rights claims affect the practice of democratic citizenship, we need a more

[21] For a good discussion of the distinctive circumstances of the Roma, see Gheorghe and Mirga (1997). For that of the Russians in the 'near abroad', see Laitin (1998). Both books discuss the on-going debate about whether the term 'national minority' is appropriate for these groups.

[22] This name, like others for the group in question, is problematic. The group being referred to is composed of the descendants of African slaves brought to America. Hence, it is not meant to include Caucasian immigrants from southern or northern Africa. Indeed, for many purposes, including ours here, it does not even make sense to include recent black immigrants from Africa in this category, since they fit the typical situation of immigrant groups.

fine-grained account that helps us to identify the underlying nature and logic of these claims.

One useful scheme for classifying cultural rights is developed by Jacob Levy (1997). He distinguishes eight general ways that groups within liberal democracies seek respect for their cultural (or religious) distinctiveness. These claimed cultural rights include: (i) exemptions from laws that penalize or burden cultural practices; (ii) assistance to do things the majority (or otherwise privileged group) can do unassisted; (iii) self-government for national minorities and indigenous communities; (iv) external rules restricting non-members' liberty in order to protect members' culture; (v) internal rules for members' conduct that are enforced by ostracism and excommunication; (vi) incorporation and enforcement of traditional or religious legal codes within the dominant legal system; (vii) special representation of groups or their members within government institutions; and (viii) symbolic recognition of the worth, status, or existence of various groups within the larger state community. (For Levy's summary, see Levy 1997: 25. All of these ways of respecting diversity would fall within the final three methods for managing differences in the taxonomy we adapted from McGarry and O'Leary, in Section 4, above.)

We will briefly describe each of these kinds of cultural rights, citing cases and justifications from the essays in this volume.

1. *Exemptions from laws that penalize or burden cultural practices*. As Levy explains, 'Exemption rights are individually exercised negative liberties granted to members of a religious or cultural group whose practices are such that a generally and ostensibly neutral law would be a distinctive burden on them' (1997: 25). Such exemptions have a long history in Western democracies, with a standard example being special consideration for Jewish shopkeepers with respect to Sunday-closing laws. Although exemptions need not involve conflicts with religious beliefs and practices (e.g. conscientious objectors to compulsory military service in several West European states have been able to cite secular beliefs), most do. As such, these rights are typically justified with arguments highlighting freedom of conscience and religion, and the unfair burden placed on those whose religious obligations differ from the majority's. The most detailed discussions of exemptions in this volume are in chapters by Callan and Spinner-Halev over the issue of whether religious parents should be allowed to exempt their children from certain classes in public schools: either by allowing them to attend state schools part-time (Spinner-Halev's solution), or by allowing for public funding of religious schools, at least in the early years (Callan's solution).

2. *Assistance to do things the majority (or otherwise privileged group) can do unassisted*. Assistance rights are also a familiar feature on the landscape of most liberal democracies. Often justified on grounds of equality in the face

of special disadvantages, they are routinely accorded to members of 'non-cultural' groups, such as the mentally or physically disabled, and cultural groups alike—most controversially in the form of affirmative-action policies. In this volume three very different sorts of assistance rights are defended on grounds of both equality and citizenship. As we just noted, Callan makes a case for public funding of parochial primary schools, since he thinks that religious communities are discriminated against if public funding is available only for secular public schools. Although he acknowledges that this compromises the ideals of civic education within the framework of common schools, he explains at length why he thinks public support for some religious education would be a reasonable way of balancing the values of citizenship and equality. Réaume considers one of the classic forms of assistance, minority-language rights. In particular, she explores the implications of meaningful support and respect for official-language minority groups within one of the institutional pillars of citizenship rights in a free society: the courts of law. Borrows argues for the importance of expanding educational opportunities for Aboriginal people not merely because they face discrimination or historical disadvantages, but because such policies would make it easier for Aboriginals to enhance their sense of citizenship within the larger community.

3. *Self-government for national minorities and indigenous communities.* Self-government rights are in many ways the ultimate minority rights, and can even include demands by groups to secede from the larger state in order to escape the status of being a minority altogether. All of the cases examined in this volume, however, involve claims for self-government powers within a pluralistic state. In either case, self-government rights are argued for in a variety of ways, for example: (*a*) with claims that a self-governing community, such as an indigenous group, was historically self-governing and never relinquished its rights; (*b*) with claims that a minority community is systematically mistreated by the majority, or that its special needs and interests are misunderstood or ignored within the larger political community; (*c*) with the belief that, in general, small, local governments are more democratic than distant central governments; and (*d*) with reference to the so-called nationalist principle, that the cultural and political communities ought to be 'congruent' (to recall the expression on the opening page of Gellner 1983). A common theme in the four chapters that discuss self-government at length is that territorial-based forms of autonomy, such as federalism and self-governing Aboriginal reserves, are insufficient once we consider the competing demands of justice and common citizenship. Bauböck emphasizes the need to combine federal autonomy with other non-territorial forms of cultural rights (such as minority-language rights) as well as a healthy respect for traditional individual rights. And looking at the recent history of the Russian federation, Smith considers the perils of allowing radically asymmetrical federal arrange-

ments that give some national minorities significantly more political auto-nomy than others. Both Levy and Borrows consider the challenges of finding appropriate forms of self-government for indigenous peoples, and the necessity of combining self-government with measures that will facilitate participation in the larger society.

4. *External rules restricting non-members' liberty in order to protect members' culture.* It is uncontroversial for all but radical cosmopolitans that nation-states can act in certain ways to protect their culture by limiting the liberty of non-citizens, especially non-residents—for example, by imposing restrictions on immigration or on foreign ownership of mass media. It is usually a matter of high controversy, however, when a cultural group within a democratic state demands the right to limit the liberty of fellow citizens who are not members of their group. In general these rights are justified in the name of protecting potentially fragile elements in minority cultures; and the need to protect cultures is often justified with the idea that a healthy cultural context is a necessary condition for individual autonomy and self-respect. Probably the most widely discussed example of such external rules concerns the infamous Quebec language laws which, among other things, have banned the use of languages other than French on commercial signs within Quebec, a province with more than 1 million non-francophone citizens.[23] Pierre Coulombe's chapter discusses this case within the broader context of linguistic politics and language rights throughout Canadian history.

5. *Internal rules for members' conduct that are enforced by ostracism and ex-communication.* As Levy explains,

Many rules and norms governing a community's members are not elevated into law. There are expectations about how a member will behave; one who does not behave that way is subject to the sanction of no longer being viewed as a member by other members. This sanction may take the form of shunning, excommunication, being dis-owned by one's family, being expelled from an association, and so on. (Levy 1997: 40)

What is interesting about these rules is that they would usually be clearly unjust if imposed by the state. For example, a state may not exclude women from decision-making offices, yet the Catholic church is allowed to, and Catholics who challenge this principle may be subject to informal or formal but non-coercive sanctions by the church. Most of the cases discussed in this volume are concerned with the state's response to the challenge of diversity, and hence issues regarding such internal rules are not directly addressed. However, it is increasingly recognized that these internal sanctions, even if informal or non-coercive, can none the less have a very significant impact on the freedom and well-being of group members. It may therefore be necessary

---

[23] This law has since been softened to allow the use of other languages as long as French is more prominent.

for the state to intervene to protect vulnerable members of groups from particularly oppressive internal rules. In Chapter 9 Saharso discusses a tragic case involving state attempts to protect Hindustani women in the Netherlands from internal cultural norms that undermined their ability to exercise their basic liberal rights.

6. *Incorporation and enforcement of traditional or religious legal codes within the dominant legal system.* There is nothing inherently contradictory about having two or more systems of law operating within a single political jurisdiction: it happens in Canada and the United States—where the former French colonies of Quebec and Louisiana have retained civil law traditions alongside the common law of the larger state—as well as in the United Kingdom, Switzerland, and of course the European Union. It is usually argued, however, that in all of these cases the legal systems involved have similar origins and forms of legal reasoning. The same cannot always be said about two more radical forms of bi- or multilegalism: the incorporation of religiously based family law, and the incorporation of traditional indigenous legal traditions. Arguments for incorporation of minority legal systems are closely linked to arguments for self-government, especially in the case of indigenous territories. In religiously divided societies, like the Ottoman Empire or modern-day Israel and India, differentiating family law among religious communities can be justified as a form of consociational autonomy or multicultural toleration. These cases of incorporation of religious family law and indigenous law are explored at length, respectively, in Chapters 8 and 12, by Ayelet Shachar and Levy. Both Shachar and Levy argue in favour of the principle of this significant cultural right for ethnoreligious and indigenous groups. But they also warn of the dangers for the groups themselves or for some of their members (especially women) if traditional legal systems are incorporated within states' legal systems in the wrong way.

7. *Special representation of groups or their members within government institutions.* This form of group right is as old as representative government itself, where it has always been entirely without controversy that territorial units are given representation in major government institutions, particularly within decision-making bodies. (Indeed, it pre-dated democratic government, when the aristocracy and religious groups demanded rights to share the spoils of power with absolute monarchs.) It is rather more controversial when cultural or religious groups, or women, demand special or guaranteed representation in the same government bodies. Nevertheless, these claims to representation are unlikely to fade, for as we noted in Section 2, issues of 'voice' and 'public reasonableness' have become central to debates about democratic citizenship, and these are inextricably tied to representation. These issues are the primary focus in the chapters by Williams and Mansbridge, which carefully weigh the benefits and costs (in terms of justice and citizenship) of various forms of special representation for historically disadvantaged groups. In his

chapter Modood suggests that some form of religious-corporate representation may actually be more conducive to social stability and intergroup harmony in a country like the United Kingdom than would a policy of presumed neutrality.[24]

8. *Symbolic recognition of the worth, status, or existence of various groups within the larger state community.* This is a catch-all category for a wide variety of forms of group recognition within the institutions, symbols, and political culture of the larger state. At stake are such matters as 'the name of the polity, its flag, its coat of arms, its national anthem, its public holidays, the name by which a cultural group will be known, or the way a group's history is presented in schools and textbooks' (Levy 1997: 46). Even such apparently functional issues as the distribution of federal powers may carry symbolic importance if a national minority controlling one of the provinces interprets an asymmetrical distribution of powers in its favour as recognition that it deserves special status as being more than 'just another province'.[25] Furthermore, as several authors in this volume emphasize, to say that a form of recognition is symbolic is not to say that it is somehow superfluous. Recognition may in fact be more important to a group than many of the other more substantive cultural rights discussed above. As Levy illustrates,

From the minority culture's perspective, the absence of interpreters [i.e. an assistance right] at a particular government office might be viewed as an inconvenience, whereas the elevation of the majority tongue to the official status, or the denial of that status to the minority language, might be viewed as an open declaration that some are not wanted as members of the state. (Levy 1997: 47)

Symbolic gestures granting or denying recognition can have profound and continuing effects within a political culture in ways that directly affect the well-being and self-respect of citizens of minority cultures, as well as their enthusiasm to participate in the political life of the larger state. Both Réaume and Coulombe discuss the dynamic impact of according a minority language full official status, and Modood does the same for the case of the recognition of immigrant communities, especially those with a different religion.

---

[24] Issues of representation are also present, implicitly, in Réaume's and Coulombe's discussion of the implications of a well functioning policy of official bilingualism (or multilingualism) in the institutions of state. In practice this provides opportunities for greater representation of members of the minority language group in, for example, the civil service and the courts; and in doing so, they argue, it improves the quality of public deliberations and makes government bodies seem less like alien forces of control for members of these groups.

[25] The symbolic value of asymmetrical federalism, which accords somewhat more autonomy to subunits controlled by a national minority, has loomed large in the demands of Quebecois and Catalan nationalists seeking constitutional revisions in Canada and Spain (see Requejo 1996). A similar issue has arisen regarding federalism in Russia, where the so-called 'ethnic republics' associated with national minorities have greater powers than the 'regions' dominated by members of the Russian majority (see Smith 1996).

We should also remember that symbolic recognition is not simply a matter of members of the majority acknowledging the special status of minority groups with whom they share a state. It also requires members of the majority to rethink their own group's identity and relation to the state. So an Englishman would recognize not only that Britain now contains large numbers of citizens of Asian, African, and Caribbean descent (in addition to the Scots, Welsh, Northern Irish, and Manx); but also that this requires rethinking what it means to be British—probably in ways that would have been inconceivable for his grandparents fifty years earlier. He may have to distinguish more clearly than he had before between an ethnic English identity and a civic British identity, and to recognize that 'Britishness' must be defined in a way that is accessible to both the new immigrants and the historically settled peoples who share the British Isles.

This is the other half of what is involved in the project of multicultural integration: where all individuals and groups strive towards a new 'transcendent identity', to recall the expression used by McGarry and O'Leary; an identity that for many will coexist with older ethnic or religious identities. These themes are explored most thoroughly here in the chapters by Modood and Waldron. A more specific example can be found in Williams's discussion of how the majority cannot simply impose its own conception of 'public reason', but must be sensitive to different culturally derived notions of reasonableness.

7. Fears about Citizenship in the Face of Minority Rights

Having compiled a list of minority groups and of minority rights claims, we can now return to our original question: how do minority rights affect democratic citizenship? This is not a simple question, since talk about citizenship, particularly in the English language, can refer to an astonishingly wide variety of ideas, concepts, and values. More to the point, talk about disintegration, fragmentation, or weakening of citizenship can be expressing any number of quite distinct political worries; from concerns about restrictions on individual rights to fears about the secession of a substantial part of the state. Just as we believe it is helpful to distinguish several distinct kinds of minority rights and different kinds of minority groups, it is surely necessary to start to disaggregate these many citizenship worries.

At the individual level talk of a person's 'citizenship' can refer to three distinct ideas or phenomena: (*a*) her *status* as a legal citizen, defined largely by a panoply of civil, political, and social rights as well as a relatively small number of duties (e.g. to obey the law, pay taxes, perform military service); (*b*) her *identity* as a member of one or more political communities, an identity that is often contrasted with her other more particular identities based on class, race, ethnicity, religion, gender, profession, sexual preference, etc.; or (c) her *activity or civic virtue*, such as the four kinds of virtues listed by Galston in our discussion in Section 2, above. These three ideas are conceptually and empirically linked in a variety of ways. Obviously, the exact rights citizens have will partly define both their citizenship status and identity, as well as the range of political and social activities available to them. The form of citizenship identity they have will have an impact on their motivations to participate virtuously in civic and political activities; and so on. Similarly, if one of these aspects of citizenship is eroded, then the others may be affected as well.

If it makes sense to think of citizenship in terms of these three categories—status, identity, and activity—then, as a first step, it should be useful to distinguish various worries about the erosion of citizenship in terms of the aspect or aspects of citizenship that are supposedly endangered by various cultural rights. Before discussing a series of these 'citizenship worries', however, it is worth adding a fourth aspect of citizenship that is clearly in the minds of critics worried about multiculturalism and cultural rights. This is an ideal or goal of citizenship that applies, not at the individual level, but at the level of the political community as a whole: it is (d) the ideal of *social cohesion*, which may include concerns about social stability, political unity, and civil peace. All of the worries about the erosion or fragmentation of citizenship, then, can be traced to worries about the vulnerability of one or more of these four ideas: citizenship status, citizenship identity, citizenship activity, and citizenship cohesion.

Worries about the Loss of Equal Citizenship Status

Minority rights usually involve some form of differentiated citizenship status: they grant certain groups or their members rights or opportunities not available to other groups or citizens. But when does differentiated status become unequal status? Some people say 'Always!', and claim that the very idea of 'differentiated citizenship' is an oxymoron. According to these commentators, citizenship is, by definition, a matter of treating people as individuals with equal rights under the law, and so the basic rights of citizenship cannot vary among citizens. This, it is sometimes said, is what distinguishes democratic citizenship from feudal and other pre-modern views that determined people's political status by their religious, ethnic, or class membership. Hence 'the organization of society on the basis of rights or claims that derive from group membership is sharply opposed to the concept of society based on citizenship' (Porter 1987: 128).

As we argued earlier, however, we believe that this claim, that minority rights are inherently in conflict with the very concept of citizenship, is untenable. Virtually every modern democracy recognizes some form of group-differentiated citizenship. One result of the new-found interest in minority rights has been an explosion of work uncovering the myriad forms of special-status or asymmetrical rights or group-specific exemptions accorded to indigenous, ethnic, racial, or ethnoreligious groups in most Western democracies. Several essays in this volume bring to light yet more cases of such differentiated citizenship, and show how familiar and widespread such minority rights have been in Western democracies. As Bhikhu Parekh puts it, citizenship in fact 'is a much more differentiated and far less homogeneous concept than has been presupposed by political theorists' (Parekh 1990: 702).[26]

So differentiated citizenship is not a contradiction in terms, nor even particularly uncommon. Our question is, when do differentiated rights involve some real disadvantage or stigmatization (and not just difference) in citizenship status—e.g. some inequality in respect, or in life chances, or in influence over government policy? That is, when does differentiated status start to create first- and second-class citizens?

In so far as we are concerned with threats to equal citizenship status *per se*, it is important to distinguish the reality of inequality and the oppression and stigmatization it fosters, on the one hand, from the *perception* of unequal status, on the other. Members of the majority often complain that special rights for minorities reduce others to being second-class citizens. If this perception is deep and widespread, it can erode the sense of common identity and solidarity. We will deal with these worries in the following subsections. At this point, however, our concern is not with feelings or perceptions, but with the actual impact of minority rights on equal citizenship status. Do citizens (whether members of the majority community or of subgroups within the minority community) have *good reasons* for thinking that certain minority rights reduce them to second-class citizens?

Some of the essays in this volume suggest that this may indeed be the case. In some cases, this threat arises for reasons internal to a particular policy of minority rights. Shachar explains, for example, how allowing religious communities to control some aspects of family law—such as rules for marriage and divorce—can have devastating implications for the rights of women in ways that are clearly incompatible with the norms of equal citizenship in a liberal democracy. Similar arguments, as Coulombe notes, were made against Quebec's language law, which at one stage banned the use of English on shopkeepers' windows. Anglophone-rights advocates claimed that this law amounted to a limit on the fundamental right of all citizens to free speech (although the courts tended not to agree). These cases both suggest that minority claims to cultural recognition threaten equal citizenship status when the

---

[26] The claim that citizenship by definition requires a common set of rights is, in effect, a variant of the claim that justice by definition requires 'colour-blind' institutions and policies, and it suffers from the same flaws.

costs and benefits of minority protection are unfairly distributed—i.e. when one subgroup within the minority (e.g. women), or when selected non-members (e.g. anglophones in Quebec), are asked to bear most or all of the costs of cultural reproduction, while others enjoy the benefits.

In other cases, the threat to equal citizenship status may arise as an unintended consequence of the minority right. For example, Mansbridge ponders the implications for democratic citizenship of having selective electoral districts to ensure the election of more African Americans. Her worry is not that these are inherently unfair (far from it!), but rather that there is evidence that this policy leads to a loss of influence for minority groups outside these districts, and hence may be reducing political equality for members of designated groups in the process of trying to enhance it.[27]

These threats to equal citizenship should be of major concern. But there is no reason to think that they are intrinsic to all minority rights claims. On the contrary, most defenders of minority rights insist that it is the *denial* of minority rights that poses the greater threat to real equality. They argue that minority rights are needed to prevent the ongoing stigmatization of ethnocultural minorities, and to remedy the disadvantages they suffer in the larger society. Substantial evidence for this claim can be found in several of the chapters in this volume. For example, the strengthening of official-language rights for French Canadians, along with a substantial degree of autonomy for the French-speaking province of Quebec, have surely played an important role in the transition for French Canadians from being an economically disadvantaged and politically under-represented group in the 1950s, to being roughly in a position of social, economic, and political equality with English-speaking Canadians today. Similarly, while certain forms of group representation may unintentionally erode a group's political equality, Williams and Mansbridge both argue that other forms of group representation are vital to genuine political equality. And, as Levy notes, in so far as the historic conquest of indigenous peoples and the stripping of their self-government rights were grounded in racist and imperialist ideologies, then restoring rights of self-government can be seen as affirming the equal standing and worth of indigenous peoples. In these and other ways, one can argue that, far from eroding equal citizenship status, 'the accommodation of differences is the essence of true equality'.[28]

---

[27] Mansbridge is also concerned about the apparent loosening of political accountability for representatives of these special districts. If she is right, this is a problem not of an erosion of equal citizenship status, but of civic or political virtue, a problem to which we shall turn presently.

[28] This phrase comes from the judgement of the Canadian Supreme Court in explaining its interpretation of the equality provisions of the Canadian constitution. See *Andrews v. Law Society of British Columbia* 1 SCR 143; [1986] 56 DLR (4th) 1.

Worries about the Fragmentation or Weakening of Citizenship Identities

Let us turn now to the effects of cultural rights on the second aspect of citizenship, the *identity* that citizens share as members of a political community. This identity will always coexist for every individual citizen with numerous other identities based, as we noted already, on class, occupation, region, race, ethnicity, religion, gender, sexual preference, generation, mother tongue, hobbies, and so on. And, furthermore, it will differ in relative importance for each individual. Civic republicans would like to insist that the citizenship identity be each individual's primary and highest identity, and it is a major aim of the politics of civic republicanism to try to bring this about. But we know that this will never be true for many people. If forced to choose, some religious people would flee their country rather than give up practising their faith. And even many scholars we know would much rather take a job in a distant country, and live their whole lives there, than give up their profession for want of opportunities at home. Moreover, it is hard to think that there is anything politically sinful about people deciding to have these sorts of priorities with respect to their different identities, or that a modern state should be permitted to act in a heavy-handed way to make its citizens all fervently patriotic.

None of this is to deny, however, the significance of common citizenship identities in a democratic state—particularly in states shared by groups that already have strong identities based on different religions or ethnicity. It may be unreasonable to expect people to cherish their citizenship identity more than any of their other identities, but it is important for people to be motivated to act as citizens first and foremost when debating and acting in the public realm, at least for a broad range of issues. It would be an obvious sign of ill health in a democracy if a politician could get away with publicly 'justifying' his actions in parliament by announcing that he knew a certain policy was bad for the country, but that he supported it because it would enrich his family. It would be hardly less worrying if political leaders could get away admitting that a policy they supported was bad for the country but in their own ethnic group's best interests.[29]

One could question how tight the connection really is between having a strong citizenship identity and being motivated to act as a responsible citizen. For example, identifying themselves as 'an American' seems quite important to most Americans, at least as important as their other social identities. Yet

---

[29] Of course it is perfectly acceptable to justify a policy that benefits one's own group (say, American Indians, or Spanish gypsies) on grounds of justice; say, because it helps rectify a historical injustice. This is because such a policy can and should appeal to every citizen's sense of justice and citizenship solidarity.

this strong identification with a shared political identity has not translated into either high levels of solidarity for co-citizens, or high levels of political participation. By contrast, being 'Belgian' seems rather less important to most Belgians, who may emphasize instead their supranational identity as 'Europeans' or their substate identity as 'Flemish' or 'Walloons'. Yet the fact that being Belgian is not of prime importance has not (yet) undermined either the generous Belgian welfare state or the relatively high levels of political participation. Citizenship identity and motivation to act as a citizen may be less closely related than many people assume.

Still, it is surely true that if ethnic, regional, or religious identities crowd out a common citizenship identity, there will be difficulty maintaining a healthy democracy. And many critics worry that this sort of fragmentation of identity is a likely consequence of multiculturalism. As Vertovec argues, in a passage quoted by Modood, multiculturalism can be interpreted as 'a picture of society as a "mosaic" of several bounded, nameable, individually homogeneous and unmeltable minority uni-cultures which are pinned onto the backdrop of a similarly characterised majority uni-culture' (Vertovec 1995: 5). In such a society, where there is no common citizenship identity bridging or transcending the various group identities, politics is likely to be reduced to a mere *modus vivendi* amongst groups that barely tolerate, let alone co-operate with, each other. There is little hope for the sort of mutual understanding, deliberation, trust, and solidarity required by a flourishing democracy.

How might minority rights make such a picture come true? For one thing, some of the most far-reaching cultural rights—especially those concerning self-government and the symbolic recognition of national minorities and indigenous peoples—are directly concerned with legitimizing cultural identities that are distinct from, and potentially in competition with, common citizenship identities. Moreover, in the case of self-government and the extending of federal autonomy for minority groups, minority leaders are given institutions and legislative jurisdictions (e.g. control of education) with which they can progressively strengthen the minority cultural identity at the expense of the statewide citizenship identity. There is no question that the recognition of self-government for indigenous peoples and the adoption of what Philip Resnick calls 'multinational federalism' for stateless nations can have these sorts of effects (Resnick 1994).

Of course, many kinds of minority groups, such as immigrant groups or African Americans, rarely ask for the kinds of territorial autonomy and recognition that national minorities seek. But even here, the sorts of cultural rights claimed by 'non-national' minority groups can place strains on the bonds of a common citizenship identity. One fear is that certain sorts of policies that are intended to promote greater participation in society by a disadvantaged minority, such as affirmative-action programmes, will instead lead to a 'politicization of ethnicity'. Self-appointed group leaders, it is argued, have an incentive to mobilize their group members to demand or maintain special treatment, and the best way to do this may be to perpetuate the sense of vulnerability or persecution the group feels in order to strengthen the group identity; again, at the expense of the larger citizenship identity. The fear then is that group leaders will be successful in 'freezing' an essentialist identity that acts as a barrier to participation by members of the group in a wider citizenship identity that is not based on their group's supposedly essential characteristics.[30]

These are legitimate concerns. But here again, there is no reason to assume that the crowding out of a common citizenship identity is intrinsic to minority rights. Whether minority rights will have this result depends on several factors. For example, Mansbridge recognizes that her proposal to have representative bodies 'mirror' some aspects of the ethnic (and gender) composition of the society at large could be seen as presupposing or promoting an essentialist view of group identities. But she insists that this fear can be mitigated by stressing the non-essentialist, contingent arguments for mirrored representation: on her view, group representation is desirable, not because certain fixed groups have an eternal right to representation, but rather because mirrored representation under certain conditions would produce a higher quality of democratic deliberation (including deliberation about the contingent nature of group identities). Whether minority rights will generate essentialist and exclusive identities will depend, she argues, at least in part on the sort of public justification that is given for them.

Of course, even if the public justification for minority rights eschews essentialism, the unintended result may be to reinforce a picture of society as a 'mosaic of . . . bounded, nameable, individually homogeneous and unmeltable minority uni-cultures'. This is an empirical question, and so we need to ask: is there any empirical evidence that minority rights promote frozen essentialist identity? One of the few cases where this has been systematically studied is in Britain, and the results are discussed in Modood's chapter. Few have studied and tracked the evolution of ethnic and religious identities in contemporary Britain more closely than Modood, and in his opinion the evidence simply belies the fear. Studies suggest the existence of much more fluid and internally complex identities among immigrant minority groups, in which a sense of pride in their ethnic heritage mingles with a developing

---

[30] In order to justify affirmative measures to enhance the representation of African Americans in mainstream institutions, for example, leaders may implicitly appeal to a conception of the 'authentic' black identity or 'essential' black experience, and emphasize how difficult it is for whites to understand (and to represent) these experiences. The unintentional and paradoxical result of this strategy, however, may be to encourage the idea that participating in mainstream institutions involves 'acting white', and that it is a sell-out to compromise or adapt this authentic black identity in order to co-operate with others.

sense of being British. Moreover, there is some evidence that the fluid and inclusive nature of these immigrant identities exists, not in spite of multi-cultural policies, but rather because of them. Precisely because they have secured public recognition and support for their ethnic identity, they have the confidence to interact with others in an open way; whereas those groups whose identities lack this sort of public recognition tend to be more defensive about their culture, and more fearful about the consequences of cultural interchange.[31] This shows, once again, that the impact of minority rights on identity cannot be deduced a priori, but requires actual empirical investigation.

In any event, the concern that minority rights will crowd out a common citizenship identity presupposes that such a common identity already exists, or would exist were it not for the presence of minority rights. But of course, in many contexts, this is not true. Many members of minority groups—whether they be new immigrants or conquered national minorities—do not identify with the state in which they live, and instead feel quite alienated from it. This is particularly true of groups that have faced discrimination or prejudice, and who therefore feel unwanted. Granting such groups minority rights can hardly erode a sense of common citizenship identity, since it does not yet exist. Indeed, minority rights may be the best way to encourage alienated groups to come to identify with the larger political community. As Coulombe, Réaume, Bauböck, and Modood all discuss, the refusal to grant recognition and autonomy to such minorities is likely to provoke even more resentment and hostility, alienating them further from their identity as citizens of the larger state. By contrast, minority rights may confirm for minorities that they are full members of the larger society whose contributions will be welcomed. In all of these ways, then, minority rights have the potential to enhance, as well as to erode, a common citizenship identity.

Fears about the Erosion of Civic Virtue and Participation

There is obviously a close link between, on the one hand, worries about the weakening of citizenship identity and, on the other, fears that citizens will lose some of the virtues of democratic citizenship as well as the motivation or capacity to participate in wider public deliberations. Many possible relations between fragmented citizenship identities and poor civic virtue and practices come to mind.

A classic example is the fear that allowing or funding schools for particular religions will destroy one of the most effective forums of citizenship education—the state school system, where children learn to play and work

---

[31] For similar evidence in the Canadian case, see Kymlicka (1998a, ch. 1).

with children whose parents have different religions, ethnic backgrounds, and values. Both Callan and Spinner-Halev discuss at length this conflict between rights to religious education and the promotion of citizenship virtues necessary for deliberative democracy.

One reason why this is a 'classic' case is that it combines several different possible threats to citizenship. First, religious schools are seen as potentially eroding children's *motivation* to act as citizens, by privileging a particularistic religious identity at the expense of a common civic identity. Secondly, even if religious schools actively encourage their students to affirm a larger civic identity, and hence their motivation for citizenship, they may potentially erode children's *capacity* for good citizenship, since the curriculum of these schools may not teach the virtues of tolerance and public reasonableness. Thirdly, even if these schools promote both the motivation and capacity for citizenship, they can be seen as eliminating the *opportunity* to act as citizens: since all students share the same faith, there is no need or opportunity for students to step outside their role as religious believer and adopt instead their role as citizens.

As Callan and Spinner-Halev both note, it is important not to exaggerate the scope of these dangers, or to presuppose that they are inherent in any system of publicly funded religious schools. But these concerns do help us to identify the sorts of criteria we can use for evaluating other minority rights: to what extent do minority rights erode either the motivation, capacity, or opportunity for people to act as democratic citizens? This questions arises, not only for schools, but also for many other public institutions, including the media, courts, electoral systems, and deliberative bodies. One can easily imagine forms of minority rights that undermine these three preconditions of citizenship—e.g. forms of minority rights that enable minority-group leaders to exercise authoritarian control over group members, and that ensure that members of the minority can interact with the larger society only though these leaders. This is a common fear about proposals to incorporate religious law (discussed by Shachar), or about certain forms of indigenous self-government (discussed by Borrows). In such cases, members of the minority may lack not only the motivation to participate as citizens, but also access to shared political forums in which they can participate.

What is interesting to note, however, is that concern for citizenship virtue and participation is often invoked by *advocates* of minority rights. They argue that special attention must be paid to the circumstances and needs of diverse groups if they are to feel like full members of the society, and to acquire the capacity and opportunity to participate in society.

For example, citizens who do not feel part of a common community or political project will have a harder time trusting each other and making the occasional sacrifices and principled compromises that are part and parcel of democratic citizenship. Immigrant groups that feel alienated from the larger national identity are likely to be alienated from the political arena as well. Conversely, when the majority identity is not able to adapt in ways that enable immigrants or other cultural minorities to feel a sense of full membership in the society, then individuals from these groups are often stigmatized and treated in ways in which the majority does not treat its own members (think of the official harassment and intolerance of gays in many countries, the violent attacks on Turks in Germany, or the disproportionate 'attention' that the police in many predominantly white cities devote to black youths).

There is a parallel here with concerns about the erosion of a citizenship identity. Just as we cannot assume that there is a pre-existing common citizenship identity that is threatened by minority rights, so we should not assume that the motivation, capacity, and opportunity to participate as a virtuous citizen already exists. So far from eroding such pre-existing conditions, some minority rights may instead help create them.

Fears about Weakening the Bonds of Social Cohesion and Political Unity

In most of the cases we have discussed so far, concerns about threats to citizenship are, we believe, overstated. The impact on citizenship of minority rights, in most cases, is mixed and ambiguous, both enhancing and threatening aspects of democratic citizenship. Under these conditions, it is clearly unhelpful to talk as if there is a zero-sum relationship between minority rights and citizenship; as if every gain in the direction of accommodating diversity comes at the expense of promoting citizenship.

But there is one case where this sort of zero-sum approach may seem applicable—namely, the case of territorially concentrated national minorities who may contemplate secession. If the cultural identity for most members of a minority group is stronger than their citizenship identity in the larger state —e.g. if they feel more Scottish than British or more Catalan than Spanish— then it may come to feel natural for them to have their own state, or at least most of the autonomy of an independent state. And, as we noted earlier, the goal of minority nationalists is precisely to legitimize and strengthen this sense of separate nationhood. Providing rights of self-government or extending federal autonomy gives minority leaders institutions and legislative jurisdictions with which they can progressively strengthen the minority cultural identity at the expense of the statewide citizenship identity. Can we not say, at least in this instance, that minority rights directly threaten citizenship cohesion?

As we learn from the ethnic-conflict literature, the most common response to this threat, even in democratic countries, has been to deny national minorities the kinds of autonomy and recognition that would encourage the development of their own identities. However, as the authors who discuss this problem here show, this is an incomplete picture of the mechanisms that lead to strengthening or weakening citizenship attachments among the citizens belonging to national minorities. For one thing, as Coulombe, Réaume, and Bauböck all emphasize, refusal to grant recognition and autonomy to such groups is often likely to provoke even more resentment and hostility from the members of the national minorities, alienating them further from their identity as citizens of the larger state. In addition, Coulombe highlights the way minority nationalist movements can be driven not only by minority-led regional governments exercising their powers of self-government, but also by heavy-handed attempts from the central government to promote a statewide identity that national minorities find threatening. Finally, both Bauböck and Smith emphasize the importance of balancing the centripetal forces of recognition and autonomy with other federally guaranteed individual rights and non-territorial group rights. Such a 'cocktail' of rights would reduce opportunities for injustice and could reinforce the sense of citizenship in the larger state for members of national minorities as they come to see both the central and regional governments as guarantors of their rights.

In sum, whether we are concerned with citizenship status, identity, virtue, or cohesion, the relationship between minority rights and citizenship is more complicated than it might initially appear. We can see legitimate worries about the potential impact on citizenship, but also countervailing arguments showing that some minority rights can actually enhance citizenship. It is impossible, therefore, to make any sweeping generalizations for or against the impact of minority rights on citizenship.

This is not, of course, an argument for ignoring or discounting the relevance of citizenship when evaluating minority rights. It is important to determine not only whether particular proposals for minority rights are consistent with principles of justice, but also whether they would enhance or erode desirable qualities of democratic citizenship. The shift from justice-based to citizenship-based arguments about minority rights is a useful and necessary broadening of the debate. Our argument is simply that this question must be examined empirically, in specific contexts, rather than prejudged on the basis of a priori speculation or anecdotal evidence.

8. Conclusion

Throughout this Introduction we have tried to give an overview of the range of cases where minority rights and citizenship interact, and of the sorts of potential (or perceived) threats that minority rights can pose for citizenship. Perhaps the key lesson we have learned is the sheer complexity of the issues.

No one can rest content with the sort of rhetorical generalizations that characterized the 'culture wars' of the 1980s and early 1990s. Critics of minority rights can no longer claim that minority rights inherently conflict with citizenship ideals; defenders of minority rights can no longer claim that concerns about civility and civic identity are simply illegitimate attempts to silence or dismiss troublesome minorities.

What, then, is the way forward? In principle, one *might* be able to imagine a research project that set itself the mammoth undertaking of examining how each sort of minority right claimed by each sort of group affected each aspect of citizenship in every given political culture. Needless to say, our aim in this volume is not to give such an encyclopaedic examination of these issues. We do hope, however, that the chapters in this volume provide a representative sample of the debates, drawing on a wide range of groups, rights, and citizenship ideals; not to mention academic disciplines and intellectual traditions. They embody the sort of fine-grained analysis that we believe is required in this area, where theory and practice learn from each other in turn.

PART I

Citizenship Education and Religious Diversity

PART II

2

Discrimination and Religious Schooling

EAMONN CALLAN

> After all, if we're concerned with identity, then what is more legitimate
> than one's aspiration that it never be lost?
>
> (Charles Taylor)

I. Ontario's Policy Dilemma

Policies that accord public recognition to cultural minorities are commonly
represented as a relatively recent strategy for coping with the deepening
pluralism of liberal societies. They are also routinely condemned for eroding
a sense of shared citizenship and departing from the norms of impartial
treatment that befit free societies. But these views are both historically and
morally dubious. For example, in Canada and elsewhere group recognition
for religious minorities has been an integral part of educational policy since
the very beginnings of mass schooling in the middle of the nineteenth century. To be sure, denominational school rights raise hard questions about
discrimination, as well as the maintenance of civic cohesion. But these rights
have served important social ends, and it is an open question whether the advantages they create for minorities must militate against common citizenship
or arbitrarily bestow privileges on some groups at the expense of others. My

---

This chapter is a coda to the argument about religious schooling I make in ch. 7 of *Creating
Citizens* (Callan 1997). I claim there that parents have no basic right to publicly funded religious
schools, although I note as an aside that the benefit of publicly funded education might
nevertheless be distributed in discriminatory ways. When I made that aside, I did not think
religious discrimination in the allocation of educational resources was as difficult a problem as
I now do. The argument of the chapter differs from the book in another way. In the book, I
defend a specific conception of civic or common education that draws heavily on the work of
John Rawls, and that conception is the basis for my argument for the common school. Here I
work with more general premisses about the relation between civic education and deliberative
democracy, and many who accept the general premisses might reject my Rawlsian conception.

purpose in this chapter is to explore the normative foundations of policy on the funding of religious schools in liberal democracies, using the case of Ontario, Canada's largest province, to elucidate considerations that have relevance beyond Canada.

To understand the problems that currently beset the state's relation to religious schools in Ontario, we need to understand the historical origins of existing policy. In nineteenth-century Ontario and Quebec religious differences marked deep political fissures, and a common education that prescinded from religious conviction was acceptable to scarcely anyone. Common schools in both provinces would cater to the creed of the majority. But since the religious majority in each was the minority in the other, almost everyone had reason to support a *modus vivendi* that would cater to minority demands in both provinces. Agreement on school rights for the Protestant minority in Quebec and the Catholic minority in Ontario was critical to the very creation of the Canadian state (Axelrod 1997: 30–1). These rights could be cogently defended on civic grounds, as a means of establishing the rudiments of political cohesion and a public culture of mutual toleration.

But this civic argument for state-sponsored religious education is inevitably weakened in the wake of secularization. Once religious antipathies are softened and schools that encourage the mingling of children across divisions of creed become a widely practicable undertaking, policies that favour them will seem to many people to be more congruent with the core values of liberal democracy. Solidarity and mutual understanding for a diverse people are best served by the experience of non-denominational schooling, or so one familiar line of argument goes. Less high-minded considerations play a role here as well. If public support for religious schools is no longer needed to keep civil peace, it is condemned as wasteful when government must be frugal (Patterson 1992). These arguments have not won the day in Ontario. But they have some appeal wherever denominational school rights are the legacy of a society more pervasively religious than the one in which they currently obtain.

Yet the cultural context of educational policy in Ontario has changed in another way as well. Guarantees of support for Catholic schools, combined with common schools that taught the creed of the Protestant majority, once ensured that almost everyone could send their children to a school consistent with their faith. Other religious groups were not sizeable enough to be of any political consequence. But as religious diversity has grown in Canada, in large part as a consequence of immigration, so too has the political significance of groups who are not beneficiaries of state support for religious schools. The increasing public assertiveness of minorities, coupled with a heightened awareness of the evils of exclusion and discrimination, have fuelled demands for the extension of state funding beyond those who were its original beneficiaries. Moreover, the same processes of secularization that have weakened the civic argument for religious schools have also swelled the ranks of those who cannot reconcile common schooling with their most basic beliefs. The ubiquity of secularization means that any common school will tend to reflect a culture repugnant to many who are religiously devout. In recent decades the solidly Protestant orientation of Ontario's common schools has gradually given way to what is now a thoroughly secular ethos, and this in turn has spurred the growth of Christian private schools (Stamp 1985: 201–2). Conservative Protestants now often look to these schools to find an education congenial to them, and the state's failure to sponsor their choice is condemned as oppressive.

So Ontario's traditional practice of state sponsorship for Catholic but no other schools outside its common system is under siege from two opposing directions. Some say the tradition has outlived its original civic purpose and must give way to a thoroughly secular educational system, committed to both shared educational purposes that unite citizens and a steadfast neutrality towards the many differences that divide them. Alternatively, others say Ontario must enlarge the range of religious schools it sponsors, extending equal recognition to those whom policies designed for earlier times now unjustly exclude. This is Ontario's policy dilemma.

I approach the dilemma through a case decided by the Supreme Court of Canada in 1996. In *Adler v. Ontario*, the court rejected the argument of Jewish and Protestant parents that the Ontario Education Act, which restricts public funding of education to non-denominational public and Catholic separate schools, violated their rights under the Canadian Charter of Rights and Freedoms. Whether the court's decision was correct on the best interpretation of Canadian law is a question I am not competent to answer. My interest is confined to the principles of public morality that the case illuminates.

I begin by examining Justice L'Heureux-Dubé's closely reasoned dissenting opinion in *Adler*. L'Heureux-Dubé argued that the plaintiffs were indeed victims of discrimination, given the equality guarantees specified in s. 15 of the Charter.[1] The nerve of her argument was a principle of group recognition according to which the state should interpret the demands of equality. I want to assess the moral force of that argument. I suggest that so far as group recognition is morally relevant to public support for religious schools, it is best construed as a matter of respect for the rights of individual parents who seek access to such schools. I then consider how respect for those rights can be accommodated in public policies that eschew discrimination and are yet duly responsive to the importance of civic education.

---

[1] S. 15 (1) reads: 'Every individual is equal before and under the law and has the right to equal protection and equal benefit of the law without discrimination and, in particular, without discrimination based on race, national or ethnic origin, colour, religion, sex, age, or mental or physical disability.'

II. *Adler* v. *Ontario*

According to the majority holding in *Adler*, the Ontario Education Act did not discriminate against religious minorities. The financial disadvantage incurred by supporters of private religious schools was self-imposed because it could be avoided simply by sending their children to public schools. L'Heureux-Dubé disagreed. For the plaintiffs, the choice to send their children to religious schools was no mere preference; it was a matter of sincere religious conviction that they were required to do so. If claims of religious discrimination were dismissed once a disadvantage could be avoided by acting against religious conviction, then 'discrimination on the basis of religion will become an empty concept' (*Adler* v. *Ontario* 1996: 413). This meant that the funding provisions of the Education Act denied the plaintiffs the equal benefit of law guaranteed by s. 15 of the Charter. They did not enjoy the equal benefit of a publicly funded education because the public schools which purported to confer that benefit were institutions to which they had serious religious objections, not merely some whimsical aversion.

For L'Heureux-Dubé, what made the denial of equality a paradigmatic instance of discrimination in *Adler* was the moral centrality of the interest in perpetuating group identity that the law invaded and the socially marginal status of those who were harmed by that invasion:

At issue here are the efforts of small, insular religious minority communities seeking to survive in a large, secular society. As such, the complete non-recognition of this group strikes at the very heart of the principles underlying s. 15 . . . The distinction created under the Education Act gives the clear message to these parents that their beliefs and practices are less worthy of consideration than those of the majoritarian secular society . . . we cannot imagine a deeper scar being inflicted on a more insular group by the denial of a more fundamental interest; it is the very survival of these communities that is threatened (*Adler* v. *Ontario* 1996: 418)

Why should a reading of s. 15 be so sensitive to the circumstances of marginal social groups and the interest in perpetuating identity? Part of L'Heureux-Dubé's answer was that the equality guarantees are primarily intended to protect vulnerable groups, such as dissentient religious minorities, against majority tyranny (*Adler* v. *Ontario* 1996: 418). The other part is to be found in s. 27, which requires that the Charter be 'interpreted in a manner consistent with the preservation and enhancement of the multicultural heritage of Canadians'.[2]

---

[2] Although L'Heureux-Dubé emphasized the 'insularity' of the religious groups from which the plaintiffs came, there is no indication that these groups evinced the degree of civic

A legislative infringement of s. 15 may yet be constitutionally justified under s. 1 if it is 'demonstrably justified in a free and democratic society'. The judge acknowledged that the funding provisions of the Education Act did serve a legitimate purpose in a free society. Partiality for schools that are 'universally open and free to all' was intended to foster the virtues of a pluralistic and democratic society. But she insisted that the denial of all public support to private religious schools was too grievous a breach of the equality guarantees to be defensible. An acceptable course would instead be partial funding of private schools, including religious private schools. That practice was already implemented in five other Canadian provinces without adverse consequences for the public ends of a free and democratic society (*Adler* v. *Ontario* 1996: 419–27).

I return in Section VII to the question whether partial accommodation to demands for publicly funded religious schools might be morally fitting. I want now to examine L'Heureux-Dubé's more basic argument regarding discrimination.

III. Discrimination and Group Identity

A striking feature of the argument is the weight put on what the law *says* to people about their worth or comparative lack thereof. The financial prejudice endured by people who must pay for religious schools without any public support is no trifling matter. But L'Heureux-Dubé argued that the deeper issue was the 'complete non-recognition' of minority interests that the financial prejudice symbolized (*Adler* v. *Ontario* 1996: 417). She quoted from an earlier Supreme Court decision that captured the connection between equality and recognition on which her own argument depended: 'The promotion of equality entails the promotion of a society in which all are secure in the knowledge that they are recognized at law as human beings equally deserving of concern, respect and consideration' (*Andrews* v. *Law Society of British Columbia* 1986: 174). The plaintiffs in *Adler* could not be secure in that knowledge because the Ontario Education Act took no account of the interest in cultural survival at stake for them in access to religious schools.

But if the critical issue in discriminatory legislation is what the law says about the comparative standing of citizens, what is not immediately clear in L'Heureux-Dubé's judgment is how we are to distinguish between laws that honour equal moral standing and laws that do not. For the language in which her argument was framed alternates between seemingly incompatible

detachment that would make them 'partial citizens' in Jeff Spinner's sense. The education of partial citizens raises special problems for the liberal state which are not relevant here (see Spinner 1994: 87–112).

interpretations of what was fundamental to the plaintiffs' demands: an individualist depiction that stressed the educational needs of particular children and the rights of their parents; and a collectivist account, which gave primacy to equal group recognition and the preservation of group identity.

This makes it a curious argument for those of us familiar with Charles Taylor's influential distinction between a liberal polity shaped by the ideal of free and equal citizenship, with its perseverant focus on individual rights, and one in which group recognition is affirmed alongside a commitment to basic rights but is irreducible to them (Taylor 1992; 1993b: 174–9). Taylor says that it is precisely when political morality must reckon with questions about identity that friction arises between the two models of liberal society. The first can supposedly give no moral weight to policies aimed at sustaining an identity across time. It can support the preservation of cultural resources which future generations might have the 'opportunity' to use. But only on the second model can we justify policies that are 'a matter of making sure that there is a community of people in the future that will want to avail itself of this opportunity' (Taylor 1992: 176). Taylor's argument focuses on questions of linguistic identity, although his binary conception of liberal politics is presented as if it were widely applicable to the politics of identity.

On Taylor's conception, L'Heureux-Dubé's argument vacillates between the two versions of liberal society. Her emphasis on group recognition and its intimate connection to policies enabling the transmission of identity across generations would appear to make sense only on Taylor's second, mildly collectivist model of liberal society. After all, religious schools are hardly in the business of preserving a cultural resource which future generations will merely have the 'opportunity' to use; they are designed to reproduce communities of faith whose members see the meaning of their lives in terms set by those very communities. Nevertheless, the judge's allusions to respect for the dignity of persons as the very core of s. 15 points to the first, austerely individualistic model of liberal politics.

But this blurring of claims about respect for individuals and recognition for groups might not signal any equivocation in L'Heureux-Dubé's reasoning. Perhaps the point is that to give equal respect to individual human beings whose very identity is constituted by different religious commitments, the state must, in its educational policies, accord recognition to the religious groups with which they identify. Group recognition becomes the necessary vehicle of respect for the individuals who belong to them. Whether or not this is the most faithful interpretation of L'Heureux-Dubé's judgment, I suggest it is the only morally credible one that could be ascribed to her.

On the standard liberal interpretation of our interest in religious freedom and non-discrimination, it has to do with the centrality of religion to different, but equally respect-worthy ways of life (e.g. Richards 1986). The respect due to individuals is partly a matter of an impartial accommodation to the divergent religious beliefs and practices in which so many find their identity.[3] This does not mean that to engage in religious discrimination is always to impair the ability of its victims to keep their faith. A religious group subject to slightly higher taxes than others, for example, might be well able to pay them. But the symbolic force of discriminatory taxation still counts for much as a denial of equal respect. By attaching a social penalty to a particular identity, the law says that those who belong to the penalized group are second-class citizens. Nevertheless, the wrong done will increase so far as the penalty of discriminatory taxation does impair the capacity to continue practising the faith. If the penalty is substantial enough to encourage defection among younger and less committed members, say, then that makes matters worse.

Notice that the evil of discriminatory taxation can be explained here strictly in terms of the ideal of free and equal citizenship and the rights that common status entails. At the same time, the evil is aptly described in a language that makes explicit the importance of group recognition and its denial, as well as the interest that religious believers have in the continuance of their way of life across generations. That interest is crucial. For only very rarely does religious practice take the form of a purely hermetic devotion, indifferent to others and their future; it is far more commonly embraced through identification with a particular community of faith that one hopes to prosper over time. That hope is in turn nourished by the conviction that the relevant community embodies some unique and compelling truth about the proper conduct of human life. Whenever a scheme of taxation confers a second-class political status on those who belong to particular religious groups, and worse still, does so in a way that endangers their very survival—and hence, by their lights, the survival of understanding about how human beings should live—then we have a grave injustice.

The intuitive appeal of L'Heureux-Dubé's argument can be brought out by noting the parallels between the predicament of the plaintiffs in *Adler* and my imaginary case of discriminatory taxation. (The analogy is as misleading as it is illuminating, as we shall subsequently see. But it does help to make clearer why arguments like L'Heureux-Dubé's are so appealing to many.) In both cases, the law puts some religious minorities at a disadvantage relative to other citizens simply because of their religious identity. Thus, the law might reasonably be taken to express a lesser concern or respect for those who must bear the disadvantage than for others, and the injustice escalates so far as the disadvantage threatens the ability to perpetuate a cherished way of life. But if that is the wrong the law does in both cases, we are still firmly

---

[3] Michael Sandel has distinguished between a liberal conception of religious liberty which exalts freedom of choice and an older republican conception that expresses the centrality of conscience to religious identity. In what follows I make no basic distinction between matters of religious choice and matters of conscience or identity. I have argued elsewhere that Sandel's distinction is confused (cf. Sandel 1996: 62–7; Callan 1997: 53–5).

within the boundaries of Taylor's first model of liberal society. What is at issue is a putative affront to the equal dignity of some citizens because of their membership in minority religions. We do not need to appeal to any ideal of group recognition that would compete with the claims of individuals *qua* free and equal citizens.

In fact, any appeal of that kind is deeply counter-intuitive, and not merely unnecessary. If group survival mattered to policy regarding religious minorities in some way independent of respect for individuals, we would have reason to discourage through law any choices that would threaten the future of minority religions. But no one is arguing for discriminatory taxes against people who freely choose to abandon minority religions. Similarly, the plaintiffs in *Adler* were not arguing for compulsory religious schooling for children from Jewish or evangelical Christian families, regardless of their parents' wishes, and no one would have taken them seriously had they done so. The interest in the perpetuation of religious identity was a critical element in their case. But this was no more than the interest of individual parents in maintaining a faith that, on their understanding of its requirements, obliged them to provide a separate religious schooling for their children. Child-rearing is typically undertaken as one of the central, meaning-giving tasks of human life, and for religiously devout parents, no expression of faith is more fundamental than discharging the educational responsibilities it imposes.

A plausible demand for state-sponsored religious schools on grounds of non-discrimination has to be understood within a liberal framework of rights rather than a collectivist politics of group recognition. But that being so, the charge of discrimination cannot be vindicated merely by showing that certain religious groups are culturally vulnerable, and that ready access to religious schools is critical to their survival. In any culturally variegated free society, some established communities of faith will fade over time, others may expand, and new ones emerge. No doubt some marginal groups can explain their precarious condition in terms of oppression, and if they sue for state support that would help them survive, the justice of their case may be compelling. But the bare fact that a given community of faith is weak, and its survival is in doubt without some costly measure that the state does not currently provide, cannot itself make the denial of provision unjust. And if it is not unjust, it cannot be discriminatory in any sense that implies injustice.

To suppose otherwise is to assume that justice for a pluralistic society is, in part at least, a matter of trying to freeze communities of faith in their current forms. But that is an untenable assumption for a society of free and equal citizens. A certain fluidity of religious identity across generations is to be expected there as the rule rather than the exception. This holds good even in a democracy constitutionally committed to 'the preservation and enhancement' of its multicultural heritage. Under modern conditions of freedom, members of the same community of faith will routinely disagree about the form in which their community is worth preserving or what would enhance its future prospects. These disagreements will be evidenced in divergent choices that parents make about their children's education. Not all evangelical Christians, for example, want alternative Christian schools for their children. And divergent choices will contribute to the processes by which communities of faith wax and wane over time. By itself, the goal of preserving and enhancing the multicultural character of a society gives the state no reason to favour either orthodox or dissident views about what form of religious upbringing would be best in any given community of faith. But if we are considering what that goal might mean in a liberal democracy, then such decisions must be left to the free play of individual choice. The alternative would be to ride roughshod over parental choice, and that would surely violate basic rights in a manner that even Taylor's collectivist model disallows. The decline and disappearance of some communities of faith is a virtually inevitable consequence of the free exercise of choice under multicultural conditions, and so even if we prize diversity as a matter of public principle, that gives us no reason to infer that whenever a community's future is threatened, the failure of the state to mitigate the threat must be discriminatory.

The interest in the survival of communities of faith is one whose importance we can and should acknowledge within the basic structure of individual rights. But no clear deductive path can be found from premises about the fragile condition of this or that religious group to conclusions about the discriminatory character of educational policies that do not protect the group from future decline. So far as L'Heureux-Dubé's argument suggests otherwise, it is wrong.

IV. Three Types of Discrimination

What then would be a reasonable basis for identifying religious discrimination in educational funding policy? I want to concentrate on the most morally basic reasons that apply to that question, and so I set aside circumstances in which the charge of discrimination might be escaped just by showing that prohibitive financial costs would be incurred by acceding to demands for state-funded religious schools.

The charge of discrimination will be telling when any of three general 'types of discrimination' apply. The first is straightforward, but the second and third create serious obstacles to the development of morally defensible funding policies. First, discrimination holds when some religious schools are sponsored and others are not, and that discrepancy does not serve the legitimate ends of civic education. The second type will apply when the ethos of available common schools promotes contempt for some communities of faith who are denied support for their own schools. Thirdly, even if common schools are in fact open to all on terms of respect, partiality for them in funding policy may implement a trade-off between very slight or speculative gains in civic education against substantial losses in the efforts of religious minorities to reproduce their faith across generations. In that event, the policy is discriminatory, or so I shall argue. What is plainly distinctive of this approach is the prominence given to the ends of civic education.[4] The reason for this can be understood by contrasting my approach with L'Heureux-Dubé's.

As I noted earlier, L'Heureux-Dubé did not think a complete accession to the plaintiffs' demands in *Adler* was constitutionally required. Denying religious minorities full funding for their schools could be justified by the aim of fostering the virtues of a pluralist and democratic society 'including the values of cohesion, religious tolerance, and understanding' (*Adler* v. *Ontario* 1996: 421). Some fiscal partiality for secular public schools might serve those values better than any feasible alternative policy, and to that extent, partiality was defensible.

If we take this as an argument of public morality, it makes the ends of civic education relevant to the moral assessment of law only *after* the occurrence of discrimination has been established, and we are then asking if, all things considered, an infringement of equality rights is the best course to take. This will seem right if we assume with L'Heureux-Dubé that funding policies are discriminatory whenever they leave fragile communities of faith at a disadvantage in their efforts to survive. But that assumption has been refuted. My alternative approach makes civic education relevant to whether denying state support to religious schools is discriminatory in the first place. Why?

Citizens typically have an interest in the perpetuation of their religious identity, and for those who are parents, that interest will profoundly affect the educational choices they want to make on their children's behalf. The strength of L'Heureux-Dubé's argument is her sensitivity to the moral importance of that interest. But no less important than that is the common stake we have in the success of civic education. The government of a free people is a project that education must carry into the future in that children need to acquire the knowledge, capabilities, and virtues of citizens who bear the responsibility of collective self-rule. On no defensible conception of civic education for the complex circumstances of contemporary liberal democracies are its ends easily reconciled with all creeds and cultures that abound in our midst. Ideals of civility or mutual respect that sustain free government

---

[4] I do not assume a priori that civic education is the only basic moral consideration that might tell against acceding to demands for state-funded religious schools. The educational rights of children could also count against accession. But I think these rights are such that they can be adequately protected in a suitably regulated system of separate religious schools. It is less clear that the more onerous ends of civic education can always be served well enough in that context. (See Callan 1997: 147–61, 178–93.)

cannot be divorced from the development of critical reason in public deliberation, and not all ways of life will thrive when children learn to think critically
about what mutual respect demands of them.[5] (I explore an example of this
kind of learning in Section VI.)

If some partiality for common, secular schools serves civic education, then
the partiality is not morally arbitrary. And this is where the analogy between
discriminatory taxation and the denial of publicly funded religious schools
unravels. The victims of discriminatory taxation will rightly say that they are
singled out to bear a special disadvantage for no other reason than the contempt they elicit among those with the power to make law. But if a given
policy effectively serves the ends of civic education, and yet does so in a way
that leaves some at a disadvantage relative to others in the perpetuation of
religious identity, the case for claiming discrimination is at least incomplete.
The purpose that informs the policy is as legitimate as any other, and it
remains to be shown why we cannot endorse the policy by virtue of that
purpose without foisting a degraded standing on those for whom it creates
some special burdens.

This does not mean that the charge of discrimination could never be telling
against a funding policy that serves civic education better than any alternative.
My claim is that respect for particularistic religious identities and the imperatives of civic education are distinct and potentially conflicting considerations to
be balanced in just educational policy. The third type of discrimination makes
it clear that these can sometimes be weighed so as to deny equality to religious
minorities. Of course, once the truth of claims about discrimination are seen
to hinge on a judicious balancing of rival considerations, they must also be
recognized as often more indeterminate, and hence more open to reasonable
disagreement, than we might ideally like them to be. But I fail to see how any
alternative approach can encompass the moral complexity of the issue.

V. Discrimination in *Adler*

I want now to look systematically at the three types of discrimination I have
identified and to consider what appropriate remedies might be. The context
of *Adler* includes a flagrant example of the first type.

---

[5] The extent to which an acceptable civic education engages critical reason is rightly emphasized by Spinner: 'The intellectual capacities of liberal citizens must be developed; they
should be given the tools necessary to make intelligent decisions about government and
politics. Without the development of these capacities, citizens will not be able to watch over
government very well; they won't be able to participate intelligently in politics' (Spinner 1994:
93). Spinner goes on to note that these capacities will inevitably affect how citizens conceive
and pursue their own good in private life as well. (See also Callan 1997; Macedo 1995a.)

   The original terms of Canadian Confederation in 1867 protected existing rights to publicly funded schools for the Catholic minority in Ontario and the Protestant minority in Quebec. According to s. 29 of the Charter, its provisions cannot detract from these rights. But until the middle of the 1980s public support for Catholic schools in Ontario had excluded the final three grades of secondary education. The provincial government then introduced legislation ensuring equal funding between Catholic and non-denominational public schools for all grades. Nothing was done to extend support to other religious schools. The Supreme Court eventually found not only that the government of Ontario had acted within the law; full funding for Catholic schools was constitutionally required because it restored to Catholics rights that had been guaranteed at Confederation and subsequently denied (Lawton 1989). A revealing passage from the judgment of the Ontario Court of Appeal on the same case was quoted, with approval, at the end of the Supreme Court decision: 'These educational rights, granted specifically to the Protestants in Quebec and the Roman Catholics in Ontario, make it impossible to treat all Canadians equally. The country was founded upon the recognition of special and unequal educational rights for specific religious groups in Ontario and Quebec' (*Reference re an Act to Amend the Education Act* 1986: 64).

   The plaintiffs in *Adler* tried to revive the argument that the privileged position of Catholic schools was discriminatory. But the argument was unsuccessful, even with L'Heureux-Dubé. Suppose for the moment that the argument is indeed without merit in Canadian law. The inequality that the Supreme Court legitimized is still discriminatory on any morally credible reading of equality.

   The discrimination at issue here does not result from the mere fact that some religious schools are publicly supported and others not. On the contrary, under any defensible funding policy, public support for religious as for other schools will come with strings attached, and inequality is the predictable outcome. Schools will have to show, for example, that they are adequately preparing children for the rights and responsibilities of citizenship. Some will not pass the test of adequacy, and then the state must decide whether they should be closed or merely unfunded but tolerated. This will almost certainly mean that some communities of faith enjoy publicly supported religious schools and others do not. That inequality is not unjust so long as the standards of educational adequacy tied to sponsorship are defensible and fairly applied. But this is not at all like the discrepancy we find between Catholic and other religious schools in Ontario. The special position of Catholic schools does not derive from their meeting politically enforced standards of educational adequacy that the others fail to meet; it derives only from the fact that they are Catholic and the others are not. The status quo *says* that only Catholics, along with those sufficiently secularized to find non-denominational schooling congenial, are deserving enough or trustworthy enough to receive public support for their schools, no matter how good by any relevant measure other schools might be. This is morally indefensible religious discrimination if anything is.

Why not end such discrimination simply by ending all support for religious schools? Something like this possibility was broached in the British government's Swann Report, *Education for All*, over a decade ago. The inquiry which produced the report was in part prompted by demands from Muslims in Bradford and Brent for state-aided Muslim schools. Catholics, Anglicans, and Jews could have state-aided schools in Britain. Why not Muslims? Swann did not directly recommend the withdrawal of state support from all religious schools. But he did suggest that the best solution would be the development of a religiously pluralistic ethos in all existing state schools, so that Muslim children could be welcome there and the demand for separate schools obviated (Swann Report 1985: 474–5, 508–9).

John Haldane's baffled response to Swann's proposal is worth quoting:

How could it satisfy the Muslim wish for their own religious schools, to be required to send their children to secular institutions? And what view should they form of a society that would respond to their expression of deep attachment to tradition by casting off its own inheritance? Of course, the latter gesture is a demonstration of tolerance and respect for pluralism; but, if the host society has so little respect for its own culture as no longer to require transmission of its religious traditions and the associated system of values, might one not doubt the seriousness of its regard for Muslim and other essentially religious immigrant cultures? (Haldane 1986: 164).

Now the crucial question is not whether Muslims would be 'satisfied' by the solution proposed by Swann. Little is more common in democratic societies than citizens being less than satisfied by the state's failure to give them all they want. The crucial question is whether the kind of solution proposed by Swann could treat Muslims with due respect.

I think Haldane would agree. The thrust of his argument is that all religion is trivialized when the inheritors of rival creeds are cast together in a common educational environment, and religious scruples and practices are celebrated as so many charming ornaments of ethnicity rather than the lineaments of 'profound religious-cum-ethical commitments' (Haldane 1986: 164). Moreover, it would be the height of naïvety to suppose that in that environment everyone would, at last, be treated without discrimination. For the environment as described is one in which no one is treated with respect who invests religious commitment with the gravity it entails inside traditional communities of faith. Contempt does not always take the shape of hostility or even explicit disagreement; it can be registered in the smiling faces of those who find us perfectly agreeable but cannot or will not take seriously our own self-understanding.

This is where the second type of discrimination becomes applicable. We do not treat members of religious minorities (or majorities) with respect when we deny everyone's demands for publicly funded religious schools and supply an alternative that cannot be squared with serious faith. Haldane is wrong to assume that common schooling must come to grief in the trivialization of religion. The very fact that many religiously devout people choose to send their children to such schools, even when other options are readily available, suggests that the trivialization of faith is not inevitable. But Haldane is right to the extent that common schooling is susceptible to that evil, and liberals are often myopic about the difficulties of avoiding it.

VI. Diversity, Respect, and the Common School

What is needed to treat members of different religions with respect in common educational institutions? It will help to proceed indirectly, by way of an example.

Patricia White has argued for compulsory sex education in schools that would, among other things, address the vexed issue of homosexuality in a morally partisan manner. The basis of her argument is a principle of respect for persons, which she presents as fundamental to democracy. White distinguishes between an affirmative, emotionally embracing respect that ministers to the flourishing of others, and the more grudging, 'stand-offish' attitude that qualifies as respect only in a thinner sense. After laying waste to a number of bad but commonly endorsed reasons for condemning homosexual sex, she concludes that 'if a democratic community is to live up to its name, its educational provision must ensure not only the tolerating of, but the flourishing of these [gay and lesbian] minorities' (Patricia White 1991: 407). So democracy requires that a morally affirmative attitude to homosexual activity prevail in state-mandated sex education; that at least is what I assume to be the point of White's insistence on the need to get beyond mere tolerance.

What attitude to those who identify with religious traditions that condemn homosexual sex would be expressed through the sex education White prescribes? She concedes that religious views on homosexuality can be taught in the school as part of comparative religion. 'The school can teach . . . that Christians hold that homosexuality is sinful. What it cannot do, is to teach that homosexuality is not only contrary to certain religious doctrines (as e.g., the eating of certain foods might be) but is *for that reason* morally wrong' (Patricia White 1991: 403–4). Indeed, White does not merely want schools to avoid instructing students to make that inference; she must want students to learn the inference is a mistake because, without that lesson, her final conclusion about the need to encourage a positive moral attitude to homosexuality could not be sustained. The trouble is that all children would thereby have to learn that the concept of sin has no moral relevance. An antipathy to sin could permissibly operate only within the interstices of moral requirements, as secular reason defines these. Religious believers are thus granted a certain acceptance. But that is conditional on the inculcation of a reading of their faith that makes it scarcely recognizable to them. 'Morally irrelevant religious taboo' simply will not do as even a rough synonym for 'sin'.

White resists the traditional understanding of sin as a centrally important moral category for religious believers because it appears to stand in the way of her conclusion that children must be taught that nothing is wrong with homosexual acts. But agreement on the moral status of homosexual acts is no more necessary to reasonable consensus on how homosexuals should be treated in the polity and civil society than is assent to the one true faith necessary to consensus on how religion should be accommodated by the state. The relevance of homosexuality to issues of public morality is integral to an acceptable civic education. And religious conservatives who are not cavalier about persecution and discrimination, whoever the victims of those evils might be, will agree. Their agreement does not, however, require them to endorse a comprehensively liberal sexual ethic or to divorce all morality from religion.

Now White is right to this extent: we cannot simply bracket the question of whether homosexual sex is wrong in order to address political questions about gays and lesbians that arise at the intersection of sex education and civic education. We cannot do that because many students will think homosexual sex wrong for reasons (including religious reasons) that they think suffice equally for legal prohibition, discrimination, or worse. Treating these students with respect will mean addressing their reasons with due charity *and* due criticism; it may even mean introducing arguments better than the ones they adduce themselves, especially when—as I suspect will often be the case—all they can offer in support of pre-reflective judgement is a visceral aversion to homosexuality or a bare appeal to sacred texts. Still, we have no reason to force this process towards closure on whether or not homosexuality is indeed innocent or wrong, all things considered, and the effort to do so will needlessly impugn convictions that prevent no one from living in mutual respect with others. No one has to abjure all religious authority on moral matters to be a decent citizen, even if everyone must think long and hard about the limits of that authority in a world where many people cannot fairly be expected to heed its deliverances.[6]

6 The argument I make here differs from White's in that she focuses directly on the relation between sex education and the overall well-being of children, whereas my narrower concern is the civic aspect of sex education. The wider and narrower perspectives might yield different

Yet so far as arguments are canvassed that purport to warrant public condemnation of homosexuality, as opposed only to the adverse judgement of the devout conscience, they are placed before the bar of common deliberation. If the deliberation is competently conducted, it is difficult to envisage the arguments faring well under conditions of pluralism. Stephen Macedo's generous assessment of a sophisticated natural law argument for state action intended to discourage homosexuality is the best that might be expected: 'These reasons are too open to reasonable disagreement to furnish a basis for demarcating fundamental rights and liberties in a regime properly dedicated to the authority of public reason' (Macedo 1995b: 329).

Macedo's appeal to 'the authority of public reason' here is crucial. I take it that what he has in mind is something like this. There is a moral discipline in learning to think about the shared world of politics and civil society with fellow citizens (or future fellow citizens) whose creed, culture, or sexual orientation may mark them as profoundly different. Mutual respect in that setting cannot evade sharp disagreement, nor can identity be insulated from the doubts—and sometimes the transformations—that new thoughts bring in their train. Arguments that seem compelling inside some more parochial shared world may fall apart once they are transposed to that larger arena, where the scrutiny of people with whom one shares fewer assumptions and less history will shake cherished certainties. But one cannot just ignore these people, because they too are fellow partners in a community of free and equal citizens, and they too must speak and be listened to with respect. The argument that Macedo dismisses might secure the confident assent of all in some more ethically homogeneous political environment than the one in which he writes. But ethical homogeneity is not the hallmark of the contemporary liberal state.

To give respect to someone is to make what Bernard Williams calls 'the effort at identification' that we owe that person: 'he should not be regarded as the surface to which a certain label can be applied, but one should try to see the world (including the label) from his point of view' (Bernard Williams 1969: 117). For many people, that 'point of view' is one in which faith is no mere label attached to the surface of the self; it is a constituent of the self, and the judgements regarding sin and piety that faith informs shape their moral outlook. Yet under pluralism, the effort of identification required of all will impose strains on identity even as identity is honoured. The religious

conclusions if the right to an adequate education were infringed whenever the school did not teach that homosexual sex is morally innocent. But I do not think that is true. Children certainly have a right to an education that will help them to think in an informed and critical way about homosexual sex and much else. They have that right because such learning is basic to their well-being. I also think that when that right is respected, not many will end up thinking there *could* be anything wrong with homosexual sex. But that is not the same as saying that all must be taught that homosexual sex is morally innocent.

believer to whom the effort is owed also owes it to the infidel, and mutual identification will modulate into mutual criticism, as well as the self-criticism that can take our lives in unpredictable directions. The criticism is intrinsic to the respect, since we give and receive respect as beings amenable to reason, not merely as bearers of a fixed identity, irrevocably sundered from our capacities for choice and understanding. The critical edge of respect means that we cannot always endorse the other's identity; it will sometimes even fall short of the 'stand-offish' tolerance to which White alludes. I may be treated with all due respect in learning that what I have believed is politically intolerable.

When religious believers demand respect for their beliefs and practices in public institutions, they will often have in mind something very different from the potentially subversive mutual respect I have been describing. They want their religious identity celebrated, and anything short of celebration will be rejected. The proposal that the respect they want could be given in common schools that encourage the mutual respect of equal citizens will then seem preposterous. But here again, we need to distinguish between policies that give people what they want and policies that answer to what is legitimate in their grievances. Common schooling of the sort I have been describing is vulnerable to an important objection that has to do with legitimate grievances, not just thwarted preferences. The objection takes us to the third type of discrimination.

The picture of common deliberation I have sketched is alluring perhaps only so far as we grant certain assumptions about those who deliberate. We are invited to imagine interlocutors with robust but very different, and often religiously informed, identities. These particularities of identity will dispose them to see questions of social co-operation in ways that may provoke conflict. But they are mindful of this, and they are also aware that they owe others an effort of identification in the joint venture of devising terms of co-operation that would be mutually acceptable. Participation in that venture may precipitate changes in their own identity, and although these may be emotionally wrenching, they are the fruit of uncoerced rational thought, and hence not to be regretted in any sense that could justify forgoing shared deliberation.

This rather idealized model might work well for an ecumenical seminar at the Yale School of Divinity. But perhaps it bears little relation to what is typical or widely feasible in non-denominational schools as we know them. Children or even adolescents from devout families do not necessarily have much understanding of the dialogical resources of traditions into which they have, as yet, only been very partially inducted. What they can say on their own behalf when faith bears on some matter of common deliberation may be easily discredited by adults or other students who have even less understanding of the relevant traditions. Especially when students belong to some small, embattled religious minority, the confidence even to say what others will think foolish or antiquated will be hard to find. The obvious worry here is that religious identity will be lost even before it is achieved. That will happen not because conviction has succumbed to the force of the better argument in colloquy among free and equal citizens; it will be lost because without yet understanding the life of faith, children have come to feel it is something odd or shameful in a world whose predominant values declare it to be so.[7]

The concern I have described could no doubt often be allayed with better common schools. To the extent that it could, the second type of discrimination would be circumvented, and many religious people who are currently averse to common schooling might come to find it acceptable. But even with the best common schools, attendance might still have significant corrosive effects on some communities of faith that flowed not from the legitimate pursuit of civic education but from the sheer pressures of cultural conformity that such institutions will perhaps inevitably exert on minorities.[8] This is speculative, but not, I think, unreasonably so. Where these conditions hold, we cannot simply dismiss demands for state-supported religious schools on the grounds that common schools are available to all in which diverse faiths are treated with respect. If some communities of faith are still denied the benefit of a publicly funded education, except on terms that gravely threaten their ability to perpetuate their identity, they can rightly complain that this is unjust unless the policy demonstrably serves an important social purpose and secures a reasonable trade-off between that purpose and the special burdens they are made to bear. Because those burdens impinge heavily

---

[7] Assimilative pressures may be powerful, irrespective of how tactfully religious differences are treated. For example, Eleanor Nesbitt describes the predicament of a British girl of Punjabi origin who enjoyed participating in an important Hindu ritual that involves staining the hands with henna. At school the girl endured the incomprehension of teachers who did not understood why her hands were sometimes 'dirty' and the scorn of other children who said she 'stank'. The moral of the story for Nesbitt is that teachers of Hindu children must have a sympathetic understanding of Hindu culture (Nesbitt 1993: 88–9). That is excellent counsel of a kind that is relentlessly belaboured in the literature on multicultural education. But it obviously does not solve the whole problem, and perhaps nothing can within the confines of the common school. For even with suitably enlightened teachers, it will take more than a little courage to come to school with stained hands when the school is part of a culture in which almost everyone makes a great fuss about cleanliness.

[8] Shelley Burtt has argued that religious misgivings about the common school often stem not from any aversion to individual autonomy or other liberal ideals but from fears about the 'aggressive secularism' of mass culture and the pervasiveness of that culture within common schools (Burtt 1996). For a sober and disturbing analysis of the way in which the curriculum may come to embody an anti-religious secularism, see Strike (1990). Concerns of the sort that Burtt and Strike raise are obscured by the widespread thesis that the civic purposes of schooling have a lexical priority over other values. My account of discrimination denies that civic purposes have any such priority.

on a morally fundamental interest, a willingness to impose them on some groups for the sake of slight or highly speculative social gains smacks of discrimination.

VII. The Value and Limits of the Common School

The third type of discrimination compels us to think hard about the rationale of common schooling. What purpose is served by systematic partiality in educational policy for schools that attempt to welcome the children of all citizens, regardless of religious or other social cleavages, and which reflect in their composition the diversity of the citizenry itself? I have suggested that the justification must lie in the ends of civic education. But that justification is far less transparent than many friends of the common school suppose.[9] Some well-functioning liberal democracies do not favour the common school,[10] and in Canada and the USA there is often more rhetoric than substance in our commitment to that particular institutional form. We also know that some religious schools seem to be effective in promoting civically important abilities and dispositions.[11] So what is the point of the partiality?

The best argument connects the common school as a vehicle of civic education to the ideal of deliberative democracy. That connection has already been intimated in what I said about learning to think in civically defensible ways about issues such as homosexuality. But I do not think the best argument for the common school can always be decisive, and reconciling the value of common schooling with non-discrimination may often, given the importance of the third type of discrimination, warrant substantial concessions to those who demand state support for separate religious schools.

The phrase 'deliberative democracy' is of fairly recent vintage, and it will

---

[9] A widely held assumption among defenders of the common school is that claims for 'culturally segregated schools' are prompted by a rejection of liberal democratic values (e.g. Gutmann 1996: 165). No doubt that is often true. But no claim on the state is fairly assessed merely by dwelling on the worst reasons for making the claim.

[10] The most interesting example here is the Netherlands, which provides full funding for all religious schools. The Dutch system is routinely invoked as the very model of desirable change by devotees of schools choice elsewhere in the world. Less often noted is that Dutch law offers support to religious schools at the price of exacting state regulation. Twenty-eight of the thirty-two hours that comprise the school week must be devoted to the mandatory state curriculum, which includes such contentious matters as sex education; only certified teachers can teach; and although teachers may be hired partly on the basis of religious criteria, they cannot be fired for religious reasons (see Walford 1995; Sweet 1997: 131–4).

[11] American Catholic high schools appear to be an example. See the remarkable study by Bryk *et al.* (1993). A cogent philosophical defence of the compatibility of separate religious schooling with liberal civic values is offered in McLaughlin (1992).

mean little to people outside the boundaries of contemporary political theory.[12] But the ideal it names animates a current of thought that runs deep in the political culture of secure democracies. According to the ideal, the political self-rule worth having is deliberative in that the institutions through which self-rule is enacted must elicit widespread, reflective participation of a particular kind. The necessary participation is a distinctive moral engagement in which citizens, through open discussion in which diverse views are voiced and collectively evaluated, make, apply, and revise the norms by which their community lives.

What educational institutions might best serve the ideal? Consider an idea that is not specifically about the kind of schools we should have but about the more general problem of creating suitable institutional vehicles for common deliberation:

deliberative arenas which are organized exclusively on local, sectional or issue-specific lines are unlikely to produce the open-ended deliberation required to institutionalize a deliberative procedure. Since these arenas bring together only a narrow range of interests, deliberation in them can be expected at best to produce coherent sectional interests, but no more comprehensive conception of the common good. (Cohen 1989: 31)

The point here is not that exclusive deliberative settings will always tend to encourage intolerance or indifference towards outsiders. But since the purpose of common deliberation is to devise and interpret a mutually acceptable framework for social co-operation, and that framework must be adjusted to the many reasonable differences among us, parochial deliberative institutions will not lend themselves to a sufficiently 'open-ended' discourse. The common school, so far as it welcomes all on terms of equal respect, would seem to be just the kind of inclusive deliberative setting Cohen thinks we have reason to favour. Religious schools may encourage much else that is laudable from a civic standpoint, but they *cannot* be arenas for inclusive deliberation by virtue of their exclusive religious identity. For example, if we want inclusive deliberation on the standing of gays and lesbians in the polity and civil society, then a deliberative arena in which all take it for granted that homosexual sex is sinful, and therefore reprehensible, does not fill the bill. (By the same token, a setting in which everyone is compelled to agree that sin is morally irrelevant *also* does not fill the bill.) No doubt common schools as we know them are often less than impressive institutions

---

[12] The literature on deliberative democracy is large. Some important contributions are Manin (1987); Cohen (1989); Hurley (1989: 314–82); Fishkin (1992); Gutmann (1992); Gutmann and Thompson (1996); Christiano (1996). A very important investigation of the educational significance of deliberative democracy is Strike (1994), although the phrase 'deliberative democracy' does not figure in the article. The theory of deliberative democracy has obvious affinities with much older ideas of republican citizenship (see e.g. Pitkin 1981: 342–9).

according to the norms of deliberative democracy. Nevertheless, the ideal of common schooling is well adapted to the practice of inclusive deliberation; what defines the educational mission of religious schools must curtail that same practice.

But this argument for the common school cannot by itself parry the objection raised in the last section; it merely brings the objection into sharper focus. For the objection is partly about what makes a deliberative arena truly inclusive. We do not create the conditions of genuinely inclusive discussion merely by bringing together children or adolescents with different, partially formed identities, and getting them to talk about the public norms by which we should live. A prominent theme in the literature on deliberative democracy is the educational value of deliberation itself, its power to teach us about ourselves and the good of the political community in which we belong (e.g. Manin 1987: 354; Christiano 1996: 255–7). Yet that is only a half-truth, because deliberation that aspires to be inclusive may fail to be so in more than a nominal sense, and in that failure it may also be profoundly miseducative. If deliberation begins in an environment in which certain voices—religious voices, say—are just not taken seriously at all, then it is liable to end there as well, and its effects may be to reinforce culturally dominant voices in their sense of superiority and to degrade and silence others.[13] So the importance of inclusive settings to deliberative democracy can be readily conceded. But

[13] Lynn Sanders argues against deliberative democracy as an ideal for the USA in current circumstances because entrenched prejudices and inequalities will tend strongly to corrupt deliberation (Sanders 1997). I think Sanders confuses the need to promote a better understanding of inclusive deliberation with the need to reject the practice altogether until other political ends are accomplished. But her article is a potent corrective to complacency about the edifying effects of deliberation. Sanders focuses on differences of race and gender. Religious differences create some special difficulties for a conception of inclusive deliberation. A vexed question in contemporary political theory is what role (if any) religious argument might properly have in public deliberation (e.g. Audi 1989; Perry 1991; Greenawalt 1995). This is hardly the place to answer the question. But I do not think any plausible answer could simply silence the distinctively religious voice in public discourse. First, even if the search for arguments about the use of state power that are mutually acceptable will tend to squeeze out distinctively religious (and anti-religious) premises, the interest in expressing and perpetuating religious identity is so important to so many people, and, at the same time, such a powerful source of social friction given religious differences, that public morality will always have to reckon with how the interest is to be justly accommodated. And to whatever extent collective deliberation is about how different religious identities can be justly accommodated, we cannot expect it to achieve its end if we all must talk *qua* citizens as if we had no religious identity. Secondly, the distinction between political reasons widely acceptable to reasonable citizens and reasons that can carry weight only within a religious tradition is more elusive than it might seem at first glance. Secular liberal morality has deep historical roots in Christian tradition, and its development has commonly been enriched by alliance and dialogue with those who still belong within that tradition. The American civil rights movement is the most striking recent example. Insisting that we cannot even begin to engage in public deliberation without effacing religious identity threatens to impoverish us all. On the latter point, see Waldron (1993b).

it does not follow that everyone has reason to trust common schools to be inclusive. Moreover, as we saw in the case of the third type of discrimination, even if that worry could be laid to rest, common schools might still impose heavy costs on religious minorities that cannot be adequately justified by considerations of civic education.

No one political response to this impasse can be deemed best, always and everywhere. But I want to indicate a possible response that acknowledges both the value of common schooling as a potentially inclusive deliberative setting and yet seeks to ease the reasonable anxieties religious minorities may have about the risks to identity that the same institution poses.

The school is among the very first significant associations which children enter beyond the family, and when they leave twelve or so years later, they are at the threshold of full citizenship if they are not voting already. Over the long transition from child to citizen, schools must somehow honour both the interest in identity formation that rightly belongs to parents and the interest we all share as members of a civic community. That being so, we might expect that a different balance between those interests will rightly be struck at different stages. For younger children in religious families, whose lives are still remote from the responsibilities of citizenship, and whose hold on their received religious identity is weak, a form of schooling that takes its bearings primarily from religious tradition may represent the most just balance between familial and civic interests in identity formation. Conversely, for the same children at a later stage of education, the moral demands of a public world in which many do not share their faith impinge urgently on their lives, and a school that takes the student directly into that world is perhaps the best course.

I do not suggest either that our interest in the formation of civic identity is irrelevant to the early stages of schooling or that concerns about religious identity count for nothing later on. The early stages of formal education might inculcate attitudes that are civically unacceptable, and these might be so deeply entrenched that later attempts to overcome them are likely to be unsuccessful. But a policy that combined state sponsorship of religious schools with careful regulation could surely address that problem. Similarly, if common schooling is the politically favoured institution later on, we must still secure an ethos that embodies equal respect for all and limits assimilative pressures that cannot be justified by civic education. But I think that task is at least more manageable when we can take for granted that religious students have in general some real understanding of and attachment to the religious traditions they bring into the common school.

The kind of policy I am recommending here, in which generous funding for religious schools during the early stages of formal education is combined with strong partiality for the common school during its culminating years, was the road not taken by the Ontario government when it established equal funding for Catholic and public schools in 1985.[14] If its purpose was to undo discrimination, then the government was addressing the wrong inequality. It was not the fact that Catholic schools were unfunded for the final three grades that was the problem; it was and is the fact that other denominational schools receive nothing. Perhaps granting the support already enjoyed by Catholics to other communities of faith, while continuing to withhold funding for the final grades of secondary schooling, would have pleased even fewer people than the course that the government did take. But I think in the long term the road not taken might have contributed something important to the ideal which L'Heureux-Dubé invoked as the very purpose of the Charter's equality guarantees: 'the promotion of a society in which all are secure in the knowledge that they are recognized at law as human beings equally deserving of concern, respect and consideration' (*Andrews* v. *Law Society of British Columbia* 1986: 174).

The aspiration that religious identity never be lost cannot be fully satisfied even in that ideal society. Some of the argument of this chapter is intended to show why that is so. And because religious identity is scarcely separable from the aspiration that it never be lost, educational policy regarding religious schools in liberal societies will always cause some conflict and much disappointment. Yet we can sometimes go further in meeting what is honourable in the aspiration than many contemporary democracies seem willing to go. A principled rejection of discrimination requires no less.[15]

[14] The Supreme Court's decision that full funding for Catholic schools restored rights that were established at the time of Confederation means that the policy I recommend here is not now feasible in Ontario, barring constitutional change. But that may not be an insuperable obstacle. Recent changes to the constitutional guarantees of denominational school rights in Quebec and Newfoundland indicate that the status quo in Ontario need not be irrevocable.

[15] I am very grateful to Shelley Burtt, Gordon Davis, Bill Galston, Will Kymlicka, Wayne Norman, Ken Strike, Lois Sweet, and Pat White for comments on an earlier version of this chapter.

3

Extending Diversity: Religion in Public and Private Education

JEFF SPINNER-HALEV

I want to begin by describing the spectre hanging over this chapter. It is an elementary or high school where students work by themselves in cubicles separated by partitions, studying—or memorizing—their lessons. Class discussions are not held; group projects are not undertaken. Teachers do not ask the class any questions. Instead, silence permeates the school, broken only by the occasional question to an adult monitor, who is usually not a certified teacher or even a college graduate. Before taking an exam, which a student takes when she is ready, a monitor will kneel and pray with her. When students pass the exam for one lesson, they go on to the next one.

This is a typical Accelerated Christian Education (ACE) school. ACE is a company in Texas that supplies schools with assignments and tests for students. These schools are low-cost, since teachers are not needed and most work is done alone by students.[1] ACE schools are one kind of the increasing number of parochial and private schools in the United States. A little over 100,000 students attended evangelical and fundamentalist Protestant schools in 1964–5; by 1988–9 that number had increased to nearly 1 million. Enrolments in non-denominational private schools increased during the same time period from nearly 200,000 to over 900,000 (Lieberman 1993: 19).[2]

ACE schools—and other parochial schools that emphasize memorization and obedience—should worry liberals on three grounds: what they teach in class, how they teach it, and to whom they teach it. Most accounts of education by political theorists emphasize the curriculum. They discuss the importance of learning about core liberal values, like mutual respect and equality. It is important to teach these values, but the ACE schools bring into sharp relief that how the curriculum is taught, and to whom it is taught, are also important. When some liberal theorists argue that teaching liberal

---

[1] One ACE school is described in Rose (1988).

[2] I am concerned here with parochial schools, but since my proposals apply to both parochial and (non-religious) private schools, I tend to use the terms 'private' and 'parochial' interchangeably.

values in public schools is so important that exemptions or accommodations for students who want to opt out of particular classes cannot be made, they do little to reach students whose parents yank them out of public schools and put them into private ones.

Not all parents who enrol their children in private schools do so to shield their children from liberal values. Some parents want their children to grow up within a particular community, while having their children exposed to the outside world. The private schools they send their children to may be quite different from the ACE schools, and emphasize critical thinking and mutual respect for all. This is a moderate separatist argument because it calls for shielding children from outsiders for a limited time. Once they reach the early teens it becomes time to expose them to the diversity of contemporary liberal societies. There is much to this argument, and I defend a version of it below, but I am wary of it when it leads to the conclusion that private schools deserve state funding. Some private schools pose little threat to liberal values, but others are like the ACE schools, and schools like these should not receive any state support.

Even without state support, however, parochial schools are growing. While some are worrisome from a liberal point of view and some not, their growth means liberals do need to rethink their arguments about civic education and diversity. Liberal arguments that emphasize the curriculum in public schools and ignore the fact that many religious students now attend parochial schools too often fall short of their goal to teach the liberal virtues to students. If parochial schools are allowed to exist, then that affects how we look at public schools. I argue below that the state should do more than grudgingly tolerate parochial schools. The guiding principle I employ here is one of inclusion. Inclusion does not always mean making every institution inclusive in the same way. It can mean acknowledging the importance of different kinds of schools, since a diverse polity may very well have both inclusive common schools and homogeneous parochial schools. These latter schools will often worry liberals who are concerned about raising good liberal citizens. I do not want to minimize this concern, and it is something I take into account as my argument unfolds.

Still, I argue that diversity should be extended in three ways. First, public schools should co-operate with parochial schools and home-schooled children, though I argue against direct public funding for parochial schools. Secondly, religious students and perspectives need to be fairly included in the curriculum and life of public schools. Though we hear much talk about diversity and multiculturalism in educational matters, religion wrongly often drops out of these discussions. Thirdly, when it is feasible, religious students ought to be given alternative assignments or texts if they ask for this accommodation. When religious perspectives and students are not included in school life, and when religious students are not accommodated, many religious students feel pushed into homogeneous parochial schools, where few liberal virtues are taught. My aim here is to allow for separate schools, while enticing parents to send their children to common, public schools, on a full- or part-time basis. This extension of diversity is the best way to aid liberal citizenship. A diversity that excludes religion and religious students is not very diverse and does little to help religious students learn the virtues of good liberal citizenship.[3]

1. The Case for Diverse Public Schools

One important problem with parochial schools (and with home schooling, which I will presume to be part of the private school option), is that they are not diverse. I am thinking here of diversity of ideas and diversity of ways of life. While it is true that many public schools have homogeneous student bodies in some ways—student bodies that are mostly white or black or middle-class—these schools can and often do have a large diversity of ideas. Students will have different religious backgrounds and come from families with different political affiliations in common schools. These students will learn that there are other ways of thinking about the world than what their parents tell them. They will have to consider the practices and ideas of others. They will (hopefully) learn to think for themselves and learn to respect those with whom they disagree. Diversity of ideas is one of the goods that common schools offer their students. A racially diverse school is an even better idea, since it means that students from different backgrounds can learn from each other—but it must be noted that some desegregated schools are permeated by hatred between members of different groups, and so their diversity doesn't really benefit many people.[4] Class diversity is similarly a good idea, but some schools are located in primarily poor or wealthy neighbourhoods, and so mostly draw their student body from one income class. Sometimes the best

---

[3] Before I begin my argument in earnest I want to make a note about the context of my argument. My setting here is the United States, but my argument works for liberal democracies that include immigrant societies and at least several religions. I assume here that religious identities are not tied to national identities, as they sometimes are around the globe. The combination of religion and nationality is often combustible, and complicates the matter of education. This is the case, for example, in many parts of the Middle East, the former Yugoslavia, Sri Lanka, and India. I also assume that there is no constitutional reason or long-standing tradition of providing direct state support for religious schools, as there is in Canada and Great Britain. Cases of this sort raise different issues from those I want to raise here, though parts of my argument may very well apply to the two latter cases.

[4] Enforced bussing sometimes only creates resentment among both whites and blacks who stay segregated within schools. Bussing also leads to whites fleeing public schools.

we can expect is a public school with diverse ideas and practices. While a school with a student body that is diverse by race and income would be better, a school with diverse ideas and practices could still encourage its students to think creatively and critically. It would encourage the virtue of liberal autonomy.

Parochial schools that are established to preserve a community need not be homogeneous. They can allow for diverse ideas; they can encourage their students to think critically about many issues. Still, the diversity in this sort of school will be less than in a common school. A school where all the students come from the same community, whose parents share certain key organizing principles in their lives, will not get students to see a wide variety of lives up close. In principle, the variety in many parochial schools that are meant to serve a particular community of believers will be less than in a common school that is meant to serve people with different beliefs. This should not be surprising, since this is the point of many parochial schools.

What common schools also show is that what matters in schools is not only what is taught, but also to whom it is taught. The same curriculum taught in a Jewish day school and in a common school does not mean students in both schools will emerge with the same sense and understanding of the lives of others. If students are to see up close other ways of life, this will mean talking on a regular basis with people who are different; it means befriending those with different ideas. Schools with a diverse student population give children the opportunity to learn about others in a real way, not just through books. Diverse schools enable students to learn how to co-operate with others and the importance of compromising with those who are different. Part of the purpose of public schools is to get children from different backgrounds together.

Heterogeneous schools allow different students to learn about one another and to learn how to work together. When students learn these sorts of things, they make for better citizens. The virtues that citizens have are learned in a complex world, which they learn when they confront people who are different from them. Learning about others is surely important. But learning *with* (and from) others is a better way to learn about other kinds of people and ideas. People who face others will, it is hoped, learn the liberal virtues of how to co-operate and compromise with people who are different; they learn how to listen to others and how to respond to them. They learn that others have different views from themselves, and that occasionally there are good reasons for these different convictions, and so they are worthy of respect. When they act as citizens, good citizens will not only think of themselves or their primary group (if they have one). Rather, they will think of the people who will be affected by different public policies and laws, and consider them when taking a position on an issue. They will learn that others have interests, and sometimes democracy calls for a compromise between those with different interests. Listening, negotiating, compromising, and thinking are all skills that are learned in diverse settings, including common schools.

The case for diverse public schools has informed considerable discussion about a recent court case, *Mozert* v. *Hawkins*. The case has been much discussed by liberals because it highlighted a radical religious challenge to a liberal education (*Mozert* v. *Hawkins* 1987). In this case, fundamentalist parents were told by the court that the schools did not have to exempt their children from courses they found offensive. The fundamentalist parents objected to these courses because they taught their children 'role-reversal' and exposed them to a variety of viewpoints and lifestyles without insisting that the fundamentalist interpretation of the biblical way of life was superior. The debate among liberal theorists about *Mozert* has centred around authority and curriculum in the public schools. Liberals argue about who should control a child's education, what kind of harm is done by exempting some children from certain classes, and what sorts of things should be included in the curriculum (Macedo 1995*a*; Gutmann 1995; Burtt 1994).

These debates are important, yet they typically and oddly omit a crucial fact: fundamentalist parents are increasingly taking matters into their own hands by yanking their students out of the public schools and sending them to private ones, or by home-schooling their children. When this happens, the debate between liberals about what exactly should be taught to students in public schools becomes meaningless, because few if any liberal virtues are taught in fundamentalist schools or by fundamentalist parents.[5] There is something curious in the lack of liberal concern about private schools and home-schooling. Liberals argue over how much responsibility the state and parents have to educate children, but if parents decide to opt out of public schools altogether, most liberals agree, the role of the state drastically decreases.[6] Parents can teach their children almost anything they want, with only a few restrictions, in private schools or at home. The much-discussed case about the Amish *Wisconsin* v. *Yoder* would probably not have taken place today. If the Amish were told by a state they had to send their children to school, they might very well decide to home-school them. Since the early 1980s many states have eased their restrictions on home-schooling, making this a possibility for most parents. While political theorists still argue about whether the Amish should have to send their children to public schools, the rise of home-schooling makes this issue purely academic.[7]

---

[5] Macedo (1995*a*) mentions the private school option in passing.

[6] Gutmann, for example, supports private schools, but with the caveat that they teach democratic values to their students (Gutmann 1989: 115–23).

[7] The theoretical issues at stake in *Yoder* still remain important, however. More theorists than I can list have discussed the *Yoder* case. See Spinner (1994, ch. 5); Macedo (1995*a*); Gutmann (1995); Macleod (1997); Shapiro with Arneson (1996); Dagger (1997). On the easing of restrictions on home-schooling, see Devins (1992).

2. Defending Parochial Schools

Current discussions of civic education and diversity do not recognize the growth and importance of parochial schools. Before I discuss how such schools should change liberal thinking about education and diversity, I first want to defend them. I want to put aside the curriculum in this defence, and argue that a good reason to send children to a religious school is to situate them in a community. A minority community that wants to retain its identity may very well have good reason to establish its own school. This community may want to teach their children to be autonomous, good liberal citizens; but they also would like to increase the odds that their children will remain part of their community. To give minority children a real choice about what community they will be a part of when they are adults may mean to stack the deck in favour of the minority community early on. Liberal diversity undermines particular communities, and so some communities may want to take extra measures to protect themselves.

Religious communities are marked by rituals and celebrations of faith, but public schools make it harder for the children of some communities to participate in their celebrations. Celebrations and rituals are not always private matters that can be performed in the evening. Some of them are celebrated or observed among the relevant community. Jewish holidays, for example, come at several times during the year (and never on the same date from year to year) and children who want to celebrate them have to miss school to do so. Typically, they will be one of a few students who do. Jewish students who keep kosher will not be able to eat at cafeterias in public schools. These students will also not be able to attend after-school events on Friday nights—football games, school dances, and so on.

Public schools are based on a weak Protestant model. The school calendar fits the needs of (some) Christians, as does the food. Recently there have been moves to accommodate minorities in public schools, but there are limits to these accommodations. Muslim students who want to skip lunch during the month of Ramadan will have a harder time keeping their daytime fast when they see their fellow students munching away at lunchtime. These students *can* skip lunch if they choose, but it would surely be easier to do so in a school where all students skipped lunch, and where lunch hour was temporarily suspended during the month. Jewish students that cannot attend schools on Jewish holidays will probably feel more comfortable at a school where the school is closed down on the holidays. If a school has only a handful of Jewish students that keep kosher, it may be extremely expensive to accommodate their needs in the cafeteria. Moving the high school institution of football to a different night is like trying to move a mountain. Schools may not be able to close for every religious holiday celebrated by their students—in some places there will be too many of them.

Some Jewish students try to maintain their practices despite their differences with the norms and practices of the public schools. For many, however, maintaining these differences is too hard, and conformity slowly sets in. Accommodating a minority doesn't change the fact that the minority will have different norms and practices from the majority. A community's practices are best kept up within the community. If Jewish students attend a Jewish school, they will not constantly find themselves at odds with the practices and norms of their school or their classmates. Instead, they will fit in; they will be able to celebrate their traditions without the everyday threat of their community's boundaries corroding.

The idea of maintaining a community and of maintaining faith are surely connected. One could, however, want one's children to attend a parochial school not (only) because of a belief in God, but to give the children a sense of belonging to a community enriched by a certain tradition. The default position in schools is the majority culture. Children may be taught in schools that they can lead many kinds of life, but their choices will surely be shaped by those around them. The idea for some Jewish students that they cannot attend football games because they happen to occur on Friday night may cause them considerable distress and confusion.[8] When most students talk about a popular television show that a Protestant fundamentalist is forbidden to watch because of its sexual nature, he will feel left out or perhaps ridiculed. Children are particularly impressionable, and the impressions they get in public schools will often lead them away from their minority community. The adults in these kinds of religious communities may rightly think that their children will have to figure out how to navigate between their faith and community and public norms when they are adults, but the longer this navigation can be postponed, the better chance the community has to survive.

Diversity, Community, and Individuality

Like any bureaucratic enterprise, schools must have some things that are standard: classes, the school calendar, and so on. But there is more to the matter than the calendar. A diverse school will stimulate individuality among students, an individuality that often works to undermine religious communities. In many ways, liberal diversity and liberal citizenship move hand in hand: liberal citizens are parts of different communities. Liberal citizens will come into contact with other kinds of people, which will expose them to different ideas and different practices. People who consider new ideas and practices are, in turn, autonomous. Autonomous citizens do not simply live

---

[8] High school football in some states takes place on Saturday nights.

by reason; they see up close different ways of living, and they talk to and spend time with people with different ideas about the good life. They will come to justify their way of life, or more likely they will change their way of life, sometimes in large ways and sometimes in small ways, as they encounter different ways of living and different ideas. This is what liberals hope will happen in diverse schools. Different (future) citizens will combine the ideas and practices they encounter in different ways. Each citizen will have a unique combination of practices and ideas, which will make up her individuality. The autonomous person lives her own life, a life she chooses, not a life given to her. Autonomous people live not by the dictates of public opinion but by their own dictates. Autonomous people 'use the resources of a pluralistic and tolerant culture critically to develop a valuable individuality'. They are 'immanent, interpretive critics of themselves, others, and their culture' (Macedo 1990: 226).9

This version of autonomy is familiar from Mill's *On Liberty*. Though Mill does not use the word autonomy, he clearly thinks of it in terms of individuality. He says that individuality need not mean eschewing all tradition: 'It would be absurd to pretend that people ought to live as if nothing whatever had been known in the world before they came into it; as if experience had as yet done nothing towards showing that one model of existence, or of conduct, is preferable to another.' Mill, however, clearly hopes that autonomous people will redefine tradition in their own individualistic ways: 'It is the privilege and proper condition of a human being, arrived at the maturity of his faculties, to use and interpret experience in his own way.' Mill wants people to have character, and to have character means making one's own choices, choices that come from the inside, not from the outside. People, on Mill's influential view of autonomy, should be inner-directed, not outer-directed. 'A person whose desires and impulses are his own—are the expression of his own nature, as it has been developed and modified by his own culture—is said to have character. One whose desires and impulses are not his own, has no character, no more than a steam-engine has character' (Mill 1991: 64, 67).

Here we see how diversity aids autonomy: citizens who confront one another, and learn from each other, will (hopefully) construct their own individuality. Yet this individuality, aided by diversity, works to subvert many religious communities. It is true that some religious communities want to shield their members, and particularly their children, from outside influences. It is these kinds of communities that especially trouble liberals. Living within a community, however, does not have to stifle autonomy, even if it sometimes does. It depends on how tightly the community is drawn. It is wrong to think

---

9 My discussion of autonomy here is indebted to Levey (1997). I should be clear here that individuality is not the same as individualism. A society that encourages people to discover and remake their identity in their own way is not necessarily encouraging people to look out for themselves while ignoring others.

that community and autonomy are always opposed to one another. For children 'to learn what it is have a way of life, they must first be given a way of life' (Gilles 1996: 971; emphasis removed). Children who grow up within a community—or communities—will have a deep understanding of a way of life. A child who grows up with a way of life can reflect on this life and decide what parts she would like to retain, what to reject, and what to alter. She can look at other ways of life and compare them to her own. A child who is given many different options about how she wants to live, and often chooses differently, will not experience any way of life deeply enough to give her a basis for comparison.

We can't experience every community in order to decide if we want to live within one. We can only deeply experience so many things in our lives. Religious conservatives will expose their children to a certain set of values. Religious and secular liberals will expose their children to a different set. Liberals worry that religious conservatives do not give their children enough choices about how to live, or allow their children to experience other ways of life. But religious conservatives can rightly ask how many liberals allow their children to experience a conservative religious life. To do so means more than attending church once a week. It means spending time living a life according to the rules of the church. A child raised within the church will eventually see that there are other ways of life out there. These children may see that their neighbours or schoolmates live differently from them.

Like religious conservatives, many liberals raise their children in a certain way with certain values. Their children see other ways of life, but they have a strong base in one particular way of life. It may be that the liberals try to expose their children to many kinds of life, but that they are still raised in a certain way with specific values. Some communities in which people are raised will be 'thicker' than others; some will expose their children to outsiders more than others. The worry, however, shouldn't just be about children raised in relatively closed communities. If the children will eventually be exposed to the lives of others, then in my view there is not much to worry about. We should worry when children are not raised with any values. When children have lots of choices, how will they be able to choose? How will they know how to value certain things and disdain others? People who are raised without any values, who are told they can choose any life they wish, may very well not know how to choose anything. We can't choose our way of life as we choose clothes; it is not something we try on for a few minutes and decide whether it fits after a quick look in the mirror.

Experiencing life in a community in a deep way does not need to mean teaching strict obedience to one way of life. Certainly this is what some people teach their children. Some religious communities, however, have traditions of debate about all kinds of matters; not every subject is up for dispute, of course, but those areas that are, are often debated rather vigorously. Both

Catholics and Orthodox Jews have traditions of strict obedience to their religious leaders—but also of spirited debate on many issues. This does not make those Catholics and Jews who are raised in sheltered communities good liberal citizens, but it does mean that they may very well learn the important debating skills that good liberal citizens have.

Living in a community can support autonomy; it also shapes the choices we have in our lives. This is true for liberals and religious conservatives alike. Community can be thought of as an 'enabling constraint': it enables us to be autonomous just as it restricts the choices we have. Enabling constraints are fairly common in our lives. Think of the rules of chess. The rules enable us to play the game, just as they restrict the way we can move the pieces. The rules of grammar work similarly. They restrict what we say and how we say it, but without some rules we would not be intelligible to others. People raised in a community are given values and a way of life that they can reject or revise when they are older. To say that children are raised in a community with a tradition, and not exposed to all the alternatives, is not to argue that they are not autonomous or to argue against community. Growing up within a secure tradition gives people the background to examine their choices and the choices of others.

My defence of religious schools assumes that these schools are not all-encompassing—it assumes that these are moderate and not conservative religious communities (see also Callan 1997, ch. 7). A community that tries to prevent its children from having any contact with outsiders, even as they become teenagers, is not combining autonomy and community. It is using the community to stifle autonomy. Such conservative communities are not the only communities committed to passing their way of life down to their children. A moderate community strives to pass its way of life down to its children, while still exposing them to the modern world so they can function within it as full members. It is possible that parents who send their children to parochial schools to situate them in a community may find other venues for their children to learn about and befriend others. They may be part of a softball or soccer league, or attend a camp that is not parochial. They might join the boy or girl scouts. Parents who are open to other communities but send their children to a parochial school for the first six or seven grades, or who send their children to both parochial and public schools on a part-time basis, are not threatening liberal citizenship.

Diverse schools can both encourage diversity and sometimes make it harder to maintain differences. This is not a paradox. There are different conceptions of diversity and difference at stake here. Liberal diversity supports an individuality that is antagonistic towards some ways of life. There are limits to diversity, limits that liberals should recognize. These limits are not just a matter of saying that those who have illiberal or anti-democratic practices have little or no place within a liberal democracy. Liberal diversity runs counter to the desire of some people to maintain minority religious communities. Yet the diversity within these communities will often be minimal. A pluralistic society, it seems to me, will allow for both diversity and group difference. This means having both common and parochial schools.

3. Financing Schools

It is to be hoped that more rather than fewer of these parochial schools will be moderate. I have defended here the idea of a middle ground, of those that want to give their children a grounding in a religious community without stifling their individuality. However, policies that defend the right of a moderate religious community to have its own schools can also be used to defend the schools of conservative religious communities. Parents whose children attend ACE schools are not moderate separatists who want to situate their children in a community before they encounter the world. Rather, they want to shield their children from the world for as long as possible.

ACE schools are not the only parochial schools that should worry liberals. One Protestant fundamentalist pastor explained his school's pedagogical philosophy: 'We come at it from an authoritarian point of view. The very first verse in the Bible doesn't endeavor to prove that God exists; it just assumes that God exists.' Different kinds of living are not explored: 'This is not a place where there are alternative world views, competing and confronting cosmologies. Christianity claims to be the only way.' Questioning the teacher is often seen as a form of disobedience. Boys are supposed to learn to craft skills, work habits, leadership, and economics, while girls should learn cooking, housekeeping, household management, sewing, growing flowers, and child care. In one school girls are not allowed to have positions in school government that are higher than the boys. Fundamentalist schools do not try to teach just at school; they often try to become 'total worlds'. These schools are typically associated with a church which has social activities for the schoolchildren after school and on the weekends. Between the two they take up most of the time the students spend away from their family (Peshkin 1986: 8, 9, 44, 127).

It is these sorts of schools that inform my opposition to direct funding to parochial schools. Here I am in agreement with many liberal theorists who are concerned to defend civic education and diversity and are generally suspicious about state funding to parochial schools, while I am in disagreement with those separatists—moderate and otherwise—who are interested in providing state funds to parochial schools. Common public schools encourage liberal citizenship. This is true for good common schools, and not all public schools are good. Their failure, though, is a matter of practice, a matter of bad planning, of scanty resources, or perhaps too many bureaucratic rules. The reason to support parochial schools is that some of them can encourage liberal citizenship, and they help maintain a community. Others do not support liberal citizenship, however, and the reason is not a failure of practice. Rather, some parochial schools deliberately do not teach the liberal virtues. Direct funding to such schools would harm the important cause of creating and sustaining a common citizenship.

Yet this may not be enough to deny funding to parochial schools. Because some of them do a bad job, why should all be denied public funding? Indeed, it is possible to make public funding contingent on adhering to certain standards, so that schools like the ACE schools do not receive public funding but better parochial schools do. The voluntary school system in Britain is an example of this: parochial schools can receive public funding as long as they meet certain standards and teach certain subjects.

My resistance to public financing for parochial schools is not a philosophical opposition (or a constitutional one), but a political one.[10] In other words, support for public funding for parochial schools should depend on the particular circumstances of the state in question. Imagine a mostly homogeneous state where, say, 97 per cent of the population is Lutheran, but where there is a small and poor Muslim community. The only way in which the latter support their own schools—which would be important to their survival —is to be given state funding. Such funding is compatible with but not mandated by liberalism. It would be a policy matter for the legislature, not a constitutional matter for the courts. The people may decide that it would like to help the Muslim community maintain its identity, believing that the survival of the Muslim community will enrich their state in a variety of ways and that support for Muslim schools is one good way to help it survive. In my view liberalism neither insists that this support be given, nor prohibits it.

The state has an important interest in encouraging citizenship, and it should not go out of its way to do otherwise. In states with an extensive immigrant tradition and with considerable diversity, supporting citizenship becomes even more important. In a diverse society people have to work harder to

---

[10] The First Amendment says that Congress 'shall make no law respecting an establishment of religion or prohibiting the free exercise thereof', but this does not say that there shouldn't be any connection between church and state. Indeed, when the Amendment became law, some states had established churches, though these state churches were on their way out. I think it is constitutional for the state to subsidize parochial schools directly as long as it supports all parochial schools (or those that meet criteria that do not inherently favour one religion over another). The Supreme Court has declared otherwise, but this would not be the first time the court erred in its interpretation of the Constitution. Funding parochial schools does not mean that government is establishing a religion—which is what the First Amendment is concerned with—*if* it funds different kinds of religious schools and public schools. A government that funds Jewish, Mormon, Protestant fundamentalist, Islamic, Methodist, and non-parochial schools is not establishing a religion. Rather, it is supporting many religions.

understand one another and to act together politically. Co-operation and trust cannot be assumed among citizens in an immigrant society; these virtues have to be encouraged. This is where the clash between liberal diversity and religious conservatives is apparent. Liberal diversity taps into the liberal virtues; diversity is usually grounded in the idea that people ought to be exposed to different ideas and different practices. People should be exposed to different practices so that they better understand their fellow citizens. Exposing people to different cultural practices is contingent on living in a culturally diverse society.

This, of course, describes the United States, where there are two further reasons to be wary of state support for parochial schools. Too often, particularly, but not only, in the South, private schools of all sorts sprang up in response to the desegregation of public schools. The state should avoid supporting these racist choices if it can. (It is true, though, that these choices have also left many public schools in poor shape, so that many people today—unlike the late 1950s and 1960s—send their children to private schools for educational reasons rather than racist ones.) Moreover, class becomes an issue in the financing of schools. If the state gave financial support to parochial schools, support for public schools would probably decline dramatically. This would leave poor or disabled students, and students with parents who did not care enough about them, in public schools. The problem of class is an important one when talking about public schools: any move away from support for public schools would almost certainly hurt lower-income people more than the wealthier. This is not to say that all public schools are in good shape; some are not, including many that serve poorer students.

What is needed is to find ways to strengthen public schools so that we can come closer to equality of opportunity, not ways to weaken them. This is an important goal that liberal society is far from reaching, and it should not move further away from it. However, the problem with the arguments of liberal theorists on education has been their almost exclusive focus on public schools and their neglect of parochial schools. Even if we do not give direct support to the latter, avenues for co-operation with religious schools and accommodation for religious students in public schools should be sought.

4. Co-operation between Public and Parochial Schools

Michael McConnell argues that parochial schools should be given financial support by the state for their secular classes. He is clear that there should not be support for the religious part of the parochial school's curriculum.

McConnell gives two reasons for such partial public financing of religious schools. First, the state has an interest in ensuring that children are well educated; whether they attend public or parochial schools is immaterial. What is material is a good education, and funding both kinds of schools would further this important end. Secondly, McConnell argues that it is unfair (and unconstitutional) to make religious parents pay for the secular education their children receive when they attend parochial schools. He complains that 'if a family chooses to integrate a religious element into primary or secondary schooling, not only must they bear the costs of the religious education, but they also forfeit *all* public subsidy for education, including secular subjects' (McConnell 1991: 1017). Because they provide a couple of classes in Talmud or the Gospels each day, religious schools lose public funding for courses in maths, science, and English. McConnell maintains that taxpayers should be indifferent to private schools as long as they meet the same objective educational standards as public schools.

The state has an important interest in ensuring that its children are well educated, as McConnell notes, and giving public funds or lending public teachers to parochial schools would help towards this end. The best argument for having public teachers in parochial schools is that it would improve the quality of teaching in some of them. Although the teaching in many parochial schools is excellent, and help from public school teachers is hardly needed, in schools such as the ACE schools this assistance would surely help to raise the quality of their education. Why make the children suffer by refusing to have public school teachers teach in parochial schools? Furthermore, these public teachers could in fact ensure that the subjects they taught were not invaded by religious themes, so that the state would not be funding religious education.

The problem with placing public school teachers in parochial schools is that it deepens, rather than alleviates, one of the basic worries about them: the more parochial schools there are, the less students of different backgrounds will mix with one other; the less they will learn how to co-operate with one another or realize that others with different views exist. This leaves the children in private schools isolated. To leave them at the mercy of bad teachers because they are not in a diverse public school is hardly fair.

Instead of directly supporting parochial schools, the liberal state should try to entice parents to send their children to common schools. My governing principle here is inclusion: the liberal state should encourage families to use common public schools, even if this use is partial. My argument against McConnell is not an argument against co-operation between public and private schools. My objection is aimed against co-operation that takes place within the grounds of the private schools. Co-operation that allows different children to get together in one setting ought to be supported by public school systems, and co-operation that does not foster this inclusion should be avoided. Such inclusive co-operation may satisfy parents of minority students who want their children to be taught about their tradition, but who also want them to be educated in a diverse setting. It may also satisfy their wish to have their children learn about their tradition and about subjects that are less religious at a lower cost. This co-operation would allow for religious and other children to meet and interact, enhancing a common citizenship. It would also add to the pluralism of public schools, bolstering the idea of diversity in public schools. It would help out many 'moderate separatists', who do not threaten the state at all, and it would allow a diverse education to reach students in parochial schools, a population that liberal theorists and public educators should no longer ignore.

Co-operation can take several forms. I will suggest two by way of illustration, but there are probably more. One form of co-operation would be to allow students to attend public schools in the morning and parochial schools in the afternoon or vice versa. Students attending both schools might end up taking two biology courses, or they may receive a secular education in the morning and learn theology in the afternoon. Parents who do not want to be penalized by having no state funding for their children's education merely because they want their children to receive a religious education can be accommodated by this scheme. The difference between a split-day programme and funding teachers for secular subjects in religious schools is that the split-day programme teaches students who attend parochial schools alongside public school students. It encourages the ideals of inclusion and diversity. It encourages students from different backgrounds to face one another and examine the animating principles behind each other's lives. This is not only helpful to the parochial school students. Those who spend all day in public schools may very well be enriched by their encounters with students who are deeply rooted in a religious tradition.

Split-day programmes would also alleviate some of the pressure to conform felt by some religious students. Having their religious identity and beliefs taught and reinforced during half the day, they will be better equipped to withstand the pressure to conform. Or they may feel pressure to conform in different ways during the day's two halves; then they will be confronted with the need to decide for themselves what to believe.

Allowing for split days may result in an indirect subsidy for parochial schools since their costs will be lower if they do not have to teach certain subjects. This may induce more parents to send their children to religious schools. Parents who want their children to have both a public and a religious education may also be more apt to use religious schools under a split-day programme. I don't see either of these possibilities, however, as a cause for worry. These parents will still support public schools since their children attend them. Split days may also encourage parents who send their children to parochial schools for a full day to send their children to public schools for half a day. This will further increase support for public schools. More importantly, it will increase the likelihood of having more inclusive schools.

Co-operation should also take place with home-schooled children. Public schools should allow children who are taught at home to attend some courses or after-school activities if they want. Being home-schooled is not the same as attending a private school, and not all children that are home-schooled are there for religious reasons, but the principle of inclusion applies to all home-schooled children just as it does to private schools. Some home-schooled children want to attend one or two courses, because their parents do not think they can teach those courses well. Some school activities, like team sports or band, cannot be done alone. The cost and time of field trips may be too much for a family, and so home-schooled children may want to join a public school's trips. The argument against this sort of co-operation seems to be motivated by spite: since these students do not enrol in public schools, they should be completely barred from them. This is hardly a matter of principle, however. More co-operation with schoolchildren who are home-schooled would benefit these children, and would probably also benefit the schools by increasing their diversity.

Co-operation between parochial and public schools is one important way to reach out to moderate separatists. Moderate separatists want their children to live in a world with porous boundaries, where they spend some time in their own community and some time in the diverse world about them. Split-day programmes and co-operation with home-schooled children allow for this, while withholding help from conservative separatists. Some parochial schools will not want to co-operate with public schools in any way, and it will often be hard to reach conservative separatists. The state can try to invite parents to use public schools, both by co-operating with parochial schools and by accommodating the beliefs of parents in public schools. Little can be done, however, about parents who refuse this invitation.

5. Multiculturalism in the Public Schools

Co-operation between parochial and public schools does not say much about how religion should be treated in public schools. Many religious parents will send their children to a public school and will want religion to be discussed in the classroom; some will object to how some courses are taught. Education cannot be value-neutral, so it will not do to say we should treat religion neutrally. The curriculum cannot be both secular and religious. It inevitably teaches some values, both directly through the curriculum and indirectly through how things are taught and to whom. But religion can be treated more fairly in public schools, and some religious children should be accommodated if they or their parents object to parts of the curriculum. If there is more accommodation of religious students in public schools, then we may see less demand for parochial schools and a corresponding reduced threat to a common citizenship.

Treating Religion Equally

I want to add my voice briefly to the chorus that is saying that religion should be taught in schools. It need not and should not be taught simply as a separate course. It will surely come up in history, social science, and literature courses. This seems like an obvious enough point, since the role of religion historically and in the modern world is rather large, but many schools shy away from any mention of it.[11] This is partly because religion is so controversial that it is easier to omit it than to discuss it openly and incur the wrath of religious parents who object to how it is taught. This does not, however, excuse writers on multicultural education who almost always pass over it while tackling other controversial subjects. At best, religion gets a passing nod from multiculturalists (Fullinwider 1996). Any account of a multicultural society that omits decent discussion of religion is surely severely flawed.

Incorporating religion into the curriculum will not make every religious parent happy. The fundamentalist parents in *Mozert* were not happy with the doctrine of several religions being taught in the school—the schools their children attended were among the minority of schools that taught religion— since they thought that this would confuse their children about the true religion. Religion is an important part of a well-rounded academic education; teaching about it is important to any understanding of the history of the world and of the world today. Studying another religion does not force students to engage in a practice that violates their beliefs. Religions often allow the study of other religions, if only to point out to non-believers the error of their ways.

Too often public school officials think that any mention of religion in public school violates the First Amendment. I can explain what I mean by looking briefly at a court case, *Settle* v. *Dickson County School Board* (1995). In this case a teacher, Mrs Ramsey, assigned a research paper on any topic of the students' choice; each student had to get the teacher's approval and use four sources in the paper. One student, Brittney Settle, wrote on Jesus Christ, which Ramsey rejected. The case is complicated by the fact that Settle received permission to write on drama, but then decided to change topics without getting permission. Thus the case was enough opaque to make the court probably right in its decision not to interfere in the teacher's decision.

---

11   This is a theme in Nord (1995). Nord is one who calls for incorporating religion into the curriculum in the name of a liberal education.

Yet Ramsey also indicated that one of the reasons she rejected the paper was that 'we don't deal with personal religion—personal religious beliefs. It's just not an appropriate thing to do in a public school'. Ramsey also added that she thought it would be hard to grade the paper since any criticisms might be taken too personally.

What would happen, though, if a Muslim student wanted to write about Jesus Christ? That would not be dealing with personal religious beliefs. Or if Brittney Settle had wanted to write about Muhammad? Another student may decide to write about Martin Luther King Jr. He may not think King is divine, but he may certainly have strong feelings about him and think him above reproach. Should he be prevented from doing so since he may not take well to criticisms of his work? Christ is certainly an important historical figure, and a student should be able to write about him if doing so falls within the guidelines of the assignment.

Treating religion as an academic subject will not please all religious conservatives. Some want other subjects to be taught from a religious perspective —they just don't want religion to be taught. They may object that to teach religion as an academic subject is to treat it within a liberal framework, and not a religious one, and they are certainly right about this. The real test for religious conservatives is the content of biology courses, where the emphasis on evolution is proof for many that religion is not taken seriously. Teaching the biblical account of creation in a religion course, but not in science, separates the sacred from the secular. For many religious people, however, this is an artificial separation. The sacred permeates all aspects of life—biology included. If a student wrote a biology paper that attempted to prove the Genesis account of creation by quoting the Bible, he would probably receive a bad grade. The reason for the low grade should not be that religion has no place in public schools, but that the paper was bad science. Of course, if the paper gave a good account of the problems of evolutionary theory, then a bad grade would be inappropriate.

Science courses should teach the best account available on any particular subject, and most scientists believe that evolution is the best account we have of human origins, while some place it as a central organizing principle in biology. Biology teachers can and probably should discuss the fact that some people do not believe in evolution, that the question of human origins is a controversial one in our society, and that students may want to look elsewhere for alternative explanations. I don't think any liberal could object to letting students know that the theory of evolution is disputed by some, but it is important to explain how scientists test and falsify hypotheses. The biology teacher should note that because most scientists believe in evolution, and the weight of scientific evidence supports the theory, that is what he will teach in his course. Exposing students who believe in the biblical account of creation in Genesis to the idea of evolution is not forcing students to engage in a practice that violates their faith; it merely exposes them to an alternative belief. Parents who object to this exposure, and who believe that the sacred permeates everything, *and* want their children taught accordingly, will not receive satisfaction in the public schools. Their objection is not only to evolution, but to the idea of a secular education, even one that accommodates religion. These parents, and not all religious conservatives are like these parents, have to turn to parochial schools or home-schooling to have their children taught as they would like.

Another way in which a connection between religious groups and public schools make some liberals queasy is when religious groups use school facilities. The issue usually is this: if a school opens its facilities to community or student groups, can and should it also do the same for religious groups? Sometimes school officials think that if they do so, they will violate the First Amendment. School officials would do better, however, to treat religious student groups the same as other groups. If different student groups can use school facilities before or after school, then so too should student religious groups. Religious students should not have to work harder than others to be able to get together; the state should merely avoid facilitating religious groups more than others.

Both the Supreme Court and Congress support equal access to public school facilities, but some liberals see such a law as rather ominous.[12] Congress passed the Equal Access Act to ensure that religious groups are treated the same as other groups. Greg Ivers thinks that this decision, and the Supreme Court's efforts to uphold it, are disastrous: they 'interfere with the special obligation of public schools to enforce the Establishment Clause . . . such a posture lends the government's prestige and support to religion in an unconstitutional manner' (Ivers 1993: 39). Ivers's argument here is hard to follow since the Equal Access Act does not promote religious activities. It says that if a school allows its building to be used by the chess club before or after school, then the Christian Students' Fellowship ought to be able to meet as well. If this promotes religion, it also promotes chess. But promote is the wrong word here. Schools are supposed to be neutral about which student groups use its facilities. The Equal Access Act means that schools have to treat religious clubs like other clubs. This is not promotion. It is neutrality.

This neutrality includes clubs of gay and lesbian students. Next to the chess club and the Christian fellowship might be the association of gay and lesbian

---

12 In *Widmar* v. *Vincent* 454 US 263 (1981) the Supreme Court ruled that a public university that opened up its facilities to non-curriculum-related clubs created a public forum which must be open to secular and religious clubs alike. In 1984 Congress passed the Equal Access Act, which extended this idea of the public forum to public schools. The Supreme Court upheld the Act in *Westside* v. *Mergens* 496 US 226 (1990). In *Lamb's Chapel* v. *Moriches School District*, 508 US 385 (1993) the court ruled that if community organizations could use school facilities after hours, then religious organizations could as well.

students. Though the Equal Access Act was passed with religious clubs in mind, in an ironic twist gay and lesbian clubs have successfully used the Act to demand meeting space at schools. The school can forbid all clubs from meeting, as a school district in Salt Lake City did to deprive gay and lesbian students from having a forum to meet. This school district did not violate the law, but schools ought to help students who want to form clubs by letting them use their facilities. The students certainly thought this, as they marched to protest the banning of all student clubs. Students who want to meet voluntarily to discuss or practise a common interest are already learning the virtues of citizenship. That they want to meet to discuss their sexuality or spirituality, or to offer support to one another as a minority, is mostly irrelevant from the point of view of democratic citizenship.

Teaching Values

The harder issue concerning multiculturalism and religion involves teaching about respect and appreciation for others, which are important themes for multiculturalists. Multiculturalists want students to appreciate that there is more than one way to see the world. They want students to appreciate that there is more than one truth in the world:

[Students] have to understand that there is not only one way of seeing things, nor even two or three. A handy number to keep in mind, simply because it reflects how complex a process of reality is, is 17. There are at least 17 ways of understanding reality, and until we have learned to do that, we have only part of the truth. (Nieto 1992: 219)

The difficulty with this account is that it easily slides into relativism: we all have different beliefs which need to be respected. Part of what multicultural educators want is to 'promote an understanding and appreciation of America's cultural diversity' (Grant and Sleeter 1989: 144). To multicultural educators (whom I will simply call multiculturalists here) assimilation is a dirty word. Education should promote understanding between groups; it should help students understand why some groups have power and others do not.[13] Education should not, however, enable students to lose their cultural identity and become assimilated Americans. Take the matter of the family. Multiculturalists want to teach that different kinds of family are equally acceptable: 'Through contrasts and comparisons of alternative family structures and educational patterns, for instance, students can come to appreciate and accept the wide diversity of life-styles, value systems, and communication

---

[13] Differences in power among groups is an important theme for multiculturalists. I won't say much about that here, except to note that to divide the United States into groups, the oppressed and the powerful, as many multiculturalists do, is a sophomoric simplification.

patterns which characterize many members of differing cultural and racial backgrounds' (Grant and Melnick 1977: 220).

Few multiculturalists actually mean that all assimilation is bad, and they often qualify their arguments against it by noting that all groups must conform to democratic ideals and 'major school and societal goals' (Banks 1992: 277, 280). These are huge qualifications, of course, the importance of which is rarely noted by multiculturalists. They hardly ever explain what are major school or societal goals. Since most societies in the world are not democratic, most immigrants in the United States will come from cultures that have at least some anti-democratic tendencies. Most cultures are patriarchal, many are racist, and few are egalitarian. A multicultural education that is predicated on democratic ideals like equality and respect for cultural diversity will find that much cultural diversity isn't worthy of respect. We need not expect immigrants and their progeny to completely assimilate, but we can rightly expect them to conform to democratic values. Many of their other cultural practices will be transformed in their interaction with the mainstream culture. Unsurprisingly, few multiculturalists tackle this issue; few want to say directly that certain aspects of an oppressed culture are not worthy of respect. Until they do so, the argument that students should learn to respect and appreciate cultural diversity will be rather empty.

Their approach also leaves multiculturalists vulnerable to the charge of relativism; and relativism is something that rankles religious conservatives. The family is a good example, since many religious conservatives believe that the traditional nuclear family is preferable to single parenthood. Death of a spouse is one thing of course, but divorce is quite another. These religious conservatives do not want their children to be taught that divorce is just as acceptable as remaining married. For some, remaining married is a matter of fulfilling of God's command. (To be sure, you need not be a religious conservative to be wary of divorce. There is plenty of reason to believe that divorce is bad for the children, though a marriage that is not working may also be bad for the children.)

Similarly, many religious conservatives think that gay people are living immoral lives. They may also be concerned about courses that teach about religion. Few will demand, as did some parents in *Mozert*, that if schools teach religion, they should teach that one particular religion is true. A more common objection may be to schools that teach that all religions should be respected as if all are equally true. It is one thing to teach about the beliefs of another religion; it is a different thing to teach students that each person has the right to choose the religion that suits them best, and that no religion is truer or better than the alternatives.

The problem I am describing here is this: how do we teach mutual respect and appreciation for others without teaching that every way of life is equally acceptable? Schools and teachers are in a particularly tough spot. If they teach values, they are bound to anger the parents who have different values. If they refuse, and teach instead that each student should decide for herself what her values are, then schools will be accused of lacking any moral compass and of teaching relativism. If they teach that everyone's perspective is valid, as some multiculturalists advocate, and that we all have our own understanding of reality, then they will again be accused of relativism.

Relativism on some issues, though, is a bad idea. Schools should teach some values, whatever the response of some parents. Yet they should not be on an ideological crusade. Schools should teach core democratic ideals and the liberal virtues, and if there is a clash between a particular culture or religion's values and these ideals, then so much the worse for the culture or religion. However, the school should not single out a particular religion or culture as undemocratic and so worthy of condemnation: it should let students draw their own conclusions from any clash with liberal democratic ideals.

The liberal virtues it should teach and encourage are those of trust, autonomy, and the value of political participation. These values have subsidiary values, and implications for other values. If we are to trust another one another, then we need to teach that stealing and lying are generally wrong. Included in the idea of autonomy are the ideas of mutual respect and equality. All citizens should be treated as autonomous, and should be encouraged to act autonomously. Just as I need people to treat me with respect if I am going to be able to pursue my plans and goals, so too must I in turn treat others with respect. Autonomous citizens are encouraged to think critically about a wide variety of issues at school. Political participation is important because it is one way in which liberal citizens can pursue the common good. Indeed, students should be taught to pursue the common good and not their own selfish interests.

These values are important, but they are not all-encompassing. The virtue of trust is, one hopes, rather uncontroversial. That politics should be used to pursue the common good will not be very contentious, as long as the content of the common good remains vague enough. The idea of autonomy, and its subsidiary value of treating all people, including women and gays, with equal respect, will be more controversial. Some parents will also scoff at modern science and its method, at least in part. Clearly, however, these are key liberal virtues and should be taught. These virtues are limited, however, and they leave plenty of values under- or undetermined. Which beliefs will lead to salvation? How many children should one have? Is abortion murder? How should the country balance care for the environment against jobs that are in pollution-creating industries? What about cloning?

There are many questions that remain after the liberal virtues are taught. In these areas schools need to tread carefully. They can teach the different beliefs about salvation, but not that each answer is equally true. They should teach that people will come to different conclusions about salvation, and what some of these different conclusions are. They should also teach that some people may be right about their beliefs and others wrong, and that each person has to decide for him- or herself what is correct. The same is true of pollution and cloning. Schools should, of course, provide students with relevant information, and encourage them to discuss their ideas with others, including their parents, and provide evidence for their views. On some matters, of course—such as which is the best path to salvation—evidence is rather hard to come by. But evidence about pollution and jobs that can be gathered and discussed. Teachers should teach students to respect the right and ability of their fellow students to form their own beliefs, but they need not respect the conclusions their fellow students reach.

Liberalism has certain core values that should be taught. The more controversial of these values, such as the idea of autonomy, partly concern how one goes about arguing, discussing, and deciding on various matters. Moral ideas are inherent in these matters, and liberals do better not to pretend otherwise. Yet these values are limited, and teaching them will leave many moral issues for students, often in consultation with their parents, to decide.

6. Accommodating Religious Beliefs

This sort of formula will not ease all tensions between religious conservatives and public schools. Schools that teach values will offend some people. (Schools that teach no values will offend other people.) Some religious conservatives will maintain that teaching that gay people deserve respect, even if schools do not teach that any particular kind (or all kinds) of sexuality is correct, offends their values. When religious conservatives object to school practices and the curriculum, the school should try to accommodate them. I have in mind two kinds of accommodation. First, accommodation should almost always mean that religious students should not have to engage in any practices that violate their beliefs. This is the easy kind of accommodation. Secondly, accommodation should be granted even when it means exempting students from being be exposed to beliefs that are at odds with their own faith when it is feasible to do so. Accommodation in these sorts of cases need not be granted as readily as in the first instance.

Public schools often refuse to accommodate religion because of a slippery-slope argument: if one person objects to a rule for a religious reason, why won't others object for other reasons? School officials sometimes avoid accommodating religious practices because they think doing so violates the First Amendment. In many cases, however, these worries are not enough to justify avoiding accommodation of religion. At other times they may think that important values are at stake, and they should be taught. How can a school exempt a student from a course that teaches about equality or mutual respect? This is at the heart of the concern that most political theorists have about accommodation.

Steve Macedo and Amy Gutmann disagree on the nature of liberal education, but they agree that in the *Mozert* case the school district was right not to allow fundamentalist children to opt out of courses in dispute (see Macedo 1995a; Gutmann 1995; Spinner 1994: 106–7). Along with Dennis Thompson, Gutmann says if the parents who sued the school district in the *Mozert* case had been successful, 'their children (and perhaps others) would fail to receive the education that is necessary for developing their capacities as democratic citizens' (Guttman and Thompson 1996: 65). Eamonn Callan agrees, saying that 'children have a right to an education that includes an understanding of ethical diversity that the parents in *Mozert* wrongly wished to block' (Callan 1997: 158). Shelley Burtt, in her laudable attempt to argue for a more inclusive polity, rather surprisingly says that 'religious parents and secular schools share the end of an education in the basic skills and virtues of a liberal democracy' (Burtt 1994: 62). Because of these shared ends, Burtt argues, the children in *Mozert* should have been accommodated. Burtt's conclusion is correct, but for the wrong reason: it is particularly important to try to accommodate fundamentalist parents because they *do not* share many liberal beliefs. Many fundamentalist parents do not want their children to be autonomous citizens in any robust kind of way; having them attend public schools is one way to subvert their parents' wishes in a way that supports liberal citizenship.

I agree with Callan, Macedo, Gutmann, and Thompson that the education the parents wanted in *Mozert* was by no means a liberal education. But their conclusion, that the accommodation the parents sought was rightly denied, is mistaken. These arguments reduce the number of students who receive a liberal education, rather than enlarge it. Gutmann and Thompson contend that if the parents in *Mozert* had won, their children would have failed to receive a liberal education. This is wrong: their children would have failed to receive a liberal education *in one class*. The parents lost the case, and many sent their children to a parochial school, and now their children fail to receive a liberal education *in all their classes*.

Arguments that focus on the curriculum—which encompasses most liberal arguments on education—note that what the parents objected to in *Mozert* are important liberal beliefs, including equality and mutual respect. This seems to me rather indisputable. Parents that object to girls being taught that they are equal to boys want to subvert a key tenet of liberal citizenship and autonomy. Yet if the refusal to accommodate leads the parents to pull their children out of the public schools and put them in ACE or similar schools, what has this tough line accomplished?

I will briefly look at easier cases first. For some religious students (or their parents) looking at members of the opposite sex in 'immodest dress' is against their beliefs. Where the rule in gym class is that everyone must wear shorts and T-shirts, religious students should be exempt from the class, or be put in an alternative class. There is little academic gain in goggling at one's scantily clad classmates, and if doing so is against someone's religious practice, they should be accommodated. A clothing rule that mandates shorts is not designed to ensure good academic performance. If many students want to wear more modest clothing, then perhaps the clothing requirement should be rethought.[14]

Parents should also be allowed to exempt their children from sex education classes, which are not academic courses; exposing students to birth control pills and condoms is not an important part of a good education. Since pre-marital sex is a practice that violates some people's religious beliefs, there is no reason to insist that their children attend sex education courses. It is true that these courses do not condone pre-marital sex, but they often discuss sex graphically, and teach students how to have sex without getting (anyone) pregnant. Making an exception to this general rule will not hurt the academic education of any student.

There are a variety of other ways in which students may need to be accommodated so that they do not violate their religious beliefs. For example, schools should not penalize any student for missing classes on a religious holiday; exams that fall on holidays should be rescheduled for the believers who spent the day in church or synagogue. I cannot canvass all the possible accommodations, since this is too local a practice. Generally, schools need to have a very good reason to make a student transgress a religious belief.

Students should also be accommodated if they or their parents object to the content of a particular assignment or course, even if this means exempting the student from learning about evolution or mutual respect. Liberals argue about the importance of teaching liberal ideals like mutual respect or equality, but these ideals are lived as much—if not more—than taught. We should not think that learning takes place only through teaching, through the curriculum. Habituation is one way to teach; surely example is another important way. A school whose ethos is one of mutual respect, where all students are treated respectfully by teachers and teachers ensure that students treat one another respectfully in the classroom, is teaching mutual respect, not (necessarily) through books but by example. It is not so important for students to learn by reading that gay people deserve respect if they see their fellow students and teachers treating gays in this way. Students will learn a great deal if they see their teachers ridicule Sikh students who wear turbans; conversely, students who are tempted to mock the Sikhs, but see others treating them with respect, may be reluctant to engage in ridicule. Though parents may not want

---

[14] A US District Court agreed in *Moody* v. *Cronin* 484 F. Supp 270 (1979).

their children to be taught that women and men are equal, they may learn the lesson anyway from the way girls are treated in school. They may even learn this lesson better through the ethos of a school than through books.

Students will not, however, learn about evolution by example, but I want to argue that students who want to be exempted from classes on evolution should still be accommodated. They should be given alternative materials and assignments, and will not then reject all the tenets of modern science. If they took their beliefs to their logical conclusion, that may be where they ended up, but how many students would do so? Many will believe in creationism, and also in carbon-14 dating. These beliefs may be incompatible, which is why they should not both be taught in public schools, but many people have contradictory beliefs that do not seem to inhibit their daily lives or their belief in science. Accommodating students who do not want to learn about evolution may keep them in public schools. They can still learn about science and its method, directly and indirectly, in their other courses. If scientific method is a guiding force in the school, exemption from one part of one course will not mean that students will fail to learn about modern science and its method. They will simply not learn about one application of it.

Students are also more likely to confront different ideas and ways of life in common schools than in fundamentalist schools. This remains the case even if students are given an alternative assignment in one class each day. They would still remain in a diverse school; they would still learn about other ways of life from other students. They would be able to befriend children with different beliefs. Furthermore, they could learn from the method employed by their teachers. Good public school teachers do not ask their students simply to memorize; they encourage their students to think and question. This is true in many kinds of classes, so if the students remained in the public school, even if they had alternative arrangements in other classes, they could still be taught the liberal virtues. They might still be confronted in ways that would get them to think deeply about their and their parents' beliefs.

The dialogue between students that Gutmann, Thompson, and Callan (and I) favour occurs many times during the school day. It takes place in classes, at lunch, and on the way home with one's fellow students. An exemption from one class might reduce the dialogue that takes place, but it hardly means that students will no longer confront different beliefs from the ones they hold. Certainly a small reduction in the way a few students confront liberal ideas that depart from their own is considerably better than complete withdrawal.

Inclusion of religious conservatives in public schools strengthens liberal citizenship, even where religious conservatives are exempted from some classes. Many liberals are too quick to condemn any accommodation in the curriculum, as if doing so is automatically a defeat for liberal citizenship. This is mistaken, however. A few accommodations can be made without sacrificing liberal citizenship, and if the alternative is fundamentalist parochial schools, then the accommodation will often bolster liberal citizenship. I do not think that anything more than accommodation is called for: certainly, the entire curriculum should not be changed in an illiberal direction, whatever some parents want. Rather, some exemptions and accommodations should be granted, instead of an immediate rejection of any deviation from the liberal curriculum.

This accommodation might decrease pluralism in society. I argued above that co-operation between public and private schools may work to support pluralism, by indirectly giving public support to parochial schools. Accommodation, however, will sometimes have the opposite effect. If students of fundamentalist parents attend common public schools rather than fundamentalist schools, their differences from mainstream society will probably decrease rather than increase. This is hardly a reason to withhold support from accommodation, though. It is a positive development when illiberal communities are influenced by the mainstream liberal society. Pluralism for its own sake should be not supported by the liberal regime.

Would such an accommodation have satisfied the parents involved in *Mozert*? It mostly depends on how relentlessly consistent with their beliefs the parents wanted to be. The ideas that the parents objected to were taught in many classes, not just the one that became the focal point of the court case. Vicki Frost, the parent who was the driving force behind the case, eventually admitted that she would have found many classes in the school objectionable. When parents like Frost come to that conclusion, they either enrol the children in private schools or try to force the public schools to change their curriculum. Many fundamentalist and evangelical parents have tried (some successfully) to change the way public schools treat many subjects (Provenzo 1990). The fundamentalist parents in *Mozert* received help from organizations that often try to change the curriculum in public schools to reflect better the views of fundamentalists, which is why Burtt's comments that these parents did not want to impose their view of education on others has to be treated rather warily. Burtt is right that this is what some parents want, but other parents have an agenda that is more far-reaching than she admits.

Accommodation has its limits: if a parent wants her child to be given alternative assignments in four classes, then that parent is really asking for an alternative education for their child. When that happens, accommodation should be refused. I cannot say exactly when accommodation is reasonable and when it should be refused. Public school officials will have to make that judgement. The point here is that they should try to accommodate reasonable requests for alternative classes instead of assuming that every request for an accommodation is an attack on their school. In a little-noticed part of the *Mozert* saga some parents actually received the accommodation they wanted for their children in the one course that parents objected to, and the school met their modest request with little difficulty (Bates 1993).

A policy of inclusion should not mean telling religious parents that they either accept public schools and its curriculum or that they flee. Inclusion means that public schools should try to co-operate with parochial schools, and try to accommodate religious students when feasible. Inclusion is not just a nice thing to do. It promotes liberal citizenship and helps to expose students to different ideas and practices. This is true for religious and non-religious students alike: in good common schools they will learn from one another and maybe benefit from the encounter. This is one reason why the most conservative and insular religious groups shy away from most kinds of co-operation with public schools and why accommodation won't interest them. They do not want partial exclusion, but exclusion that runs very deep.

PART II

Political Participation and Group Representation

4

What does a Representative Do? Descriptive Representation in Communicative Settings of Distrust, Uncrystallized Interests, and Historically Denigrated Status

JANE MANSBRIDGE

For at least three functions, disadvantaged groups may want to be represented by individuals who in their own backgrounds 'mirror' the typical experiences and outward manifestations of belonging to the disadvantaged group.

First, representatives serve as instruments of ongoing consultation and communication, not only with constituents from their districts but also with constituents elsewhere and members of interest groups. The representatives are thus part of a deliberative process that is organized vertically, from citizens and their interest groups up to representatives and from the representatives down to citizens and their interest groups. Yet members of groups embedded in a tradition of domination and subordination often experience faulty communication: The dominant group has not learned to listen and the subordinate group has learned to distrust. Members of subordinate groups may thus often find that effective substantive representation depends on their being represented, both in constituent communication and in interest group communication, by members of their own group, with whom they can communicate easily and by whom they can reasonably expect to be better understood.

Secondly, representatives form part of a horizontally organized deliberative process at the legislative level. The representatives in assembly need to communicate effectively with one another. Yet subordinate groups often

This work was completed while the author was a fellow at the Center for Advanced Study in the Behavioral Sciences, supported by National Science Foundation Grant #SBR-9601236. Further support came from the Institute for Policy Research at Northwestern University. I am grateful for suggestions on an earlier and more comprehensive study from William Bianco, Carol Swain, Melissa Williams, Iris Marion Young, and particularly Benjamin Page. Another version of the work appeared as 'Should Blacks Represent Blacks and Women Represent Women? A Contingent "Yes"', *The Journal of Politics*, vol. 61 (August 1999): 628–57, sections reprinted by permission.

need to put new issues on the political agenda. These issues are by definition 'uncrystallized'—that is, they have not gone through a process of pre-election deliberation and position-taking. When issues are uncrystallized or when nuances of a deliberative issue require an understanding gained primarily through personal experience, representatives who are not personally in touch with the typical experiences of their constituents will often not contribute adequately to the deliberation of these issues. Moreover, when an issue has not been fully discussed and digested in the larger public deliberative process, legislators who represent disadvantaged groups but are not themselves members of the group sometimes have difficulty persuading representatives from more advantaged groups of the salience of the disadvantaged group's problem. This deliberative task is facilitated if the representative, being a member of that group, can spontaneously formulate issues, draw examples, and stress key components for legislation from the typical experiences of that group, and can bear witness from personal experience to the salience of the problem.

Both of these considerations bear on substantive representation through the deliberative process. A third consideration, unrelated to substantive representation, is that representatives who are members of one of the polity's subgroups can change the social meaning of membership in that group through their actions and presence in the body authorized to make laws for the polity as a whole. A proportional representation of members authorized as lawmakers confirms that members of this group are capable of that function and expected to fill it. That confirmation in turn increases the *de facto* legitimacy of the polity for members of these groups. This positive effect on political status is particularly important when the polity has a history of legally excluding members of a specified group from the vote or other political rights. Such a legal exclusion usually leaves historical traces of the dominant culture's past conclusion that members of the group so specified were not fit to rule.

The benefits achieved by 'mirror' or 'descriptive' representation in these three contexts may not outweigh other costs of such representation, but those benefits deserve to be counted in the balance.

1. Descriptive Representation

In 'descriptive' representation, representatives are in their own lives and persons in some sense typical of the larger class of persons whom they represent.[1] Black legislators represent black constituents, women legislators represent women constituents, and so on. The word 'descriptive' in this

---

[1] Birch (1993: 72); see also Birch (1964: 16). The term 'descriptive representation', coined by Griffiths and Wollheim (1960), was adopted by Pitkin (1967). In the two best recent treatments of the issues, Phillips (1995) uses the term 'politics of presence' and Williams (1998) the term 'self-representation'.

context can have two meanings, both of which I intend to denote. Most commonly the word refers to visible characteristics, such as colour of skin or gender. It can also, however, refer to shared experiences, so that a representative with a background in farming is to the appropriate degree a descriptive representative of his farmer constituents.

In describing a representative as 'descriptive' I do not mean to suggest that the representative need be no more than descriptive. I mean instead to denote one characteristic of the representative, usually in addition to other characteristics of good representation.

The most common criticism of descriptive representation contrasts this form of representation with 'substantive representation'. The first part of this chapter acknowledges that substantive representation is the most important goal in the representative process. It argues that descriptive similarity, like party identification and susceptibility to re-election, is best seen as one among many characteristics of a given representative that make it more likely that the representative will represent the constituent's substantive interests and perspectives accurately. Descriptive similarity also gives constituents accessible cues that the representative is more likely than others without those characteristics to engage in such accurate substantive representation.

The analysis in this chapter will stress two specific contexts in which shared descriptive traits allow a representative to represent constituents' substantive interests better than, say, a shared party label. These contexts are: (1) when communication between representative and constituent would otherwise be undermined by mistrust, and (2) when the legislature must decide on 'uncrystallized' issues, that is, issues that did not appear on the political agenda at the time of the representative's election. In the first context, of distrust, descriptive representation can promote vertical communication between representative and constituents (and the constituents' intermediaries who share these descriptive traits). In the second context, of uncrystallized interests, descriptive representation can promote horizontal communication among representatives. If we judge representation by deliberative as well as aggregative criteria, we will find that in the two contexts I have identified, descriptive representation often furthers the substantive representation of interests.

2. Deliberative Arguments for Descriptive Representation

Focusing on the two contexts of communicative distrust and uncrystallized interests derives from shifting our normative attention in the representative process from an exclusive concern with traditional accountability to an additional concern with the quality of deliberative interaction between representative and constituents and among representatives in the legislature.

Descriptive representation is not popular among normative theorists. Indeed, most normative democratic theorists have rejected descriptive representation relatively summarily (Griffiths and Wollheim 1960; Pitkin 1967; Pennock 1979; Grofman 1982: 98), often with some version of Pennock's trenchant comment, 'no one would argue that morons should be represented by morons' (Pennock 1979: 314, based on Griffiths and Wollheim 1960: 190). Even among explicit advocates of group representation the ideal of descriptive representation finds little support. Will Kymlicka (1995a: 139) writes, 'the general idea of mirror [descriptive] representation is untenable', and Iris Marion Young (1996: 354) concurs: 'Having such a relation of identity or similarity with constituents says nothing about what the representative does.'

Empirical political scientists studying women and black legislators have had similar negative assessments. Irene Diamond, the first empirical political scientist to investigate in depth the actions of women legislators, reported, for example, that in New Hampshire, the state with most women legislators, most women legislators did not see themselves as 'acting for' women in Pitkin's phrase. Rather, New Hampshire's low salary ($200 a year in 1972) and high representative–constituent ratio (with its consequent low competitiveness) brought to the legislature a high proportion of older homemakers. With little self-confidence or desire for a career in politics, they did not see themselves as representing women's interests (Diamond 1977). On the basis of this kind of evidence, women political scientists often concluded that descriptive female gender had no predictable relation to support for women's substantive interests (e.g. Schlozman and Mansbridge 1979).[2] The first empirical political scientist to investigate in depth the actions of black legislators, Carol Swain, similarly concluded that in the United States Congress, 'More black faces in political office (that is, more descriptive representation for African Americans) will not necessarily lead to more representation of the tangible interests of blacks' (Swain 1993: 5).

These normative theorists and empirical researchers make an important, incontrovertible point. The primary function of representative democracy is to represent, through both deliberation and aggregation, the substantive interests of the represented. Descriptive representation should be judged primarily on this criterion. When non-descriptive representatives have, for

---

[2] Sapiro (1981: 712), however, argued that in the case of women descriptive representation was 'a necessary condition, but it is not sufficient'. Her argument for necessity rested on the grounds that (1) having women rather than men in office demonstrably makes government somewhat more responsive to women's interests; (2) participation in government is intrinsically valuable; and (3) increased representation of women will undermine the perception that politics is a male domain. I will reproduce most of these arguments here, while both moving them from the domain of necessity to contingency and agreeing that the contingent circumstances that make some descriptive representation beneficial for women obtain now and in the foreseeable future.

various reasons, greater ability to represent the substantive interests of their constituents, this is a major argument against descriptive representation. My argument here will be that in the two contexts of historical mistrust and uncrystallized interests, descriptive representation can contribute to, rather than detract from, substantive representation.

3. The Deliberative and Aggregative Functions of Substantive Representation

Ideally, substantive representation has two functions: deliberation and aggregation. The *deliberative* function of democratic representation is aimed at achieving understanding of which policies are good for the nation, which policies are good for a representative's constituents, and when the interests of various groups within the nation and constituency conflict. It is also aimed at creating commonality when that commonality can be genuinely good for all. In its deliberative function, a representative body should ideally include a representative who can speak for *every group that might provide new information, perspectives, or ongoing insights* relevant to the understanding that leads to a decision.

The *aggregative* function of democratic representation is aimed at producing some form of relatively legitimate decision in the context of fundamentally conflicting interests. In its aggregative function, the representative assembly should, in moments of conflict, ideally represent the interests of *every group whose interests conflict with those of others*, in proportion to the numbers of that group in the population.

The questions of which perspectives will contribute to understanding and which interests conflict will, of course, often be contested, as will the question of how close in any given case an issue comes to either common or conflicting interests. Nevertheless, the two criteria of useful perspectives and conflicting interests provide answers to the oft-repeated criticism that democratic theorists 'provide few guidelines for selecting which social characteristics merit representation' (Morone and Marmor 1981: 437; see also, on descriptive representation, Pitkin 1967: 87–8; Grofman 1982: 98; Voet 1992: 395). In *deliberation*, the perspectives of left-handers (to take an example from Marone and Marmor 1981: 437) should be represented when their *perspective is relevant to the decision*—in, say, decisions regarding the design of surgical instruments. Similarly with redheads, Lithuanians, Italians, Jews, the uneducated, and all other groups. In *aggregation*, the interests of left-handers should be represented when their *interests conflict* with those of right-handers.

In theory, for the deliberative function only one representative from a group might be needed to contribute a useful perspective to the collective decision. To contribute to the appropriate understanding, a group may need only a 'threshold' presence in the deliberation (Mansbridge 1983; Kymlicka 1993: 77–8; Phillips 1995: 47, 67 ff.). In practice, however, disadvantaged groups often need the full representation that proportionality allows in order to achieve deliberative synergy, critical mass, and a range of views within the group.

Deliberation is often synergistic. For this reason, up to the point at which a group acquires too many representatives for fruitful interaction, the more individuals representing a given opinion, interest, or perspective, the better. More representatives usually produce more information and more insight. Groups whose members will be affected by a decision might therefore legitimately demand, even under deliberative criteria, as many representatives as reflect their numbers in the population.

In actual deliberations disadvantaged groups may also need more than one representative to produce the critical mass necessary to generate a willingness among those representatives to enunciate positions that diverge from those of the majority in the deliberative assembly. In addition, they may need this critical mass to convince others—particularly members of dominant groups—that the minority perspectives or insights they are advancing are widely shared, genuinely felt, and deeply held within their own group.

Finally, because the content and range of any deliberation is often unpredictable, as many representatives as proportionality allows may be needed to represent the range of views within the represented group. One representative of African American perspectives in a representative body, for example, will not usually be able to present adequately the characteristic insights of poor and well-off, female and male, urban and rural African Americans. Although these members of the group share some perspectives, opinions, and interests, each will bring different, and sometimes conflicting, shades of insight to the shared experiences and perspectives. They will also bring to the polity different political experiences and commitments. These varied inflexions and internal oppositions together constitute the complex and internally contested perspectives, opinions, and interests characteristic of the group. They are not easily represented by one individual, whether descriptive or not.

Thinking only of descriptive representation for a moment, this analysis suggests that African Americans in the United States are far more richly represented by a Congress that includes William Gray III (a black member of Congress who did not support the Congressional Black Caucus's alternative budget because he was chairman of the budget committee in the House) and George Crockett (a black member of Congress who condemned the State Department for refusing to grant Yasser Arafat an entry visa and who supported the legalization of marijuana) than by a Congress that included only one of these two.[3]

In short, no matter how purely deliberative the assembly, reasons of synergy, critical mass, and internal diversity ensure that in practice each group will usually want to claim as many representatives on that body as is justified by its proportional limit. The demand for proportionality is accentuated by the fact that in practice almost all democratic assemblies are aggregative as well as deliberative, and achieving the full normative legitimacy of the aggregative function requires that the members of the representative body cast votes for each affected conflicting interest in proportion to the numbers of such interest-bearers in the population (see Mansbridge 1983, 1994, 1996, for a fuller exposition of these ideas).

These criteria help resolve the problem in traditional theories of representation of having no guidelines for specifying what *groups* should be represented in a democratic decision. They do not yet resolve the problem of when such groups should be represented *descriptively*. That is the goal of this chapter.

4. Two Forms of Descriptive Representation

Descriptive representation can take two forms, a 'microcosmic' and a 'selective' form. In the microcosmic form, the entire assembly is designed to form a microcosm, or representative sample, of the electorate.[4] In the far more frequent selective form, institutional design gives selected groups greater descriptive representation than they would achieve in existing electoral systems in order to bring the proportions of those groups in the legislature closer to their percentages in the population. The costs of these two forms differ in important respects. Their benefits are more similar.

The Microcosmic Form

The microcosmic form of descriptive representation was the ideal of John Adams, James Wilson, Mirabeau, and certain other eighteenth-century theorists (see Pitkin 1967). Almost all of Hanna Pitkin's argument against descriptive representation is explicitly or implicitly directed against this form. After Pitkin's argument against it, few democratic theorists have argued for

---

[3] See Swain (1993: 41, 49–71) for Gray and Crockett, and (1993, *passim*) for the diversity in opinions and styles within the spectrum of African American representation in Congress in the 1980s and early 1990s. See Young (1996) for the concept of diversity of opinion within a single 'perspective'.

[4] The term 'microcosmic' comes from Birch (1993: 72); the term 'selective' is my own.

this form. Instead, without ever referring to the concept of descriptive representation, theorists have simply suggested adding to existing electoral systems some component of microcosmic representation.

More than twenty-five years ago Robert Dahl urged adding a third assembly, chosen by lot from a nation-wide population, to advise the United States Senate and House of Representatives (Dahl 1970: 149; 1977: 17; 1985: 86–9; 1992: 54–7). More recently (Dahl 1997) he has suggested creating smaller deliberative bodies, drawn by lot from a nation-wide population, to consider specific issues, such as health care, on which the re-election incentives of politicians and the desire to benefit without paying costs among the populace combine to curtail appropriate deliberation. John Burnheim (1985) has suggested replacing all elective institutions with institutions based on lot and a mixture of nomination and lot. Ned Crosby (1991, 1996) has induced the state of Minnesota and private foundations to commission 'citizen juries', bodies of citizens chosen by representative sampling from a state-wide population, to deliberate and decide on contested issues, then advise the public and elected legislatures on their deliberations. Dennis Mueller and colleagues (1972) and Benjamin Barber (1984: 290–3) have proposed election of officials by lot, and Jack Nagel (1992) has proposed that, on thorny issues such as triage in health care, governments create a 'deliberative assembly on a random basis'. James Fishkin (1991, 1995, 1996) has promoted the similar theory and practice of 'deliberative opinion polls', in which representative samples of a nation-wide population deliberate on issues in a context designed to influence public debate and political party decisions.

All of these authors are motivated by a desire to make decisions more democratic—that is, to incorporate greater political equality and better citizen deliberation in the process. All are also motivated by a desire to make the decisions more responsive to the needs of constituents and more able to serve the public good. Some argue implicitly that participation in government is intrinsically valuable, and thus, all other things equal, should be spread equally among descriptive groups (see Sapiro 1981 and Phillips 1995 for an explicit argument). Some are further motivated by a desire to make decisions more legitimate in the perceptions of the citizenry (increasing *de facto* legitimacy). Among the theorists who recommend adding to the governmental structure some form of assembly drawn on a random basis from the citizenry, I have not found one who uses the term 'descriptive' (or 'mirror') representation, or evaluates the costs and benefits of the recommended forms in explicit response to the literature critical of descriptive representation. The issue has therefore not been fully joined.

The costs of descriptive representation depend on its form. If microcosmic representation replaced elected representative assemblies, the chief costs lie in the strong likelihood that choosing the members of a ruling assembly at random from the population would produce legislators with less ability, expertise, and possibly commitment to the public good than would choosing those legislators through election. In current electoral systems many of those who run for election have chosen lawmaking as their vocation. They have spent much of their adult lives acquiring the skills needed for the job. The voters then select among these individuals, guided in part by the ability and training of the candidates in their chosen field. Representatives so selected arguably have greater abilities and training in this field than individuals selected through a representative sample. Representatives who have chosen politics as a calling and who have been selected in competitive elections may also have a greater commitment to the public good than individuals chosen through a representative sample (see Madison 1987), although some election and re-election incentives work in the opposite direction.

My own experience with town meeting democracy (Mansbridge 1983) leads me to conclude that the ability, expertise, and commitment to the public good of ordinary members of the public are sufficient to make a random sample of citizens a plausible, if distinctly not ideal, representative assembly. In contrast to Pitkin, who argued that there is simply 'no room' in a descriptive concept of representation for 'leadership, initiative or creative action' (1967, 90), I do not find it hard to envision a representative sample of the United States population producing the kind of leadership, initiative, and creative action of which the average New England town meeting is capable. The capacities of such leaders, initiators, and creators would undoubtedly not reach the level of those who now guide the nation in the United States, but I am not sure that they would be incapacitatingly worse.

Nevertheless, because lawmaking in large states and at the national level usually requires considerable talent and acquired skill, no current democratic theorist in the United States advocates substituting microcosmic representation for electoral representation. Even the Australian John Burnheim, who advocates microcosmic representation (Burnheim 1985), does not expect his suggestion to be put into practice within our lifetimes in any of the world's current democracies. The suggestions with a greater likelihood of being adopted in practice add to existing electoral systems some component of microcosmic representation.

The costs of adding a descriptive advisory assembly to existing representative systems include the straightforward monetary cost of paying for the additional representatives, their staffs, and their infrastructure, and the institutional costs of adding another layer of deliberation, responsibility, and compromise to what is on the US national level already an unwieldy bicameral legislature embedded in a system that distributes power among three separate branches of government and three major levels of decentralization (national, state, and local). *Ad hoc* advisory systems, such as citizens' juries, deliberative opinion polls, and deliberative assemblies on a random basis, incur far fewer costs.

The Selective Form

Selective descriptive representation is the more common form of descriptive representation advocated and practised today both in the United States and in other existing democracies. It is not the form to which Pitkin addressed most of her attention. In the most common versions of the selective form, geographical district lines are drawn to encourage the election of descriptive representatives, and parliaments or parties set aside a number of seats for members of specific descriptive groups, such as scheduled castes or women.

Selective descriptive representation works quite differently from the microcosmic form. While microcosmic representation guarantees almost all conceivable groups proportional representation through its explicitly randomized selection procedure, selective descriptive representation requires developing criteria that specify which groups should be descriptively represented. Moreover, while microcosmic representation requires something approaching a random sample of the population, no better or worse than that sample in knowledge, experience, or character, selective descriptive representation requires adding descriptive characteristics to an existing list of criteria for accurate substantive representation. Those criteria will undoubtedly include knowledge, experience, and character.

Like any of the criteria for accurate substantive representation, trying to ensure descriptive representation often entails some costs in other criteria. In selective descriptive representation, the necessity for specifying any one descriptive characteristic generates the first major cost. Insisting that women represent women or blacks represent blacks implies an essential quality of womanness or blackness that all members of that group share. Insisting that others cannot adequately represent the members of a descriptive group also implies that members of that group cannot adequately represent others (Phillips 1992, 1995; Kymlicka 1993, 1995a; Swain 1993; Young 1996).

This problem of essentialism haunts every group that hopes to organize politically around a facet of identity, including descriptive characteristics such as gender and race. Essentialism involves assuming a single or essential trait, or nature, that binds every member of a descriptive group together, giving them common interests that, in the most extreme versions of the idea, transcend the interests that divide them. Such an assumption leads not only to refusing to recognize major lines of cleavage in a group, but also to assimilating minority or subordinate interests in those of the dominant group without even recognizing their existence (Spelman 1988; Fuss 1989; see Young 1994a, 1996, for ways of conceiving of group existence with a minimum of essentialist thinking).

At its most basic, of course, the process of thought itself encodes a form of essentializing. Most of us cannot think 'table' without unconsciously conjuring up a four-legged brown piece of furniture, thereby marginalizing in our considerations the many tables with more or fewer legs and different colours. The problem of simple categorization becomes much worse when, as is often the case in human affairs, one group is socially dominant and becomes the norm, setting expectations and structuring institutions so that those who do not conform to that norm are perceived as deviant or lesser beings, perceive themselves as deviant, and cannot function as well in the structures designed for the members of the dominant group.

Even political groups based on descriptive identity that challenge the hegemony of the dominant group cannot escape this internal dynamic. Feminist organizations that appeal to 'sisterhood' have portrayed that sisterhood primarily in terms that reflected the concerns of the dominant (white middle-class) groups in the movement (cf. e.g. Spelman 1988; Harris 1990). Black feminist writers who have challenged that dominance within feminism have themselves portrayed black women as having a singular 'Afrocentric standpoint' (e.g. Collins 1990). Although human cognitive processes prevent our eliminating this tendency to assume homogeneity within a group, we can fight that tendency by cultivating avenues of dissent, opposition, and difference within our organizations, struggling to appreciate contradictions within a larger perceptual standpoint, and using plurals rather than singulars in our writing.

The advocacy of descriptive representation can emphasize the worst features of essentialism. When an extreme descriptivist writes, 'it is impossible for men to represent women' (Boyle 1983: 797),[5] that statement implies the corollary, that it is impossible for women to represent men. It also implies that any woman representative represents all women (and all women equally), regardless of the women's political beliefs, race, ethnicity, or other differences.

The essentializing feature of descriptive representation can be mitigated by stressing the non-essentialist and contingent reasons for selecting certain groups for descriptive representation. The selection process should begin by asking what features of the existing electoral process have resulted in lower proportions of certain descriptive groups in the legislature than in the population—a result that one would not expect by chance and that suggests the possibility that 'certain voices are being silenced or suppressed' (Phillips 1992: 88; also 1995: 53, 63). The next screening question should be whether the members of that group are able adequately to represent themselves. If the answer is yes, the third question might be whether the dominant group in the society has ever made it illegal for members of that group to represent themselves. If the answer to that third question is also yes, the group appears

---

[5] See also a group of Frenchwomen in 1789, cited in Phillips (1995: 52) ('a man, no matter how honest he may be, cannot represent a woman'), Beverley Baines, cited in Kymlicka (1993: 67), and Antoinetre, L. Brown; cited in Williams (1998: 133).

to be a good candidate for affirmative selective representation, on the grounds that the social, political, and economic processes that allowed one group in the past legally to forbid the political participation of another may well have their sequelae in the present, working through informal social, political, and economic structures rather than through the law.[6]

A formulation like this points backward to contingent historical processes rather than inward to an essential nature. It also implies that when the systemic barriers to participation have been eliminated through reform and social evolution, the need for affirmative steps to ensure descriptive representation will disappear. The institution of descriptive representation itself becomes contingent.

A second, and related, cost of selective descriptive representation involves the way developing institutions that encourage citizens to see themselves as members of a subgroup may erode the ties of unity across a nation, a political party, or a political movement (see e.g. Phillips 1995: 22 ff.). This serious cost has greater or lesser weight depending on the precise institutional arrangements. In some contexts, institutions that encourage subgroups tear deeply at the connected fabric of the whole. In other contexts, subgroups become the experiential anchors for participation that links the individual to the whole. As work on 'civil society' progresses, scholars may distinguish better than they have to date the characteristics and contexts that incline some institutions to the disintegrative, others to the integrative, function.

A third cost of selective descriptive representation applies specifically to a particular method for achieving this result—drawing electoral boundaries to create relatively homogeneous districts. This cost is the potential loss of influence in other districts. If, for example, white Democrats represent many substantive interests of black voters much better than white Republicans, and if concentrating black voters in black districts produces a few more black representatives at the cost of many more Republicans elected from other districts, then in some historical circumstances, such as when the percentages in a majority-rule legislature are almost tied between Republicans and Democrats, the substantive impact of losing those Democratic legislators will be high and the cost perhaps not worth paying (see e.g. Swain 1993: 7–19).

A fourth cost of selective descriptive representation lies in the possibility of

---

[6] The intent of this argument is not to restrict groups designated for selective representation to those who have been legally deprived of the vote or other rights of citizenship, but to signal this characteristic for particular attention in the contest for selection, because such a strong marker of historical discrimination tends to create communication impaired by distrust as well as a social meaning of lesser citizenship. See Phillips (1992, 1995), Kymlicka (1993, 1995a), and Williams (1998) on historical and systemic disadvantage. Guinier (1994: 140), however, points out that her argument does not rely primarily on the historic context of group disfranchisement.

reduced accountability. The descriptive characteristics of a representative can lull voters into thinking their substantive interests are being represented even when this is not the case. As one black representative to the US Congress told Carol Swain, 'One of the advantages, and disadvantages, of representing blacks is their shameless loyalty to their incumbents. You can almost get away with raping babies and be forgiven. You don't have *any* vigilance about your performance' (1993: 73).[7] One would expect this danger of blind loyalty to be eased as more descriptive representatives entered a representative assembly, allowing constituents to compare more easily the virtues of one descriptive representative against another. The appointment of Clarence Thomas to the Supreme Court of the United States may have served as a milestone in the evolution in this process in the black community, as some African American organizations (e.g. the Congressional Black Caucus and the NAACP) opposed Thomas's candidacy in spite of his descriptive characteristics (see Swain 1992; also West 1992; Crenshaw 1992). The decision of many women's groups not to support all women candidates for election represented a similar milestone among US feminists (Mezey 1994: 261).

Against these costs, one must weigh the benefits in enhanced deliberation of descriptive representation. These benefits, I argue, are greatest in contexts of communicative distrust and uncrystallized interests.

5. Contexts of Communicative Distrust

The quality of the mutual communication between representative and constituent varies from group to group and era to era. Historical circumstances can interfere with adequate communication between members of one group and members of another, particularly if one group is historically dominant and the other historically subordinate. A history of dominance and subordination typically breeds inattention, even arrogance, on the part of the dominant group and distrust on the part of the subordinate group.

In conditions of impaired communication, including impairment caused by inattention and distrust, the shared experience imperfectly captured by descriptive representation facilitates communication between representatives

---

[7] The representative's lack of vigilance derives in part from the fact that 'Black representatives from historically black districts are essentially guaranteed reelection if they survive their primaries' (Swain 1993: 220), a condition that in turn derives partly from the almost uniform commitment of black voters 'to the party, faction, or individual candidate that is most supportive of racial reform' (Pinderhughes 1987: 113). See Guinier (1994: 35, 58–60, 82) and de la Garza and DeSipio (1993) on the importance of designing representative systems that increase political participation and attentiveness among the electorate, and the problems of majority–minority districts in this respect.

and constituents. Representatives and voters who share some version of a set of common experiences and the outward signs of having lived through those experiences can often read one another's signals relatively easily and engage in relatively accurate forms of shorthand communication. Representatives and voters who share membership in a subordinate group can also forge bonds of trust based specifically on the shared experience of subordination.

Claudine Gay's (1996) data, for example, indicate that African American constituents in districts represented by an African American legislator are more likely to contact their representative than African American constituents in districts represented by a white legislator. As Representative Donald Payne, a black congressman, commented to Carol Swain, 'Black constituents feel comfortable with me, and see that I feel comfortable with them' (Swain 1993: 219). Groups that are disadvantaged in the electoral process differ, however, on this dimension. Replicating Gay's study but looking at women representatives, Elizabeth Haynes (1997) has shown that women in districts represented by a woman are *not* more likely to contact their representative than women in districts represented by a man. Problems in communication between men and women certainly exist, but the size of the male–female gaps in communication may well be smaller than the size of gaps in communication created by nationality, class, or race.[8]

In the United States voters have many of their most vital interests represented through the 'surrogate' representation of legislators elected from other districts. Advocates of particular political views who lose in one district, for example, can hope to be represented by advocates of those views elected in another district (Mansbridge 1998). Surrogate representatives do not have to be descriptive representatives. Adversary democratic norms are satisfied when the interests of a given group are represented equally aggressively by any representatives, so long as those interests are represented in proportion to the number of interest-bearers in the population. Deliberative democratic norms, as discussed earlier, require at least a 'threshold' presence in the deliberation, and perhaps proportionality as well, for reasons of synergy, critical mass, and the diversity of views within any given perspective. In this surrogate process, descriptive representation often plays its most useful role, allowing representatives who are themselves members of a subordinate group to circumvent the strong barriers to communication between dominant and

---

[8] See Williams (1998) on 'trust' for the history of African Americans' justified mistrust of whites in the U.S. See Tannen (1994: 73, 188) for implied comparisons of gender and ethnicity differences and Hyde (1990) on size of difference as well as existence of difference. Psychologists have now begun to include measures of size of difference in their studies. Many linguists have not yet adopted this strategy. In neither field are comparisons between the size of gender and other common differences standard—an omission that contributes to the common magnification of gender differences (Mansbridge 1993).

subordinate groups. Black representatives, for example, are likely to be contacted by blacks 'throughout the region' and not just in their own districts. The district administrator for Mickey Leland, a black Texas Democrat, told Carol Swain: 'What people don't understand is that Mickey Leland must be the [black] Congressman for the entire Southwest' (Swain 1993: 218).

One example will illustrate the communicative advantages of descriptive representation, even for women, whose barriers to communication with men are probably not as high as the barriers between blacks and whites. In 1970, before the current slight increase in the number of women representatives in the US Senate, Birch Bayh was arguably the progressive senator most sympathetic to the Equal Rights Amendment (ERA). One of his roles was, therefore, to act as a surrogate representative for the women proponents of the ERA. Bayh served the ERA activists, who consulted him both as mentor, through his commitments to progressive causes, and as gatekeeper, through his role as chair of the judiciary committee.

Early in the constitutional amendment process Senator Bayh suggested to the proponents an alternate wording for the ERA, based on the words of the existing Fourteenth Amendment to the constitution, which guaranteed equal rights based on race. The ERA proponents rejected Bayh's proposed wording as 'weakening' the force of the Equal Rights Amendment. It is not clear in retrospect, however, that the alternative wording would have weakened the Amendment. And the wording Bayh suggested would undoubtedly have greatly clarified the uncertainty that eventually became one main cause for the ERA's failure to be ratified in the states.

The history of the interaction between Birch Bayh and the ERA proponents reveals considerable distrust of Bayh among the proponents—a distrust greatly increased by the young male Ivy League staffer assigned to the project, who reportedly described the ERA proponents as 'hysterical' women. Had the Senate at that time included a powerful progressive female legislator such as Patricia Schroeder, the ERA proponents would undoubtedly have chosen her as their mentor. The female legislator in turn would almost certainly not have assigned such an insensitive staff member to the project. A female legislative mentor might even have been able to convince the ERA supporters to adopt a wording parallel to the Fourteenth Amendment, which in turn would very probably have resulted in the ERA's being ratified in the states. This ratification would have induced the Supreme Court to make gender a 'suspect category' in their analyses, which it is not now.

The failure of Birch Bayh to communicate with the ERA proponents in an atmosphere of mutual trust exemplifies the importance of descriptive representation in the larger system of surrogate representation. It suggests the following rule: the deeper the communicative chasm between a dominant and a subordinate group, the more descriptive representation, on both a surrogate and territorial basis, is needed to bridge that chasm.

6. Contexts of Uncrystallized Interests

In certain historical moments citizen interests on a given set of issues are relatively uncrystallized. The issues have not been on the political agenda long, candidates have not taken public positions on them, and political parties are not organized around them. In Central Europe after the fall of communism, for example, many political interests were relatively uncrystallized, as hundreds of new political parties struggled to define themselves on the issue map. (One Polish party called itself the 'Party X', using a consciously contentless signifier; another defined itself, with almost as little content, as 'slightly West of centre'.) When interests are uncrystallized, the best way to have one's most important substantive interests represented is often to choose a representative whose descriptive characteristics match one's own on the issues one expects to emerge. One might want to elect a representative from one's own geographical territory, class, or ethnicity. Then, as issues arise unpredictably, a voter can expect the representative to react more or less the way the voter would have done, on the basis of descriptive similarity. The original geographic representation of voters in the United States was undoubtedly intended in part to capture this form of descriptive representation.

In political systems where many issues such as those involving economic class are relatively crystallized, other issues, such as those involving gender, are surfacing and evolving rapidly on the political agenda. When this is the case, individuals for whom these relatively uncrystallized interests are extremely important may get their best substantive representation from a descriptive representative.[9]

In the United States, where party discipline is weak and representatives consequently have considerable autonomy, legislators often vote by what I have called elsewhere 'introspective representation', asking themselves what they think is the right policy for their constituents and the nation (Mansbridge 1998; see also Kingdon 1981: 45; Bernstein 1989; Stimson *et al.* 1995). In introspective representation, voters exercise power not by changing the behaviour of the representatives, as suggested in traditional mechanisms of accountability, but by electoral selection. In this form of representation, the voters often use descriptive characteristics, as well as party identification and indicators of character, as cues by which to predict whether a particular

---

[9] Two of Anne Phillips's four 'key arguments' for descriptive representation turn on this issue. One is 'the need to tackle those exclusions that are inherent in the party-packaging of political ideas' and the other 'the importance of a politics of transformation in opening up the full range of policy options' (1995: 25; see also 43–5, 50, 70, 151 ff.). Her analysis, particularly of transformative politics, goes much farther than I have the opportunity to do here.

candidate, if elected, will represent their interests, both crystallized and uncrystallized.

In 1981, for example, when the Illinois legislature was about to vote on the Equal Rights Amendment, I asked several legislators how they determined what their constituents thought about the Amendment. One rural legislator explained that he knew what his constituents felt because they felt the way he did: 'I come from my district, and they were brought up the same way that I am, or was, and worked the same way I always have' (Mansbridge 1986: 152).[10] As a descriptive representative of his constituents, he believed he could know their reactions to the ERA without the ERA having been on the political agenda when he was elected, and without consulting his constituents subsequently. He took himself to be 'one of them', and was presumably so taken by most of his constituents, by virtue of a cluster of descriptive characteristics, not one.

In the United States Congress, one Midwest Republican made a similar descriptive argument, assuming a similar homogeneity within another member's district:

I could take you down the hall and introduce you to a member who just drips his district, from his shoes to his straw hat. You don't have to go to his district to know what it's like, you just have to look at him. . . . Congress represents its districts because each member comes from his district much more so than because he tries to adapt his personal philosophy [to what his constituents want]. (Bianco 1994: 39)

Focusing on what seems more like a single descriptive characteristic, a black legislator told Richard Fenno, 'When I vote my conscience as a black man, I necessarily represent the black community. I don't have any trouble knowing what the black community thinks or wants' (Fenno 1978: 115). This legislator's stance of introspective representation in fact derived from far more than the colour of the legislator's skin. 'His own identification with the black community', Fenno commented, 'is obvious and total. Every expression he gives or gives off conveys the idea, "I am one of you"' (1978: 115). This representative assumed that he and his constituents shared a set of experiences that generated specific perspectives and interests requiring representation in the legislature. His constituents in turn used not only his skin colour but his body language, choice of words, accent, and other external

---

[10] Or, as member of Congress put it to John Kingdon: 'I grew up with these people and I guess I reflect their thinking' (1981: 45). Because of this, almost complete attitudinal identity with a majority of their constituents, members of Congress will say and believe, 'You'll find congressmen most of the time will want to vote according to their obligations and principles as they see them. The political considerations are less important' (1981: 46). As one journalist summed up the relationship: 'They [the members of Congress] just reflect where they came from' (1981: 47). Such statements reflect assumptions of a relative homogeneity of interests and perspectives within the majority that elected the representative (Bianco 1994).

signals to predict the likelihood of a large body of experience shared with them and other African Americans.[11]

When unable to select a representative with reliable descriptive characteristics, voters often select for what I call 'pseudo-description', mimicking descriptive behaviour. Samuel Popkin recounts President Gerald Ford's adventures on campaign in Texas, as Ford tried unsuccessfully to eat a tamale in order to show the Texas Mexican voters that he was 'like them' to the extent of appreciating their food. Popkin comments that familiarity with a culture's food is 'an obvious and easy test of ability to relate to the problems and sensibilities of the ethnic group and to understand and care about them' (Popkin 1994: 3). Later he confirms that:

Demographic facts provide a low-information shortcut to estimating a candidate's policy preferences. . . . Characteristics such as a candidate's race, ethnicity, religion, gender and local ties . . . are important cues because the voter observes the relationship between these traits and real-life behavior as part of his daily experience. When these characteristics are closely aligned with the interests of the voter, they provide a basis for reasonable, accessible, and economical estimates of candidate behavior. (1994: 63–5)

The accuracy of these cues, and the degree to which they predict 'identification' (Fenno 1978: 58–9) or 'common interests' (Bianco 1994), depend on the degree to which the descriptive characteristics are in fact aligned with the interests of the majority of voters in their districts, so that representatives engaged in introspective representation will reflect the policies their constituents would choose if they had greater knowledge and time for reflection.

In introspective representation both post-election communication and traditional accountability between the representative and the constituent can be non-existent, and the relation still fulfil democratic norms. Because this is not a traditional principal–agent relation but rather a relation only of selection, democratic norms requires that in the selection process communication be open, accurate, and likely to help participants achieve a better understanding of their interests. We can also judge the relationship normatively by making a third-person estimate of the substantive interests of the constituents and the degree to which the representative actually promotes those interests effectively in the assembly (Mansbridge 1998).[12]

When legislators are engaged primarily in introspective representation, descriptive representation will enhance that representation most when

---

[11] Conversely, both the West Indian background of General Colin Powell and other signals in his language, deportment, and political identification led some African Americans not to see him as a descriptive representative whom they would expect to act 'like them'.

[12] I use interests rather than opinions or preferences in this analysis because of the number of times, acknowledged by representatives and constituents themselves, that voter preferences do not match their deeper interests (see e.g. Bianco 1994: 17).

interests are relatively uncrystallized—that is, when party identification and campaign statements provide poor clues to a representative's future actions. On the many issues relating to gender, for example, where views are changing and policies developing in a relatively *ad hoc* way to meet a rapidly evolving situation, descriptive representatives are, other things equal, more likely than non-descriptive representatives to act as their surrogate constituents would like them to act.

Issues of race, which are somewhat more crystallized in the United States than issues of gender, also produce moments when a descriptive representative acts in a context of relatively uncrystallized interests. In 1993, for example, Carol Moseley-Braun was the only black member of the US Senate. Senator Jesse Helms had attached to some legislation an unrelated amendment renewing the design patent of the United Daughters of the Confederacy—which featured the Confederate flag. 'With many senators unaware of what they were voting on', the *New York Times* reported, Helms had won a test vote on his amendment, 52 to 48. Senator Moseley-Braun, who had earlier tried to bury Helms's attachment in committee, now argued vehemently against the Senate's legitimizing the flag by granting this patent. 'On this issue,' she contended, 'there can be no consensus. It is an outrage. It is an insult. It is absolutely unacceptable to me and to millions of Americans, black or white, that we would put the imprimatur of the United States Senate on this kind of idea.' After Moseley-Braun's impassioned speech, several senators reversed themselves, killing the measure. Some senators found themselves in the position of Robert F. Bennett, Republican from Utah, who, in offering the motion to reverse, told the Senate that he 'didn't have the slightest idea what this was about' when he had voted for the amendment the first time, and had joined the majority in a simple effort to keep Democrats from killing a Republican amendment (Clymer 1993: B6).

As an African American, Moseley-Braun was undoubtedly more likely than even the most progressive white representative to notice and feel it important to condemn the use of the Confederate flag on the design patent of the United Daughters of the Confederacy. The flag issue had not previously appeared on the active political agenda of either the nation or the state of Illinois, Braun's constituency. She undoubtedly had never mentioned the issue in her election campaign. Nor could she have feared re-election sanctions on this point, since without her intervention the amendment would have passed unnoticed. She did use the issue to consolidate her position with her black voters in the next election, but one can imagine a less dramatic issue in which this would not be the case. The most important reason for her action seems to have been the particular sensibility, created by experience, that led her to notice the Confederate flag and be offended by it. Her descriptive characteristics—going beyond skin colour to her use of language and ties to her church—had earlier signalled that sensibility to her black constituents.

Experience as an African American made Braun the only member of the Senate not only to notice this issue and fight for it, but also to find words to describe it that would convince the other senators to change their minds. Had other African Americans been with her in the Senate, those legislators might have helped Braun keep the amendment in committee, or have seconded her speech, making it easier for her, as a freshman senator, to speak out against Helms, one of the most senior members of the chamber. Greater representation of that sensibility would probably have produced an even better deliberative process.

With respect to gender, many issues relating to sexual harassment and violence against women are politically salient but have not become sufficiently crystallized that the two main parties in the United States have developed distinctive and opposing positions in regard to them, or that candidates usually mention their positions on these issues in their campaigns. It is not surprising, then, that women legislators have usually been the ones to bring these issues to the legislative table. In Illinois, for example, the Commission on the Status of Women, a bipartisan legislative group including a few non-legislators such as the anti-feminist Phyllis Schlafly, brought to the legislature a bill that, among other things, changed the burden of proof in rape (requiring the alleged rapist rather than the victim to show that the victim had consented) and instituting the crime of rape in marriage. This pattern of distinctive attention has been repeated in legislature after legislature. Having more women in office unquestionably makes government policies more responsive to women's interests.[13]

Disadvantaged groups also may need descriptive representation in order to get these uncrystallized substantive interests represented with sufficient vigour (see Phillips 1995: 69 and *passim* on the 'degree of vigorous advocacy that people bring to their own concerns'). As Pamela Conover observed in a different context, 'When it comes to thinking about social groups it matters enormously whether we are part of that group. Try as hard as we can, the political sympathy that we feel for other groups is never quite the same as that which they feel for themselves or that which we feel for ourselves' (Conover 1986: 17). In the case of Anita Hill versus Clarence Thomas, for example, an issue involving sexual harassment (which could not have been on the agenda of the members of the United States House of Representatives when they ran for election) emerged in the Senate hearings on the nomination of Thomas for the Supreme Court. It was the women in the House of Representatives, where the percentage of women had reached a critical mass, who took decisive action. The famous photograph of five women legislators from the

---

13 Thomas (1994) and Mezey (1994) point out that although on several feminist issues party affiliation predicts feminist position better than female gender, gender has its own independent effect). See also Berkman and O'Connor (1993), Skjeie (1991), Jonasdottir (1988).

House of Representatives charging up the Senate steps to demand a delay in the Thomas nomination captured for many women voters the need to have representatives of their own gender in the legislative body.

7. Beyond Substantive Representation: Changing the Social Meaning of Group Membership

Two other benefits of descriptive representation do not enhance substantive representation, but nevertheless deserve consideration in any discussion of the costs and benefits of descriptive representation. These benefits, both involving status, arise from the representative assembly's role in constructing social meaning.

The Construction of Social Meaning

In certain historical conditions what it means to be a member of a particular social group includes some form of 'second-class citizenship'. Operationally, this is often the case when the group has at some point in the polity's history been legally excluded from the vote. In these conditions, the ascriptive character of one's membership in that group often carries the historically embedded meaning 'Persons with these characteristics do not rule', with the possible implication, 'Persons with these characteristics are not able to (fit to) rule'.[14]

Whenever this is the case, the presence or absence in the ruling assembly (and other ruling bodies, such as the executive and judiciary) of a proportional number of individuals carrying the group's ascriptive characteristics shapes the social meaning of those characteristics in a way that affects most bearers of those characteristics in the polity.

A parallel outside the polity may clarify the process of meaning construction. Before the Second Wave of the women's movement in the United States and the revolution in women's sports that it brought about, it was part of the definition of 'female' to be non-athletic. The definition was not all-encompassing: some women found ways of being female and athletic. But most women were expected, and expected themselves, to be poor athletes. Today, women's sports in schools and universities have begun to be funded, although not usually at levels comparable to those of men's sports. Women athletes are in the news—although again, not to the same degree as men. These social facts change the definition of being female in regard to athletics in a way that affects every female regardless of her own orientation and actions.

---

[14] In German, *Regierungsfähig*: 'fit to rule'.

Similarly, when descriptive characteristics signal major status differences connected with citizenship, then a low percentage of a given descriptive group in the representational body creates social meanings attached to those characteristics that affect all holders of the characteristics. Low percentages of blacks and women, for example, create the meaning that blacks and women cannot rule, or are not suitable for rule.

In 1981 Virginia Sapiro (1981: 712) argued that increased descriptive representation of women in the legislatures would undermine the perception that politics is a 'male domain' (see also Phillips 1995: 39, 79 ff.). In 1976 Mack Jones reported that the growing number of black elected officials in the South had changed that region's political culture: 'The idea of Blacks as political participants rather than subjects is becoming the norm' (1976: 406). In 1989 a black member of the Arkansas House of Representatives said he worked to help blacks get elected in local races because he wanted to dispel 'the myth that some white kids might have that blacks can't serve or shouldn't be serving at the courthouse' (trial transcript from *Whitfield* v. *Democratic Party*, cited in Guinier 1994: 54; see also 34, 36).

This is a historically specific and contextual dynamic. Normatively, making a claim for descriptive representation on these grounds requires historical grounding for the factual contention that the social meaning of membership in a given descriptive group incorporates a legacy of second-class citizenship. Such a claim could point, for confirmation, to a history of being legally deprived of the vote.

A major cost to this claim, in addition to the problem of essentialism discussed earlier, involves the way the very process of making a claim of historical disability to some degree undermines claims on other political tracks that members of the group have currently achieved the status of first-class citizens. As in any claim for justice based on disadvantage, signalling that disadvantage in public erodes the public presentation of the group as fully equal. This cost must be balanced against the benefit of creating new social meanings that include members of the group as truly 'able to rule'.

Claims like this one, based partly on the concept of reparations, do not in theory entail the cost of painting a group as disadvantaged, because—as in the restitution of property in the countries of the former Soviet bloc—claims for reparations can be and are made by political, economic, and social equals (or superiors). But claims for reparation do require both establishing a history of intentional injustice and arguing convincingly that a particular form of reparation (in this case establishing some form of descriptive representation) is the best way of redressing that injustice.[15]

---

[15] Distinguishing between minority 'nationalities' within a nation-state and minority 'ethnic groups', Kymlicka (1995a) makes a convincing case on the basis of reparations for nationalities having forms of representation separate from those of the majority population. Although he

The argument here for the creation of social meaning is an argument not for a right but for a social good. The argument is simply that if the costs are not too great, any measure is good that increases the degree to which the society as a whole sees all (or almost all) descriptive groups as equally capable of ruling.

De facto *Legitimacy*

A second and related benefit to descriptive representation comes in the increased empirical (or sociological, or *de facto*) legitimacy of the polity. Seeing proportional numbers of members of their group exercising the responsibility of ruling with full status in the legislature can enhance *de facto* legitimacy by making citizens, and particularly members of historically under-represented groups, feel as if they themselves were present in the deliberations (Gosnell 1948: 131, cited in Pitkin 1967: 78; also Minow 1991: 286 n. 69, 291; Guinier 1994: 35, 39; Phillips 1995; Kymlicka 1993: 83). Seeing women from the House of Representatives storming the steps of the United States Senate, for example, made some women feel actively represented in ways that a photograph of male legislators could never have done.

These feelings are deeply intertwined with what might be called the 'psychological' benefits of descriptive surrogate representation to those voters who, because of selective bias against their characteristics, are less than proportionately represented in the legislature. The need for role models, for identification, and for what Charles Taylor (1992) has called 'equal dignity' and 'the politics of recognition' can be assimilated under this rubric. In many historical moments, these factors may be of great importance to a particular constituency.

I stress the creation of social meaning and *de facto* legitimacy rather than, say, the need for role models on the part of individuals in the descriptively under-represented group[16] because points like these have often been presented as questions of individual psychology. Instead, I want to point out that the social meaning exists outside the heads of the members of the descriptive group, and that *de facto* legitimacy has substantive consequences.

I agree that social relations among and between groups can have major

does not espouse descriptive representation for minority ethnic groups or women, the same kind of case could be made for temporary forms of selective descriptive representation. A full analysis of historical exclusion from rights of citizenship would encompass, among other groups, Jews, Asians, young people, and the propertyless. See Williams (1998) on 'memory'.

[16] e.g. 'Some time in the past it was necessary to have black faces in Congress to serve as role models for other young people who would aspire to be elected officials . . .' (Representative Craig Washington, interview with Carol Swain, 1991; Swain 1993: 193); 'Blacks need role models in government . . . they need to know that good leadership (or bad) is not dominated by one race or group' (Preston 1978: 200).

effects on individual identity. It is important that members of a disadvantaged group not be given, in Taylor's (1992: 65) words, 'a demeaning picture of themselves'. From this perspective, if the costs are not too great, we should promote diversity in all positions of authority and excellence. Young people in particular need these kinds of 'role models'. I have no quarrel with this point. Yet I consider of even greater importance the effects of social meaning on the perceptions and actions of members of the more advantaged groups. There are sometimes more of them, and they are more powerful. My aim, in short, is changing the psychology of the oppressor far more than the psychology of the oppressed.

For similar reasons I do not contrast 'symbolic' and 'substantive' representation. In political contexts the word 'symbol' often bears the unspoken prefix 'mere'. Moreover, symbols are often perceived as being 'only' in people's heads rather than 'real'. Psychological needs are intangible, and it is easy to contrast the 'intangible' to the 'real' (cf. Swain 1993: 211, but *per contra* 217). In most writing on this subject the structural consequences of descriptive representation have been de-emphasized in favour of psychological ones in ways that I believe does not reflect their actual relative influence in contemporary political life.

8. Institutionalizing Fluid Forms of Descriptive Representation

Because there are always costs to privileging any one characteristic that enhances accurate substantive representation over others, voters and institutional designers alike must balance those benefits against the costs. And because I have argued that the benefits of descriptive representation vary greatly by context, it would be wise, in building descriptive representation into any given democratic institutional design, to make its role fluid, dynamic, and easily subject to change.

This analysis suggests that voters and the designers of representative institutions should accept some of the costs of descriptive representation in historical circumstances when (1) communication is impaired, often by distrust, and (2) interests are relatively uncrystallized. The contextual character of this analysis suggests strongly that any institutionalization of descriptive representation is best kept fluid. Full-assembly forms of descriptive representation are best kept advisory and experimental for a good while, as they currently are. Selective forms are also best kept experimental. Permanent quotas are relatively undesirable because they are both static and highly essentializing. They assume, for example, that any 'woman' can stand for all 'women', any 'black' for all 'blacks'.

Drawing political boundaries to produce majority–minority districts is also both relatively static and essentializing. Cumulative voting in at-large districts (Guinier 1994) is far more fluid, as it allows individuals to choose whether they want to cast all their votes for a descriptive representative or divide their votes among different representatives, each of whom can represent one or another facet of the voters' interests. Such systems, however, have their own costs in party collusion to produce non-competing candidates and the consequent voter demobilization.[17] Systems of proportional representation with party lists have well-known costs, but are still a relatively flexible way to introduce selective descriptive representation, as those lists can change easily in each election.[18] Similarly, experimental decisions by political parties to make a certain percentage of candidates descriptively representative of an underrepresented group are preferable to quotas embedded in law or constitutions. Such *ad hoc* arrangements can be flexible over time. Less obtrusive, but also undoubtedly less immediately successful, are other 'enabling devices', such as schools for potential candidates (Phillips 1995: 57), scholarships to law schools for members of groups that are both historically disadvantaged and proportionately underrepresented, and other reforms aimed at reducing the barriers to representation.[19] At any given level of effectiveness, the more fluid the mechanism the better, so that it can respond to changing contexts.

This chapter represents a plea for moving beyond a dichotomous approach to descriptive representation. It argues that descriptive representation is not always necessary, but rather that the best approach to descriptive representation is contextual, asking when the benefits of such representation might be most likely to exceed the costs. Contexts of communication impaired by distrust and of relatively uncrystallized interests should alert both voters and the designers of institutions to the possibility that descriptive representation will further democratic ends. Operationally, one key trigger for raising the possibility of both these contexts is the historical fact of a descriptively coded group having been deprived in the past of one or more of the rights of citizenship.

---

[17] The state of Illinois practised cumulative voting until the process was eliminated in 1982 in a cost-cutting effort that reduced the size of the assembly. The system produced greater proportional representation in the state legislature but not a great degree of voter choice, because often for strategic reasons the two major parties ran altogether only three candidates for the three seats available in each district (Sawyer and MacRae 1962; Adams 1996).

[18] See Zimmerman (1992, 1994) for the positive and negative features of cumulative voting and different forms of proportional representation.

[19] E.g. those studied by the Canadian Royal Commission on Electoral Reform: 'caps on nomination campaign expenses; public funding of nomination campaign expenses. . . . the establishing of formal search committees within each party to help identify and nominate potential candidates from disadvantaged groups; financial incentives to parties that nominate or elect members of disadvantaged groups; and so on' (Kymlicka 1993: 62).

5

The Uneasy Alliance of Group Representation and Deliberative Democracy

MELISSA S. WILLIAMS

In recent years a number of democratic theorists have converged on the conclusion that democratic justice towards minority or disadvantaged groups requires that they be adequately represented in processes of political decision-making.[1] When policies are formulated without the active participation of members of such groups, they are likely to be biased or incomplete in various ways. Where relations of social and political inequality have long been structured along the lines of group identity, there is an inadequate foundation of trust between citizens who belong to marginalized groups and representatives who belong to privileged groups. Without this trust, the flow of communication which is a precondition of effective representation is unlikely to exist. Moreover, these groups' experience of marginalization yields an understanding of social practices and institutions which is not readily available to individuals who lack that experience. Membership in a marginalized group often brings with it a distinct political voice, and effective representation for such groups requires that this voice receive a hearing in the political process.

Even if marginalized groups achieve self-representation in decision-making processes, however, their mere presence may do nothing to shape the outcomes of those processes. If decision-making is competitive and majoritarian, there is nothing to prevent the more powerful and numerous participants from ignoring marginalized-group voices.[2] Assuming that democratic

An earlier version of this essay was written during my fellowship year at the Program in Ethics and the Professions at Harvard University. It is part of a larger research project for which I have received funding from the Social Sciences and Humanities Research Council of Canada. I am grateful to both institutions for their support. I would also like to thank Edward Andrew, Joseph Carens, David Kahane, Will Kymlicka, Dominique Leydet, Patchen Markell, Wayne Norman, Alec Walen, and David Welch for their thoughtful comments on earlier drafts.

[1] See esp. Young (1990: 185–91; 1994); Guinier (1994); Phillips (1995); Williams (1995, 1998).

[2] For further discussion of this problem, see Beitz (1989: 135); Guinier (1994: 105–8); Williams (1998, chs. 4 and 7).

principles of individual equality preclude the systematic over-representation of minorities in decision-making bodies, this means that the only hope that marginalized-group presence will have a lasting effect on policy outcomes is that decisions are based not only on the counting of votes but also on the sharing of reasons. Thus the defence of group representation depends importantly upon encouraging the deliberative features of democratic decision-making—those aimed at reaching principled agreement—and discouraging the log-rolling or competitive features, in which small numbers and limited resources translate into a failure to secure trade-offs from other actors.

As this suggests, defenders of group representation and theorists of deliberative democracy are natural allies. The challenge of pluralism to political legitimacy lies at the heart of the project of deliberative democracy. Both moral pluralism and social diversity undercut the liberal state's claim to neutrality and require an alternative foundation of legitimacy. Deliberative democrats extend the liberal notion that legitimate government is based on consent by arguing that the terms of social and political co-operation should be the outgrowth of a reasoned exchange among citizens. To sustain the claim to legitimacy, however, the processes of deliberative democracy must include all relevant social and political perspectives. Just as difference theorists have argued that justice towards marginalized groups requires deliberative processes of political decision-making, deliberative democrats have argued that a full account of just and legitimate deliberative processes must give some attention to the place of marginalized-group needs and identities in discursive exchange. (See e.g. Sunstein 1988; Habermas 1996a: 183.) Thus the connection between group representation and deliberative democracy is internal to both bodies of democratic theory.

Despite these close affinities between arguments for group representation and defences of deliberative democracy, they are not coextensive; there are also important tensions between them. Some of these tensions have been traced out in recent feminist engagements with deliberative theory, and have been answered by deliberative democrats. Although I am deeply sympathetic with the project of deliberative democracy, I am not persuaded that its defenders have adequately addressed the challenges of social difference—difference defined along the lines of gender, race, ethnicity, class, sexuality, and so on—to a deliberative conception of legitimacy. Indeed, if we take the challenges of social difference seriously, we find that they threaten to undermine the very notions of reasonableness and reason-giving upon which deliberative theory depends for its conception of legitimacy. In particular, we find that whether or not citizens will recognize others' reasons *as* reasons may be a socioculturally contingent matter. Moreover, it seems likely that the contingency of this recognition may tend to be resolved in a manner that systematically disadvantages the reasons of marginalized groups in a discursive exchange. The theory of deliberative democracy, while the best account of legitimacy we have going, remains incomplete until it addresses this problem.

Theorists of group difference have been highly critical of the liberal state's claims of neutrality and impartiality: claims of impartiality, they argue, are always purchased at the price of suppressing social difference. One of the central aims of deliberative theory is to redeem the ideal of impartiality by defining political processes in a manner which avoids bias against valid social interests. The next part of this essay presents the broad outlines of theories of deliberative democracy and explores the place of the concept of impartiality in those theories.[3] There we see that, for deliberative democrats, impartiality is a virtue both of institutions and of individual citizens. In Section 2 I explore the different kinds of contributions that marginalized-group perspectives make to democratic deliberation. In Section 3, drawing on and extending recent feminist critiques of deliberative democracy, I explore two interrelated challenges to deliberative theory, one focused on the standard of reasonableness and the idea of reason-giving and the other on the contingent social and political circumstances under which marginalized-group perspectives may sway the judgement of other citizens. Finally, I explore the implications of these changes for our more general notions of the virtues and responsibilities of citizenship. The essay also includes an Appendix summarizing a debate in the United States Senate that illustrates the contingency of reason-giving in public discourse.

1. Deliberative Democracy and the Ideal of Impartiality

Theories of deliberative democracy rely—in several ways and with varying degrees of explicitness—on the ideal of impartiality as a regulative principle.[4] Before turning to a discussion of the place of impartiality in models of deliberative democracy, though, it will be helpful to present a brief sketch of what deliberative democracy is.[5] First and foremost, theories of deliberative

---

[3] This discussion connects this essay to a broader project, tentatively titled *Reconstructing Impartiality*, of which it will be a part.

[4] Thus one of the two pillars of Jürgen Habermas's theory of discourse ethics, the discourse principle, 'is only intended to explain the point of view from which norms of action can be *impartially justified*' (Habermas 1996a: 108). The discourse principle provides that 'Just those action norms are valid to which all possibly affected persons could agree as participants in rational discourses' (1996a: 107). See also Sunstein (1993: 17).

[5] In the following discussion I include a broad range of contemporary theorists in the category of 'deliberative democrats'. There are obvious differences among these theorists, particularly according to whether the work of John Rawls or that of Jürgen Habermas has had the stronger influence on their work. On the themes which most concern me here, however, the similarities among these theorists are more pertinent than their differences.

democracy are concerned with the problem of political justification in the face of moral disagreement, and aim to provide a solution to that problem. According to the ideal of deliberative democracy, Joshua Cohen tells us, 'justification of the exercise of collective political power is to proceed on the basis of a free public reasoning among equals' (Cohen 1996: 99; see also Cohen 1989; Manin 1987). Not every form of political discourse conforms to the ideal of deliberative democracy; the idea of free public reasoning among equals constrains both the context and the content of discussion. Most importantly, deliberative democracy requires that the context of political discussion is one in which participating citizens stand in a relation of equality to one another and aim at reaching moral agreement on the important features of their shared social and political life. As expressed by Amy Gutmann and Dennis Thompson, the core idea of deliberative democracy is the principle of reciprocity, which 'calls on citizens to continue to seek fair terms of cooperation among equals' (Gutmann and Thompson 1996: 53).

As regards the content of political discourse, theories of deliberative democracy impose several further important constraints. Participants in democratic deliberation must defend their preferred understandings of the public interest or common good on the basis of *moral or ethical reasons* which are acceptable to all participants. This view of democratic legitimacy stands in contrast, in particular, to understandings of politics grounded in strategies of mutual advantage.[6] The legitimacy of political action turns not on whether it serves all citizens' interests equally well, but on whether it is grounded in reasons that all can accept as valid. What constitutes mutually acceptable reasons? Most importantly, such reasons should not appeal to premises on which there is fundamental and reasonable disagreement, i.e. premises whose plausibility cannot be established through 'relatively reliable methods of inquiry' (Gutmann and Thompson 1996: 56). Insistence on such premises (of which the clearest examples are the dictates of revealed religion) destroys the equal positioning of the participants in the discussion by privileging the moral commitments of some over others. (See Cohen 1996: 101.)

On the phenomenological level, deliberative democracy looks something like this: We make arguments to one another about the requirements of the common good, and try to persuade one another of our understanding of that good. Our arguments are grounded in reasons which we believe others can accept, and they are aimed at what is *common* rather than what is particular to individual or group. Thus we do not make appeals to divine authority or to controversial understandings of human nature as the ultimate ground of our claims on other citizens. The claims we make regarding particular individuals

---

[6] For critiques of conceptions of justice grounded in mutual advantage, see Barry (1995, ch. 2), and Gutmann and Thompson (1996: 57–8).

or groups must be framed not in terms of their narrow interests, but in terms of shared commitments to public ends, including the public end of justice. In speaking, then, we take up our identity as citizens concerned with the common good, not (except in so far as it sheds light on shared ends) that of bearers of particular interests. Finally, deliberative democracy makes demands on our character as well as on our public self-presentation: we must enter the conversation with sufficient open-mindedness that we can be persuaded by the arguments of others.

How does such persuasion come about? We hear ways of characterizing issues of joint concern that are novel to us, that cause us to see those issues in a different light, and that do a better job of making sense of the facts of the case and of our own conflicting moral intuitions than do the accounts we had hitherto affirmed.[7] We narrow the range of disagreement through this process, and our collective decisions reflect a greater degree of a common sense of the matter than we had possessed in advance of the discussion. To the extent that no voices were silenced in the deliberative process, and everyone's arguments were listened to open-mindedly, the decision we arrive at has a greater legitimacy than it could have had through any other method of decision-making.

Getting at the ways in which the ideal of impartiality is implicated in theories of deliberative democracy is complicated by the multiple meanings of the term 'impartiality'. Indeed, some theorists eschew the term altogether because of its strong association with notions of deductive reasoning, with the ideal of the impersonal judge, and with unsustainable claims to moral authority—in short, with characteristic features of what I have called the juridical model of justice (Williams 1995).[8] But these do not exhaust the available ways of thinking about impartiality, and several other understandings of impartiality permeate every discussion of deliberative democracy. The meaning of impartiality as an essential (if not the sole) element of justice in a democratic society is illuminated, in particular, by examination of the dual meaning of its opposite, partiality. The justice of a judgement or policy depends, first, upon its not being partial in the sense of 'incomplete': it must take all relevant evidence, perspectives, and persons into account. Secondly, justice depends

---

[7] As this formulation suggests, it seems to me likely that deliberative democracy's phenomenology of persuasion bears important similarities to the idea of reflective equilibrium on which Rawls's views of justification rely so heavily.

[8] See especially Gutmann and Thompson's distinction between the principle of impartiality and the principle of reciprocity, and their rejection of the former in favour of the latter (1996: 53–4, 59–63). At the same time they acknowledge that what they mean by 'reciprocity' is closely akin to what Brian Barry defines as 'justice as impartiality', namely, 'principles and rules that are capable of forming the basis of free agreement among people seeking agreement on reasonable terms' (Barry 1995: 11); see Gutmann and Thompson (1996: 373–4 nn. 1–3). Cf. Sunstein (1993: 24): 'the principle of impartiality requires government to provide reasons that can be intelligible to different people operating from different premises'.

on judgements and policies that are not partial in the sense of 'biased': they must not favour some over others on morally arbitrary grounds. As Benhabib puts it, 'What is considered impartial has to be "in the best interests of all equally"' (Benhabib 1996: 83; see also Chambers 1996: 100–1). Further, impartiality so understood may be a virtue of individuals as they deliberate, a virtue of institutions and practices, or a virtue of laws and policies.

The principle of impartiality permeates characterizations of the ideal of deliberative democracy in at least six ways:

1. *Impartiality as inclusiveness: persons*. All theories of deliberative democracy make the inclusiveness of democratic processes central to their normative ideals. Democratic decisions should in principle be based on the deliberation of all (Manin 1987: 352). As John Dryzek articulates the ideal, 'No concerned individuals should be excluded, and if necessary, some educative mechanism should promote the competent participation of persons with a material interest in the issues at hand who might otherwise be left out' (Dryzek 1990: 43). It is important to note that inclusiveness as an element of impartiality is substantively related to absence of bias as the essence of impartiality. As Jürgen Habermas notes, 'nothing better prevents others from perspectivally distorting one's own interests than actual participation' (Habermas 1990: 67). In any case, deliberative democracy aspires to a polity in which public decisions are justifiable to all citizens, and in which all public actors hold themselves accountable to give publicly acceptable reasons in defence of their actions. Although there may some limitations on the degree to which this aspiration can be met, even in theory, it remains the regulative goal of deliberative democracy.[9]

2. *Impartiality as inclusiveness: issues*. Deliberative democrats seek to structure political institutions and processes so that all relevant considerations are brought to bear on political decisions. The quest for inclusiveness operates on two levels. First, deliberative democracy aims to ensure that all of the reasons and evidence that are relevant to a particular decision are brought to bear on the deliberative process.[10] (See e.g. Manin 1987; cf. Cohen and Rogers 1995: 42–3.) Secondly, there is no subject-matter which is immune, in principle, to public discussion. In contrast to Rawlsian liberals, deliberative democrats

---

[9] See esp. Gutmann and Thompson (1996: 128), where they address the challenges of achieving such universal accountability, both at the level of theory and at the level of practice. See also Chambers (1996: 197–8).

[10] In part, as I will discuss further below, inclusiveness with respect to issues is important because the *soundness* (as distinct from the *justice*) of public decisions depends on a thorough consideration of all relevant evidence. In part, though, this form of inclusiveness is an important addendum to the inclusion of all relevant persons in the deliberative process in cases where inclusiveness as regards persons does not automatically ensure inclusiveness as regards reasons. This is particularly likely in areas where citizens are not able to act as effective advocates of their own interests, as is frequently the case with children and the mentally disabled.

would not take even basic rights and liberties 'off the political agenda'.[11] The openness of the political agenda means that previously addressed issues are always potentially subject to public debate. (See e.g. Gutmann and Thompson 1996: 83.)

3. *Impartiality as absence of bias: institutional structure.* The structure of the deliberative situation is itself impartial, in so far as participants are characterized as standing in relations of perfect equality to each other. None has any structural advantage in getting her views heard sympathetically by others; everything turns on the persuasiveness of the arguments themselves. '[P]articipation in . . . deliberation is governed by the norms of equality and symmetry; all have the same chances to initiate speech acts, to question, to interrogate, and to open debate' (Benhabib 1996: 70). In short, relations of power have no place within the deliberative process.

4. *Impartiality as absence of bias: reasons.* The core principle of deliberative democracy is that the reasons relied upon to justify political decisions are acceptable to all. Thus, reasons participants offer in defence of their interpretations of shared ends are themselves 'impartial' reasons, in two senses. First, as discussed above, reasons must not rely upon premises which can only be affirmed by some participants, of which premises grounded in revealed religion are the most clear-cut example. Secondly, reasons should appeal to the interests that all participants share rather than to the partial interests of some subset of participants. In a deliberative process the argument that what is good for General Motors is good for the country, without a more specific account of how other social actors will benefit from the flourishing of General Motors, simply carries no persuasive force. Finally, the impartiality of reasons should function as a constraint on the public presentation as well as the development of deliberative decisions. As Seyla Benhabib puts it, 'some moral ideal of impartiality is a regulative principle that should govern not only our *deliberations* in public but also the *articulation* of reasons by public institutions' (Benhabib 1996: 83).

5. *Impartiality as absence of bias: participants.* The impartiality of deliberative democracy depends importantly not only on the structure of institutions and on the content of political discourse, but also on the character of democratic citizens; it is a virtue of individuals as well as of institutions and practices. Participants in democratic deliberation should give 'full and impartial consideration' to various alternative principles and courses of action before them

---

[11] See esp. Benhabib (1996: 79–80), where she argues that the content of basic human and civil rights is always essentially contested in a democracy. Benhabib offers this statement both as an (accurate, in my view) empirical account of the contestation of basic principles, but also as an element of the normative theory of deliberative democracy. This is not to say, of course, that deliberative democracy would allow such contestation to make basic rights susceptible to change by simple majoritarian procedures, as Benhabib reassures us. The point rather is that deliberative democracy does not seek to shelter any principles from reasoned critique and review.

(Cohen and Rogers 1995: 96). Thus, impartiality is a feature not only of the spirit in which participants should *speak*, but also of the spirit in which they should *listen* and *judge* each other's speeches (see Williams 1995: 85–7). Most importantly, perhaps, democratic deliberation depends upon citizens' possessing qualities of character that include open-mindedness and a willingness to be persuaded by reasons different from the ones they brought to the public forum. 'Open-minded citizens try to break personal and institutional habits that would discourage them from accepting an opposing position at some time in the future, or at least from modifying their position in that direction. Both the political mind and the political forum should be kept open to reconsideration of decisions already made and policies already adopted' (Gutmann and Thompson 1996: 82–3).

6. *Impartiality as absence of bias: outcomes*. Deliberative democracy takes as both its premiss and its conclusion that political decisions should not systematically favour some persons or interests over others. This is not to say that deliberative decisions will not sometimes require the unequal distribution of benefits or burdens, but that whenever such inequalities exist they will be justifiable through reasons which all could accept.

I find this ideal of democracy very appealing, and I am among those who have argued that some model of deliberative democracy is a necessary presupposition of any coherent defence of marginalized-group representation (Williams 1998). Yet for a number of reasons I remain uneasy about the adequacy of existing accounts of deliberative democracy as a model of justice towards marginalized groups. The remainder of this essay will continue to explore some of the reservations I have about the capacity of deliberative democracy to serve the end of justice towards marginalized groups, and to see what resources we might have for answering them. It proceeds by asking a general question: How does attention to the perspectives of marginalized groups contribute to the legitimacy of political decisions reached through democratic deliberation?

2. Marginalized Group Perspectives in Democratic Deliberation

A plurality of social perspectives is a necessary presupposition for deliberative democracy; otherwise, there would be nothing to be gained from discussion.[12] Pluralism enhances deliberation because it expands the number of alternative understandings of a problem we can entertain in attempting to

---

[12] Cf. Phillips (1995: 151): 'Deliberation matters only because there *is* difference; if some freak of history or nature had delivered a polity based on unanimous agreement, then politics would be virtually redundant and the decisions would already be made.'

resolve it. In particular, the presence of a plurality of points of view or of opinions within political discourse presumably strengthens our judgements and our decisions by allowing us to anticipate some of the weaknesses and pitfalls that attend any particular perspective. It allows decisions to be more complete, to comprehend a greater array of social and political possibilities, and to foresee a greater number of social and political consequences of our decisions.

So far, it is clear that many different forms of social diversity will enhance the deliberative process, and that marginalized-group perspectives constitute a dimension of pluralism which will contribute at least as much to the comprehensiveness of political decisions as any other. Indeed, there may be good reasons to suppose that they will contribute more, since their perspectives have historically tended to get ignored in the political process. They may see things about social forces that are not readily apparent to others, and what they see may turn out to be extremely valuable for the formulation of good public policy (see Cohen and Rogers, 1995: 42–3; Young 1997b). This notion lay behind some of the strongest arguments for the extension of the franchise to women in the US woman suffrage movement at the beginning of this century. Activists, notably Jane Addams, argued that changes in industrial production and the dynamics of increasing urbanization meant that social functions (hygiene, waste disposal, health) which formerly had been performed within the household now needed to be addressed as matters of *public* policy. Because women were the agents within the household who had performed these social roles, Addams argued, they had a knowledge about such needs that men generally did not possess. Women should have an equal place in politics, therefore, because the formulation of good public policy depended crucially upon their input into the decision-making process (Addams 1914).

While the foregoing account makes a great deal of sense of the ways in which a more inclusive deliberative politics serves our interest in the *soundness* of political judgements, however, it does not tell us much about the ways in which a deliberative politics of difference can serve the end of *justice*. That is, while it presents reasons why the perspectives of marginalized groups might improve social policy, it does not give an account of how including those perspectives within the deliberative process will help to ameliorate groups' systematic marginalization in the society at large, i.e. to increase the justice of social and political arrangements. The dynamics of deliberation through which marginalized-group perspectives could reshape public understandings of justice in ways that help to dismantle the social structures of inequality, I believe, must be somewhat different from the dynamics of deliberation that existing models of deliberative democracy presuppose (and which I have roughly sketched above). It is here that my concerns about the limitations of the deliberative model arise.

To explain, let me begin by sketching a description of the dynamics of a deliberative politics which includes the voices of marginalized groups and serves the end of ameliorating the structures of inequality that sustain their identity as such. In such a process members of marginalized groups explain how an existing practice functions to reproduce their marginalization and prevents them from being able to participate as full and equal members of society. For example, women might undertake to explain to men how sexual harassment impedes their ability to perform their work or to rise through the ranks in their careers. People with disabilities might try to explain how much time it takes them to navigate their way through a city that was not built with them in mind, and how participating in some spheres of social life and employment is simply impossible for them, not because of the nature of their disabilities but because they are physically prevented from entering the relevant spaces. Other participants in the discussion—men, or persons without disabilities—listen to their accounts, and learn to see their own practices from a new angle. But there is more to it than this: for in order for the arguments to have any impact on the social structure of inequality, the listeners must also learn to see their own practices as oppressive to others, as unjust. Finally, they must be willing to change those practices, even though doing so will almost certainly be damaging to their own interests as they have understood them until now. As Iris Young expresses this dynamic in a defence of group representation,

Group representation unravels the false consensus that cultural imperialism may have produced, and reveals group bias in norms, standards, styles and perspectives that have been assumed as universal or of highest value. By giving voice to formerly silenced or devalued needs and experiences, group representation forces participants in discussion to take a reflective distance on their assumptions and think beyond their own interests. When confronted with interests, needs and opinions that derived from very different social positions and experience, persons sometimes come to understand the limitations of their own experience and perspective for coming to a conclusion about the best policy for everyone. (Young 1994*b*: 136)

If we examine more closely the relationship between the assumptions of deliberative democracy and the requirements of a deliberative process that can ameliorate group-structured inequality, however, we discover that social difference poses two broad challenges to deliberative theory. First, attention to the distinctive perspectives on political issues that follow the lines of social difference raises several doubts about deliberative theory's standard of 'reasonableness' and about how participants decide what counts as a reason for purposes of political deliberation. Some difference-based critics of deliberative democracy argue that its norms of public reason themselves are biased against the modes of communication characteristic of marginalized groups. Whatever one makes of those critiques, which I will discuss further below, it does seem clear that because deliberation's propensity to ameliorate group-structured inequality depends upon marginalized groups' critique of the practices which reproduce their disadvantage, and because those critiques turn on contested interpretations of the social meaning of those practices, the recognition of marginalized groups' reasons *as reasons for (or acceptable to) other citizens* is a highly contingent matter, and that there are good reasons for thinking that privileged groups will have a systematic tendency to reject marginalized group interpretations of social practices as unreasonable (even in cases where that rejection is not a product of overt prejudice).

The second general area of tension between marginalized-group participation and deliberative theory follows naturally from the first. As we will see below, the demands of a deliberative process that is responsive to social difference are even greater than the demands of deliberative democracy generally. Yet the capacity of deliberative democracy to deliver on its promise of impartial political decisions depends upon its capacity to meet these demands; otherwise deliberative theorists must concede the systematic tendency of the processes they recommend to reproduce unjust systemic patterns of inequality. Consequently, deliberative theory would appear incomplete so long as it neglects to articulate the conditions under which its aspirations can be realized.

The remainder of the essay explores these two broad challenges to deliberative theory from the theory of social difference.

3. Social Difference and Justice Claims: Two Problems for Deliberative Theory

The Standard of Reasonableness and the Norms of Deliberation

Some critics have focused on the constraints on speech that theories of deliberative democracy impose on participants and have argued that those constraints are biased against marginalized groups in two ways. First, they argue, some models of deliberative democracy call upon participants to speak in their capacity as citizens, articulating their arguments in terms of shared or general interests, rather than as bearers of particular identities and interests. Yet it is only by focusing on the *divergent* interests of privileged and marginalized groups that the latter's contribution to deliberation can contribute to the end of justice towards those groups. Participants in a difference-sensitive deliberative process are present as bearers of distinct and identifiable interests, and not simply in their (generalized or universalized) role as citizens. (See Benhabib 1992.) The diversity of perspectives that are brought to bear on discussions of public policy is not simply the diversity that comes from participants' mastery of different bodies of knowledge and experience, but is a diversity that specifically reflects social structures of inequality, the lines of group difference along which positions, wealth, opportunity, political influence, etc. are unevenly distributed. To the extent that the speech norms of deliberative democracy discourage arguments grounded in partial interests, therefore, they obstruct justice. (See esp. Young 1990: 104–6.) Anne Phillips summarizes the point nicely: 'When oppressed groups are called upon to put their own partial interests aside—to address the shared concerns of all humanity, to think beyond their own interests and needs—this injunction can lock them into the very structures they are trying to dislodge' (Phillips 1995: 147).

Most theorists of deliberative democracy would now concede that the generalizability of interests should not apply to every level of argumentation, and that arguments grounded in justice claims have a rightful place in democratic deliberation whether or not they refer to a divergence of interests among citizens. Another way of putting this is that citizens share an interest in the justice of their political arrangements, and any argument that bears on considerations of justice therefore belongs in the public forum. Moreover, as Gutmann and Thompson argue, 'Individuals and groups are not obligated to deliberate if others refuse to do so, and if doing so would put them at a further disadvantage. Citizens engaged in cooperative institutions do not have moral obligations to do their share unless they have reasonable assurance that others will not take advantage of them' (Gutmann and Thompson 1996: 72–3).

A second critique launched by difference theorists against theories of deliberative democracy concerns the tendency of the latter to favour forms of expression which are not characteristic of marginalized groups, nor best suited to the articulation of their perspectives. 'The norms of deliberation are culturally specific and often operate as forms of power that silence or devalue the speech of some people' (Young 1996: 123). The cultural specificity of the norms of deliberation, Young argues, takes several forms. In contrast to the assumptions of deliberative theory, most actual arenas of deliberation are the sites of agonistic struggle, not places where people seek agreement. Such forums favour 'speech that is assertive and confrontational' over speech that is 'tentative, exploratory, or conciliatory'. Because the latter is more often characteristic of marginalized groups than of privileged groups—and especially of women as compared to men—actual political deliberation tends to favour already privileged participants (Young 1996: 123).

The response of deliberative theorists to this critique is that there is ample skill and talent among members of marginalized groups to provide effective advocates for their positions. This is particularly true, Gutmann and Thompson suggest, in representative institutions in which participants in deliberation have been chosen from a large pool of citizens. 'Disadvantaged groups', they argue, 'have usually found representatives from within their own ranks who could speak for them, and who could articulate their interests and ideals, at least as reasonably and effectively as representatives of established groups' (Gutmann and Thompson 1996: 132–3).

But Young argues further that deliberative theory conceives of democratic communication too narrowly by resting on the exchange of reasons. Consequently, she argues, deliberative theory forecloses alternative forms of expression—including 'greeting, rhetoric and storytelling'—that may be more conducive to understanding across the boundaries of social difference than the presentation of reasoned arguments. She thus favours what she calls 'communicative democracy' over 'deliberative democracy' as a theory which gives a central place to the forms of expression that can help to ameliorate group-structured inequality. In contrast to the reason-giving norms of deliberative theory, she argues, communicative democracy validates these discursive forms, together with the embodied and affective aspects of human existence to which they give expression. Communicative democracy, she argues, is committed to 'an equal privileging of any forms of communicative interaction where people aim to reach understanding. While argument is a necessary element in such effort to discuss with and persuade one another about political issues, argument is not the only mode of political communication' (Young 1996: 125).

Deliberative theorists respond that, whatever the forms of expression necessary to arrive there, the aim of democratic politics must be to meet a standard of legitimacy whose measure is the defensibility of public institutions in terms of reasons that all can accept. While impassioned rhetoric may motivate others to listen, and powerful narratives may constitute evidence for a speaker's arguments,

Young's attempt to transform the language of the rule of law into a more partial, affective, and situated mode of communication would have the consequence of introducing arbitrariness, for who can tell how far the power of a greeting can reach? . . . rhetoric moves people and achieves results without having to render an account of the bases upon which it induces people to engage in certain courses of action rather than others. (Benhabib 1996: 83)

Moreover, as Victoria Kamsler suggests, there is no reason to suppose that powerful rhetoric and engaging storytelling will not serve the interests of privileged groups as much as or more than it will serve marginalized groups. 'Like shared jokes, shared stories can function to establish the fact of shared identity, experience and interest [among members of dominant groups], and as such have played an important role in the rhetoric of [such groups] from Pericles onward' (Kamsler 1996: 17).

In a similar vein, Gutmann and Thompson argue that deliberative theory's emphasis on the exchange of reasons does not banish passionate speech from the political forum. Indeed, they acknowledge that passionate speech may play a critically important role in democratic deliberation, because there may be circumstances in which it is the only means of getting an important issue on the deliberative agenda. As an example, they discuss African American Senator Carol Moseley-Braun's passionate speech to the Senate concerning legislation to renew a design patent on the emblem of the Daughters of the Confederacy, an emblem which includes an image of the Confederate flag. Moseley-Braun had earlier persuaded the judiciary committee not to renew the patent, but Senators Jesse Helms and Strom Thurmond attached the patent as an amendment to a national service bill that they expected to pass. The amendment passed in a test vote without substantial floor debate, despite Moseley-Braun's protest and presentation of the well-reasoned arguments she had given in the judiciary committee. After that vote Moseley-Braun rose from the floor in a threatened filibuster and, 'match[ing] reason to passion' (Gutmann and Thompson 1996: 136, quoting 'Ms. Moseley Braun's Majestic Moment') launched a three-hour debate on the merits of the patent. Because of the close association between the history of slavery and the symbolism of the Confederate flag, she argued, the amendment was 'an outrage. It is an insult. It is absolutely unacceptable to me and to millions of Americans, black and white, that we would put the imprimatur of the United States Senate on a symbol of this kind of idea'. At the end of the debate she sparked with this speech, the amendment was defeated by a substantial margin.

Gutmann and Thompson conclude from this example that 'Nondeliberative means may be necessary to achieve deliberative ends': the Senate had not given reasoned consideration to the issue until Moseley-Braun spoke passionately. Further, they suggest, immoderate speech may communicate important information (in this case, the intensity of African Americans' concerns over the symbolism of the Confederate flag) more effectively than dispassionate, calmly reasoned arguments. (See Gutmann and Thompson 1996: 135–6.)

I find these arguments persuasive, and ultimately agree with deliberative theorists that the ideal of democratic legitimacy must make political choices rest on reasons that are acceptable to all citizens. None the less, the place of marginalized-group perspectives in deliberation does raise questions which Benhabib's and Gutmann and Thompson's arguments do not resolve. In particular, it raises questions about the standard of reasonableness that lies at the heart of deliberative theory, about how we judge what counts as a reason in political discourse. I would like to suggest that the judgement that another's arguments are reasonable is a much more contingent matter than deliberative theory suggests, and that the contingency of such judgement is strongly conditioned by membership in groups structured along the lines of social privilege and disadvantage. What deliberators could accept as reasons may turn out to depend importantly on who they are and on who is presenting the reasons to them. This unsettles the premisses of deliberative democracy, which appears to contain an implicit supposition that the reasonableness or unreasonableness of others' arguments will be self-evident.[13]

The status of reasons as reasons becomes particularly problematic in circumstances where the subject of disagreement is the *social meaning of existing practices*, particularly where those practices (allegedly) reinforce current unjust structures of social privilege. For it is especially in such circumstances that the social meanings that marginalized groups attach to a practice diverges from the social meaning that privileged groups attach to it. In those circumstances, the reasons that undergird marginalized groups' critique of the practice *do not function as reasons for members of privileged groups*, because the social meaning of the practice for the marginalized group is (at least initially) inaccessible to them. When the eradication of structures of unjust inequality depends upon affirming the social meaning of a practice for marginalized groups, rather than reinforcing the practice's social meaning for privileged groups, the justice of deliberative outcomes depends not only upon participants exhibiting the virtues of open-mindedness and mutual respect (as deliberative theory emphasizes), but also upon their possessing the virtue of empathy,[14] and of giving marginalized-group claims the particular advantage of their empathy. There are good reasons to believe that privileged groups will be predisposed to perceive marginalized-group interpretations of social practices as unreasonable where such interpretations diverge from their own, particularly in circumstances where the privileged group's interpretation of the practice has the consequence of reinforcing their position of relative advantage (as, for example, has historically been the case for the actions which now fall under the heading of 'sexual harassment').

The contingency of what counts as a reason in deliberation becomes clear if we return to the example of the Senate debate over the design patent for the Daughters of the Confederacy. The Appendix to this essay summarizes that debate as it was reported in the *Congressional Record*. A focused reading of the debate reveals that it turned on whether a majority of senators accepted Moseley-Braun's interpretation of the social meaning of the Confederate flag (as an emblem of slavery) rather than Southern white senators' non-racist interpretation of the flag (as a remembrance of sacrifices for one's homeland). While some of the Southern white senators were undoubtedly disingenuous in their invocation of a non-racist meaning for the flag, it does not seem fair to dismiss all of them as racist. Some undoubtedly did affirm a non-racist interpretation of the flag's meaning, and did not identify the flag with slavery. Why should the social meaning of the flag to African Americans count as a reason for them, when the content of that meaning is not the content they

---

[13] On the problematic character of the standard of 'reasonableness', see Moore (1996: 171–2).

[14] For a related discussion, see Kymlicka (1995*a*: 141), citing Minow (1991).

perceive or affirm? Deliberative theory does not, as it stands, appear to provide any bar against their responding to Moseley-Braun as the *Plessy* court responded to arguments concerning the stigma of segregation: 'We consider the underlying fallacy of the plaintiff's argument to consist in the assumption that the enforced separation of the two races stamps the colored race with a badge of inferiority. If this be so, it is not by reason of anything found in the act, but *solely because the colored race chooses to put that construction upon it*' (*Plessy* v. *Ferguson* 1896: 551; emphasis added). Yet disagreements of this sort— over the meaning of social practices that marginalized groups experience as oppressive—are very likely to be among the most important issues for marginalized groups in the deliberative process. Without some account of the standard by which we should judge privileged groups' reception of arguments over social meanings, deliberative theory remains inadequate to the goal of justice towards marginalized groups.

Habermas and Rawls have not overlooked this difficulty altogether in their accounts of political discourse, though they address it only obliquely and neither has offered a solution to it. Habermas acknowledges that there are modes of argumentation (including the aesthetic mode) which coexist with practical discourses but which do not aim at rationally motivated agreement. This coexistence of modes of argumentation that appeal to a standard of rationality with those that do not, he concedes, 'represents a liability for the former, a liability that originates in the sociohistorical situatedness of reason' (Habermas 1990: 106). I take this to signify that what motivates agreement in *actual* discourses is some combination of an appeal to reasons, an appeal to aesthetic judgements, and so on, and that the precise mix of arguments that will generate actual agreement is likely to be contingent on the particular socio-historical circumstances in which the discourse occurs. Moreover, Habermas acknowledges that social conflict inflects practical discourses because 'contested norms tend to upset the balance of relations of inter-subjective recognition' (1990: 106) Again, this point reinforces my argument that in order for marginalized-group perspectives to have an influence on political decisions, they have to be *recognized* as reasonable by other participants. Yet there are strong incentives for privileged groups to withhold that recognition, particularly where their own entrenched interests are at stake. (I address this point further in the next section.) There are good reasons to suppose, then, that the 'liability' of practical discourses to be affected by contingent factors of social identity and social power is more likely to accrue to marginalized than privileged participants in a discourse.

The notion that reason underdetermines political judgement receives similar affirmation from John Rawls in *Political Liberalism*. This is not surprising; all the defenders of deliberative democracy leave some space for 'reasonable disagreement' among citizens even after they have engaged in a discourse aimed at reaching agreement. Rawls labels the sources of reasonable disagreement the 'burdens of judgment'. Among the burdens of judgement, Rawls notes, is the fact that:

To some extent (how great we cannot tell) the way we assess evidence and weigh moral and political values is shaped by our total experience, our whole course of life up to now; and our total experiences must always differ. Thus, in a modern society with its numerous offices and positions, its various divisions of labor, *its many social groups and their ethnic variety*, citizens' total experiences are disparate enough for their judgments to diverge . . . on many if not most cases of any significant complexity. (Rawls 1993: 56–7; emphasis added)

At the same time, Rawls also recognizes that there are 'sources of unreasonable disagreement', and that these include 'prejudice and bias, self- and group interest, blindness and willfulness' (1993: 58). Yet in the context of an actual discourse in which there is disagreement, how are participants to distinguish reasonable disagreement grounded in radically different group experiences from unreasonable disagreement grounded in group interest? The Senate debate over the Confederate flag, again, presents a situation in which what is at stake is precisely whether Moseley-Braun's interpretation of that symbol constitutes a reasonable or an unreasonable source of disagreement, a valid representation of the distinctive experience of African Americans or an attempt to score political points by choosing to take offence at an innocuous piece of legislation. The ambiguities of the case suggest that the 'burdens of judgment' may tend to fall disproportionately on the shoulders of the disadvantaged.

In any event, it is clear that the norms of deliberation that must govern exchanges between privileged and marginalized groups are somewhat different from the norms of deliberative theory as discussed above. Indeed, because of the more immediate relationship participants bear to identifiable interests, the aspiration to impartiality is much more demanding within the second model of deliberation than within the first (although that, too, is quite demanding). Let us place ourselves in the role of a participant in deliberation whose presuppositions are being challenged by another participant. The first model asks us to listen to the other's account of the common good and to evaluate it in a spirit of impartiality, without attending to the question whether or not our interests would be served by such a conception. The second model asks us to go beyond that, to listen sympathetically to another's claim that our practices treat them unjustly. Indeed, it asks us to listen sympathetically to the claim that the fulfilment of our interests comes at the cost of a just regard for their interests. Where the other's arguments are strong, it asks us to revise our evaluation of our own practices, to judge them unjust, and to forgo the interests they serve for the sake of justice. Whereas in the first model of deliberation we can 'bracket off' the question of how our interests might be affected by a change in policy, in the second model we cannot avoid attending to that question, since the point of the other's claim is that current arrangements unjustly prefer our interests to theirs. The stringency of these moral requirements leads naturally to the question whether a theory of democratic communication which depends upon them is hopelessly idealistic. This leads us to the second general challenge to deliberative theory from the standpoint of social difference.

The Social and Institutional Conditions of Deliberative Legitimacy

Although participants in deliberative democracy may be equally situated with respect to one another, a deliberative process that ameliorates structural inequality must make power relations a central feature of the deliberative agenda. It is only by making the unjust consequences of their power visible to privileged groups that marginalized-group perspectives can have any chance of transforming prevailing understandings of the requirements of justice. Yet models of deliberative democracy generally are silent on the relationship between inequalities of social power and the process of deliberation. This omission is traceable to some degree to the influence of Habermasian theory upon views of deliberative democracy: Habermas's theory of communicative action explicitly abstracts from relations of power to construct an 'ideal speech situation' which is free from the relations of power which inhibit 'systematically undistorted communication'. Although it is true that there is nothing in deliberative theory to preclude giving priority on the political agenda to issues of structural inequality, neither do theories of deliberative democracy reliably make those issues central to their account of political legitimacy. Perhaps most importantly, they tend to neglect the question of how to achieve deliberative forums in which marginalized and privileged citizens can participate on a basis of equality.[15]

Gutmann and Thompson have addressed this problem in a preliminary way without resolving it. As they acknowledge,

Those who benefit from . . . background inequalities are not likely to support the policies that would mitigate their effects. It is difficult to deliberate dispassionately about the laws that might bring about the end to one's own chance to deliberate as a lawmaker. The results of deliberative representation are skewed, but not therefore determined, by the very inequalities that the deliberative process of representation is supposed to correct. (Gutmann and Thompson 1996: 134)

---

[15] Anne Phillips makes this point very nicely: 'Explorations of deliberative or communicative democracy often refer rather grandly to a principle of equal access to decision-making assemblies or substantive equality in resources and power, but they do not give much consistent attention to how these conditions would ever be achieved' (Phillips 1995: 154).

Their defence of deliberative democracy against this critique is that 'Deliberation must be part of any strategy to break out of the cycle of injustice created by background inequalities,' and that there are features of actual legislative institutions that make factors other than social status—political skill, collegiality, and a spirit of reciprocity itself—important in determining how likely it is that a given individual will get a fair hearing from colleagues (1996: 134). These points have merit, but one might question whether the theory of deliberative democracy is complete without some further account of the circumstances—both sociological and institutional—under which deliberative processes can avoid structural bias against already disadvantaged groups.

All things considered, the outcome of the deliberative process that is specifically responsive to group difference is impartial in a different sense from the impartiality of outcomes in most extant models of deliberative democracy. It is still impartial in the sense that it does not favour some groups over others, but it goes beyond this in that it must also be *transformative*; it must *correct* the past biases of social arrangements in ways that other models of deliberative democracy seldom contemplate.

Cass Sunstein's critique of what he calls 'status quo neutrality' is an important exception in the literature on deliberative democracy in this regard. As Sunstein argues, much of contemporary liberal and legal discourse 'defines neutrality by taking, as a given and as the baseline for decision, the status quo, or what various people and groups now have. . . . A departure from the status quo signals partisanship; respect for the status quo signals neutrality' (Sunstein 1993: 3). But we need not accept this presumption in favour of existing practices and distributions, even in circumstances where there is disagreement over what alternative practices are most desirable. To the contrary, when the status quo entrenches unjustifiable inequalities among groups, maintaining it constitutes an injustice. A commitment to deliberative democracy, which requires the defence of political practices on terms justifiable to citizens, entails abandoning status quo neutrality. (Sunstein 1993: 6, 353.)

For a number of reasons, then, the view of deliberation that emerges if we focus on the contributions of a discourse involving marginalized groups to collective understandings of justice appears more radical than the more common views of deliberative democracy would seem to admit. A deliberative politics of difference makes sense only as a transformative politics, one which contemplates not only 'a fairer distribution of resources and power between groups we expect to remain hostile' but also the emergence of 'a more comprehensive understanding that validates the worth of each group' (Phillips 1993: 160). But at the same time as it presents a more radical view of democracy than most other deliberative models, it also seems to run the risk of being even more naïvely utopian than those models, which have themselves often been criticized for their lack of realism concerning human psychology and motivation, for making 'heroic assumptions about participants' (Johnson 1998: 25–6). If participants in deliberative democracy as normally described are 'heroic', then participants in a deliberative politics of difference would seem to have to be divine.[16]

In fact, I do not believe that the ideal of a deliberative politics of difference *is* naïvely utopian under all circumstances; the trick is to be more specific about the circumstances in which it is conceivable that privileged groups will relinquish some of their privilege in response to marginalized groups' justice claims. What, then, could possibly motivate a disposition in privileged groups to listen impartially to claims of marginalized groups in the manner I have described?

It seems to me that there are there are two principal sources of the motivation of the powerful to listen empathetically to the voices of those who are less powerful: (*a*) the desire to be just, or at least to be able to justify one's position (both in the sense of one's beliefs and in the sense of one's social standing) to others (see Scanlon 1982); and (*b*) the need to stem conflict in order to avoid its costs. Both of these can serve as motives to listen and to try to understand a situation from the standpoint of another, even a less powerful other. In fact, if we look to the most profound historical moments of the inclusion of oppressed groups into democratic politics—the civil rights amendments, the women's suffrage amendment, the Civil Rights Act, South African democracy, the inclusion of First Nations in Canadian constitutional negotiations—all have in common the fact that a new responsiveness to oppressed groups arises with *both* a failure to be able to justify current practice *and* a social mobilization of the oppressed which threatens potentially high costs to the dominant group or class should it fail to resolve the conflicts.

What this suggests, however, is that the motive of a common good of justice and the motive of interest are in fact much more closely intertwined than prevailing models of deliberative democracy admit. It is a threat to the interests of privileged groups that sometimes inclines them to be open to a redefinition of the requirements of justice. The same connection between interest and justice is of course present for marginalized groups as well, though it appears in a different form: as many opponents of group recognition have noted, acknowledging group-based claims of injustice creates a motive for groups to assert disingenuous claims, and to wield a 'victim' status as a tool of political power. This is not a dynamic I wish to deny, although I do not draw the same conclusion from it as do opponents of the 'politics of difference'.

---

[16] Cf. Rousseau's description of democratic self-government: 'If there were a people of gods, it would govern itself democratically. So perfect a government is not suited to men.' (Rousseau 1978: 126).

Thus, by examining the tensions between the claims of marginalized-group representation and the ideal of deliberative democracy we can bring to the surface some important lacunae in the latter. In particular, models of deliberative democracy are imperfect tools for deepening our understanding or advancing the end of democratic egalitarianism so long as their character-ization of the norms of deliberation and of the relationship among delib-erators remain within the realm of ideal theory, and so long as they continue to assume a sharp disjuncture between a politics of interest and a politics of deliberation. Instead, this exploration suggests that we should conceive of politics as consisting of a continuum between perfect solidarity and the unbridled battle of interests.

If we choose to think of politics and of the possibilities for egalitarian deliberation in this way, I believe that we will find that the capacity of political processes to approximate the ideal of impartiality depends crucially upon (a) social circumstances, in particular the degree to which marginalized groups are politically mobilized; and (b) the structure of political institutions. Both of these factors can create pressures upon privileged groups to co-operate in a deliberative mode with less privileged groups. The political mobilization of marginalized groups creates pressures in the manner I have described above. Political institutions can themselves create incentives for deliberation through decision rules that move in the direction of consensus or unanimity as a re-quirement of legitimate or binding political decisions (as in John C. Calhoun's system of concurrent majorities, or as with supermajority rules), as well as through norms of public discourse themselves. As Jon Elster has recently argued, the publicity of political argument can, by itself, have the effect of moderating the play of interests in political decision-making even where in-terest is what motivates participants, a dynamic he describes as 'the civilizing effects of hypocrisy' (Elster 1995).

Some recent theorists of deliberative democracy have begun the work of moving from the realm of ideal theory towards a theory of democracy which is responsive to the imperfections of the societies in which they hope to enhance political deliberation. (See especially Cohen and Rogers 1995; Gutmann and Thompson 1996; Habermas 1996a.) While ideal theory has an important place in our understanding of justice and our aspiration to im-partiality, a focus on the requirements of a deliberative politics of difference brings out some of the inherent limitations of ideal theory, and directs us to focus as well on questions of institutional design and to seek empirical gen-eralizations about the historical relationships between privileged and margin-alized groups.[17] The recent efforts of democratic theorists to move beyond ideal theory are laudable, but a great deal of further work remains to be done.

---

[17] For an instructive account of the relationship between ideal and non-ideal theory, see Carens (1996).

4. Conclusion

My starting-point in this exploration is a claim about citizenship: that the full and equal citizenship of members of marginalized groups depends upon their participation in processes of political decision-making, and that these processes must be conducted in a manner that is open to the reasons that marginalized groups bring to them. To a certain extent, institutions themselves may be redesigned to encourage a more inclusive deliberation among diverse citizens. But inclusion in decision-making institutions, by itself, is unlikely to ensure that political outcomes reflect the needs and concerns of citizens from marginalized groups. The arguments I have raised here support the familiar notion that the justice and legitimacy of democratic societies depends upon the qualities of citizens as well as on the design of institutions.

Most importantly, the capacity of processes of democratic deliberation to ameliorate structural injustice towards marginalized groups depends on citizens' willingness to listen to others' arguments in a spirit of impartiality. As I have argued, though, this capacity is even more demanding than deliberative democrats have tended to suppose. For relatively privileged citizens engaging in a discourse with marginalized citizens, it requires a willingness to interrogate one's own judgements about the unreasonableness of others' arguments, particularly where recognizing the validity of those arguments would jeopardize one's material or cultural interests. One might even go so far as to say that a spirit of impartial political discourse sometimes requires a sort of 'difference principle as applied to reasons'.[18] By this I mean a willingness to regard the reasons offered by marginalized groups as the reasons that sustain a collective decision even when those reasons are not immediately available from within one's own social or cultural experience. As the Senate debate over the Confederate flag shows, Carol Moseley-Braun's speech motivated many of the white senators to do precisely this.

My account of democratic deliberation also posits an empirical relationship between the level of social and political mobilization of a group and the responsiveness of democratic discourse to a group's distinctive experience. If such a relationship exists, it carries further implications for our understanding of citizen virtue. Political apathy and passivity undercut the legitimacy of democratic processes for all citizens, but the realization of democratic justice towards marginalized citizens appears to be especially dependent upon their active involvement not only in the central institutions of political decision-

---

[18] The reference is to the second part of John Rawls's second principle of distributive justice, which provides that 'Social and economic inequalities . . . are to be to the greatest benefit of the least advantaged members of society' (Rawls 1993: 6).

making, but also in broad-based social movements.[19] A commitment to ameliorating group-structured inequality, then, carries with it a commitment to the increased democratic participation of disadvantaged citizens.

Appendix
Senator Carol Moseley-Braun and the Confederate Flag Debate

On 12 May 1993 the US Senate Judiciary Committee, of which Senator Carol Moseley-Braun was a member, considered an application from a prominent Southern social and charitable organization, the United Daughters of the Confederacy (UDC), for the renewal of a special design patent for its insignia. The insignia included an image of the Confederate flag; the organization's membership is based on ancestral links to individuals who fought for the Confederacy in the US Civil War. Moseley-Braun had conducted considerable research into the insignia and the connections between the Confederate cause and the history of slavery in the United States. She opposed the renewal of the design patent in the committee's proceedings and presented her findings that the insignia was amply protected under other patent legislation, and that the conferral of a special design patent by the Senate was an extraordinary and rare measure. The judiciary committee voted 13 to 2 against renewing the design patent. Subsequently, Senator Jesse Helms of North Carolina quietly added the design patent to a national service bill. On 22 July the vote for the amendment arose without advance notice. Moseley-Braun, who had not anticipated the amendment, decided on the spur of the moment that she must oppose it on the Senate floor for the same reasons why she had opposed it in committee.

Moseley-Braun's opening speech culminated in her motion to table the amendment, i.e. to delete it from the bill. She began by emphasizing that the UDC emblem did not require the protection of a design patent approved by the Senate, as it was already amply protected under general patent legislation. Nor is the work of the organization dependent in any way upon having a design patent. She emphasized that a design patent 'is not just a matter of simple recognition. It is a rare honor given to an organization.' She emphasized that fewer than ten organizations have received them in the last century.

> [T]he United Daughters of the Confederacy have every right to honor their ancestors and to choose the Confederate flag as their symbol if they like. However, those of us whose ancestors fought on a different side in the Civil War, or

---

[19] The sort of political activity I have in mind here includes the organization of citizens into what Nancy Fraser calls 'subaltern counterpublics', social subcultures within which marginalized groups develop a political self-understanding and the organizational strength from which to enter constitutionally defined political institutions (Fraser 1997a: 80–5; see also Mansbridge 1996).

who were held, frankly, as human chattel under the Confederate flag, are duty bound to honor our ancestors as well by asking whether such recognition by the U.S. Senate is appropriate. (*Congressional Record*, 22 July 1993, s9253)

The members of the organization, she argued,

have a right to use whatever insignia they want, they have a right to organize in any way they want, they have a right to conduct whatever business they want. But at the same time it is inappropriate for this Senate, this U.S. Congress, to grant a special, extraordinary imprimatur, if you will, to a symbol which is inappropriate to all of us as Americans as this one is. (ibid. s9253)

Moseley-Braun emphasized that it was because of the racist symbolism of the flag that the Senate should refuse to endorse it.

The fact of the matter is the emblems of the Confederacy have meaning to Americans even 100 years after the end of the Civil War. Everybody knows what the Confederacy stands for. Everybody knows what the insignia stands for. . . . When a former Governor stood and raised the Confederate battle flag over the Alabama State Capitol to protest the Federal Government support for civil rights and a visit by the Attorney General at the time in 1963, everybody knew what that meant. Now, in this time, in 1993, when we see the Confederate symbols hauled out, everybody knows what that means. (ibid. s9253–4)

She continued by stressing the importance of focusing on symbols that unite rather than divide Americans:

the Stars and Stripes forever is our flag, whether we are from North or South, whether we are African-Americans or not—that is our flag. And to give a design patent, that even our own flag does not enjoy, to a symbol of the Confederacy seems to me just to create the kind of divisions in our society that are counterproductive. (ibid. s9254)

Moseley-Braun included in the record of the Senate a letter from the US Patent Office confirming her claims about the rarity of design patents and the protection of insignia under other legislative provisions.

Following Moseley-Braun's argument and presentation of evidence, South Carolina Senator Strom Thurmond and Senator Howard Metzenbaum of Ohio debated the question whether a design patent offers any needed protection to the organization's insignia. Helms intervened to argue that the motion to table the amendment was a 'punitive action' and an 'abuse' for which 'These fine, gentle ladies' were 'singled out' (ibid. s9256). Senator Patti Murray of Washington rose in solidarity with Moseley-Braun, invoking their shared position as women in the Senate and noting that Moseley-Braun was the lone African American in the body. 'We will not allow deference to notions of tradition to hide racism or any other form of discrimination or intolerance' (ibid. s9256).

At this point in the debate, a vote was taken on Moseley-Braun's motion to table the amendment, and it was defeated, 52–48.

Following the vote, the Senate chamber was filled with a buzz of conversation as Moseley-Braun rose again to speak, this time in less moderate tones. Over the noise, Moseley-Braun stated, 'I have to tell you this vote is about race. . . . It is about racial symbols, the racial past, and the single most painful episode in American history.' Once the Senate was brought to order, Moseley-Braun continued to speak about the Confederate flag, becoming more impassioned as she went on. She became so agitated that she felt the need to apologize:

> I am sorry, Madam President. I will lower my voice. I am getting excited, because, quite frankly, that is the very issue. The issue is whether or not Americans, such as myself, who believe in the promise of this country, who feel strongly and who are patriots in this country, will have to suffer the indignity of being reminded time and time again, that at one point in this country's history we were human chattel. We were property. We could be traded, bought, and sold. Now, to suggest as a matter of revisionist history that this flag is not about slavery flies in the face of history.

She emphasized that she had tried, in her earlier speech, to be 'dispassionate' rather than 'inflammatory', and that she had consciously chosen not to introduce a part of her research into the Confederate flag and its symbolic connection to slavery. But now she saw no reason for such restraint, and she read from an 1861 speech of the vice-president of the Confederacy, entitled, 'Slavery: The Cornerstone of the Confederacy', in which he stated that 'Our new Government is founded upon . . . the great truth that the Negro is not equal to the white man, that slavery, subordination to the superior race is his natural and moral condition.' Moseley-Braun continued, 'It is an absolute outrage that this body would adopt as an amendment to this legislation a symbol of this point of view.' She emphasized that she had, in her seven months in office, attempted to adopt a conciliatory manner with her colleagues. 'But I say to you, Madam President, on this issue there can be no consensus. It is an outrage. It is an insult. It is absolutely unacceptable to me and to millions of Americans, black or white, that we would put the imprimatur of the United States Senate on a symbol of this kind of idea.' She chided members of her own party for voting in favour of the amendment.

Moseley-Braun urged her colleagues from both parties to give the amendment the attention it deserved and to reconsider their judgement that it was 'no big deal'. She urged them to realize:

> what a very big deal indeed it is—that the imprimatur that is being sought here today sends a sign out to the rest of the country that that peculiar institution has not been put to bed for once and for all; that, indeed, like Dracula, it has come back to haunt us time and time and time again; and that, in spite of the fact that we have made strides forward, the fact of the matter is that there are

those who would keep us slipping back into the darkness of division, into the snake pit of racial hatred . . . and of support for symbols of the struggle to keep African-Americans . . . in bondage. (ibid. s9258)

Some of Moseley-Braun's Democratic colleagues began now to enter the debate and reinforce her arguments. Dianne Feinstein of California appealed especially to Southern colleagues to listen to Moseley-Braun's comments 'about the impact of the Confederate flag . . . on a major portion of the American constituency those who are African-American; those who carry with them the heritage of a nation which at one time and to a great extent still has a certain racism and bias in much of what we do' (ibid. s9258). Bill Bradley also spoke in support of Moseley-Braun, and urged his colleagues to reconsider their vote. He also reminded Republicans that they belonged to the party of Lincoln, and urged all his colleagues not to dismiss her speech because of its emotion: 'It is emotional. It is emotional as anything is that goes to the very depths of our humanity and that hopes for the best in all of us to prevail every day, as Americans' (ibid. s9259).

Moseley-Braun again joined the debate, reminding the Senate that the amendment had been defeated in the judiciary committee by a vote of 13–2, and expressed how surprised she had been to see it attached to the current legislation. The strategy of the amendment's sponsors had been to suppose that the amendment would never be noticed. This belief, she argued, reflected a failure to 'understand the implications of what this means, not only to me personally, but what it means to every descendant of that peculiar institution'.

Senator Exon (Nebraska) intervened at this point to argue that the issue was not simply a matter of racism. 'I know very well most of the people who voted against' the tabling motion 'did not do it . . . from their heart on racial grounds.' 'Rather, I suspect it was from the old attitude of the South—the South shall return. . . . I suspect in all sincerity, that the vast majority of those who failed to vote for the tabling motion had no concept or understanding of the very legitimate background and concerns that have been made by the Senator from Illinois' (ibid. s9260). But this, he continued, should not prevent the Senate from recognizing that it 'has made a mistake'.

Democratic senators Moynihan (NY) and Biden (NJ) next intervened to emphasize the momentous importance of Moseley-Braun's speech, stressing that it had led them and others to see a dimension of African American experience that had not been apparent to them before. Moynihan stated that her speech was the most moving he had heard in his seventeen years in the Senate, and characterized her insights about the meaning of the Confederate flag as an 'epiphany' (ibid. s9260). Biden emphasized her congenial collegiality, her lack of dogmatism, and her ability to act as a conciliatory force in the Senate. He continued to say that her speech demonstrated the importance of the presence of minorities in the Senate:

I think we saw here today on the floor of the Senate one of the reasons why I and others have been saying for so long there is a need for diversity in this body

. . . whether it is as a native American, a black African-American, or as an Irish-American, or as an Asian-American, to be able to bring the one thing that is most needed at this moment in this country, and that is civility and a sense of understanding of the other person's point of view. (ibid. s9260)

[T]he Senator from Illinois has pointed out something today that has been sorely missing in this body: that one single voice speaking for millions and millions of voices in this country who feel disenfranchised, and in many cases are; who feel like this body does not understand their problems, and in many cases they do not; who know that most of us do not come from a background or circumstance that allows us not only to understand but feel and taste the problems of an entire segment of this country; finally, who have a voice that has two purposes, not only to represent their point of view but to sensitize us to that point of view, because, hopefully, all of us in here share the vision of healing of the Senator from Illinois. (ibid. s9261)

Senator Ben Nighthorse-Campbell, the only Native American senator, also intervened to express his solidarity with Moseley-Braun as a member of a minority group that continues to be subject to discrimination and racism.

At this point in the debate Republican senators began entering the discussion again. Senator Simpson of Wyoming, who had voted against Moseley-Braun's motion, noted that the design patent had been unanimously renewed, four times throughout the century. He raised the question whether Moseley-Braun thought that the Senate, by renewing the patent so many times, had engaged in 'some form of racist decision making'. Moseley Braun responded by denying any racist motives of past or present Senates, saying that 'It just happened. It just happened because there was nobody around to bring attention to what was clearly and obviously a mistake' (ibid. s9262).

The next intervention was an emotional and moving speech and a turning-point in the debate. It was from Senator Howell Heflin of Alabama, who began by invoking his love of the South and his own family roots in the Confederacy, as well as his family ties to the Daughters of the Confederacy. He emphasized that he did not believe that the organization had racist intentions. And he recounted his remark to his legislative director, whose great-great-grandfather was a slave, that 'if I vote with Senator Moseley-Braun, my mother, grandmother, and other ancestors will turn over in their graves'. He said, 'Well, likewise, my ancestors will turn over in their graves [if you do not].' 'But the whole matter boils down to what Senator Moseley-Braun contends—that it is an issue of symbolism. We must get racism behind us, and we must move forward.' Therefore, he said he supported a reconsideration of the motion to table the amendment. 'I feel that, today, this is a symbolic step. If we move forward to put the stamp of approval of the U.S. Senate and the Congress on a symbol that is offensive to a large segment of Americans, I think we will not be moving in the right direction, and it is a wrong approach to the ideals for which this country must stand' (ibid. s9263).

After Heflin's speech other senators who had voted against Moseley-Braun began to switch sides. Senator McConnell of Kentucky stated, 'It never occurred to me in casting my vote a while ago that it would be interpreted as somehow an endorsement of racism or slavery, but rather I did it out of respect for my ancestors and their roots which ran deep in the South' (ibid. s9264). Senator Riegle of Michigan remarked on the power of both Moseley-Braun's speech and Heflin's in explaining his change of heart. He invoked the military service of African Americans, and suggested that when citizens have put their lives on the line for their country, they should not be repaid with symbols that they regard as degrading.

Several Democratic senators again joined the discussion to support Moseley-Braun. Senator Kerry of Massachusetts stated,

> What is remarkable to me, as I stand here, is that there is a real discomfort as I think about the fact that we are 96 white men and women debating whether or not we ought to be sensitive to the expression of one African-American and one native American. If that does not tell us what the problem is, then nothing will. (ibid. s9265)

Senator Barbara Boxer of California spoke in high praise of Senator Heflin's remarks. 'For what he has done today, and the way he did it, speaks to the best in every American. If ever there was proof that diversity in this institution is important, we got that proof today.' 'I truly believe if the Senator from Illinois had not been sent here by her very wise constituents, this vote just may have gone by' (ibid. s9265).

Senator Chafee, who had voted against Moseley-Braun's motion, stated,

> It is apparent from this debate . . . that a group in our society feels very deeply about this matter, and those views have been very powerfully enunciated by the extraordinarily excellent speech of the distinguished Senator from Illinois. . . . I must say, regrettably, rarely on this floor are minds changed. All too often nobody is here listening . . . But I have been persuaded by the views that I have heard expressed today, especially by the Senator from Illinois. (ibid. s9267)

Senator Bennett of Utah stated that he, together with other Republican colleagues, 'did not realize the greater implications of what we had just done' (ibid. s9267).

After a few interventions concerning parliamentary procedure, a motion was made to reconsider the motion to table the amendment. It passed with a vote of 76–24. Immediately afterwards, a vote was again taken on Moseley-Braun's motion to table the amendment, and it passed, 75–25.

Following the vote, several senators who had again voted against the motion spoke to clarify their reasons for doing so. Senator Mack stated,

> I reject the notion that the issue before the Senate was one of racism. Rather, I view the amendment as designed to preserve the heritage of those who are proudly descended from the ranks of those who fought and died in the Civil War. . . . This was not a vote about racism. It was a vote about allowing a group of elderly women the privileges of honoring their emblem. I voted for that privilege. (ibid. s9268)

Moseley-Braun spoke to thank Heflin for his graciousness, as well as others who had supported her in the debate. Senator Danforth spoke in apology for his vote in favour of the motion, saying,

> I was almost sick to my stomach when I cast that vote, and the reason was that in order to prove in a symbolic way my feelings about how disgusting racism is, I had to tar with the brush of racism innocent people who are members of an organization . . . that they feel strongly about . . . and their motives have nothing to do with racism and nothing to do with approval of slavery. (ibid. s9270)

He continued by noting that on the White House lawn, after Lee's surrender, Lincoln asked the band to play two songs: 'Yankee Doodle' and 'Dixie'. 'I take it that if April 10, 1861 occurred today, we would be having symbolic votes on the floor of the U.S. Senate to the effect that the band should not have played "Dixie" on that occasion' (ibid. s9270). Senator Byrd also spoke to express his view that the Confederate flag symbolizes Southerners' sacrifice for their homeland, not an attachment to slavery. Byrd quoted a documented conversation between a Confederate prisoner and his Yankee captor, who asked the soldier, ' "Why are you fighting us like this?" To which the Confederate soldier replied, "Because y'all are down here." ' Byrd continued, 'That was not racism. That was not a defense of slavery. That was a man protecting his home, his family, and his people. . . . Americans of Southern heritage need not defend slavery in order to memorialize the legacy of which they are a part' (ibid. s9271). He concluded by castigating those Republicans who changed their votes as 'turncoats who ran for cover for political reasons'.

PART III

Immigration, Identity, and Multiculturalism

6

Cultural Identity and Civic Responsibility

JEREMY WALDRON

1. Civic Responsibility

The inhabitants of any country have a duty to deliberate responsibly among themselves about law and public policy. Each has a duty to play his part in ensuring that those around him—those with whom he lives, in Kant's phrase, 'unavoidably side by side' (Kant 1991, paras. 43, 121)—come to terms with one another, and set up, maintain, and operate the legal frameworks that are necessary to secure peace, resolve conflicts, do justice, avoid great harms, and provide some basis for improving the conditions of life. I shall call this the duty of civic participation.[1]

Like many duties, the duty of civic participation is not just a duty to do X but a duty to do X carefully and responsibly. In the case of this duty, the burden of responsibility—civic responsibility—has at least two aspects to it. It means (1) participating in a way that does not improperly diminish the prospects for peace or the prospect that the inhabitants will in fact come to terms and set up the necessary frameworks. And it means (2) participating in a way that pays proper attention to the interests, wishes, and opinions of all the inhabitants of the country. (Correlative to this aspect of civic responsibility is

I am grateful to Joseph Carens, Will Kymlicka, Alan Musgrave, Gerald Neuman, and Richard Sutton for comments on and criticisms of earlier versions of this paper presented at a conference in Toronto and as a public lecture at the University of Otago, New Zealand, in summer 1998.

[1] Calling it 'civic participation' connects the duty to the idea of citizenship. But it is citizenship in a broad and informal sense: whether or not one is legally a citizen of the state that governs the country in question, one has the duty I am talking about simply as an inhabitant of the country. I believe this duty stands in a sort of ur-relation to the duties of citizenship as they are more commonly understood. Certainly it is deeper than (it is arguably foundational to) the more familiar notion of legal citizenship, for the duty I am talking about is the duty to make it possible that there be a state and a legal system in the country one inhabits; i.e. it is a duty to make it possible that there be something around here to be a (legal) citizen of. For the importance of keeping clear about the different uses of the term 'citizenship' in jurisprudence and political philosophy, see G. L. Neuman (1992: 1283 ff.).

a fundamental right of each of the inhabitants that his interests, wishes, and opinions be properly attended to.)

In both (1) and (2) I used certain place-holder language. I talked about participating in a way that does not *improperly* diminish the prospects for peace etc., and I talked about paying *proper* attention to the interests, wishes, and opinions of others. People will disagree about how to fill out these formulations; for example, there will be at least as many rival conceptions of *proper attention to others' interests, wishes, and opinions* as there are theories of justice. Still, the formulations that I have given are not empty. Someone's holding a conception of *proper attention* that I disagree with is different, to my mind, from his not thinking that there is any issue about what attention is properly due to others' interests, wishes, and opinions.

This chapter addresses a question that arises when we try to fill out these formulations. One plausible and attractive conception of *proper attention to other's interests etc.* involves the idea of the inviolability of the individual—the idea expressed in modern doctrines of human rights. We think that although people will inevitably have to bear some costs, risks, and disappointments for the sake of peace, justice, and the common good, still we should not set up laws and policies that sacrifice individuals themselves or that require individuals to give up their very being to secure some social good. Each person has fundamental interests in life, freedom, and well-being (his rights), and these impose constraints on what counts as the proper pursuit of the goals of civic participation. If a conception of this kind is accepted, then of course there will be disputes about *which* individual interests fall into this category; i.e. there will be disputes about what rights we have. Contributing to and resolving these disputes will be part of what civic participation involves. This too is a part that must be played responsibly: one of things each of us should bear in mind as we advance our list of rights is the impact of that list on the overall civic enterprise. Each must ask himself whether a given demand that he makes as a matter of 'rights' will undermine or preclude altogether the fundamental settlement which is the goal of civic participation. I am not saying that if the answer is 'Yes', then the demand should be abandoned. But if the answer *is* 'Yes', then that is a very serious matter, and accordingly the proponent should think long and hard about the basis and provenance of the demand.

2. Identity

The idea of *identity* plays an increasing role in modern politics. It affects the way people perform their duty of civic participation; and it affects their conception of what it is to perform that duty responsibly.

In 'The Politics of Recognition' (Taylor 1992), Charles Taylor linked *identity* with the notion of authenticity, the demand for recognition, the idea of difference, and the principle of equal dignity. *Authenticity* connotes the idea that each of us should live in a way that is true to himself, not conforming to a way of life simply because it is accepted by others. *Recognition* is the idea that others should be sensitive to my quest for authenticity. They have a responsibility to interact with me on the basis of who (as far as they can tell) *I* think I really am; they have a responsibility to respect me as the authentic self I think I am and am striving to be, rather than as the person they think it convenient for me to be. The idea of *difference* begins with the fact that the sort of being I think I am and deserve to be recognized as may not be the sort of being you think you are and deserve to be recognized as. From this fact, proponents of difference infer that the requirements of interpersonal respect may not be the same across persons. There may be a difference between what it is for me to respect you and what it is for you to respect me. Accordingly different people may have different rights; we are not entitled to assume that one size fits all. Nevertheless, the principle of *equal dignity* implies that in some sense everyone's identity is entitled to *the same* respect: there should be no second-class citizens in a liberal democratic society. (This presumably means that there is some sort of metric of equality—against which we can determine whether X's identity is being accorded the same respect as Y's identity—despite the exigencies of difference.)

I am not going to comment on the sense or coherence of these ideas, except to say that they all look very challenging. I want to consider a couple of further steps that are commonly taken down this road, and their implications for the thesis about civic responsibility that I set out at the beginning of this chapter. As outlined in the previous paragraph, the connections between authenticity, respect, difference, and equal dignity which constitute the modern notion of identity seem to be rooted in romantic individualism. Each of us is a unique individual, with an identity particular to himself. Each must discover his own voice, character, vocation, and destiny and (like Rousseau or Byron) live in a way that is true to that identity (Rosenblum 1987). But romantic individualism has often had a hard time holding its own in modern politics against the idea of national, ethnic, and cultural identities. In fact, the heroic ideal of authentic individual self-creation, of radically individualized difference, has not been found plausible as the basis of most people's identities, and is often rejected as fanciful, élitist, and parochial.[2] It is much more plausible sociologically and, to many, much more comfortable to assume that people forge their identities in the crucible of the nation, culture, or *ethnos* in which they are reared and raised. On this view, individual identities are moves

---

[2] Parochial in the sense of being an idea peculiar to a certain phase of culture and literature in Western Europe and its colonial outposts, and far from uncontested even there.

within particular cultures,[3] and to that extent they are shared and collective rather than heroically solitary and individualized.

This does not, however, diminish the challenge of 'difference'. Almost all modern societies are multicultural. Despite the best efforts of nationalism,[4] most states rule over people and peoples of a variety of national backgrounds; they comprise communities of many different ethnicities and cultures. In these circumstances it is often thought more important (from the point of view of respecting a given individual, X) to find out (a) which culture X's identity was forged in than to find out (b) what particular identity X forged as an individual within that culture. Indifference or misapprehension at level (a) is often thought to be a much worse affront to X's dignity than indifference or misapprehension at level (b). Or, to put it the other way round, the most common basis for the most egregious affronts to people's identities is thought to be hatred of a particular culture or ethnicity rather than disrespect for the particular identity an individual has crafted for himself within his culture or ethnicity. Accordingly, the strongest demand that is made in modern identity politics is that we should respect the distinctive dignity of the cultural or ethnic background that each individual has or claims as his own.

In a recent discussion K. Anthony Appiah has called for a more 'recreational' conception of ethnic identity (Appiah 1996: 103). He suggests we should 'live with fractured identities; engage in identity play; find solidarity, yes, but recognize contingency, and above all practice irony' (1996: 104). In the modern world, however, identity is anything but recreational. It is deadly serious politics—identity politics—and it is played out for high stakes and with serious ramifications not only for who ends up with what, but also for the terms on which the basic social settlement is framed.

One way of understanding this seriousness is to see that identity claims are often put forward in the spirit of the claims about individual rights that were discussed at the end of Section 1; indeed they are often put forward explicitly as versions or instances of rights. Like claims of rights, identity claims are presented as essentially non-negotiable. One says: 'I can give up many things for the social good, but I will not give up my identity. I should not be required to sacrifice *who I am* for the sake of the benefit to others.' Thus identity, like rights, connotes in politics the idea of certain reservations which one is entitled to insist on for oneself and which others have to recognize as constraints. When I say that some issue is crucial to my identity, I present my view of that issue (my interests in it, my needs, my preferences) as both interpersonally and socially non-negotiable: I imply that accommo-

---

[3] For an excellent account of this view, see Kymlicka (1989, ch. 8).

[4] I take nationalism to be the thesis that states should be organized, boundaries drawn, peoples moved about, and educational and cultural enterprises undertaken with the eventual aim that those with a common nationality should have a state of their own.

dating my interests, needs, or preferences in this matter is crucial to respecting *me*.

3. Compossibility

As I said in Section 1, liberal political philosophy has always proceeded on the basis that *some* such claims are appropriate. But the viability of the liberal enterprise depends on claims of this sort being fairly limited and being disciplined by a norm of compossibility.[5] Let me elaborate. It is assumed, first, that only a very small number of such claims *need* be put forward—i.e. that fundamental respect for persons (their rights and their identities) is not infinitely demanding, and that most individual preferences and interests can be dealt with on a fair basis that *does* allow negotiation and trade-offs. There is a modest list of rights, and the idea of rights is not all there is to political morality so far as the interests of individuals are concerned.

Secondly, so far as the small number of interests that *do* require this special non-negotiable treatment are concerned, liberal theory is committed to the expectation that all such interests will pass the test of compossibility. If I claim non-negotiably that some interest of mine simply *has* to be respected, my claim is thrown in question—not refuted necessarily, but thrown in question —by a showing that it could not possibly be accommodated in a political union along with the similar claims of others people. The liberal conception of rights and justice would be gravely embarrassed by a showing that the special non-negotiable respect we have been talking about could not com-possibly be accorded (in a single system of rights) to all the interests for which it might properly be demanded.[6]

[5] 'Compossibility' is a technical term, which originates, I believe, with Leibniz. The idea is that two things, each of which is possible, may not be *com*possible, i.e. possible together: the existence of one may preclude the existence of the other or even presuppose that the other does not exist. Thus a world without sin is possible; and a world in which there is forgiveness is possible: but forgiveness and the absence of sin are not compossible. (For a useful discussion, see Steiner 1994: 2.) In ethics and politics compossibility refers to joint practicability. Suppose there is one lifeguard, *A*, at a beach, and that two swimmers, *B* and *C*, at opposite ends of the beach get into difficulties. Then although we may say that *A* has the duty to rescue *B* and that *A* has the duty to rescue *C*, the two duties may not be compossible inasmuch as *A* can rescue only one of them.

[6] Note that '. . . may properly be demanded' and '. . . can compossibly be accorded' are *independent* constraints on liberal theories about the special treatment due to certain individual interests. We are not entitled to modify the former simply for the sake of the latter. For example: either respect for the importance of *A*'s freedom of worship requires accommoda-tion *X* or it does not; it does not *cease* to require *X* or require something *less* than *X* simply because we discover that it is impossible to furnish *X* to everyone on whose behalf the case for it can be made.

4. The Difficulty Posed by Cultural Identity

It is widely—I think correctly—believed that this liberal task of securing proper respect for all the interests that demand it becomes immeasurably more difficult when identity is associated with culture whilst retaining the flavour of rights. It is hard enough to set up a legal framework that furnishes respect for persons as individuals, and which ensures that the interests and freedoms basic to individual identity are not sacrificed for the sake of the common good. But if respect for an individual also requires respect for the culture in which his identity has been formed, and if that respect is demanded in the uncompromising and non-negotiable way in which respect for rights is demanded, then the task may become very difficult indeed, particularly in circumstances where different individuals in the same society have formed their identities in different cultures.

The reason for this extra difficulty is not always well understood. It is not just a matter of inconvenience, as when a school or college is required to accommodate an array of different holiday observances for a variety of students' religions. Nor is it simply a matter of extra expense, as it would be (say) if unisex toilet accommodation (in small restaurants or offices) were opposed by those brought up in particular cultures or religions. It is not even a matter of the *unfamiliarity* of cultural identity claims made by one who does not identify with the dominant culture in a society. Some political philosophers have made great play of the difficulty that is involved when people of different backgrounds try to bring disparate types of reasons into some sort of commensurate relation with one another in public deliberation. They argue that deliberation needs to be disciplined by norms of 'public reason,' which will exclude, for example, appeals to religious revelation or to other reasons whose contents or appeal are in some other peculiar sense private or limited (cf. Rawls 1993: 212 ff.). I believe that this problem is greatly exaggerated, and I have argued against 'public reason' restrictions elsewhere.[7] The real difficulty has little to do with inconvenience, expense, or the antinomies of public reason. It arises primarily because of what a culture is or aspires to be.

Though it is arguable that people form their identities in particular cultures (Kymlicka 1989; Waldron 1992), cultures are not like hairdressers, set up in order to furnish individuals with diverse and colourful identities. In the sense in which the term is used in identity politics, a *culture* is (something like) an enduring array of social practices, subsisting as a way of life for a whole people. Moreover, a culture is not like an array of clubs and hobbies; it represents the heritage of a particular people's attempts to address and come to

---

[7] See Waldron (1993b). I discuss the point further towards the end of this section.

terms with the problems of social life—problems that are serious and have to be addressed. A culture will comprise a particular way of dealing, for example, with relations between the sexes, the rearing of children, the organization of an economy, the transmission of knowledge, the punishment of offences, and in general the vicissitudes that affect all the stages of human life and relationship from conception to the disposition of corpses, and from the deepest love to the most vengeful antipathies. So when a person talks about his identity as a Maori, or a Sunni Muslim, or a Jew, or a Scot, he is relating himself not just to a set of dances, costumes, recipes, and incantations, but to a distinct set of practices in which his people (the people he identifies with when he claims this as his identity) have historically addressed and settled upon solutions to the serious problems of human life in society.

Identity claims, I said, are made in politics—often in the politics of a larger multicultural society. That larger society also has to deal with the ordinary problems of social life among its inhabitants. It too will be trying to set up practices and rules to govern relations between the sexes, the rearing of children, the organization of an economy, the transmission of knowledge, the punishment of offences, etc. When it arrives at and tries to implement a set of solutions to these problems, those solutions will implicitly contradict some of the solutions arrived at as part of the heritage of the smaller cultures that make up the fabric of the larger society's multiculturalism.

Let me illustrate with a crude example. In response to the enduring question of what rules are to be set up to govern the organization of families and households, culture *A* may answer 'Polygyny', culture *B* may answer 'Polyandry', and culture *C* may answer, 'Monogamy'. If the larger society *S* (which includes individuals who self-identify as *A*s, *B*s, and *C*s) opts for monogamy, then clearly it is opting for an answer which directly contradicts the answer given in *A* (not to mention the answer given in *B*). Now officials of *S* may criticize the beliefs associated with *A* as exploitative or unholy (they may well adopt the rhetoric of *C* in this regard), and the elders of *A* are likely to return the compliment, criticizing monogamy as repressively puritanical or perhaps as subversive of patriarchal authority. My point is that these solutions are *rivals*: they constitute alternative and competing answers to what is basically the same question. Not all cases are as straightforward as I have made this one, of course. Often it will not be quite the *same* question that *A*, *B*, and *C* are addressing; or their respective solutions may vary only because they were predicated originally on quite different social conditions. But still in many cases there will be enough of an overlap, so that there is evidently some degree of *opposition*, not just difference, between the two ways of life.[8]

---

[8] This will be particularly so when one makes *holistic* comparisons between cultures: assumed differences in background circumstances (which might otherwise explain away some perceived rivalry between a given pair of customs) may in fact reflect opposing solutions that the cultures in question have given to other common problems that they face.

I don't mean opposition in the sense that the cultures are necessarily competing for territory, power, or resources. I mean that each of them *disagrees with* the other's solution to the problem that each of them faces: each of them thinks that the other's solution to this common problem is silly or unholy or just plain wrong.

The previous paragraph took a static approach: culture *A* has its solution, culture *B* has its solution, and culture *C* has its solution (which has been adopted by the overarching society *S*). Considered as abstract propositions, the three solutions contradict one another. But now we must also consider the matter dynamically, for what really interests me are the implications of identity politics for the way in which the members of *S* (who include some *A*s and *B*s and *C*s) go about discussing and settling upon a solution. (Remember: we are interested ultimately in the bearing of identity politics on the way in which people discharge their civic responsibilities in the larger society in which they live.) Suppose that the respective heritages of cultures *A*, *B*, and *C* are reasonably settled, but that (for whatever reason) it is still an open question what rules society *S* should have or persevere with in this regard. How should we expect someone who self-identifies as an *A* to participate in this debate?

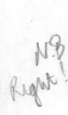

1. He may, first of all, insist that whatever view the larger society finally takes of the merits of different family regimes, it should at least leave room for *A*s like him to practise their own distinctive customs. This is something like a claim for religious accommodation.[9] In many cases, this may be all that is asked for, and often it will be a perfectly reasonable proposal. I have little to say here about the issue of accommodations for cultural differences, except that of course it should always be the first recourse in any situation of the sort we are considering. If mutual accommodation and toleration are in fact available, then the rest of what I shall say in this chapter is inapplicable. (And this may be one legitimate use of the rhetoric of identity: to invigorate the search for a system of mutual accommodation, with the urgency of something like a rights claim.)

But accommodation is not always practicable. And a system of mutual accommodations will not count as a solution if the disagreement between the *A*s and their opponents is in fact a disagreement about what people may be permitted to do. Many opponents of polygamy think it wrong, not just to practise, but to permit, polygamy (just as many opponents of racism think it wrong not just to practise, but to permit, discrimination).[10] In that case, the

---

[9] Of the sort that was rejected (to say the least!) in *Reynolds* v. *United States* 98 US 145 (1879).

[10] Similarly, the dispute about abortion cannot be solved on the basis of accommodation in the way that pro-choice slogans sometimes disingenuously suggest—e.g. 'If you oppose abortion, don't have one.' What the pro-life faction maintains, and what their opponents deny, is that abortion is a form of murder and is to be prevented and prosecuted as such. The pro-choice faction is no more prepared to accommodate the practice of this view by those who

society cannot finesse the issue through mutual accommodations: the As, the Bs, and the Cs must confront their disagreements directly.

2. Secondly, then, assuming that mutual accommodations are not available, we should expect someone who self-identifies as an A to contribute his heartfelt opinion as to what the policy of S ought to be on this matter. As a good A, he believes in polygyny, and he may presumably be expected to try to explain to his fellow citizens why polygyny is not only not wrong (as the Cs suggest), but in fact positively desirable. And we expect that the Bs and the Cs will have something to say in response. Civic deliberation is now under way on a matter of common concern.

But precisely because it is *deliberation* that is now under way, the individual from A cannot expect any special weight to be attached to his opinion simply because of its connection with his identity. His opinion will be responded to in civic debate on the basis of its content. Has he made a good argument? Are his facts right? Do the major premises of his account point to values that are of real importance? Could the important values he points to be secured by any other means? Having been put forward as a contribution to debate, his opinion must now take its chances in relation to the other opinions milling around[11] in the market-place of ideas.

I mentioned earlier the worries expressed by some theorists that reasons and arguments drawn from different cultures may bog down deliberation in some sort of incommensurable stalemate, and I said that I thought that prospect had been exaggerated (Rawls 1993; Waldron 1993b). I do not think we should underestimate the curiosity of human beings and their ability to conduct conversations across the barriers allegedly posed by the most disparate conceptual schemes. Perhaps over-influenced by the Wittgensteinian idea that effective communication presupposes some sort of agreement in judgements (Wittgenstein 1974: 88e, para. 242), we theorists tend to think that deliberation requires a framework of common concepts and understandings; and we are less embarrassed than we ought to be when, time and again, various seafarers, and traders, and migrants prove us wrong. At any rate, I think it is a serious mistake to approach the problem of intercultural deliberation *first* with the idea of deliberative discipline and the exclusion of certain lines of argument on the basis of some Rawlsian idea of public reason (Rawls 1993: 220–2). Our first responsibility in this regard is to make whatever effort we can to converse with others on their own terms, as they attempt to converse with us on ours, to see what we can understand of their reasons, and to present our reasons as well as we can to them. The a priori conviction that stalemate is bound to result and that 'there is no talking to these people' is

believe it than the pro-life faction is prepared to accommodate the practice of abortion itself by those who think it permissible.

11 'To mill around' here means 'to interact with other opinions' in the manner suggested by J. S. Mill in ch. II of *On Liberty* (1956).

itself a violation of the duty of civic participation. (And, one should add, it is a violation most often committed by members of the majority or dominant culture in the kinds of societies we are talking about.[12])

Admittedly when one presents an unfamiliar view in deliberation with others, one takes the risk that, even if it is understood, it will not be persuasive. Certainly we are not entitled to say that its being rejected is a *sign* of its not being understood, for if two or more such views are really at odds with one another, it must in principle be the case that one at least of them may be rejected by a person who understands them both. That is why deliberation—and mutual understanding—are necessary; and that is why those things—rather than the tendentious and usually one-sided discipline of 'public reason'—are what the duty of civic participation requires.

3. At this point, faced with these risks and responsibilities, our protagonist may ponder a third move—and it is this third move which poses the greatest difficulty for the liberal enterprise and which is, in my view, the greatest abuse of civic responsibility. Instead of presenting his view or his culture's view of family organization as a contribution to civic deliberation in society S, he may demand respect for it—the opinion—as an element of respect for *him*. If someone else criticizes his views about polygyny—refutes his empirical assumptions, denies his major premiss, or exposes the fallacies in his reasoning—he may see this as a personal affront, as an attack on him, and an assault on his identity. 'This is the view associated with culture *A*,' he may say, 'and membership of culture *A* is an important part of my identity. An *A* is essentially what I am. If you criticize or refute the *A* view on this matter, then beware!—it is me, and my fellow *As*, that you are criticizing and refuting. If you want to respect me and people like me, you had better take my *A*-ish view seriously and give *to it* the sort of respect in deliberation that my personhood and my identity command.'

We are all familiar with this as one of the ways in which discussions about religion can go badly wrong; suddenly one becomes aware that what was previously the critical evaluation of someone's view is being treated as a personal affront or an insult. And it happens distressingly often in modern academic life as well: scholars increasingly protest that they are 'offended' by an opposing view in social or political theory, when in times past they would have said that they *disagreed* with it and would have tried to explain why. Of course this happens mostly in cases where people feel very deeply about their beliefs, and often the offence complained of is unnecessary, in the sense that there may have been no need for the antagonists to push their disagreement to this extreme. In the context that we are dealing with, however, in this chap-

---

[12] Compare John Stuart Mill's account of who is most likely to be guilty of the 'intemperate' presentation of a view—the dominant majority or the dissident minority?—at the very end of ch. II of *On Liberty* (Mill 1956: 64–7).

ter, the complaint of disrespect (and the deliberative moves that elicit it) are made in a debate that *is* necessary—in circumstances where the inhabitants of S *do* have to figure out what they as a society are going to settle upon in this matter, on which the As (and others) have such strong views.

5. From Opinions to Interests

One way of understanding what is going on when the As make their complaint about disrespect is that, by virtue of their complaint, an *opinion* of theirs is being converted into or treated as an *interest*. (And not just any interest, but a vital interest that demands the special non-negotiable treatment that is properly accorded to rights.)

In liberal democratic societies it is often very important to keep interests and opinions separate, at least so far as political understandings are concerned. Suppose the people of a society disagree about what rights the inhabitants of that society have; suppose in particular they disagree about what rights a certain minority have. Such disagreement is of course a disagreement *about* interests; but it is a disagreement *of* opinion. Faction F_1 believes that a certain interest of a minority group, M_1, should be given special weight against the interests of the majority, M_2, while the opposing faction F_2 denies this. Clearly the matter has to be settled—by a vote, perhaps, or by some sort of authoritative ruling. If it is settled by a vote and if F_1 loses, may the members of that faction complain legitimately about tyranny of the majority? The answer is 'Not necessarily.'

To begin with, if there is a legitimate complaint about tyranny of the majority, it is to be made by or on behalf of the members of M_1, not the members of F_1. Nothing tyrannical happens to a person *simply* by virtue of the fact that his opinion is not acted upon by a community of which he is a member. Furthermore, we are not entitled to assume that the membership of the two groups is the same: F_1 may comprise many members of M_2 and may not include all of the members of M_1. People often organize themselves politically in ways that do not correspond exactly with their interests.[13] Certainly tyranny of the majority is a danger if the votes of those who compose the differing factions represent nothing more than the particular interests or

[13] An example may help. Affirmative action in the United States is opposed by some of those whose interests it is intended to advance, and supported by many of those whose unfair advantages it is intended to offset or remedy. So if a majority decides that the rights of racial minorities do not generate an entitlement to affirmative action, we are not in a position to assume that *that* is the very majority whose actions and interests the minority rights in question were supposed to constrain.

satisfactions of the voters. On that assumption, allowing a majority to prevail *means* allowing the interests of the minority to be sacrificed to those of the larger group. But nothing similar need happen between majorities and minorities if we assume the members of the society are addressing some controversial issue about rights in good faith, for on this assumption a vote may represent, not an individual interest, but a sincerely held individual opinion on a matter of common concern.

Even if the memberships of F_1 and M_1 *do* overlap, it does not follow that defeat for F_1 at the hands of a majority counts as tyranny of the majority. Unless we want to say that each group and each individual has whatever rights it thinks it has, we must accept that claims of rights will have to be subject to political decision of one sort or another, and that some of them may have to be rejected as ill founded. It simply cannot be the case that someone is wronged every time an opinion about rights is rejected in politics. Sometimes a wrong is done because the rejection is unjustifiable; but even then the most that can be said is that the victims are wronged *qua* members of the interest group M_1, not that they are wronged *qua* members of the opinion group (even the overlapping opinion group) F_1.

All this seems to be indispensable for understanding political decisions about rights, in the context of good-faith disagreement in society over what rights we have (Waldron 1993*a*, 1998). As we analyse such disagreements and think about the constitutional structures that are to house them, we must be very careful to distinguish between the individual or minority interests which are the subject of the disagreement and the opinions held by an individual or a minority about their interests or the interests of others. But of course it is exactly this distinction that is confounded when people start demanding special respect for a view associated with a particular culture as part of the respect they demand for their identity. What was an opinion is now being treated as an interest—as a symbolic interest going to the heart of the identity of the person who puts the opinion forward.

6. Compleasance

Suppose the members of more than one group make the move that we imagined the *A*s making (near the end of Section 4). And suppose those moves are taken seriously as putting on the table important facts about those people's identities. The *A*s put forward their view about polygyny, and they indicate that they will regard any criticism or refutation of this view as an affront to their identity; and the *C*s put forward their view about monogamy and they say that *they* will regard any criticism or refutation of their case as an affront to *their* identity. Now a society which takes these identity claims seriously will be simply paralysed, unable to settle on a view about the regulation of family arrangements. The identity claims which we are imagining—the demands that the *A*s and the *C*s are making that their opinions should be respected—are incompossible. Moreover, they are, by virtue of the issue posed in the society, incompossible in principle, not simply as a matter of cost or resources. The aspects of identity for which respect is now demanded began life as *opposing opinions*; that is why they cannot *both* be respected now in the way their proponents demand.

Does it follow, from this incompossibility, that claims of this sort should never be made? I certainly believe they should never be made. People should advance their opinions and, even when those opinions are deeply treasured artefacts of a culture they identify with, the most that should be demanded for them in the way of respect is that people listen to the opinions, take them seriously, not make fun of them, but rather respond to them in practical deliberation, making the best effort they can to see whether there is anything in them that is true, insightful, or persuasive. I don't think anyone should insist, as a condition of respect *for him*, that his opinion on a matter of common concern be accepted or implemented or treated as immune from criticism in political debate (Waldron 1989b). However, I do not think that this belief of mine follows straightforwardly from the point about incompossibility.

Thomas Hobbes seemed to think it did, or rather he came close to thinking that something like this followed. He believed that people had a responsibility to change themselves if they could, and change the tenor (and if need be the contents) of their most cherished views and desires, so that they could fit into a peaceful society. Indeed he thought this was a *law of nature*:

A fifth Law of Nature, is COMPLEASANCE; that is to say, That every man strive to accommodate himself to the rest. For the understanding whereof, we may consider, that there is in mens aptnesse to Society, a diversity of Nature, rising from their diversity of Affections; not unlike to that we see in stones brought together for building of an Edifice. For as that stone which by the asperity, and irregularity of Figure, takes more room from others, than it selfe filles; and for the hardnesse, cannot easily be made plain, and thereby hindereth the building, is by the builders cast away as unprofitable, and troublesome: so also, a man that by asperity of nature, will strive to retain those things which to himself are superfluous, and to others necessary; and for the stubbornness of his Passions, cannot be corrected, is to be left, or cast out of Society, as combersome thereunto. (Hobbes 1988, ch. 15, 106)

This seems to imply that if one can do without the assertion of a rights claim or an identity claim that is going to pose a compossibility problem, then one has a duty to try and do without it. For if the claim really is 'superfluous' to the person who makes it, if it really would not be unreasonable to require him to give it up, his persistence in asserting it makes him 'combersome' to the process of securing peace and building a commonwealth. Or to put it in more straightforward language, the maintenance of such identity claims seems incompatible with one's duty to participate responsibly in civic affairs.

The trouble is, however, that we have not yet established that it *is* possible or reasonable for people to give up claims of this sort without sacrificing their identity. Certainly, identity should not be expanded to cover every demand that a person makes, every opinion he has, every preference he wants fulfilled. But it does not follow that identity claims can be shrunk to order, so to speak, simply to meet the requirements of compossibility.[14] Respect for individuals and compossibility are *independent* constraints on a liberal order; the one is not merely the reflex of the other.[15] We are not entitled to dismiss out of hand the view that respect for persons really does require this sort of respect for their opinions, simply because it would be a structural embarrassment to liberal society if it did.[16]

7. Cultural Engagement

Fortunately, an argument can be made that the sort of identity claims that are worrying us are not claims that their proponents need to make in order to vindicate their cultural identities. By this I mean, not that they are politically unnecessary (I will discuss briefly some exigencies of the political second-best in Section 8)[17] but that they are not what participation in a culture as such inherently requires. Indeed, I want to go further and argue that claims of this sort represent quite inauthentic ways of engaging and identifying with a culture. They not only exaggerate but distort the way in which a person relates to the culture which is part of his identity.

The key here is the air of self-consciousness that pervades the cultural engagements and self-presentations associated with identity politics. I noted earlier that the modern idea of identity associates cultural context with individual authenticity. One forms oneself, yes—but one does so in the context of a particular culture; and the reality of that culture is therefore essential to the self which one forms and to which one has a responsibility to be true. The trouble is that, at the individual level, the authenticity requirement involves

---

[14] Cf. Rawls's suggestion that it *is* reasonable to require individual conceptions of the good to be tailored to fit the requirements of a compossible social order (Rawls 1971: 30–1). Indeed, in Rawls's later work, this is one of the meanings of 'reasonable' (Rawls 1993: 48–54).

[15] See n. 6, above.

[16] Also, there's another difficulty with the Hobbesian view. It takes *two* to establish incompossibility; so which of them is required to make the adjustment? (Example: does the pornographer make life impossible for a devout person or is it that the devout person, with his sensitivities, makes life in a liberal order impossible for the pornographer?)

[17] See below, text accompanying n. 19.

a supreme effort of self-consciousness—as one struggles to catch the urgings of one's inner voice or whatever—while at the cultural level such intense self-consciousness might be quite inappropriate and distracting.

Think for a moment about involvement in a given culture in a *non*-multicultural setting, i.e. involvement with a culture in the culture's natural habitat, so to speak. One is living as an *A*, with a bunch of other *A*s, and the frame of culture *A* is all any of us has been used to. In this setting it is doubtful whether thoughts *about* one's culture—how marvellous it is; how colourful and distinctive; how important it is to the identity of each of us—will loom very large in people's involvement in the life of their community. In this situation what one does is simply speak or marry or dance or worship. One participates in a form of life. *Proclaiming* or *advertising* that this is what one is doing would be viewed by the other *A*s as rather strange. Certainly it would be to participate in a different form of life—a form of life only problematic-ally related to the first. As I said, what one does in straightforward cultural engagement is simply speak or marry or dance or worship. In doing so, one does not say anything about the distinctive features of, say, the Irish heritage, or the peculiarities of the Maori wedding feast. One keeps faith with the mores of one's community just by following them, not by announcing self-consciously that it is the mores of one's community that one is following.

The point is of some general importance, for I think it helps explain why self-conscious engagement with a culture or a national identity often seems so artificial, compared to the life of the culture or nation itself. Consider a suggestion by Isaiah Berlin in his essay on nationalism. Berlin suggested that nationalism involves:

the notion that one of the most compelling reasons, perhaps the most compelling, for holding a particular belief, pursuing a particular policy, serving a particular end, living a particular life, is that these ends, beliefs, policies, lives are ours. This is tanta-mount to saying that these rules or doctrines or principles should be followed not because they lead to virtue or happiness or justice or liberty . . . or are good and right in themselves . . . rather they are to be followed because these values are those of my group—for the nationalist, of my nation. (Berlin 1981: 342–3)

I am sure Berlin is right to see this as an aspect of explicit nationalist conscious-ness. It seems to me that it is characteristic, too, of a great deal of modern cultural identity politics. People say: 'I dress this way or I speak this language or I follow these marriage customs because they are the ways of my people.'

But when you think about it, this is a very peculiar attitude to take—to insert the cultural provenance of a norm or value into what H. L. A. Hart called its 'internal aspect' (Hart 1994: 88 ff.). It seems very odd to regard the fact that this is 'our' norm—that this is what we Irishmen or we French or we Maori do—as part of the reason, if not the central reason, for having the norm and for sustaining and following it.

N.B.

For consider a point I made earlier: social norms and practices do not exist in order to make up a colourful, distinctive culture for us to immerse ourselves in. They exist in a context of reasons and reasoning. There is always a story to be told, a story internal to the norm—part, as I say, of its 'internal aspect'—as to why this way of doing things is better or appropriate or efficient or obligatory or required. If I ask an elder of the group to which I belong why we have and follow a norm of monogamy, he may tell me a story about the need for reciprocity and equality between lovers and explain why this is difficult or impossible in polygamous relationships, or he may tell me a story about the sun and the moon and about there being only one of each. Either way, *that* is the sort of thing that counts, in the group, as a reason for following the monogamy custom. I may not accept the reasoning that the group associates with the norm; or I may find the sun and the moon story bewildering or unsatisfying. But if I do, then that is all there is to say about the matter: I no longer respect the norm on the basis on which it claims my respect. I certainly do not show any respect for it—rather I show a vain and self-preoccupied contempt for the norm itself—by gutting it of *its* reasons, and replacing them as reasons with *my own* need to keep faith with my cultural roots. That is not the point of the monogamy requirement at all, and to think of it as the point (or even as one reason among others) may be to give a quite misleading impression of how important the norm is supposed to be in the culture and what that importance is based on.

In other words: if there are norms and practices that constitute 'our' way of life, and that matters to us, then the thing to do is embrace them wholeheartedly, not in a way that leaves it open for us to comment to others in the sort of stage-whisper that characterizes modern identity politics: 'I am following the practices of my culture' or 'What I am doing here is revisiting my roots'. It is not and has not been the nature of *our* moral practices to go around saying that sort of thing about them—one doesn't say this as one refrains from dishonesty, for example—and I doubt that it is the practice of very many other groups either. On the contrary, to congratulate oneself on following 'the norms of my community' is already to take a point of view somewhat external to those norms, rather than to subscribe wholeheartedly to the substantive commitments that they embody.

Once this is accepted, then I think it is also clear that one cannot legit-imately regard criticism and discussion as a simple *affront* to some aspect of one's cultural identity. Humans and human groups take their norms seriously, and to take them seriously is to think of them as embedded in something like a structure of reasons and reasoning. Whatever we think of them from the outside, from the inside they are not like the rules of games or the norms of fancy dress—things one can cast off as soon as it seems no longer important to display oneself as a member of a particular group. They make deep claims, powerful claims about what is important in the world (and beyond it) and what sort of things are at stake in the areas of life that they govern; and those claims are usually held to be true, which means that they offer a better account of what really matters than the reasoning associated with the different norms and practices of the society next door or across the sea. Now, that reasoning may bewilder and disconcert us; it is no part of my argument that it should be familiar or congenial or just like our reasoning over here.[18] But it is like ours at least in this: that it represents or claims to represent some repository of human wisdom as to the best way of doing things. As such it necessarily makes its reasoning available—though, as I have said now several times, not always easily or comfortably available—to understanding and assessment on the basis of, and in comparison with, what else there is in our society in the way of human wisdom and experience on questions such as those that the norm purports to address.

8. Others

The common legal framework that I mentioned at the beginning of the chapter is needed in relation to whoever we find ourselves living with, interacting with, or potentially quarrelling with. In the phrase I quoted from Kant, we have a duty to come to terms with those with whom we find ourselves 'unavoidably side by side' (Kant 1991, paras. 43, 121). In recent communitarian political philosophy there has been a tendency to insist that a well-ordered society should be thought of as something constructed among those who *share* certain fundamental understandings and beliefs (cf. Walzer 1983). By contrast, the great virtue of Thomas Hobbes's work and Immanuel Kant's work in political philosophy is that they begin from *the opposite assumption.* They assume that we are always likely to find ourselves, in the first instance, alongside others who disagree with us about justice; and they argue that if there is to be community or a common framework for living, it has to be created in the form of positive law, constructed out of individual views or views sponsored by particular cultures that are given initially as disparate and opposed. That seems both more realistic in the mixed-up circumstances of the modern world, and less dangerous than the communitarian view—less dangerous, certainly, when one thinks what is likely to be done—what has in fact been done—to turn the communitarian assumption into a self-fulfilling prophecy.

Of course, since I am putting so much emphasis on real-world conditions (finding ourselves unavoidably side by side with uncongenial others), my

---

[18] But, as I said earlier, it is possible to exaggerate the implications of this unfamiliarity (Rawls 1971, 1993; Waldron 1993b; Wittgenstein 1974).

analysis invites the question: why do I not also consider the real-world pre-dicaments of most cultural minorities? For often—perhaps even characterist-ically—dominant majorities make no attempt whatsoever to *debate* the merits of (say) monogamy versus polygyny with the members of groups which hold contrary views. They simply *impose a view*, and then disingenuously accuse the dissident minority of failing to live up to its civic responsibility. In these circumstances—which are equally circumstances of the real world—appeals to identity politics are introduced by cultural minorities as a sort of last resort, in a desperate attempt to simply *get a hearing* for their side of the case. In the face of the majority's refusal even to consider minority practices as an alter-native, the minority says, 'We refuse to accept the status quo, in which the majority ignores the reasons for our practices. We need to show the majority that we are deadly serious in our cultural commitments—that it is not just a game we are playing or a costume we are wearing—and that we find their ob-stinacy on this point intolerable.'[19] And it is on this basis that they introduce move 3 outlined at the end of Section 4 above.

Nothing in my analysis is intended to show that that strategy is morally or politically inappropriate. But it does seem to me important to distinguish two levels of 'real world' analysis: there are (*a*) the real-world circumstances in which talk of civic responsibility makes sense in the modern world; and (*b*) the problems posed by imperfect compliance with the principles appropri-ate for (*a*). (This distinction corresponds to John Rawls's distinction between (*a*) the circumstances of justice, such as moderate scarcity, and (*b*) the prob-lem of partial compliance, such as the entrenchment of injustice.)[20] We cannot know how far or in what respects the majority are failing in the duties they owe to cultural minorities without an analysis of the kind I have undertaken in Sections 1–7. Some of what the majority may think is fair is revealed by such an analysis to be unfair—such as the a priori imposition of constraints of 'public reason'. (See Rawls 1971, 1993; Waldron 1993a; Wittgenstein 1974.) And much of what majorities are accused of doing unfairly—such as contra-dicting or debating minority practices—is revealed by such analysis to be not after all inappropriate. And our philosophical willingness to sort through the accusations in this way should not be mistaken for doubt about the pro-position that *on the whole* real-world majorities have tended to act unjustly and oppressively in this business. But the truth of that proposition does not make it any less urgent to ascertain whether the positions characteristically associ-ated with identity politics are positions that are inherently appropriate in the circumstances of modern society, or whether they should only be regarded

---

[19] This is Will Kymlicka's formulation (in a letter to me). I am grateful to him for the em-phasis he has put on this point.

[20] See Rawls (1971: 8 and 245 ff., strict versus partial compliance; and 126–30, circumstances of justice).

as fall-back strategies, designed as effective tools to combat injustice despite their inherent inauthenticity.

9. Conclusion

Civic responsibility—this business of coming to terms responsibly with others—is relative to what is more or less a geographical relation of being unavoidably side by side with others. In the circumstances of modern life, that geographical relation—being unavoidably side by side with others—is no guarantee whatever that common moral views and shared understandings can be taken for granted. We are not in a position to pick and choose those with whom we are required to come to terms. Of the people who surround us, competing for the use and control of the same action-space and the same resources, we cannot say 'We will enter into civil society with the As, but not the Cs because the Cs do not share our views or traditions'. The discipline of politics is that there is no alternative to our coming to terms with the Cs if they live and interact with us. Since humans have fanned out haphazardly over the face of the earth, a way has to be found, when they cluster together in particular fertile or hospitable territories, to bring into deliberative relation with one another the views of all the individuals and all the groups in that vicinity as to what is a proper way to respect one another's interests. And they cannot do that—they cannot discharge that responsibility—if some (whether they are the majority or the minority) think from the beginning that their deeply held opinions are polluted by juxtaposition with others' or affronted by being introduced into a deliberative process at all.

Because we hold disparate views and come from different cultures, this business of coming to terms with one another is not bound to succeed. It is a fragile enterprise, and we have often seen it fail. Accordingly, it is a matter in which we are morally required to take care. Our need to come to terms with the others around us, and the vulnerability of that process to various sorts of impossibility, has an impact on the way in which it is reasonable for us to present ourselves as partisans of different views or participants in disparate traditions.

Earlier I attempted to distinguish a mode of allegiance to the traditions and practices of a particular culture that is in principle incompatible with this civic responsibility—namely, the presentation of one's engagement with a particular set of norms and practices as though it were a brute aspect of one's identity, like one's sex or one's colour, and therefore non-negotiable by anyone who himself takes seriously and respects himself. I contrasted this with a mode of engagement with the norms and practices of one's community or culture which is engagement with them, and reasoning about them, as norms. To treat a tradition or practice of one's culture as a norm means to treat it not simply as a costume, but as a standard which does some work in the life of one's community. And that means treating it as a standard with a point: a standard which does work which might, in principle or as a matter of at least logical possibility, have been performed by *other* norms, *alternative* standards, and which therefore cannot be understood except in terms of its association with an array of reasons explaining why it is in fact *this* norm rather than *that* norm—monogamy, for example, rather than polygyny— which is the standard we uphold.

I think that only if one's initial allegiance to the practices of one's culture is held and presented in that sort of spirit can it be presented to others of different cultures (others who hold different norms) as a responsible first move in the complicated political business—which includes bargaining, deliberation, compromise, authority, and voting—the difficult business of coming to terms with those with whom we *have* to come to terms (as opposed to those with whom we would like to come to terms). Or, to return finally to our theme of identity: only if one's allegiance to the practices of one's culture is held and presented as a matter of reasons, rather than as a matter of identity, can the presentation of these practices count as a way of discharging one's duty as a citizen to participate responsibly in deliberation about policy and law.

7

Anti-Essentialism, Multiculturalism, and the 'Recognition' of Religious Groups

TARIQ MODOOD

1. Anti-Essentialism

It is only in the last few years that the discourse of multiculturalism has become respectable. Yet, initially seen as a progressive discourse, it is today already seen by many academic commentators as conservative, even reactionary. Arguments for political multiculturalism are directed against essentialist or monistic definitions of nationality, for example, definitions of Britishness which assumes a cultural homogeneity, that there is a single way of being British. Multiculturalists have emphasized internal differentiation (relatively easy in the case of Britain, which encompasses up to four national or semi-national components, England, Scotland, Wales, and Northern Ireland) and fluidity, with definitions of national belonging being historical constructs and changing over time. In this way it has been possible to argue for the incorporation of immigrant groups into an ongoing Britishness and against those who prophesied 'rivers of blood' as the natives lashed out against the aliens perceived as threatening national integrity.

In this political contest the ideas of essential unity, integrity, discreteness, and fixity have been seen as reactionary, and internal differentiation, interaction, and fluidity as progressive. Yet in recent years when multiculturalism has come to be respectable, at least in terms of discourse, academic critics have attacked multiculturalism in terms very similar to those used by multiculturalists against nationalism or monoculturalism. The positing of minority or immigrant cultures which need to be respected, defended, publicly

The work on which this chapter is based was made possible by the ESRC award R00222124, for which I am grateful. I would like to thank Joe Carens for his comments on an earlier version of the chapter and Bhikhu Parekh for several beneficial discussions. This chapter originally appeared in the *Journal of Political Philosophy*, Vol. 6, No. 4, 1998, pp. 378–99.

supported, and so on is said to appeal to the view that cultures are discrete, frozen in time, impervious to external influences, homogeneous, and without internal dissent; that people of certain family, ethnic, or geographical origins are always to be defined by them and indeed are supposed to be behaviourally determined by them (Gilroy 1987; Anthias and Yuval-Davis 1992). The underlying assumptions of multiculturalism, at least in its non-reflective moments, have been identified in this way:

The premise of sorting populations by ethnic origins according to presumed cultural essence is that a culture is a community of deep-seated values. For values one may also read social roles and meanings, or customs and traditions. But what makes cultural origin a category of population is the additional assumption that a culture is a community of original identity, to which individuals belong by birth. By the common sense of being and belonging which sets the tone of this cultural recognition, all those born into a community absorb and ineradicably sediment within themselves its customary ways of thinking, feeling and being. Even if they do not so identify themselves, they are nevertheless properly identified with that community, whatever subsequent layers of other cultures they may have absorbed to cover over the original sediment. (Feuchtwang 1990: 4)

In this anti-essentialist critique, in which the target is sometimes labelled 'ethnic absolutism' (Gilroy 1992), 'culturalism' (Dirlik 1990), 'culturalist differentialism' (Al-Azmeh 1993: 4, after Taguieff 1987), multiculturalism is interpreted as 'a picture of society as a "mosaic" of several bounded, nameable, individually homogeneous and unmeltable minority uni-cultures which are pinned onto the backdrop of a similarly characterised majority uni-culture' (Vertovec 1995: 5). Despite its crudeness—or perhaps because of it— it is argued that throughout Europe many public policies and wider political discourses surrounding multiculturalism tend to employ just such a picture (Vertovec 1995: 1). In Britain this critique and the charge that multiculturalism supports reactionary community leaders is associated with activists and academics connected with Women against Fundamentalism. This is an organization set up by the Southall Black Sisters as a response to the political Islamism of the Rushdie affair to 'challenge the assumption that minorities in this country exist as unified, internally homogeneous groups' (Women against Fundamentalism 1990: 2; see also Yuval-Davis 1992: 284), and in particular to oppose the idea of the 'seemingly seamless (and supra-racial) Muslim consensus in Britain' (Connolly 1991: 4–5).[1] Although anti-essentialism is a relatively recent position, the position it attacks, however much it may be assumed in our unreflective moments, is so manifestly absurd that few would want to

---

[1] It has been difficult for an organization which has few Muslim members to have credibility as a critic of a coercive, essentialist, political concept of 'Muslim' when it supports a coercive, essentialist, political concept of 'black' (Modood 1994, 1995). I am, however, here concerned with the logic rather than the politics of this position.

defend it. In fact, it has recently been said that 'opposition to essentialism is a near-universal characteristic of the debate on identity' (Kirton 1995: 5).

The British anti-essentialists have proposed the ideas of hybridity and of new ethnicities as an alternative to essentialist ethnic identities. The thrust of these positions is that ethnic identities are not simply 'given', nor are they static or atemporal, and they change (and should change) under new circumstances or by sharing social space with other heritages and influences. They typically cite factors such as the consequences of post-colonial immigration, the movement of populations, the mixing of cultures, and the critiques of old ideas of racial superiority. As a result there are many individuals who have fused identities, whose lifestyles reflect a variety of ethnic heritages, who refuse to be defined by their ethnic descent or any one group, but who consciously create new identities for themselves (Rushdie 1991; Bhabba 1994; Hall 1992a; Gilroy 1993; for a debate, see Werbner and Modood 1997). For some the power of cultural essentialism is such that it is implicit in even these attempts to oppose it. Ayse Caglar, in a recent article, points out that while theorists of hybridity are able to show how cultures can mix, the presumption is that prior to the mixing there were two different cultures à la essentialism. Moreover, even if hybridity theory shows the crassness of the idea of 'one group, one culture' and allows for fluidity and change, the cultures that it speaks of are still anchored in territorial ideas, for the underlying assumption is that 'one space, one culture' is the norm to which hybridity is the exception (Caglar 1997).

Yet the fear of essentialism can push one too far the other way. Stuart Hall writes that because of factors such as migration and the globalization of economics, consumption and communications, societies can no longer be constituted by stable collective purposes and identities organized territorially by the nation-state. In its most radical version, not only does politically constituted multiculturalism become impossible, but the idea of a unified self becomes an unrealistic dream:

> If we feel we have a unified identity . . . it is only because we construct a comforting story or 'narrative of the self' about ourselves . . . The fully unified, completed, secure and coherent identity is a fantasy. Instead, as the systems of meaning and cultural representation multiply, we are confronted by a bewildering, fleeting multiplicity of possible identities, any one of which we could identify with—at least temporarily. (Hall 1992b: 277)[2]

This radically multiple self has a penchant for identities, but prefers surfing on the waves of deconstruction to seeking reconstruction in multiplicity. It is post-self rather than a multi-self. Even in less radical versions, the self is no

---

[2] Hall does not always argue as if the contemporary self was radically decentred (Hall and Held 1989).

more connected to one location, society, or state than another, any more than the typical consumer is connected to one producer or the goods of one country. Reconciled to multiplicity as an end in itself, its vision of multi-culturalism is confined to personal lifestyles and cosmopolitan consumerism and does not extend to the state, which it confidently expects to wither away (Modood 1997b).

It seems then that anti-essentialism is inherently destructive. Each escape from its grasp (for example, in the celebration of hybridities) proves to be illusory, while thoroughgoing embrace seems to leave us with no politics, no society, not even a coherent self. There seems to be a relentless and unstoppable logic that takes us from nationalism or social monism to the self as a comforting fiction. What promised to be an emancipatory, progressive movement seems to make all political mobilization, with its 'deconstruction' of the units of collective agency (people, minorities, the oppressed, etc.), rest on mythic and dishonest unities. Hence some of those who embrace philo-sophic anti-essentialism argue, nevertheless, that the pragmatic power of essentialism must be salvaged from the destructive logic. Hall, for example, analyses racial identity as a fiction, but one which is necessary in order to make 'both politics and identity possible' (Hall 1987: 45). Others, especially some feminists, speak of a 'strategic essentialism' in which one knows that essentialism is false but in some politically favoured contexts may act as if it was true (Spivak 1987; Brah 1992; cf. Fuss 1989). Hence the conceptual polit-ical unity of women or blacks—though not, as we saw earlier, of Muslims—is protected from radical anti-essentialism.

There must clearly be something wrong with an intellectual movement that leads to such counter-intuitive conclusions (the self as fiction) and to contortions in order to protect favoured political projects from the results of consistency. I think that the social theoretical movement I have been de-scribing is based on the wrong kind of anti-essentialism. The starting-point, the suspicion about some discourses of culture, is right, but it does not follow that the ordinary, non-theoretical discourses are incoherent. In talking about other people's cultures we often assume that a culture has just the kind of features that anti-essentialists identify. When non-Chinese people, for example, talk of 'Chinese civilization', their starting-point often is that it has a coher-ence, a sameness over centuries, and a reified quality. Sometimes, as Caglar notes of minority intellectuals, one slips into such a mentality when talking of one's own cultural traditions (Caglar 1997). One is particularly prone to this when one is producing a systematic summary or ideological justification for those traditions. Hence, rich, complex histories become simplified and collapsed into a teleological progress or a unified ideological construct called French culture or European civilization or the Muslim way of life.

In cases where we essentialize or reify someone else's culture, no antidote may be to hand, for we lack the knowledge to overturn the simplifications. In the case of a living culture that we are part of, that we have been inducted into, have extended through use, and seen change in our own lifetimes, it is easier to appreciate better the processes of change and adaptation, of borrowings from other cultures and new influences, and yet at the same time appreciate what is the *subject* of change. For change implies the continuation of something that has undergone change. It is the same in the case of a person: at the end of one's life one might reflect on how one's personality changed over time and through experience, and see how all the changes constitute a single person without believing that there was an original, already formed, essential 'I' prior to the life experiences. As with a person, so with a culture. One does not have to believe that a culture, or for that matter an ethnic group as the agent of culture, has a primordial existence. A culture is made *through* change; it is not defined by an essence which exists apart from change, a noumenon hidden behind the altering configurations of phenomena. In individuating cultures and peoples, our most basic and helpful guide is not the idea of an essence, but the possibility of making historical connections, of being able to see change and resemblance. If we can trace a historical connection between the language of Shakespeare, Charles Dickens, and Winston Churchill, we call that language by a single name. We say that it is the same language, though we may be aware of the differences between the three languages and of how the changes are due to various influences, including contact with and borrowing from other languages, and without having to make any claim about an 'essence'.

In the points that I have been making, I have been influenced by Wittgenstein's anti-essentialism. In the 1930s and 1940s Wittgenstein thoroughly revised the philosophy of his early work the *Tractatus* (1994). In the *Tractatus* Wittgenstein had assumed that all languages aspired to a single ideal structure. In his later work he argued that languages were of many different kinds, reflecting different histories, purposes, and forms of life and could not be judged against an ideal standard. But he did not think it followed that *anything* could be a language; he thought that specific languages could have a unity in the way that different elements of a game hang together and makes sense to the players. The key point is that one did not need an idea of essence in order to believe that some ways of thinking and acting had a coherence; and so the undermining of the ideas of essence did not necessarily damage the assumption of coherence or the actual use of a language (Wittgenstein 1967, para. 108). The coherence of small-scale activities (e.g. games) is, of course, easier to see and describe than those of histories and ways of life, but as long as we do not impose an inappropriately high standard of coherence (e.g. the coherence of a mathematical system, as assumed to be the ideal of language in the *Tractatus*), there is no reason to be defeatist from the start.

The lesson I draw from this is that we do not have to be browbeaten by a dogmatic anti-essentialism into believing that historical continuities, cultural groups, coherent selves do or do not exist. Nothing is closed a priori; whether there is sameness or newness in the world, whether across time, across space, or across populations, are empirical questions.

2. Ethnic Minority Identities in Britain

Let us then try to proceed by locating ourselves within some empirical data. I shall present here some findings from the Fourth National Survey of Ethnic Minorities in Britain, of which I was the principal researcher. Fieldwork was undertaken in 1994 and covered many topics besides those of culture and identity, including employment, earnings and income, families, housing, health, and racial harassment. The survey was based on interviews of roughly about an hour in length, conducted by ethnically matched interviewers, and offered in five South Asian languages and Chinese, as well as English. Over 5,000 people were interviewed from the following six groups: Caribbeans, Indians, African Asians (people of South Asian descent whose families had spent a generation or more in East Africa), Pakistanis, Bangladeshis, and Chinese. Additionally, nearly 3,000 white people were interviewed, in order to compare the circumstances of the minorities with that of the ethnic majority. Further details on all aspects of the survey are available in Modood et al. (1997).

As might be expected, the survey method has many limitations, especially in relation to complex topics like those of identity. Nevertheless, if we bear in mind that all research methods have their limitations and cannot be substituted for each other, so that no one is *the* method, then this survey has the potential to offer what small-scale ethnographic studies, armchair theorizing, and political wishful thinking cannot. The survey explored only certain dimensions of culture and ethnicity. For example, it did not cover youth culture and recreational activities such as music, dance, and sport. These cultural dimensions are likely to be as important to the self- and group identities of some of our respondents, especially the Caribbeans, as the features we gathered data on. Moreover, almost all the questions asked in the survey provided indications of how closely people affiliated to their group of origin. We did not explicitly explore ways in which members of the minorities had adopted, modified, or contributed to elements of ways of life of other groups, including the white British.

We found that members of minority groups, including those born and raised in Britain, strongly associated with their ethnic and family origins; there was very little erosion of group identification down the generations. But, while individuals described themselves in multiple and alternative ways, it was quite clear that groups had quite different conceptions of the *kind* of group identity that was important to them. The important contrast between groups was that religion was prominent in the self-descriptions of South Asians, and skin colour in the self-descriptions of Caribbeans. Despite the various forms of anti-racist politics around a black identity of the last two decades—an identity which politicians and theorists have argued is *the* key post-immigration formation (Modood 1994)—only a fifth of South Asians think of themselves as black. This is not an Asian repudiation of 'the essential black subject' (Hall 1992*a*) in favour of a more nuanced and more pluralized blackness, but a failure to identify with blackness at all.

N.B.

The South Asian identification and prioritization of religion is far from just a nominal one. Nearly all South Asians said they have a religion, and 90 per cent said that religion was of personal importance to them. In some ways this cleaving to religion extends to the Caribbeans too. It is true that as many Caribbean as white people, nearly a third, and even more Chinese, do not have any religion, and that the general trend down the generations within every ethnic group is for younger people to be less connected to a religion than their elders (though perhaps to become more like their elders as they age). Nevertheless, while only 5 per cent of white 16–34 years old said that religion was very important to how they led their lives, nearly a fifth of Caribbeans, more than a third of Indians and African Asians, and two-thirds of Pakistanis and Bangladeshis in that age group held that view. Non-white Anglicans are three times more likely than white Anglicans to attend church weekly, and well over half of the members of black-led churches do so. Black-led churches are a rare growth-point in contemporary Christianity. Indeed, the presence of the new ethnic minorities is changing the character of religion in Britain not simply by diversifying it, but by giving it an importance which is out of step with native trends.

Ethnic, racial, or religious identification was of course not universal. For example, one in six British-born Caribbean-origin people did not think themselves as being part of an Afro-Caribbean ethnic group; this was quite unrelated to the growing issue of mixed ethnicity: nearly half of all 'Caribbean' children had a white parent, a development which is bound in due course to impact on conceptions of Caribbean and black identities. For East African Asians their job was as important an item of self-description as any other. Whilst over a third of Caribbeans and about a quarter of South Asians wished to send their children to schools where half the pupils were from their ethnic group, only a tenth of Chinese wished to do so.

These identities, various as they are, do not necessarily compete with a sense of Britishness. Half of the Chinese but more than two-thirds of those in the other groups also said that they felt British, and these proportions were, as one might expect, higher amongst young people and those who had been born in Britain. The majority of respondents had no difficulty with the idea of hyphenated or multiple identities, which accords with our prior study and other research (Hutnik 1991; Modood *et al.* 1994). But there was evidence of alienation from or a rejection of Britishness too. For example, over a quarter of British-born Caribbeans did not think of themselves as being British. This too accords with our in-depth interviews at the development stage. We found that most of the second generation did think of themselves as mostly but not entirely culturally and socially British. They were not, however, comfortable with the idea of British being anything more than a legal title. In particular they found it difficult to call themselves 'British' because they felt that the majority of white people did not accept them as British because of their race or cultural background; through hurtful 'jokes', harassment, discrimination, and violence they found their claim to be British was all too often denied (Modood *et al.* 1994, ch. 6).

Distinctive cultural practices to do with religion, language, marriage, and so on sometimes still command considerable allegiance. The case of religion has already been mentioned. A further example is that nearly all South Asians can understand a community language, and over two-thirds use it with family members younger than themselves. More than half of the married 16–34-year-old Pakistanis and Bangladeshis had had their spouse chosen by their parents. There was, however, a visible decline in participation in distinctive cultural practices across the generations. This was particularly evident amongst younger South Asians, who, compared to their elders, are less likely to speak to family members in a South Asian language, regularly attend a place of worship, or have an arranged marriage. Yet, as has been said, this did not mean that they ceased to identify with their ethnic or racial or religious group. In this respect the survey makes clear what has been implicit in recent 'identity politics'. Ethnic identification is no longer necessarily connected to personal participation in distinctive cultural practices, such as those of language, religion, or dress. Some people expressed an ethnic identification even though they did not participate in distinctive cultural practices. Hence it is fair to say a new conception of ethnic identity has emerged.

Traditionally, ethnic identity has been implicit in distinctive *cultural practices*. This is still the case, and is the basis of a strong expression of group membership. Additionally, however, an *associational* identity can be seen which takes the form of pride in one's origins, identification with certain group labels, and sometimes a political assertiveness. The ethnic identities of the second generation may have a weaker component of behavioural difference, but it would be misleading to portray them as weak identities as such. In the last couple of decades the bases of identity formation have undergone important changes, and there has come to be a minority assertiveness. Identity has moved from that which might be unconscious and taken for granted because implicit in distinctive cultural practices to conscious and public projections of identity and the explicit creation and assertion of politicized ethnicities. This is part of a wider sociopolitical climate which is not confined to race and culture or non-white minorities. Feminism, gay pride, Quebecois nationalism, and the revival of Scottishness are some prominent examples of these new identity movements which have come to be an important feature in many countries in which class politics has declined. Identities in this political climate are not implicit and private but are shaped through intellectual, cultural, and political debates and become a feature of public discourse and policies, especially at the level of local or regional government. The identities formed in such processes are fluid and susceptible to change with the political climate, but to think of them as weak is to overlook the pride with which they may be asserted, the intensity with which they may be debated, and their capacity to generate community activism and political campaigns. In any case, what is described here as cultural-practice-based identities and associational identities are not mutually exclusive. They depict ideal types which are usually found, as in this survey, in a mixed form. Moreover, a reactive pride identity can generate new cultural practices or revive old ones. For some Caribbean people a black identity has come to mean a reclaiming of the African-Caribbean cultural heritage and has thus stimulated among some younger people an interest in Patois–Creole languages which was not there amongst the migrants. A similar Muslim assertiveness, sometimes a political identity, sometimes a religious revival, sometimes both, is evident in Britain and elsewhere, especially amongst some of the young.

Some of the group differences mentioned above can be partly explained by place of birth, period of residence in Britain, or occupational class, or by a combination of these and related factors, but underlying them was an irreducible difference between groups. The contrast between South Asians and Caribbeans has already been mentioned. A further important difference between groups, perhaps related to the influence of religion, is between African Asians and Indians (about 90 per cent of whom are Sikhs and Hindus), and Pakistanis and Bangladeshis (over 95 per cent of whom are Muslims). On a range of issues to do with religion, arranged marriages, choice of schools, and Asian clothes, the latter group take a consistently more 'conservative' view than the former, even when birth or age on arrival in Britain and economic position are taken into account.

Group differences of this kind used to be regarded by anti-racists as of negligible significance for public policy, for it used to be argued that the important policy goal was to eradicate racism and that all the non-white groups in Britain experience the same racism. As the research evidence of differential stereotyping has accumulated over the last decade, the leading theorists discovered what they alleged was a new racism, though the differential stereotyping and treatment of Asians and blacks seems to be as old as the presence of these groups in Britain (Modood 1997c). The Fourth Survey strongly supports the contention of differential prejudice targeted at different groups.

NB.

The survey found that there is now a consensus across all groups that prejudice against Asians is much the highest of any ethnic, racial, or religious group; and it is believed by Asian people themselves that the prejudice against Asians is primarily a prejudice against Muslims.

The perception of these groups' cultural practices and the extent to which they are adhered to no doubt is a determinant of the prejudice against them such that the important prejudice in Britain is a cultural racism rather than a straightforward colour racism. But it would be wrong to assume that groups which are most culturally distinct or culturally conservative are least likely to feel British and vice versa. It has already been mentioned that the Caribbeans, of all non-whites the culturally and socially closest to the white British, had the highest proportion who dismissed identification with Britishness—more than the Pakistanis and the Bangladeshis, the most culturally conservative and separate of these groups. This certainly should not be taken to imply that the cultural conservatism consists in simply wanting to be left alone as a community and not making political demands upon the public space, say, in the manner of the Amish in Wisconsin. For example, half of all Muslims wanted state funding for Muslim schools, something which was only granted in December 1997 and against which there is presumed still to be considerable white opposition (not necessarily from committed Christians: the survey found that nominal Christians and agnostics or atheists were more likely to express prejudice against Muslims than committed Christians). The political demands of Muslims such as these are not akin to conscientious objections, to principled exemptions from civic obligations, but—akin to other movements for political multiculturalism—are for some degree of Islamicization of the civic; not for getting the state out of the sphere of cultural identities, but in some small way for an inclusion of Muslims into the sphere of state-supported culture.

At the same time, the trend in all groups, however, is away from cultural distinctness and towards cultural mixture and intermarriage. As can be guessed from above, the trend is not equally strong in the various groups. For example, among the British-born, of those who had a partner, half of Caribbean men, a third of Caribbean women, a fifth of Indian and African Asian men, a tenth of Pakistani and Bangladeshi men, and very few South Asian women had a white partner.

3. 'Recognizing' Hybridity

The above brief description of some of our survey findings about ethnic identities and group consciousness in Britain suggests a number of points that could be further discussed. The key implication I wish to draw here is that while there is much empirical support for those theorists who have emphasized the fluid and hybrid nature of contemporary post-immigration ethnicities in Britain, the suggestion that groups are so internally complex that they have become 'necessary fictions' is much exaggerated, and that the theoretical neglect of the role of religion reflects a bias of theorists that should be urgently remedied. The political challenge, I believe, is to reach out for a multicultural Britishness that is sensitive to ethnic difference and incorporates a respect for persons as individuals and for the collectivities that people have a sense of belonging to. That means a multiculturalism that is happy with hybridity but has space for religious identities. Both hybridity[3] and ethno-religious communities have legitimate claims to be accommodated in political multiculturalism; they should not be pitted against each other in an either–or fashion as is done all too frequently by the anti-essentialists and by some liberal political philosophers (e.g. Waldron 1992).

I want to focus here on an aspect of the political recognition of religion, for this is largely absent from cultural studies, and from sociological and political science discussions. Before I do so, I would just like to make the point that the recognition of hybridity does not suffer if multiculturalism includes a recognition of religious and other communities. Indeed, while the two may not require the same political structures, it may be that hybridity can actually benefit from some recognition of communities. What I have in mind can be illustrated by reference to an Anglo-Canadian comparative study (Ghuman 1994). Ghuman looked at the multicultural context and school provision in relation to some South Asian children in a part of Birmingham and a part of Vancouver. He found that there was much less official multiculturalism in Birmingham than Vancouver, but that the Indo-Canadian adolescents felt much more 'mixed' and 'hyphenated' (as the official ideology encouraged them to do), whilst the British Asians identified much more with their communities and the norms and mores of those communities rather than, as did the Indo-Canadians, with the values and lifestyles of their white peers. Much more than the ideologies of multiculturalism and assimilationism was relevant here; the Birmingham sample were more from poorer homes, and were more residentially concentrated, for example. Nevertheless, I draw the implication that the influence of parental or communal conservatism upon children can be stronger than that of official monoculturalism in schools. Conversely, official recognition of communal heritages facilitates hybridity, national inclusivity, and positive attitudes to change amongst minorities—and majorities. This seems to me to parallel the phenomenon that Barbara

---

[3] 'Hybridity' is a less than satisfactory term, suggesting as it does that hybrids are something lesser than the 'species' from which they are derived. I reject that implication, but use the term as it has gained currency in the literature, not least from those who wish to celebrate their own hybridity (Rushdie 1991; Bhabba 1994).

Lal has called 'the ethnicity paradox' to describe the conviction of some early twentieth-century United States sociologists that allowing European immigrants and Southern black migrants to cities such as Chicago to form communal organizations was the most satisfactory way of promoting long-term participation in the institutions of the wider American society (Lal 1990, ch. 5). This does not necessarily ghettoize or 'freeze' immigrant communities, but may allow them to adapt in an atmosphere of relative security as opposed to one of rootlessness and powerlessness, where each individual is forced to come to terms with a new society in relative isolation and, therefore, exclusively on the terms of the majority (Modood 1992a: 57–8).

It is also worth noting that recognizing hybridity has quite different implications from those that multiculturalism is sometimes taken to have for citizenship. For example, in one prominent liberal account of multicultural citizenship, the cultures in question are assumed to be discrete societal cultures, typically a 'nation', and the political significance for liberals of these cultures is that they are a context of choice for their members, without which capacity for autonomous individuality would be affected (Kymlicka 1995a). It is true that Kymlicka primarily has in mind indigenous, historical, or territorial nationalities in what he takes to be multinational states, rather than post-migration identities, the subject for discussion here. But this only serves to reinforce the point that justifications for different forms of multiculturalism (in the case of Kymlicka's subject-matter, 'multinational citizenship' seems the more apposite term) may be such that a claim that they are covered by a single theory cannot be substantiated. Certainly, British hybrid or hyphenated identities, such as black British or British Asian, do not depend on discrete societal cultures (such cultures are neither available nor sought); their political significance is less to do with 'contexts of choice' than with exclusion–inclusion, for the political issue it raises is the definition of the community of 'Britishness'. Moreover, while the community at issue is a nationality, it is not a nationality to be contrasted with one's group identity but a nationality which the hybrids wish to make a claim on and so to be a part of. Hybridity, then, is not a substate nationality (in the way of Scottishness or Catalan); it is a form of complex Britishness. This is particularly worth emphasizing because in Britain there are people who want not just to be black or Indian in Britain, but positively want to be black British or British Indians (Hall 1998; Jacobson 1997). They are less seeking civic rights against a hegemonic nationality than attempting to negotiate politically a place in an all-inclusive nationality.

Such political demands create argument and debate and unsettle identities, sentiments, symbols, stereotypes, etc., especially amongst the 'old' British. Yet it should be clear that the empirical evidence of hybridity suggests that this is a movement of inclusion (at least from the side of those excluded) and social cohesion, not fragmentation. Translated into policy, it could be a contribution to a renewal of British nationality or national-rebuilding of the sort exhorted by Prime Minister Blair, especially in his Labour Party conference speech of September 1997 (Jacques 1997). In so far as an inclusive nationality is a precondition of or facilitates a sense of citizenship (Miller 1995), it is a positive contribution towards citizenship.

Hyphenated nationality seems, then, to pose no major issues of principle for citizenship, as long as we are not committed to an essentialist definition of nationality, or the wrong kind of anti-essentialism, or a theory that bases multicultural citizenship on a 'context of choice' argument. My own suggestion is that it points us towards a theory of multiculturalism in which we respect and recognize people's sense of belonging regardless of whether that identity is a context of choice or not.

There is a lot more that can be said about recognizing hybridity, but as there is already quite a lot of literature on the topic and very little on what I believe is equally important, the recognition of religious minorities, I would like to give more space to the latter.

4. 'Recognizing' Religious Communities

In some West European countries, notably Britain, policy demands based on religion are increasingly being made and religious groups are often the basis of political mobilization and lobbying. In Britain these demands include the modifications of school curricula, dress codes, provision of halal meat and vegetarian meals, separate worship in the generality of state-funded schools, and also state funding for privately established Muslim schools in the same way that Christian and Jewish schools are funded (MET 1997). Parity has also been sought in relation to the law on blasphemy and/or the incitement to racial hatred (Modood 1993a), and there is a general demand to outlaw discrimination on the basis of religion and to incorporate the cultural needs of religious minorities in social and health services (UKACIA 1993). Ethno-religious minorities have also sought to become political actors through the setting up of syndicalist institutions such as the Muslim parliament, or by demanding sectional representation in existing institutions such as the House of Lords or the Labour Party, usually on the model of a form of representation already achieved by Jews or blacks or women (Modood 1993b).

Most theorists of difference and multiculturalism exhibit very little sympathy for religious groups; religious groups are usually absent in their theorizing and there is usually a presumption in favour of secularism. Yet we must not be too quick to exclude religious communities from participation in the political debates etc. of a multicultural state. Secularity should not be embraced without careful consideration of the possibilities for reasonable dialogue between religious and non-religious groups. In particular, we must beware of an ignorance-cum-prejudice about Muslims that is apparent amongst even the best political philosophers (Modood 1996: 178–9).

Charles Taylor is at fault here in his argument for a politics of recognition. He presents a moderate version of a 'politics of difference', and part of his moderation consists in his recognition that not everybody can join the party: there are some groups to whom a politics of recognition cannot be extended within a liberal polity. However, the only example he gives of those that cannot be included are Muslims. While he refers to the controversy over *The Satanic Verses*, the only argument he offers for the exclusion is: 'For mainstream Islam, there is no question of separating politics and religion the way we have come to expect in Western liberal society' (Taylor 1994: 62). Similarly, in her argument for a plural politics Chantal Mouffe asserts that modern democracy requires an affirmation of a 'distinction between the public and the private, the separation of church and State' in ways not granted by Islam (Mouffe 1993: 132). These I believe, however, are odd conclusions for at least two reasons.

First, it seems inconsistent with the starting-point of the argument for multicultural equality, namely, it is mistaken to separate culture and politics. More to the point, it all depends on what one means by 'separation'. Two modes of activity are separate when they have no connection with each other (absolute separation); but activities can still be distinct from each other even though there may be points of overlap (relative separation). The person who denies that politics and religion are absolutely separate can still allow for relative separation. In contemporary Islam there are ideological arguments for the absolute subordination of politics to religious leaders (e.g. Khomeini; even then the ideology is not always deemed practical), but this is not mainstream Islam, any more than the model of politics in Calvin's Geneva is mainstream Christianity.[4]

Historically, Islam has been given a certain official status and pre-eminence in states in which Muslims ruled (just as Christianity or a particular Christian denomination had pre-eminence where Christians ruled). In these states Islam was the basis of state ceremonials and insignia, and public hostility towards it was a punishable offence (sometimes a capital offence). Islam was the basis of jurisprudence but less so of positive law. State legislation, decrees, law enforcement, taxation, military power, foreign policy, and so on were all regarded as the prerogative of the ruler(s), of political power, which was regarded as having its own imperatives, skills, etc., and was rarely held by

---

[4] Ayatollah Khomeini is, of course, regarded by many Muslims as one of the most important Muslim leaders of this century. My point is that his concept of rule by religious scholars, *vilayati faqih*, is a radical innovation and not mainstream Islam (Ayubi 1991).

saints or spiritual leaders (Piscatori 1986; Ayubi 1991; Khaldi 1992). Moreover, rulers had a duty to protect minorities.

Just as it is possible to distinguish between theocracy and mainstream Islam, so it is possible to distinguish between radical or ideological secularism which argues for an absolute separation between state and religion, and the moderate forms which exist throughout Western Europe except France. In nearly all of Western Europe there are points of symbolic, institutional, policy, and fiscal linkages between the state and aspects of Christianity. Secularism has increasingly grown in power and scope, but it is clear that a historically evolved and evolving compromise with religion is the defining feature of West European secularism, rather than the absolute separation of religion and politics. Secularism does today enjoy a hegemony in Western Europe, but it is a moderate rather than a radical, a pragmatic rather than an ideological, secularism. Indeed, paradoxical as it may seem, Table 7.1 shows that mainstream Islam and mainstream secularism are philosophically closer to each other than either is to its radical versions. Muslims, then, should not be excluded from participation in the multicultural state because their views about politics are not secular enough. There is still a sufficient divide between private and public spheres in Islamic faith and practice to facilitate dialogue with other (contending) religious and non-religious communities and beliefs.

TABLE 7.1.

Religion and state	Radical secularism	Radical Islam	Moderate secularism	Moderate Islam
Absolute separation	Yes	No	No	No
No separation	No	Yes	No	No
Relative separation	No	No	Yes	Yes

There is an alternative argument, however, for a multiculturalism which explicitly embraces radical secularism. Versions of this argument are quite popular with reformers as well as academics in Britain at the moment (Modood 1994, 1997a). This argument recognizes that in a country like Britain religion and state are not separate, the constitution gives the Church of England (and Scotland), with its links with the monarchy and parliament, a privileged position, often referred to as 'establishment'. Moreover, it is asserted that an institutional privileging of one group is *ipso facto* a degrading of all the others, allowing them only second-class citizenship: establishment 'assumes a correspondence between national and religious identity which marginalises non-established churches, and especially non-Christians as only partial members of the British national collectivity' (Yuval-Davis 1992: 283).

It is maintained that if we are to take multicultural equality seriously, the Church of England ought to be disestablished: public multiculturalism implies radical secularism, regardless of whatever compromises might have been historically required. This argument relies upon three different assumptions which I would like to consider in turn.

Neutrality

It seems to be assumed that equality between religions requires the multicultural state to be neutral between them. This seems to be derived from Rawls's contention that the just state is neutral between 'rival conceptions of the good'. It is, however, an appeal to a conception of neutrality that theorists of difference disallow. For a key argument of the theorists of difference is that the state is always for or against certain cultural configurations: impartiality and openness to reason, even when formally constituted through rules and procedures, reflect a dominant cultural ethos, enabling those who share that ethos to flourish, while hindering those who are at odds with it (Young 1990).

This objection seems to have particular bite for secularism; for, even where it is not avowedly atheistical, it seems not to be neutral between religions. For some people, religion is about 'the inner life', or personal conduct, or individual salvation; for others, it includes communal obligations, a public philosophy, and political action (for example, as in the Christian socialism favoured by the British Labour prime minister, Tony Blair, not to mention the various Christian Democratic parties in Western Europe). Radical secular political arrangements seem to suit and favour the private kind of religions, but not those that require public action. It is surely a contradiction to require both that the state should be neutral about religion, and that the state should require religions with public ambitions to give them up. One way out of this difficulty is to restrict neutrality to certain kinds of cases. Thus, for example, it has been argued that the liberal state is not and ought not to be neutral between communalistic and individualistic conceptions of the good. Liberals should use state power to encourage individualistic religions over those orientated to shaping social structures; what they ought to be neutral between are the various individualistic religions (Waldron 1989a: 78–80). But this leaves unclear why non-liberals, in particular those whose conception of the good is not confined to forming a coherent individual life for themselves, should be persuaded that the liberal state is the just state; and, if they are not, and the pretence of meta-neutrality is dropped, how is the liberal state to secure its legitimacy? Even this, however, is a less arbitrary use of the idea of liberal neutrality than is found among multiculturalists such as Taylor or Amy Gutmann. After recognizing that multicultural equality between groups can take a neutralist or interventionist version, Gutmann suggests that the former is more suited to religious groups and the latter to non-religious educational policy (Gutmann 1994a: 10–12). Yet she offers no justification for this differential approach other than that it reflects United States constitutional and political arrangements.

It has been argued that, even where absolute neutrality is impossible, one can still approximate to neutrality, and this is what disestablishment achieves (Phillips 1997). But one could just as well maintain that, though total multicultural or multi-faith inclusiveness is impossible, we should try and approximate to inclusiveness rather than neutrality. Hence, an alternative to disestablishment is to design institutions to ensure those who are marginalized by the dominant ethos are given some special platform or access to influence so their voices are heard. By way of illustration note that while American secularism is suspicious of any state endorsement of religion, Indian secularism was designed to ensure state support for religions other than just those of the majority. It was not meant to deny the public character of religion, but to deny the identification of the state with any one religion. The latter is closer to what I am calling moderate rather than absolute secularism. In the British context, this would mean pluralizing the state–religion link (which is happening to a degree), rather than severing it. It is interesting that Prince Charles has let it be known that as a monarch he would prefer the title 'Defender of faith' to the historic title 'Defender of *the* Faith' (Dimbleby 1994: 528).

Autonomy of Politics

Secondly, implicit in the argument for the separation of the spheres of religion and politics is the idea that each has its own concerns and mode of reasoning, and achieves its goals when not interfered with by the other. (I am here only concerned with the autonomy of politics.) The argument is that politics has limited and distinctive goals and methods, these relate only to a dimension of our social world, and can best be deliberated over in their own terms, not derived in a lawlike way from scriptures, dogmas, or theological arguments. The focus of political debate and of common political action has to be defined so those of different theologies, and those of none, can reason with each other and can reach conclusions that are perceived to have some legitimacy for those who do not share a religious faith. Moreover, if people are to occupy the same political space without conflict, they have mutually to limit the extent to which they subject each other's fundamental beliefs to criticism. I think such arguments became particularly prominent in seventeenth-century Western Europe as people sought to put an end to the religious wars of the time.

I have already suggested that this idea of relative autonomy has shaped statecraft both in the Muslim world and in the constitutional structures of contemporary European states. Nevertheless, I do not think the autonomy of politics is (or could be) absolute, nor that it supports radical (as opposed to moderate) secularism. The point I wish to make here is that this view of politics is not just the result of a compromise between different religions, or between theism and atheism, but is part of a style of politics in which there is an inhibition, a constraint on ideology. If politics is a limited activity, it means political argument and debate must focus on a limited range of issues and questions rather than on general conceptions of human nature, of social life, or of historical progress. Conversely, to the extent that politics *can* be influenced by such ideological arguments, for example, by their setting the framework of public discourse or the climate of opinion in which politics takes place, then it is not at all clear that religious ideologies are taboo. While it is a contingent matter as to what kind of ideologies are to be found at a particular time and place, it is likely that ideologically minded religious people will be most stimulated to develop faith-based critiques of contemporary secularism where secular ideologies are prevalent and, especially, where those ideologies are critical of the pretensions of religious people.

Of course, we cannot proscribe ideology, secular or religious. My point is simply that the ideological or ethical character of religion is not by itself a reason for supposing that religion should have no influence on politics. Rather, institutional linkages between religious conscience and affairs of state (as through the twenty-six bishops who by right sit in the House of Lords at Westminster) are often helpful in developing politically informed and politically constructive religious perspectives that are not naïvely optimistic about the nature of politics.

Democracy

Proponents of a radically secular multicultural state maintain that establishment, even a reformed establishment (e.g. a council of religions), is a form of corporatist representation and is therefore open to the charge of being undemocratic. Advocates of multicultural equality are skating on thin ice here, for it is not uncommon for them to argue for special forms of minority representation. While in practice this often means special consultative committees, the preferred method is usually some form of constraint on an electoral process (a device, for example, that reserves certain seats for women or a minority in a decision-making forum). In any case, there is no reason to be a purist in polities where mixed forms of representation are the norm and are likely to remain so. We are, after all, talking about bodies with very little power. One would, therefore, have to take a practical view of how damaging it would be for an institution with such little power to remain independent of the franchise.

There are certainly advantages in allowing organized religion corporatist influence rather than encouraging it, or obliging it, to become an electoral player. Some examples of when a religion deprived of state influence seeks an electoral intervention and joins the party competition, as in Pat Buchanan's bid for the Republican Party presidential nomination in the United States, or the emergence of Islamist parties in various countries, or in the effects of electoral Hindu chauvinism on the Indian state, suggest that the radical secularist's concern with democratic purity may in the end be counterproductive. Of course, one could argue that organized religion should not be allowed to support electoral candidates (Audi 1989), but advocates of this restriction typically fail to explain why churches and other religious organizations are significantly different from ethnic associations, businesses, trade unions, sport and film stars, and so on. It is also difficult to see how such restrictions are democratic: denying religious groups corporate representation while at the same time requiring them to abstain from electoral politics—all in the name of democracy and so that 'the nonreligious will not feel alienated or be denied adequate respect' (Audi 1989: 295)—seems to compromise democracy more seriously than the maintenance of the current weak forms of corporate representation.

The goal of democratic multiculturalism cannot and should not be cultural neutrality but, rather, the inclusion of marginal and disadvantaged groups, including religious communities, in public life. Democratic political discourse has perhaps to proceed on the assumption that, ideally, contributions should be such that in principle they could be seen as relevant to the discourse by any member of the polity. This may mean that there is a gravitational pull in which religious considerations come to be translated into nonreligious considerations, or are generally persuasive when allied with non-religious considerations. What it does not warrant is the relegation of religious views to a private sphere. Neither my intention nor my expectation is the demise of secularism. The argument for inclusion is aimed at keeping open the possibility of dialogue and mutual influence. It does mean, however, as pointed out by Graham Haydon, that:

> there is no reason to assume that religious points of view must entirely give way to secular ones. For the entry of non-secular views into the debate does at least make it more possible for secular thinkers to appreciate the force which the other points of view have for those who adhere to them. Secular thinkers may pragmatically be willing to make some accommodation to the views of religious thinkers: movement need not be all the other way (as it would be, by default, if religious viewpoints were to remain only in a private realm). (Haydon 1994: 70)

N.B.

In arguing that corporate representation is one of the means of seeking inclusiveness, I am not arguing for the privileging of religion, but recognizing that in the context of a secular hegemony in the public cultures of contemporary Western Europe, some special forms of representation may be necessary and more conducive to social cohesion than some other scenarios.

The implications of the recognition of religious groups for civic identities are, however, less clear to discern than in the case of hybridic ethnicity. In various societies religious sectarianism, communalism, or fundamentalism produces social cleavages which undermine the conditions of civic solidarity. It is equally clear that similar effects are produced by cleavages associated with ethnicity, nationality, race, class, and so on. If religion is a potential danger to civic pluralism, it is not peculiarly so. On the other hand, religion can be a source of renewal of community to overcome social divisions and can provide an underpinning of compassion, fairness, justice, and public morality—to refer once again to Tony Blair's Christian socialism for illustration—on which civic solidarity and civic duties rest. Ethnoreligious formations, such as Muslim political assertiveness in Britain, are intrinsically neither friend nor foe to multicultural citizenship and hyphenated nationality. It all depends on how the civic order responds to them and modifies them. To reject them outright on the basis of an alleged definition of Western political culture is neither theoretically nor practically justifiable. What is important is that we eschew the contemporary bias against religious groups when discussing these matters.

5. Conclusion

The anti-essentialism that has become a virtual orthodoxy in identity studies is right to emphasize that minority identities are continually changing and reinventing themselves through fusing with elements of majority cultures and that this process of mixing, of hybridization, will increasingly be the norm where rapid change and globalization has made all identities potentially unstable. However, it is a misunderstanding of anti-essentialism to conclude that all collective agency rests on mythic and dishonest, albeit strategically necessary, agency. Unities, continuities, resemblance, groupness are not a priori banished, but remain the object of empirical inquiry. One such inquiry in Britain suggests that the minorities are not of a single generic type. A multiculturalism that is not biased towards non-white minorities of a particular kind (those defined by colour; those defined by transatlantic youth culture) should aim to find political space for hybridity and religious communities.

I have suggested that there is a theoretical incompatibility between multiculturalism and radical secularism. That means that, in a society where some of the disadvantaged and marginalized minorities are religious minorities, a public policy of multiculturalism will require the public recognition of religious minorities, and the theoretical incompatibility will become a practical issue. In such situations moderate secularism offers the bases for institutional compromises. Such moderate secularism is already embodied in church–state relations in Western Europe (France being an exception). Rather than see such church–state relations as archaic and as an obstacle to multiculturalism, we should be scrutinizing the compromises that they represent and how those compromises need to be remade to serve the new multicultural circumstances.

PART IV

Gender and Ethnic Diversity

8

Should Church and State be Joined at the Altar? Women's Rights and the Multicultural Dilemma

AYELET SHACHAR

> Family law not only defines the legal options for individuals caught in the flux, but in more subtle as well as more obvious ways, shapes their societies.
>
> (Barbara Stark, 'Forward: Rappaccini's Daughters?')

> There is a proposition in economics, less familiar elsewhere than it should be, called the 'general theory of the second best.' Simply stated, that theory says that a vision of what one would ideally like may not be a very good guide at all to the choice among non-ideal options where the ideal is unobtainable. The best we can do, when the very best is impossible, may be something very different indeed.
>
> (Robert E. Goodin, 'Designing Constitutions')

In recent years, political and legal theorists have argued that liberal democracies should accommodate distinctive religious or cultural groups within their borders by granting them special rights and exemptions, or by offering them some measure of autonomy in matters of self-governance. Such accommodations, or 'differentiated citizenship rights' in Will Kymlicka's terminology (Kymlicka 1995a: 26–33), generally aim to ensure that minority groups have an option to maintain what Robert Cover calls their *nomos*: the normative universe in which law and cultural narrative are inseparably related (Cover 1983). Multicultural accommodation presents a problem, however, when pro-identity group policies aimed at levelling the playing-field between minority cultures and the larger society systematically allow the maltreatment of individuals *within* the religious or cultural group—an impact which is in certain cases so severe that it nullifies these individuals' status as citizens. Under such conditions, well-meaning accommodation by the state may leave members of minority groups vulnerable to severe injustice within the group, and may in effect work to reinforce some of the most patriarchal and hierarchical elements of a culture.[1]

One of the most important areas in which multicultural accommodation can have this effect is family law. Close-knit religious or cultural groups often demand respect for their customs regarding marriage and the family, on the grounds that their enforcement is essential to the group's continued cultural existence. (I call such groups, whether religiously or culturally aligned, 'nomoi groups'.) In diverse societies around the globe, proponents of multicultural accommodation and minority group leaders alike are pushing for legal reforms in the family law arena that would make the state adapt its institutions and traditions to reflect the cultural diversity of the citizenry. While this trend is controversial, and raises old questions about the appropriate relationship between 'church and state',[2] it still looms large on the public policy agendas of many democratic countries. In fact, various liberal democracies have already begun to reallocate legal powers in matters of family law to nomoi groups. In the United States, for example, the Indian Child Welfare Act has removed jurisdiction over Indian child welfare issues from state courts to tribal courts, the latter being designated as the exclusive or preferred forum for certain custody proceedings involving Native American children.[3] Similarly, Canada, Australia, and (most recently) Britain are also revisiting their family law policies, exploring different ways in which state law can be sufficiently pluralistic, so as to allow different communities to be governed by their own religious or customary institutions on certain matters of marriage and divorce proceedings.[4]

Surprisingly, while theoretical debates have raged in recent years over whether to adopt multicultural accommodation policies—arguing over how such policies should be determined and to which groups such policies should apply—little consideration has been given to the complex arena of family law. Although multicultural accommodation policies mean well in that they aim to respect nomoi groups' cultural norms and practices, such policies may, ironically, impose disproportionate injury upon a specific category of group

---

[1] Elsewhere, I call this phenomenon 'the paradox of multicultural vulnerability', by which I mean to call attention to the fact that traditionally subordinated categories of group members may bear disproportionate costs for their *nomos*, and that their vulnerability may, ironically, be exacerbated by the very accommodationist policy aimed to promote their status as multicultural citizens. See Shachar (forthcoming *a*).

[2] For a brief historical analysis of the history of church and state relations in the family law context, see Weisbrod (1987–8).

[3] The Indian Child Welfare Act of 1979, 25 USC §§1901–1963 (1994). See also the case of *Matter of Adoption of Halloway*, 732 F. 2d 962 (Utah 1986); *Mississippi Band of Choctaw Indians* v. *Holyfield*, 490 US 30 (1989). A policy of deference to tribal marriage, divorce, and gender-biased membership rules was also adopted in the case of *Santa Clara Pueblo* v. *Martinez*, 436 US 49 (1978).

[4] For analyses of these changes cf. Parkinson (1994); Syrtash (1992); Bainham (1996); Pearl (1995).

insider, in this instance women. More specifically, the family law policies designed to accommodate the practices of different minority cultures can act to *sanction* the maltreatment of women according to the rules of their own *nomos*. Women play central roles in creating and preserving the collective identities of many nomoi groups, and these roles are often the most rigidly defined by their communities' 'essential' family law traditions.[5] As these intragroup traditions are respected by the wider society, their oppressive nature is implicitly condoned. Unfortunately, the problem of intragroup oppression of women is rarely analysed in the literature. However, when it is raised, it is often presented as an *unavoidable* consequence of tolerating cultural differences in the liberal state.[6] I believe this view is misguided,[7] and suggest that the real challenge facing proponents of multicultural accommodation is to acknowledge the potential tension between respecting cultural differences and protecting women's rights[8]—a phenomenon most evident in the family law arena, and to seek new viable legal approaches to resolve this tension. Focusing on religious communities, this chapter uses the example of family law to explore how jurisdiction is currently split between 'church and state', and how that legal authority can be best divided between them. I analyse how different models for allocating legal authority affect both women's intragroup status and their communities' ability to maintain their cultural distinctiveness in a diverse society.

My discussion proceeds in three steps. Section 1 demonstrates why women living in minority groups are more vulnerable than men to maltreatment in

---

[5] I have addressed this issue in greater detail in Shachar (1998).

[6] Chandran Kukathas, for example, defends the right of nomoi groups to impose many internal restrictions upon their members, as long as they allow members a right of exit (Kukathas 1992a). Susan Okin, on the other hand, suggests that 'no argument can be made on the basis of self-respect or freedom that female members of the culture have a clear interest in its preservation'. In Okin's view, 'they *may* be much better off if the culture into which they were born were . . . to become extinct' (Okin 1997: 28). I view both Kukathas's 'non-intervention' policy and Okin's simplified dichotomy between promoting group-based interests and women's rights as misguided. Both writers fail to address the complexity of women's lived experiences—the *multiplicity of their affiliations*. As individuals with multiple affiliations, female group members may legitimately wish to preserve their cultural identity and, at the same time, to fight for greater gender equality.

[7] I discuss this point in greater detail in Shachar (forthcoming *c*).

[8] This tension is addressed by Will Kymlicka in *Multicultural Citizenship*, where he suggests that it can be overcome by a distinction between two kinds of multicultural accommodation: those that promote justice between groups ('external protections') and those that restrict the ability of individuals within the group to revise or abandon traditional cultural practices ('internal restrictions'). He endorses the former type of accommodations but rejects the latter (Kymlicka 1995a: 34–44). While this distinction is attractive and seems to offer a clear rule for decision-makers, it fails to provide a viable solution for a set of real-life situations in which the 'external' and 'internal' aspects of accommodation are interwoven, and the very multicultural policy that promotes justice between groups also exposes certain categories of group members to *sanctioned* intragroup oppression. For further discussion of this problem, see Shachar (forthcoming *b*, ch. 2).

the family law context, a vulnerability which I describe in terms of the two main functions of family law: the demarcating function and the distributive function. In Section 2 I summarize and critique the two extant approaches to family law accommodation which exemplify the current family law arrangements adopted in numerous legal democracies.[9] These two approaches, which I call the 'secular absolutist' model and the 'religious particularist' model, are evaluated in light of the following two questions: First, how well does the division of legal authority implied by this model preserve the cultural uniqueness of nomoi groups? Secondly, how does this model's allocation of legal authority affect the intragroup status of women?[10] My analysis illustrates that *neither* model provides an adequate balance between cultural preservation through family law accommodation and the protection of women's rights as citizens in the liberal state. In Section 3, I develop the contours of a new alternative multicultural approach to family law accommodation which I call the 'joint-governance' model. Unlike the secular absolutist and the religious particularist models, the joint-governance model respects the crucial identity-preserving function of family law, but at the same time seeks to provide women living in nomoi groups with the legal protections guaranteed to them as state citizenship. Hence, the joint-governance model can effectively ease the maltreatment that women often suffer at the hands of their own groups' traditions, by allowing them to function simultaneously as citizens with state-guaranteed rights *and* as group members with participatory status in an accommodated nomoi community.

1. Women and Family Law

Women as Cultural Conduits

Recently, feminist scholars have began to investigate seriously the tangled relationship between gender and the reproduction of collective identities. Although this relationship is obviously complex, writers from various disciplines agree that women occupy a special position in constituting collective identities: 'On the one hand, they are acted upon as members of collectives, institutions or groupings . . . On the other hand, they are a special focus of . . . concerns as a social category with a special role (particularly

---

[9] These two approaches take slightly different forms in different countries. I will briefly describe the key features of each model and refer to its typical practical legal implementation.

[10] I restrict my analysis in this chapter to the effect of family law accommodation upon the relations between husbands and wives. The analysis of the intragroup effect of family law accommodation upon children requires a separate discussion which is beyond the scope of this chapter.

human reproduction)' (Yuval-Davis and Anthias 1989: 1, 6).[11] Yet women's unique position in nomoi groups as cultural conduits gives rise to an ironic problem: these crucial cultural roles have traditionally been expressed in the realm of the family, through adherence to a set of gender-biased norms and practices which often subordinate women.[12] Laws pertaining to the family are central to the self-concepts of nomoi groups. However, these very same laws and practices often subordinate women to such an extent that when their groups' practices are accommodated by the state, women living in nomoi groups risk losing their basic rights as state citizens.[13]

Scholars have focused on particular case-studies which examine how women become emblematic of political positions and of cultural identity in particular local or historical processes.[14] Of particular interest to my discussion here are case-studies of religious communities, which have shown that women are assigned 'the role of bearers of cultural values, carriers of traditions, and symbols of the community' primarily because they carry out the tasks of nurture and reproduction (Moghadam 1994*a*: 4). As I will show in the next subsection, a group's family law policies incorporating women's roles as cultural conduits into the group's *nomos* tend, at the same time, to solidify a system of unequal power relations which subordinates women.

The Anatomy of Family Law

There are two perspectives one may take to the body of family law. One is more outward-looking or externally focused. This can be described as family law's 'demarcating' function, which maintains a group's membership boundaries *vis-à-vis* the larger society. The other perspective is more interpersonal or inwardly directed. This can be called family law's 'distributive' function, which shapes and allocates rights, duties, and ultimately powers between men and women within the group. The distinction between these two

---

[11] Note that Anthias and Yuval-Davis's analysis of women's unique position is not aimed at essentializing their role as child-bearers and care-givers (i.e. as biological and cultural reproducers of collective identities), nor does it express the view that all 'human reproduction' experiences of women are similar. Anthias and Yuval-Davis therefore differ from cultural feminists who glorify mothering as the epitome of an ethics of care. Cf. e.g. West (1988). For a critique of West's 'essential woman', see Harris (1990).

[12] For example, the personal status options of women are often officially determined by a 'male guardian—a father, husband, brother or uncle' (cf. Freeman 1990).

[13] I focus my remarks on 'citizens', as the prime beneficiaries of the rights and protections of modern citizenship. Under this category I include all persons who permanently reside in a given territory. Other groups of individuals, for example, non-citizens, may also be entitled to certain basic rights and protections by the state. However, defining the exact scope and limits of such protections is beyond the scope of this chapter.

[14] Of the rapidly growing body of literature which treats the relationship between gender and the construction of collective identities, see Afshar (1987); Grewal and Kaplan (1994); Kandiyoti (1991); Moghadam (1994*b*).

functions parallels the distinction between two legal aspects of marriage and divorce proceedings: personal status and property relations. Divorce proceedings generally involve both aspects: a change in personal status (the demarcating function) and a determination of property relations between the spouses (the distributive function). While often intermingled in practice, personal status and property relations are legally two distinct subject matters (cf. Vestal and Foster 1956: 23–31).

Family Law's Demarcating Function

First, the demarcating function of family law—that is to say, the centrality of family law in defining and regulating a group's membership boundaries—can best be understood in terms of the two basic means through which group identities are maintained. These two means, which are often intertwined, have been generally categorized as 'the racial, ethnic, biological and territorial, on the one hand, and the ideological, cultural and spiritual on the other' (Ben-Israel 1992). Anne McClintock stresses the former, emphasizing that collective identities 'are frequently figured through the iconography of familial or domestic space' (McClintock 1993: 62–3). Moreover, she observes that even the term nation derives from *nasci* (Latin): ' "to be born", and that national collective identities are also symbolically figured as domestic genealogies' (McClintock 1993: 62–3).[15] Benedict Anderson also suggests that communities are best viewed as akin to families and religious orders (Anderson 1991: 7, 143–4). Such communities are understood by their members as having 'finite, if elastic boundaries, beyond which lie other nations' (1991: 7). Defined in this fashion, group membership derives its meaning from a system of 'differences',[16] which must be demarcated by membership boundaries.

Family law demarcates membership boundaries in two related ways: first, by developing complex lineage rules which determine who, by virtue of birth, is eligible for acquiring full membership in the group, and secondly, by defining who by way of marriage can become a group member.[17] Given the fact that nomoi groups (as well as nation-states) acquire members first and foremost by birth (cf. Eisgruber 1997; Cott 1996) (rather than by consent, for

[15] Note that the analogy I propose here between identity groups and nations is limited to the mechanisms of biological and cultural reproduction. I focus here on the situation of nomoi groups which exist within the framework of a larger political entity (the state), rather than on that of groups seeking national independence or secession from the larger body politic. The nomoi groups which I analyse seek accommodation for their differences *within* the boundaries of a state composed of a diverse citizenry.

[16] For a general discussion about the construction of 'difference' as a relational term, see Minow (1990); Parker *et al.* (1992).

[17] Accordingly, a family law tradition loses its opportunity to set the legal terms for membership if a nomoi group permits anyone interested in joining the group to become a full member.

example),[18] it is not surprising that nomoi groups have developed various social and legal mechanisms for controlling the personal status and the reproductive activity of women—for women have a central and potentially powerful role in procreating the collective (Klug 1989: 31).[19]

Intragroup policing of women,[20] if encoded in the group's *nomos*, is partially achieved via the implementation of personal status laws and lineage rules which clearly state how, when, and with whom women can give birth to children who will become full and legitimate members of the community.[21] In nomoi groups which stress the 'biological descent' element of identity, legal marriage is a necessary but not sufficient condition for granting group membership by birth. Therefore, a child may be born into a marriage legally recognized by the nomoi group, but still not be considered a 'blood' member of the community.[22]

For example, although there is no genetic distinction between children born of mixed marriages, whether the 'full blood' parent is the father or the mother, in many nomoi groups the gender of the 'blood' parent determines whether or not the child of a mixed marriage can legally and socially belong to a given community.[23] Clearly, personal status laws and lineage rules are a

[18] For a position which advocates the model of political membership or citizenship by consent rather than by birthright, see Schuck and Smith (1985).

[19] I consider reproduction and mothering as, like other human relationships and institutions, to be constructed by law, history, and society, rather than imprinted by biological drives. For similar views on reproduction and mothering, see Glenn (1994).

[20] Men, too, are controlled by such laws, but not in a similarly discriminatory and oppressive fashion.

[21] Yet even within this legal paradigm, there is leeway in defining the specific legal means through which membership boundaries are codified in a nomoi group's traditions. Although sharing the notion that group membership is legally transmitted by birth, different religious traditions have developed different 'membership transmission procedures'. The Jewish tradition, for example, dictates that membership by birth is transmitted along matrilineal lines, while other religious traditions, such as Islam, dictate that group membership be transmitted along patrilineal lines. Yet other traditions recognize both matrilineal and patrilineal lines. For a feminist critique of the social and legal regulation of women's 'legitimate' reproduction of children, see M. O'Brien 1981; Iglesias 1996.

[22] Consider, for example, the Santa Clara Pueblo's membership rules which were upheld by the US Supreme Court decision in the case of *Santa Clara Pueblo v. Martinez* 436 US 49 (1978): 1. All children born of marriages between members of the Santa Clara Pueblo shall be members of the Santa Clara Pueblo. 2. . . . children born of marriages between male members of the Santa Clara Pueblo and non-members shall be members of the Santa Clara Pueblo. 3. Children born of marriages between female members of the Santa Clara Pueblo and non-members shall not be members of the Santa Clara Pueblo. 4. Persons shall not be naturalized as members of the Santa Clara Pueblo under any circumstances. I discuss the *Martinez* case in greater detail in Shachar (1998).

[23] Similarly, in virtually all democratic countries the husband's nationality traditionally determines the nationality of the children of a mixed marriage, as well as the wife's nationality. According to this principle, a native-born woman who married a foreign national lost not only her legal personality (as a *femme couverte*) but also her own nationality and independent

product of a particular group's history and established traditions; yet they are none the less perceived as reflecting a real 'biological' distinction between children worthy of being granted full membership and those excluded from the group. The Halakhah (Jewish religious law), for example, constructs 'blood' taboos with regard to the status of children born to a Jewish father who marries outside the faith. Since according to the Halakhah, group membership in the Jewish community is transmitted along matrilineal lines, a child born to a Jewish husband and a non-Jewish wife cannot become a member of the Jewish community at birth.[24] In order to acquire full membership (that is, religious affiliation as a Jew), a child of a Jewish father and a non-Jewish mother would have to go through formal, although simplified, procedures of conversion. As in other religious nomoi groups, the act of conversion requires rites of passage which constitute a symbolic 'rebirth' into one's new religious affiliation. The analogy to birth, is of course, not accidental. Even in the United States an 'alien' has to go through a 'naturalization' process in order to become a full member in the political community, i.e. to 'fill in' for what has not been acquired 'naturally' by birth.[25]

Interestingly, under Jewish family law a child born to a Jewish father and a non-Jewish mother *after* she has converted to Judaism becomes a full member of the Jewish community *at birth*. As the authors of *The Myth of the Jewish Race* observe, the distinction between the status of children born to a non-Jewish mother and those born to a non-Jewish mother who has converted to Judaism simply cannot be explained in 'blood' terms; for, as they put it, 'the genetic make-up of the children born to such mixed couples [between a Jewish father and a non-Jewish mother who has or has not converted into Judaism] remains the same' (Patai and Wing 1975: 91–2). Hence, the distinguishing factor here is cultural—i.e. the mother's conversion is perceived as an indication that her children will grow up in a Jewish home.

However, even if we accept the argument that many biological categories are socially constructed (as I think we should),[26] we must none the less recognize that a group's transmission of membership by birth has meaning only

citizenship status. For further discussion, see International Law Association (1998). In the American context, for example, from 1855 to 1934 an American woman who married a foreign national was automatically (and often involuntarily) deprived of her birthright citizenship. On this troubled period in US history, see Sapiro (1984). Today only a minority of nation-states continue to uphold gender-biased citizenship laws, specifying that the nationality of children born to a mixed marriage is determined by the father's nationality (Stratton 1992).

[24] The legal situation is different in Israel, where Jewish nationality for the purposes of the national public register is not identical with the Jewish Orthodox definition of religious affiliation (Akzin 1970; Ginossar 1970).

[25] 'Nature' and its cognates also come from *nasci*, to be born, so that 'nature' and 'nation' share an etymological, if not historical, root.

[26] Of the growing literature on this subject in the context of race, see Harris (1995); Lopez (1994). More generally, see Delgado (1995); Crenshaw *et al.* (1995).

N. B.

under a group's specific family law, and lineage rules are an important factor in the maintenance of the group's self-concept. Thus, family law has crucial importance in the construction of a shared identity among group members who constitute, as Benedict Anderson says, an 'imagined community' (Anderson 1991). Family law matters for the preservation of collective identities, then, not because of one group or another's characterization of 'blood' membership. Rather, it has value as a political expression of legal and cultural sovereignty, i.e. a self-defined procedure for demarcating membership boundaries.[27]

Family Law's Distributive Function

Family law does more than demarcate a group's membership boundaries, however. It also defines property relations between the spouses, and, in the event of divorce, determines the economic and custodial consequences of this change in personal status. Through the distributive aspect of family law, a group's governing property rules shape the allocation of resources and obligations between spouses during a marriage, and between an ex-husband and ex-wife after the marriage ends. Property relations relate to a wide range of issues which need to be settled upon divorce, such as a spouse's right to post-divorce support, ownership in matrimonial property, or entitlement to child custody. Unfortunately, in many nomoi groups the distributive function of family law helps to solidify power inequalities between men and women within the community. In instances of divorce, for example, women living within accommodated nomoi groups often find that they have limited or no legal rights to property, post-divorce financial support, or even custody of their children.[28] In other words, upon the termination of a marriage women who observe the group's tradition may find that they are entitled to little

[27] In the common law tradition, this sovereignty was recognized under the doctrine of 'marriage good where celebrated is good everywhere'. That is, as a general principle of conflict of laws, a country should grant any marriage validity in the parties' home country (or under the parties' personal laws) the fullest recognition. The logic behind this principle is aptly summarized by Richard Cleveland: 'From the time of clan and kin communities to the twentieth century, status has been and still is the true expression of the fact that there are different ideas about fundamental relations strong enough to obvious advantage of wholesale dealings. Status is still a serene monument to the originality of independent political communities' (Cleveland 1925). For further discussion, see Clarkson and Hill (1997: 295–319). In the American context, for example, tribal courts have retained (formally, at least) a limited sovereignty to make their own substantive law in certain matters of self-determination, such as family law. See e.g. *United States* v. *Wheeler*, 435 US 313, 321 (1978); *Santa Clara Pueblo* v. *Martinez*, 436 US 49 54 (1978): 'membership rules were no more or less than a mechanism of social . . . self-definition, and as such were basic to the tribe's survival as a cultural and economic entity.'

[28] In some Muslim communities, for example, although an ex-wife is entitled to the return of her dowry (or *mehar*), she is not necessarily entitled to alimony payments for more than three months after a divorce (the *iddat* period). For a concise overview of these family law distributive rules, see Nasir (1986).

if any compensation for years devoted to the family, and therefore, for the cultural preservation of the community at-large.[29] Thus, although women as cultural conduits can, in theory, establish a dominant position within their respective nomoi groups, in practice the emphasis on women's unique role in the task of procreating the group has had exactly the opposite effect. In fact, under circumstances such as those described above, the legal autonomy granted to nomoi groups in the family law arena has a detrimental effect on women's basic rights. Hence, while state accommodation of nomoi groups' family law practices permits minority cultures to preserve their identities (i.e. their 'differences') on the one hand, it also implicitly sanctions the restriction of women's entitlements to economic and cutsodial rights in the event of divorce, on the other hand.[30]

That nomoi groups should struggle for autonomy in the family law arena is not surprising. Yet family law policies in certain nomoi groups have a particular, often detrimental, effect on women, who stand at the fulcrum of legal rules and policies encoded in their groups' family law traditions.[31] Precisely because family law partakes in shaping 'internal restrictions' within a given group, multicultural theorists cannot treat the delegation of legal powers in the family law arena solely as a matter of 'external protections'.[32] Rather, scholars, legislators, and public policy-makers must recognize and compensate for the ways in which well-meaning accommodation policies burden women.

2. The Multicultural Accommodation Dilemma

The second phase of my discussion considers the two ways in which legal authority over marriage and divorce matters is currently divided between the

---

[29] In Kenya, for example, 'divorce under both African customary and Islamic laws can be extrajudicial; one party can unilaterally bring about the divorce without any requirement that a court hear the dispute. . . . In the case of divorce, women married under Islamic and African customary laws are almost never entitled to marital property and are rarely provided with a maintenance' (Muli 1995). See also Freeman (1990). In other cases, distributive family laws specify a child's father is his/her natural legal guardian, and that only in the event of his death or disappearance can the mother assume the role of legal guardian. For a concise discussion of this problem in the context of the Hindu Guardianship and Minorities Act of 1956 in India, see Singh (1994).

[30] For a discussion of the potentially negative effects of family law accommodation on women in specific country contexts, see e.g. the articles in Moghadam (1994b); Cook (1994).

[31] Clearly, however, not all women within a given nomoi group suffer intragroup injuries, even if they are subject to the same family law code. This is partly because women in religious or ethnic communities, as elsewhere, differ in social status, wealth, or age.

[32] I am referring here to Will Kymlicka's 'external protections/internal restrictions' distinction (Kymlicka 1996). See also n. 8 above.

church (nomoi groups) and the state. (Note that my usage here of the term 'church' does not refer only to Christian religious institutions. Rather, it is used as a generic name for the institutions of religious or cutomary communities.) The two approaches, which I call the secular absolutist model and the religious particularist model, are evaluated in terms of their impact on women's rights, on the one hand, and on a group's sense of cultural and legal autonomy, on the other. As will be shown, neither model provides an adequate balance between the protection of women's rights as *citizens* of the liberal state and the preservation of a group's *nomos*. In each model one of these aspects suffers. In an attempt to resolve this imbalance, I propose an entirely new model, which I call the joint-governance model. The joint-governance model, though still theoretical, promises to be more effective than the secular absolutist and religious particularist models, in that it ensures that women are given protection of their basic rights as citizens while at the same time allowing nomoi groups to enhance their self-governing powers and hence their sense of autonomous identity.

The Secular Absolutist Model

The secular absolutist model is based on a strict separation between church and state. Under this model, the state has the ultimate power to define legally what constitutes 'the family' and to regulate its creation and dissolution. The secular absolutist approach is practised, for example, in civil law countries such as France, Belgium, and the Netherlands, where a uniform, secular, state law is imposed upon all citizens in family law matters, regardless of those citizens' group affiliation. Under the secular absolutist model, religious officials have no formal role in defining or celebrating marriages. Even if a religious marriage ceremony takes place, it has no validity in the eyes of state law. The couple may, of course, decide to perform a religious ceremony because of its symbolic or emotional value.[33] However, the only way to change *status* formally (e.g. from single to married, or from married to divorced) is under the provisions of state law.

In its ideal form, the secular absolutist model does not grant legal recognition to a marriage or divorce performed by a representative of a religious or customary family law tradition. This refusal to grant recognition to cultural or religious authorities erodes nomoi groups' power to preserve their cultural distinction through the autonomous demarcation of their membership boundaries. The secular absolutist model also does not acknowledge the distributive aspect of religious or tribal family law traditions. In other words, the state does not allocate *any* legal authority to the church (nomoi groups)

---

[33] Thus, even when a state consolidates its exclusive authority over a person's marital status, religious ceremonies are not necessarily abolished.

over issues of status or property relations, preserving for itself the *ultimate* regulatory power over the citizenry in matters of marriage and divorce.

In theory, the major apparent advantage of the secularist absolutist model is that it creates a legal regime in which the state equally burdens all churches or nomoi groups. That is, all forms of religious or customary marriage and divorce proceedings, whether Christian, Muslim, Jewish, Hindu, or of any other religious or customary origin, have *no* legal validity under state law. Prima facie, this approach prevents nomoi groups from claiming that the state supports only the religious practices of the majority in the family law arena.

In practice, however, the allocation of legal authority set by the secular absolutist model clearly does not encourage the preservation of nomoi groups through the accommodation of their differences, as it fails to address both the demarcating and the distributive aspects of 'other' family law traditions. The secular absolutist model is based on the presupposition that religion or customary practices are relegated to the 'private' realm (having no formal, and in this sense, 'public' validity in legal terms). This public–private (or universal–particular) distinction, as has already been observed by many political theorists, does not permit minority groups to be on an equal footing with the dominant culture (Young 1989), since minority cultures often 'come to the game after it has already begun' and do not define the governing standards of a society's institutions (see Spinner 1994). In the context of marriage and divorce regulation, this problem has particular salience given that 'in the West, [at least] the link between Christianity and state law has long been particularly visible in the area of family law' (Weisbrod 1987–8: 753).

Among the conflicting claimants to sovereignty in the history of family law, it is the state rather than the church which is the newcomer (McReavy 1959, quoted in Weisbrod 1987: 746). In fact, the very character of marriage as a public, regulated institution evolved with the rise of Christianity in the West. The church used its dominant position during the late Middle Ages to formalize a set of rules regulating marriage. These rules were formally pronounced and expounded by ecclesiastical courts which enforced canon law. Through marriage, church authorities regulated individuals' conduct, with regard to both the requirements for its valid celebration and the rights and obligations which this change in status entailed for the parties (Rheinstein 1953: 9). Under this ecclesiastical family law regime, a marriage could no longer be terminated by the informal, private act of the parties.[34] Rather, a divorce, if at all possible under church rules, could not have taken place without the official co-operation of a functionary of the church. The

---

[34] In the 16th century it became necessary 'to institute formal proceedings in a court, to submit to an official investigation, and to obtain a formal decree' in order to terminate a marriage (Rheinstein 1953: 9).

state did not wrest jurisdiction over marriage and divorce from the church until the late eighteenth century, when the vesting of power over family law matters in secular authorities was seen as a symbol of modern European nation-building. As Nancy Cott observes, 'for as long as the past millennium in the Christian West, the exercise of formal power over marriage has been a prime means of exerting and manifesting public authority' (Cott 1995: 108). Hence, although today we take it for granted that marriage and the family are subject to regulation by the state, the state's involvement in creating the laws governing the creation and dissolution of marriage is a fairly recent phenomenon.

The emerging concept that the family constituted a topic of concern for the regulatory power of the state permitted, at least in principle, the termination of marriage by a civil official. Yet, the secular concept of '*fault* divorce' (dominant in most Western countries' family law codes until about three decades ago) is rooted in the Christian concept of marriage as a sacrament, and, 'for that reason . . . [is] indissoluble by man' (Rheinstein 1953: 8).[35] Since the inception of the modern Western state Christian underpinnings of marriage have significantly influenced the 'secular absolutist' notion of family relations. A stark example of this underlying connection between religious and secular perceptions of marriage can be found in the famous 1878 US Supreme Court anti-polygamy decision in *Reynolds* v. *United States*, where the court held that 'marriage, while from its very nature a *sacred* obligation, is nevertheless, in most civilized nations, a civil contract, usually regulated by [state] law' (*Reynolds* v. *United States* 1878: 165; emphasis added). In fact, monogamous marriage was conceived by secular authorities as 'the most crucial precondition of public order —as a "pillar of the state"'.[36] This view was 'naturally' viewed as appropriate to the state, 'in essence because it was the view of the [prevailing] Christian Churches' (Weisbrod 1987: 754).

Family law has not remained unaffected by twentieth-century trends of secularization and liberalization. Most significantly, in most Western countries women have finally achieved nominal, though not always *de facto*, equality in the family law arena. Yet in a world of profound and accelerating change, the institution of marriage, as Max Rheinstein observes, 'has been standing out as a pillar of stability' (Rheinstein 1953: 3); while apparently neutral, the defining precepts and principles regulating marriage and divorce under the secular absolutist model still impose a greater burden on citizens whose

---

[35] In the past three decades, however, the regulation of the family has become increasingly 'divorced' from religious morality, or, in Max Rheinstein's terminology, family law has undergone two major changes—those of secularization and liberalization.

[36] See also Weyrauch *et al.* (1994: 578): 'Polygamy is often seen as an issue dividing West from East, Christian from Muslim, or modern civilization from older, less civilized times. . . . polygamy has from time to time in our [US] history been considered a moral question of enormous importance. In England and in some states in the US, it was a capital offense.'

family law traditions are not based 'on the view of the Christian Churches'. This model, in short, fares poorly when judged by its success in accommodating nomoi groups.

The secular absolutist model fares better in respecting women's rights, however. Because this model provides no accommodation in the family law arena, nomoi group members are subject to state law (rather than their groups' family law traditions) in matters of both status and property relations. As I mentioned earlier, many religious and customary family law traditions sanction gender-biased rules that systematically disadvantage women within the community and threaten their entitlement to basic economic and parental rights at divorce. Hence, while the regulation of marriage and divorce by the secular state is *not* neutral in its effect upon nomoi groups (since it prescribes greater obstacles for groups who seek to preserve their cultural identities), the formal separation of church and state has the advantage of better protecting the rights of female group members by removing marriage proceedings from the 'sacred' realm. Once in the secular realm, the content, rationale, and definition of marriage and divorce law can be challenged by the citizenry and transformed via regular channels of democratic politics. It seems reasonable to suggest, then, that the secular absolutist approach, even if far from perfectly protecting the rights of women undergoing divorce proceedings,[37] at least ensures their formal entitlement to equal treatment, unlike some nomoi group traditions, which uphold marriage and divorce laws that clearly discriminate against women.[38]

While some countries have preserved the rigid application of the secular absolutist model, multicultural societies such as Canada, Australia, the United States, and Britain have in recent years introduced a modified version of the secular absolutist model. Under this version of the secular absolutist model, the state stills retain its *ultimate* authoritative power to regulate citizens' marriage and divorce affairs; however, state family law codes have been reformed to permit greater cultural diversity. For example, civil authorities may grant religious officials with concurring authority to solemnize marriages. Under the New York Domestic Relations Law, for example, a religious ceremony that has taken place in New York State and which was solemnized by an authorized religious official would be recognized as valid in the eyes of state law. Similarly, the draft American Uniform Marriage and Divorce Act, to be adopted state

---

[37] Note that although state regulation of the family in the USA is now based on equal protection jurisprudence, gender-neutral rules may fail to ensure the needs of the traditionally weaker parties in the family, i.e. women and children (Weitzman 1985). Weitzman shows that following divorce men's living standards rise by 42 per cent, while those of women fall by 73 per cent. Other scholars have challenged these figures, claiming the relevant figures to be a 10 per cent improvement for men and a 27 per cent decline for women (Peterson 1996). There is no dispute, however, that women and children suffer a substantial decline in living standards following divorce.   [38] See nn. 19–32 above, and accompanying text.

by state, suggests that the solemnization of marriage may be accomplished either by a civil authority or 'in accordance with any mode of solemnization recognized by any religious denomination, Indian Nation or Tribe, or Native Group' (Uniform Marriage and Divorce Act, §206; cited in Krause 1995).

Though permitting greater legal diversity in marriage proceedings, the state under this variant of the secular absolutist model reserves for itself the regulatory power over the act of divorce—in both demarcating (status) and distributive (property relations) arenas. This modified version of the secular absolutist model has, ironically, even further expanded the power of state law over minority cultures by creating a formal linkage between the civil proceedings of divorce and the removal of all religious or customary barriers to remarriage.[39] That is, 'the machinery of the state' can now be used, for example, in the case of Jewish Orthodox divorce proceedings to compel a recalcitrant spouse, within whose power it is to grant a religious divorce, to do so. To implement this new legal arrangement, civil authorities in the above-mentioned countries were given discretionary power to refuse making a secular divorce decree absolute or to adjourn property proceedings until satisfied that all religious or customary impediments to remarriage have been removed.[40]

To sum up, the secular absolutist model, in its different variants, is attractive in that it ensures, at least formally, that women living in nomoi groups have access to all the rights and protections guaranteed to all other citizens at divorce. However, the model fails to address the identity-preserving function of family law, and may also systematically discriminate against minority cultures by tacitly enforcing the norms of the dominant culture in the family law arena.

The Religious Particularist Model

The religious particularist model, on the other hand, better addresses the problem of respecting cultural differences by granting religious communities the authority to pursue their own traditions in the family law arena. Under this model, the state does not intervene in or regulate citizens' marriage and divorce affairs. Instead, recognized religious or customary communities are vested with legal power over matters of personal status. In extreme versions

---

[39] See e.g. New York State's Domestic Relations Law, s. 253 (also known as the 1983 New York *get* law), enacted by the Law of 1983 c. 979, §1, eff. 8 Aug. 1983. In 1992, s. 236B was added to New York's Domestic Relations Law, in order to provide more effective tools for civil authorities to pressure an otherwise recalcitrant husband.

[40] Such state-imposed removal of barriers to remarriage may, under certain circumstances, enhance the bargaining power of women who want to preserve their cultural identity but have no legal powers under their nomoi groups' traditions to force their spouses to follow the 'proper' proceedings of a religious divorce. This problem arises particularly in relation to the *get* proceedings in Jewish law. See e.g. Washofsky (1981). But see Reitman (1997) for a critical analysis of this variant of the secular absolutist model as it plays out in the context of English family law.

of this model there is no state law which governs matters of marriage and divorce. Rather, different nomoi groups are recognized by the state, and their autonomous courts are designated as the exclusive or preferred forums for adjudication of certain family law matters.

Arguably, the religious particularist approach is attractive from a multicultural standpoint, because it provides a pluralistic legal system in which each community self-governs a crucial aspect of its *nomos*: family law. Given the role of marriage and divorce law in preserving collective identities, it is clear that the recognition of different communities' norms and practices enhances the status of minority cultures within a diverse society. Unlike the secularist absolutist model, which is exercised in countries where the regulation over matters of family law has already been 'won' by the state, the religious particularist model is exercised in countries where the state never directly challenged (or 'divested') religious authorities of their power to regulate citizens' marriage and divorce affairs.

Historically, the religious particularist model was manifested in the Ottoman Empire's *millet* system. It is less often recognized that a related method of 'indirect rule' was also practised by the British colonial administration in certain conquered overseas territories.[41] In the majority of African and Asian overseas colonies, for example, matters of family law were particularly often left to the autonomous jurisdiction of different religious and customary community.[42] Today countries such as India, Kenya, and Israel, which prior to independence had been subject to Britain's 'indirect' colonial rule, still preserve this essence of a pluralistic system of family law.[43]

In Kenya, for example, the state has enacted a set of statutes which recog-

[41] In contradistinction to settled territories, where the *terra nullius* (vacant land) legal fiction permitted the colonizers to ignore existing tribal legal systems (as was the case in the British colonies of North America and Australia, for example), in most African and Asian conquered territories the colonial administration did not try to replace the Islamic, Hindu, or unwritten tribal customary family law with the rules of the English common law (Shachar and Hirschl 1999).

[42] It is important to note, however, that the British colonial administration never adopted a *carte blanche* non-intervention policy. Instead, it formally reserved for itself the power to refuse to recognize specific customary practices, if these practices were (in the eyes of the colonizers) incompatible with 'morality, humanity or natural justice'. This regime of differentiation as fashioned in colonial Africa (and reformed after independence) has been criticized by several contemporary writers as a reflection of the colonizers' narrative of a clear (and hierarchical) divide between Europeans and Africans, marked by separate systems of law which are defined in opposition to one another (Mamdani 1996). See also Hooker (1975). My discussion in this section focuses on the post-independence period, exploring the different ways in which an institutionalized religious particularist model may allow religious and customary communities to preserve their unique family law traditions in deeply divided societies.

[43] In countries previously governed by the Ottoman *millet* system or by British indirect rule, the post-independence state legislator often clarified the scope of jurisdiction granted to different religious and tribal communities by codifying the multiplicity of legal sources which govern family law issues.

nize the diversity of personal laws applicable to different groups of citizens through the African Christian Marriage and Divorce Act c. 151, the Hindu Marriage and Divorce Act c. 157, and the Mohammeddan Marriage and Divorce Act c. 156 (Kabebery-Macharia 1992: 195). Marriages celebrated in accordance with these statutes must follow the formalities and procedures for marriage and divorce in accordance to Christian, Hindu, and Islamic personal law.[44]

Similarly, in Israel the legislature has gradually codified the arena of family law with its multiplicity of legal sources, which date back to the Ottoman Empire's *millet* system. Israel, however, has no state marriage and divorce law. Rather, each religious community's autonomous courts hold exclusive jurisdiction over its respective members' marriage and divorce affairs.[45] Therefore, 'In matters affecting their families, Israelis must function as Jews, Muslims, Druzes, etc.' (Edelman 1994: 121).[46] While the Israeli state has preserved the sphere of autonomy granted to religious courts in adjudicating matters of marriage and divorce, it has taken over the regulation of other matters of personal status, such as adoption (Adoption of Children Law 1981), guardianship (Capacity and Guardianship Law 1962), and matrimonial property (Spouses (Property Relations) Law 1973), as well as succession, wills, and estates (Succession Law 1965). Legislative attempts to 'divest' religious communities of their legal authority to determine status issues (i.e. marriage or birthright membership) failed after they met formidable resistance from both members of minority groups (Arab Muslims in particular) and Israeli representatives of Orthodox Jewry.[47]

In India, legal struggles over the scope of religious communities' regulation of personal status matters reflect the bitter dissent between the Hindu majority and Muslim minority. The complex system of personal laws in India was recognized by the British colonial administration, and was largely preserved

[44] Customary law, which remains unwritten and uncodified, nevertheless continues to apply to a majority of Kenyans. In case of doubt, spouses must swear affidavits stating that they are married in accordance with customary law. For critique of this policy, see Kabebery-Macharia (1992: 195).

[45] A district court has authority to dissolve a marriage only if the spouses belong to different religious communities.

[46] Israeli state law preserves the various degrees of exclusive jurisdiction in matters of family law, as granted to different religious courts by the Ottoman and the British. The widest jurisdiction is enjoyed by Sharia (Muslim) courts. Christian denominational courts have more limited mandates, and exercise jurisdiction over matters of marriage, divorce, and maintenance. Rabbinical courts have exclusive control only over matters of marriage and divorce. Druze courts' exclusive jurisdiction is similar in scope to that exercised by rabbinical courts. As mentioned above, this multiplicity of legal sources dates back more than five centuries, to the Ottoman *millet* system, which was later codified by the British colonial administration through the Palestine Order in Council of 1922.

[47] See the debate in the Knesset prior to the enactment of the Women's Equal Rights Law 1951.

at independence (see Everett 1997 passim). Today, religious communities in India still govern a broad range of family law issues, including marriage, divorce, maintenance, guardianship, adoptions, wills, intestacy and succession, joint family and partition.[48] As in Kenya and in Israel, matters of personal status are basically divided along religious lines, permitting each religious community to demarcate its membership boundaries through birth and marriage.

As explained earlier, nomoi groups often use family law as a way to construct their membership boundaries, and also as a way to allocate rights, duties, and (ultimately) power between men and women within the community. Under the religious particularist model, identity groups' 'differences' are fully recognized and solidified by state law.[49] Each community is given autonomous powers to demarcate its membership boundaries and to preserve its cultural distinctness. However, minority cultures often use these powers to perpetuate an unequal distribution of rights, duties, and powers between men and women, enforcing gender-discriminatory rules which would never have passed constitutional muster outside the 'protected' realm of religious law, because they clearly violate women's basic rights as full and equal citizens.

Thus, while the religious particularist model maintains the autonomy and sovereignty of different minority cultures (upholding the demarcating function of family law), it is problematic in terms of women's rights, particularly because it extends jurisdiction to nomoi groups beyond pure *status* issues to matters of *property relations* between spouses (the distributing function of family law). As we have seen, property relations relate to a wide range of issues which need to be settled upon divorce, such as a spouse's right to post-divorce support, ownership in matrimonial property, or entitlement to child custody. In the three examples of multicultural family law systems for Kenya, Israel, and India, women are theoretically guaranteed full and equal citizenship rights by state law. But in practice, these women's basic rights may be circumscribed by their groups' accommodated family law traditions. Such circumscription of basic entitlements applies, for example, to a woman's right to change her personal status, the right to exercise her legal capacity as natural guardian of her children, the right to purchase, register, and own property in her name, and the right to acquire a share in matrimonial property.

---

[48] Hindus in India are governed by the Hindu Marriage Act of 1955, the Hindu Succession Act of 1956, the Hindu Guardianship and Minorities Act of 1956, and the Hindu Adoption and Maintenance Act of 1956. Muslims are governed by the Sharia Act of 1937, the Muslim Women's Dissolution of Marriage Act of 1939, the Muslim Women's (Protection of Rights on Divorce) Act of 1986, and uncodified Muslim personal laws. Christians are governed by their own Christian Marriage Act, the Indian Divorce Act, and the Indian Succession Act. Parsees, too, have codified laws of marriage, divorce, and succession (Singh 1994: 378–9).

[49] I analyse the different ways in which state law defines and in certain circumstances reconstructs a group's 'authentic' expression of its own cultural heritage, often fostering an overly rigid, 'reactive' assertion of cultural identity (Shachar forthcoming *b*, ch. 2).

Hence, the preservation of nomoi groups' cultural distinctness through family law accommodation imposes severe, systematic, and *sanctioned* injuries upon women, violating their basic rights as state citizens. The religious particularist model therefore compromises women's citizenship status by upholding the structural impediments imposed upon them by their own groups in the family law arena.

What makes this situation so complex is that women's gender-specific subordination is justified in the name of preserving their group's collective identity. Thus, female insiders who criticize their group's gender-biased family law policies can be seen by the group as threatening its most cherished traditions.[50] Even attempts to transform the *distributive* aspect of family law, which is regarded by most nomoi groups as secondary to the *demarcation* function, can be easily blocked in the name of a group's *nomos*. Under such conditions, the religious particularist approach to multicultural accommodation inevitably has injurious intragroup effects: it partakes in silencing alternative voices within nomoi groups, and tacitly endorses systemic intragroup violations of women's basic rights. In short, the religious particularist model effectively protects nomoi groups' membership boundaries, but it also propagates systemic inequalities within an accommodated group. What is more, it fails to provide institutional or political incentives for religious courts or nomoi group leaders to lessen the disproportionate burden imposed upon women by their groups' family law traditions.

3. A Suggested Synthesis: The Joint-Governance Model

An altogether different and better way to divide jurisdiction between nomoi groups and the state over matters of family law is the joint-governance model, which is consciously designed as an alternative to both the secular absolutist and the religious particularist models. As discussed above, women's rights are relatively secure under the secular absolutist model but the state fails to accommodate their nomoi groups' family law traditions. On the other hand, the state fully recognizes the authority the church (nomoi groups) in regulating matters of marriage and divorce under the religious particularist model yet unjustly threatens women's basic individual rights in the name of protecting their groups' *nomos*. Since both of these models spring from a dichotomous understanding of legal authority, under which either the group or the state *exclusively* governs matters of marriage and divorce, neither model succeeds in recognizing the significance of family law without compromising women's basic rights as state citizens. Yet legal authority can be divided differently. Instead of having *either* the state *or* the group control the full range

---

[50] For further discussion of this problem, see Shachar (forthcoming *b*, ch. 4).

of issues that arise in marriage and divorce, as is currently the case under both the secular absolutist model and the religious particularist model, the joint-governance approach suggests a new, *multicultural* separation of powers between group and state. Under this new model, neither entity would have ultimate control over both the demarcating and the distributing aspects of family law. Rather, as in various federal legal systems, legal authority over citizens would be *shared* by the different membership communities to which they belong, in this case their religious nomoi group and the state.

The starting-point of the joint-governance model is the recognition that identity group members living within the boundaries of a larger political community, the state, possess at least two different types of identity: their identity as citizens of the state and their identity as members of the particular nomoi group to which they belong. Each of these two membership communities has an interest in overstating its jurisdiction over the individual. Neither the church nor the state, however, can adequately protect the different facets of an individual's identity as *both* a group member and a citizen. Such a fresh approach to this division of powers enables the striking of a certain balance between two sets of competing norms. This would in turn permit legal students from radically different domains to remain distinct while still on speaking terms. The goal of the joint-governance model is to build precisely such a system of cooperation between the state's law and the group's tradition, which would result in *simultaneous* governing of group members' family law affairs.

Instead of operating on the basis of an oversimplified 'either/or' understanding of legal authority, the joint-governance model divides the legal jurisdiction between the church (nomoi group) and the state along lines of *subject-matter* jurisdiction. That is, the joint-governance model allocates legal authority between group and state by allowing certain aspects of a single dispute (such as divorce proceedings) be governed by the group, while others are subject to the jurisdiction of the state. In this respect, the joint-governance model institutes the 'no monopoly' rule as its key governing rationale: neither the state nor the group has sufficient power to resolve legal disputes in the family law arena without *co-operation* from the other authority.

The joint-governance model resembles existing federal legal systems in that it divides authority between a larger polity and a smaller, somewhat autonomous unit existing within that polity. Most federal systems, however, allot legal powers in accordance with different 'layers' of authority,[51] requiring some judicial entity to stand at the apex of the legal system (in the American context, for example, the US Supreme Court has the *ultimate* legal power to determine legal disputes, whether they have originated under federal or state law). The joint-governance approach diverges from a purely federalist stance,

---

[51] I discuss this point in greater detail in Shachar (1998).

however, because the specific powers it grants to nomoi groups are not hierarchically evaluated; that is, with regard to different aspects of a particular legal dispute, the nomoi group and the state each possess a complementary authority. The joint-governance model therefore holds that both the nomoi group and the state must each have an input in governing legal disputes that affect group members in their identity as adherents of their *nomos* and citizens of their state. To address this multiplicity of affiliations, joint-governance establishes a more diverse and *decentralized* legal system which requires a 'dialectical federalism' between the state and the different nomoi groups to which its citizens belong (see Cover and Aleinikoff 1977).

In the family law context this dialectical federalism must rest on a new separation of legal powers between church and state. As I mentioned earlier, every divorce proceeding consists of two elements: a legally valid change in status which dissolves the marriage and permits the parties to remarry, and a divorce settlement which specifies the property relations between ex-husband and ex-wife. Because these two subject-matters are interwoven in reality, under the joint-governance model neither the group nor the state could resolve a family law dispute which involves different facets of the individual's multicultural identity without co-operation from the other legal authority. For example, if the group is granted control over matters of personal status which determine, among other things, who by way of birth and marriage is entitled, by the group's own family law traditions, to full and automatic membership in the community (family law's demarcating function), then the state is given complementary jurisdiction over the distributive aspect of family law, that is, over property matters such as the right to post-divorce support, ownership in matrimonial property, or entitlement to child custody. When property relations are regulated by the state, rather than the church (nomoi group), a civil authority can apply the more egalitarian principles encoded in state law in lieu of the often gender-biased religious and customary family law traditions enforced by nomoi group traditions. On the other hand, by granting jurisdiction over status matters to the group, the joint-governance model permits minority cultures a crucial opportunity to define autonomously their membership boundaries and maintain their unique *nomos* within a diverse society.

In an ideal world, the recognition of cultural differences would not jeopardize women's citizenship status. But the question of how to facilitate cultural diversity while protecting at-risk group members' rights is not merely a theoretical concern. Particularly in the family law realm, we are constantly confronted with non-ideal situations: in the case of the religious particularist model, a *carte blanche* devolution of state power over matters of status and property to the group is complicit in imposing a disproportionate burden upon women for the sake of preserving their group's *nomos*. As crucial agents in the process of cultural reproduction, women are highly valorized, but they are forced at the same time to bear social, legal, and economic hardships that their male counterparts are not subjected to by virtue of their status as husbands and fathers. The secular absolutist model better addresses the problems of women's rights in the family arena by imposing uniform state laws upon all citizens, regardless of their group affiliations. While not sensitive to cultural differences, the secular absolutist model at least formally (though not always substantively) protects the interests of women at divorce by imposing compliance with the more gender-egalitarian demarcating and distributive family law principles encoded in state laws.

Neither of these two extant models provides an adequate balance between cultural preservation through family law accommodation and the protection of women's rights as citizens in the liberal state. Each model opts instead to satisfy one or the other tension, offering little hope to high-risk group members who may legitimately wish to preserve their affiliations with minority cultures while at the same time exercising their hard-won citizenship rights to transform power hierarchies from within their different communities of faith. Instead of choosing between these two non-ideal options, we must turn 'to something very different indeed' (Goodin 1996).

By nominally 'splitting' property from status in the family law arena, the new joint-governance approach I propose may allow women to gain greater leverage within their communities, even under restrictive traditional family law regimes that have long diminished women's ability to acquire independent means of livelihood or to resist dominant cultural scripts, but without forcing nomoi groups to abandon their traditional procedures for defining who is 'inside' and who is 'outside' their boundaries. With state protection of their property rights during divorce, for example, women living in nomoi groups can gradually gain greater autonomy in determining their personal status, and may be able to pursue more freely gender-specific interests *within* their own religious or customary communities. Moreover, female group members under the joint-governance model have an opportunity to alter the distributive laws which govern their intimate affairs, because state law, unlike religious or customary law, is subject to change through democratic channels.[52] Nomoi groups' traditions are also susceptible to change. Such transformation, however, is not likely to be achieved by popular vote. Rather, it would require an internal process of revisiting dominant interpretations of sacred texts, and subsequent rulings upon these texts, which have historically been the almost exclusive preserve of men (Goodman-Thau 1993: 45). Women's access to such texts is still an extremely controversial and contested

---

[52] To achieve this goal, women might establish cross-nomoi group coalitions, attempting to encode into state law new provisions to address their gender-specific concerns. For example, to avoid destitution or dependency after divorce, such coalitions might lobby for state-underwritten job training or adult education programmes that would help women get on their feet after many years devoted primarily to the family.

matter. However, religiously observant women around the world are gradually trying to promote the reinterpretation of sacred texts, by assuming spiritual leadership, revitalizing the faith, and offering alternative historical and theological readings of their different communities' entrenched traditions (compare Hélie-Lucas 1994: 401–2; Goodman-Thau 1993: 45–53).

These are important processes. The joint-governance model recognizes that any attempt to alter culturally entrenched gender biases is an extremely difficult task. No magic jurisdictional formula can fully overcome the obstacles involved in the process of intragroup transformation. Yet by ensuring that neither the state nor the group possess ultimate or exclusive control over all matters of family law, the joint-governance approach (if carefully crafted to suit different legal arenas and particular group circumstances) can effectively assist in productively altering the incentive structure operating within a given minority group, so that female group members' indispensable contribution to the group can serve as a source of empowerment, rather than a rationale for their continued oppression. Space does not permit a detailed description of how the new joint-governance model can fully achieve this goal (see Shachar forthcoming), yet it is sufficient to outline a guiding principle: rather than tacitly condoning the problem of intragroup oppression by providing jurisdiction to minority cultures in the name of respecting differences, the joint-governance model utilizes the contemporary rethinking of the troubled relations between church and state, minority cultures and the larger society, to challenge entrenched power relations not only *between* groups but also *within* them. A brief example may help clarify this last point.

Given that many minority communities conceive of their *nomos* in direct relation to the roles women play within the group, female group members have tremendous potential power: without them, the group cannot survive. Their continued participation is crucial for the group's cultural reproduction, for its social and economic well-being, and politically, in terms of sheer number of participants in a given minority community. Responsible group leaders must be concerned with regeneration—that is, with ensuring that a nomoi group will have enough members in the foreseeable future to preserve its practices over time. The maltreatment of women by the group, therefore, becomes a self-defeating strategy as soon as it starts to threaten their continued membership in the group, or their children's qualification for, or interest in, full group membership. From this point onward, it is in the interest of the minority group—as a *collective* which is struggling to preserve its membership boundaries—to find ways to ensure that women continue to adhere to the group's demarcating marriage and divorce traditions. The idea here is not that intragroup change will occur solely because of the 'good will' of a given minority group's leaders. Rather, the joint-governance model draws upon a realpolitik consideration that it may be better to accommodate women, so as to ensure they follow the group's self-defined traditions, than to run the risk of losing significant numbers of group members, who may choose to high-light the citizenship aspect of their identity and break their loyalty to the group altogether. The state's accommodation of a minority group's cultural practices will thus be ideally structured, so as to allow (and in fact facilitate) a process of intragroup transformation which will permit traditionally mar-ginalized group members to exercise more freely and fully their voice and agency *within* the context of their own nomoi communities.

Thus, once we reject the misguided premise directing the secular absolutist and the religious particularist models that a single entity be granted exclusive jurisdiction over the individual in all aspects of a given legal arena, it becomes apparent that there are many possible ways to reallocate powers between the state and the group to accommodate the different facets of a citizen–group member's identity. Because the joint-governance model creates a legal scheme of checks and balances in which *neither* the state *nor* the group has sufficient legal authority to govern all aspects of marriage and divorce, its implementa-tion will require the state, in countries where the secular absolutist model governs, to relinquish, to some degree, its legal power and delegate it to nomoi groups operating within its borders. In the absence of political pressure, no reasonable state would voluntarily give up its regulatory powers. In countries where the religious particularist model governs, it is also unlikely that nomoi groups will voluntarily give up their regulatory power over family law. Moreover, the deeper the cleavages between nomoi groups comprising a body politic, the more difficult it will be to alter the current balance of power between church and state. All this goes to show that serious political com-mitment is required in order to implement the joint-governance model—whatever the relationships between church and state in a given polity. If political theorists, legislators, and public policy-makers do not work to imple-ment different yet better legal arrangements which recognize the significance of group members' cultural identity while protecting women's basic rights as citizens, who else will?

Conclusion

In this chapter, I have offered a theoretical framework which explains the significance of family law in preserving cultural identities, while also per-petuating a damaging intragroup subordination of women. Family law thus presents a challenge to proponents of multicultural accommodation: on the one hand, it is a crucial forum in which nomoi groups construct and assert their *nomos* in a diverse society, and, on the other, it imposes disproportionate burdens on women, often violating their basic rights as citizens. Having analysed the two extant models for dividing legal authority between church and state in family law matters, I have shown that while the secular absolutist model better protects women's rights, it fails to accommodate their nomoi groups' family law traditions. The religious particularist model, for its part, permits nomoi groups to preserve their family law traditions; but by often reinforcing the most patriarchal elements of a given culture, it fails to protect women's basic rights as state citizens. Unfortunately, neither of these models succeeds in both respecting cultural differences and protecting women's rights.

In an attempt to create an accommodationist model which meets both these requirements, I have sketched the contours of a new approach to multicultural accommodation—the joint-governance model. This model allocates legal authority between 'church and state' along lines of subject-matter jurisdiction, utilizing mutual input from both value systems—i.e. state law and religious or customary family law—in resolving a single legal dispute such as divorce proceedings. More specifically, the joint-governance model grants preferred jurisdiction to nomoi groups over the crucial issue of status demarcation, while the distributive aspects of family law disputes, i.e. decisions regarding property relations, are subject to the jurisdiction of the state. This subject-matter division of legal authority requires engaging in a 'dialectical federalism' between the state and the church (nomoi groups), because neither community under the 'no monopoly' rule has sufficient legal power to fully resolve a family dispute, without the co-operation of the other membership community to which the citizen–group member belongs.

While the model I propose does not fully resolve the tension between respecting cultural difference and protecting women's rights, it goes further than existing models in allowing nomoi groups to preserve their cultural distinctness (or *nomos*), while protecting the interests of women within nomoi groups. Perhaps most importantly, in recognizing group members' multiple affiliations, the joint-governance model does not force women into an unjust zero-sum choice: your rights or your culture. Instead, it grants female group members the leverage to renegotiate oppressive family law traditions *from within* their cultural communities, armed with their hard-won rights as state citizens.

9

Female Autonomy and Cultural Imperative: Two Hearts Beating Together

SAWITRI SAHARSO

On 18 April 1988 a 23-year-old Dutch Hindustani woman took her life by drinking a bottle of concentrated acetic acid.[1] Her reason for committing suicide was frequent maltreatment by her husband, whom she had married four years earlier. This might have been one of those tragic incidents that initially shock us but which we soon forget, were it not for two extraordinary developments. First, the woman's family requested that the public prosecutor reconsider his initial decision not to prosecute, and the case went to trial. And secondly, a noted anthropologist was called as an expert witness at the trial, and later published his thoughts about the case in a Dutch law journal (see Lamur 1992). On 11 August 1992 the trial began. The husband was tried on two charges: that he had frequently maltreated his wife and deliberately incited her to commit suicide, and that his maltreatment of his wife led to her death. (Hence for a conviction on the first charge, deliberate intention is required, while for the second it is not.) It was the first, and to my knowledge the only, case in Dutch criminal law of a charge of incitement to suicide. The assumption underlying the accusation was that in inciting his wife to commit suicide the husband had not only used physical power (the frequent mal-treatment), but had also relied on the cultural power given to him as a Hindustani husband. The accusation hinged on three claims: (a) that her culture required of the victim that she obeyed and stayed with her husband, (b) that she was not able to act against this cultural norm, and (c) that her

Research for this chapter was carried out within the framework of the Incentive Programme of Ethics and Policies, which is supported by the Netherlands Organization for Scientific Research. I would like to thank Kathy Davis, Kees Everaars, Will Kymlicka, Yvonne Leeman, and Odile Verhaar for their helpful comments. I am especially grateful to Wayne Norman for his help.

[1] Hindustanis are a group that migrated in the 19th century from India to Surinam, at that time a Dutch colony. In the 1970s, the years surrounding Surinamese independence, many Hindustanis took up residence in the Netherlands.

husband knew this and had acted on this knowledge. All of this made the cultural background in the case highly relevant, and that is why the court had asked for the report of a cultural expert.

According to this cultural expert, Surinamese anthropologist Humphrey Lamur, neither maltreatment of the wife by the husband, nor suicide, as a way for the wife to end her sufferings, are uncommon among Hindustanis. Traditional social norms sometimes leave the woman little choice: Hindustani women were typically brought up to believe that a wife is to obey her husband, that divorce and remarriage are not an option (since no Hindustani man would want a divorced woman for a wife), and thirdly, that going back to her own family was no solution (because this was considered a disgrace to the family; women who sought refuge from spousal abuse with her parents were often simply returned to the husband).

In the case at hand, the husband was living in the Netherlands before he returned to Surinam for the marriage, which had been arranged by the parents. The woman had, previous to her marriage, spent her life in rural Surinam. After the wedding the couple moved to the Netherlands, where a year later a son was born. The husband admitted that during their marriage, and even on the day that she committed suicide, he had regularly beaten up his wife. Using interviews with the woman's family, Lamur found that the woman had received a traditional Hindustani upbringing, which includes, in the words of the woman's mother, that 'a wife has to accept that now and then she receives a blow' (Lamur 1992: 158). The woman herself was considered by her relatives to be someone who remained faithful to these values. The husband was aware of this, for he too shared these values. He considered himself the authority in the family and as such entitled to beat his wife. Both husband and wife were also traditional in their view that after marriage the wife belongs to her husband and his family, more so than to her own kin, and that, except for occasional visits, she cannot return to her parent's home. When questioned by the court, it appeared that the husband found it unthinkable that his wife could leave him.

Lamur's conclusion for the court was, first, that maltreatment indeed often occurs among Hindustanis (but is therefore not yet defensible), and secondly, that it is very plausible that the victim, led by her traditional Hindustani upbringing, was not able to decide to leave her husband. Under these conditions she had no other way to escape her sufferings but to take her life; hence the validity of the accusation of incitement to commit suicide. The cultural expert's report suggests that the woman's culture restricted her autonomy to such an extent that she was psychologically not able to act against its imperatives.

I believe that this case illustrates well how intercultural value conflict often revolves around gender inequalities. What is at stake in these conflicts is ultimately women's autonomy. In this chapter I shall explore some relations between cultural conflicts and gender inequalities by focusing on the way different cultures shape the forms and extent of the autonomy available to women. Much liberal thinking about cultural rights and toleration suffers from its failure to take these matters into account. It becomes evident that different conceptions of self thrive in different cultures, and that these in turn partly determine both the form and extent of autonomy available to individuals in these cultures. We simply cannot presume that the autonomous individual in much abstract liberal theory is a universal category. Beginning with some of the lessons from the suicide case discussed above, I shall inquire about whether it is possible to find a conception of autonomy for women that is both worthy in the eyes of Western liberals and compatible with Asian cultures, particularly for Asian communities transplanted into the West. Next, I think that a modified conception of autonomy might also be of some value not only to accommodate minority cultures, but also to address another concern among liberals: that is, the concern that civic virtue and public-spiritedness amongst citizens are in decline—that individualization has progressed so far that people no longer feel responsibility for the community. Relying on insights from psychoanalysis on the 'structure' of Western and Asian personalities, I will argue that it is helpful to begin our search for such a conception of autonomy by understanding the relations between what I shall call 'intrapsychic' and 'interpersonal' autonomy. By focusing only on the latter concept, liberal theorists and policy-makers are likely to ignore an important psychological resource in their attempts to reconcile commitments to both cultural toleration and individual autonomy.

Before proceeding I want to make a remark of a more methodological nature. My case deals with Hindustanis as a Dutch immigrant population that originates from South Asia. I thereby assume that notwithstanding the transition from India to Surinam, and then later to the Netherlands, and notwithstanding the processes of creolization and hybridization that have taken place, the core values in Hindustani culture concerning gender relations remained relatively intact (Mungra 1990). In short, it makes sense to think of this as an essentially Asian culture, and to draw on numerous studies in psychology and the social sciences that attempt to elucidate general differences between South Asian and Western cultures.

1. Cultural Conflict as Gender Conflict?

Most Western societies today harbour within their boundaries minority groups whose cultures are distinct from the culture of the majority. Many liberal political theorists have argued that these groups should have extensive, though not unlimited, rights to live in accordance with their culture. The accommodation of cultural practices often necessitates some revision of rules and regulations, and this has given rise to the question whether and on what grounds an exemption to the general rule should be allowed. Hence there is an increasingly vast literature that explains, among other things, why it is justifiable for Sikhs to drive their motorbikes without wearing a helmet (Poulter 1987) or why the Amish should be allowed to drive horse-drawn buggies on American highways (Spinner 1994). Were these the only sort of cases, then the road to intercultural toleration in liberal states would be an easy one to follow. Many intercultural value conflicts, however, are less inno-cent, and the proper metaphor is not a clear road but a thorny path. In the name of culture, girls and women can be denied the right to education; virginity rules may mean that their behaviour and freedom of action are strictly regulated; and clitoridectomy is intended, and sometimes even openly defended, to control women (Okin 1997). All of these are examples in which individual's basic civil rights and liberties are violated and all of them are examples of gender inequalities.

This is no mere coincidence. Intercultural value conflict is very often a conflict over gender inequalities, and the Hindustani suicide case is but one example of minority cultural practices that limit women's autonomy (Okin 1997, 1998).[2] Of course, gender inequalities are not characteristic of non-Western minority cultures only. Feminist movements would not have arisen in the West if everything was peaches and cream. This being said, I do think that some cultures (and some periods within the same culture) are more oppressive to women than are others and that feminists and liberals alike have a responsibility to speak out against gender injustices—particularly when the persistence of such injustices might be encouraged by liberal commitments to toleration and cultural rights.

My further contention is that what is at stake in these cultural conflicts is ultimately women's autonomy. All of the above-mentioned practices are examples of cultural practices that limit women's right to *act* autonomously. What I want to suggest, however, is that there still is a second sense in which women's autonomy can be restricted by their culture. What troubles me

---

[2] This is also the basic assumption underlying the research I am conducting, together with my colleague Odile Verhaar. To Susan Moller Okin's argument I wish only to add that one important reason for minority groups to limit their female members' rights and liberties is that the proper conduct of women is often what distinguishes them from others. Women's conduct becomes one of the symbolic markers of religious or ethnic identity (Meznaric 1994; Papanek 1994; Saghal and Yuval-Davis 1992b; Zarkov 1997). This is one reason, I think, why cultural minority groups are reluctant to give up these practices. I want to stress that it is also the dominant society that does this boundary-marking. In the Netherlands, for example, Islamic prescriptions on the clothing and conduct of women are often misused to construct immigrant groups of Islamic background as the ultimate Other that can have no place in this democracy. Hence politicians who normally never show much concern for the well-being of women, when it comes to Islamic women, all of a sudden show up as their great liberators.

about the cultural expert's report is that, although it does explain that Hindustani culture does not value autonomy for women, it does not explain why the woman's culture was so deeply ingrained in her that she was not able to deviate from it. What exactly kept her from deviating? It seems that it was not because of the social pressure exercised upon her (although in other cases this might also play a role). What I want to suggest, therefore, is that people—and in particular women raised in a culture that does not value autonomy—may find themselves hampered in their *psychological ability* to act autonomously. That is to say, even when there would be no social constraints on them, and in that sense they would have the right to act autonomously, they still might feel an inner constraint not to do so. Before we can draw further lessons from cases like that of the Hindustani woman, it is necessary to look at how liberal theory in recent years has tried to reconcile the values of individual autonomy and cultural pluralism.

2. A Typical Hard Case?

The case with which we began seems to be a perfect example of a 'hard case'. Since the group practice in question leads to the infringement of the civil rights and liberties of individuals (Hindustani women), it pits liberal commitments to cultural toleration and individual autonomy against each other, leaving open the difficult question of how a liberal state should respond to such practices. In this section I shall examine a number of liberal answers to the question of toleration, concentrating on how they deal with personal autonomy. Since my aim is to get a better understanding of how we can account for the limitations to autonomy apparent in the suicide case, and to enhance women's capacity for autonomy *vis-à-vis* the cultural demands of their community, it is particularly relevant to know (*a*) how willing the liberal state should be to restrict minority cultural practices when they do not respect the autonomy of the group's members, and (*b*) to what extent it is recognized that a person may not be capable of acting autonomously.

Let us begin with a basic understanding of the nature of autonomy within contemporary liberalism. It is typically defined as 'the idea that individuals should be free to assess and potentially revise their existing ends' (Mendus 1989: 56), or as 'the vision of people controlling, to some degree, their own destiny, fashioning it through their own decisions throughout their lives' (Raz 1986: 369), or as the view that 'individuals should be free and equal in the determination of the conditions of their own lives' (Held 1987: 290). For my argument it is relevant to note that what these definitions all point to is that autonomy requires certain conditions. According to Raz, these are 'appro-

priate mental abilities, an adequate range of options, and independence'
(1986: 372).

For many theorists individual autonomy is liberalism's core value.
Although they are not insensitive to the fate of minority cultures—on the
contrary, their work shows great concern for the cultural needs of minority
groups—the right of autonomy is what for them defines the limits of
toleration.[3] It cannot be tolerated that cultural groups impose restrictions on
their members' autonomy. For 'what distinguishes *liberal* tolerance is precisely its commitment to autonomy' (Kymlicka 1995a: 158) and hence 'it is
neither possible nor just to allow all conceptions (of the good) to be pursued'
(Rawls 1988: 258). Still, this does not mean that these authors unconditionally
license intervention in a community's culture. This is, in part, because as
liberals they are also committed to protecting the private sphere from
intrusion. Hence, it is 'with regret' that John Rawls (1988: 268) accepts the
interceding in Amish culture that is implied by the civic education he thinks
Amish children should get.[4] Similarly, Jeff Spinner holds that as long as there
is evidence that the Amish do choose their way of life, they should be granted
a 'grudging tolerance', entailing, amongst others things, that 'the state does
not need to worry about the political education of Amish children' (1994:
102–3). Although authors may differ on where exactly to draw the line, there
seems to be great unanimity about the bottom line, that at the very least
cultural minority groups must leave their members an exit option (cf.
Fitzmaurice 1993: 14; Kymlicka 1995a: 170; Spinner 1994: 102).

Critics of the autonomy-based approach to toleration take as their starting-
point the fact that many cultural groups hold conceptions of the good that
do not value personal autonomy. Bhikhu Parekh, for instance, writes in a
critique of Will Kymlicka that to expect these groups to let their members
freely and self-consciously affirm their membership, that is to say, to relate to
their cultures in a way that the liberal does to his and to tolerate them only
to the extent that they behave as respectable liberals, is to deny them in their
authentic otherness (Parekh 1997: 59; cf. Kukathas 1995: 241–5). Moreover,
according to these critics, theories that take personal autonomy as a central
liberal value are bound to treat a culture that encourages autonomy and
choice as morally superior to one that does not (Kukathas 1997: 76; Parekh
1997: 56). This, and a general wariness about state intervention in minority
groups' cultures, is the concern lying behind Chandran Kukathas's efforts to
develop a defence of toleration that does not rest on a notion of autonomy.
His proposal entails that cultural groups may exert great power over their
own members, including the freedom to restrict their members' rights to

---

[3] See amongst (many) others Fitzmaurice (1993); Green (1995); Kymlicka (1995a); Leader
(1996).

[4] The Amish are yet another group that grants its members, particularly its women, little
personal autonomy.

autonomy. The only proviso Kukathas makes is that individual members must have the freedom to leave the community.

In short, this debate among liberals is about the importance of the individual's right of autonomy as against the group's right of autonomy. Here the debate seems to pose cruel choices: either one places the individual's right of autonomy first, and hence sanctions cultural interference; or one places the group's autonomy first, and does not intervene even when individual autonomy is threatened. As both positions express legitimate concerns, one is drawn to ask if we cannot have both. I shall return to this question presently. But let us turn first to my second question, above, concerning the recognition or appreciation of the possibility that people will be in some sense psychologically unable to act autonomously even in situations where they are not literally constrained.

Rawls and Kukathas do come close to discussing this question. For example, Rawls notes that citizens 'may regard it as simply unthinkable to view themselves apart from certain religious, philosophical and moral convictions, or from certain enduring attachments and loyalties' (1985: 241). Similarly, Kukathas notes that 'if an individual is so completely settled in the way of life of a community that the idea of leaving is inconceivable, this person is in a sense "unable" to leave' (1992b: 677). These two statements come close to a recognition that people are not always psychologically able to exercise their freedom of choice. However, neither author pursues the implications of this fact, and indeed both go on to minimize the problem. Rawls, for example, assumes that people who are unable to leave or change their relationships in private life are none the less capable of exercising autonomy in their public lives, and that this is all a 'political' conception of liberalism should be concerned with. If people's autonomy in the public sphere is respected, then Rawls assumes that the inability to exercise autonomy in the private sphere is benign. Similarly, Kukathas argues that so long as people have a formal right of exit, then it does not matter whether they are 'in a sense unable to leave'. People who are 'settled' may be psychologically unable to leave, but so long as there is a right of exit, then Kukathas assumes that this person's 'settlement' is freely chosen. In different ways, then, both Rawls and Kukathas ignore the question about what sorts of 'appropriate mental abilities' are needed to ensure that people's 'settlement' in particular ways of life does not become a source of oppression or harm.

Why is it so important to focus on the 'psychological preconditions' or 'appropriate mental abilities' for the exercise of autonomy? The case of the Hindustani woman's suicide shows that we cannot take proper account of the impact of cultural practices on autonomy unless we broaden our understanding of autonomy to include these basic psychological preconditions. In the suicide case we simply cannot assume that the young woman was capable of exercising the degree of autonomy that she was granted within the context of the Dutch state. For in the Netherlands there are shelters for battered women. Secondly, she was not a socially isolated woman who was ignorant of Dutch society. So, it seems that it was not material conditions or ignorance, but her own psychological inability to distance herself from what her culture had taught her, that prevented the woman from taking a more viable escape from her anguish. This premiss makes the case more poignant, and also—for liberal theorists used to presuming a basic capacity for autonomy in all citizens—potentially harder to deal with.

3. Into the Heart of Darkness: Psychoanalytical Understandings of the Asian Self

Of course, it is standard for critics of liberalism to question its reliance on abstract conceptions of autonomy and individuality. These critics range from communitarians, who reject the idea of an autonomous self capable of stepping out of its ends and the culture that constitutes it, to postmodernists, who emphasize the idea of the individual as an invention and the subject as a socially constituted self. Among cultural anthropologists it is commonly understood that the notion of the self as an autonomous individual is a culture-bound, Western notion that is not applicable to non-Western cultures. This is the background to Clifford Geertz's remark that:

The Western conception of the person as a bounded, unique, more or less integrated motivational and cognitive universe, a dynamic centre of awareness, emotion, judge-ment, and action organized into a distinctive whole and against a social and natural background is, however incorrigible it may seem to us, a rather peculiar idea within the context of the other world cultures. (Geertz 1973: 48)

Since my case deals with people who originate in South Asia, what do scholars of South Asia have to say about South Asian notions of personhood? Before going on, let me remark that in comparing cultures the focus is necessarily on differences between them rather than on differences within them. I realize that this of course runs the risk of unjustly homogenizing cultures. With respect to South Asia the prevailing view that individuality and autonomy are not valued is explained, amongst others, by reference to the Hindu world-image. In Hinduism, it is claimed, the notion of an individual separate self is considered as an illusory concept that keeps us from reaching the ultimate aim of existence which is a state in which all distinctions between subject and object, between that which is felt to be inside the person and that which is outside, have been transcended (*moksha*). Another central idea in Hinduism is that every person has his own particular life task, which he has to fulfil (*dharma*). What is for a particular person the proper moral behaviour is given. Hence, a person is thought ideally to live in conformity to his *dharma*, not to determine his own good or fashion his own destiny. (Cf. Allen 1997; Carrithers *et al*. 1985; Kakar 1978, ch. 3.) Others point to the far more hierarchical structure of relationships in South Asian families, as compared to Western families. A South Asian family member is to a far greater extent expected to act in conformity with the behaviour considered proper to his position in the family hierarchy. This again leaves the individual little scope for autonomous action. It had led some authors, such as Dumont (1965, 1980), to assert that in South Asians the capacity for personal autonomy is just not developed.

If we combine the insights offered by this literature, then the answer to my problem seems clear: the Hindustani woman in question had behaved in accordance with what was culturally expected of her as a wife, and was then not able to act against these expectations, because as a member of this Asian culture she had simply not developed the individuality and capacity for autonomy that is needed to do that. But, as it stands, I am not happy with this answer at all. What the literature describes is basically cultural notions of the self and social expectations regulating behavioural patterns. While I do not want to dispute the correctness of these descriptions, what I do dispute is the direct correspondence between, in particular, the cultural notions of the self and the actual intrapsychic structuring of the self that is implied by the answer (and indeed by the writing of some of the authors). The mixing up of cultural notions and psychological categories would render people mere cultural dopes and South Asian women as merely passive victims of cultural socialization.

Like many liberal theorists in the last decade or so, I want to account for how people are capable of acting as socially constituted yet autonomous individuals. So I would like to keep open the possibility that some people may have no conscious understanding of themselves as individuals while still having developed (some) individuality. Equally, while conformity may be the culturally valued behaviour, this does not have to mean that a person is devoid of all autonomy. What the case of the Hindustani woman does show is that the capacity for autonomy is clearly more developed in some people than in others. To learn more from this case, therefore, we must consider how this capacity is developed. I believe that there is an important body of insight into this question that is largely unknown to contemporary liberal theorists, namely, the writings of contemporary psychoanalysts, especially those who deal directly with cross-cultural comparisons. In the language of psychoanalysis the question of the development of a capacity for autonomy is understood in terms of the organization of personality. And within this framework, it makes sense to talk in general terms about 'the Western personality or self' or 'the Asian personality or self'. Again, this is not meant as a form of stereotyping, or as a denial that there is great variation in the organization of individuals' personalities within cultures, as well as important similarities between all humans. It is no more than a useful shorthand to highlight some of the psychological implications of different cultural structures.

One will look in vain for the word 'autonomy' in the vocabulary of classical Western psychoanalytic theory (Laplanche and Pontalis 1973).[5] The *idea* of autonomy, however, is captured well by the twin lemmas of 'ego' and 'identification'. The ego is the product of identifications. 'Identification' is, in Laplanche and Pontalis's *The Language of Psychoanalysis*, a 'psychological process whereby the subject assimilates an aspect, property or attribute of the other and is transformed, wholly or partially, after the model the other provides. It is by means of a series of identifications that the personality is constituted and specified' (1973: 205). According to classical psychoanalysis, the normal outcome of the identification process is an individual with firm ego boundaries who experiences himself as a differentiated, but organized, unity, who exists independent of and differentiated from his environment. The capacity for autonomy is developed out of this process of separation (from the mother) and individuation. In short, the normal outcome of the identification process is the autonomous individual.[6]

Psychoanalytic studies of South Asians dispute the universality of this finding.[7] They stress that the Asian personality is characterized by more permeable ego boundaries that make for a more relational and less individualistic self. This is partly explained by the fact that in infancy and early childhood South Asian mothers tend to accede to their children's wishes and inclinations rather than to try to mould and control them. In effect the original symbiotic relation with the mother tends to be continued longer and hence 'the child's differentiation of himself from his mother . . . is structurally weaker and comes chronologically later than in the West' (Kakar 1978: 104). This is further explained as functional in the setting of close-knit extended family relations. These are characterized by 'an intense emotional connectedness

---

[5] It was Hartmann (1958) who introduced the term in psychoanalytical theory.

[6] Lack of firm ego boundaries is in classical psychoanalysis a sign of pathology, notably of schizophrenia.

[7] Actually the classical psychoanalytical account of the ego is also qualified by feminist interpretations. They claim that Western women normally do develop ego boundaries, but that these are relatively weaker than are men's boundaries. Next, their claim is that women have a conception of the good that is more relational and situational than that of men and that holds care rather than autonomy as a central value. Hence the autonomous individual is, according to them, essentially a male individual and liberal morality—a male morality (cf. Chodorow 1978; Gilligan 1982; Tronto 1993). In my account of the Asian psyche, I draw on the work of notably Sudhir Kakar (1978), Katherine Ewing (1991), and Alan Roland (1996). A note on terminology: Kakar speaks of Indian and Hindu personality interchangeably, Ewing speaks alternatively about Pakistanis and South Asians, and Roland discusses Indian and Japanese identity formation. Since there seems to be a substantial difference with Japanese identity, but no important difference between Indian and Pakistani identity in these studies, I shall refer simply to South Asian identity.

with a constant flow of affect and responsiveness between persons; by a strong mutual caring, dependence and interdependence, with a greatly heightened, reciprocal asking and giving in an emotional atmosphere usually of affection and warmth; and by a highly empathic, nonverbal sensitivity to one another's feelings and needs without the other having to verbalize them' (Roland 1996: 32). In relationships characterized by such close emotional engagement, boundaries between people tend to get blurred and leave less room for personal autonomy. Nevertheless, this aspect of South Asian family life is usually highly valued by South Asians, and shows up in the statements of people who, for whatever reason, have become outsiders to their culture. Take, for instance, British Pakistani author Hanif Kureishi's reflection on his visit to his family in Pakistan:

the family scrutiny and criticism was hard to take, as was all the bitching and gossip. But there was warmth and continuity for a large number of people; there was security and much love. Also there was a sense of duty and community—of people's lives genuinely being lived together, whether they liked each other or not—that you didn't get in London (1986: 22).[8]

Yet, another characteristic of the extended family, already mentioned, is that family relations are hierarchical, this hierarchy being organized along lines of age and gender. This does not mean that the senior has no obligation towards the junior—he is expected to be nurturing and supportive to the junior and thus feel responsible for the junior's well-being (cf. Roland 1996: 28–35)—but obviously there are greater expectations of the junior to comply with the needs and wishes of the senior than the other way around. What kind of effect these expectations can have on women is clearly illustrated in a speech of a British Asian woman who, after ten years of life in a violent marriage, killed her husband.[9] She explains,

My culture is like my blood—coursing through every vein in my body. It is the culture into which I was born and where I grew up, which sees the woman as the honour of the house. In order to uphold this false 'honour' and 'glory' she is taught to endure many kinds of oppression and pain in silence. In addition, religion also teaches that

---

[8] The question arises whether Asian family life is equally valued by men and women. I know of little research in this area, so it is hard to say. Nevertheless, it is interesting to look back at feminists' debates from the 1980s to see how Asian feminists, in Britain and in the Netherlands, criticized the feminist conceptualization of the family as a site of oppression only. They claimed that for them the family offered also much support and security. This suggests that Asian women at least have mixed feelings about Asian family life. See e.g. *Feminist Review*, 17 (1984) or the reactions to Barrett and McIntosh (1985) in *Feminist Review*, 20 (1985).

[9] The speech is rendered for us by Gita Saghal (1992), who was involved with two women's groups in Britain, Southall Black Sisters (SBS) and the Brent Asian Women's Refuge. In 1990 SBS launched a campaign to obtain the release from prison of this woman, Kiranjit Ahluwalia. The speech was taped while she was in prison.

her husband is her god and fulfilling his every desire is her religious duty. A woman who does not follow this path in our society has no respect or place in it. She suffers from all kinds of slanders against her character; and she has to face much hurt entirely alone. She is responsible not only for her husband but also for his entire family's happiness. (Saghal 1992: 188)

Her words again suggest that South Asian cultural norms leave individuals, and in particular women, relatively little scope for autonomous action. The internalization of these cultural norms ('my culture is like my blood') seems to generate a psychological disposition that limits women in their capacity for autonomy.

In understanding what is distinct about the capacity for autonomy of women raised in traditional South Asian communities, however, it is not sufficient to think only in terms of their having less of it than, say, middle-class women raised in the West. Following Katherine Ewing (1991), I want to argue that we make the distinction between interpersonal and intrapsychic autonomy, according to which in Asian women the first is indeed often diminished while the second can be highly developed.[10] Intrapsychic autonomy is 'the ability to maintain enduring mental representations of sources of self-esteem and comfort, permitting a more flexible adaptation to the vicissitudes of the immediate environment' (Ewing 1991: 132). We might, then, consider intrapsychic autonomy as the psychoanalytical equivalent for what Raz referred to as 'appropriate mental abilities'. Ewing does not provide a formal definition of 'interpersonal autonomy', but from the context I make out that it must refer to the right to act autonomously in the social world, which may or may not be culturally curtailed. About 'interpersonal autonomy' Ewing writes that it 'is valued by middle-class Americans as the ideal mode of relationship among adult family members, but is not valued in the same way among groups of other cultural backgrounds' (1991: 136-7). Of the two, intrapsychic autonomy is, for Ewing, clearly more fundamental. It means that 'in many South Asian families, individual family members do in fact act in an autonomous fashion intrapsychically, while . . . accepting the demands for conformity within the family' (1991: 139). Hence conformist behaviour does not always reflect a conformist inner world.

The next step Ewing takes is that she claims that it is not only *possible* that a low degree of interpersonal autonomy goes together with a high degree of intrapsychic autonomy, but that the latter is even *necessary* to survive without psychological damage in these situations. It is through the firmly consolidated inner world of self and object representations that the experience of

---

[10] Intrapsychic autonomy seems to be a universal psychoanalytical category, to be found both in South Asians and North Americans, but in particular Roland (1996: 19) suggests that this 'highly private self', as he terms it, is more developed in South Asians than in North Americans. Ewing leaves this matter more undetermined.

merger of self and social role is never total, and that the individual is less dependent on his or her environment.[11] Thus intrapsychic autonomy is also described by Ewing as 'the ability to maintain a conscious awareness of one's inner thoughts and feelings when these differ from one's overt actions and may be socially unacceptable' (1991: 141). This is particularly important, essential even, for the functioning of a South Asian woman, 'who typically spends her whole life in [the] interpersonal dependency relationships' of the extended family (1991: 132).

So, the claim of psychoanalytical studies is that the personalities of South Asians are indeed different from that of the average Western person in that they have developed more permeable ego boundaries and a greater capacity for empathy. This is in part a rephrasing in different terms what the cultural studies also maintain. Yet, since for the development of autonomy a certain degree of individuation is required, their claim is not that South Asians completely lack individuality. On the other hand, while in classical psychoanalysis the capacity for autonomy is considered as conditional on individuality, this is qualified by the insight that intrapsychic autonomy is also possible in individuals that have not developed a highly individuated personality and under conditions that leave little scope for autonomous action. Moreover, Ewing's valuable insight is that the capacity for intrapsychic autonomy gives people, especially women, the psychological resilience needed in conditions where they have limited interpersonal autonomy. I think that this distinction allows for a better understanding of why the Hindustani woman I began with was not able to act against her culture's expectations. It may also offer us clues to how we can enhance the capacity for autonomous action in women like her. To this I now turn.

4. Autonomy Regained

If my discussion so far has shown anything, it is that autonomy is a many-layered concept, and a liberal concern for autonomy must be prepared to engage with these various levels. Let me recapitulate the steps in the argument thus far:

1. Traditional Asian cultural conceptions of the self do not put great value on individuality and autonomy.

2. This is paralleled by typical South Asian family structures, which do not include much interpersonal autonomy; this is explained by the close emo-

---

[11] An example to illustrate the point: a woman's actual environment, say, her new family in law, may transmit to her that she is a person not worthy of love or esteem; yet if the mental image of, say, her mother's love and esteem for her is held firmly with her, her self-love and self-esteem will remain untarnished.

tional engagement between family members and by the limited scope for autonomous action that they allow, particularly for women.

3. In so far as women have internalized these cultural notions of womanhood, this constitutes a psychological disposition that limits their ability to act autonomously.

4. The traditional Asian family structure is reflected in the psychological make-up of South Asians, first, in their empathic capacities, which enable close emotional ties, and secondly—of particular importance for South Asian women —in a highly developed capacity for intrapsychic autonomy that enables them to cope with the fact that they have limited interpersonal autonomy.

Before proceeding with the argument, let me first state that I do not think that there is anything objectionable about close emotional family ties. They may be a culturally shaped mode of relationship among family members that is different from that in most Western families (see Meissner, in Ewing 1991: 138: 'The goal of a normal family (by Western standards) is to promote the development of well-differentiated and individuated identity in offspring'). But this mutually engaged family life does not necessarily preclude the right of autonomy that liberals care about. Moreover, it is highly valued by the people within these cultures. What I want to ask is whether there is a way to enhance the ability to act autonomously that also respects the relational qualities necessary for the close emotional engagement between family members.

It is time to return to the Dutch court case with which I began. The husband was found guilty of frequent maltreatment of his wife, and this was not considered by the court to be culturally excusable. But for the charge of incitement to suicide, the court ruled that evidence was lacking. This will probably come as no surprise, since sustaining this last claim would have required the court to acknowledge that some cultures leave their members with so little capacity for autonomy that these individuals have no choice but to follow their culture's imperatives. Such a claim, even in this case, is highly questionable (see Maris 1995); and besides it would have opened, as Deborah Woo put it, 'a Pandora's box of nearly infinitely excusable offenses' (1987: 420), because then the court would equally have had to accept the husband's defence that he had only acted as his culture had socialized him to, for which he could not be held responsible.

Does this now mean: case lost, all lost? Not at all. The case gained a high profile within the Dutch Hindustani community and stimulated much discussion about gender relations. The anthropologist Lamur was—to his own embarrassment—hailed by many women as a protagonist of the women's cause, and according to him it made Hindustani women realize that maltreatment is an offence that can be reported (Lamur 1992: 157).[12] This points to the

---

[12] This was also confirmed by him in a telephone conversation I had with him on 15 Jan. 1998.

importance of a public discussion of cultural notions of womanhood, both within and in dialogue with the community. Secondly, the case points to the importance of the social conditions that enable women to exercise effectively their right of autonomy, including, minimally, their need to be informed about their legal rights.

It is doubtful that a better understanding of her rights would, by itself, have kept the Hindustani woman from committing suicide. Her problem was, I think, that her gender role left her little interpersonal autonomy, that is, little scope for autonomous action and to that extent her suicide can be blamed on her enculturation. Next, her capacity for intrapsychic autonomy, that is, her capacity to keep in touch with her inner thoughts and feelings, may have been underdeveloped. If that was the case, she was atypical of women in her culture. This would mean then that she experienced a merger of self and social role to such an extent that she continued to live up to that role, even when she was no longer able to. Still, even if she had developed a strong sense of intrapsychic autonomy, it remains to be seen if she would have acted autonomously, for the capacity for intrapsychic autonomy is explained as functional in conditions where there is limited scope for autonomous action. I consider intrapsychic autonomy an important form of autonomy and I would expect it to be a precondition for autonomous action, but in itself not a sufficient precondition. Intrapsychic autonomy refers to the ability to stand back from the actual situation and to be able to reflect on it critically. Important for its development is that the individual has been able to establish a firmly consolidated inner world of self and object representations (object constancy). It does not say, however, which objects inhabit this inner world. I would expect that, in order to act autonomously, it should entail an under-standing of oneself as an autonomously acting person. As long as that is not the case, a person is not exactly incapable of acting autonomously (in the sense of a lacking faculty), but is less inclined to do so and in that sense her capacity is limited.

So the question remains: what can and should the liberal state do for women like her from minority cultures that constrain their autonomy? In the space that remains I could not even begin to sketch an abstract, general answer to this question. Instead, I will discuss briefly what has already been tried by the Dutch government. Interestingly enough, there are already several policies in place that promise to enhance women's psychological capacity for autonomy, even if they are not yet recognized as such. I shall discuss one of these: the programme of family intervention.[13]

---

[13] This paragraph relies on information bulletins from the Averroes Foundation (which co-ordinates the programme) known as the Stap (Step) series. I have also used Eldering and Kloprogge (1989), Eldering and Vedder (1993), and two special issues on the family interven-tion programme of the Dutch pedagogical journal *Vernieuwing* ('Renewal'), 50/8 (1991) and 56/9 (1997).

The family intervention programme takes its inspiration from the Head Start project that was launched in the United States in the 1960s. It was adapted in the Netherlands some years ago to address the fact that children from certain cultural minorities, as well as those from some segments of the Dutch working class, were failing dramatically at school. More specifically, the programme targets Turkish, Moroccan, Surinamese, and Dutch groups. The underlying assumption was that these groups' traditional child-rearing practices, characterized as non-inductive, obedience-orientated practices, provide insufficient preparation for school. The programme has both cognitive and socio-emotional objectives. The main goal in the socio-emotional realm is to promote children's individuality and capacity for autonomy by modifying the mothers' child-rearing practices. The project includes a range of programmes for the age groups ranging from 0–2 years to 6 years old. They are designed as home-based and hence mother-focused programmes. This entails that a project co-worker comes to visit the mother in her home to give her instruction and supervision. In addition to this there are group sessions where mothers and professionals meet. Should the programme prove successful, we would have here an instrument for the promotion of the capacity for autonomy in children, and *ipso facto* in girls and women. Perhaps not surprisingly, though, the results so far have been disappointing.

Even if this programme were successful in achieving its goals, however, it is not clear that it would be morally justified. For one thing, it constitutes a major intrusion in the private sphere. Within certain limits (for example, to protect against child abuse) child-rearing is usually considered the private affair of the parents. Secondly, the assumption that mothers from minority and working-class backgrounds are incompetent is weakly founded, if not insulting; the programme is not based on an evaluation of components in the culturally shaped child-rearing patterns of the mothers that could be built upon. It claims to be culturally sensitive, but we have already seen that it cannot possibly be so if it is based on the assumption that autonomy requires a highly individuated personality (i.e. Meissner's 'normal family'). It thus offers only one model of personality development, notably a Western one, in which autonomy and individuality are interlinked, and it expects the mothers to comply with that model. Were the programme to succeed in this, then at least in the case of the South Asian group, it would dramatically change their rearing patterns, the personality structure of their children, and eventually the group's culture. Is this justifiable? I do not think so, because it is not at all clear that all of these dramatic changes are required for the enhancement of women's capacity for autonomy or that there is no alternative.

I think that there is such an alternative. It suggests itself when we look at why the programme is so ineffective. One plausible explanation is that it does not link up with existing rearing practices, and is therefore able to realize only ephemeral and superficial changes in the way mothers raise their children.

But what would it mean to link up with existing practices? In the case of South Asians, this 'linking up' would mean that the programme would build on existing resources, such as the capacity for intrapsychic autonomy. As this capacity is acquired in the context of the extended family and seems to go well with the relational qualities that make for close emotional family ties, it suggests that it is possible to enhance their capacity for autonomy, while respecting these qualities.[14] An example may illustrate the point. As it is, the intervention programme, and Dutch institutional pedagogical interference in general, is based on an understanding that South Asian mothers (and for that matter Turkish and Moroccan mothers), are over-indulgent and spoil their children (cf. Van der Zwaard 1995). This is considered as hampering their children's individuation and autonomy. We are now able to see that acceding to the child's wishes (i.e. 'indulgence') enhances the mutuality of mother and child and that this again is functional for the development of a relational personality. Since this acceding attitude does not necessarily preclude the development of (at least an intrapsychic) capacity for autonomy, there is no reason why it should be discouraged. The problem is rather that it needs a certain sensitivity to sit on this particular fence, and that at the moment Dutch policy-makers and programme-designers are prevented from developing such sensitivity by their adherence to their culture-bound ideal of a highly individuated autonomous individual. Although many problems still remain unresolved, such as how the programme is to avoid being unjustifiably paternalistic, my argument is notably an argument against certain kinds of intervention programmes, but not against family intervention *per se*.

5. Conclusion

The problem I started with was how we can account for the limited psychological ability to act autonomously that appeared from the suicide case of a Hindustani woman in the Netherlands, and how the state can enhance that ability.

Much of the liberal debate on cultural rights and the limits of toleration has proven not to be very helpful in addressing these questions, because it focuses too narrowly on the right to autonomy, and thereby ignores the fact that this right is of little worth without the ability to act autonomously. We also have to get beyond the false dichotomy according to which respecting

---

[14] Actually, this was precisely the aim of the Turkish Early Enrichment Project that was developed in the 1980s. And they claim that it was successful in this respect (see Kağıtçıbaşı 1996: 158–60).

group autonomy and individual autonomy come to be seen as almost mutually exclusive goals.

My wanderings through academia and the world alike have shown that the basic liberal assumption of the autonomous individual may indeed be liberalism's 'necessary fiction'. It is commonplace to argue that neither Asian cultural conceptions of the self nor traditional South Asian family life place much value on individuality and autonomy. The distinction proposed here between intrapsychic autonomy and interpersonal autonomy makes it possible to qualify this image. It makes clear that South Asian family life allows for the first, but leaves little room for the second, particularly for women. Insomuch as women have internalized this cultural imperative, this constitutes a psychological disposition that hampers their ability to act autonomously. Yet, there is also a second sense in which the assumption of the autonomous individual is a fiction, in that it takes the capacity for autonomy for granted, thereby naturalizing it and preventing us from inquiring how it is brought about. I think that psychoanalysis gives a good account of how the capacity for autonomy is achieved in the individual. Yet it also makes clear that there is not just one capacity, or rather that a capacity for autonomy is not necessarily always tied up with a highly individualistic personality. The capacity for intrapsychic autonomy is developed within the context of the extended family, which requires a personality structure that is highly empathic to the feelings and psychological needs of others, in short, a relational self. These studies on Asian personality further suggest that, as it is, the capacity for intrapsychic autonomy functions as a mechanism to cope with a situation characterized by little interpersonal autonomy. The psychic well-being of traditional South Asian women seems to rest to a great extent on this capacity.

Still, we might want to enhance their capacity to act autonomously—the tragic death of the Hindustani woman I began with serves as a very powerful argument for this obligation. A series of Dutch family intervention programmes intends to do just this, but it is unclear whether they can do what they promise. If they could, however, then the promotion of the ability to exercise autonomy in women could be a powerful argument for their justification. These programmes are not as yet justified on these grounds, but I would welcome it if arguments about women's autonomy were taken into consideration. It is possible to imagine a programme that, while enhancing the capacity for autonomous action, is more respectful of the relational qualities that are characteristic of traditional South Asian personalities and family life. It must be built on existing psychological resources, like the capacity for intrapsychic autonomy. Although there are still other reasons that make it questionable if such a programme is morally justified, my argument is not an argument against family intervention *per se*.

My proposal entails a conception of the person that is both capable of exercising autonomy and capable of concern with the well-being of others. This person, though not identical with the typical liberal individual, does seem compatible with liberal citizenship. Moreover, in the light of the growing concern that the civic virtue and public-spiritedness of citizens is in decline, my relational individual may have certain advantages, in that she seems better qualified to attune to these 'habits of the heart' than is the liberal individual. She thus seems to be a nice 'go-between', able to accommodate both the demands of liberal citizenship and those of the cultural group. So, while I began with the observation that female autonomy and the cultural demands of minority groups often seem strange bedfellows, I would like to end with the prospect of two hearts beating together.

PART V

Language Rights

10

Official-Language Rights: Intrinsic Value and the Protection of Difference

DENISE G. RÉAUME

There has been considerable theoretical debate about how to understand the value of culture so as to determine what, if any, protections for minority cultural practices are warranted in a multicultural society. The backdrop for this debate is a dominant liberal tradition that has assumed that the sorts of individual interests that are capable of grounding claims must abstract from particular cultural affiliations, thereby leaving no normative space for the protection of culture. This perspective is tied to a conception of citizenship as the equal enjoyment of a set of individual rights common to all members of society. Such a conception automatically prompts suspicion of claims that do not apply universally—that is, that seek protection for practices or attributes that are not uniformly participated in by all members of society. By contrast with traditional human rights claims, like freedom of expression and freedom from arbitrary detention, which protect human interests enjoyed by each person, cultural rights seek to protect 'special' interests, ones peculiar to the members of a specific group.

One popular argument for cultural protections presents the value to individuals of their own culture in instrumental terms: use of one's own cultural practices, it is argued, better enables one to achieve objectives that are important independently of those practices; particular group practices should be protected for the sake of the objectives they help achieve. Since the independent objectives relied on are capable of being formulated in a universal fashion, this argument can easily reconcile the protection of particular cultural practices with the traditional liberal commitment to a universalistic conception of citizenship. I shall argue, however, that this form of argument misses an important aspect of the value of particular cultures: it fails to grasp the intrinsic rather than instrumental value to people of their own cultural heritage, and this intrinsic value is the key to justifying the 'special' character of minority cultural rights. Any account of the value of culture that treats it as merely instrumental to extrinsic ends can only provide a very insecure foundation for cultural protections. In particular, it is unlikely to provide a strong justification for understanding such rights as articulated by their advocates: as rights to the maintenance of cultural difference rather than merely to assistance in integrating into the society's dominant practices. It is the former that require an adjustment to the conventional liberal notion of universalistic citizenship. The maintenance of cultural difference involves ongoing protection of practices that deviate from the mainstream, and this requires 'special' treatment— the application of different standards to the minority from those applied to members of the majority. Measures designed to help minorities ultimately to be able to assimilate into the majority involve an element of group differentiation, but it is temporary and in the service of eventual uniformity of treatment.

I will begin with a general critique of an account of the value of culture rooted exclusively in its instrumental usefulness, and provide an alternative account of its intrinsic value. The philosophical debate has focused on the value of culture, rather than language *per se*, but given the relationship between the two, arguments about the value of one should be readily transposable to the other. I then turn to a concrete language rights issue in order to illustrate the dangers of instrumental accounts of minority cultural rights in the absence of an understanding of the intrinsic value of culture. My example concerns recent constitutional jurisprudence in Canada about the right to use either French or English before federal and some provincial courts. I shall argue that the singular lack of interpretative generosity exemplified in the dominant approach, established in the leading cases of *MacDonald* and *SANB* (*MacDonald* v. *City of Montreal* 1986; *Société des Acadiens du Nouveau-Brunswick* v. *Minority Language School Board No. 50* 1986), is explained by the court's failure to recognize the intrinsic value of mother tongue language use in the judicial setting.

1. Intrinsic versus Instrumental Conceptions of the Value of Language

Culture has been recognized as important because it is the context within which other important individual choices are made (Kymlicka 1989, ch. 8; 1995*a*, ch. 5). This in the context of the argument that it is the ability to plan one's life, to choose one's commitments and pursuits, that makes life worth while for human beings. On this account, planning one's own life is not valuable merely because it promotes some further valuable end, but rather is good in itself. It does not derive its value from its contribution to some other end, but rather itself accounts for the value of a particular life. In other words, the self-directed life is intrinsically good. So far, this argument could be interpreted to attribute intrinsic value to culture as well because it treats the cultural context of choice as a logical condition of the making of life choices.

It is not merely causally related to the ability to make choices, but a constitutive element of that ability (Raz 1986: 178). To say that the use of culture is a logical condition of something else that has intrinsic value is to make the cultural context for choice itself intrinsically valuable. The pursuit of a life plan cannot be regarded as an objective independent of a context giving it meaning. Thus, the argument might go, if individuals are entitled to the protection of their ability to choose a life plan, the context that makes choice possible must deserve protection. To the extent that language is an aspect of culture, this sort of argument can be applied more narrowly to provide an account of the grounds for protecting language.

This may appear to yield a conclusion in favour of protecting *particular* languages—my ability to live my life using *my* language—but this appearance is an illusion. This sort of explanation of the value of language as an account of its intrinsic value works only when it remains at the abstract level—focused on the value of language in the abstract. It is true that access to language *per se* is a logical condition of, not merely causally related to, the planning of a life. The living of any recognizably human life requires some linguistic context. But this is insufficient to establish the intrinsic value of a particular linguistic context. The English linguistic context is not a logical condition of planning a life, any more than German, Cantonese, or Tagalog is. A life can, in principle, be equally satisfactorily planned in any language. Once we move away from the abstract context, it is plain that the more usual environment of the claim to linguistic protection is one in which there is more than one linguistic context present. The question, then, is whether people can lay claim to the use of their own when an alternative is available and there are legitimate reasons, such as convenience and cost, in favour of the alternative. Demonstrating the intrinsic value of some linguistic context does not tell us enough about the value of people's particular language to answer this question.

A familiar argument designed to respond to this challenge relies on the difficulty for individuals in transferring from one culture or language to another. This may be offered as a way of linking language or culture to personal identity. Both play a role in establishing personal characteristics that are relatively deeply ingrained and therefore hard to change. The difficulties of transfer can indeed be diverse and substantial.[1] To begin with, there is the personal effort involved in learning the new way of life. This is often a lengthy process and frequently one marked by imperfect achievement. The complexity and subtlety of such comprehensive social practices as language are notorious. The difficulty in mastering them means that in so far as one needs to use new cultural forms to achieve independent objectives—using a new

---

[1] These sorts of difficulties are canvassed by Kymlicka (1995a: 82 ff.) and also adverted to by Raz (1994: 71).

language to get a job, or using a new conception of relationships with co-workers to gain acceptance on the job, for example—these independent objectives may be impaired. The consequences may include the foreclosure of many options that one might have wished to pursue, as well as attendant economic and social disadvantage. This, in turn, will have consequences for one's self-esteem as one finds oneself relegated to less skilled jobs and marginalized from important currents in social and political life. The costs of cultural transfer are considerably and painfully compounded by including the damage to familial relationships caused by parents, children, and grand-children being integrated to different degrees in a given culture and therefore unable fully to share all of it (Raz 1994).[2]

These arguments about the difficulty and cost of transfer rely on the in-strumental connection between culture and language and other human ends. The difficulty of operating in a second language or culture is simply the flip side of the instrumental ease of the accomplishment of one's independent goals in a familiar one. The slide simultaneously from the abstract to the particular and intrinsic value to instrumental value is easy to understand. It is hard to think about language instrumentally as long as we are thinking about it in the abstract, about the possession and use of language itself rather than any particular language. Since it is difficult, if not impossible, to separate language in the abstract as a tool from the other ends it is used for, its value will be bound up with the value of these other ends. They are not thinkable as meaningful activity without language. In a unilingual society isolated from the speakers of any other language, this is also how the value of its own language would be understood. In this kind of context, language will be regarded simply as intrinsically valuable because of its integral connection to the human activity it makes possible.

Once we postulate contact between language groups, however, the picture changes. Once an alternative is available—we can contemplate using this language or that—it becomes easier to distinguish language as a tool from the ends it makes possible. For a person who speaks French and not English, the use of French is instrumentally valuable in participating in those language-using activities that take place amongst other speakers of French. This gives one access to all the independently valuable ends that language is used for: forming relationships, playing games, learning a craft, carrying on a pro-fession, keeping up with the news or the gossip, buying groceries or shares on the stock market, formulating rules for social conduct. But it is no longer

---

2 For example, Raz argues that one aspect of many people's life plan to which they are deeply committed involves intergenerational relationships grounded in the kind of under-standing that requires a common culture. This seems to be a specific application in the family context of Raz's more general argument that it would be an infringement of autonomy to eliminate a life option for someone who was already deeply committed to it because it would be harder for such a person to substitute another life plan for the one denied (Raz 1986: 411).

true that this particular tool, French, is the only means of access to these activities. *This* language is not intrinsically connected to the value of all those activities that language in the abstract makes possible. In so far as it is difficult to learn a second language and even more difficult to achieve fluency, one's own language is simply a better means to accomplish one's independent objectives. The instrumental value, or liability, of one's own language can depend upon with whom one wants, or needs, to communicate. It is instrumentally very valuable in communication with other speakers of the same language, but instrumentally a handicap if one has reason to communicate with speakers of a different language.

But the instrumental nature of the connection between language and other ends is precisely the weakness in the cost-of-transfer argument for protecting particular languages. Identifying the value of language to individuals in this way suggests that if we were to find a way to eliminate these costs, or perhaps if we could even significantly reduce them, this would seriously weaken the claim to accommodations designed to allow a minority to maintain its linguistic practices in the face of policies designed to achieve assimilation of the minority into the majority.

Let's start with the difficulties of transfer. It is true that for many people this takes a great deal of effort. For others it is relatively easy. It is easiest for those whose home culture is not very different from the proposed new culture. Does this mean that, if we could identify those who would be able to make the change easily, we would be justified in making at least these people do so, or at least refusing to accommodate their different practices so that they have an incentive to adapt to majority practices? One of the costs of transfer that has serious consequences for self-esteem is that very often one is treated as a second-class citizen until one has mastered the new cultural system at a certain level of accomplishment. But this is not a necessary part of the process, merely a lamentable fact about the way most societies 'welcome' newcomers. If we could change this, putting in place a very careful process of integration designed to support the self-esteem of members of the minority as they learn their new culture, would it then be permissible to enforce such a policy rather than designing policy around the ongoing protection of cultural difference? Similarly, the economic consequences of having to master a new culture or language are not inevitable either. If the majority were prepared to make good the economic losses of the adult members of the minority, knowing that their children, raised within the new culture, will not suffer this cost, could change be required?

The cost to intergenerational family relationships is more complicated, at least for those families including adults who find the obstacles to transfer insurmountable despite society's best efforts to help. But even this argument, itself a pretty thin thread to hang an entire multiculturalism policy on, will not take us very far. First, it suggests that cultural or linguistic continuity has value only for members of intact families, so that we would do no wrong in automatically placing orphaned or abandoned children in homes outside their community of origin. More importantly, since there is no iron law of human nature that says that human beings can only ever master one culture or language at a time, and since we know that children can readily absorb more than one, this argument grounds protection for only one generation. If children of the minority are taught their parents' culture and language and also integrated into those of the majority, there would be a sufficient basis of mutual understanding between parents and children for healthy family relationships. At least, we need a further argument why the intergenerational sharing of world-view must be complete and completely symmetrical to be satisfying (since even within families belonging to a dominant culture there are often important generational differences of world-view). Could we legitimately expect minorities to raise their children biculturally and then expect the bicultural children of these families to complete the transfer to the majority culture and language with their own children? Even if we wanted to extend the protection of this argument to relationships between grandparents and grandchildren, this simply delays the completed integration process by one generation.

This programme of supportive, gentle, gradual transferral of people from one culture to another may well be utopian. The difficulties of transferring may be more intractable than it suggests. Or the political will necessary to create a genuinely supportive and relatively costless process of integration may be lacking. Since my primary focus is on the protection of language, it is interesting to note that the idea of relatively painless transfer is less utopian with respect to language considered on its own. Because children can be raised to speak more than one language fairly comfortably, a fairly smooth transition could be accomplished in two generations. But the point is not how realistic this is; the important question is: if we *could* significantly reduce or eliminate the costs of transfer, would it then be permissible to expect people to transfer rather than allowing them to maintain their own culture and language? An account focusing on language as an instrument lacks the resources to argue not merely for a right to help in transferring from one language or culture to another, but a right not to have to transfer—a right to support in the continuance of their language practices.

In the context of a plurality of languages, the intrinsic value of any particular language can no longer piggy-back on the value of the activities it is used for. But there is another way of understanding the intrinsic value of each particular language—as a human accomplishment, an end, in itself. Each language is itself a manifestation of human creativity which has value independent of its uses. Although it may express ideas, concepts, myths, traditions that have approximate equivalents in other languages, it is a unique form of expression and valuable as such. The same may be said for culture more generally.[3] It is this aspect of the importance of language that is missed by an exclusive focus on language as a tool of effective communication.

Most people value their language not only instrumentally, as a tool, but also intrinsically, as a cultural inheritance and as a marker of identity as a participant in the way of life it represents. Their language is a repository of the traditions and cultural accomplishments of their community as well as being a kind of cultural accomplishment itself. It is the vehicle through which a community creates a way of life for itself and is intrinsically bound up with that way of life. Participation in these kinds of communal forms of human creativity is an intrinsic part of the value of human life. The particular form it takes for a particular group of people takes on intrinsic value for them because it is *their* creation. For the group as a whole, its language is a collective accomplishment. An individual member's use of the language is at once a participation in this accomplishment and an expression of belonging to the community that has produced it. Because this participation has intrinsic value, members of a language community identify with that language—they take pride in its use and in the cultural accomplishments it represents and makes possible. This sort of intrinsic value, attributable to particular languages and reflected in the expressive interest in identification with them, comes to the fore when two or more linguistic communities are in contact. It is in being conscious of an alternative to one's own linguistic way of life that one begins to identify the latter as a distinct form of human creativity in which one can take pride.

This intrinsic value of language, as a manifestation of human creativity with which its speakers identify, is the key to understanding the claim to its protection in its particular manifestations. At the same time the fact that language has an instrumental dimension should not be ignored in an analysis of the form protections should take, precisely because this instrumental dimension makes language vulnerable to the manipulation of its usefulness. The extrinsic purposes for which language is useful are themselves extremely important to people. Therefore, the best way to weaken a language and effectively force the adoption of another is to lessen its usefulness in achieving these other ends. Likewise, battles for the protection of language will revolve around maintaining or improving its usefulness in important domains. However, what motivates this desire to protect the usefulness of one's language is the attribution to it of intrinsic value independent of its uses. Thus, although we will have occasion to focus on language as a tool, we must not lose sight of people's underlying attribution of intrinsic value to their mother tongue.

---

[3] This does not necessarily mean that all cultures are good. It is theoretically possible for a culture to exhibit such defects as to be unworthy of allegiance. My claim about intrinsic value is merely that, if a culture is valuable, it is intrinsically valuable to its members as the form that their human creativity has taken.

A normal sign of the intrinsic value placed on cultural or linguistic affiliation is the desire to use it in the conduct of one's life as well as to transmit
one's heritage to one's children and thus to see it carry on into future generations. Recognition of this value requires the creation of a minimal threshold
of security which people enjoy as members of a linguistic group (Green 1987:
658; Réaume and Green 1989: 779–85; Réaume 1991: 45). Linguistic security
consists in two sets of conditions. First, a linguistic community must enjoy
recognition by others of the intrinsic value of its language. This requires that
use of its language not be made a ground of liability or otherwise publicly
denigrated. Such treatment causes members to lose their self-esteem and
abandon their mother tongue because it is associated with inferiority and
second-class status (Taylor 1992: 25–6, 1993b). Secondly, linguistic security
requires support for the instrumental usefulness of the language, not merely
for the sake of other ends considered extrinsically, but out of respect for the
intrinsic value of a life lived within a particular linguistic milieu. This second
component, in turn, involves the existence of a substantial array of contexts
for the use of the language, but, in addition, it is promoted by ensuring that
the instrumental use of the language for extrinsic purposes is not disrupted—
that is, that use of the language is not rendered unduly detrimental to the
pursuit of other ends.

Against the backdrop of this account of the value of a language for its
speakers, I turn to a consideration of one aspect of the Canadian language
rights regime—the right to use French or English before the courts—to
illustrate the difference it makes to the interpretation of concrete rights when
courts fail to grasp the notion of intrinsic value outlined here.

2. Official-Language Use Rights in the Constitution

The official-language use rights[4] in the judicial setting exemplify the characteristic feature of the Canadian language rights regime.[5] Although they do

---

[4] These protections are found in various constitutional provisions: s. 133 of the Constitution Act 1867, s. 23 of the Manitoba Act, and s. 19 of the Charter of Rights and Freedoms,
reiterating the effect of s. 133 with respect of federal institutions and extending these to New
Brunswick. I shall refer to these collectively as the official-language use rights.

[5] The right to use either official language in the courts is merely one element of the
Canadian official-language regime. The other rights are the right to use either language in the
federal legislatures and those of some provinces, the right to the publication of statutes in both
languages, the right to communicate with government agencies at the federal level and in some
provinces, and the right to minority-language education across the country. These provisions
regulate linguistic relations between citizens and the state; they do not require or even seek to
foster personal bilingualism. For an overview of the Canadian regime, see Bastarche (1987).

not apply uniformly across the country,[6] in those jurisdictions to which they do apply they accord the right to speakers of both official languages—French and English—to use their own language in judicial proceedings. This contrasts with the approach more characteristic of the territorial model of language policy:[7] dividing a country up into linguistic regions and designing institutions to match the linguistic preferences of the regional majority, and leaving it up to citizens to locate in an area that will enable them to enjoy access to these institutions in their preferred language. The territorial model requires members of regional minorities to adapt to the practices of the majority should they decide to take up residence in an area dominated by another language group.[8] In other words, the territorial model does not really accord language rights to minority communities or their individual members.

The Canadian approach is based on a rights model. A member of the minority francophone population of Manitoba or New Brunswick or the minority anglophone population of Quebec is entitled to the use of her own language in judicial proceedings rather than being forced to conform to the language of the provincial majority population. Likewise, a litigant from anywhere in the country has the right to the choice of her official language before federal courts and tribunals. The Canadian approach makes the securing of official language use rights potentially costly for the state. Jurisdictions in which the majority population is anglophone, for example, and in which most members of the bench and Bar can be expected to be anglophone, must

[6] Canada's federal system of government along with the history of different provinces joining Confederation at different stages and on different terms from one another complicates the description of the official-language rights regime. In the judicial setting, the right to use either official language applies in all courts falling exclusively under federal jurisdiction and in the courts of some, but not all, provinces. In Manitoba and Quebec these rights were introduced provincially at the time they each joined Confederation; in New Brunswick these rights were introduced by the Constitution Act 1982. Similar rights were originally included in the legislation creating the Northwest Territories, out of which Alberta and Saskatchewan were created, but were not entrenched in the constitutions of those two provinces and have since been repealed. Official-language rights in the judicial setting have never been constitutionalized in any of the remaining provinces.

[7] For the distinction between the 'territorial' and 'personal' models, see Laponce (1987, ch. 7). Laponce describes the personal model as the attempt to establish language rights that are fully portable, that is, they accompany the citizen anywhere she may reside within the country (1987: 165). Because the regulation of the operation of the courts is in part a matter of provincial jurisdiction in Canada, and because not all provinces are officially bilingual, the right to use French or English before the courts is not a fully portable right. Nevertheless, it has more in common with the personal model than the territorial model. However, I prefer not to use Laponce's label to describe the Canadian regime, largely because it presupposes an individualistic conception of the rights described. Instead, it seems more accurate to characterize non-territorial regimes as language *rights* regimes, since their distinguishing feature is that they accord some language use rights to members of more than one linguistic community within a given political unit.

[8] Laponce offers the Swiss model of unilingual cantons as an example (Laponce 1987: 174).

nevertheless provide some accommodation for speakers of the other official language. By contrast, the territorial model allows institutions within each region to operate unilingually and imposes the cost of minority status on members of the minority.

The general analysis above of the inadequacies of a purely instrumental foundation for the protection of language or culture sheds light on the Canadian Supreme Court jurisprudence concerning the right to use French or English before certain courts. The interpretation placed on these constitutional provisions has been roundly criticized from a variety of quarters for its wild departure from normal constitutional canons of interpretation prescribing a purposive, large, and liberal approach. I want to join in that criticism and suggest that the mean-spiritedness of the Supreme Court's approach is best explained as grounded in the failure to see any intrinsic value in the use of one's own language in the judicial setting. The discussion in the court about the rationale for the official-language use rights relies too heavily on instrumental considerations. These are insufficient to explain and therefore provide a robust account of precisely the 'special' characteristics of the official-language rights—the respect in which they protect the right to be different. Paradoxically, however, the court's interpretation defines a right that is so devoid even of valid instrumental purpose that its use is likely directly to impair the independent ends litigants pursue when involved in litigation. Thus, this approach impairs linguistic security by frequently making it costly to use one's own language in the judicial setting.

The upshot of the Supreme Court judgments in *MacDonald* and *SANB* can be simply described. In response to MacDonald's claim that he was entitled under s. 133 to be served with a summons in respect of a traffic offence in the official language of his choice, the court held that the rights encompassed by the section are only those of speakers, not recipients of communications. Thus, the government official issuing the summons was entitled, as speaker, to use his own language whether or not that language was also MacDonald's. In response to the argument of La Société des Acadiens de Nouveau-Brunswick that it was entitled under s. 19 of the Charter to a judge who was capable of understanding its official language, the court held that the right is merely a negative liberty not to be interfered with in speaking either official language and imposes no positive obligations on anyone to understand one's speech. Taken together these litigants were advocating that the official-language use rights be interpreted as 'comprehensive use rights', encompassing the right to speak, understand, and be understood directly in one's own official language. According to the court's interpretation, the right consists of a bare liberty to speak one's own official language.

Two rationales were canvassed to try to explain and justify the official-language use rights. The plaintiffs argued in favour of a natural justice model: just as natural justice requires that any litigant must be able to understand and be understood by a court in order fairly to be able to put his case and respond to arguments made against it, so official-language speakers must have the right to understand and be understood in their language. This would be to interpret the official-language use rights as a sort of official-languages version of the natural justice rights. This argument was rejected, the court holding that the two sorts of rights are conceptually distinct and cannot be combined without distorting each (*MacDonald* v. *City of Montreal* 1986: 500–1). Instead, the court appealed to a categorization of the official-language rights as a 'political compromise' grounded in the historical 'deal' between the two most powerful linguistic groups amongst the settler population at the time of Confederation. Neither rationale is satisfactory. Both, in different ways, fail to grapple with the intrinsic value of the use of one's own language in the judicial setting.

The Natural Justice Model: Language as Instrument

Anyone before a court is there to make a claim, or defend against one, or to contribute to the court's ability to adjudicate one. It is essential to the court's ability to judge these issues fairly that relevant messages are effectively communicated between participants. Natural justice is concerned with the fairness of trials. Fairness requires that a litigant understand the charge or claim made against him and have a chance to tell his side of the story. In other words, fairness requires effective communication between litigants and between litigants and the court. Mutual comprehension is not merely instrumentally related to the pursuit of a fair trial; it in part constitutes fairness. The plaintiffs in *MacDonald* and *SANB* were trying to invoke natural justice in the cause of extending official-language use rights by arguing that effective communication would be served by a comprehensive interpretation of the official-language use rights to include being able to communicate in one's own official language to a judge who understands that language. However, the argument failed to take account of the fact that, although effective communication is intrinsic to fairness, there is no particular language whose use is necessary to effective communication and which is therefore intrinsic to fairness. In other words, natural justice conceives of the relationship between language and effective communication instrumentally—some means must be employed to that end, but it need not be *this* means. Fairness dictates the threshold of accuracy necessary to count communication as effective, but beyond that threshold it has nothing to say about the choice of roughly comparable means to that end. This makes the natural justice model an unfortunate choice in the effort to establish an entitlement to use a particular means of communication with the court.

That natural justice, in so far as it has been concerned with mutual comprehension across language barriers, has always understood the connection between language and fairness instrumentally can be demonstrated through a brief survey of the accommodations that have been developed. In the normal context involving a litigant whose mother tongue is neither official language, it is evident that some means must be found of enabling the litigant to understand and be understood. However, rather than use the litigant's language, a means that is not usually convenient to the court, effective communication is ensured through the provision of interpretation services. When the litigant or witness can understand and be understood by using the court's language, even if it is not her mother tongue or preferred language of expression, the law holds that effective communication is adequately served by using the court's language. Natural justice provides no further entitlement. We can infer from this that natural justice does not independently value the use of the litigant's own language for purposes of communication. The litigant's language is regarded as an obstacle to be overcome through interpretation if she cannot use or understand the court's language. Use of the litigant's language is regarded as a luxury at best, a nuisance at worst, if the litigant is able to use the court's language. From the point of view of natural justice, effective communication is the sole objective; the use of the litigant's language is merely one amongst other means to this end. If other equally effective means are available—*a fortiori*, if effective but more convenient and less expensive means are available—natural justice provides no basis for a claim to the comprehensive use of the litigant's own language. In other words, the implicit benchmark for effective communication in the conventional natural justice jurisprudence is the use of the court's language by all participants. Only if that is not possible is accommodation made, and then the most expeditious alternative available—use of interpreters—is the standard means adopted to protect fairness.

Thus because of the instrumental relationship of the use of any *particular* language to the end of achieving natural justice, one must go beyond this rationale in order to justify an entitlement to the use of French and English, in particular. Worse, in the absence of some further rationale, the natural justice argument is open to an uncomfortable inference that it creates two classes of natural justice rights—one for official-language speakers and one for everyone else. If the sort of effective communication required to ensure a fair trial is held to mandate, for French and English speakers, use of one's own language before a court capable of understanding it, yet non-official-language speakers are, at best, entitled to interpreters, it looks as though the latter are entitled to a lesser degree of fairness in their trials (Newman 1993: 178). As long as the objective of language rights is taken to be an enhanced variation of the rationale of natural justice rights, it is bound to seem objectionable to say that French and English speakers are entitled to a higher level of natural justice than anyone else. After all, natural justice rights are a quintessential example of the sort of right that is supposed to apply equally to all persons. But no one contemplates reading the additional protections afforded to speakers of the two official languages back into the general natural justice rights. The constitution explicitly grants official-language rights that go beyond natural justice rights in a number of ways, making them special rights. If not, the official-language use provisions would be entirely superfluous, a bit of legal frippery. It does not take much boldness of interpretative spirit to hold that these provisions must mean something.

This opens up a second objection to the use of the natural justice model: the effective communication rationale underlying the language-related accommodations made under the rubric of natural justice cannot explain the official-language use rights in so far as they are special. At a bare minimum, the text of the various official-language use provisions unambiguously accords French and English use rights that are wider than natural justice rights in four respects. First, whereas the general freedom to speak one's own language is ordinarily confined to those cases in which the litigant is incapable of speaking the language of the court,[9] this restriction does not apply to official-language speakers. If a Cantonese- or Ukrainian-speaking litigant can speak English, for example, he will be required to do so; a francophone who can speak English is still entitled to use French if he chooses. Secondly, natural justice rights are limited to parties and witnesses, while the official-language rights apply to anyone involved in judicial proceedings. For example, courts have required lawyers appearing before them to speak the language of the court, even when they cannot so require a party or witness. However, a lawyer is a person for purposes of s. 133 and therefore enjoys the same right as a litigant to choose between French and English. That is, a lawyer may speak French before an anglophone bench unimpeded, whereas he could be prevented from speaking Cantonese. Thirdly, litigants have the right, under ss. 133, 23, and 19, to submit documents in either official language. There is no right, provided by natural justice or otherwise, to submit documents in any other language. If documentary evidence in a non-official language is submitted, it is up to the litigant to produce an accurate translation for the benefit of the court. Finally, the right to use French or English includes the right that one's representations be included in the court record in their original tongue (*R. v. Mercure* 1988). The communications of speakers of other languages will appear only in the translated version.

These rights held by French and English speakers go beyond natural justice and cannot be explained by appeal to the effective communication objective that informs natural justice rights. Effective communication can be served adequately, often better, by requiring anyone who is able to speak the court's

---

[9] *R. v. Berger* (1975), 27 C.C.C. (2d) 357 (B. C. C. A.); *R. v. Reale* [1973] 3 O.R. 905, aff'd [1975] 2 S.C.R. 624 (S.C.C.). Failure to provide an interpreter does not deny a fair trial if it is found that the litigant was capable of understanding what went on, even if he or she had some difficulty. *R. v. Kent, Sinclair and Gode* (1986) 40 Man R. (2d) 160 (Man. C. A.).

language to do so; by expecting litigants to hire lawyers capable of and willing to use the court's language; by requiring litigants to adduce documents in the court's language; by incorporating translations into the court record. The effective communication rationale cannot explain any of these special features of the official-language use rights. After examining the Supreme Court's explanation of the official-language use rights, I will come back to an alternative understanding that goes beyond the instrumental and incorporates the sense in which the use of one's own language in a public setting like a court has intrinsic value.

The Political Compromise Model: Language Rights as Constitutional Horse Trade

The alternative rationale for the official-language use rights offered by the court is implicit in its characterization of them as 'based on a political compromise rather than on principle' (*MacDonald* v. *City of Montreal* 1986: 500–1; *SANB* 1986: 578). This seems to justify, in the judges' minds, giving these rights a very restrictive interpretation. In so far as the text unambiguously requires some special right for French and English speakers, the courts will have to respect it, but there is no need or warrant for interpreting the text generously from the point of view of the rights claimant, as is typically done in the interpretation of other constitutional rights. Unfortunately the court said very little to flesh out this idea of political compromise rights that would explain why this justifies second-class status (Green and Réaume 1990: 564). While a variety of features of language rights are identified that distinguish them from traditional rights, none of these justify engaging in a narrow and restrictive interpretation. What further understanding of the notion of a right based on political compromise might explain the court's interpretative attitude? In what sense are s. 133 and related rights a political compromise?

Rights created by law can represent a compromise in at least two different senses. First, the legal provision may represent a compromise between two conflicting principles, both of which are valid. The compromise may then involve incorporating some play for each of the principles without giving either full sway. It is hard to see, though, how this could justify the sort of automatic restrictive interpretation employed in *MacDonald* and *SANB*. Why should anyone think that such a narrow reading is guaranteed to respect the compromise? Instead, one would expect the courts to investigate the two conflicting principles to understand the sweep of each and then to look to the text for indicators as to the scope to be given to each in order simultaneously to respect the other to the extent possible. So this cannot be the kind of compromise Beetz J had in mind, since he articulates no competing principles and engages in no such process of reciprocal tailoring. Indeed, the fact that these rights are referred to as representing a *political* compromise, and that they are explicitly distinguished from constitutional rights grounded in principle, suggests another interpretation.

The idea must be more like this: the inclusion of these provisions reflects a political power struggle between two interest groups as a result of which one side mustered enough power to insist on a provision in its interests, forcing the other side to compromise its own objectives.[10] The interest group behind the provision may not have been strong enough to get everything it would have liked; thus there may be compromise on both sides. On this understanding of compromise the only normative foundation for the com- promise provision is the raw political power of the interest group capable of forcing its inclusion. There may be nothing morally wrong in a group pursuing its interests in this way, but nor would there have been anything wrong in not including the provision if the 'other side' had had the political power to resist. While this conception of compromise is fraught with con- ceptual ambiguity (Posner 1982: 584–9), the intuition grounding a restrictive interpretative policy for such provisions is clear. Concessions that were wrested by force of political strength might have to be observed to the letter, but one would have no reason to read them any more generously than neces- sary. A generous interpretation would illegitimately give one party more than it was able to negotiate.

It is worth fleshing out some of the assumptions underlying this con- ception of linguistic political compromise. Despite the use in the constitution of generic phrasing guaranteeing *any person* the right to use *either* official language, the purpose of these rights must be to enable speakers of English and French when they are in a minority to use their own language rather than the majority language. The prospect of a federal court or a Manitoba court requiring an anglophone to speak French or a Quebec court requiring a francophone to speak English is so fantastic as to make ridiculous the idea that constitutional protection against it is necessary. The notion of political compromise articulated above implies that these minority linguistic commun- ities mustered the political power to wrest this concession from the majority community. To see this as a concession without foundation in principle, one would have to argue that the majority would have been perfectly justified in creating public institutions such as the judicial system exclusively in its linguistic image, but was forced by the minority to include some scope for use of their own languages. Thus the argument assumes that linguistic homo- geneity in such institutions is the norm and legitimately so, and that the language used should be the majority's. The more strongly it is assumed that unilingualism is legitimate, the more it will make sense to interpret restrict- ively any departure from that norm. Missing from this picture is any sense

---

[10] For an analysis of such an 'interest group theory' of legislation generally, see Posner (1982).

that the minority may have a legitimate intrinsic interest in the use of its own language. Instead, the image is one of arbitrary wilfulness coupled with the political strength to enforce it.

The Intrinsic Value of Linguistic Recognition in Public Institutions

A more unattractive picture of the foundation of official-language use rights than that described by the Court can scarcely be imagined. But there is another way to tell the story that highlights the intrinsic value to a community of its language and the significance of its use in key public contexts, while still acknowledging its more instrumental value.[11] The flourishing of a minority linguistic group includes its participation in public life in its language. This is integral to its ability freely to define itself as a collectivity and fairly to participate in Canadian society. The various concrete rights in the constitution implementing linguistic security can be seen to advance both the intrinsic and instrumental interests in language. On the instrumental side each set represents an important sphere of activity valuable independently of the language in which it is conducted—political institutions, government services, education, and the judicial system. Beyond the achievement of aims that can be understood independently of the language in which they are accomplished, each of these spheres is also a component of the life of a language community and as such is intrinsically related to its well-being. An important part of this picture is the language of the public life and public institutions of one's society.

From this perspective it makes sense that the constitution seek to make the most important aspects of the country's political institutions accessible to minority-language communities. The scope of life which can be conducted in one's own language is thereby importantly expanded to include interaction with government agencies and participation in political institutions, including the courts. In so far as this interaction has instrumental value—improving one's ability to win one's court case, for example—communication in one's own language obviously serves this instrumental purpose. More importantly, the operation of public institutions in a minority language advances the intrinsic expressive interest in language use by making the state and its institutions a full participant in the life of the community and the members of the group full participants in public life. In this respect access to public institutions has an important participatory dimension. Bilingualism makes important governmental bodies seem less like alien forces which control the minority without being accessible to them (Breton 1986) and more like parts of the community. There is no better way to devalue a community and encourage resentment than to force its members to use the majority language

---

[11] This account recapitulates and builds on the one I outlined in Réaume (1991: 53–4).

in order to be able to participate in the public life of their country. Thus the symbolic importance of access to public institutions is enormous, even for those who will never end up before a court.

Recognition of this intrinsic value in the ability of minority official-language communities to use their own language in court argues in favour of requiring the government to meet the specific responsibilities imposed upon it in a spirit of becoming a full participant in the linguistic life of both official-language communities. From this perspective it is insufficient merely to refrain from interfering with the language use of the minority. The flourishing of a language community means that there must be full communication in that language within the community. If government is to be a part of this community, it must be prepared to communicate with its members in their own language. The more fully this is realized, the more the minority can feel comfortable with these institutions as representative of their linguistic community; the more they can feel that public institutions are open to them, belong to them. If official participation in the linguistic life of the minority is too grudging or artificial, this will cut off from the minority a crucial aspect of social life. Because of the range of benefits that can accrue in this way—instrumental and non-instrumental—linguistic security is best served if government services, including judicial services, are organized within minority language communities so that they are provided largely by members of that community.

Adoption of this rationale for the official-language use rights should also have led to a different response to the argument that s. 19 of the Charter must be read in light of s. 16's declaration of the equality of the two official languages and interpreted in this spirit of equality. Although recognizing that s. 16 contains some principle of equality of status between the two languages, Beetz J, in *SANB*, nevertheless concluded that this equality was not violated by his interpretation because either language could be used, in his narrow sense, before the courts (*SANB* 1986: 578). There was no acknowledgement that a majority-language speaker who exercises his right will be much better off than a minority-language speaker who does so; that the court will seem a much less alien environment to the former than to the latter. In other words, Beetz J interprets the equality principle in s. 16 in the most formalistic way imaginable, failing to consider the impact of the equal right to use one's language in his narrow sense. He does not consider the possibility that the declaration of equality was meant to indicate that the aim of the drafters was a broader equality of respect between the two official-language communities. If this is the interpretative stance dictated by the idea of language rights as political compromise rights, it makes all too painfully obvious where the balance of political power actually lies.

A recognition of the intrinsic value of official-language use should lead us to the conclusion that these provisions are designed to guarantee each language community, when it is in the minority, substantially the same access to these institutions in their own language as the majority enjoys. These institutions are meant to be integrated as fully as possible into both communities. This calls for access to court staff and judges who are capable of dealing with litigants in their own language. Section 16 of the Charter, which recognizes the equality of status of Canada's two official languages, should have been seen as reinforcing this interpretation.[12] This equality cannot be the hollow one of the equal freedom to make one's own phonetic noises before a court. If it were, the result would clearly be that local majorities would be greatly advantaged over local minorities. One is not only more comfortable with and better able to communicate with others who speak one's own language, but also more likely to feel affinity for state institutions capable of providing service in one's own language.[13]

Salt in the Wound: Useless Language Use Rights

The intrinsic value description of the rationale of the official-language use rights puts them in the context of the other language rights guaranteed by the constitution to reveal a whole that is arguably greater than the sum of its parts. It also highlights the intrinsic importance to people of their own language, while recognizing that this intrinsic importance is to some extent bound up with the use of the language for instrumental purposes. By contrast, the Supreme Court's approach is not only devoid of a conception of the intrinsic importance to minority linguistic communities of the use of their language before the courts, but defines a right that in fact has no instrumental benefits and indeed will often impair the right-holder's ability to further her

---

[12] That these rights must be informed by the principle of equality between our two official language communities was also recognized by Wilson J in *MacDonald* v. *City of Montreal* (1986: 538): 'The purpose of the constitutional guarantee . . . would appear to be to put the two languages on an equal footing . . . and afford protection to each of the two founding linguistic groups from the intrusion and ultimate dominance of the other . . . This purpose is not satisfied by imposing an obligation on the province to deal with an English speaker in either English or French. Indeed, the only type of obligation that can fulfill the purpose underlying s. 133 is one which requires the province's courts to deal with an English speaker in English and a French speaker in French.'

[13] This requirement of equal treatment is obvious with respect to parliament. Despite Beetz J's blindness to the point, if francophone members had no assurance that provisions would be made to enable others to understand them in the House, the potential for meaningful participation would be eliminated. Of course we cannot require that all Members of Parliament be directly able to understand members of the other language group, but personal bilingualism is not necessary. It is significant that without any prodding from the courts the government has recognized its obligation to provide translation for Members of Parliament. This surely is not only for political reasons in the narrow sense, but because it is accepted that members legitimately expect both to be understood and to understand as a necessary condition of being able to participate—both in the sense of getting their message across and in the sense of feeling a part of the institution.

objective in being before the court in the first place. The combined effect of the attribution of the right only to speakers or issuers, the idea that the corresponding duty is one of non-interference, and the conceptual segregation of language rights and natural justice rights results in the definition of official-language use rights that end up protecting very little of even instrumental value. Natural justice provides the protections that are most important, obviating an appeal to official-language use rights. Where natural justice runs out, the special rights provided by the constitution are virtually useless. Let me demonstrate.

Official-language use rights give participants in a judicial proceeding the right to use French or English as they choose, without limitation. According to the Supreme Court, however, these rights give one no right to comprehension. For this, one must look to natural justice, which provides for the right to an interpreter. This positive right, however, is confined to those who *cannot* understand or speak the language in which the trial is conducted. Applied to the case of minority francophones and anglophones, this will mean that, in most cases, those exercising minority official-language rights will not be entitled to an interpreter because many members of the two minorities are functionally bilingual.[14] A strictly negative interpretation of the official-language rights means that although a party or witness who wishes to speak a different official language from the court is entitled to do so, the court is under no obligation to provide translation.

Secondly, the natural justice right to an interpreter is confined to parties and witnesses.[15] Thus it has been held that a lawyer who cannot understand the language used by the other party (or the court) is not entitled to an interpreter.[16] Litigants' right to an interpreter is based on the right to be 'present' at one's trial and to be able to respond to the case against one. Witnesses are entitled to interpretation services because they are assisting the court in adjudicating the merits of the case. Neither of these rationales cover lawyers

---

[14] This, indeed, was the approach taken in *Mercure*, in which the Supreme Court held that there had been no need for an interpreter at the trial because there was no evidence that the accused was not capable of understanding English (*R.* v. *Mercure*, 1988: 273–4). However, there are also cases holding that the person asking for assistance is the best judge of whether he is capable of understanding the court's language, and the court should not enter upon a detailed examination of the person's capacities. However much these cases extend the right to an interpreter, though, it will not be enough to cover all cases of the invocation of the s. 133 right (*R.* v. *Petrovic* (1984) 47 O.R. (2d) 97; *Roy* v. *Hackett* (1985), 9 O.A.C. 273. See also *R.* v. *Tsang* (1985), 27 C.C.C. (3d) 365 (B.C.C.A.), and *Serrurier* v. *City of Ottawa* (1983), 42 O.R. (2d) 321).

[15] In this respect it is narrower than s. 2 (g) of the Canadian Bill of Rights, which extends the right to any person involved in any proceedings (*Re Canadian Javelin Ltd. and Restrictive Trade Practices Commission* (1980), 117 D.L.R. (3d) 82).

[16] *Cormier* v. *Fournier* (1986), 69 N.B.R. (2d) 155. In this case, the lawyer was a unilingual anglophone representing a client at a trial that was otherwise to be conducted, by agreement of the parties, in French in New Brunswick.

who cannot understand the proceedings. A lawyer does have the right to use the official language of his choice, but if the court does not understand him or he cannot understand the court, he must provide his own interpreter to participate in the trial.

The denial of the right to be understood under the rubric of the official-language rights also has implications for the worth of the right to submit documents in a language other than the court's. Litigants have the constitutional right to submit documents in either official language. Documentary evidence in a non-official language must be provided in translation for the benefit of the court. In the absence of an official-language right to be understood, the minority official-language litigant is often placed, *de facto*, in the same position. Given a negative interpretation of the right, it seems that the court, while allowing the documents to be filed in their original form, could refuse to have them translated. The litigant would then have no choice but to have them translated himself, which is, in effect, to say that the litigant must file the documents in the language of the court in addition to filing them in his own language.

Let us take stock. Consider the case of a francophone litigant confronted with an anglophone court. It is almost overwhelmingly the case that the francophone community outside of Quebec is bilingual. Nevertheless, a francophone may use French before the Manitoba courts, for example, even if perfectly capable of speaking English. He may file all documents dealing with the case in French. The judge, however, will not be able to understand them, and so they will have to be translated into English, perhaps at the litigant's expense. The litigant can give evidence in French, but again, this will have to be translated, also at the litigant's expense. If we suppose that the litigant has a francophone lawyer, she too will be able to make representations in French which, again, will have to be translated. All of this will be recorded in the language originally used. In *Mercure*, LaForest J. remarked that the record of a trial has use beyond the trial itself (*R. v. Mercure* 1988: 276). The case may be appealed and the appeal court may wish to have recourse to the original words of a witness, for example. However, in the normal course of things, the appeal court judges will also be unilingually anglophone, and therefore will also have to have recourse to the translation. Thus the litigant's case will be decided entirely on the basis of the translation of the record, not on the basis of the record itself. What, then, is the practical value of these rights? They seem to serve no purpose other than providing the symbolic satisfaction of knowing that a transcript of the trial exists in some archive recording that one spoke French rather than English. The actual words that one used will have had no impact on the decision-maker.

On this description, not only is there little practical value in exercising one's official-language use rights, but there may actually be a considerable cost in doing so. First, one may worry that insisting on the exercise of this right may aggravate or annoy an unsympathetic judge.[17] Of course, no judge *should* be influenced by such considerations, but given the history of the relationship between our two largest language communities, this may indeed happen without the litigant being able to prove that the outcome of the trial was affected. Furthermore, even if most judges are in fact capable of rising above such prejudice, a litigant may reasonably fear prejudice based on his experience of hostility towards the use of a minority language in other contexts. Whether actually justified or not, this fear will clearly be a disincentive to the minority-language user to exercise his right. Indeed, as long as language use rights in general are understood purely instrumentally, judges can be forgiven for being impatient with an official-language litigant insisting on the use of her language when she does not need to. Secondly, getting one's message across through a translator is a poor second best to communicating directly with the judge.[18] This is especially so in the case of a lawyer's submissions to the court on her client's behalf. Under these circumstances the litigant would better advance his interests in winning his action if he waived his right to speak French and asked his lawyer to argue the case in English. Add to this the possibility that the minority official-language speaker would not be entitled to an interpreter provided by the court, and the costs of not deferring to the court's choice of language are overwhelming. This makes especially clear the minuscule practical advantage to a lawyer in her personal capacity of the right to use her own official language. If it would be in the best interests of her client to use English rather than French, a lawyer would be in dereliction of her duty to insist on her right to use French (and would undoubtedly quickly be replaced). Thus the lawyer's exercise of her right is tied to the client's and has only as much practical value as the latter.

This demonstrates that the instrumental benefit that accrues to minority official-language speakers because of s. 133 is very small indeed. This should immediately make one ask what the point could have been in entrenching this right in the constitution. This is the question obscured by the court's categorization of language rights as second-class, political compromise rights. The denial of intrinsic value in the ability of French and English speakers to use their own language implicit in this categorization, coupled with the negative instrumental value of the right, makes this a very curious subject for

[17] Anyone who doubts that judges are capable of being so annoyed should consider the remarks of Freedman CJ in response to M. Forest's claim that the production of the relevant statutes in an official French version was imperative to his case in *Re Forest and the Court of Appeal of Manitoba* (1977), 77 D.L.R. (3d) 445 (Man. C.A.). Dewar CJQB noted in *Forest* v. *A. G. Manitoba* [1978] 5 W.W.R. 721 (Man. Q. B.) at 725–6 that this claim had been dropped in the application made to his court. Can it be doubted that this was the applicant's rational response to the negative reaction encountered in the Court of Appeal? For further empirical evidence of litigants' fear of adverse consequences of using their own language, see Cousineau (1994).

[18] See e.g. Barristers' Society (1981). Monnin CJM voiced the same concerns in his dissenting opinion in *Robin* v. *College de St. Boniface* (1984), 15 D.L.R. (4th) 198 at 259.

constitutional protection. It is hard to avoid the conclusion that there is no meaningful point for the narrow right to use either official language. In particular, a purely negative right seems to have no point other than an empty symbolic one. Its purpose cannot even be construed as furthering the instrumental effective communication objectives of natural justice, since the official-language rights provide something more than natural justice only when the person wishing to exercise the right is capable of speaking the court's language but prefers not to. In these cases, effective communication is obviously furthered by abandoning one's constitutional rights. To accord the official-language use rights a merely symbolic purpose fetishizes the two languages rather than treating them as the lifeblood of their respective communities. This attribution of a meaningless purpose to ss. 133 and 19 must be replaced with a richer one. In my view, proper attention to the intrinsic value of the use of either official language in the courts coupled with the principle of linguistic equality requires the judicial system to aspire to being fully able to provide litigants with a judge and court staff who are capable of dealing with them in their own language.

3. How Special can Special Rights Be? Why only French and English?

So the court's account of language rights as compromise rights may be unsatisfying. Nevertheless, one might argue that what is special—not to say 'peculiar' (*MacDonald* v. *City of Montreal* 1986: 500)—about the official-language use rights and which can explain the court's reluctance to read them generously is precisely that they are confined to the use of the English and French languages. An account of the intrinsic value of being able to use one's own language and having its use fully accommodated by public institutions may be a better-rounded account of the value of language, but it can't tell us why only two language communities are entitled to this kind of recognition of their languages. Surely, one might say, one's own language is intrinsically valuable to one, *whatever* one's language is. Why, then, should only some languages be accorded official-language status?

Indeed, it follows from my earlier analysis of the intrinsic value of language that each language is valuable in this way to its speakers simply because it is their own creation. However, as I have argued elsewhere (Réaume 1988: 26; 1991: 54–5), because the use of a language in its fullest sense is a group practice and not a wholly individual endeavour, the right to official-language status depends upon there being a viable community of speakers of a particular language. If one interprets the official-language rights as going beyond the freedom to the use of one's language in private and the purely negative right to speak it in public contexts; if language rights require that certain institutions be able to operate in certain languages, size is important. A community must be of a certain size before it is feasible to provide the appropriate services by delivering them within the community itself. There must be enough francophones and anglophones in the respective jurisdictions in which they are in the minority to enable the state to provide enough judges, lawyers, and clerks to be able to handle trials in each of the official languages. Without an adequate population base within the minority community to supply the necessary officials, the state might well be faced with coercing members of the majority to become fluent in the language of the minority in order to be able to provide the necessary services. The courts are not used to taking into account the number of potential claimants there are to a particular right in order to understand its meaning and extent because most Charter rights protect fully individual interests—ones that can claim protection even if no one else benefits but the individual claimant. But in the case of language rights, to recognize the role of numbers in determining which communities are entitled to protection is merely to acknowledge the material context in which the rights exercised by individuals are situated. The good of the carrying-on of one's life in a particular language and the more concrete rights to its use in particular contexts require that there be a language community large enough to sustain a reasonably full life in that language for its members.

At the time of Canadian Confederation the French and English language communities were substantial enough nationally to justify being accorded official status, and the anglophone minority in Quebec was also sufficiently large to be considered viable for these purposes, provincially. When Manitoba joined Confederation, its population was roughly half French-speaking and half English-speaking. What basis could there have been for saying only one of these two communities was entitled to participation in public institutions in its own language? The francophone population of Manitoba has declined in proportional terms since 1870, bringing it perhaps closer to the boundary of non-viability, but this is in substantial part attributable to the part the provincial government has played since then and until very recently in deliberately denying francophone rights. If there was any element of compromise, in the derogatory political sense in which the Supreme Court seems to use it, in these early constitutional provisions, it is that the minority francophone communities in Ontario, Nova Scotia, and New Brunswick were not included in their protection. The unfairness of this was rectified for New Brunswick in 1982; franco-Ontarians and the French-speaking Acadian population of Nova Scotia are still waiting. Similar protections were provided for the francophone minorities in the prairies through s. 110 of the Northwest Territories Act, but, in what might be described as another compromise, when Alberta and Saskatchewan were created, they were given the power to amend or repeal these provisions.

If one understands the compromise involved in the formulation of the official-language rights this way, it puts a whole new gloss on the court's interpretative policy with respect to compromise rights. But the perversity in the logic whereby the right accorded to some minority communities should be read restrictively because it was not extended to all eligible minority communities should be obvious. There may be an unfairness or inequality in the fact that the minority-language communities in each province are not covered by the official-language rights, but it seems an odd way to redress it to read down the rights accorded to those who are protected. It is true that formal equality can be achieved by either levelling down or levelling up in these sorts of circumstances, and that the courts do not have the power to level up—they cannot read into the constitution an extension of the official-language rights to the minority in each province. But to respond by levelling down to the extent permitted by the text, by interpreting the right minimal-istically so as to give those who do benefit as little as possible, is to adopt the wrong conception of equality. Inclusion of a particular language in key public contexts is a right that should be accorded because it speaks to a particularly important interest of the speakers of that language. That the constitutional text does not encompass all speakers of that language or all contexts for its use does not make it any less important to the well-being of those who are covered in the contexts covered.

This same argument can be extended to defend a robust interpretation of the official-language rights even if one takes the view that their limitation to the French and English language communities is wrong.[19] If one thought either that at the time of Confederation there were other linguistic com-munities of sufficient size to warrant protection for the use of their languages in public institutions or that since then other such communities have devel-oped, one might argue that it is unfair that the official-language provisions were drafted so as not to be capable of extension to all viable language com-munities. Nevertheless, this cannot justify a narrow interpretation of the content of the existing official-language rights. To restrict the rights of some minority groups because all minority groups that should have been included were not does not serve the cause of protecting cultural or linguistic differ-ence. Rather it ensures the hegemony of (regional) majorities.

4. Language as Instrument of Nation-Building: Does Bilingualism Breed Disunity?

The objective of minority official-language communities in Canada is to maintain the viability of their language communities and resist assimilation to the majority language. This objective is fully understandable only if the

---

[19] I sought to make this argument more generally in Réaume (1991: 55–6).

intrinsic value to its speakers of their language is recognized. It is in this context that the task of interpreting the concrete constitutional rights that have been accorded to English and French speakers arises. If these rights are interpreted so as to recognize only the instrumental value of the use of one's own language, the resulting protection is unlikely genuinely to contribute to the maintenance of linguistic difference, whatever narrower instrumental benefits may accrue from the exercise of the right. The Supreme Court has started off the interpretation of official-language use rights in the courts on a very bad footing. I have argued that the root of the problem is the failure to see how the right to use either French or English in the courts is tied to the importance of public institutions in the life of a language community, which is in turn tied to the intrinsic value to that community of a full communal life in its own linguistic milieu.

Unspoken in the Supreme Court's approach is an attitude towards bi- or multilingualism that is very common. This view treats language policy as not properly a matter of human rights, but rather to be determined in accordance with considerations of efficiency or social solidarity. Both tend to militate in favour of unilingualism. It is obviously much more convenient and cost-effective if everyone in a country speaks the same language. More interesting is the argument that unilingualism is conducive to national unity. In an age, it might be argued, in which we cannot rely on direct relations between compatriots, nor on some historically effective cultural commonalities such as religious conviction, in order to provide a foundation for social cohesion, a common language could help create a sense of national identity. Fostering linguistic commonality will be conducive to political stability and a greater willingness of citizens to bear the reciprocal sacrifices necessary for the common good. Conversely, recognizing the right of a linguistic minority to live as fully as possible in its own language fosters a separate sense of identity that may ultimately lead to secessionist impulses. Canada, with its history of political wrangles over Quebec's continued participation in Confederation, it is sometimes argued, is a good example of where bilingualism leads. From this perspective, the Supreme Court might be interpreted as attempting to stem the tide of separatism.

In reply, one might first note that even if it is the case that Canadian political leaders made a mistake in 1867, and then ratified and enlarged it in 1982, in entrenching minority-language protections, it is not properly the role of the courts to correct the mistake. It was therefore wrong for the court surreptitiously to attempt to undermine existing constitutional provisions through an interpretation so narrow as to render them a liability to the groups meant to benefit from them. Beyond the politics of constitutional interpretation, however, the argument in favour of unilingualism for the sake of social solidarity is questionable. To begin with, I would take issue with the use of Canada's political history as an empirical example of the risks of bilingualism. Indeed, there is at least as good, if not better, reason to consider Canada as an example of the risks of enforced unilingualism. Despite the existence of a range of official-language rights in the constitution since 1867, they were very widely ignored except within the province of Quebec, where the rights of the economically and politically powerful anglophone minority have always been reasonably well respected. At the federal level and in the predominantly anglophone provinces, minority francophone rights were, until recently, a dead letter. It was 1958 before simultaneous translation was available in the House of Commons (MacMillan 1998: 66); until then franco-phone legislators were simply expected to use the language of the majority. It was 1969 before any serious attempt was made to introduce bilingualism into the federal civil service and to ensure the provision of government services in the language of the citizen (Official Languages Act). It was 1982 before minority-language education rights were guaranteed across the coun-try through their inclusion in the Charter. The growth of separatist senti-ment in predominantly francophone Quebec is as likely to be a reaction to the disregard for minority francophone rights as a product of the provision of those rights.

In any event, whatever the psychosocial explanation of the rise of separat-ism in Quebec as an empirical matter, the unilingualism recipe for social solidarity runs into a more serious moral obstacle. Even if it is true that it is easier to foster social solidarity in a unilingual society, the question of language policy often arises in circumstances in which a country already con-tains two or more viable linguistic communities. Advocating unilingualism for the sake of social solidarity must then entail taking measures to produce unilingualism out of multilingualism. Assuming that no community is likely to agree to abandon its language, unilingualism can be accomplished only by more or less aggressively depriving one linguistic community of the use of its language. Less aggressive measures would include refusing to support the minority language in any way, such as through the provision of services in its language; more aggressive measures would extend to the prohibition of the use of the minority language.

Prohibition might initially seem heavy-handed, but the consequences of the mere refusal of pro-active accommodations are scarcely less disturbing. People are committed to their language, not merely as a means to success in other forms, but as a valuable way of life. As long as they are allowed to use their own language whenever they can do so without calling on government resources, they will continue to try to maintain that commitment, even when it costs them access to other opportunities and goods. In the case of a sizeable linguistic minority, then, it will be many generations before the language will die out. In the meantime, members of that community will become increas-ingly marginalized from the mainstream of society: they will likely become embittered by their linguistic exclusion from public institutions; those who continue to cling to their language will likely be subjected to increasingly sub-standard education and, in turn, will suffer economic marginalization; even those sent to majority-language schools will likely find their needs ill met, leading to an education deficit at least for the first generation to undertake assimilation. The result will be the creation of an underclass, the effects of which are likely to endure for many generations even after the minority language is eliminated. One wonders how social cohesion is likely to be produced out of such systemic marginalization. But even if it were ultimately achieved, the human cost would be staggering and would extend far beyond the deprivation of the minority community of its language. Although much of this argument appeals to side-effects of denying linguistic security that go to non-linguistic interests, these speak to important aspects of the quality of life, and general principles of equality would dictate against imposing such costs. It is only by refusing to acknowledge them that the social solidarity argument for unilingualism can retain any semblance of plausibility. It is true that there are economic and potential social costs attached to official bilingualism, but so too are there economic and social costs of forced uni-lingualism.

This suggests that the strategy of benign neglect, of simply refusing to accommodate minority linguistic practices, may be no less harmful to minority groups than a direct effort to eliminate those practices. Indeed, prohibition backed up by firm enforcement measures may better serve to minimize the economic and social costs of having to adapt to a new language. Yet even strong advocates of the benefits of unilingualism are reluctant to go this far. And in that reluctance we might suspect some dim recognition of the nature of the core value of a language to its speakers. If my account of the intrinsic value of language is at all plausible, it suggests why the extermination of a language for the sake of national unity is no more acceptable than the suppression of a religious community. People find in their mother tongue a marker of identity, an expression of their belonging to a community, a unique and valuable form of human creativity. To refuse them its use, to set out systematically to devalue it and make its use costly, is to show profound disrespect for fellow citizens. When this core value of language is used to inform our understanding of the injustice of inflicting the economic and social costs of transfer to the majority language on members of the minority, it enriches it. To treat mother tongue language use as intrinsically valuable is to position language protections as a species of human rights, rather than treating language as manipulable in the service of social goals such as national unity.

If this argument is successful, it suggests that we look for other ways to foster social solidarity. It is beyond the scope of this chapter to suggest a comprehensive approach to this problem, but let me conclude with the suggestion that the recognition of comprehensive official-language use rights in the judicial setting may do more to contribute to social cohesion than not. I have argued that the best way to guarantee these rights in a way that fosters linguistic security is to organize the delivery of judicial services so that members of the minority community are served largely by members of their own community. However, in most settings it will not be feasible or necessary to segregate the two communities completely. Instead we would expect simply that enough judges and court workers be present in the system to be able to deliver services in the minority language, although they would also provide services in the majority language as well. This would produce a cadre of well-educated, bilingual professionals, able to move between the two communities. In time we would expect that they would be joined by members of the majority community who have undertaken the challenge of becoming personally bilingual. The existence of such a group—each well placed to interpret the other community to its own, each with a stake in deepening cross-cultural understanding rather than exacerbating tensions—could well have a significant trickle-down effect that would foster a form of social solidarity based on respect for difference rather than insistence on homogeneity.[20]

---

[20] Since this article was completed, the Supreme Court of Canada has had occasion, in the case of *R. v. Beaulac* ([1999] 1 S.C.R. 768), to reconsider the attitudes towards the interpretation of official-language use rights criticized here. *Beaulac* concerned the right of an accused person to a trial in the official language of his choice. The majority judgment by Bastarache J. officially rejects the horse-trade conception of language rights and with it the policy of restrictive interpretation. In doing so, the Court implicitly accepts the criticism of the political compromise idea (Green and Réaume 1990), and the general line of analysis urged in this article. We have now a clearer recognition that a narrowly instrumental account of the rationale of official-language rights is inappropriate.

The Court has made the welcome move of grounding its language rights analysis in the attribution of equal status to French and English found in s. 16 of the Charter, and of signalling its commitment to a substantive interpretation of equality. All this removes the barriers erected in *MacDonald* and *S.A.N.B.* to a meaningful interpretation of language rights. However, there remain instrumentalist tinges to the Court's new approach. There is an attitude of greater generosity, but the purpose of language rights is still expressed in terms of 'the preservation and development of official language communities' (791), and 'assist[ing] official language minorities in preserving their cultural identity' (796). This apparent adoption of the 'survival model' of language rights (Green 1987; Réaume 1991) threatens merely to substitute a new end towards which language protections are a means, opening up new avenues for argument that whenever observing a right will not serve the goal it may be disregarded. Given that the language in which any given trial is conducted can rarely if ever be said to have an appreciable impact on the goal of community survival, this means seems to be ill-suited to its alleged end (Green 1987).

Perhaps the very language of 'purposive interpretation' as a constitutional ambition naturally predisposes judges towards instrumental descriptions of the rationale of rights. But this is not without danger. To move away fully from instrumentalist reasoning, the Court's recognition of the equal status of French and English as a substantive and not merely formal ideal still needs to be more firmly rooted in an understanding of the intrinsic value of its language to the members of a community as integral to their communal self-expression.

11

Citizenship and Official Bilingualism in Canada

PIERRE A. COULOMBE

Canada's current policy on official bilingualism responds to the two challenges of citizenship and stability. The policy is grounded in the contemporary dominant discourse on the management of ethnolinguistic diversity. Because linguistic assimilation seriously harms one's identity, it is said, linguistic minorities ought to have special rights to maintain their language, as opposed to having to assimilate as a condition of full and equal citizenship. But this should only apply to sizeable linguistic minorities, such as English- and French-speaking communities. Size being somewhat of a weak criterion for the recognition of rights, though a central one for the allocation of powers, we have traditionally rescued the argument by drawing on history and in- voking the notion of historical priority. Hence there are 'national' minorities that have a special claim to the preservation of their language, and 'immig- rant' minorities that don't. Moreover, these guiding principles for determin- ing language policy are set in the context of Quebec nationalism, which constitutes one of the main threats to the stability of the Canadian state. The architects of official bilingualism were driven not only by a conception of what historical justice requires, but also by the need for counter-measures to the rising secessionist movement in Quebec.

This view of language policy in Canada raises issues that can be imported in the more general discussion on citizenship. First, that the idea of language protection only for English- and French-speaking Canadians is foreclosed by some features of citizenship and compatible with others is telling of the paradoxes of citizenship in a liberal and federal polity. Secondly, the kinds of commitments that underlie official bilingualism are an indication of the nature of the bonds that have grown between Canadians. Examining these

I would like to thank Alan Patten (McGill University, Montreal) and Boris Tsilevich (Riga City Council, Latvia) for their comments. The editors of this volume also made several useful suggestions to improve the arguments. Diane Roussel was helpful in periodically revising the form and content of the text. An earlier version of this chapter was presented during the con- ference 'Citizenship in Diverse Societies: Theory and Practice', at the University of Toronto Law School, on 5 Oct. 1997.

issues can inform us on the moral validity of Canada's federal language policy in light of theories of citizenship, but perhaps more significantly on its potential to express civic solidarity in addition to its role in maintaining the stability of the federation.

Before going any further, it is worth noting that official bilingualism is only one component of Canada's language rights regime. The division of powers between the federal and provincial levels of government means that no one level has full authority over language policy. Each of the various provincial language policies interacts with official bilingualism in complex ways so that we cannot fully understand the language rights regime in Canada by looking at a single policy in isolation. The federal nature of the constitution and the different philosophies that underlie each approach to state language planning has led to a patchwork of language policies rather than anything resembling a uniform system.

Official bilingualism at the federal level has roots in a number of laws and finds its essential principles guaranteed by the constitution.[1] Viewed in its broad applications, official bilingualism has five components. First, the constitution, as amended in 1982, defines English and French as the two official languages in Canada. Secondly, the federal government and its agencies are required to provide services in either of the two languages where demand warrants it. Thirdly, whenever feasible federal public servants are allowed to work in their own language. Fourthly, official-language minorities, that is to say, French-speaking Canadians outside Quebec and English-speaking Canadians inside Quebec, have since 1982 the constitutional right to receive primary and secondary instruction in their language where the numbers warrant. Finally, the federal government encourages individual Canadians to become bilingual by funding immersion programmes, where children receive their schooling in the minority language, and by offering civil servants second-language training. This last component, however, is marginal to the overall policy, which allows citizens to choose which official language to use in governmental settings, rather than citizens becoming bilingual themselves.

Provincial language policies vary greatly from one province to another. Most noteworthy is Quebec's desire to make French the sole public language

---

[1] The Constitution Act 1982 includes a Charter of Rights and Freedoms that entrenches important language rights. In addition to declaring English and French as the two official languages of Canada, the Charter guarantees any member of the public the right to receive federal services in either language where there is significant demand and where it is reasonable to expect such services in either language. It also gives Canadian citizens whose first language learned and still understood is that of the English or French linguistic minority of the province in which they reside, or who have received their primary education in Canada in English or French, the right to have their children receive publicly funded primary and secondary school instruction in that language, where the numbers warrant. These provisions cannot be amended unless the parliament of Canada *and* all provincial legislatures consent to do so.

in the province, which does not always sit well with the federal approach of supporting English and French as having equal status throughout the country, without distinction between Quebec and the rest of Canada.[2] Also interesting is New Brunswick's recognition of the equality of French and English *communities* in the province, somewhat of a departure from the federal government's preference for formulating its recognition in more *individualistic* terms so as to avoid any intimation of Canada being a binational state. Or again, the Northwest Territories' unique Official Languages Act, by officially recognizing six Aboriginal languages in addition to English and French, deviates from other approaches in extending official status to regional languages. The point is that there is a great deal of diversity when it comes to provincial preferences towards language planning.

In the following discussion I will focus on the principles that underlie official bilingualism viewed broadly with the objective of making sense of the interplay between citizenship in the Canadian polity and its embodiment in federal language policy. Whenever relevant, the discussion will include references to provincial policies as well.

I will first provide (Section 1) an historical overview of events that have relevance to the development of official bilingualism construed as a civic commitment. I will then discuss (Section 2) three strands of citizenship that are involved in justifications (and criticisms) of language rights for French- and English-speaking Canadians. I will also examine (Section 3) the degree to which some of these justifications can reflect moral ties between citizens. Finally, I will make (Section 4) a few concluding remarks concerning the state of these ties today. The main question of the chapter is whether we can speak of official bilingualism as reflecting a civic commitment. As we will see, how Canadians go about deliberating on the nature of their commitment and their desire to sustain it goes to the heart of what citizenship requires.

1. Historical Roots

Whether a state can accommodate cultural diversity without undermining the sense of unity and solidarity among its members is a central question in theories of citizenship and in practical policy-making. The question has been central throughout Canadian history, most notably in relation to the French–English duality. In Canada two main sets of answers have been given since the question was asked in 1763, when New France was ceded to Great Britain. The first set of answers was that cultural homogeneity is a prerequisite for

---

[2] On Quebec's language policy, see Comité Interministériel sur la Situation de la Langue Française (1996).

nation-building and for equality of opportunities. On this view, the imperial authorities, and later various provincial governments, would implement a policy of assimilation of the French community. The second set of answers was that the stability of the state requires the toleration, if not promotion, of cultural differences and that equal citizenship should not be equated with sameness. Those who shared this view believed that the building of a common nationality could only be based on the celebration of the French–English duality.[3]

Each answer had its own merit, and we can understand why each could have currency under certain circumstances and could inform British and Canadian constitution-makers. But one or the other option often proved unworkable or undesirable, as is illustrated by the history of the status of the French language prior to the foundation of modern Canada in 1867.[4] The first civilian regime following the British conquest of New France, enacted by the Royal Proclamation of 1763, attempted to impose English law on the French Canadian majority and, by requiring that all candidates for public office abjure the Roman Catholic faith, attempted to exclude them from the administration of the colony. Although the proclamation was silent on the matter of language, its effect on the French language would be detrimental in virtue of the lower status its speakers would have from now on. British immigration to the new colony was encouraged, but when it turned out to be less significant than anticipated, some French Canadians were permitted to hold office in order to ensure the smooth running of the colony. The colonial authorities came to realize that New France would not be so easily absorbed into British North America and that it was in their interest not to disrupt their way of life. Some of the more enlightened governors were also adamant in their refusal to allow the small group of English merchants to exercise dominion over French Canadians. Governor James Murray, for one, refused to create the assembly called for by the proclamation, since he knew it would serve the interests of the English minority, French Canadians having been deprived of their right to participate in public affairs. So did his successor, Guy Carleton, whose initial disposition to side with the English merchants soon gave way to feelings of esteem towards the French Canadians, who, in his opinion, were destined to survive in this portion of British North America.

This prudent and benevolent attitude on the part of some British élites was reflected in the Quebec Act of 1774. Political unrest in the British colonies of New England was growing, and so were the calls by the American Congress for the French Canadians of Quebec to take up their fight against the Crown (Middleton 1992: 37–40). Ensuring the loyalty of the French Canadians and

---

3 For a historical overview of language policy in that perspective, see Cook (1991: 73–81).

4 A good overview of language policy is found in Patry (1981: 23–33). For a very useful and detailed analysis of the various constitutional regimes since the Conquest of New France, see Reesor (1992).

their élites (the landowners and the clergy) would require making concessions. Hence the Quebec Act reinstated French civil laws and institutions and indirectly recognized the use of the French language alongside English in their application.

More changes would have to be made as the American War of Independence brought a sudden increase in Loyalist immigration to the western portion of Quebec (the territory roughly corresponding to today's southern Ontario). Still the British did not resort to a policy of assimilation of the French. They instead passed the Constitutional Act 1791, which separated Quebec into two distinct colonies, each with its own elected assembly, but controlled by a governor: the predominantly English colony of Upper Canada, and the predominantly French colony of Lower Canada—respectively today's southern portions of Ontario and Quebec. The Act meant that each community would be a majority on its own territory. If the new regime was again silent on the issue of language, French and English became the *de facto* official languages in Lower Canada's assembly.

As nationalist sentiments grew in Lower Canada during the first years of the nineteenth century, so did the desire of English merchants and British authorities to reunite the Canadas and impose English once again. Meanwhile, elected leaders in both Lower and Upper Canada felt the time had come for the British to accept responsible government in each colony, the principle according to which no government should govern without the confidence of the elected legislature. The tensions culminated with the rebellions in both Canadas in 1837 and 1838, easily crushed by the British. The solution proposed by Lord Durham, who was sent from Britain to investigate the insurrections, marked a rupture with the policy of accommodation that had prevailed since 1774. Though he sympathized with the calls for responsible government, he believed the root of the problem was to be found in the continued existence of the French community, whose way of life hindered the progress of civilization. Consequently, the solution lay foremost in assimilating French Canadians for the good of all. The British government hence passed the Union Act in 1840, which united the colonies into a single province and whose main feature, in keeping with the assimilationist scheme, was an elected assembly that under-represented the more numerous French Canadians. English was explicitly declared the sole official language of the new province of Canada, though restrictions were not placed on the use of French in the assembly's debates.

This policy was short-lived as Canadian élites of British and French origins began to co-operate in the governing of the united province. Instead of a cohesive English block that would have pursued the assimilation of French Canadians, co-operation between the two communities soon became institutionalized in the practices of government. A rather complex system of dualism characterized the administration of the colony divided in two regions:

Canada West (formerly Upper Canada) and Canada East (formerly Lower Canada). Instead of a single administrative structure controlled by the English, separate sections and ministries allowed each region to look after its own affairs. Even the location of the capital of the united Canada alternated between the two regions. A tacit agreement also provided for a system of double-majority rule, whereby no law that affected a region would be passed without the majority support of elected members from that region. Moreover, reformers on both sides, namely Canada West's Robert Baldwin and Canada East's Louis-Hippolyte LaFontaine, struggled in concert for responsible government against those who wished to uphold Lord Durham's project and British imperial control. They eventually formed the first responsible coalition government in 1847. By 1848 both languages enjoyed official status.

The question of unity and diversity also underlay the 1865 debates on a new arrangement between the French and English Canadians and other colonies of British North America. Some favoured a union of the colonies under a single assembly. John A. Macdonald, representative for Canada West, believed that a political system that absorbed regional identities into a single nation under a single government would best avoid the flaw that, in his opinion, had caused the American Civil War: states with too much powers. Some argued for a federal system that would allow each colony to preserve its identity while joining with others for common purposes. George-Étienne Cartier, representative for Canada East, put forward the idea of a political nationality that would at once transcend and safeguard the multiple identities under a federal union. Understanding that the proposal for a legislative union would lead to an impasse, Macdonald accepted federalism as the only possible compromise—though his preferences for a strong central government none the less permeated the final agreement, the British North America Act of 1867. The new regime, which forms the basis of Canada's present-day constitution, gave provinces jurisdiction over local matters, but also over those matters considered central to their identity, most notably education. Section 133 of the Act also recognized a limited legislative and judicial bilingualism in that English and French could be used in the parliament and courts of Canada as well as in the legislature and courts of Quebec.

Until the passage of the Official Languages Act in 1969 the rights of the francophone minorities were repeatedly violated by most provincial governments. In the name of uniformity, most English-speaking provinces moved to dismantle the Catholic school system or severely restrict instruction in French. For a number of political and legal reasons, the federal government and the courts were either unable or unwilling to stop the harmful actions of provincial majorities. It was not until the rise of Quebec nationalism in the 1960s that the mood of the country, with much unease, shifted to a more tolerant mode. The fear of Quebec secession persuaded the English Canadian intelligentsia that the spirit of Confederation had to be revived. Committed federalists from Quebec made their way to Ottawa in order to bring changes that would make the whole of Canada, not just Quebec, the home of French Canadians. From this emerged the policy of official bilingualism.

In short, the assimilationist project of the Royal Proclamation soon gave way to the recognition of French culture and institutions under the Quebec Act, and that of the Union Act gave way to federalist practices and an official bilingualism that would later be included in the British North America Act. After a century of infractions to the moral contract that had given birth to Confederation, official bilingualism was finally born in 1969 and its essence later entrenched in the Constitution Act of 1982. Throughout Canadian history decisions to deny or recognize the French language were most often dictated by circumstances and instrumental considerations, such as the need for stability and efficiency (Patry 1981: 31). They were also concrete manifestations of the opposite philosophies of cultural homogeneity and cultural pluralism. But as the uneasy coexistence led to closer co-operation in common achievements and the building of a political community, the status of French became tied with the issue of citizenship.

2. Three Strands of Citizenship

Debates about language rights in Canada reveal different facets of citizenship. One perspective on citizenship only allows a thin definition of language rights and is distrustful of far-reaching claims. Another view invokes an historic contract between the national communities, the terms of which ought to be accepted by recent immigrants. Yet another view emphasizes the importance of democratic deliberations in the ongoing formulation of cultural policies. These different perspectives on citizenship, from which are derived different kinds of justifications for language rights, coexist awkwardly. In order to make sense of this, I will examine three strands of citizenship to which correspond three kinds of justification for accepting or rejecting the various claims.

(i) Liberal Strand

The first strand, which can be labelled the liberal strand, speaks of the equal freedom and dignity of all human beings as moral persons. Against particularistic criteria of membership and inequality before the law, it states that all individuals should be recognized as equal members of the political community. Public institutions should be arranged in such a way that these principles are the only relevant ones in the distribution of social benefits and burdens. Derived from this idea of citizenship is the moral vocabulary of human rights, which tells us something about how we ought to relate to one another as human beings, about the things we should or should not do to each other, regardless of time and space. Rights discourse provides a vocabulary for articulating moral relations that have universal validity and a legal framework for entrenching the protection of basic interests in the constitution of a country. This view of citizenship often (though not always) rests on the assumption that certain principles have natural or supernatural origins, and therefore that they are non-negotiable, even in the context of democratic deliberation.

This liberal feature of citizenship entails particular kinds of language rights, though these can only go so far because of their implied universalism. To take an example, protection against certain forms of discrimination and interference on the basis of one's mother tongue is, and can practically be, owed to all human beings. The state can easily uphold its duty, say, not to forbid individuals from speaking their language at home; it needs only to refrain from interfering. But multiple claims to work in one's language would cancel each other out, or might require ranking according to a criterion offensive to the value of equal treatment (MacMillan 1983: 351; Coulombe 1995: 99–100). This is a subset of the familiar distinction between negative duties, where the respect of rights involves an absence of interference, and positive duties, where intervention is, on the contrary, necessary on the part of the duty-holder. A universal and equal treatment of linguistic interests is compatible with negative duties of non-interference, anything more being unfeasible. These kinds of language rights are construed as human rights on their own, or at least derived from the basic interest we all have in being treated equally and being free to express ourselves.

Of course, there is in Canada a deep-rooted respect for basic liberal values inherited from Great Britain and more recently entrenched in the constitution via the Charter of Rights and Freedoms. The problem lies elsewhere. Claims made in the name of collective interests, such as those that have been made by French Canadians, can be denied in the name of equality between individuals. French Canadians, it is sometimes said, ought to benefit from the equal protection of the law, no more, no less, just like everybody else. Communities such as French Canada, however, seek forms of accommodations that reach far beyond the rights against discrimination and interference on the basis of language. They seek a recognition of their language as members of a distinct, full-fledged society within the larger Canadian state. Since they will not allow the free market of cultures to determine the (predictable) outcome of the contact between the vulnerable French language and the powerful English language, they demand that the state intervene. Such intervention is often judged inconsistent with equality of treatment.

It is interesting to note that the Charter of Rights and Freedoms' provisions on official bilingualism are formulated in terms that are as universal as possible ('*Everyone* has the right to use English or French . . .'), and that even when they are more restrictive ('*Citizens* of Canada have the right . . .'), they still cast a wide net. These two formulations avoid any suggestion that the duties to promote either the French or the English language are owed to particular individuals, or at least to particular Canadians or communities, in keeping with the core liberal value of equality. In other words, the right-bearers are not peoples of English and French descent, but all individuals or citizens regardless of origins. Former Prime Minister Trudeau explained how 'the Charter always seeks to define rights exclusively as belonging to a person rather than a collectivity', and that 'this preference holds good even where the official languages are concerned: individuals, not linguistic groups, are ensured of their right to use any language' (Trudeau 1994: 86–7).

Still, the recognition of the French language clearly has roots in the historical entitlements of French Canadians. What seems to be a contradiction between descent-related rights and universal human rights may in fact reveal an attempt to reconcile different kinds of contracts, as we will see below.

(ii) Historical Strand

Conventional rationales for recognizing language rights for some communities and not others have their root in a different strand of citizenship. This second strand calls upon historical commitments to justify the granting of language rights to the French- and English-speaking communities, commitments that take the shape of a contract. These two groups are considered founding communities in the sense that Canada's basic political structures and institutions are the product of time-honoured compromises and collaborations between them, as was examined in Section 1. They are entitled to the preservation of their respective identity, the argument goes, because of their historical role in the construction of Canada as a political community. Henri Bourassa, one of French Canada's leading intellectuals during the first half of the century, conceived language rights for French Canadians not only as being ordained by God's natural law, but also as a result of just desert: 'The strength and extent of our rights in the Canadian Confederation', he wrote in 1902, 'are measured by neither the number of our people nor by the size of our fortunes' (Bourassa 1970: 105; MacMillan 1982). French Canada's past contribution to preserving the integrity of what was left of British North America created an obligation on the part of the British to preserve the French language. The 1867 Confederation itself could not be interpreted only as a contract between British colonies, but also as one between French and English Canadians. This tacit understanding, Bourassa believed, should be integral to the spirit and letter of the constitution and in future interpretations of it. The idea of a historical contract between French and English has always been central to French Canadian political thought. It was certainly part of the frame of mind of those who would later reflect upon the state of French–English relations in the face of growing nationalist feelings in Quebec. One such reflection took the shape of the Royal Commission on Bilingualism and Biculturalism in the 1960s, whose co-chair, André Laurendau, subscribed to Bourassa's dualism (McRoberts 1997). Though the Official Languages Act brought forth by the Trudeau government in 1969 only partly conformed to the conclusions of the commission, it too implied the idea of a historical contract.

When we examine official bilingualism in light of citizenship viewed as a contract, and address the factors that allowed these legal and moral entitlements to develop, history indeed appears to be an inescapable source of justification. Perhaps this would not be troublesome if, following the original contract, Canada's immigrants had been limited to people of French and English descent. The country's multicultural heritage, however, is such that no ethnic group, French and English included, can today claim to represent more than a quarter of the total population. In short, the multi-ethnic character of Canadian society leaves no doubt. What is less obvious is how to approach justifications for official bilingualism in the context of increasing ethnic diversity.

There is a cluster of views according to which there ought to be authoritative rules about what values are to be central to Canadian citizenship. These values would necessarily include liberal ones, such as the rule of law (and the weak language rights defined above), but also substantive values that are constitutive of the Canadian political culture. What this entails is that the equality of English and French remains a kind of founding principle of the larger political community which recent immigrants must abide by if they wish to become citizens. Immigrants would be required to cut ties with their past, and adhere to the historically defined values of their host country, which include a commitment to its cultural and linguistic continuity. When immigrants join Canada, they do so as individuals with no prior claim to the protection of their languages other than that accorded by universal human rights. In this view, Canada is, in the words of Peter White, 'a country of two and only two public or official languages and cultures; a dual melting pot, or perhaps a double-boiler, but not a mosaic' (White 1992: 6). Naturally, recent immigrants, not being members of the historical community, may be unable to feel a deep commitment to its cultural continuity. They may have instrumental reasons for respecting the terms of entry, such as benefits to be gained, but no deep-seated identification with the source of the common allegiance that gave rise to cultural policies (Weinstock 1995: 107). Regardless, this view would entail a policy of acculturation to mainstream Canadian society, construed as a bicultural state.

Canada as a historical contract between English and French communities, the terms of which include at the very least protection of the two languages, is problematic on a number of fronts. Debates surrounding the Royal Commission on Biculturalism and Bilingualism, and later proposals to amend the constitution,[5] clearly brought this out. The presence of Canadians whose ethnic descent is other than French or British and increased immigration from non-Western societies challenge the illusion of a clear-cut bicultural political community to which a dualist conception of citizenship might once have been suited. For some, dualism spells injustice for Canadians of other origins who feel that granting official status to French is tantamount to a distinction between first- and second-class citizens. The charge is not against the idea that rights can have their source in historical events, but that the singling out of one community requires a reading of history that unfairly ranks the contributions of the many peoples who also built this country. Furthermore, the original bargaining process may have been unfair given the presence of weaker parties, most notably Aboriginal peoples. Vernon Van Dyke argues that 'It is unjust to accept or assume status and rights for states, nations, and "peoples", but to reject them for ethnic communities that are also historically constituted' (Van Dyke 1995: 54). If one agrees with his statement, a logical course of action would be to expand the official list of founding peoples. Perhaps this could be done on a regional basis so that, for instance, various languages be recognized as official, but only in the regions where they are spoken.[6] The general idea is that granting language and educational rights for French Canadians would entail granting the same recognition to other groups (MacMillan 1982: 421). But the exclusive nature of far-reaching language rights renders such recognition impracticable, hence the call for an undifferentiated citizenship that abandons this ranking exercise altogether and abolishes the policy of granting official status to any group at all.

Communities tell different stories about their place in Canada's history, each revealing a facet of reality. These equally valid stories do not converge, and so each community seeks recognition of its own narrative. One such narrative that has currency today is that Canada's policy of official bilingualism reflects a distribution of rights, perpetuated in constitutional arrangements, that is the legacy of an unequal distribution of power. The existence of a given set of language rights is therefore bound up not only with common understandings about historical entitlements, but with historical power struggles as well. Quite simply, the fact that the French were a substantial national minority gave them more power than, say, the Ukrainians, who were not. Cultural forces at play since the Conquest of New France in 1760

---

[5] One constitutional reform package proposed in 1987, the Meech Lake Accord, illustrates this tension. Quebec was to be recognized as a distinct society, and linguistic duality throughout Canada reinforced. Some Canadians viewed this recognition as condoning the idea of Canada as being made up of two founding peoples, which, according to them, no longer reflects reality.

[6] Manoly Lupul, for example, argues for a more 'elastic' concept of founding peoples that would recognize regional languages. See his 'Comments' in Lupul (1991: 307–9).

congealed, as it were, and became the reference base on which can be measured various claims to recognition.

The policy of official multiculturalism, enacted by the Trudeau government in 1971, can be viewed as a clumsy attempt to address the conflict between official bilingualism and multi-ethnicity. The Commission on Bilingualism and Biculturalism had defined Canada as being composed of two distinct societies, one English-speaking and one French-speaking, though each could be considered multi-ethnic. Worried that adopting the commission's dualistic vision of the country would only reinforce the notion of two separate nations and eventually lead to Quebec's secession, Trudeau instead proposed a policy of multiculturalism within a bilingual framework. In a spirit of fairness, the policy also meant to adapt the Canadian political community to the realities of an increasingly multi-ethnic pluralist society whose complexity makes it difficult to see membership in dualistic terms.

The federal multiculturalism policy is multifarious and has evolved over time. Its main components include cultural preservation (funding cultural events, heritage retention programmes, etc.) and inclusion (removing the barriers to full participation in society). More recently, the policy on official multiculturalism has shifted its priorities away from heritage retention and towards education about principles of common citizenship, participation, and inclusion (Fleras 1995: 197–217). This is part of the overall mandate of the Department of Canadian Heritage, which is 'to provide a "sense of a country" which respects the many ways to be a Canadian', and to ensure that barriers to integration be lifted so that minorities find their way into the mainstream of Canadian life (Doré 1993: 232–3). In keeping with the 'bilingual framework', official multiculturalism does not extend to the promotion of institutional multilingualism, though it involves limited state support for heritage, non-official languages, such as the funding of bilingual school programmes (for example, English–German or English–Ukrainian in Prairie provinces) and community-based private initiatives.

Understood in this manner, official multiculturalism operates within the historical contract model of language rights. It is as if the historically based commitment to official bilingualism had been modified to accommodate multi-ethnicity. Having provided historical justice to two of the founding peoples, the state would have felt obliged to provide justice to the other peoples as well. If such is the rationale, we can understand why the relationship between official bilingualism and official multiculturalism has been criticized on both sides. Where minorities other than French and English are concerned, official multiculturalism is not as entrenched in public institutions as official bilingualism is, thus denoting inequality between communities. Section 27 of the Charter of Rights and Freedoms, for instance, instructs judges to interpret the constitution in a manner that is consistent with Canada's multicultural heritage, but does not grant substantive rights such as those of ss. 16 to 20 of the Charter pertaining to French- and English-speaking minorities. For francophone minorities, the symmetrical treatment of cultures that official multiculturalism implies translates into a rejection of the dualist model and a folklorization of their identity into the Canadian mosaic.[7]

This tension between official multiculturalism and official bilingualism reveals the difficulty of constructing citizenship when communities clash over their claims to official status and their conceptions of equality. If it is hard to avoid talk of historical priority, perhaps another strand of citizenship can help in the formulation of a different kind of contract.

(iii) Democratic Deliberation Strand

A third strand of citizenship is indeed present in Canada's language policy. This strand features the notion of a contract between citizens of a particular polity, but without any a priori reference to history. While appealing to the values of equal respect that have universal validity and to those values that are generated throughout history, it relies mostly on the public deliberations of citizens of the political community, who determine the terms of membership. These terms acquire legitimacy because they are authored by the citizens of that polity or by their representatives. Here, rights discourse will again provide the citizenry with concepts to express principles of justice so derived, but without being unduly constrained by talk of either universal or historical entitlements. Stated differently, if there are reciprocal rights and duties to be derived from our common humanity and others that we acquire through historical events, there are also those that arise from our deliberative efforts as citizens of a given political community.

The notion of citizenship as being grounded in democratic deliberation cannot admit of a contractual arrangement whose script has already been written.[8] A political community is not immutable and fixed, but fluid and forever changing. Public deliberations on basic political structures and institutions are an ongoing process. And since the choices a society makes partly depend on its sociological make-up, changes in this make-up will naturally influence the kinds of choices that are made (Leydet 1995: 128). Once immigrants become citizens, they are equally entitled to participate in the determination of the institutions and policies pertaining to language planning. The more general point is that the virtues attached to this strand of citizenship, such as the equal right of participation, conflict with practices that exclude some citizens (i.e. of origins other than French or English) from public debate on the basis that their participation will fragment the consensus and undermine the historical contract. Giving this argument a more positive slant, it

---

[7] Michel Bastarache analyses the two policies in Bastarache (1987: 63–75).

[8] This point is made by Jeremy Waldron in his chapter in this volume.

would mean that the legitimacy of the policy on official bilingualism is contingent upon the quality of the public deliberations that produce it. This last approach to justifying official bilingualism is the one that can best sustain a stable consensus. But it is also the most demanding, for it requires that there be a public reason for the policy, one that citizens would find reasonable as free and equal members of the political community. The objective is to ensure that a decision on matters of language policy would be endorsed in a spirit of civic friendship.

We need to consider briefly the sorts of reasons and arguments that would be admissible in a public deliberation about language policy. For example, should there be constraints on majority rule to avoid a situation where the majority might be tempted to adopt the thin liberal view of language rights? Should it be permissible to make a case for recognition on grounds of historical priority? One possible framework for answering these questions is suggested by James Tully, who speaks of three constitutional conventions (Tully 1995). The conventions constitute the norms that should guide our efforts at recognizing and accommodating cultural diversity. First, constitutional negotiations ought to respect each party's understanding of itself (mutual recognition). Secondly, an amendment to the constitution ought to be approved by those it affects, following the principle that what touches all must be approved by all (consent). Thirdly, mutual recognition of the parties' identities must be upheld in new constitutional arrangements, unless parties consent otherwise (continuity). These conventions can have various concrete expressions depending on the situation.

Engaging in a dialogue of this kind might assist Canadians in their search for forms of association that accommodate ethnolinguistic diversity and whose rationale would be persuasive in a spirit of civic friendship. In particular, it could shed light on how 'multiculturalism within a bilingual framework' may have contemporary moral relevance. In that regard, a promising argument is offered by Will Kymlicka. Instead of viewing official multiculturalism as a policy that was uncomfortably grafted on official bilingualism (as discussed above), its adoption has rather served to separate language from lifestyle and ethnic descent. The designation of English and French as the two official, public languages is inescapably tied to the historical fact that Canada was colonized by Britain and France. But to value two public languages over others because of the historical dominance of particular national communities does not equate with privileging their lifestyles and interests. In other words, the promotion of English and French as dominant languages need no longer be associated with the promotion of the lifestyles of citizens of English and French descent. Multiculturalism is thus seen as a means of integrating immigrants into one of the two societal cultures in Canada: francophone or anglophone. Each is characterized by its language and social institutions, but neither of them imposes common religious beliefs and specific lifestyles (Kymlicka 1998a, ch. 3).

Viewing in this way the connection between bilingualism and multiculturalism meets important objectives. It respects the continuity of francophone and anglophone societies, which no longer wish to be defined primarily in ethnic terms. It also provides a significant symbolic recognition of Canadians who do not share the same ethnic continuity with Canadians of French and English descent, but who can today share in the continuity of their respective societal cultures. Finally, it serves as an efficient mechanism for the integration of immigrants, thus removing a barrier to greater solidarity between citizens.

I mentioned that the terms of a constitutional negotiation on language policy acquire legitimacy if they are authored by the citizens of that polity or by their representatives. Democratic deliberations were until recently ill suited for the task of negotiating a moral contract between the various communities. Instead, élite accommodation managed to formulate the policy in terms of reciprocal duties acquired throughout history. It was accepted that French- and English-speaking Canadians should have little to say about it, that they should call upon the state to regulate their coexistence. In fact, the two peoples were better off not having any close interaction, thus preserving their cultural, religious, and linguistic integrity, whereas élites on each side, for their part, had the capacity for common understandings. In the words of Henri Bourassa:

On [our élites] falls the duty of learning English, of drawing close to the elite of the English majority, of thoroughly studying the temperament, aspirations and the traits of English Canada. Moreover, the English elites have the same responsibility. If the most influential and most enlightened of the two races tried to have more to do with each other and got to know each other better, our national future would not be so precarious. (Bourassa 1970: 105; LaSelva and Vernon 1997: 380)

In his view, true equality of status of the English and French languages might grow out of this 'fruitful contact' between élites. Clearly, significant changes to Canada's political culture have taken place since then. Contemporary Canadians increasingly challenge the élitism that characterizes the manner in which decisions on language issues have traditionally been made. We could perceive this as a threat to established policies, where if Canadians have more of a say, they might also be more likely to undo the delicate compromise that had been woven by élites. But we could also see this as an opportunity to nurture an ethic of public discussion and civic solidarity from which can emerge a stable consensus on language policy.

(iv) Weaving the Three Strands

Three strands of citizenship are therefore involved in various justifications for language rights. The first emphasizes the liberal value of equal respect for all human beings, which implies that all deserve equal protection and support of their respective language. Since reciprocity is impossible when claims to such protection and support are far-reaching, language rights are narrowed down to protect individuals against undue discrimination and interference on the basis of their mother tongue. Universal language rights as human rights, however, cannot satisfy the particular demands of national minorities, whose claims reach beyond individual protection. The second emphasizes the value of a historical contract among the peoples who founded the political community and the consequent recognition of their languages in the public sphere. Reliance on history alone, however, is likely to spark feelings of resentment among those who feel cheated by a selective national memory. In reaction, the federal policy on official multiculturalism can be understood as an attempt to append to official bilingualism the equal respect for the cultural heritage of each and every new arrivant. The third strand emphasizes the republican value of the democratic process that defines the terms of citizenship. It does not preclude civic education for citizens and asylum-seekers alike about the historical worth of a given language policy for the good of the overall community. But it does require that no party be excluded from public deliberations. Such deliberation might reinterpret the relation between official bilingualism and official multiculturalism in the respect of mutual recognition and continuity.

Justifications and criticisms of official bilingualism in Canada cut across these three strands of citizenship. Whether the actual policy of official bilingualism can pass the test of public deliberation is a question that remains open. Yet part of the answer would presume an understanding of the nature of the commitments that are involved in supporting the policy. Addressing this issue may tell us something about official bilingualism's potential to reflect civic solidarity.

3. Moral and Instrumental Commitments

In the previous section I touched upon some of the parameters of admissible arguments in the context of a public deliberation on official bilingualism, as well as an argument that could be persuasive to Canadians viewed as equal participants. I would now like to turn to the question of how extensive an agreement on official bilingualism should be. It will be useful to distinguish between two kinds of commitment involved in how Canadians look at official bilingualism, each corresponding to different kinds of tie citizens and communities have with each other.

The first one can be identified as a moral commitment. It is akin to the Rousseauian idea of the foundations of a just state, whereby citizens feel empathy for each other and subordinate their private interests to the public good. In Canada such civic bonds are framed in a federal context, where the recognition and celebration of the worth of each constituent community is also a foundation of justice. Official bilingualism so construed is an expression of a patriotic allegiance to the political community historically constituted. It is derived not from a prudential obligation (i.e. the desire to prevent Quebec's secession), but from a conception of justice that lies at the heart of what it means to be Canadian.[9] No doubt we cannot speak of the moral foundations of a given language policy to the same extent that we can of national social programmes or regional redistribution schemes that clearly seek social justice. Yet in so far as that policy reflects mutual goodwill, not just mutual containment, between French- and English-speaking communities and citizens of various descent, it is sound to speak of it as a moral commitment. This kind of commitment runs deep in Canadian history. It was at the root of prior endeavours at nation-building, most noteworthy when Britain's assimilation project under the Union Act of 1840 failed because of the trust and respect that had grown between the two communities, leading to an official recognition of both languages (Magnet 1995: 10). By 1848 it was evident that some Canadian leaders had achieved more than the stability of the united province and acknowledged a moral commitment. As we saw, contemporary arguments about the value of official bilingualism in a multiethnic society also reveal a renewed moral commitment.

The second kind of commitment that underlies the way we conceive of official bilingualism is instrumental in nature. It involves no moral bonds between citizens, but rather a *modus vivendi* of the sort that Hobbes introduced. Here there is a need to regulate or contain the conflicting interests of individuals, whether these are economic or ethnolinguistic. Less demanding than a moral commitment, a *modus vivendi* ensures a balance between social forces and follows a desire to reduce conflict in a divided society.[10] Viewed this way, official bilingualism becomes a policy of mutual restraint, whereby we will treat our minority well if you treat yours similarly. The policy also serves as a buffer where French and English populations conflict in majority–minority settings. Joseph Magnet shares this view:

The point is that the language rights system is premised on the inevitability of such conflict. Its contribution is to control it as much as possible, to channel it into manageable political and legal processes in order to prevent it from escaping into unmanageable inter-communal conflict which threatens to tear apart the foundation upon which the Canadian state is erected. (Magnet 1995: 83)

[9] This is not unlike the position Leslie Green and Denise Réaume take when they write that 'the claims of the French minority at the national level are based on right, not might' (Green and Réaume 1991: 10).

[10] See Norman (1994: 92). Norman also argues (1994: 92) for the need for a deeper commitment in a federal state: 'Federal partners in [a multilingual] state, then, clearly have both a material and a moral obligation to develop a language policy that will mitigate these factors which both threaten development of a stable overlapping consensus and lead to specific injustices.'

The history of French–English relations is permeated by attempts at producing a *modus vivendi*. For example, the Quebec Act of 1774 protected the social and religious institutions of the French Canadians in the hope that they would not join the rebellious American colonists. The primary goal was one of political expediency, that is, having to deal with rising instability in British North America. The architects of Confederation themselves, by according little protection to official minorities, assumed that the English majority outside Quebec would have an interest in tolerating its French minority or else place the English minority of Quebec in a predicament (Magnet 1995: 13). And later, the suggestion that official multiculturalism was designed by the Trudeau government as a way of undermining the bicultural model of official bilingualism also reflects instrumentality.

A shared moral commitment to official bilingualism is more congenial to the ideal of citizenship. When we reduce language policy to an issue of national security, we are resigning ourselves to *realpolitiks* as our ultimate framework for understanding the value of the union. But the higher goal of citizenship is quite a challenge in a multination state. The absence of a common culture and language and the lack of a common will place obstacles to the development of feelings that engender mutual goodwill. Each member nation also tends to appropriate for its own nationalist purposes feelings of fraternity and fellowship, and to condemn to failure efforts to achieve anything more than a loose association with others, if any at all (LaSelva and Vernon 1997: 35–8). Hence in Canada we often speak of 'two solitudes', of two distinct political communities who, without an identity of interests, cannot take a 'we'-perspective and who ultimately obey their own national imperatives. More accurately, we should speak of four solitudes if we bear in mind some of the barriers that exist between mainstream society and Aboriginal peoples on one hand, and between settled citizens and newly arrived immigrants on the other hand.

These obstacles make moral commitments in a multination state all the more commendable, for the very reason that they are not engendered by close ethnic, linguistic, or religious ties of nationhood, but rather are the product of civic solidarity between peoples who a priori do not share an identity. The kinds of bond involved in two nations' mutual recognition of each other's language are not the same as those of members of a national majority who legislate the promotion of their language, however justified they might be. To take a concrete example, solidarity is less involved (though other moral challenges are) when the legislature of Quebec imposes French as a public language by appealing to the preferences of the French Canadian majority in the province. Official bilingualism, on the contrary, reflects the desire of two societies to share a common political community where goodwill does not come naturally and interests often diverge. It draws from the philosophy of federalism itself, which presupposes such an endeavour.

4. Official Bilingualism as a Matter of Citizenship

While Canadians generally support the federal policy on official bilingualism, there are some who see it as a failure. One recurrent criticism among English Canadians is that they generously went along with the policy with the expectation that it would prevent national break-up. When the Quebec sovereigntist movement did not go away, they felt cheated. Why, then, persist with official bilingualism if the Quebecois are ungrateful? Criticism also comes from within Quebec. The Constitution Act of 1982, though a great achievement as far as official minorities are concerned, was sanctioned without the consent of Quebec's legislature. Fundamental components of official bilingualism were entrenched in the supreme law of the land despite Quebec's objections. The amendment entrenched a symmetrical application of official bilingualism throughout the country, which to some degree impedes Quebec's own efforts to make French the public language in the province. By promoting English in Quebec no differently from French outside Quebec, the federal government in effect privileges English as the dominant language given that the playing-field is unequal from the start. In other words, it is not the English language that needs promotion, even in Quebec, but the French language. Moreover, some critics interpret Trudeau's model of official bilingualism as being in line with a kind of Canadian nation-building that seeks to absorb the Quebecois identity.[11] Finally, considering that the assimilation rate of francophone minorities is still very high in most parts of English Canada, the efficiency of the measures taken since the late 1960s is questionable (Chevier 1997: 13–14, 44). All in all, the critique goes, the policy has failed to serve as an expression of true equality between French- and English-speaking communities. What remains, at best, is nothing but the mere expression of a *modus vivendi* between self-interested individuals or communities; at worst, it is a costly error. And since the arguments about the role official bilingualism plays in appeasing Quebec nationalism and ensuring its loyalty to the federation are somewhat suspect, even the stability rationale seems to rest on a mistake.

But these conclusions seem premature for two reasons. First, if it is problematic to claim that official bilingualism secures the Quebecois' attachment to Canada, it remains likely that abolishing official bilingualism would shake the foundations of the federation. It is a common mistake to believe that

---

[11] For an interesting critique of the impact of 'multiculturalism within a bilingual framework' on Quebec's capacity to integrate immigrants, see Labelle *et al.* (1995: 213–45). Also interesting is Marc Chevier's critical overview of the federal government's language policy (Chevier 1997: 39–44).

because official bilingualism has not prevented the growth of the Quebec separatist movement, abolishing official bilingualism would not threaten national unity any further. Canada's constitutional order, including provisions for official bilingualism, was partly designed to maintain national security and stability in a context of inter-ethnic friction. Joseph Magnet correctly argues that there is 'a tendency to ignore the national security dimension which called the official languages policy into being, and the political struggle for power, resources and survival which continues to surround it on all sides' (Magnet 1995: 81). Such instrumental considerations may not enjoy the aura of moral justifications, but they none the less constitute a sound rationale for Canada's language policy.

There is a second reason that is less tangible but telling of the bonds that exist between Canadians. This can be illustrated with a few examples. In 1988 the Quebec government faced a dilemma. The Supreme Court of Canada had just ruled that some parts of Quebec's language laws, namely the ones that restricted the use of languages other than French on commercial signs, were unreasonable limits to freedom of expression as guaranteed by the Charter of Rights and Freedoms. The government of Quebec, however, decided to invoke a controversial provision of the Charter that allowed it to shield its law from the Supreme Court ruling, and hence to continue to impose French-only signs. In reaction to Quebec's decision, vindictive municipal governments in Ontario declared themselves unilingual English. The episode reflected more than a disagreement about language planning, but a real moral failure. Each side had failed to understand the impact of their actions on the moral contract between French and English. This was not, of course, the first of such moral mistakes. Looking back on the various attacks by English-speaking provincial majorities on French Catholic schools, few are those who would today argue that 'might made it right'. Or again, had the assimilation project of the Union Act of 1840 worked, and Lord Durham's 'problem' been efficiently solved, moral harm still would have been committed. What these examples allude to is the sense of malaise which arises when reciprocal duties towards official minorities are subordinated to political expediency, for what is being harmed here are more than official minorities, but the political community itself, 'like a recurrent virus infecting the Canadian body politic' (Magnet 1995: 15). It may be that Henri Bourassa's 'marriage of convenience' (Bourassa 1970: 103), after all, gave rise to the moral bonds of citizenship.

When we try to redefine some of the terms of belonging in Canada, namely those that pertain to the recognition of identity, we invariably come face to face with the issue of linguistic duality, as witnessed during the debates surrounding various proposals to amend the constitution. We are then confronted with the two questions of solidarity and stability. The first invites us to consider what civic fraternity requires in the federation, while the second warns of the risk of national break-up. These are contemporary versions of old questions. They were the questions asked by Governors Murray and Carleton and leaders of the church following the conquest, by LaFontaine and Baldwin in the aftermath of Durham's report, and by Macdonald and Cartier during debates on a new union. The policy on official bilingualism, very much like federalism itself, evolved into a civic commitment alongside its instrumental purpose. In that sense, recognizing the French–English linguistic duality has been not only a matter of state stability, but one of citizenship as well.

PART VI

The Rights of Indigenous Peoples

12

Three Modes of Incorporating Indigenous Law

JACOB T. LEVY

> It is the folly of conquerors to want to give their own laws and customs
> to all the peoples they conquer. This accomplishes nothing.
>
> (Montesquieu, *Considérations sur les causes de la grandeur des Romains*)

Indigenous minority groups often seek (or have already secured) recognition of their customary legal systems in the law of the wider state. On land use and possession, marriage and family life, inheritance, and a variety of other issues indigenous peoples have legal traditions of their own. They do not wish to see those traditions supplanted or ignored by the laws of the states in which they live.

States can respond in a number of ways. Some of these are morally un-justifiable; to neglect indigenous law completely, or to persecute those who attempt to live by it, are unjust responses. There is, however, a range of more appropriate responses, a variety of policies and legal systems that recognize or incorporate indigenous law in different ways. Once the decision has been made to make *some* accommodation of indigenous law, there remain serious questions about how this is to be done, how best to balance goals like respect for indigenous traditions, protection of the rights of indigenous persons, legal clarity and simplicity, and peaceful and co-operative coexistence with the wider society.

This chapter describes three broad kinds of incorporation of indigenous law: common law, customary law, and self-government. These modes of incorporation have different internal logics, different moral and political implications, and different resulting legal rights of indigenous people. The chapter discusses those differences with reference to the experience of some societies that have incorporated indigenous law in these various ways.

Indigenous law incorporated within the common law is not quite recognized as *law* at all, but as a social situation which creates the kinds of facts which trigger the law of the wider society. The state recognizes indigenous forms of common law rights and statuses. Indigenous land rights might gain legal status though the concept of adverse possession, and indigenous marriages might gain legal status through the concept of common law marriage.[1]

More status is given to indigenous law, and accordingly less to the idea of law common to all citizens, when indigenous law is incorporated as a separate system of customary law, parallel (or at least not entirely subordinate) to the common law. In this case the standards to be invoked, the concepts to be applied, the meanings to be imputed are those of the indigenous legal tradition. Legal decisions are to be reached in accordance with the demands of customary law, however modified or constrained that law might be.

Indigenous law is accorded the greatest status when self-government forms the foundation of the recognition of indigenous law, which implies that indigenous peoples have at least in principle been recognized as sovereign nations. Indigenous law is respected in a way analogous to the respect accorded the laws of foreign states.

As I will argue at greater length below, the fact that one model accords greater status to indigenous law than another does not necessarily mean that indigenous people have more or preferable rights under that model. Customary incorporation characteristically yields legal rights to use traditional lands as they have traditionally been used; that is, it generates usufruct rather than proprietary rights. Common law incorporation, on the other hand, characteristically generates stronger property rights in the form of collective freehold ownership; as far as the law of the state is concerned, indigenous people are free to use their land traditionally or otherwise and still retain it as their own land.[2]

Most states use elements of more than one mode of incorporation; but there are differences of emphasis. The self-government mode of incorporation is most important in the United States, and is also significant in Canada. Customary incorporation plays at least some part in most states that accord any status to indigenous law, but is relied on almost exclusively in South Africa. Australia places greater emphasis than other states on common law incorporation.

I do not intend to deny the important historical, legal, and logical connections among these three ways of incorporating indigenous law. All three found some expression in the nineteenth-century opinions of John Marshall in US Indian cases. The common law and customary law modes have enough in common that an advance in one is often taken as precedent for the other.

---

[1] I should note at the outset that my use of terms like 'common law incorporation' or 'common law recognition' does not correspond to the usage of James Tully (1994, 1995). Tully generally advocates what I refer to as customary law recognition, in which indigenous law is considered a system parallel to the common law rather than being subsumed within it.

[2] In this chapter I generally use the term 'freehold' except when the courts of a given state use 'fee simple'. The differences between these terms for private property ownership (i.e. the slightly more general character of 'freehold') are not particularly relevant to any of the questions being addressed.

All are responses to similar sets of facts and circumstances. But without disputing any of this I still suggest that there are three different logics, that (for example) conceiving of indigenous land rights as ownership, customary use, and sovereignty are importantly different and in some ways incompatible.

Typically, these three different logics of incorporation have emerged through different mechanisms. Common law incorporation has characteristically taken place judicially, for example, and self-government has typically been recognized in treaties. There is, however, no necessary correspondence between the logic of incorporation and its mechanism.[3] Legislation as well as judicial decision has moved Australian law towards the common law logic. Customary incorporation often takes place through a state's constitution rather than through judicial recognition of a parallel system of law. And treaties with indigenous peoples, while they are a common incident of recognizing indigenous peoples as sovereign, are neither necessary nor sufficient for the self-government mode of incorporation. Sometimes (e.g. New Zealand's Treaty of Waitangi) a treaty is the mechanism for *surrendering* the sovereignty that has been recognized.

In some sense common law recognition accords the least status to indigenous law and self-government recognition the most; it might seem sensible to begin the discussion with one of those and move steadily to the other end of the scale. Customary recognition, however, in some ways provides the conceptual framework for all three modes, and common law and self-government will be easier to discuss after customary recognition.

1. Customary Law

> The relations of [Indians] to their ancient sovereign or government are dissolved, but their relations to each other, and their customs and usages remain undisturbed.
>
> (Justice Badgley, *Connolly* v. *Woolrich* [1869])
>
> [T]here are indigenous peoples whose legal conceptions, though differently developed, are hardly less precise than our own. When once they have been studied and understood they are no less enforceable than rights arising under English law.[4]
>
> (Lord Sumner, *Re Southern Rhodesia*, [1919])

Incorporation of indigenous law as customary law was common throughout

---

[3] I had failed to notice this before Patrick Macklem pointed it out, resulting in significant confusion in an earlier draft of this chapter.

[4] This passage immediately follows the passage made famous and infamous by its use in *Milirrupum* v. *Nabalco* (1971) at 151, insisting that some indigenous people are 'so low on the scale of social organization' that there is no point in imputing ownership of land to them.

the British Empire, and remains so in its successor states.[5] In customary incorporation, the state recognizes the survival of law based on customary rules and usages of the indigenous community, without conceding sovereignty to that community. That is, indigenous people have the right to be governed by their own traditional law, without having the right to self-government. They may marry, inherit, adopt children, hunt, fish, and use their lands as they did before colonization. The sovereign state might claim the right to override customary law by explicit legislation, just as it can legislatively override the common law. For example, the constitution of Hawaii says that 'The State reaffirms and shall protect all rights, customarily and traditionally exercised for subsistence, cultural and religious purposes and possessed by ahupua'a tenants who are descendants of native Hawaiians who inhabited the Hawaiian Islands prior to 1778, subject to the right of the State to regulate such rights' (article XII, (7)). In the absence of such an override, though, customary law is presumed to remain in effect. The British routinely restricted the customary law of the inhabitants of its colonies by preventing its operation when it violated (British interpretations of) the principles of 'natural justice'. A distant descendant of that restriction is the limitation of customary law by a written constitution or bill of rights. While the South African constitution of 1996 explicitly provides for and protects the various indigenous systems of customary law (s 211), it also holds that those systems are subject to that constitution's bill of rights (s 39 (2)).

   Land rights are central to all three modes of incorporation, and the differences among the three models can be clearly seen by their differing treatments of land. Under customary recognition, the questions of what lands indigenous people have rights to and of what rights they have to them are both answered with reference to indigenous custom and law. This notably means that indigenous land rights include neither freehold nor sovereignty, but specific rights of usage and exclusion, e.g. rights to fish, hunt, forage, hold religious ceremonies, occupy, and/or exclude others. As Justice Brennan of the Australian High Court put it in his *Mabo* opinion, 'Native title has its origin and is given its content by the traditional laws acknowledged by and the traditional customs observed by the indigenous inhabitants of a territory. The nature and incidents of native title must be ascertained as a

---

[5] For the most part, in this chapter I discuss states operating under the English common law, due to my greater familiarity with English legal concepts than with, for example, Roman ones. But I do not think that any of the three modes of incorporation is specific to English law. Occupancy can give rise to property rights under Roman law, and this is a key aspect of common law incorporation. Self-governing incorporation is possible in any state that considers its indigenous population sovereign; customary incorporation is possible in any state that recognizes the indigenous law without recognizing indigenous sovereignty. For examples of customary incorporation in non-common-law states, see the Constitution of Paraguay, c. V, and the Constitution of Guatemala, §66.

matter of fact by reference to those laws and customs' (*Mabo* v. *Queensland* 1992: 429).

For more than a century Canadian courts have held that customary indigenous law continues to affect such matters as marriage, divorce, and inheritance. A customary marriage, for example, was held to be a legally valid marriage as early as 1867 in *Connolly* v. *Woolrich*. While the trial court suggested that there was a continuing Indian right of self-government and so moved down the path towards the self-government mode of incorporation, the court of appeal (in the passage which began this section) flatly denied that and grounded its affirmation in the validity of indigenous customary law.

Indigenous law can be incorporated as customary law by the general courts or by specifically indigenous ones. Often, both will be true to some degree within the same state, so that (for example) a dispute between two indigenous persons will be handled in the first instance by indigenous institutions and, if it is subsequently taken to the general courts, the latter will attempt to apply customary laws as best it understands them.

In addition to land use and family law, customary criminal law may be incorporated by the state, which may grant customary authorities the authority to punish offences against customary law. This is extremely controversial, and is most likely to invite concerns about human rights violations, as in the 1994 case of an Australian judge who authorized the customary punishment of a spearing through the leg in lieu of a punishment by the state (Foster 1994; Jamrozik 1994).

In North America, however, the customary laws of criminal justice are more likely to emphasize restitution and/or reconciliation, compared with the focus on punishment of the states' legal systems. In 1994 two members of the Alaskan Tlingit tribe were sentenced to banishment on coastal islands, where they were both to gain rehabilitation through living off the land and cut timber to sell to pay for restitution for the medical bills of the man they had beaten and robbed. A Washington state judge gave formal approval to the banishment, though both men were required to serve prison time as well.[6] Canada has given some legal standing to the 'sentencing circles' of First Nations communities, communal procedures involving both victim and offender and typically resulting in fines or restitution (or, more rarely, banishment for a period of time) rather than imprisonment.[7]

---

[6] Only a small fraction of the restitution owed has yet been paid, one of several reasons why the experiment has not been regarded as a success and is unlikely to be repeated in the United States for some time. I discuss this case in more detail in my unpublished 'Multicultural Dilemmas'.

[7] In contrast to the criticism of the brutality of the Australian spearing, North American critics have complained that banishments and restitution are too lenient compared with prison. After a Cree man was sentenced to a year-long banishment in the woods followed by three years' probation for sexual assault, the *Toronto Sun* (1995) editorialized, 'where can we sign up for punishments like that?'

2. Common Law

> In some territories . . . a customary system of real property law might
> not have existed, or might be incapable of proof. If the territory was
> inhabited, this does not mean that the indigenous people living there
> would have no legal rights to the lands occupied by them after the
> Crown acquired sovereignty. In this situation, English law would apply
> to give them a 'common law aboriginal title'.
>
> (McNeil 1989: 192)

The common law mode of incorporation recognizes customary ways of
using powers or establishing legal situations for which the dominant culture
has a different set of procedures. A customary marriage might be recognized
as creating a real marriage in law, bringing with it all of the benefits the state
has attached to that legal status. Customary wills, gifts, property convey-
ances, or even establishing of initial property rights can be the subjects of
such recognition. These are typically recognitions not of customary ways of
making law, or of the content of customary law, so much as customary ways
of establishing legal conditions and situations. Thus, common law incorporation might recognize customary marriages as common law marriages,
meriting some or all of the privileges which the law accords to marriage; but
not recognize, for example, polygamous marriages where these are authorized by customary law but not by the general law. Common law incorporation would generate no *right* to inherit according to customary rules of
succession, but would grant the expectations formed by custom the same
status as other expectations of support have in the law of estates. No state
relies exclusively on common law incorporation, but it plays an especially
important part in Australian law.

Turning again to the central issue of land rights: common law indigenous
title is grounded in the facts of indigenous occupancy of land. Indigenous
ownership of traditional lands is recognized; but what is recognized is
ownership. As far as the law of the general state is concerned, it does not
matter whether the indigenous people traditionally used their land for
cultivation, hunting, gathering, fishing, or religious ceremonies; they own it.
As Justice Toohey put it in his *Mabo* judgment, 'It is presence amounting to
occupancy which is the foundation of the title and which attracts protection'
(*Mabo* at 486). At common law the fact of possession significantly contributes
to a claim of ownership, and the fact of occupancy contributes to a claim of
possession. While the *Mabo* decision did not quite wholly articulate or endorse
a common law understanding of native title, the subsequent Native Title Act
(1993) moved Australia even more towards common law recognition by

allowing native title to be traded for freehold, even when alienation was not possible under customary law.

While generally the collective freehold ownership of common law incorporation offers wider control over land to indigenous landholders than do customary rights, there is an important qualification to be made. The common law logic has no space for exemptions from general regulations concerning land use, hunting, fishing, or the environment. If the customary use of the land is restricted or prohibited by a general statute, common law recognition may not offer any defence. Something similar is true in other areas of law. Common law incorporation offers those married according to indigenous law all the legal privileges of marriage according to the general law—or at least all the privileges of common law marriage—rather than limiting the rights of customarily married couples to those they held under customary law. (Income tax benefits were not a right arising under customary law for married couples; common law recognition allows customary marriages to attract the benefits that the state accords to all marriages.) As noted above, however, it need not allow for any special rights, privileges, or duties which arise under customary law but which are prohibited by the general law, such as a right to enter into polygamous marriages.

The widely cited Australian Law Reform Commission (ALRC) report (1986) on the recognition of Aboriginal law largely recommended incorporation within the common law, with some elements of customary law. The comprehensive statute proposed by the commission explicitly stated that customary law was to be recognized as a matter of fact, not as a matter of law.[8] Recognition for a variety of purposes such as marriage and inheritance was described as 'functional'. Customary marriages were to be recognized for a variety of specified purposes within Australian law (e.g. the tax code), not declared to be valid marriages *tout court*. Expectations of support arising because of custom were to be granted the same standing as other reasonable expectations of inheritance, but the customary law of inheritance was not itself to be incorporated. Customary criminal law was to be taken into account by the Australian judicial system; it was not to replace it.

Incorporation through the common law leaves very little space for recognition of indigenous criminal law. 'Little', however, is not quite 'none'. Certainly, common law incorporation means that indigenous persons are subject to the general criminal law. This is unlike the customary and self-

---

[8] When a court recognizes a body of law *as law*, that body of law is directly binding. When a body of law is recognized *as a matter of fact*, the law being applied remains unchanged; the alien body of law is taken into account as a set of circumstances that help answer the questions of which laws have been triggered, which laws apply. The ALRC did not recommend that the Australian courts become forums for the adjudication of customary law, only that they take customary law and Aboriginal adherence to it into account when deciding questions of common law.

government modes, in which there is at least some presumption that matters between indigenous persons are to be governed by indigenous law. Still, indigenous criminal law needs to be recognized at least as a matter of fact by the courts. In many cases matters such as intent and reasonableness cannot be wholly determined without reference to the indigenous law.

The ALRC recommended further accommodation of the general criminal law to Aboriginal law, still considerably short of customary incorporation. (For one thing, the proposed legislation explicitly stated that Aboriginal law was to be recognized as fact and not as law.) Thus, it urged that persons be able to refuse to testify in the general court if their testimony would reveal that they had violated Aboriginal law. Moreover, judges were to be empowered to empanel single-sex juries if a defendant had to reveal matters about Aboriginal law which the other sex was forbidden to know. It also made extensive recommendations regarding judicial discovery of the content of Aboriginal law; the ALRC intended for common law incorporation to be taken seriously.

The distinctness of the common law mode of recognition is often overlooked. It is commonly said that *Mabo* brings Australian law into line with the law of states like Canada, New Zealand, and the United States; but this is not quite right. Australia has relied more heavily than the other states on incorporation through the common law, while the other states use various mixtures of all three types (but are especially distinguished from Australia by their recognition of indigenous sovereignty, discussed below). Commentators as knowledgeable as Henry Reynolds and Garth Nettheim have fallaciously assumed that *Mabo* is compatible with or even entails recognition of some form of Aboriginal sovereignty. Reynolds asks:

If, as the High Court determined, indigenous land rights and land law survived the arrival of the British why didn't other aspects of the local law? If property rights continued until they were extinguished in a clear and plain manner why didn't other elements of Aboriginal law, custom, and politics? If interest in land ran on into the colonial period and beyond why didn't the right of internal self-government? (Reynolds 1996: 9)

Nettheim similarly suggests that:

There seems . . . no reason why the High Court's approach should not be extended from real property to intellectual property, or into the area of criminal justice, or into the domain of self-government. If the laws of Aboriginal peoples have survived for some purposes, there is no reason in principle why they may not have survived for other purposes. (Nettheim 1995)

If, however, I am right that there is a distinct common law mode of incorporation, then there is no inconsistency between, say, *Mabo's* finding in favour of land rights and the subsequent finding in *Coe* v. *Commonwealth* (1993) and *Walker* v. *NSW* (1994) that there is no surviving Aboriginal sovereignty. In *Coe* a request was made (and denied) for a declaration of the sovereignty of an Aboriginal tribe. In *Walker* a criminal charge against an Aboriginal man was contested on the grounds that the general criminal law was inapplicable to Aboriginal peoples who had not requested or accepted it, that only customary criminal law could be applied. This claim, too, was rejected: 'Such notions amount to the contention that a new source of sovereignty resides in the Aboriginal people. Indeed, *Mabo (No. 2)* rejected that suggestion' (s. 2). I do not think that Chief Justice Mason was right to suggest that recognition of customary criminal law necessarily violates the very ideas of a criminal law and of equality before the law; but he was certainly right that Australian law under *Mabo* does not extend such recognition. 'Interest in land' has status within the common law; 'the right of internal self-government' does not.

Australian law seems to fluctuate between common law and customary incorporation. The *Mabo* court was divided on the basis of native title, with Brennan considering it customary, Gaudron and Deane finding that customary title was extinguished with the English acquisition of sovereignty, then 'reignited' as common law native title, and Toohey adopting an intermediate position that emphasized occupancy (see Mulqueeny 1993: 168). *Walker* and *Coe* decisively rejected any claim that Aboriginal law or—especially—Aboriginal sovereignty survived colonization, but the *Wik* v. *Queensland* (1996) judgment seems to treat at least some native title as grounded in customary rights rather than common law title.

3. Self-Government

> The Indian nations had always been considered as distinct, independent political communities . . . The constitution, by declaring treaties already made, as well as those to be made, to be the supreme law of the land, has adopted and sanctioned the previous treaties with the Indian nations, and consequently admits their rank among those powers who are capable of making treaties. The words 'treaty' and 'nation' are words of our own language, selected in our diplomatic and legislative proceedings, by ourselves, each having a definite and well-understood meaning. We have applied them to Indians, as we have applied them to the other nations of the earth. They are applied to all in the same sense.
>
> (John Marshall, *Worcester* v. *State of Georgia*, 1832)

A quite different relationship between the settler state and indigenous peoples is posited by the self-government model. There, indigenous peoples are considered (semi-sovereign) states or (domestic dependent) nations, self-governing except with regard to foreign affairs and alliances.[9] The self-government mode of incorporation is most prominent in the United States and Canada.

The self-government model grants or recognizes what neither of the other two models does: territorial sovereignty. It is the only mode to recognize a *lawmaker* in addition to, or instead of, *laws*. The tribal governments are acknowledged as legitimate rulers (or at least legitimate intermediate rulers) over indigenous people. Put another way, indigenous people are seen as having a right to give themselves laws rather than simply to live according to their laws.

Land rights grounded in the self-government model thus look more like political territory rather than like private property, which explains why such land is often seen as inalienable. Indigenous peoples have sovereignty, and only other sovereigns stand as their equals. Private persons can no more purchase indigenous lands than they could purchase sovereign power over England. '[T]he Crown (or other European crowns) was the only agent with the authority to negotiate with the Aboriginal peoples, considered as nations, and to secure non-Aboriginal title to property in North America' (Tully 1996: 170). In the United States it is typically the case that the tribal governments which have sovereignty over their territory do not have title to it as property; the land is owned by the United States government, which holds it in trust for the tribe.[10] Indeed, on many reservations individual non-Indians own much of the land, without legal detriment to Indian sovereignty—though at some periods there was much political detriment, and the non-Indian landowners were the opening wedge for the ultimate undermining of sovereignty.

At least since Marshall's time on the Supreme Court, the self-government mode of incorporation has held a prominent place in the law of the United States. While the federal government has cyclically strengthened and weakened the powers of tribal governments, they have always been recognized as being of some importance (Sharon O'Brien 1989, chs. 4–5). Some sovereignty, some rights of self-government, have generally been considered to reside in Indian tribes. Tribal governments are to a significant degree free from interference by the various states. They may establish criminal courts (to try only Indians), family courts, marriage laws, and land use laws. They may allow commercial gambling even when that is prohibited by the state within which the tribal reservation is located. Tribal laws are incorporated into the general law in a manner similar to the incorporation of one state's law by another. The two legal systems must acknowledge the validity of one another's acts,

---

[9] On the distinction I draw in Levy (1997) between the recognition and enforcement of minority law and self-government, the treaty mode is an instance of the latter, while the other two modes are instances of the former.

[10] This is not true for all tribes; the Five Civilized Tribes, the Senecas, and the Pueblos all own title to their lands as well as having sovereignty. See Sharon O'Brien (1989: 215).

grant those acts 'full faith and credit' (in the terms of the constitution), and co-operate or at least reach agreement on jurisdictional matters. Disputes between the legal systems are regulated by the federal courts, since indigenous sovereignty is always subordinate to federal sovereignty, but the federal courts are often obliged to protect Indian law against state incursions.

Canadian law has ordinarily not gone quite as far down this path as American law. If tribal governments in the United States have powers close to those of states, tribal governments in Canada have tended to be more like municipalities. Under the Indian Act, provincial laws generally do apply to Indians and other indigenous people; and band councils have delegated authority over matters like traffic regulations, building codes, and public health (Indian Act, 1985, s. 88, 81). Representatives of Canada's First Nations have long argued that their rights of self-government are inherent rather than delegated, and are much more extensive than is recognized in the Indian Act.

This pattern changed dramatically with the August 1998 signing of an agreement between the Nisga'a nation, on one hand, and the governments of Canada and British Columbia, on the other. This agreement, the first modern-day Canadian Indian treaty, not only secures possession of 750 square miles to the Nisga'a. It also provides for the creation of a new level of self-government, a level with powers much more extensive than those of the Indian Act band councils. The treaty has yet to be ratified, but is already being pointed to as a possible precedent for agreements between Canada and fifty other First Nations, whose claims taken together cover most of British Columbia.

The creation of Nunavut changed the pattern even more significantly for the Inuit. On 1 April 1999 the eastern half of what was the Northwest Territories became a separate, partially self-governing territory, Nunavut—a territory that will have an Inuit majority. The creation of Nunavut was part of a negotiated settlement of land and sea claims between the Inuit and the Canadian government. Nunavut comprises about one-fifth of the Canadian land mass, and title to about one-fifth of Nunavut itself will be restored to the Inuit as a result of the agreement. Ownership and sovereignty remain distinct, however, and non-Inuit continue to be able to own land, subject to the regulations of the Nunavut and federal governments.

Customary law and customary rights sometimes superimpose on common law recognition and common law rights rather than strictly replacing them. Similarly, treaties can be superimposed over both. In Canada, for example, the fact that many tribes have land rights recognized by treaty does not change the fact that tribes without treaties may have common law or customary title.

For a decade and a half there was considerable activism in support of a treaty (or 'Makaratta') between the Australian government and Aborigines (Department of the Prime Minister and Cabinet 1991; Baker 1988). A prominent group of non-Aboriginal Australians formed an Aboriginal Treaty

Committee in 1979 to lobby for such action. In 1982 a Senate committee recommended an amendment to the constitution which would give the Commonwealth the power to enter into a 'compact' with Aborigines. By 1987 then Prime Minister Bob Hawke supported the idea, urging that a treaty or compact be agreed upon in time for the bicentennial of English settlement in 1989. Instead, in 1991 the Council for Aboriginal Reconciliation (CAR) was created with a ten-year mission to promote greater understanding between Aboriginal and non-Aboriginal Australians, possibly leading to a final written document by the hundredth anniversary of Australian federation in 2001.

The treaty movement had its greatest momentum before *Mabo*, and supporters typically assumed that a treaty would be a, or the, way to secure native title. Non-Aboriginal critics, like then Opposition Leader John Howard, accepted the link between a treaty and land rights and used this as an argument against a treaty. (By contrast, Aboriginal critics saw a treaty as most likely symbolic and a distraction from the struggle for land rights.)

Subsequent developments, however, have shown this to be a mistake; native title can be grounded perfectly well within the common law, without a treaty. Given *Mabo*, the Native Title Act, and *Wik* v. *Queensland*, any treaty of more than symbolic value would seem to involve primarily self-government rather than land rights. As the deadline for the CAR's work draws nearer, Australia may have to confront the question of whether to continue developing common law and customary law incorporation or to switch emphases dramatically to self-government. The latter course of action seems unlikely.

4. Inconsistencies and Hybrids

The point of distinguishing the three modes of incorporation is not to recommend one over the others, or even to suggest that no state can coherently use more than one of them. One reason for distinguishing these categories, however, is that the failure to do so has often been unfairly disadvantageous to indigenous peoples. That is, they have received the worst of two or more categories at the same time; the inconsistency in their treatment has not been random and neutral but detrimental.

In *Baker Lake* v. *Minister of Indian Affairs* Justice Mahoney laid out a plausible test for common law native title. He said that claimants of such title must prove that they and their ancestors were members of an organized society; that the organized society occupied the specific territory over which the title was claimed; that the occupation was to the exclusion of other organized societies; and that the occupation was an established fact at the time of colonization. No reference here is made to customary law in any form; these criteria clearly test occupation and possession, not the existence or content of Indian law. That Mahoney was thinking in terms of common law title is further borne out by his dictum that 'the coexistence of an aboriginal title with the estate of the ordinary private landholder is readily recognized as an absurdity' (*Baker Lake* 1979: 565). There is nothing absurd about the coexistence of a customary usufruct right with freehold title; but of course one title of exclusive possession cannot coexist with another. Yet Mahoney held that the Inuit of Baker Lake, who satisfied his four criteria, held only a right to hunt and fish over the land, not a right to possess the land or to exclude others from it. This he seems to have based on his supposition that only rights to hunt or fish existed under *customary* law; but he did not otherwise refer to the existence of Inuit law, much less prove what it contained. Under *Baker Lake*, then, Indians and Inuit land rights are incompatible with 'the estate of the ordinary private landholder'; this is one of the disadvantages of common law title. That title includes too much to coexist with private property, and so has often been extinguished where customary usufructuary rights might have continued to exist. Yet under *Baker Lake* aboriginal title has all the disadvantages of customary title as well; it is limited to (the judicial reading of) the traditional uses of the land. Having met the burden of proving exclusive occupation, the Inuit did not gain the right to exclude or to occupy!

Similarly, the self-government mode of incorporation, and its underlying logic of territorial self-government, logically implies recognition of indigenous criminal law, and recognition that tribal governments have authority to punish anyone on tribal land who violates that law. Since the Supreme Court decision *Oliphant v. Suquamish Tribe* (1978), however, the United States has held that tribal governments have *no* authority over non-members in criminal matters, even in the case of crimes committed against Indians on reservation territory. The jurisdiction of Indian law is held to include only Indians, as if that law were personal customary law. The disadvantage to Indians of this inconsistency is not only formal or procedural. When a non-Indian commits crimes against an Indian on a reservation, only a federal court may try the case. US Attorney-General Janet Reno (1995) has noted the real difficulties this has created for the maintenance of law and order on reservations. Federal prosecutors rarely make the prosecution of misdemeanours a priority, and federal courts are typically located far from the reservations over which they have jurisdiction.

As a result, misdemeanor crime by non-Indians against Indians is perceived as being committed with impunity. This implicit message of lack of accountability deters victims from reporting crimes, and police from making arrests because they know there will be no prosecution. This, in turn, encourages the spread of crime and ultimately, the commission of even more serious crime.

Given this, it is perhaps unsurprising that American Indians suffer violent crimes at a rate more than twice that of other Americans, and that (unlike violence against whites or against blacks) these crimes are mostly interracial rather than intraracial (see Claiborne 1999). The inconsistency that *Oliphant* gives rise to actually endangers Indians, making them more vulnerable to violence.

Some recent Canadian and Australian jurisprudence on land rights has attempted to hybridize the customary and common law modes; I do not think that it has succeeded, and it has repeated with greater sophistication some of the disadvantages of *Baker Lake*. In *Mabo* the Australian High Court held that the content of native title varies depending on the content of Aboriginal customs and traditions. In this respect under *Mabo* native title appears to be customary; but it is entirely extinguished with freehold private property over the same land, the burden that logically follows from common law title. In other respects *Mabo* came close to articulating fully a jurisprudence of common law title, especially in so far as it rejected any linkage between the survival of native title and the continuation of traditional or customary ways of life. If Aborigines have a customary right to possess a piece of land and to exclude others from it, their continued enjoyment of that right does not depend on the maintenance of customary religious practices or of the technological or economic conditions of their ancestors. Moreover, Aborigines were recognized to have the right to do much with their land which was not part of their traditions. The break, however, was incomplete: native title was held to be inalienable, on the grounds that the traditional Aboriginal understanding of land did not allow for its sale. Thus Aborigines were prevented from the sale of any piece of their land, and (perhaps more importantly) prevented from using it as collateral for mortgages or credit. So, in *Mabo* as in *Baker Lake*, indigenous rights were extinguished like common law title, without being replaced by the full legal rights of that title.

The recent Canadian case of *Delgamuukw* v. *British Columbia* (1997) explicitly tries to rationalize this discrepancy. Chief Justice Lamer's majority opinion argues that the Delgamuukw and Haaxw indigenous peoples, who argued for aboriginal title as fee simple ownership,[11] and the British Columbian government, which argued that aboriginal title was nothing but a cluster of customary use rights, were both mistaken:

The content of aboriginal title, in fact, lies somewhere in between these positions . . . its characteristics cannot be completely explained by reference either to the common law rules of real property or to the rules of property found in aboriginal legal systems. As with other aboriginal rights, it must be understood by reference to both common law and aboriginal perspectives. (paras. 111, 113)

[11] To be specific, they accepted the jurisprudence holding that aboriginal title was inalienable but otherwise argued that it included full fee simple ownership. I return to inalienability below.

To be specific: aboriginal title:

is a right in land and, as such, is more than the right to engage in specific activities which may be themselves aboriginal rights. Rather, it confers the right to use land for a variety of activities, not all of which need be aspects of practices, customs and traditions . . . However, that range of uses is subject to the limitation that they must not be irreconcilable with the nature of the attachment to the land which forms the basis of the particular group's aboriginal title. (para. 111)

Lamer argues that the nature of the aboriginal attachment to land is, among other things, premissed on the transfer of the land from generation to generation. The limitation to which he refers thus prevents activities ranging from strip mining to the spoilage and wasting of the land to the sale of the land.

I don't mean to deny that *Delgamuukw* is a very favourable ruling for Canada's First Nations, or that it is conceptually much clearer than much of the jurisprudence that preceded it. Yet one is left wondering why the court goes so far but no farther in renouncing the status of guardian of indigenous traditions and understandings. Aboriginal title is considered a title to the land, one which includes the right to do much that was not traditionally done and not dependent on any continuity of customs or practices. Why then stop short of recognizing fee simple rights?

Part of the answer seems to be that Canadian courts, like their Australian counterparts, view the law as absolutely settled on the inalienability of aboriginal or native title, and think that they must articulate doctrines which make sense of this settled point. The major sources for this position, however, are the Royal Proclamation of 1763 and the United States Supreme Court decisions of John Marshall—both grounded in the self-government mode of incorporation—or, in the case of the proclamation, perhaps not in 'incorporation' at all but in the recognition of Indian nations as foreign sovereign units. The exclusive right of purchase of Indian lands which Marshall found vested in the United States had more to do with their status as partially foreign states than with the traditional communal character of land tenure, more to do with the right of each 'discovering' or colonizing power to exclude the others than with the protection of indigenous custom.[12]

By contrast, the Nisga'a treaty holds that 'the Nisga'a Nation owns Nisga'a Lands in fee simple, being the largest estate known in law' (Nisga'a Final

---

[12] This is especially true of the last of Marshall's important Indian opinions, *Worcester v. State of Georgia* (1833). The earlier *Johnson v. M'Intosh* (1823) did make reference to the communal character of traditional title as part of a secondary argument; but in that opinion, unlike in *Worcester*, Marshall viewed the Indians as having little more than a right of occupation. *Johnson* may be good precedent for customary incorporation, as *Worcester* certainly is for the self-government mode; but neither is binding on or even particularly relevant to the common law mode.

Agreement, ch. 3, s. (3)). As far as Canadian law is concerned, the Nisga'a are free to do as they wish with their lands, including selling the fee simple title; they do not lose sovereignty over the land when they sell the title. (I return to the issue of separating ownership from sovereignty in Levy (forthcoming).) The Nisga'a constitution and Nisga'a law can constrain alienation, but federal and provincial law cannot. The Nisga'a may register their land as inalienable with the federal government, but retain discretion to withdraw that registration and return the land to fee simple ownership.

5. Religious Law

The standing given in some countries to the law of religious minorities, or the laws of all religious groups, is in important ways similar to the incorporation of indigenous law discussed here. Israel and India are well-known examples; family law, inheritance law, and the like are specific to each religious community. There have been disputes about the relationship of those religious legal systems to the civil law, including disputes over the right of the civil system to override the religious law in the event of (perceived) human rights violations.[13]

Typically, though, religious law only lends itself to customary incorporation. In certain minor ways common law recognition is possible, as when a state recognizes all religious leaders as having the authority to create (legally identical) marriages. Religious minorities might be recognized as national minorities with rights of self-determination and self-government, as Serbs and Croats have sought within the Bosnian state; but this accords no particular standing to the *content* of religious law. Actually incorporating religious law as state law requires the customary mode of incorporation. (It is interesting to note that indigenous custom has sometimes been categorized as 'religion' in order to deny it the standing of 'law', as in *Milirrupum*.) India can serve as an example.

At the time of British colonization Muslim law was in force through large parts of India. Britain constrained the Muslim princes and allowed more or less free reign to Hindu practices; the Muslim criminal law in particular was entirely superseded. But Islam was not pushed out of law altogether; Muslim 'personal law' was allowed to govern relations between Muslims. Some similar provisions were made for Sikhs, Buddhists, Jains, Christians, and the tribal peoples of the north-east, but the size and centrality of the Muslim

---

[13] J. N. Matson (1993) notes some of the historical links and parallels between British recognition of Muslim law in some colonies and British recognition of indigenous customary law in others.

minority makes it a case of particular interest. Islam has a rich and complex legal tradition which originated outside the Hindu sphere of influence (unlike, say, the Sikh or Buddhist religions), and continuation of Muslim personal law into post-independence and post-partition India has sometimes been a matter of serious controversy. The Indian state openly considers the reform of Hindu social traditions and practices a legitimate state purpose; customary Muslim leaders strenuously deny that it should view Islamic law in the same light.

N.B.

Muslim men may marry up to four women at a time, the limit prescribed in the Koran. They may also divorce their wives at will (divorce by *Talak*), and need not follow judicial divorce proceedings; Muslim wives seeking divorce against the will of their husbands must show cause. Muslim couples may divorce extrajudicially by mutual consent, a power not available to others. The apostasy of a Muslim man from Islam results in the automatic dissolution of a Muslim marriage, though the same is not true for the apostasy of a Muslim woman.

The support of divorced wives has been a contentious issue. The Muslim law in force holds that an ex-husband must ordinarily support an ex-wife for three months after the divorce and children raised by the ex-wife until they are 2 years old as well as returning the wife's dowry. The criminal law holds persons of means responsible for the support of their indigent relatives, including aged parents, handicapped adult children, and ex-wives. In the important and controversial *Shah Bano Begum* case, the Supreme Court in 1985 held that the relevant section of the criminal code was applicable to Muslims. Legislation passed in response effectively reversed that judgment. Now Muslim men are liable for support only for three months, unless at the time of divorce both husband and wife declare that they would rather be governed by the general criminal code. Responsibility for support of an indigent Muslim ex-wife now lies with those relatives who would be able to inherit from her under Muslim law (parents, siblings, adult children), not with the ex-husband (Bhattacharjee 1994: 150–9, 179; Das 1994: 125–37).

Only one-third of a Muslim's property may be disposed of by will. Daughters receive only half the share of sons on inheritance (Bhattacharjee 1994: 180). Non-Muslims cannot inherit from Muslims, except when they are apostates. This may not apply to testamentary disposition of property; but that cannot exceed one-third of the estate in any event (Bhattacharjee 1994: 109–17).

In general, land and property law is not included under 'personal law', an obvious difference from the indigenous cases. In one significant respect, however, personal law determines the rules concerning landholdings. When two or more Muslims jointly own a piece of land, or when one owns land and another has some legal right concerning it (e.g. a right of passage over it), or when one owns land and another owns an adjoining plot, there is a right of pre-emption of sales. When one Muslim seeks to sell his or her (share in the) property, the co-owner, possessor of a non-proprietary right, or owner of adjacent property must be given the opportunity to buy it first. When there are a number of Muslims with such interests, the Muslim seeking to sell land (or other real property) must get all of them to refuse explicitly to buy the land before selling to an outsider. Those exercising their right of pre-empting a sale do not actually have to buy the land in order effectively to block the sale. If they refuse either actually to purchase the land or to explicitly waive their right to do so, then any outside purchaser is faced with the prospect of litigation which may well be lost. All of this results in a kind of community veto over sales to outsiders, and indeed the point of pre-emption is to allow a community to retain its character (Bhattacharjee 1994: 163–75, 180). This device perpetuates communal concentration ('segregation' to critics, 'the viability of communities' to sympathizers) in a way similar to rules that members of indigenous tribes may only sell their lands to other tribe members.

Muslim criminal law in general does not have legal standing, and on matters defined by the Indian state as criminal, confessional differences are typically not observed. That is not to say that there are no distinctions drawn. A Hindu man who marries more than one woman not only does not have a legally valid plural marriage; he is subject to criminal prosecution for bigamy. The criminal code of India, not merely its family civil law, dictates that adequate alimony be paid from a divorced husband to a divorced wife; this is no longer applicable to Muslims. But there is no Muslim community which is entitled to inflict coercive punishment for violation of its rules, no Muslim jurisdiction to compete or conflict with the general jurisdiction in criminal cases, no talk of having Muslims police Muslims and deal with lawbreakers internally—much less self-government that would allow criminal jurisdiction over local non-Muslims.

The legal foundation for recognition in India is entirely statutory. The key piece of legislation is the Muslim Personal Law (Shariat) Application Act 1937; important revisions and additions came in the Dissolution of Muslim Marriage Act 1939 and the Muslim Women (Protection of Rights on Divorce) Act 1986. Substantial case law has developed around the statutory provisions, of course; but there is no constitutional right to confession-specific personal laws. Indeed, the constitution of India instructs the 'State [to] endeavour to secure for the citizens a uniform civil code throughout the territory of India' (s. 44). Britain established the custom of allowing multiple systems of personal law, but the custom has legal standing only in so far as it was codified and the codification remains in force. There is substantial dispute over the degree to which the fundamental rights provision of the constitution limits the various systems of personal law; but there is no question that the Indian legislature could eliminate all recognition if it saw fit. The relevant statutes often make reference to Muslim (or Mohammedan) law, leaving to the courts the task of identifying that law. The courts in turn are inclined to defer to the Hadith and the Imamia, authorized traditional commentaries on and interpretations of the Koran, rather than directly engaging in Koranic interpretation.[14] Courts also rely on previous courts' declarations of what the relevant Muslim law requires. This is customary incorporation; until and unless India abolishes the confessional personal legal codes, the courts are supposed to rule according to their understanding of the relevant religious laws.

The 1937 legislation instructs courts to apply Muslim law to personal relations between Muslims. There is legal controversy about some of the implications of this. Muslim law dictates that a marriage be dissolved when the husband apostatizes; but when he has apostatized, he is arguably no longer Muslim and it is unclear whether Muslim law should still apply as far as Indian law is concerned. In some areas Muslims can opt out of Muslim law; for example, a couple at divorce may declare themselves bound by the general code and not by Muslim law. But there is no general Indian code of personal law, only enactments of Hindu and Muslim (and Sikh and Buddhist and . . .) personal laws. There are some statutory provisions for how to handle a case that falls between the cracks, but often it is a matter for judicial discretion.

The British courts retained the right to interpret, apply, and limit customary law in Africa, and to do the same with religious customary law in India. By contrast, the Ottoman *millet* system and its successors in contemporary states like Israel and Lebanon do not allow secular courts to interpret religious law. Religious officials and institutions within each community, such as rabbinical courts, have the authority which the British system reserved for British courts. Religiously specific courts raise the danger of giving too much secular power to religious officials, like Israel's chief rabbinate; but the general courts might distort religious law, as the Indian courts have been accused of with reference to Muslim law. Of comparable importance is whether there is a general civil code accessible to those who wish to opt out of the religious courts. There is not in Israel, and in India there is only for certain very limited purposes. In both states, however, there are vocal advocates of such a code. The impossibility of a non-religious marriage in Israel, for example, has been a matter of serious controversy.

If we are more concerned with preventing internal cruelty and abuses of

---

[14] There are similarities between constitutional interpretation and interpretation of a religious text. Levinson (1990) analogizes the usual precedent-bound legal approach to the Catholic tradition and the periodic demands to free interpretation from case law and return to the constitutional text to Protestantism. In the Indian Muslim case the analogy becomes a near-identity. The Koran, like a constitution, is a founding source of law, ostensibly supreme. In both cases, though, many think that there is often good reason to build or even rely on previous interpretations rather than beginning anew with the original text. The Hadith might perhaps be compared to the Federalist Papers, though they are both taken more seriously and are less certain in their origin.

power than with procedural authenticity—and the multiculturalism of fear argues that we should be—we have good reason to prefer the British Indian model. If, however, we have strong reason to suspect bad faith or lack of sufficient knowledge on the part of the dominant group's courts, as was arguably true of British courts in Africa and was certainly true of apartheid era courts in South Africa, we have reason to prefer leaving interpretation in the hands of the community whose customs are being interpreted. In either case, both the concern to protect individual members of communities and the need for a stable legal framework that can survive intermarriage, assimilation, secularization, and so on call for a civil code accessible to all who choose it.

6. Evaluations and Limitations

One could agree with everything that has been said until now and not agree with what follows; the conceptual distinctions made could be valid even if all of the evaluations made below are invalid.

Much of what is accomplished by common law incorporation, and some of what can be accomplished with customary incorporation, can also be accomplished by individualization of the law generally. For example, a state with mandatory primogeniture might allow a minority with other traditions to abide by their customs allowing women or subsequent sons to inherit—a form of customary recognition. But it might also abandon mandatory primogeniture in favour of the purely testamentary disposition of goods; this would allow members of the minority as well as members of the majority to follow rules other than primogeniture. Now, it might still be the case that neither members of the majority culture nor members of the minority culture thought that the legitimate disposition of goods was determined by choice; both might think that there is a binding cultural rule which they must follow in drawing up their wills. But that is no different from laws on freedom of religion which claim to allow people to practise whatever religion they choose even if no one experiences either inherited belief or conversion as a *choice*.

Marriage law—in particular, *divorce* law—has been individualized to a certain degree in some states by the growing use of prenuptial agreements. Some of what minorities seek through the incorporation of customary marriage law might be accomplished with further individualization of marriage contracts, including the ability to set in advance the permissible terms of divorce. Louisiana has, controversially, increased the number of available options by one; couples may choose to enter 'covenant marriages', from which divorce is more legally difficult. If still wider discretion were granted, then the perceived need for the incorporation of culturally specific legal codes might well be less.

Even some unusual property rules (e.g. the Indian Muslim rule of pre-emption and some indigenous inalienability rules) could be generated under a regime that allowed restrictive covenants on land titles. Something similar is true of many demands for exemptions from general laws; repeal of the law accomplishes the same purpose. Jews and Catholics do not need special exemptions from prohibition for their ceremonial wine once prohibition is repealed; Sikhs do not require exemption from motorcycle helmet laws if none such are in place.

I think this is a strategy worth pursuing. It allows for cultural differentiation without freezing any particular customary understandings or communal affiliations into law. There are a few reasons, however, for thinking that this will not always be enough (though, of course, one might think that it is all that is morally justifiable). Every system of law has default rules, rules that come into play when a problem has not been foreseen or provided for in advance. Testamentary disposition does not solve the problem of what to do in cases of intestacy; and when two cultural communities have significantly different family patterns and expectations, the minority may well seek incorporation of its rules for intestacy. Similarly, even the most elaborate of prenuptial agreements cannot predict every subject of dispute in a divorce. Courts must have rules on which to fall back; and those rules may be dependent on one cultural understanding of family obligations but be quite inappropriate in another. The ALRC recommended allowing not only customary Aboriginal wills but customary intestate inheritance and even challenges to wills on the basis of legitimate customary expectations; this sort of result obviously could not be reached simply by allowing individual choice of law to rule.

Will Kymlicka (1995a: 192) has noted a catch-22—I do not think it is a paradox—in the problem of developing a shared sense of citizenship in multi-national states:

Self-government rights . . . do pose a threat to social unity. The sense of being a distinct nation within a larger country is potentially destabilizing. On the other hand, the denial of self-government rights is also destabilizing, since it encourages resentment and even secession. Concerns about social unity will arise however we respond to self-government claims.

The dilemma is not limited to self-government rights as I describe them here. Self-government and customary recognition both partially legally detach indigenous peoples from the state and the general law, and so potentially undermine their sense of belonging to that state. Common law recognition, on the other hand, may well not satisfy the feeling among indigenous peoples that they ought to be recognized as distinct peoples. It may leave many members of indigenous communities feeling alienated and distant from a state that does not grant them their due. Perhaps they will never feel like full citizens in a state which does not fully acknowledge their distinctive status.[15]

It is important to note one more aspect of the impasse. Even partial detachment from the state can undermine the feeling, however weak it may be to begin with, among non-indigenous peoples that their indigenous neighbours are fellow citizens engaged in a common social or political enterprise. That is, if social unity and shared citizenship are important goals—if we really care about the experienced feelings of shared citizenship rather than some unanswerable questions about which collectivities individuals *ought* to feel loyal to—they cannot only be measured with reference to the feelings of indigenous citizens. Now, even if indigenous peoples were simply resident aliens trapped in states not of their own making, or citizens of enclave polities surrounded by those states (think of Lesotho and South Africa), those states would owe them much better treatment than they have often received. Even such aliens have a right not to be exterminated, not to have their goods expropriated, not to have their children stolen away. And even such aliens would have a right to restitution or compensation for many of those past wrongs. But they would *not* have any right to special representation in the political organs of the state, or to ongoing non-compensatory financing by that state, or to special assistance in entry into the life of the wider society. Why would anyone offer affirmative action in the civil service or universities to such aliens, if their just moral claims have essentially to do with separateness? If non-indigenous citizens are made to feel that indigenous peoples are not really part of the state, then they will have little reason to support such integrative benefits. This does not get us any closer to solving the problem Kymlicka notes; indeed, it takes us farther away.

It seems to me, though I cannot show this in any scientific fashion, that this dilemma of membership afflicts New Zealand somewhat less than it does Canada, the United States, or Australia, to say nothing of more deeply divided states like South Africa and India.[16] But if this is true, it is probably

---

[15] Chandran Kukathas has argued that the liberal state has no legitimate concern with social unity in this sense that it is my sense of my own identity is none of the state's business. I am sympathetic to his worries about making social unity and identity-shaping too central to our political morality; I don't think that the liberal state should try to shape its citizens' identities so that identification with the state takes some unmitigated *priority* over identification with other collectivities. But surely the liberal state legitimately can be *as* concerned as churches, ethnic groups, and the rest with the identity of their members; it may try to ensure that there is *some* attachment, though it is of course constrained in the means it may use. See Kukathas (1996, 1997).

[16] South Africa's constitution and current official self-understanding—'We, the people of South Africa . . . believe that South Africa belongs to all who live in it, united in our diversity'— describe the hope of shared citizenship rather than a formula for attaining it, much like the American *E pluribus unum*.

true for non-replicable reasons. The Maori can be convincingly understood as one people with status as co-founder of the state, while the indigenous peoples of the other states are much more diverse among themselves. New Zealand can have Maori and English as joint official languages. Canada could not make every indigenous language an official language and have that status retain any meaning at all.

Similarly, the Treaty of Waitangi arguably does involve a voluntary waiving of sovereignty on the part of the Maori. Even complete compliance with the treaty on the part of the New Zealand government would not create differentiated citizenship. The British did not think that Australia's Aborigines were competent to sign treaties, and the North American treaties generally retained or merged rather than waived sovereignty. So the feeling of shared citizenship between Maori and Pakeha (if I'm right that there is such a feeling) flows from a real jointness of the polity that may not be available to the other states under discussion.

I don't suppose that this classification, or any classification, can cut this knot; the problem is a real one that can not be clarified away. But I can suggest some additional considerations to be put into the balance. Transparency, simplicity, and clarity are virtues of a legal system, though, of course, a legal system must also be complicated enough to take many morally relevant nuances and details into account. The incorporation of customary law undermines all these virtues; it multiplies the fundamental legal philosophies as well as multiplying jurisdictions and interpreters.

Perhaps these problems are easily manageable. After all, civil law and common law jurisdictions coexist in the United States (Louisiana adheres to the civil law) and Canada; South Africa has always relied on both common law and Roman–Dutch legal systems; and Switzerland survives and thrives with its marriage of Roman and German legal traditions. Customary law might coexist with English law just as easily. We have, however, some reason to doubt this. The European legal traditions have common roots; the civil law and the common law, for example, have both been critically influenced by Roman legal traditions. That substantially aids mutual comprehensibility between the two traditions. No such common roots exist between European and indigenous traditions. Adding to the difficulties are the multiplicity of customary laws within a state; customary law is not Indian or Aboriginal but Cree or Navajo or Pitjantjatjara or Waanyi. As jurisdictions and legal concepts multiply, the comprehensibility of the legal system as a whole can be maintained only by restricting the range of activities subject to customary law. Legal transparency, it should be noted, also aids in social and cultural mobility. Those bound by a system of customary law which is itself difficult and complicated to master will be that much less likely to invest the time to learn about the law of the wider state, their rights under that law, and the possibility of using it rather than customary law for some purposes. I think that such mobility, the possibility of accessing the law of the wider state, is important for any sense of shared membership in that state. The possibility of a choice of jurisdictions is one of the advantages, or compensations, that liberal multi-ethnic states can offer indigenous peoples whose ancestors did not voluntarily join those states. And the more often customary legal incorporation is used instead of common law incorporation, and the more complex and differentiated customary law is, the less real that choice of jurisdictions becomes.

Self-government incorporation might present fewer such difficulties, though it depends in part on what decisions the sovereign indigenous peoples make about their laws. In general, though, this kind of recognition creates a legal environment similar to federalism, the complications of which are well known but also manageable. Territorially based federalism has well-known advantages and disadvantages regarding the promotion of a shared identity. It sometimes creates a base and a structure for future secession; but it sometimes gives members of ethnic minorities an institutional tie to the political order.

The point of common law incorporation, of course, is to recognize indigenous rights within a common legal and conceptual framework, so it creates the fewest difficulties of legal complication; though it certainly also gives indigenous peoples less reason to think that they have been recognized as fully distinct. In some sense common law incorporation can bolster a common citizenship only to the degree that the sense of political separateness is already weak. If the distance felt from a given state by the indigenous people in that state has to do with the discriminatory application of the general law, the denial of land rights, and the actual suppression of custom, then common law incorporation can be a viable solution.

Each mode of incorporation has further virtues and drawbacks as measured by liberal democratic principles. Common law incorporation preserves the possibility of one law before which all can be equal, once that law has been understood in suitably generous ways. It eliminates (or at least mitigates) the culturally discriminatory aspects of the general law, without limiting the access of indigenous people to the rights offered by that law. On the other hand, it clearly subordinates indigenous law and generally leaves the law of the settlers' state as the framework for all legal relations. The common law model does not attempt to undo historical wrongs (such as conquest), except in so far as it demands compensation for unjust takings of indigenous property in land.

Customary law recognition involves the fewest legal fictions; indigenous traditions are not forced into either the concepts of European common law or those of European international law but are recognized (as far as possible) on their own terms. Customary recognition also emphasizes the traditional aspect of indigenous traditions, however, and leaves little space for innovation, reform, or democratic alteration even by indigenous people themselves. Customary recognition may bind indigenous people to old ways, and even make their rights conditional on their adherence to the old ways.

For example, holders of common law title own their land under few conditions. The greater the reliance on customary law, however, the greater the conditionality of ownership might become. Customary law might identify who has rights to use a piece of land for what purpose; but it also identifies who has what *responsibilities* to the land, and what uses are impermissible for anyone. A legal regime in which indigenous peoples held their lands primarily under customary law rather than common law title, and which took customary law seriously, would result in indigenous peoples being significantly more restricted in the use of their lands than other members of the society are in the use of theirs. It is arguable that, under such a regime, refusal to fulfil responsibilities about land logically entails a forfeiture of rights to the land. Using such reasoning, the Queensland Aboriginal Land Rights Act makes customary Aboriginal responsibilities for land an essential part of the land claims process:

A land claim application must include, among other things, a statement of the responsibilities in relation to the land that the claimants agree to assume if the land is granted because of the claim. If the claim is made on the ground of economic or cultural viability, the claim must also include a statement of the specific proposal for the use of the land claimed . . . The deed of grant must specify . . . the responsibilities that the group of Aboriginal people have agreed to assume in relation to the land. (Neate 1993: 196–7)

Enforcement of customary law by the criminal law system of the state can even more obviously bind members to observance of traditional rules. Will Kymlicka terms rules binding members of minority cultures to their cultural traditions 'internal restrictions' and criticizes them as incompatible with liberal principles (1995a, ch. 3). While I do not think that all such internal rules are illiberal (see my discussion in Levy 1997), we surely have some grounds to worry if the state enforces such customary norms or makes legal rights conditional on their observance.

This problem may be exacerbated by customary legal enforcement by state courts (rather than by a parallel system of indigenous courts). The state courts typically have only the blunt instrument of a 'natural justice' exception with which to override customary law, and no mechanisms for its reform or evolution. Outsiders have limited access to the kind of information that would allow a judge to say, 'this has been the rule, but that is the underlying principle, and in new circumstances the principle can be better satisfied with a new rule'. While the common law changes and grows by judicial action, the judiciary is likely to take a more static view of customary law, in part because they have a better chance of being true to the customs if they do, in part because if the indigenous law is not customary, then it has no particular standing on this model.

The converse of the fear that state recognition will artificially freeze customary law is that such recognition will distort the customs (see Woodman 1988). Whether the state courts are the only forums for adjudication of customary legal claims or the forums of last resort, final authority for the interpretation of indigenous law is taken out of indigenous hands. Sometimes the distortion is intentional, as it seems to have been by the apartheid regime's codifications of African customary law. But even the best-intentioned of interpreters may be handicapped by being raised in (and having legal training in) a different cultural background.[17]

This problem may be inescapable under customary incorporation; the problem of the freezing of customary law can at least be mitigated in its effects. A general, liberal legal code accessible to all, and accessible on a case-by-case, issue-by-issue basis, helps make exit or partial exit possible for members of customary communities. If there is not a liberal civil code, or if members of some communities do not have access to it because the state considers them bound by customary law, then the possibility of exit (and the check it creates on group membership) does not exist. Although Kymlicka (1995a, ch. 8) and Kukathas (1992a, b) disagree to a certain extent about the validity of conservative rules within a minority group when exit *is* possible, they certainly unite in condemning such rules when it is *not*.

Conversely, *if* the law of the wider state is easily accessible to indigenous people,[18] customary recognition might help promote liberal goals in a way similar but preferable to federalism. Offering a choice of jurisdictions, a choice of laws, over a wide range of activities creates a kind of competition among legal systems. Under federalism, some change of place is typically necessary in order to move from a more to a less restrictive law. Since customary law is personal, not territorial, if indigenous people can choose the law under which they live—and especially if they can choose on a case-by-case, issue-by-issue basis—pressure might be placed on both legal systems to more closely match their needs and choices. On the other hand, this assumes that there is some valid mechanism for the change or reform of customary law, which we have seen to be a difficult assumption to make.

A self-government foundation is most in accordance with norms concern-

---

[17] All of this, of course, assumes that lawyers and judges are much less likely to be members of indigenous cultures. That is a contingent fact, but so far a generally true one. Bruce Clark (1990: 4) offers that fact as a reason why indigenous leaders in Canada might prefer political negotiation to forcing judicial recognition of (what he claims are) existing rights of self-government.

[18] Customary recognition might itself make the wider law less accessible in fact, even if it is formally available, because of the difficulty in learning about one's rights and duties under two or more deeply different legal systems.

ing the right of peoples to self-government; it also leaves the least space for liberal human rights constraints. Only the self-government model accords to indigenous people the right to determine their political status as they see fit. Only the self-government model allows them to stand as the final interpreters of their own law. And only the self-government model allows them to change and reform their laws as they see fit. Assuming that the tribal governments are internally democratic, self-government seems to meet democratic requirements at least as well as common law incorporation and rather better than customary law.

Liberal values are somewhat less well served. When an indigenous sovereign violates individual rights—by restricting religious liberty, by unjustly discriminating against women, and so on—the logic of the self-government model gives the wider state little space to intervene. As Kymlicka puts it, recognizing the self-government rights of a national minority (a category which includes indigenous minorities) requires liberals in the wider state to view rights violations within the minority nation the same way they would view rights violations in, say, Saudi Arabia: something to be criticized and agitated against, but not something they have legitimate authority to prevent. Joseph Carens suggests that this might be for the best, in a discussion of the possible application of the Canadian Charter of Rights and Freedoms to indigenous governments, because 'people are supposed to experience the realization of principles of justice through various concrete institutions, but they may actually experience a lot of the institution and very little of the principle' (Carens 1996–7: 117). That is, the ostensibly liberal institutions of the wider state (e.g. courts) have done such a poor job of promoting liberal values with respect to indigenous people that we have reason to deny those institutions jurisdiction. If this is so, it only says that self-government is the least bad alternative from a liberal perspective given current constraints, not that it is an affirmative good.[19]

Some argue that a self-government or sovereignty model is the only one which is logically coherent. How can laws be recognized without recognition of a lawmaker? How can indigenous ownership of land be acknowledged without acknowledging indigenous sovereignty over that land? These questions in a sense assert what they attempt to prove: the reality and continuing validity of indigenous sovereignty. If there is no such sovereignty, of course, there is nothing inconsistent about not realizing it. But if we suppose that at the moment of settlement Europeans did or should have viewed indigenous peoples as sovereign nations under the terms of European international law, even that does not prove the existence of continuing sovereignty. If adverse

[19] Will Kymlicka has suggested that one solution to this problem might lie in indigenous peoples submitting to international human rights conventions and tribunals, thereby gaining the advantages of judicial review without having to submit directly to the state that has broken promises to them in the past.

possession is a good rule for ownership,[20] it is an indispensable rule with regard to sovereignty. Even in the complete absence of any legally valid extinguishment of sovereignty, full sovereignty cannot be thought to endure unexercised for ever. A case can be made for the rights of living members of cultural minorities to self-determination, or to secession in certain circumstances; but that case cannot simply be based on the putative sovereignty of their ancestors. I argue elsewhere that the case must be made instrumentally in terms of defence of liberal values or protection from violent states, because any general defence of an inherent right to self-government rests on implausible claims about the external reality of some category like 'nation'.

At the risk of over-repetition, I am not sure that it makes sense to try to identify 'the best' or even 'the preferred' mode of incorporation; but it does make sense to identify the characteristic dangers, difficulties, and opportunities of each. Customary incorporation without a commonly accessible civil law is dangerous to members of the indigenous community.[21] Customary incorporation *with* a general civil law creates dangers of opportunistic choice of jurisdiction; but the possibility of such choice is generally salutary and the danger of, for example, an indigenous criminal opportunistically choosing the more lenient jurisdiction can be taken into account. Territorial self-government carries well-known dangers concerning the treatment of local minorities, possible incentives for secession, and the protection of individual rights. Common law incorporation risks understating the distinctiveness of indigenous peoples.

Neither is the joining of all three modes a solution. The risks that a territorial government will be oppressive are hardly lessened by making it sole owner of, as well as sovereign over, all of its land, or by justifying its authority in terms of its ability to preserve forcibly customary ways of life.

From the perspective of indigenous groups, consistency is a virtue; inconsistency, at least, has too often been to their disadvantage. From the perspective of the wider state, clarity and simplicity are advantages; I have argued that they are advantages for the indigenous minority as well. All of these needs, at least, common law incorporation can satisfy. Elements of customary incorporation are often necessary; but the more customary law is constrained by the possibility of members opting out of it, perhaps the more like common law incorporation it becomes. For contingent historical reasons, some indigenous communities have clear legal claims to consistently observed self-government rights; but those rights are not and should not be too tightly linked with the other modes of incorporation. Where there is not yet a strong claim or need for self-government—as in Australia—it seems to me that it can

---

[20] I argue that it is, especially in a multicultural society (Levy forthcoming).

[21] Jeremy Waldron (1993a) notes, though using different terminology, that it is also dangerous to the peace of the wider community.

be treated as a last resort, after good-faith efforts have been made to meet indigenous aspirations and needs through common law and then customary incorporation.

Drawing on Shklar and Montesquieu, I argue elsewhere (Levy 1996, forthcoming) for a multiculturalism of fear which makes the avoidance of cruelty and violence (whether intercommunal or intracommunal) the central goals of liberal multiculturalism. From the perspective of a multiculturalism of fear, many of the considerations noted above weigh heavily on the side of common law recognition, and limit customary recognition to cases in which there is a general civil law available. Territorial models of ethnocultural self-government are systematically prone to conflicts over borders and local minorities. The non-territorial models, by contrast, actually diminish the incentives for certain kinds of conflict. Local minorities are obviously less aggrieved than under a territorial model; the indigenous (or religious) minority gains legal rights which diminish its members' sense that only their own state can protect them. However, non-territorial customary recognition, when that recognition excludes access to any civil code, creates grave dangers of its own, both to those bound by customary law and to others.

Jeremy Waldron (1993a) uses the example of Romeo and Juliet to show the dangers created when the only laws or governing norms belong exclusively to neighbouring but separate communities. The absence, as it were, of a common law allowing intermarriage within the city forces the pair out of the city and out of the protection of laws altogether as well as generating conflict between the communities. This violates two central prescriptions of the multiculturalism of fear: to mitigate communal conflict and to protect individuals from the dangers of complete exclusion. Shklar (1991: 4) reminds us that 'to be a stateless individual is one of the most dreadful fates that can befall anyone in the modern world'; as much as liberalism fears the power of the state, it also fears the status of statelessness in a world of states. (Compare Walzer 1983: 32; Arendt 1973: 276–90.)

13

'Landed' Citizenship: Narratives of Aboriginal Political Participation

JOHN BORROWS

My grandfather was born in 1901 on the western shores of Georgian Bay, at the Cape Croker Indian reservation. Generations before him were born on the same soil. Our births, lives, and deaths on this site have brought us into citizenship with the land. We participate in its renewal, have responsibility for its continuation, and grieve for its losses. As citizens with this land, we also feel the presence of our ancestors, and strive with them to have the relationships of our polity respected. Our loyalties, allegiance, and affection is related to the land. The water, wind, sun, and stars are part of this federation. The fish, birds, plants, and animals also share this union. Our teachings and stories form the constitution of this relationship, and direct and nourish the obligations this citizenship requires. The Chippewas of the Nawash have struggled to sustain this citizenship in the face of the diversity and pluralism that has become part of the land. This has not been an easy task. Our codes have been disinterred, disregarded, and repressed. What is required to re-inscribe these laws, and once again invoke a citizenship with the land?

Close to thirty years have passed since Harold Cardinal wrote an influential book entitled *The Unjust Society* (Cardinal 1969). His work catalogued the troubling conditions Indians found themselves in during the late 1960s.[1] He described the denial of Indian citizenship, and wrote as a response to the Trudeau government's plan to eliminate Indian rights.[2] His message captured the feelings of Aboriginal people everywhere. He chronicled a disturbing tale of how Indians were marginalized in Canada through bureaucratic neglect, political indifference, and societal ignorance. He labelled Canada's treatment of Indians as 'cultural genocide' (1969: 139), and in the process gave widespread literary presence to the absence of Indian rights. In convincing tones he outlined thoughtful solutions to overcome threats to our underlying citi-

---

[1] For a description of these conditions see Hawthorn (1966).

[2] The government set out this plan in the 1969 White Paper (see Department of Indian Affairs and Northern Development 1969). The White Paper was a policy designed to reduce and minimize political and 'lawful obligations' owed to Indian people. The leading work examining the White Paper is Weaver (1981).

zenship, organized around the central theme of Indian control of Indian affairs. He called for action to protect special Aboriginal connections with the land. He advocated the strengthening of Indian organizations,[3] the abolition of the Department of Indian Affairs (1969: 163), educational reform,[4] re-structured social institutions,[5] broad-based economic development,[6] and the 'immediate recognition of all Indian rights for the re-establishment, review and renewal of all existing Indian treaties'.[7] Cardinal's ideas resonated throughout Indian country and parallel proposals became the mainstay of Indian political discourse for the next three decades.[8] He articulated a revolutionary message in a transformative time.

Fast-forward to the massive five-volume Report of the Royal Commission on Aboriginal Peoples released in 1996 (Royal Commission on Aboriginal Peoples 1996). Same story: an account of the violation of Aboriginal rights, and a call for their immediate recognition and renewal. The report records the continued excision of Aboriginal relationships with their lands. It demonstrates that the problems Cardinal profiled stubbornly remain. Despite some notable achievements in the intervening years, such as constitutional recognition and affirmation of Aboriginal rights, it illustrates how indigenous citizenship with the land is increasingly tenuous. In their broad outlines, Cardinal and the commission's messages are notable for their similarity. Aboriginal people are suffering, their rights are being abrogated, and the answer to this challenge is Aboriginal control of Aboriginal affairs. Like Cardinal, though more elaborately and expansively, the commission recommended a series of legislative and policy goals such as the strengthening of Aboriginal

[3] Indian organizations were to 'restore and revitalize a sense of direction, purpose and being for Indians', and 'work to weld communities together into dynamic, growing forces that can participate in their twentieth century environment' (Cardinal 1969: 162–5).

[4] Cardinal observed: 'Since the introduction of formal white education to the Indians of Canada, their original educational processes have either been shunted completely aside or discouraged. The only purpose in educating the Indian has been to create little brown white men, not what it should have been, to help develop the human being or to equip him for life in a new environment' (1969: 166).

[5] On the restructuring of social institutions Cardinal wrote: 'there must be created, within these communities, structures that attack the problem at their source. Ideally, most of the services within a community should be provided by the community itself. Before this can happen, huge sums of money must be provided, aimed at community problems. No outside bureaucracy, whether in Ottawa or in a provincial capital, is flexible enough . . .' (1969: 168).

[6] Economic development was to require 'huge sums of money . . . to enable Indian groups to take advantage of . . . opportunities on our own reserves' (Cardinal 1969: 169).

[7] In securing Indian rights through existing and renewed treaties Cardinal suggested: 'The negotiations for this must be undertaken in a new and different spirit by both sides. The treaties must be maintained. The treaties must be interpreted in light of needs that exist today. . . . The Indian simply cannot afford to allow the government to renege on its obligations because, if he does, he commits cultural suicide' (1969: 166).

[8] Writing representative of this approach can be found in Little Bear et al. (1984); Boldt and Long (1985); Long and Boldt (1988); Richardson (1989); Cassidy (1991).

nations,[9] the abolition of the Department of Indian Affairs,[10] educational reform,[11] restructured social institutions,[12] broad-based economic development,[13] and the immediate recognition of all Aboriginal rights for the re-establishment, review, renewal, and creation of treaties.[14] Same story, same solutions. A revolutionary message in a reactionary time.

Why the same approach? If the message didn't have the desired effect the first time, why repeat it? Does the call for Aboriginal control of Aboriginal affairs stand a greater chance in the spirit of the late 1990s than it did in the late 1960s? While there are hopeful signs on the horizon,[15] there is also cause for concern.[16] Despite the wisdom of the message, so far the reaction to the commission has been as feeble as the response to Cardinal. All the while, Aboriginal citizenship with the land is being slowly diminished. The disfranchisement of our people (and our spirits) from the land, water, animals, and trees continues at an alarming rate. Do we need a new story, new solutions? We do. We no longer need a revolutionary message in a transformative time; we need a transformative message in a reactionary time.

To preserve and extend our participation with the land, it is time to talk also of Aboriginal control of Canadian affairs. Aboriginal people must work

---

9 Recommendation 2.3.27 of the Royal Commission states: 'The Parliament of Canada enact an Aboriginal Nations Recognition and Governance Act to (a) establish the process whereby the government of Canada can recognize the accession of an Aboriginal group or groups to nation status and its assumption of authority as an Aboriginal government to exercise its inherent self-governing jurisdiction; (b) establish criteria for the recognition of Aboriginal nations, including . . . [there follows a list of six criteria]; (c) authorize the creation of recognition panels under the aegis of the proposed Aboriginal and Lands Tribunal to advise the government of Canada on whether a group meets recognition criteria; (d) enable the federal government to vacate its legislative authority under section 91 (24) of the Constitution Act, 1867 with respect to core powers deemed needed by Aboriginal nations and to specify which additional areas of federal jurisdiction the Parliament of Canada is prepared to acknowledge as being core powers to be exercised by Aboriginal governments; and (e) provide enhanced financial resources to enable recognized Aboriginal nations to exercise expanded governing powers for an increased population base in the period between recognition and the conclusion or reaffirmation of comprehensive treaties.'

10 Recommendation 2.3.45 of the Royal Commission states: 'The government of Canada present legislation to abolish the Department of Indian Affairs and Northern Development and replace it by two new departments: a Department of Aboriginal Relations and a Department of Indian and Inuit Services.'

11 See recommendations 3.5.1 to 3.5.44 of the Royal Commission.

12 See recommendations 3.2.1 to 3.4.15.

13 See recommendations 2.5.1 to 2.5.52.

14 See recommendations 2.2.2 to 2.2.17.

15 For instance, in early Jan. 1998 the Minister of Indian Affairs responded to some of the Royal Commission's recommendations regarding residential schools. She stated that the government of Canada 'expresses profound regret' for past actions which have contributed to some of the difficulties Aboriginal people currently experience.

16 See e.g. R. v. Pamajewon [1996] 2 S.C.R. 1025, where the Supreme Court of Canada refused to consider broad rights to self-government under s. 35 (1) of the constitution.

individually and as groups beyond their communities to enlarge and increase their influence over matters that are important to them. We need an Aboriginal prime minister, Supreme Court judge, and numerous indigenous CEOs. We need people with steady employment, good health, and entrepreneurial skill. They should be joined by Indian scientists, doctors, lawyers, and educators; and be coupled with union leaders, social activists, and conservative thinkers.[17] We need these people to incorporate indigenous ideologies and perspectives into their actions, including ideas about the federalism we should enjoy with the earth. These people could join with compatible existing groups, or they could form new political organizations, research institutions, and corporate enterprises to expand Aboriginal influence. These people should stand beside reserve-based teachers such as Aboriginal elders, chiefs, grandmothers, aunties, hunters, fishers, and medicine people as bearers and transmitters of culture. For too long the burden of cultural transmission has been placed on reserve-based teachers and leaders. While their knowledge will always remain vitally important in the expansion of ideas, other Aboriginal people in different settings within Canada also have to shoulder some of this responsibility. Aboriginal people must transmit and use their culture in matters beyond 'Aboriginal' affairs. Aboriginal citizenship must be extended to encompass other people from around the world who have come to live on our land.

After all, this is *our* country. Aboriginal people have a right and a legal obligation as a prior but ongoing indigenous citizenship to participate in its changes. We have lived here for centuries, and will for centuries more. We will continue to influence the land's resource utilization, govern its human relationships, participate in trade, and be involved in all of its relations—as we have done for millennia. Fuller citizenship requires that this be done in concert with other Canadians—as well as on our own, in our own communities. Aboriginal control of Aboriginal affairs is a good message, and it has to be strengthened—but it is also limiting. It is not consistent with holistic notions of citizenship that must include the land, and all the beings upon it. When we speak of Aboriginal control of Aboriginal affairs, it is evident that Canadians feel they do not have much of a stake in that message,[18] except maybe what 'they' think 'we' take from 'them' in the process.[19] Canada's

---

[17] It is not that the message of greater participation within Canada did not appear in Cardinal and the commission's proposals; it is just that this message did not receive the same emphasis and pursuit as 'Aboriginal control of Aboriginal affairs'.

[18] See Brian Schwartz (1990: 78–80), where he argued that 'separatism leads to indifference from the larger community instead of supportive interaction'.

[19] A survey conducted by Southam News and Compas Poll asked: 'Do you feel the federal government should put more money in the following areas.' It then listed sixteen categories and elicited a response which gave national defence and Aboriginals the lowest priority; see Gherson (1997).

stake in Aboriginal peoples, in the land, has to be raised: at radical, liberal, and conservative levels.

Our world is bigger than the First Nation, reserve, or settlement. Approximately half of the Aboriginal population live outside these boundaries (Royal Commission on Aboriginal Peoples 1996: i. 17–20). Certainly our traditional lands and relationships lie outside these boundaries. Even if the reserve is where we live, national and international forces influence even the most 'remote' or seemingly local time-honoured practice. In fact, an autonomous Aboriginal nation would encounter a geography, history, economics, and politics that requires participation with Canada and the world to secure its objectives. Aboriginal control through Canadian affairs is an important way to influence and participate in our lands. Without this power we are left outside significant decision-making structures that have the potential to destroy our lands. This is a flawed notion of citizenship. Canadians must participate with us, and in the wider view of polity that sustained our relations for thousands of years.

If we pursue this notion of citizenship, what will this new narrative sound like? How will its constituent stories be arranged? How does this new narrative relate to the former? What is lost, and what is gained? The development of another narrative may severely undermine those who have invested their aspirations and energies in the former, even if the message is complementary. Some have spent a tremendous amount of time and effort developing messages of an exclusive citizenship and measured separatism for Indians, through a form of self-government. These real human interests need recognition. But that approach, while appropriate and helpful, is not rich enough to encompass the wide variety of relationships we need to negotiate in order to live with the hybridity, displacement, and positive potential that our widening circles represent.[20] The extension of Aboriginal citizenship into Canadian affairs is a developing reality because of their increasingly complex social, economic, and political relations. Intercultural forces of education, urbanization, politics, and intermarriage each have a significant influence in drawing indigenous people into closer relationship with Canadian society.[21] The impulse behind the call for this refocused narrative is suggested by these changing dynamics in the Indian population. Since 1961 our populations have quadrupled (Royal Commission on Aboriginal Peoples 1996: i. 14),[22] rates of urban residency have climbed to 50 per cent of the total Aboriginal population (Royal Commission on Aboriginal Peoples 1996: i. 17–20), and one in every two Aboriginal people marries a non-Aboriginal person (Statistics

---

[20] An excellent compilation of writers addressing issues in simultaneous cultural participation is found in Ashcroft et al. (1996).

[21] The intercultural nature of Canadian society has been examined in Tully (1995).

[22] In 1961 the Aboriginal population was estimated to be 220,000.

Canada 1996). Moreover, our health has improved,[23] and incomes have increased.[24] While these indicators hide the continuing individual and collective pain of too many Aboriginal people, numerous Aboriginal people frequently interact with Canadians in a very significant way.

I have taught at three of Canada's larger universities in the past seven years, and my experience at each of them indicates that an increasing number of Aboriginal people are graduating from them prepared to contribute at the First Nation, provincial, national, and in some cases the international level. Over 150,000 Aboriginal people now have or are in post-secondary education (Department of Indian and Northern Affairs 1994). That is a significant development, since in 1969 there were fewer than 800 Aboriginal post-secondary graduates (Department of Indian and Northern Affairs 1994). When 150,000 is measured against our overall population of approximately 1 million, it is apparent that Aboriginal citizenship is expanding—and that Aboriginal control of Aboriginal affairs, while necessary, is not enough to reflect the simultaneous cultural participation occurring. I have directly supervised and watched graduate 100 Aboriginal law students, and have spoken to and visited with hundreds more. I have watched them fill jobs as entrepreneurs, managers, lawyers, teachers, politicians, researchers, and public servants. In the wider university setting I have witnessed a similar phenomenon. In May 1997 I watched the graduation of the top medical student at the University of British Columbia, who was an Ojibway woman. A few months earlier I was an external reviewer of the Native Indian Teacher Education programme at UBC and discovered that some of the province's most respected educators, and a good number of principals, graduated from this programme. UBC also has similar programmes in forestry, business, health, engineering, and arts that demonstrate similar success. These deep changes that can be statistically and anecdotally noted show that Aboriginal narratives on citizenship have to be transformed.

Yet, I have also witnessed the struggles some of these same students experience. Racism (Royal Commission on Aboriginal Peoples 1996: ii. 817), cultural alienation, family tragedy, poor academic preparation, insensitive teachers, and unresponsive curricula conspire to rob many Aboriginal people of the benefits education can bring. Furthermore, I know that there are many more who could be participating who are not; some out of choice, but most do not because of the colonial pathologies that continue to resonate within

[23] 'Although the life expectancy of Aboriginal people throughout North America as measured from birth is significantly lower that for non-Aboriginal people, it has improved since the second world war' (Royal Commission on Aboriginal Peoples 1996: iii. 119).

[24] However, this expansion in income did not keep pace with that experienced by non-Aboriginal people (see Frideres 1993: 159–62). Also disturbing is the fact that Aboriginal unemployment increased in this period (Royal Commission on Aboriginal Peoples 1996: ii. 804).

our communities. The backdrop of these and other continued challenges may generate a cool reaction to assertions of Aboriginal control of Canadian affairs. As such, I anticipate that the account I am suggesting will meet with some resistance.

For example, it may be thought that I am advocating assimilation. I am not. Assimilation implies a loss of political control, culture, and difference. Aboriginal control of Canadian affairs has the potential to facilitate the acquisition of political control, the continued development of culture, and respect for difference because it could change contemporary notions of Canadian citizenship.[25] Citizenship under Aboriginal influence may generate a greater attentiveness to land uses and cultural practices that are preferred by many Aboriginal peoples. Canadian notions of citizenship might not only develop to include greater scope for people's involvement in sustenance activities, but these ideas of citizenship might also further reduce the tolerance for land uses which extirpate these pursuits. A recognition of the importance of these objectives could thus shield Aboriginal peoples from assimilation by ensuring sufficient space for the pursuit of preferred Aboriginal activities. Moreover, Canadian citizenship under Aboriginal influence may expand to recognize the land as a party to Confederation in its own right. Many Aboriginal groups have well-developed notions in their philosophies and practices about how to recognize the land as citizen. They may be able to influence other Canadians to consider the adverse impact of their activities on the land itself, as an entity in its own right.[26] Aboriginal values and traditions could help shape these changes and reframe the relationships within our polity. Aboriginal peoples would resist assimilation with such a recognition because their values concerning land could be entrenched in Canada's governing ideas and institutions, and help to reconfigure Canada in an important way.

Tradition can be the dead faith of living people, or the living faith of dead people.[27] If indigenous traditions are not regarded as useful in tackling these present concerns, and applying in current circumstances, then these tradi-

[25] The potential for the narrative of Aboriginal control of Canadian affairs to affect these changes will be strengthened as the notion of Aboriginal control of Aboriginal affairs remains strong and vibrant. I am not advocating that Aboriginal control of Aboriginal affairs be neglected.

[26] I recognize that considering land as a party to citizenship in its own right would initially seem strange to many people who were not used to considering land as having an agency of its own. There would be questions and concerns about how to detect this agency and protect its functioning in the light of demanding, competing interests. After all, even if Aboriginal peoples were able to exercise enough influence to momentarily convince other Canadians that land should have a place of its own in decision-making, it may be fairly asked who would articulate the land's concerns. Aboriginal peoples have some answers to these questions (see Borrows 1997a); and there is a substantial non-native literature that concerns itself with these questions in the non-Aboriginal context: an influential, thoughtful, and representative piece is Stone (1987).   [27] For a general discussion of this issue see Pelikan (1984).

tions are the dead faith of living people. On the other hand, if our people, institutions, and ideologies are relevant for participation beyond our boundaries, this marks the living faith of our ancestors—the living traditions of dead people. Aboriginal peoples can resist assimilation by applying their traditions to answer the questions they encounter in the multifaceted, pluralistic world they now inhabit.

When my great-great-grandfather placed his name and totemic symbol on a treaty that surrendered 1.5 million acres in southern Ontario, he did not assent to assimilation (Borrows 1992). He sought control over his life amidst changing cultural circumstances. He knew that Chippewa–Anishinabe culture could benefit from the promises of non-Aboriginal education, employment, housing, and medicine. These were pledged to us in return for other people participating in citizenship with our land. We have fulfilled our part of the agreement: other people enjoy our land; it is now time for Aboriginal peoples to access promises related to Canadian affairs. This is not to extinguish Aboriginal culture through its interaction with Canada; it is to enrich it by allowing for its development and application to our current needs. There is contemporary worth in indigenous traditions which consider all the constituent parts of the land related (see J. D. Hughes 1983; Vescey and Venables 1980). While I regard this knowledge as imperfect and incomplete, it is also insightful and wise. There is much to be gained by applying this knowledge—within Aboriginal communities—and within Canada. Our intellectual, emotional, social, physical, and spiritual insights can simultaneously be compared, contrasted, rejected, embraced, and intermingled with others. In fact, this process has been operative since before the time that Indians first encountered others on their shores.[28]

Concerns about assimilation may not be the only grounds on which others may object to a narrative of Aboriginal control of Canadian affairs. Participation within Canada may not sound or appear to be 'Aboriginal'. It may be said that this notion violates sacred treaties and compromises traditional cultural values.[29] Yet, it should be asked: what does it mean to be Aboriginal or traditional? Aboriginal practices and traditions are not 'frozen'. Aboriginal identity is constantly undergoing renegotiation. We are traditional, modern, and postmodern people. Our values *and* identities are constructed and reconstructed through local, national, and sometimes international experiences. The meaning of Aboriginal is not confined to some pristine moment prior to the arrival of Europeans in North America (Borrows 1998). Similarly, the

---

[28] The Supreme Court of Canada failed to recognize and protect as rights any practices that developed from the interaction of Aboriginal and non-Aboriginal peoples in *R. v. Vanderpeet* [1996] 2 S.C.R. 723. A critique of this test is found in Barsh and Henderson (1997).

[29] It is first important to note that what is 'traditional' or constitutes a central cultural value will differ between First Nations. These differences make it difficult to anticipate which precise issues may be of concern in Aboriginal control of Canadian affairs.

notion of Canadian, or any other cultural identifier, is not fixed.[30] As Edward Said observed about identity and culture:

No one today is purely *one* thing. Labels like Indian, or woman, or Muslim or American are not more than starting-points, which if followed into actual experience for only a moment are quickly left behind. Imperialism consolidated the mixture of cultures and identities on a global scale. But its worst and most paradoxical gift was to allow people to believe they were only, mainly, exclusively, white, or Black, or Western, or Oriental. Just as human beings make their own history, they also make their cultures and ethnic identities. No one can deny the persisting continuities of long traditions, sustained habitations, national languages and cultural geographies, but there seems no reason except fear and prejudice to keep insisting on their separation and distinctiveness, as if that was all human life was about. (Said 1993: 336)[31]

As Said implies, the formation of culture and identity is contingent on our interactions with others. This insight makes it difficult to object to the point that an assertion of Aboriginal control of Canadian affairs is not 'Aboriginal'. Aboriginal values and identity develop in response to their own *and* other cultures' practices, customs, and traditions.[32] As such, 'Aboriginality' is extended by Aboriginal control of *both* Canadian and Aboriginal affairs. Since important aspects of Aboriginal identity are influenced by Canada, Aboriginal control of Canadian affairs is one way to assert more control over what it means to be Aboriginal. In the process, such assertions may even shape what it means to be Canadian.

Some, however, may not be impressed with this more fluid notion of what it means to be Aboriginal. There may be objections that I have gone too far, that the idea that Aboriginal citizenship could include non-Aboriginal people inappropriately stretches tradition. For example, it might be claimed that Aboriginal control of Canadian affairs violates sacred cultural traditions such as the two-row wampum belt. The Gus Wen Tah, as the belt is called, was first adhered to by my people, the Ojibway, in 1764, when the British made an alliance with the Indians of the upper Great Lakes (Borrows 1997*b*).[33] The belt consists of three parallel rows of white beads, separated by two rows of purple. To some, the belt suggests a separate nation-to-nation relationship between First Nations and the Crown that prohibits Aboriginal participation

[30] While I have observed that identity is not fixed (see Wolf 1982: 387), I would not argue it is not infinitely fluid. People's interpretations of their cultures' meaning is restrained by their sense of 'how we do things here' (see Taylor 1992).

[31] I would like to thank Natalie Oman for bringing this quotation to my attention (Oman 1997: 42).

[32] For a discussion of how identity is formed through this interactive, dialogical process, see Bakhtin (1981: 354).

[33] The principles represented in the two-row wampum were over 100 years old by the time they were received in this area. They were first established by the Haudenosaunee with the Dutch in 1664, and with the English not too many years later.

in Canadian affairs. This interpretation flows from a focus on the purple rows. One purple row symbolizes the British going down a river, politically navigating their ship of state; while the other purple row represents the Indians going down their river, politically controlling their own ship of state. Some have said 'these two rows never come together in that belt, and it is easy to see what that means. It means that we have two different paths, two different people' (Haudenosaunee Confederacy 1983: 13). This reading of the belt centres on the autonomy of each party, as the parallel purple lines are thought to signify that neither party was to interfere in the political organization of the other. In this symbolism is rooted the idea of Aboriginal control of Aboriginal affairs. In fact, according to this description Aboriginal control of Canadian affairs seems to violate a fundamental tenet of the Gus Wen Tah.

In considering the potential of the Gus Wen Tah for embracing a notion of citizenship that includes non-Aboriginal people, two important observations deserve attention. First, the Gus Wen Tah contains more than two purple rows. The three rows of white beads represent a counter-balancing message that signifies the importance of sharing and interdependence. These white rows, referred to as the bed of the agreement (Haudenosaunee Confederacy 1983: 13), stand for peace, friendship, and respect. When these principles are read together with those depicted in the purple rows, it becomes clear that ideas of citizenship also have to be rooted in notions of mutuality and interconnectedness. The ecology of contemporary politics teaches us that the rivers on which we sail our ships of state share the same waters. There is no river or boat that is not linked in a fundamental way to the others; that is, there is no land or government in the world today that is not connected to and influenced by others. This is one reason for developing a narrative of Aboriginal citizenship that speaks more strongly to relationships that exist beyond 'Aboriginal affairs'. Tradition, in this case represented by the Gus Wen Tah, can support such an interpretation.

A second observation that speaks to the Gus Wen Tah's potential to encompass Aboriginal control of Canadian affairs is that its interpretation must be made by reference to other belts exchanged in the same period. The Gus Wen Tah cannot be read in isolation from these other instruments, which clarify the meaning of the two-row wampum. Just as one should not read a treaty according to its written words alone, one should not interpret the Gus Wen Tah solely according to its woven characters. For example, at the time the Gus Wen Tah was exchanged at Niagara in 1764, another belt accompanied it which emphasized the interdependence between the Indians of the Great Lakes and the nascent settler population. A ship was woven into one end of the belt with its bow facing towards Quebec. At the other end of the belt is an image of Michilimackinac, a place in the centre of the Great Lakes regarded as the heart of the Chippewa–Anishinabe homelands. Between the two objects were woven twenty-four Indians holding one another's hands, with the person furthest to the right holding the cable of the ship, while the one on the extreme left has his foot resting on the land at Quebec. Representatives of the twenty-two First Nations assembled at Niagara in 1764 touched this 'Belt of Peace' as a symbol of friendship and as a pledge to become 'united'.[34] This strong imagery conveys the connection between Aboriginal and non-Aboriginal peoples and the lands they occupied. In fact, in this belt the Indians are holding onto the ship to pull it over to receive and participate in the benefits from the non-indigenous population. These wider understandings demonstrate that tradition can support a notion of citizenship that encourages autonomy, and at same time unifies and connects us to one another and the lands we rely on.

Concerns about Aboriginal control of Canadian affairs, however, will probably not end at borders of Indian reserves, Inuit lands, and Metis settlements. The idea may also cause some concern among the broader Canadian public. The radical approach to Aboriginal control of Canadian affairs could be troublesome as some wonder about the potentially wrenching nature of this kind of action. If Aboriginal people are going to participate in Canadian and global politics, this will require a great deal of change within the country. An assertive and aggressive stance for control may bring to mind ethnic and racial strife in other countries where groups are attempting to seize control of the state. Canadians have already in a small measure experienced such conflict where, in select instances, Aboriginal peoples have taken direct action to maintain their place with the land. Some Aboriginal peoples may be willing to pursue this challenging course to control Canadian affairs if their underlying concerns about their continuing relationships with the land are not respected. However, even more conciliatory liberal or conservative approaches could create difficulties, as some within the current establishment will not be prepared to cede or share power. There is a need to overcome this near-exclusivity. The chairs, corridors, and halls of legislatures, universities, courts, law societies, unions, and corporate boards of directors have been sluggish in responding to the influx of Aboriginal people. To my knowledge, though this needs to be supplemented with further research, there are approximately ten Aboriginal legislators, twenty tenured Aboriginal professors, seventeen Aboriginal judges, one law society bencher, no national Aboriginal union executives, and no Aboriginal members of boards of directors in Canada's twenty-five largest corporations. These levels of representation have to change. Indeed, it is required if Canada is ever to enjoy an inclusive citizenship.

Such a change would not require the grant of any special numeric weight to Aboriginal peoples participating in these institutions beyond their proportionate representation of 5 per cent of the general population. If Aboriginal peoples were to have their proportionate participation reflected in national

---

[34] Thomas G. Anderson (1858).

institutions, there could potentially be over fifty Aboriginal legislators, 1,700 tenured Aboriginal professors, 100 Aboriginal judges, and hundreds of Aboriginal union and corporate executives. Participation at this level could result in significant changes to the way land in Canada is treated and allocated. Aboriginal people could bring their views of land, formed through contemporary and centuries-long teachings about its place in community citizenship, to the attention of Canada's institutions. There is no doubt that the exercise of Aboriginal participation in decision-making power in these settings would result in the control of Canadian affairs being different from what it is today. While I appreciate that not all Aboriginal peoples working in these positions would adhere to the notions of citizenship outlined in this chapter, my experience and knowledge in dealing with Aboriginal peoples across the country convinces me that their participation would enfold many of the ideas developed here.[35] Many of these people would help to reformulate ideas about the place of land in our conceptions of citizenship. While some would function without attentiveness to the values formed through interactions with the people who hold the philosophies and values described herein, others certainly would, because such ideas and experiences have a central place in many Aboriginal communities.[36] As such, Aboriginal participation even at a level proportionate to their population in Canada would have an unparalleled effect on the functioning of our society and our conceptions of citizenship.

Yet, in accomplishing this change, there could be another concern among the broader Canadian public about the equity and fairness of Aboriginal control of Canadian affairs. After all, if Aboriginal peoples represent approximately 5 per cent of Canada's population, and have exclusive control of land on their reserves, it may be asked why they should have any interest and influence over land use outside of their reserves. It may be said that Aboriginal peoples cannot expect both to control their own affairs and also to exercise significant influence over others.[37] The seeming inequality in this

[35] For example, I know most of the Aboriginal judges in Canada. Almost every one of them undertakes their role on the bench in a way which upholds and respects Canadian legal values, while at the same time infusing the system with their insight and understanding formed through their educational and life experiences.

[36] My identification of widespread agreement on certain precepts among Canadian Aboriginal peoples does not come from some essentialized notion of the Aboriginal psyche. Rather, it is only to note that Aboriginal peoples have been positively socialized and negatively racialized to interpret the world in ways that differ from many non-Aboriginals. If exposed to different contexts, Aboriginal peoples can have as many different views on life as other people, if they are nurtured and educated in such environments. However, the process of socialization and racialization currently operating structures the formation of ideas and identity for Aboriginal peoples in certain ways. While many Aboriginal peoples may be able to question or separate themselves from these influences, strong societal forces nevertheless exist both within and outside Aboriginal communities to structure their development. For readings about the social nature of racialization, see Li and Bolaria (1988, esp. ch. 1).

[37] It would be interesting to examine the irony of those who would question Aboriginal

approach to citizenship may cause some concern because it may appear as if Aboriginal peoples would enjoy rights in Canada that others do not possess. One response to this matter may rest on Aboriginal people's legal status under Canadian property and constitutional law. Most Canadians do not demonstrate great concern over the law's recognition of property and civil rights; in fact, such guarantees are an important part of the country's most cherished values. An argument can be made that the protection of Aboriginal off-reserve property and civil rights merely (and belatedly) extends the benefits of Canadian property and civil rights law to Aboriginal peoples. Simply speaking, Aboriginal peoples may not have surrendered these rights over land outside their reserves. For example, in those areas of the country where Aboriginal peoples never entered into agreements with the Crown, they maintain a relationship with land outside their reserves that flows from their pre-existing use and occupation of that land (see *Delgamuukw* v. *British Columbia* 1997). Furthermore, in those areas of the country where Aboriginal peoples entered into treaties with the Crown, the oral history and text of these agreements often contains guarantees of Aboriginal land use outside reservation boundaries for numerous livelihood purposes.[38] These examples illustrate that many Aboriginal peoples have never consented to sever all relations with the land outside their reservations. Thus, on equitable and legal principles Canadian law may support the notion that Aboriginal peoples have a right to influence decisions outside their reserves, on their traditional lands, even if they have control over their own affairs.

Another response to concern about the fairness of Aboriginal peoples having exclusive control over their own lands—and at the same time participating in the control of lands outside their boundaries—involves the recognition that federalism as a political system should operate to encourage the simultaneous integration and separation of communities.[39] An exclusive focus on Aboriginal control of Aboriginal affairs does not equally facilitate these principles in the relationships Aboriginal peoples have with others. Aboriginal control of Aboriginal affairs focuses on the idea of autonomy to the exclusion of interdependence. The concurrent assertion of Aboriginal control of Canadian affairs rebalances interdependence with autonomy.

peoples' right to participate in the control of their own and others affairs, especially in light of the fact that many people have not found any problems with Canadians controlling their own and Aboriginal affairs.

[38] *R. v. White and Bob*, (1964) 50 D.L.R. (2d) 613; aff'd. (1965) 52 D.L.R. (2d) 481n (S.C.C.); *R. v. Taylor and Williams* (1981) 62 C.C.C. (2d) 228 (Ont. C.A.); *R. v. Simon* (1985) 24 D.L.R. (4th) 390 (S.C.C.); *R. v. Horseman*, [1990] 1 S.C.R. 901 (S.C.R.); *R. v. Badger*, (1996) 133 D.L.R. (4th) 324 (S.C.C.); *R. v. Sundown* [1999] 1 S.C.R.; Henderson (1994); Cardinal (1997).

[39] See the Supreme Court of Canada's comments in *In the Matter of Section 53 of the Supreme Court Act, R.S.C., c. S-26*; and *In the Matter of a Reference by the Governor in Council Concerning Certain Questions Relating to the Secession of Quebec From Canada, as Set out in Order in Council P.C. 1996–1497, Dated September 30, 1996* (Quebec Secession case) at paras. 55–60.

Other Canadians have long enjoyed autonomy *and* interdependence through their participation in provincial and national communities that somewhat represent both their local and nationwide concerns. Aboriginal peoples have never participated with other Canadians in this way. At the local level their position has been largely ignored, and at the national level their interests have been repressed by centuries-long colonial control. Thus, the notion that Aboriginal peoples should control Canadian affairs is, at some levels, a claim for Aboriginal peoples to enjoy the same rights as other Canadians, and participate as citizens in the country with appropriate federal structures and representation. There is no unfairness in such a claim; in fact, it would be unfair to prevent Aboriginal peoples from participating in Canada's federal structures in a manner similar to other regional and national communities. While from this perspective it may hardly seem transformative to speak of Aboriginal control of Canadian affairs given the well-entrenched notions about federalism in Canada, sadly, this discourse is ground-breaking when dealing with Aboriginal peoples. Their historical treatment and recent narratives have focused ideas of citizenship on principles that facilitate autonomy, to the exclusion of other more interdependent models of citizenship.[40]

However, even if Aboriginal peoples do have rights concerning land outside of their reservations through the application of legal rights and the principles of federalism, non-Aboriginal people may still wonder about the fairness of Aboriginal peoples qualifying for citizenship in their political system, when they cannot qualify as citizens in Aboriginal peoples' systems. This question may be especially poignant when other institutions of federalism guarantee mobility rights between various jurisdictions (*Black* v. *Law Society of Alberta* 1989), as membership in other federal structures is not restricted by ethnicity. In response to this question many Aboriginal peoples would argue that their circumstances are different, and that they must be able to place restrictions on citizenship based on ethnicity to preserve the existence and survival of the group (see *Jacobs* v. *Mohawk Council of Kahnawake* 1998). While I think restrictions on Aboriginal citizenship are necessary to maintain the social and political integrity of the group, I must admit that I am troubled by ideas of Aboriginal citizenship that may depend on blood or genealogy to support group membership. Scientifically, there is nothing about blood or descent alone that makes an Aboriginal person substantially different from any other person.[41] While often not intended by those who

---

[40] The fact that this discourse has developed in the face of strong holistic perspectives that many Aboriginal peoples possess makes this exclusion even more striking.

[41] There are numerous scientific and sociological studies that make the point that blood or race creates objective biological categories. The United Nations Educational, Scientific, and Cultural Organization (Unesco) has hosted many conferences where the participants have repudiated the biological notion of race (see Rex 1983; Montagu 1972). For a general overview of the literature and arguments, see Satzewich (1990: 251, 252–6).

advocate such criteria, exclusion from citizenship on the basis of blood or ancestry can lead to racism and more subtle forms of discrimination that destroy human dignity.

However, while I do not favour limits on citizenship on racialized grounds, it may be appropriate to have rigorous citizenship requirements on other grounds, to protect and nurture these communities. Aboriginal peoples are much more than kin-based groups. They have social, political, legal, economic, and spiritual ideologies and institutions that are transmitted through their cultural systems. These systems do not depend exclusively on ethnicity, and can be learned and adopted by others with some effort. Therefore, Aboriginal peoples could consider implementing laws consistent with these traditions to extend citizenship in Aboriginal communities to non-Aboriginal people. If non-Aboriginal people met certain standards that allowed for the creation and reproduction of these communities values, then these people should have a way to become Aboriginal citizens. The extension of this responsibility would respect the autonomy of Aboriginal communities, while at the same time recognizing the need to consider our interdependence as human beings. Thus, it is possible to develop answers to concerns people may have about Aboriginal control of Canadian affairs.

In the end, however, perhaps the most profound concern in adopting the discourse outlined in this essay is the multidimensional nature of the power imbalance Aboriginal peoples experience. Control in Canada is not exercised merely through people and institutions. Both are governed by deep-seated global and national tenets that animate and direct the 'acceptable' bounds within which people and institutions can exercise power. Aboriginal notions of citizenship with the land are not among these accredited ideologies. Assertions of Aboriginal control of Canadian affairs will encounter a matrix of power that works to exclude notions of 'land as citizen'. This will be especially evident when its economic implications are understood. In some cases the application of indigenous traditions might require that Aboriginal people share the wealth from the land with other Canadians; in others it may mean that a proposed use would have to be modified or terminated. A reorientation of this magnitude is not likely to occur without substantial opposition from those who benefit from the prevailing ideologies currently allocating power. To surmount this challenge Aboriginal people must employ many complementary discourses of control. This is the reason that Aboriginal control of Canadian affairs must join prevailing narratives of Aboriginal control of Aboriginal affairs in preserving and extending citizenship with the land.[42]

---

[42] Aboriginal control through Canadian affairs also has the potential to check the nepotism, abuse, and disregard for women that can occur within communities. Enough of our people have now raised these concerns to respond to them. Of course, nepotism, abuse, and disregard of women's rights occur in wider Canadian society, and Aboriginal people taking control in Canadian affairs will not end this. But it may diffuse its most poignant effects if alternatives for

Conclusion

There exists a 'special bond' between Aboriginal peoples and the lands they have traditionally occupied (*Delgamuukw* v. *The Queen* [1997] 153 D.L.R. 193). These bonds should be reflected in the discourses of Aboriginal citizenship. To only speak of Aboriginal control of Aboriginal affairs would disfranchise most Aboriginal peoples from their traditional lands. Measured separatism would separate many from places they hold dear. Why should an artificial line drawn around my reserve prevent me from participating in the vast areas my ancestors revered? This focus could prevent the acknowledgement and strengthening of the continuing Aboriginal reliance, participation, and citizenship with the lands they use outside these lines. Aboriginal peoples still honour the places made meaningful by an earlier generation's encounters. They still travel through these places and rely on them for food, water, medicine, memories, friends, and work. Many are hesitant to relinquish their relationship with them in the name of Aboriginal self-government merely because non-Aboriginal people now live there and also rely on this land. Aboriginal control of Canadian affairs provides a discourse which simultaneously recognizes the meaningful participation of Aboriginal people with one another, and with their non-Aboriginal neighbours. It contains a deeper commitment to preserve and extend the special relationship Aboriginal peoples have with the land. It does not abandon age-old territorial citizenships merely because non-Aboriginal people are now necessary to preserve the land's ancient relations.

In 1976 my grandfather died on the same shores he was born on seventy-five years earlier. He did not live his whole life there, however. His life's experiences were not completely bounded by the artificial borders of a colonial department's Indian reserve. As a young boy he hunted with his father in traditional territories recently made into rich, fertile farmlands. As a young man he worked in Wiarton, Owen Sound, Windsor, and Detroit as a plasterer and labourer. At the same time he fished in the waters of Georgian Bay and Lake Huron (and, in later years, taught his grandson about this practice when I was growing up). He then went on to Hollywood, California, acted in hundreds of films, and married a non-Aboriginal women from this state while he was there. As a middle-aged man he came back to the reserve when Pearl Harbour was bombed and resumed his practice of working off-reserve as a labourer, and hunting off-reserve to support his family. He

shelter, participation, and criticism lie within both Aboriginal and wider Canadian circles. While the potential for criticism on these issues may trouble some Aboriginal leaders, this may not be a bad result if these reproaches result in greater attention and accountability. For further discussion, see Laroque (1997).

received an honorary doctorate from the University of Kentucky because of his knowledge of plants and medicines throughout the 1.5 million acres of land his grandfather treatied over. Everywhere he went, including California, there were always people around with whom he could speak Ojibway, fluently. During the last twenty-five years of his life he alternatively lived on the reserve with my grandmother in their old cabin, on our hunting grounds north of the reserve, or with some of his eight children, who lived off the reserve in non-Aboriginal towns throughout the traditional territory. Discourses of Aboriginal citizenship must be enriched to reflect this fuller range of relationships with the land. Aboriginal culture is not static and, at least in southern Ontario, develops and redevelops through a wider variety of interactions than is recognized in conventional narratives of citizenship. Narratives of Aboriginal political participation should be transformed to reflect this fact.

PART VII

Federalism and Nationalism

14

Sustainable Federalism, Democratization, and Distributive Justice

GRAHAM SMITH

Of all the forms of governance that political theorists interested in the relationship between multicultural diversity and distributive justice have considered, federation has attracted the most attention. Yet the desirability of structuring federations to accommodate national or ethnic minority-defined constituent units and the compatibility of such governance with a defensible form of distributive justice are issues that continue to provoke considerable debate. Those opposed to structuring federal governance along national minority lines focus on two sets of arguments.

First, it is claimed, institutionalizing the federation along such lines is more likely to promote a primordial nationalism, which in politically unstable polities increases the likelihood of inter-ethnic violence and even civil war. Not only do such arrangements tend to solidify and make permanent what might be temporary or partial group identities, they also allow key policy areas to be hijacked by highly partisan titular élites and thus increase the probability of tyranny by the minority, which, it is contended, acts as an impediment to liberty for all.

Secondly, it is argued that by empowering particular national minorities such a federal arrangement is likely to impose limits on genuinely pluralist interests, since the demands and concerns of other groups or individuals will be downgraded or hidden from the gaze of federal politics. Within late modern federal democracies, despite the rise and increasing political prominence of new social movements, the capacity of the federal system and its political parties to represent forms of collective identities other than those of the dominant regional norm are invariably disadvantaged. When combined with consociational practices, federation can further reinforce limits on a more genuinely pluralist politics by highlighting inter-ethic politics and by delimiting entry-points and downgrading the politics of the marginalized to the more local arena.

In short, for the liberal theorist and proponent of federalism, the most effective way to secure minority rights is through non-ethnically based constituent units in which the appropriate framework and guarantor for ensuring the protection of minority rights are constructed around the human rights of individual citizens, regardless of ethnic, racial, or other backgrounds.

Those who defend federal-based minority-group recognition hold that, instead of furnishing the conditions for ethnic instability, federation can provide a means of managing intergroup conflicts that might otherwise develop into violence and lead to the proliferation of mini-statelets of limited viability. Thus while the Yugoslav federation was imperfect, when contrasted with the events following its collapse, it could be regarded as providing an effective means of preventing tribal wars. In Spain federalizing minority-group recognition has played a vital part in ensuring that country's relatively smooth transition from authoritarian to democratic rule. The other defence focuses on federation as a means of accommodating minority demands for political recognition and group liberty. On the grounds that minority cultural self-preservation (as well as political representation) is of fundamental importance for individuals because belonging to a minority culture provides 'a meaningful context for choice', the retention of group rights through federal supports is defended as an antidote to majority-group cultural assimilation. Any conception of entitlement should therefore be extended to protecting the right to be culturally different (Kymlicka 1995a; Taylor 1992). While such institutionalized protection could be seen as an infringement upon liberal rights, it might better be interpreted as providing immunity for such ethnoregional groupings. Thus such an arrangement can be justified so long as the basic rights of citizens who have different commitments to that of the ethnoregional majority, or no such commitments at all, are protected.

For the post-communist world, such questions have a particular poignancy. With few exceptions, post-communist polities are driven by a need to resolve serious ethnic conflicts in countries where traditions of individual freedoms are either non-existent or weakly developed and where demands for group recognition are being played out with often tragic consequences. Indeed few scholars would dissent from the view that central to their successful democratization is the recognition of certain liberal values embodied in the idea of the civic state. Of the post-communist multi-ethnic polities, Russia commands particular interest. Not only is it different in being the only post-soviet state to experiment with federation as a means of accommodating its national minorities, it has also had to reconcile a multinational diversity—with over sixty officially recognized minority nationalities—on a scale far greater than any other post-communist regime. Moreover, Russia is also unique amongst contemporary federations in that it was born out of a former federation, the Soviet Union. While post-soviet Russia's experiment with federation is generally interpreted as a means of ensuring that the country makes a successful transition to democracy and retains its territorial integrity, doubts have been expressed as to whether it can rightfully claim to be a federation based on democratic principles. After all, despite the introduction in December 1993 of a federal constitution and its proclamation (chapter 1, article 1) that 'Russia is a democratic federate rule-of-law state', a sovereign state's claim to federal status lies in more than an assertion that it constitutes a federation. The move towards greater presidential-style governance following the September 1993 *coup d'état* and the increasing powers that the president has secured in relation both to the Federal Assembly and to regional and local governments cast doubts upon Russia's progress towards establishing a democratized federation. In particular, some of the distinctive executive functions of the federation, as secured by the president, do not derive from the entrenchment of regional representation at the centre through a national legislature.

None the less, Russia does contain many of the features generally associated with a federation (King 1993; Graham Smith 1995). Its representation is preponderantly territorial; Russia comprises eighty-nine 'federal subjects', twenty-one higher-status ethnorepublics, and sixty-eight lower-level subjects: forty-nine regions (*oblasts*), six territories (*krais*), ten autonomous districts (*okrugs*), the Jewish autonomous *oblast*, and two 'federal' cities (Moscow and St Petersburg). Territorial representation is secured on at least two subnational levels, namely, local and regional government; and constituent units are incorporated electorally into the decision-making process of the national centre through representation in both the upper (Council of the Federation) and lower (State Duma) chambers of the Federal Assembly. The 178-member strong Federal Assembly comprises the heads of state of the ethnorepublics and regional governors, all of whom, following a 1996 decree, are elected by their constituent units.

While the federation is partly based on accommodating national minorities largely through representation at the ethnorepublic level, doubts have been expressed as to whether the federal process has developed in tandem with a coherent policy on minority rights. Thus Deputy Premier Ramazan Abdulatipov, in taking up ministerial responsibility in August 1997 for issues of ethnic relations, federal policy, and regional issues, asserted that 'to this day . . . there has been no federal nationalities policy' (*Nezavisimaya gazeta*, 21 August 1997). Abdulatipov's comments notwithstanding, this chapter asks whether Russia can accommodate a federal solution that is driven in part by a commitment to minority representation or whether it is adopting self-defeating structures liable to the very centrifugal forces federalism is trying to manage. It also looks at whether the adoption of what might be described as a mixed-rights approach to federal politics—that is, one which attempts to reconcile liberalism and nationalism—can provide the basis for a sustainable federalism that is not only grounded in the usual elements highly valued in democratic federations—toleration, respect, compromise, and bargaining— but also allows for mutual recognition of the right to be culturally different as well as safeguarding equality and social justice. The chapter is divided into three main parts. First, it explores the federal process. Secondly, it examines attempts, especially since the ending of the Chechen crisis, to develop a more coherent federal nationalities policy. Thirdly, focusing on the ethnorepublics, it argues that a democratized federation offers the most effective antidote to both minority and majority primordialist nationalisms. The chapter concludes by briefly exploring the implications of Russia's particular experiment for our understanding of multicultural federalism more generally.

The Federal Process

Central to shaping federal formation in Russia are three tensions, each of which is explored in turn: refederation, which entails conflict over the appropriate designation of powers between the centre and the ethnorepublics; federal asymmetry, which raises questions concerning the principles of equality and differentiation between the federation's constituent units; and the politics of the subject, that is, whether to structure the federation on the basis of individual or group rights.

Refederation—that is, the process of refederalizing Russia following the collapse of the Soviet federation in 1990 and Russia's declaration of state sovereignty—has been shaped in large measure by tensions between efforts to preserve Russia's territorial integrity and the empowerment of the ethnorepublics. In effect, it has reflected a struggle to secure a balance of power between the centre and its constituent subjects that will preserve the sovereign-boundedness of Russia. Thus the policies of the centre are not so much a serious attempt to develop a coherent and well-thought-through politics of multicultural recognition as an exercise in the management of secession prevention. Relations between the centre and its constituent units have undergone three identifiable stages of formal reframing.

The first stage began with the March 1992 Federal Treaty, the first attempt to provide a building-block for refederation following a two-year transitional period in which Russia's first president, Boris Yeltsin, had offered the ethnorepublics 'as much sovereignty as you can stomach' (*Literaturnaya gazeta*, 15 August 1990). In supporting the autonomist demands of Russia's ethnorepublics in this initial period, Yeltsin had seen a means for strengthening his own power base and of undermining Mikhail Gorbachev's position as president of the Soviet Union. Thus Yeltsin openly encouraged Russia's own ethnorepublics to declare themselves as sovereign entities with greater political powers. In return, several of the ethnorepublics reciprocated by boycotting Gorbachev's last-minute 1991 referendum to keep the Soviet Union together. By so doing the ethnorepublics mobilized behind Yeltsin and his vision of a sovereign and territorially intact Russia. The Federal Treaty was signed by nineteen of the twenty-one republics, with only Chechnya and Tatarstan refusing to participate. It permitted the ethnorepublics to adopt their own constitutions and laws, elect their own legislatures and heads of state, appoint their own supreme courts, and have their own symbols of statehood. While the treaty, which included a scheme to raise their status in relation to the other regions and constituent units, did appease most of the ethnorepublics, it also encouraged them to enact legislation of increasing concern to Moscow. Indeed, the failure to reach a fully workable compromise was one of the reasons that led Yeltsin in 1993 to dissolve the Russian parliament and to reclaim the initiative by putting the proposed federal constitution to a plebiscite.

It was part one of the Federal Treaty, namely those provisions concerned with the delimitation of powers to the ethnorepublics, which formed the basis of the December 1993 federal constitution (*Rossiiskaya gazeta*, 25 December 1993), marking the second stage in refederation. The new Russian constitution fell short of the scale of sovereignty that many of the ethnorepublics had envisaged. Although it accepts the principle of national self-determination, it does not confer the right to secede, as is made clear by chapter 1, article 4, which states that the Russian federation 'ensures the integrity and inviolability of its territory'. This omission strikes at the heart of centre–ethnorepublic tensions. The right of the ethnorepublics to secede was built into the original 1992 Federal Treaty but was interpreted by some of the constitution's framers as an abrogation of Russia as an integral primordial-territorial entity. This, as the ethnorepublics see it, is the denial of nations to practise, if they so desire, the right of national self-determination, a right which it is noted was theoretically available even during Soviet rule to its union republics. Compared with federations in late modern democracies, the federal constitution also contravenes a basic given that the central authorities may not unilaterally redefine the powers of its constituent units. In the Soviet constitution the President had been given powers both of judicial review (that is, the right to suspend acts issued by the executive bodies in Russia's provinces) and of arbitration between federal and local bodies or between constituent members of the federation.

For many of the ethnorepublics, the constitution was therefore judged as an abrogation of many of the autonomous rights previously embodied in the Federal Treaty. In the referendum, held on 12 December 1993, it received support from only nine of the twenty-one republics. Seven republics rejected the constitution (Adygea, Bashkortostan, Chuvashia, Dagestan, Karachaevo-Cherkessia, Mordovia, and Tuva); the plebiscite was declared invalid in Tatarstan, where less than 14 per cent of the electorate voted, and Chechnya did not participate at all (*Rossiiskie vesti*, 25 December 1993). Despite protests from a number of the ethnorepublics that their consent had not been given to this pro-presidential federal variant, Deputy Premier Sergei Shakrai was adamant that its introduction was legitimate as it had received endorsement by 58.4 per cent of the electorate: 'The constitution has been approved by citizens and not by the component parts. As citizens have approved it, the constitution is now in force in all constituent parts of the Russian federation' (*Rossiya*, 19–25 January 1994, 3). The principle of majority rule stood: the ethnorepublics, including Chechnya, were unconditionally bound by the majority decision.

With all twenty-one ethnorepublics introducing their own constitutions, an escalation in the so-called 'war of sovereignties' characterized the period following the plebiscite. According to the Yeltsin administration, no less than nineteen of the twenty-one ethnorepublic constitutions violated the federal constitution, either by declaring the given republic to be a subject of international law, by outlining the parameters of republican monetary systems, or by delimiting the republic's borders with other republics and regions, and even foreign countries (*Rossiiskaya gazeta*, 4 November 1996). Specific violations included the establishment of illegal taxes and dues in a number of the ethnorepublics, the right to decide questions of war and peace in the case of Tuva's constitution, and in Karelia and Sakha (Yakutia) the right to grant citizenship. In an attempt to try and reclaim the high ground of federal politics, and prompted by fears that the pro-independence policies of the Chechen government would spur on other republics, especially in the north Caucasus, to push for secession, the federation entered the third stage of de-federation, in which the centre began to negotiate a series of bilateral power-sharing treaties while continuing to claim that the federation was based on equality between its constituent parts. Had such a policy of secessionist-management been instituted earlier with regard to Chechnya, Moscow's military intervention and consequent bloody war might have been avoided.

Russia is far from unique in the way in which an asymmetric federation has evolved as part of the federal process. As with Spain and Canada, the federal process in Russia demonstrates that 'federating' can involve 'a post-constitutional process of reaching important agreements as much as it may rely on an original compact' (Agranoff 1997: 390). Thus, as in Spain, expanding constituent governance has continued as part of a fluctuating and ongoing process in which an asymmetric form of diffused federal construction continues to unfold, although in Russia it has been far less planned or systematically thought through than Spain's transition to an *estado de las autonomías* (a state made up of autonomous regions). What also distinguishes Russia from other asymmetric experiments is the sheer extent of federal asymmetry: by April 1998 over forty of its eighty-nine constituent units had successfully negotiated varying degrees of privileged status, with 'work in progress' in a further dozen.

Not surprisingly, considerable controversy has surrounded the question of whether the federation should be based on equality or differentiation of federal subjects. Initially, many federalists had supported the idea of the so-called 'republicanization' of Russia, in which Russia's constituent units, following the recommendations of a November 1990 Parliamentary Commission, would be based on fifty or so non-ethnic-based constituent units similar to the German *Länder*. Under this scheme the Russian *oblasts* were to be transformed into republics, ensuring that citizens, irrespective of their place of residence, would be entitled to equal rights. In the event the proposals adopted by the Presidium of Russia's Supreme Soviet in January 1992 won the day, whereby a distinction was drawn between the ethnorepublics and the regions, with the autonomy of the latter limited to adopting their own charters but not their own constitutions. Although initially envisaged as a stop-gap measure, this system, which is clearly designed to appease the more bellicose ethnorepublics, has formed the basis of both the Federal Treaty and the constitution. Not surprisingly, it has attracted considerable opposition from. the regions, which see it as creating two classes of citizens: those residing in the federation (the ethnorepublics) and those who have to abide by the rules of a unitary state (the regions) (Stroev 1996). In an attempt to appease the regions (and secure their support in the 1996 Presidential elections), Yeltsin did grant them the right to elect their leading officials, including their heads of state ('regional governors'), who had hitherto been appointed by the state president. This brought them closer to the ethno-republics and went some way towards weakening the centre's patronage. However, a decree of July 1997 again upgraded the status and authority of Yeltsin's so-called presidential representatives in an attempt to reassert central-executive control over regional governors, a move which is interpreted in the regions as reinforcing the centre's commitment to an asymmetric federation.

The signing of the bilateral power-sharing treaties (beginning in February 1994 with Tatarstan, and followed by a number of the other ethnorepublics and from 1996 with some of the regions) has reinforced differentiation. Designed to build bridges and in effect to rectify what the ethnorepublics in particular see as the inadequacies of the 1993 constitution, it has resulted in greater differentiation between the ethnorepublics as well as blurring the hitherto formalized distinction between the ethnorepublics and regions. This is reflected in the language that has been used in codifying the treaties, which in its varying terminology ascribes to federation subjects differing political powers and rights (J. Hughes 1996). In this regard Tatarstan has led the way in securing significantly more powers and more concessions and advantages than other subjects of the federation. Thus while recognizing that the republic is a constituent member of the federation, there is no recognition in its treaty of the primacy of the federal constitution and of acknowledgement of article 4 (the inviolability of Russia) (Lysenko 1996). In contrast to Tatarstan, which is recognized as 'a state joined with the Russian federation', neigh-bouring Bashkortostan is 'a sovereign state within the Russian federation'. Kabardino-Balkaria is described as only 'a state within the Russian federa-tion', while Udmurtia is merely deemed to be 'a republic'.

Far from being based on a recognition that the ethnorepublics should be treated distinctively, federal asymmetry represents more the anarchy of the political market-place than considerations of a coherent nationalities policy. The greater bargaining power at the disposal of some ethnorepublics and regions compared to others, especially the resource-rich republics, has been particularly evident in influencing political outcomes. Thus, as one report cynically noted, after Yekaterinburg succeeded in being the first *oblast* to sign a power-sharing treaty, other regions were also given the opportunity to renegotiate sovereignty, although only those who were major economic donors to the federal budget and who constituted a support base in Russia's 1996 presidential campaign did so (*Moskovskie novosti*, 6–12 June 1996). The economically poorer regions, dependent on federal subsidies, seemed to acknowledge that there was little in it for them in renegotiating relations with the centre as greater sovereignty had usually meant loss of considerable financial assistance from the federal budget. What, however, bilateral treaty formation is beginning to end has been a form of fiscal federalism that, although it claimed to allocate according to need, had in effect created a system in which the richer republics and regions tended to contribute the least to the federal budget, but which in terms of federal allocations often received more than the federal average (Graham Smith 1996). In short, such developments have done much to fuel support, especially amongst Russia's regions, to extend the rights of the federation's individual subjects through equalizing their relative status, and establishing constituent units that transcend ethnic borders. As one prominent Russian federal theorist opposed to such an arrangement notes: 'Everyone knows what separating one's child-ren into those who are favourites and those who are not can result in. The effect has been analogous in producing a total lack of respect on the part of the children towards the parents and towards each other' (Valentei 1996: 30).

The federal process has also straddled an uneasy compromise concerning the question of minority rights, of whether the citizen as an individually or group-constituted subject offers the better prospects for realizing a democratized and stable federation. In referring to 'the nation [of Russia] as co-citizenship' (*sograzhdanstvo*) in a 1994 speech, Yeltsin seemed to suggest recognition of a plurality of identities and rights which seemed to reflect a vision of federation based on accommodating both individual and group rights (*Rossiiskaya gazeta*, 25 February 1994). While elements of group rights have been incorporated into and recognized by both constitutional and treaty-framers, the former has taken priority based on the premiss that the rights of minorities can best be safeguarded through promoting individual liberties. This is reflected in both the 1992 Federal Treaty, which emphasized above all the rights and liberties of individuals as being paramount, and the constitution, which is unequivocal in prioritizing the equality of all peoples and subjects of the Russian federation. Thus the declared constitutional right to practise a native language is informed largely by such liberal thinking. On the other hand, the federalizing process reflects important collectivist principles with regard to ethnic minorities, not least the right of both subunits and peoples to self-determination.

There are a number of probable reasons why minority rights have been framed in this way. In the desire to democratize, the Western liberal model, especially during the formative period in federal formation (1990–2), was held up by liberals as the only effective and proven alternative to a former state ideology that, in both institutionalizing and practising collectivism, had suppressed individualism and stifled individual freedoms. For post-soviet Russia this meant embracing a conception of liberal democracy that, as Touraine notes, tended to be summed up in terms of the economic freedom of the market-place replacing the repressive and stifling collectivism of Soviet socialism: 'the reconstruction of social life began', he notes, 'not with popular movements or new ideas, but with economic management' (Touraine 1997: 175). But it also implied creating a non-ethnic secular state in which individual citizens—for the first time in Russia's history—could participate directly in the polity irrespective of their ethnicity, which it was felt should now be relegated to the private sphere. However, for Russian nationalists, liberal individualism has also been used as a convenient mask for promoting and safeguarding a majority nationalism that wishes to relegate expressions of minority ethnicity to the private sphere but wishes to forward Russian ethnicity in the public sphere. Thus, for Russian nationalists, the rejection of group rights and the promotion of individual rights is also bound up with reclaiming their own national homeland of Russia from a Soviet regime which was perceived as promoting the territorial rights of national minorities to the detriment of Russians. In short, many Russians felt that the Soviet nationalities policy had made them an underprivileged majority in their own homeland republic (RSFSR). This was also reinforced by a widely held fear that the continuation and expansion of such preferential treatment for minorities would result in discrimination against Russians both nationally and especially in the ethnorepublics. Finally, for Moscow's federation builders, there is the recurring theme that support for minority collective rights promotes geopolitical chaos and fragmentation. In order to contain the envisaged anarchy of nation-statism, the centre has shown a willingness to entertain concessionary rights only to the presently constituted ethnorepublic federal units, in an attempt to thwart further group demands. It is a strategy that has also received a receptive audience amongst especially those ethnorepublic élites concerned about ensuring the hegemony of their own titular nations in ethnorepublics where they are not in a demographic majority (in only four of the twenty-one republics does the titular nation constitute a clear majority: Chechnya, Chuvashia, Tuva, and North Ossetia).

In actuality, then, the politics of the subject has been largely caught up in promoting the rights of either majority or minority national groups. As Ramazan Abdulatipov readily acknowledges, collectivist values are still as much part of Russia's culture as liberalism is in the West:

today, collective rights for the people of Russia have not less but probably more mean-ing than individual rights, although the priority of the latter could be recognised as more important in the future. At least in Russia, individual rights will not become an absolute value as in the West, where this was achieved through the elimination of whole peoples and tribes notwithstanding 'sacred devotion' to humanistic values. We should be grateful that the Russian nation has historically been lacking this kind of western hypocrisy. (Abdulatipov 1995: 19).

Eurasianism and Presidential Decree 909

Despite legitimate claims that Russia has still to perfect a coherent and viable nationalities policy, a series of laws and decrees towards the end of the military phase of the Chechen crisis and subsequently have been introduced that constitute an attempt to rethink the relationship between federation and diversity. The most important and wide-ranging of these attempts is summed up in Presidential Decree 909 of June 1996. Although a non-binding legal document, it represents the outcome of a compromise between the centre and constituent subjects on the most appropriate way forward to effect a fairer and more equitable form of federate justice. Rather than simply looking towards a Western-liberal model as a building-block, it reflects an attempt to develop a conception of distributive justice which encapsulates a variety of principles and solutions reflecting what might be more appropriately labelled as Russia's attempt to go beyond a liberal or nationalist solution by finding 'a third way' (Resler 1997). In addressing both equality and difference between the federation's subjects and in attempting to stake the federation's future on what can be best interpreted as a mixed-rights perspective on national minorities, it lays out a more integrated approach, albeit a schema which many Western political theorists would no doubt interpret as eclectic and contradictory.

One powerful normative conception of Russia that the decree proposes is to construct the federation around a Eurasianist vision of Russia, opening up a potentially more constructive dialogue of what citizenship should be. A term first mooted by Russian émigrés in the 1920s, it is based on the notion that Russia is a continent unto itself, located between Europe and Asia, and is geopolitically and culturally different from both (Chinyaeva 1996; also Neumann 1996). As Russia occupies a special and unique place within northern Eurasia, it is therefore held that Russia must find its own particular niche and solutions to its cultural diversity. Accordingly, the goal of a multi-ethnic Russia is to ensure 'the cultural self-preservation and further development of national traditions and co-operation of Slavic, Turkic, Caucasian, Finno-Ugric, Mongolian and other peoples of Russia within the framework of Eurasian national-cultural space' (*Rossiiskaya gazeta*, 10 July 1996, 5). Both European and Asian experiments with state-building are therefore rejected as inappropriate to what is deemed to be a more viable Eurasian way of 'harmonizing the development of nationalities'. No doubt reflecting a concession to the majority culture, what is more problematic is the part ascribed to the Russians in this process, in which 'thanks to the unifying role of the Russian (*russkii*) people . . . a unique unity and diversity and spiritual community and union of various peoples has been maintained'. And the text continues, 'inter-ethnic relations in the Russian federation will in large part be determined by the general national situation of the Russian people, a buttress of Russian federation statehood' (*Rossiiskaya gazeta*, 10 July 1996, 5).

Embedded in the ambiguity of Eurasianism are a variety of normative readings of what Russia should be. One reading conveys a sense of federation working towards multi-ethnic coexistence. Here the centuries-long intermingling of European and Asian cultures is seen as a positive, beneficial, and enriching force, providing the potential for national coexistence at a variety of scales—from the federal to the neighbourhood—based upon mutual recognition of the equal value of all national cultures. It is one which within the public sphere at least is generally supported by the political leaders of the ethnorepublics (*Nezavizisimaya gazeta*, 5 March 1996, 3). The other reading, one which ascribes to the cultural Russians 'a leading role', is more problematic. In its more extreme form, it attempts to ascribe a mission and identity to the majority nation within post-soviet Eurasian space. And herein lies much of the problem in reviving a conception of Eurasianism that, at least in terms of its original theory, draws heavily upon Slavophile thinking and on the spiritual and organic qualities of the Russian nation. It is a conception which holds that Russia's Eurasianist mission should be not only to promote the Russian language, culture, and values, but also in some versions to reallocate a special role for the Russian Orthodox Church. In defining the nature of Eurasianism, it also raises the issue of Russia's territorial boundedness. Thus, for many Russian nationalists, Eurasianism is also to do with reconnecting up with a pre-soviet and idealized tsarist empire and with celebrating the questionable claims to such Russian virtues as universal humanism and spiritual congregationalism.

More than anything else, bound up with what has become a populist vision is a crisis of national identity, of what it means to be ethnic Russian in a spatially reduced and redesignated multi-ethnic homeland. Russians, in short, have had far greater difficulties compared with the ethnorepublic titular nations in coming to terms with the loss of 'the big homeland', the Soviet empire. In contrast to Tatars or Buryats, who had their own designated homeland, the institutional–territorial frame for Russians was not so much the Russian republic (the RSFSR) but the Soviet Union. The Soviet state did not furnish the RSFSR—the cultural homeland of the Russians—with the institutional trappings of nationhood. Rather, Russians were encouraged to think of the Soviet Union as their homeland. Thus for Russians what and where is their homeland remains ambiguous in two senses. First, just as Soviet nationalist policy discouraged institutional ethnic Russian nation-building within the RSFSR, so too the post-soviet federation has worked towards constructing nation-building institutions for the minorities. For Russians, regionalization in the form of the *oblasts* has provided only limited scope for an alternative to minority nation-building. As Tishkov (1995) has noted, what ethnic Russians require more than anything else is a sense that they feel at home in their homeland and that neither their identities nor their cultures are perceived as threatened or imperilled by a federation protecting the rights and identities of national minorities. Secondly, for ethnic Russians, Eurasianism leaves fluid the sovereign-boundedness of Russia, in which the political boundaries of Russia might again encompass the full extent of the Russian historic community, including Ukraine, northern Kazakstan, and north-east Estonia. It is a conception of the boundedness of Russia which is given some legitimacy by the Presidential Decree which links domestic nationalities policy with Russia's interests in looking after its broader historic community, where it is claimed that Russia should 'defend the rights and interests of cit-izens outside the federation, and provide help for compatriots in preserving and developing the language, culture, traditions, and links with Russia' (*Rossiiskaya gazeta*, 10 July 1996, 5).

Besides emphasizing the federation's commitment to the preservation and national self-determination of the ethnorepublics, the decree also offers the prospect for further regions to enter into power-sharing agreements with the centre, thus coming closer to Spain's model of offering autonomy to all con-stituent units who desire greater control over their affairs. This, however, it is made clear, 'does not mean that the aim is the "gubernization" [regionaliza-tion] of the republics or the "republicanization" of the regions (*oblasts*) and districts (*krais*)'. Rather, the goal is to recognize 'the striving of peoples for self-determination and objective processes of integration into Russian federa-tion (*rossiiskoe*) society'. It is a statement reminiscent of the dialectical policy of the Soviet regime, which envisaged the national cultures of its ethno-republics both 'flourishing' (*ratsvet*) through federal institutional supports and at the same time moving 'closer together' (*sblizhenie*) through the fed-eration's commitment to greater socio-economic equalization between its constituent parts. The decree thus emphasizes the importance of 'equalizing the level of socio-economic development of federation subjects', of a federation allocating resources according to need and developing measures to boost especially the economy of depressed regions, notably of central Russia and the north Caucasus. Thus federation is to promote the redistribution of wealth in a manner reminiscent of the way in which the policy of *sblizhenie* purportedly functioned during the Soviet period.

The goal of rectifying material inequalities embedded in this vision of federation raises an important aspect that has become marginalized in more general discussions of 'the politics of recognition'. As Fraser (1997*b*) argues with regard to questions of social justice in late modern democracies, the dislodging of material inequalities from considerations of group rights has impoverished any coherent understanding of distributive justice; rather, 'justice today requires both redistribution and recognition'. Thus in any consideration of multinational federation, we also need to rethink group rights so that attention is paid not only to the right to be culturally different but also to ensuring that such a politics of recognition does not exclude considerations of the economically and socially disadvantaged. This is in effect where Walzer's proposition falls down: 'If some sort of union—federation or confederation—is our goal', he argues, 'the best way to reach it is to abandon coercion and allow the tribes to separate and then to negotiate their own voluntary and gradual, even if only partial, adherence to some new community of interest' (Walzer 1992: 169). Within the Russian context, such advice is an invitation to the powerful and economically more advantaged ethnorepublics to effectively renegotiate and reshape the fiscal framework of federation to their own advantage and so to the detriment of other less powerful and more economically disadvantaged constituent units. Moreover, while some of the poorest constituent units are ethnorepublics—notably Ingushetia, Dagestan, Adygeya, Tuva, and Kalymkia—many of the non-ethnic-based regions also suffer from severe economic displacement (Bradshaw and Palacin 1996). Any understanding of federate distributive justice should not, therefore, lose sight of such inequalities; to do otherwise is likely to weaken support amongst the poorer constituent units—ethnorepublics as well as the Russian regions—for recognition of the value of a multinational federation.

Finally, and probably most innovative of all, the decree attempts to broaden the remit of who qualifies for self-determination. Rather than jumping from the individual to the ethnorepublic as the appropriate unit, it addresses itself to those peoples who occupy the space in between, namely those ethnic minorities who either do not possess their own administrative homeland or live outside the homeland claimed by their co-nationals. The authors in effect broaden the concept of federation by recognizing 'multiple forms of national self-determination', including acknowledging the rights of those not represented as constituent federal subjects to national-cultural autonomy. This idea draws inspiration from the ideas of the late nineteenth-century Austrian social democrats Karl Renner and Otto Bauer, who argued that group rights of the territorially non-represented should be supported in addition to a purely territorial one. In particular, each citizen would declare her national affiliation in an electoral register, and national groups would then be represented in a second chamber of parliament that should take responsibility for matters such as language education in schools. In drawing upon such a principle, federal-builders acknowledge that the national minorities and especially 'the small scattered peoples' of the Siberian northlands should be able to decide questions concerning 'the preservation and development of their customs, language, education, culture' (*Rossiiskaya gazeta*, 10 July 1996, 5). Accordingly, the federal authorities have proposed setting up an Assembly of the Peoples of Russia which would include representatives of dispersed minorities and could provide scope for promoting the ideal of deliberative democracy amongst otherwise conflicting ethnic groups. (Through deliberative democracy, decisions are reached by open and uncoerced discussion of the issue in question where the aim of all participants is to arrive at an agreed judgement.) In addition, in proposing a form of cultural subsidiary within the localities, national-cultural autonomy signals not only the potential role that local government can play in 'directly reflecting residents' interests and allowing a more flexible response to national needs' but also the participatory role that minorities and diasporas are encouraged to perform in creating 'self-governing public organizations in places of compact settlement' and in promoting their own local language media, which, it is intended, would be buttressed through state financial support (*Rossiiskaya gazeta*, 10 July 1996, 5). One such scattered people, the German diaspora, has been singled out for special praise by the Yeltsin administration as a model to emulate. Even though they live, for the most part, in scattered grassroots communities, the German minorities have attracted considerable federal resources to help facilitate local self-government. Indeed, Russia's Germans have also succeeded in going beyond the non-territorial principle by establishing two culturally autonomous districts within Omsk and the Altai (*Rossiiskaya gazeta*, 29 March – 4 April 1997).

So far, however, the idea of national-cultural autonomy has had limited impact in capturing the imagination of minorities in a country with no tradition of promoting extra-territorial rights and where self-determination is still conceived as a territorial phenomenon. It would appear that the indigenous peoples of the northlands are also despondent. Highly mobilized organizations like the Social Organisation and Movements of the People for the North contend that despite both federal and ethnorepublic constitutions proclaiming support for indigenous rights, neither the resources nor the effort are being put into protecting their self-preservation as communities from culturally homogenizing regimes, or into providing the means necessary to safeguard their traditional lifestyles and distinctive local economies from the impact of the transition to a market economy.

Laudable as these aims may be, broadening the concept of self-determination has not gone hand in hand with addressing who qualifies for self-determination and under what conditions. The decree seems to operate on the assumption that any national group designated a nationality (a legal definition) at the time of the last census of 1989 has a right, if it wishes to exercise it, to self-determination. By extension, those minorities excluded from the census do not appear to be able to exercise this right. The problem with such vague criteria is that there is a tendency to invite highly mobilized cultural élites, whose purported imagined communities often number only a few thousand (the 1989 census included the so-called 'peoples of the north' with populations ranging from 190 to 34,675), to overplay their sense of shared cultural community and common identity when that identity is under threat. This gives the impression of communities that may not be as co-herently imagined or supported as their self-identifiers claim. If it can be proven that especially those groups of the northlands who have abandoned their native language have *chosen* to do so, then the right to linguistic self-protection might be considered less strong. If, however, individuals have been coerced into abandoning their culture, a claim made by activists with some justification given the lack of support for non-ethnorepublic-based national-ities by the previous regime, then the argument for measures to support linguistic revival should be considered supportable.

Federation and Nationalizing Regimes

There is little doubt that the ethnorepublics display many of the features of 'nationalizing regimes', a term coined by Brubaker (1996), who observed that, since the establishment of sovereign statehood, political élites in newly emergent multi-ethnic post-communist regimes have a tendency to promote the culture, language, and even political hegemony of the nominally state-bearing nation, to make the state what it is judged as properly and legit-imately destined to be, a fully realized and culturally more homogeneous nation-state. While some political élites within the ethnorepublics adhere to the primordial-nationalist principle, that national and sovereign spaces should be congruent, none the less the ethnorepublics do differ in the extent of their 'nationalizing practices', the most extreme variant being that of 'ethnic cleansing' involving the Ingush minority from the north Caucasian republic of North Ossetia. Since October 1992 an estimated 34,000–64,000 Ingush have fled North Ossetia for neighbouring Ingushetia following clashes between the two communities in which some 600 people have been killed (Rotar

1997). Such regimes display features of primordial nationalism in which the identity markers of 'national communities' are culturally essentialized and taken as absolute, in which there is no room for recognition of those individuals with overlapping or multiple senses of identity who through, for instance, inter-ethnic marriage inhabit more than one community's life-world, and where monopoly rights are claimed over the historic ethnic homeland. Such exclusivist claims imply that, for example, Russians who arrived in the ethnorepublics during recent decades should have their political rights restricted because they inhabited the region at a later historical period than the ancestors of the so-called titular nation. For those who hold with exclu-sionist principles, promoting expulsion, limiting immigration, or assimilating co-nationals are therefore often 'tactics' to ensure ethnic homogeneity and numerical dominance of the nation, to aspire to the congruity principle and to the end-stage that such a modernist understanding of national self-determination has come to mean: the sovereign nation-state. Thus part of the tragedy of nationalism is the result of reducing the notion of self-determination to the idea of the nation-state. On this basis of infringing upon the liberties of others, primordialist nationalism therefore cannot be justified with reference to group rights. In contrast, a civic nationalism (civic national identity) differs in that 'the nation is regarded as a territorial community of citizens bound by common laws and a shared public culture' in which the aim is 'to unify the citizen community in its national territory around a set of shared symbols, myths and memories and fuse it with an identifiable culture community' (Anthony Smith 1995: 111). Some encouraging signs in this direction include the way in which more or less all the ethnorepublics have reformulated their opening declarations of 'state sovereignty', from framing them in terms of a particular national group to declaring (as in the case of Sakha's revised constitution), 'We, the multinational (*mnogonatsionalnvi*) people of the Republic of Sakha . . .' (*Konstitutsiya (Osnovnoi Zakon)*, 1994).

For the ethnorepublics the most effective means of weakening such primordialist and exclusivist minority nationalisms is through federation. For weakly developed democracies, Walzer's formula therefore seems apt: 'the best hope for restraint lies . . . in federal or confederal checks and balances and in 'international pressure' (Walzer 1992: 170). This is not an argument that denies the principle of the right of nations to statehood, but rather one which acknowledges that there are grounds to suggest that nation-statehood would for the moment at least lead to far greater infringement of the rights of others. Thus if it can be shown that secession would be likely to limit the liberties of other minorities and individuals, or even through certain cultural practices the liberties of some of its own peoples, then there may be an a priori case for not granting secession to that group (Buchanan 1991).

There are two points that it is important to make in this regard. First, demands for secession are not widespread: only two republics, Chechnya and

Tatarstan, have since 1990 demanded independence from Moscow. The other ethnorepublics seek only greater autonomy (Treisman 1997). Although no referenda on secession have been held to test the ethnorepublic constituent democratic will, the absence of other possible indicators of majority support for secessionism, such as nationalist organizations, would suggest that, like their political élites, most of the ethnorepublic constituents see their future as best served as part of a federation, or, in the case of Tatarstan, possibly a confederation. The reasons why secession is so weakly developed would certainly include perceptions of economic viability and prospects of being materially worse off outside the federation. On the basis of rectifying a past injustice of involuntary incorporation, a criterion acknowledged as legitimate grounds for secession, only one republic, Tuva, would qualify. As a sovereign state between 1921 and 1944, it was incorporated into the Soviet Union without the consent of its constituent majority (Penter 1997). However, as one of the poorest republics of the federation, it is highly dependent on federal subsidies, one probable reason why secession has little support.

Secondly, the Chechen experience warrants consideration. Although Chechnya is not archetypal, its experiences before and after the war (1994–6) do illustrate the problems of secessionism in illiberal polities. It is difficult to establish whether there was a democratic mandate for *de facto* independence: both parliamentary and presidential elections did occur in October 1991, but turnout was only about 10–12 per cent and voting took place in only seventy of the 360 electoral districts (Tishkov 1997: 202). Even before the war began in December 1994, about one-sixth of the population had fled the republic, primarily ethnic Russians for whom individual and group rights had been violated. Now, after the signing of a peace accord between Moscow and Chechnya in August 1996, in which the two sides agreed to postpone a resolution to the republic's status for five years, and after presidential and parliamentary elections in January 1997, which the Organization for Security and Co-operation in Europe (OSCE) monitors deemed to be fair, neither individual nor group rights are widely respected. Although post-1996 human rights violations cannot be separated from the experiences of the twenty-one-month war, their scale and intensity should not be ignored. Of particular concern to Western human rights organizations (as well as to Moscow's politicians) has been the recent introduction and use of the Chechen criminal code, which 'allows for an alarming level of violent punishment, invasions of privacy, and violations of other basic, internationally recognised human rights' (Denbar 1997: 71). In August 1997 the Chechen parliament also passed a law making Chechen the republic's sole official language. It is the only ethnorepublic to have enacted such legislation. Of course, given the increasing impact of Islamic militarism on the making of post-war Chechnya, it is only too easy to fall into the trap of the liberal critique of minority ethnocentrism by defending the values of occidental culture and a secular federation that should be accepted by all minorities without acknowledging that such a stance mirrors the very image of fundamentalism that it perceives in minority leaders. But when such practices are conducted against those who do not share this culture (non-Chechens) or who have not consented to the election of its representatives, then the issue becomes more complex and not easily resolved. The question must be asked whether individual and group rights are more likely to be protected in a far from democratic federation than in an illiberal state.

There are a number of ways in which federation and federal politics act as a counterweight to limiting primordialist nationalism. First, there is federal intervention. The Federal Constitutional Court has acted as a means of curbing or reversing exclusivist practices. In June 1997 Khakasia was successfully brought to court for introducing a republic electoral law that required a five- to seven-year period of minimum residency in the republic for candidates to the republican legislature and the post of republican president, while federal legislation stipulated that the requirement for minimum residency could not exceed one year. (All such residency requirements have now been outlawed by the centre.) In other instances power-sharing treaties have curbed exclusivist local citizenship policies. None the less, despite federal pressures, issues that strike a fine balance between individual and group rights have not always been resolved. Thus, as part of its 1996 power-sharing agreement, Krasnodar *krai* managed to negotiate the right to regulate migration into the region (*Izvestiya*, 21 August 1997). Although not based on issues of cultural protection, but grounded in the desire to introduce a local admissions policy in a district that has received a disproportionately large share of refugees from the north Caucasus, it has triggered off a debate about the role the federal centre should play in providing resources and employment opportunities in localities of emigration and thus pre-empt encouragement by local political élites to treat membership of their ethnorepublic or region as a private club. Some other republics, however, defend such actions on the basis of providing a balanced self-preservation of cultures. In instituting republic citizenship, the Siberian republic of Sakha (Yakutia) makes it clear in article 12 of its constitution that citizenship is open to all those 'born and permanently residing within the republic': however, the same document stipulates that only a republic citizen who was born in the republic, who has lived in the republic continuously for fifteen years, and who is fluent in both state languages (Yakut and Russian) can stand for the most senior political offices (*Konstitutsiya*, Yakutsk 1994).

Secondly, renegotiating bilateral treaties with the centre has encouraged 'territorializing' rather than 'nationalizing' practices in which political élites seem more willing to play the role of *topo*cratic rather than *ethno*cratic actors. As Hanauer notes in relation to Tatarstan, where the titular nation comprises only some 49 per cent of the republic's population and in which both Russians and Bashkirs constitute large minorities, 'the fact that political struggles have been framed as centre–periphery rivalries rather than inter-ethnic ones has contributed to a strong sense of Tatarstani civic identity' (Hanauer 1996: 82). There is evidence to suggest that such strategies of communal inclusiveness —an attempt to build what Abdulatipov (1996) calls a more acceptable civic nationalism—have strengthened a sense of solidarity amongst its Russian minority of being part of Tatarstan rather than Rossiiskii (a civic loyalty to the Russian state). Other studies of civic identities also show that ethnicity is not quite the 'community of fate' that primordialist nationalists would wish to portray. In a survey of four ethnorepublics (Tatarstan, Sakha, North Ossetia, and Tuva) it was found that most Russians saw their identities as lying equally with either the ethnorepublic and Russia or with the ethnorepublic, and only a small proportion just with Russia (Drobizheva 1994). Similarly, in another survey in nineteen of the twenty-one republics more respondents placed themselves in the category of citizen with equally shared loyalties (between Russia and the republic) than in any other category (Tishkov 1997: 262). Somewhat paradoxically, the formation of such cross-cutting identities owes something to the legacy of Soviet nationalities policy, which promoted an inter-nationalizing culture leading to high levels of inter-ethnic marriage and multilingualism.

Thirdly, federation has encouraged local élites to adopt a relatively balanced approach to language issues, especially between the titular nation and Russians. Most republics have endorsed both the titular language and Russian as official state languages (the latter as the language of 'federal communication'). In the case of some ethnorepublics, a special state programme exists which defines strategies for broadening the use of the titular language in the political, economic, and cultural life of the republics, a policy that is defensible on the grounds of cultural survival and in reversing linguistic colonialism. It would seem morally right that Russians should speak the indigenous language, for, despite high levels of multilingualism amongst the titular nations (according to the last (1989) census, 70 per cent of the titular nations of the ethnorepublics could speak Russian), knowledge of other federation languages is poor. At the same time, federation has helped to protect the linguistic needs and sensitivities of Russians. In one of the most multinational republics, Bashkortostan, where Turkic-speaking Bashkirs make up 22 per cent of the population, Tatars 28 per cent, and Russians 39 per cent, the authorities purposely put off a decision concerning what languages should be adopted and encouraged a public debate. Consequently, ethnic-group representatives agreed to promote what is labelled 'the cult of the native language', in which all vernaculars—not just the three major spoken languages—'deserve equal protection and development under the law'. Moreover, while it is acknowledged that the state has a role to play in promoting the equal worth of some thirteen languages, 'the cult of the native language' is also based on the assumption that the most vital work for linguistic revival should be delegated to the family, more specifically by the mother (Graney 1997). By moving the focus of language politics and obligation for all languages from the state to the private sphere, political élites have attempted to avoid making language a politically charged issue of state politics.

Finally, international pressures have also played an important part in shaping a more democratic and less ethnic-conflict-ridden federation. Global institutions—such as the European Bank for Reconstruction and Development and the World Bank—have played a direct role in linking aid and development to ensuring Russia protects its minorities and works towards a more sustainable federalism. More specific human rights organizations, notably the OSCE and the Council of Europe, have played an important part as mediators in ethnic tensions and in ensuring that Russia complies with recognized international human rights norms, while the European Union has been effective in using punitive trade measures to insist that Russia allow the OSCE access to monitor the volatile situation in Chechnya. In short, the price of international recognition and trade is linked to minority accommodation.

Normative Lessons for Rethinking Multicultural Federalism

It would seem then that, of all the various forms of 'identity politics' in the modern world, the demands of territorially concentrated national minorities for national recognition and self-government are amongst the most difficult for democracies to accept and accommodate. Since Russia contains dozens of such minority nationalisms, it provides a particularly instructive example of how these demands should, and should not, be accommodated. Federalism has often been proposed as an appropriate vehicle for accommodating minority nationalisms within a larger state, and indeed it is difficult to imagine how Russia could have got as far as it has with democratization, or survived at all, without adopting some form of federation. However, the Russian example suggests that federalism will only accommodate minority nationalisms under two conditions. First, the boundaries of federal subunits (or republics) must be drawn so as to create units in which minority nations can exercise meaningful self-government. The proposal to create a German-style federal system in Russia, in which the federal units would be deliberately drawn so as not to correspond to the traditional homelands or ethnocultural groups, was quickly rejected, and would not have provided a mechanism for accommodating minority nationalisms.

Secondly, if a federal system contains some subunits which are vehicles for minority nations (the ethnorepublics) and some subunits which are simply regional divisions within the majority national group (the regional governments), it is likely, and perhaps unavoidable, that some form of 'asymmetry' in powers and status will arise between the nationality-based subunits and the regional units. Attempts to create a uniform status for all federal subunits in Russia have consistently failed, in part because the nationality-based subunits really do have distinctive needs and aspirations which a federal system should reflect. Critics of such asymmetrical, multinational federalism worry that it inevitably leads to secession. However, the Russian experience suggests that accommodating minority nationalisms in this way need not lead to secession, and indeed may provide the only way to prevent minority nationalisms from leading to secession. While it is important to adapt federal forms of governance to meet the needs of minority nations, it is equally important to make sure that we do not thereby promote or entrench a 'primordial' form of nationalism which is ethnically exclusive and territorially monopolist. To help avoid this danger, it is important to ensure, first, that federal subunits are defined not as the possession of one ethnic group, but rather as belonging to all residents; secondly, that a civic identity is developed which can be a source of allegiance and identity for non-dominant groups; thirdly, that in addition to recognizing any rights of groups, there is firm protection for individual rights; fourthly, that non-territorial forms of cultural diversity are recognized, and that non-territorial forms of cultural autonomy are promoted; and finally, that norms of distributive justice are enforced across federal units. With these measures in place, the legitimate aspirations of minority nationalisms can be respected through federal devolution without threatening the rights of individuals or of other ethnic and cultural groups who happen to reside in the nation's homeland, and without leading to secession or the erosion of an overarching federation.

15

Why Stay Together? A Pluralist Approach to Secession and Federation

RAINER BAUBÖCK

1. Why Theories of Secession Need a Theory of Federation

Secessionist movements raise a difficult question for political theory. Should boundaries between states be redrawn when they are challenged by significant parts of the citizenry? In recent years this question has been addressed in an impressive new literature. What has emerged from this debate is a profound disagreement among contemporary liberal political theorists.

There are those who want to reconcile liberalism with nationalism. Traditionally, nationalism attributes to collectivities called nations a right of self-determination and recommends that the borders of nations and states be congruent (Gellner 1983: 1). Three critiques have been raised against this solution to the boundary problem. First, nations are not natural categories with a well-defined membership but are themselves shaped by the cultural policies of modern states. Secondly, on any conception of nationhood, there are many more potential nations than there are territories that could be organized as sovereign states. And thirdly, drawing political boundaries along the lines of national membership ignores (or suppresses) small and dispersed minorities, as well as mixed populations and multiple individual identities. Liberal nationalists assert that respect for individuals requires also respecting national communities, membership in which is an important resource for individual autonomy and well-being (Margalit and Raz 1990; Tamir 1993; MacCormick 1996). However, this does not yet explain why boundaries of nations ought to determine the borders of states. In response to the critique of this principle liberal nationalists have adopted two different strategies. The first one may be called the civic nationalist project. It associates the nation

A first version of this chapter was presented at the Nobel Symposium 'Nationalism and Internationalism in the Post-Cold War Era', Stockholm 7–10 Sept. 1997, a second one at a conference on 'Multiculturalisme, Constitutionalisme et Citoyenneté' at the Centre Culturel Canadien, Paris, 9–11 Oct. 1997. Special thanks to Christine Chwaszcza, Will Kymlicka, and Wayne Norman for sending me extensive and useful comments.

with the public culture of a liberal-democratic polity that is open for all citizens irrespective of their cultural affiliation and ethnic origin (MacCormick 1996: 562–3). The other project is cultural nationalism, which sees national identities as fundamentally given for each individual by the fact of being born into a group. On this view the task of liberal polities is to promote the flourishing of such groups (Margalit and Raz 1990; Tamir 1993; Weiler 1997). Civic nationalists modify the nationalist principle by assimilating the nation to the liberal state, cultural nationalists by disconnecting the two. The former strategy retains the principle that the boundaries of nations and states ought to coincide as far as possible (Miller 1995: 188; Moore 1997) but would strongly reduce the number of groups that could claim nationhood (Miller 1995: 112); whereas the latter project more or less abandons the idea that nations have a claim to independent statehood (Tamir 1993: 150; Philpott 1995: 382; MacCormick 1996: 566).

An even stronger contrast exists within the traditional liberal camp that derives political legitimacy from individual rights rather than from common national identity. Choice theorists regard the wish of a regional majority to separate from a given polity as a sufficient justification for secession (provided that the same right is granted to groups in the seceding territory and provided secession does not impair the viability of the remainder state) (Beran 1984, 1998; Nielsen 1993, 1998; Gauthier 1994; Wellman 1995). Others object that easy secession would undermine international peace as well as the internal stability of democratic regimes. Moreover, it is impossible to find a rule for democratic decisions about boundaries that would be procedurally neutral between the preferences of secessionists and unionists (Bauböck 1994b, ch. 7). They conclude that legitimate secession requires a just cause: only serious grievance, rather than merely aggregated individual choices, can justify secession (Buchanan 1991, 1997a, b; Brilmayer 1991; Chwaszcza 1998; Norman 1998). In this view the legitimacy of political boundaries depends on the state's guarantee of equal individual rights for all citizens.[1]

None of the current Anglo-American theories of secession gives proper consideration to the most common grievance voiced by national minorities in multinational states: that the terms of federation are either unfair or have been violated by the majority. If this charge is indeed a plausible and necessary justification for threatening with secession, then it would also follow that a national minority is morally bound to maintain the unity of the existing state as long as fair terms of federation are respected. That is the main idea of this chapter. Liberal nationalists often see multinational federations as

---

[1] Jürgen Habermas has defended this position: 'Solange nämlich alle Bürger gleiche Rechte genießen und niemand diskriminiert wird, besteht kein normativ überzeugender Grund zur Separierung vom bestehenden Gemeinwesen' ('As long as all citizens enjoy equal rights and nobody is discriminated against, there is no convincing normative reason for separating from the existing polity') (Habermas 1996b: 171; my translation).

second-best solutions how to realize a principle of self-determination in a world where not all nations can become independent. Grievance theories of secession sometimes recommend federal arrangements for prudential reasons in order to accommodate nationalist aspirations without threatening the unity of the state (e.g. Buchanan 1997a: 53). In contrast to the former view, I will argue against a right to self-determination and assert instead a right to self-government that can be sufficiently realized in a federal framework. In contrast to the latter, I regard federal self-government by national minorities as their collective right rather than merely as a self-interested concession of governments in multinational polities.

Federalism is the combination of self-rule and shared rule in compound polities (Elazar 1987: 5, 12, 59). This broad definition applies to confederations between states as well as to federal states, to territorial federations as well as to federal arrangements between non-territorial groups. In a narrower sense territorial federalism 'is a political organization in which the activities of government are divided between regional governments and a central government in such a way that each kind of government has some activities on which it makes final decisions' (Riker 1975: 101). While government in large unitary states is always to some extent decentralized, it is non-centralized in federal ones. The powers of regional governments are not delegated by a central government but are directly derived from democratic representation (Elazar 1987: 35). The most common distinction between different kinds of federal arrangements concerns the first element of the definition: the balance between self-rule and shared rule. In confederations joint decisions are binding for the governments of the separate states only; in federal democracies regional and federal decisions both have direct impact on citizens and both kinds of governments are directly accountable to their citizens.[2] Federations thus create a nested structure of dual citizenship for all members of the polity (Kymlicka 1995a: 182).

There is a second dimension of federalism that has received less attention and refers to the units of the compound polity. These can either be mere regional subdivisions within a state or culturally distinct entities. Lijphart identifies these two types as congruent and incongruent federations. The former are 'composed of territorial units with a social and cultural character that is similar in each of the units and in the federation as a whole' (Lijphart 1984: 179),[3] whereas in the latter type internal political borders tend to coincide with ethnic and cultural boundaries. Multinational federations are by definition incongruent. However, stated in this way the contrast between the two types is not all that clear. The USA and Germany are obviously not

---

[2] See Mill (1972: 400). It is interesting to note that even the European Union, which is not a federal state, has already moved beyond confederation with many decisions having direct effect for individuals and with a rudimentary system of Union citizenship supplementing citizenship of the member states.   [3] Lijphart adopts this distinction from Tarlton (1965).

multinational federations, but Utah or Bavaria are in religious and cultural terms rather distinct from other states. More generally, any territorial division may serve as a basis for the political articulation of a particular local mix of social and cultural interests and identities (Elazar 1987: 73, 167). What is specific in multinational federations is not the mere correspondence between cultural and political boundaries, but a political representation of perceived differences of collective identity through the division of federal units so that such groups exercise powers of self-government within some or all of the units.[4] Borders between federal provinces or states are drawn to guarantee for particular groups a stable local majority of the population in that territory (Kymlicka 1998a: 135). This makes multinational federations compound polities in a specific way. In regional federations[5] the constitutive units are regarded as mere subdivisions within a single polity. '[P]olitical sovereignty resides in the people who delegate powers through constitutional devices on a limited basis to different governments as they see fit' (Elazar 1987: 231). Although the regional units are generally historical entities with a particular cultural character, their borders are contingent from the perspective of the federal constitution. The character of the federation itself would remain the same if they were drawn differently. Multinational federations are, however, composed of more than one 'people'. While these still jointly form one federal people which delegates powers to a federal government, each of them separately delegates powers to its regional government.

Federal systems of both types generally enhance regional self-government with mechanisms for the representation of the constitutive units in federal institutions (Marko 1995: 487). A common mechanism of this sort is a second chamber of parliament directly representing the regional governments (as in the German Bundesrat) or elected on a regional basis with equal numbers of mandates for every federal unit (as in the US Senate). In multinational federations collective representation is sometimes strengthened by exceptional means, such as reserved seats in government institutions or courts. This will still not prevent small nationalities from becoming permanent minorities in federal decision-making. In response to this problem special representation is sometimes reinforced by a minority-group veto while self-government can be strengthened by nullification rights.[6] All these institutional devices show the

[4] This special legitimation for multinational federations is generally ignored in the accounts of Wheare (1947) and Riker (1975).

[5] Resnick (1994) and Kymlicka (1998a) use the term *territorial* federation instead of *regional*. This is misleading because multinational federations are generally territorial, too, in the sense that they are built on a territorial division of power. In this respect they are different from consociational arrangements (Lijphart 1977), which may be seen as a non-territorial form of federalism (Elazar 1987).

[6] Veto rights allow minorities to block legislation at the federal level which would adversely affect them; nullification rights allow them to nullify federal legislation so that it does not apply in their own province (see Buchanan 1991: 38, 1997b: 307).

special significance of federal representation for multinational polities: on the one hand, it serves to integrate the various national communities into the larger political community by providing them with collective powers to shape federal policies; on the other hand, it gives them a platform to block federal policies which adversely affect their interests.

The distinction between unitary states, regional federations, and multinational ones describes the dominant structure of democratic governance and representation. There are, however, also mixed types such as the Canadian polity, which is constitutionally designed as a regional federation of ten provinces but whose historical identity is that of a multinational federation. The principles of multinational federalism can also operate in a subsidiary manner in unitary states or regional federations. An example for this are the special powers of self-government of native Indian tribes, of Puerto Rico, and some other offshore islands governed by the USA (Kymlicka 1998a: 136–8). Daniel Elazar has introduced the term federacy for such relationships which link a large power with a smaller polity 'whereby the latter has greater autonomy than other segments of the former and, in return, has a smaller role in the governance of the larger power' (Elazar 1987: 7). In mixed regimes as well as in federacies multinational federalism is asymmetrical in the sense that only the minority conceives of itself as a distinct polity whereas members of the national majority predominantly identify as individual citizens of the larger federation (Kymlicka 1998a: 141).

As pointed out by Wayne Norman (Norman 1994: 80), there are two possible shortcomings with the federal solution to nationality conflicts. First, devolving political power to minorities who form provincial majorities also turns state-wide majorities into minorities in these provinces. These latter groups will claim the same rights as their co-nationals living elsewhere in the state. Secondly, small or dispersed nationalities who are not able to form regional majorities may feel that their position worsens if they are subjected to provincial laws rather than to federal ones. The situation of Anglophones and indigenous groups in Quebec illustrates both problems. The answer should not be to abandon federal solutions, but to refine them by adding provisions of non-territorial cultural rights, federal protection, and special exemptions or powers for groups that cannot form a federal unit. This is what we might call a pluralist approach to the problem of federation and secession. I will try to show that it has its own difficulties but is still superior to the liberal, republican, and nationalist answers considered so far. Only towards the end of the following discussion will I refer to problems of ethnic diversity and cultural minority rights. While a federal structure of polities may also have beneficial side-effects for ethnic minorities, their claims are different from those articulated through federalism. Moreover, small and dispersed ethnic minorities cannot raise serious challenges to existing state borders. These emerge from groups or political entities that either already form a federal unit or autonomous province or could do so if the state in which they live adopted this solution. This is why 'an adequate theory of secession requires an adequate theory of federation' (Kymlicka 1992: 532).

In order to provide an alternative to current theories of secession we must show, first, that in addition to basic human and citizenship rights certain kinds of groups have a right to federal autonomy and states have corresponding duties to grant these rights; secondly, that the enjoyment of such rights morally binds minorities to maintain the unity of a federal state; and thirdly, that federal arrangements are not only morally legitimate or required, but also sufficiently stable. This last requirement means that federal arrangements should not create perverse incentives for federal authorities and majority representatives to recentralize the state or for minorities to break the union apart or to use secession threats to bargain for unjustified privileges. In the following section I will explore three different perspectives on federalism which could help to establish the federal rights and duties of minorities and may provide some initial responses to the more empirical question of stability.

2. Three Questions about Federation

Why Federate?

Norman suggests a contractarian approach to federation which 'recommends federal principles and institutions if they would have been selected by enlightened federal partners interested in developing a stable mutually beneficial federation for the long haul' (Norman 1994: 83). The basic situation is therefore one of 'independent nations negotiating to form a just and stable federation' (1994: 85). Such an approach seems to apply better to confederations between states (as the European Union) than to most federal states, whose provinces had never enjoyed independence. Still, some constitutional acts like the Union of 1707 between Scotland and England or the Canadian Confederation of 1867 have been interpreted as involving a contract between independent partners. In other cases, where formerly self-governing groups were forcibly included in a state but never abandoned the aspiration to self-government, we can imagine fair terms of an initial agreement that can be used as a benchmark for assessing the present arrangements. The familiar liberal device of hypothetical contract can thus justify claims for autonomy raised by many indigenous minorities. In all these cases the contract argument is quite straightforward and asks states to honour explicit or implicit agreements underlying existing federal arrangements as well as to introduce new ones for groups who should have enjoyed a right to negotiate the terms of their inclusion under fair conditions.

A contractarian test can also be applied to a much wider range of situations where a minority had not been actually self-governing before being coercively included in a wider state but where economic and political development within that state had transformed it from an ethnic into a national minority. In this situation we could imagine a Rawlsian original position (Rawls 1971) at the constitutional level with the background assumption that the parties know that they are members of a common polity and have already worked out the basic individual liberties and rights of citizens. They are then informed that groups of citizens whom they represent are faced with the danger of becoming permanent minorities in the democratic process and have developed a strong desire to govern their own affairs. Without knowing whether they themselves represent such minorities or the national majority the parties have to work out constitutional arrangements that will guarantee the fair value of political liberties for such minorities. The problem with the Rawlsian approach is that the connection between the device of representation and the principles of justice which it is supposed to yield is quite controversial. Or, to put it differently, whether parties behind such a veil of ignorance would in fact adopt federal arrangements or be satisfied with a lower level of protection of minorities is hard to say. I suggest, therefore, that we ought to look for alternative and more straightforward justifications for multinational federalism that can supplement or reinforce the contractarian argument and can help to specify the terms of fairness in such arrangements.

The starting-point for this is to consider that federalism can come about in two different ways: by union or by devolution. A normative theory of federation must therefore show under which conditions it is preferable to independent government of the separate parts as well as to centralized government. In addition to the question: (1) 'Why federate rather than stay independent?' we must then answer the further questions: (2) 'Why transform a unitary state into a federal one?' and (3) 'Why maintain a federation rather than centralize the state or break it apart?'

The answer to the first question will be motivated by the attractions of federation such as material benefits of economic integration or by threats like the superior power of some potential aggressor state.[7] These are prudential reasons rather than moral ones and they cannot explain why the terms of federation should remain binding over generations once these conditions have changed. If a contractarian theory of federation wants to show why groups that have never signed an actual contract and that have the potential

---

[7] This is John Stuart Mill's view, which has influenced many contemporary accounts. For him federation is an answer to the threat of war between states, rather than to internal diversity within states: 'Portions of mankind who are not fitted, or not disposed, to live under the same internal government, may often with advantage be federally united as to their relations with foreigners: both to prevent wars among themselves, and for the sake of more effectual protection against the aggression of powerful States' (Mill 1972: 398).

to form separate states should not secede, it must argue that there are moral reasons that oblige them to enter into a federation and that remain binding thereafter. One such argument seems to be provided by Kant, who thought that international peace can only be durably maintained by an ever-enlarging federation of republican states (Kant 1984). Joining such a federation is therefore a moral imperative. However, this reason applies only to confederations between states and not to federal states.[8] Another answer is suggested by Lord Acton: 'A great democracy must either sacrifice self-government to unity or preserve it by federalism. The coexistence of several nations under the same State is a test, as well as the best security of its freedom . . . The combination of different nations in one State is as necessary a condition of civilized life as the combination of men in society' (Acton 1907: 277). Taken literally this proposition would not only justify maintaining multinational states, but would also require the formation of new ones out of relatively homogeneous nation-states. This merely turns on its head John Stuart Mill's famous dictum that 'Free institutions are next to impossible in a country made up of different nationalities' (Mill 1972: 392).[9] While a defence of pluralistic federation must deny that liberal democracy is incompatible with a multinational structure of the polity, it certainly need not assert that the latter is a necessary condition for the former.

A second weakness of the contractarian approach is that, except in its Rawlsian variant, it cannot ground a general right to federal autonomy and a corresponding right to secession if such autonomy is denied. Explicit and implicit agreements generate only special rights.[10] Federalist constraints or justifications for secession would then apply to multinational states with a federal constitution, but not to those that consistently deny their national minorities any collective autonomy or representation. In contrast, a broader theory of federalism which mandates devolution in these cases can establish a general right to federal autonomy for certain kinds of groups as well as a right to secession when such autonomy rights are persistently violated.

Why Devolve Unitary States?

The devolution perspective of federation is thus in many cases more plausible than the contractarian one both as an empirical and as a normative account.

---

[8] Kant rules out the possibility of a single federal world-state although he remains ambiguous as to its desirability.

[9] David Miller's theory of nationality explicitly restates Mill's approach (Miller 1995: 10, 98).

[10] 'Remedial Right Only Theories allow that there can be special rights to secede (1) if the state grants a right to secede . . . or if (2) the constitution of the state includes a right to secede . . . or perhaps if (3) the agreement by which the state was initially created out of previously independent political units included the implicit or explicit assumption that secession at a later point was permissible . . .' (Buchanan 1997a: 36).

In a recent paper Juan Linz mentions three specific reasons that explain why and under which conditions unitary states are likely to be transformed into multinational federations. We could call these the 'historic record argument', the 'democratic irreversibility' argument, and the 'transition to democracy' argument. Examining the history of successful federal arrangements Linz concludes that: 'Multinational federalism is not the result of different nation-states uniting to create a new and larger multinational federal state. Multinational federalism seems to be the result of an effort to hold together within the state territories within which an old or new national sentiment, identity, exists or has emerged and becomes incompatible with an unitary state' (Linz 1997: 27). The second argument states that democracies can transform themselves by democratic means into federations whereas 'In a multinational state, it is unlikely that a democratic transition to an unitary state would be possible' (Linz 1997: 8). Liberal democratic constitutions provide national minorities and their élites with rights of free speech and association that can be used as resources for defending their aspirations to self-government. Once autonomy or special representation have been enshrined in federal arrangements, they come to be seen as elements of democratic citizenship. Democratic majorities cannot legitimately deprive any part of the polity of its citizenship rights. In federations this constraint extends beyond equal individual liberties and includes collective rights of national minorities. The third argument emphasizes another aspect in which democratic federalism is different in kind from non-democratic variants. 'Multinational federalism presumes the existence of a working state, a *Rechtsstaat*, the introduction of democracy, and then the solution of the multinational conflicts by democratic federalism. If that sequence is reversed, the prospects are very different' (Linz 1997: 47). The breakdown of the multinational empires of the nineteenth century, of the Soviet Union, and of Yugoslavia was not due to a general unsustainability of federal solutions for nationality conflicts, but to a lack of democratic institutions which could have integrated such diverse populations. The implication of this argument is that democratic federalism is not just about granting national minorities special rights, it is also about maintaining and defending democratic institutions at the level of the federation. A multinational federation with no effective common citizenship or with a central government which is not accountable to the citizenry is very likely to disintegrate into separate states once democracy gets a hold in its component parts.

The normative argument for recognizing territorially concentrated historical minorities as political communities within the larger polity can be stated like this: There is no good reason why claims to self-government should be a priori limited to sovereign states. If we find that within such states there are groups of the population that conceive of themselves as distinct political communities that wish to collectively decide matters of specific concern for their members and that form regional majorities, then there is no prima-facie reason to deny them rights to partial autonomy. In fact, the equal representation of citizens at the level of the larger polity will in these cases *require* that their affiliations to these smaller political communities be taken into account so that they are not disadvantaged compared to majority members for whom the larger state is coextensive with the only political community within which they want to be represented. Many theorists of democracy have suggested that legitimacy of majority rule depends on opportunities for minorities to become themselves majorities in competitive elections. However, this is an extremely remote possibility for a minority that defines itself as a distinct historic community within a larger society. If their members rank the interests of their own group high compared to those political issues that concern all citizens, they will see a system of political authority that denies them autonomy or special representation as illegitimate.

A manifest desire for self-government which would be continuously overridden by state-wide majorities unless protected by federal arrangements is therefore a powerful reason for transforming unitary states into multinational federations. However, this is not the only normative argument for devolution. Others reason include empowering the *individual* citizens by multiplying the levels of government where they can exert their influence, or preventing the abuse of political authority by establishing a system of checks and balances between regional and federal governments, or allowing for experimentation with various policies and forms of political representation (Elazar 1987: 102; Kymlicka 1998c: 137). All these latter reasons apply to regional federations just as to multinational ones. They may support a move from mere decentralization in unitary states to federal devolution by giving provincial levels of government some final decision-making power and making them directly accountable to their local constituencies.[11] The multinational approach turns devolution into a vehicle for integrating collectivities which could otherwise challenge the existing borders. The second group of reasons may, however, just as well be used to split up minorities and to suppress potential or manifest demands for autonomy.[12] Instead of representing diversity within the polity,

[11] Whether this should be generally seen as an improvement of democratic representation is a controversial claim. Riker (1975), for example, rejects both the normative arguments for devolution and the hypothesis that federalism makes any difference to political outcomes. In his view, it merely complicates procedures of political decision-making. While this may be sometimes true for regional federations, it is certainly wrong for multinational ones. In highly diverse societies, federalism does make a difference to the protection of minority interests.

[12] Splitting up minorities by federal boundaries may be justified as long as it does not disadvantage them with regard to a national majority. The Francophone minority in Switzerland is divided into several cantons. What is wrong is not splitting minorities but manipulating boundaries to secure regional majorities for a federal majority. Where national or linguistic

devolution can then become an instrument for transforming heterogeneous societies into apparently homogeneous polities.

Examples of this policy may be found both in unitary and in federal states. When in 1789 the National Assembly divided France into eighty-three departments of roughly equal size, this was meant to destroy the historical identities of regions many of which could be identified by cultural and linguistic difference. In the USA the borders of Florida were drawn so as to prevent a Hispanic majority, and statehood of the former Mexican territories in New Mexico and Arizona was delayed until 1912, when Anglophone settlement had overturned the previous majority (Kymlicka 1998c: 137). In a republican perspective such ethnic gerrymandering of internal boundaries could be perfectly legitimate because the federal scheme is meant to empower the individual citizen rather than groups. Ignoring historical boundaries makes it also easier to create subunits of equal size which allow for equality of collective as well as individual representation. Unequal numbers of populations of federal provinces combined with an equal number of seats for each province in a federal chamber mean that the votes of individual citizens are weighted unequally in different parts of the federation. However, such congruous-federalism-by-design is a rare exception. In federal unions the provinces or states generally do represent historic units and their self-government is justified by imagining them as constitutive building-blocks of the larger unit.[13]

Imposing congruous federalism on a society of regionally concentrated national groups may sometimes be an effective way of maintaining unity by suppressing demands for autonomy. But attempts to do so may just as well

groups are of roughly equal size or where the regions they inhabit do not form a contiguous territory, federal boundaries may well divide them all into several units as long as the minority's rights to self-government are not sacrificed to the majority's aspirations to dominate the whole federation. As in Switzerland, subdividing groups into smaller units for the purpose of federal representation may even provide additional stability to a federation. I am grateful to Will Kymlicka for pointing this out to me. However, this model cannot be easily generalized because Switzerland is a rather exceptional case and not a multinational federation properly speaking. The aspiration for self-government has historically been attached to the cantons rather than to language groups, while national identity is focused on the federal level. Language-based nationalism did cause the secession of Jura from Bern in 1979 but has not produced a desire to unite the new canton with the rest of la Suisse Romande. In truly multinational societies it would be rather difficult to artificially subdivide the units which consider themselves to be the founding nations of a federation.

13 The United States, which has been regarded as the classic example of congruous federation, shows the highest degree of inequality of representation due to unequal size of states. Wyoming, with a population of less than 500,000, and California, with 30,000,000, each elect two senators. The only reason why this is not regarded as violating standards of equality of political rights is that the states are considered to be historically distinct units with a right to govern most of their own affairs and to be represented as such units in a second chamber.

incite resistance movements to resort to violence. The irreversibility argument suggests that under democratic conditions the latter result is more likely than the former. As long as basic liberties are maintained, minority nationalists are able to voice their grievances and mobilize support. Blocking democratic channels for their representation will hardly be sufficient to force them into capitulation. This policy option should therefore be discarded for both moral and prudential reasons. The alternative solution of a self-consciously incongruous federation is by no means a simple formula for resolving national conflicts. It requires a delicate balance between federal unity and the representation of regional units and national collectivities which is sometimes difficult to achieve. Although groups that define themselves as national minorities can fit well into a federal scheme that gives them collective representation and autonomy, they may still regard their special claims as quite different from those of the other provinces. One of the major complaints of the Québécois is that their status has deteriorated from one of the two founding nations to one among ten provinces. This is why they demand recognition as a 'distinct society' on top of their rights as the majority in one province. Still, the two reasons for devolution need not be mutually incompatible. The Scottish and Welsh referenda of September 1997 illustrate how they can be combined. Labour, Liberals and nationalists who all supported the vote for regional assemblies had different reasons for doing so. The Scottish National Party saw this as a first step towards independence, Welsh nationalists merely strove for more regional autonomy within the UK, while Labour and the Liberal Democrats wanted to decentralize some areas of government and to experiment with proportional representation.

My answer to the second question about federalism is thus that historic minorities have good cause to demand a change of the present system in over-centralized states[14] as well as in federal arrangements that are skewed against them. Whether they may legitimately use the threat of secession in order to bring such transformation about is a matter that depends on contextual judgements about the gravity of their complaints.

Why Maintain Federations?

The contractarian perspective establishes a duty of states to respect explicit or implicit federal agreements, while the devolution perspective establishes a duty to create federal arrangements that satisfy legitimate claims of minorities. The third question searches for normative reasons why the unity of a federal state should be maintained. If any good reasons can be found, this places a burden of argument on the shoulders of those who would want to break up the state into its constituent parts. This goes not only for secessionist

---

[14] Such as France before the creation of the twenty-two regions in 1982.

minorities but also for currents among federation-wide majorities who think that 'one should finally get rid of the troublemakers'.[15]

The reasons given by just-cause theorists, who deny a primary right to secession, are also relevant for maintaining a federal state. First, in a well-ordered democracy citizens regard the polity as an ongoing co-operation over generations which generates public goods and benefits. Some of these goods are collective in the sense that their division into separate packages for independent states will reduce the total value. More importantly, any operation of dividing them in this way will create some injustice towards groups of citizens that could be avoided if a common polity is maintained. Among the most important of these public goods is 'the web of group affiliations . . . generated by long-time living together, intermarriage, friendship and interests. It is that web that the dichotomous choice that a decision by plebiscites implies necessarily ignores and destroys' (Linz 1997: 16). While the institutions of liberal democracy allow for an articulation of group claims, which are generally repressed in authoritarian regimes, they also promote the emergence of linkages across group boundaries and of multiple identities. Geographical mobility and intermarriage between groups generates a certain number of horizontally overlapping identities, but the federal structure itself promotes dual identities for *everybody* by adding a layer of federal citizenship to the particular memberships of the constitutive collectivities. The costs of separation are therefore generally much higher than the costs of staying separate. This is another important reason why a theory of federation cannot be reduced to the initial reasons for uniting.

It will be objected that multinational federalism facilitates separation because it already creates an internal division of the polity, recognizes particular national identities, and allocates important public goods and political powers to its subunits. This will lower the costs of ultimately dividing the state itself. A federal structure of the state may also whet the appetite of secessionists, who could be deterred by the much stronger resistance a centralized state can put up against them.[16] But the very features that are seen to threaten unity in

[15] The dominant strategy of oppressive regimes is, of course, to expel the population rather than to reduce their own territory. The various Bantustans and the mock state of Transkei created by the apartheid regime in 1976 were, of course, dependent territories within South Africa. Strategic state contraction (Lustick 1997) is nearly always a response to powerful movements for independence. However, faced with rising economic and political costs of resisting secessionist demands political leaders of national majorities have sometimes advocated separation as a minor evil. During the final months of the Czechoslovak federation the Klaus government did nothing to preserve the union or to test support for separation in a plebiscite.

[16] In the previous section I have already compared federal arrangements with unitary states and have found sufficient normative reasons for devolution in multinational societies and some empirical evidence for the sustainability of multinational federalism in democratic regimes. What we are now concerned with is how federalism compares to separation from the perspective of the various nationalities or autonomous provinces.

federal states also provide moral reasons for maintaining this unity that are not available in a unitary state. A group that considers itself a distinct minority within the state enjoys powers not merely to shape the public culture of the region where it forms a majority, but also to protect its other members who are dispersed throughout the federation. It can also influence all policies of federal authorities that may affect its interests (such as foreign policy towards other countries to which it feels culturally linked). Secession transforms its autonomy into sovereignty but deprives it of its voice in the governance of the larger state. While autonomy gives the minority a moral reason to maintain the federation by partially satisfying demands that are invoked to justify secession, collective representation involves the subunits in the government of the larger polity so that they also acquire a collective responsibility for the common good of that state.

This will not impress radical nationalists who are unwilling to compromise on the demand for full sovereignty. They will see the political involvement of their group in federal institutions either as a mere step towards independence or as an attempt by the state to appease the nationalist leadership. Pluralistic federations may be able to live with this phenomenon if they can either isolate stubborn nationalists from their broader group or can 'corrupt' part of their leadership by co-opting them into federal institutions. As long as self-consciously national groups get a fair deal from the federal government, the prospects for both strategies should not be too bad. One possible side-effect might well be that an isolated secessionist group will then resort to terrorist violence. However, it would be wrong to think that the danger of violent political action could be reduced either by resisting nationalist demands for self-government or by granting easy secession.

Whether or not these reasons for maintaining federation are sufficient to refute the claims of secessionists will of course depend on how federal arrangements live up to their promise to strike a fair balance between the collective interests of the various parts of which the state is composed. The flip side of a theory of federation that serves to deny the legitimacy of secessionist claims is that a breach of federal agreements by the representatives of the majority population gives minorities good grounds for threatening secession. The federalist approach rejects, therefore, the republican assumption that secession can never be justified as long as individual rights of citizens are maintained. It adds a distinctive justification to a grievance theory of secession which is generally absent from liberal accounts.[17] Threatening secession may

---

[17] For example, Allen Buchanan's shortlist of justifying grounds for secession consists of '(1) persistent and serious violations of individual human rights and (2) past unredressed unjust seizure of territory', to which he adds discriminatory redistribution as a third reason (Buchanan 1997b: 310). In his more extensive previous discussion he included the 'limited goals of political association' (Buchanan 1991: 35). However, he restricted this justification to the extremely rare case of federal states formed from previously independent units by explicit

be a legitimate ultimate means to defend collective rights within federal arrangements. This added reason makes the theory also more realistic than its competitors. It highlights one of the most common reasons for secessionist challenges and explains why liberal democratic constitutions are not immune to them.

Suppose a parliamentary majority in a multinational state unilaterally suspended a federal arrangement of special representation or constitutional veto for a minority without touching any of the individual rights of citizenship, such as the use of a minority language and without introducing discrimination, e.g. in access to public office. If majorities enjoyed such a licence to modify the terms of federation in their favour, then minorities would have no reason to accept them as fair and binding. What should count as a breach is difficult to specify in general terms. A well-ordered federation is not a final settlement of claims that could have been be enshrined in a foundational contract, but an institutional framework for building mutual trust in an ongoing negotiation of claims (Tully 1995: 140–82). In a modern economy and mobile society the social boundaries between subunits of a federation and their particular cultural characteristics are continuously in flux. This provides temptations for groups that gain in demographic or economic strength to change the terms of federation to their advantage and nourishes corresponding fears among the 'losers'. However, a federal agreement will become less binding over time if modifications in the allocation of powers and benefits are the outcome of bargaining procedures that merely reflect the respective strengths of the various parts. Maintaining a proper balance may require compensation for the weaker parts for a loss in demographic or economic leverage by giving them more political weight.

Sceptics will still remain unconvinced that these moral reasons carry sufficient force as motivations for political actors. In this view, 'demands for self-government . . . reflect a desire to weaken the bonds with the larger political community, and indeed question its very authority and permanence' (Kymlicka 1995a: 181). Accepting such demands 'is likely to lead to a desire for ever-increasing autonomy, even independence' (1995a: 186–7).[18] The danger is that even fair terms of federation will not be honoured by nationalists, to whom they give the power to jeopardize the unity of the state. Yet if we look at present multinational federal democracies, there is still no empirical evidence that the disuniting forces will ultimately and inevitably succeed. The Quebec referenda on sovereignty and election results in auto-

---

contract. Wayne Norman includes among just causes of secession 'that the group finds its constitutional rights grossly or systematically ignored by the central government or the supreme court' (Norman 1998: 41). This still does not fully cover those cases where the existing constitution unjustly denies self-government rights. The task of a normative theory of federalism is to specify why and when such rights ought to be constitutionally guaranteed.

[18] See also the more extensive argument in Kymlicka (1998c).

nomous provinces of Western European democracies[19] do not indicate a strong and permanent desire for independence among national minorities. While the support for regional self-government is constant and strong in most of these areas, the vacillating endorsement for secessionist parties seems to be more often a reaction to perceived breaches of promises by the central government.

There are basically four reasons which taken together may shape a widespread preference for maintaining unity in democratic multinational federations.[20] Multinational federalism can achieve integration through (1) concession: by granting partial self-government and special powers at the federal level; (2) moderation: by undercutting support for extreme nationalists through free competitive elections; (3) participation: by involving minorities and their representatives in federal schemes of power-sharing; (4) multiple identities: by allowing for geographical and marital mobility across boundaries and by promoting an overarching identity of federal citizenship.[21] None of these reasons fully removes the perverse incentives discussed above, which may push federal agencies towards infringing on autonomy and national minorities towards secession. Even the best federal arrangements cannot offer a guarantee for stability. My only claim is that alternative solutions are even more unstable. In multinational societies neither a primary right to secession nor grievance approaches which do not include a right to federal autonomy are likely to produce well-integrated democratic polities.

Let me draw some preliminary conclusions. If a democratic state consists of several territorially concentrated collectivities that conceive of themselves as distinct political communities and if the unity of the state has not been created and maintained by oppression, colonization, or recent annexation, then a federal solution will be generally preferable either to a centralized structure of government or to the break-up of such a state. This reverses the priorities shared by most nationalists. Rather than regarding homogeneous nation-states as the best realization of the principle of self-determination and accepting multinational federations grudgingly as second-best solutions, we should see border changes or the restitution of independent statehood as necessary only for colonies or annexed territories, but generally promote federal solutions within existing borders as the best possibility for building viable and just democracies. The break-up of multinational democracies is therefore to be deplored as a regrettable, and in many cases avoidable, political

[19] The first regional elections in Scotland and Wales in May 1998 confirmed the success of Labour's devolution strategy while establishing the two nationalist parties as strong democratic opposition movements within the new assemblies.

[20] This list summarizes a longer one presented by Linz (1997: 41–2).

[21] Kymlicka sees a possible basis for unity in a multinational state in the mutual recognition of identities, but tends to view this as a fortunate circumstance that cannot be easily created where it does not already exist (Kymlicka 1995a: 191).

failure.[22] As long as federal arrangements strike a fair balance between the various claims, the option of minorities to secede is constrained not only by feasibility conditions (such as geographical contiguity) but also by the commitments their representatives have accepted through co-operating in the federal institutions. A well-ordered federation may under these conditions provide a point of convergence from which the options of centralized government and separation both appear as illegitimate. Such a federation need not therefore recognize a general *right* to secede, although it may have to *tolerate* secession when it is persistently supported by a sufficient majority in a province and if it does not seriously disadvantage other groups in the province or the remainder state.

This approach avoids the reification of political community implicit in both nationalism and republicanism. By allowing for multiple levels of self-government it undermines illusions about a collective self which forms the substance of the polity and is imagined as an individual, that is, as an indivisible entity endowed with a single will. At the same time, it can assert that the very idea of democracy does imply a substantive conception of political community with a shared structure of authority, equal membership, and equal representation in collectively binding decisions. The contract theory of federation which merely considers its emergence from previously self-governing polities reinforces the analogy of union as marriage and secession as divorce which is frequently invoked by choice theories of secession (Beran 1984: 25; Nielsen 1993: 35; Gauthier 1994: 360, 371; Wellman 1995: 146). If a federation is like a marital contract, then each partner seems to have a prima-facie right to terminate the relation. However, if federal states are seen as voluntary unions, the same must hold for their constitutive communities as well. A federation is, then, in John Rawls's memorable words, a union of unions. Only nationalists can regard these groups as if they were individuals, i.e. indivisible moral agents. Adding the independent reasons for how federation can come about by devolution and why union ought to be maintained helps to correct the implicit nationalist bias of a purely contractarian view.

We can better understand this if we distinguish a right to self-government from self-determination. The latter concept refers to the idea that the collective 'self' of the national community, which is either defined objectively by a shared ancestry and culture or subjectively by a shared will of belonging

---

[22] As pointed out above, this conclusion need not apply to non-democratic multinational states. First, historical records tell us that there is a high likelihood of secession when authoritarian regimes in multinational states break down. Secondly, from a normative perspective it is impossible to justify a general duty of minorities to maintain the unity of a state that is not democratic and does not guarantee their basic liberties. A necessary dose of consequentialism should, however, oblige their representatives to search for alternative solutions if secession would involve great harms to others and a high probability of violent conflict.

to a political community, determines the borders within which the nation is to rule itself. In contrast, the idea of self-government, which is at the core of democratic legitimacy, need not imply a right to determine the borders of the territory or the boundaries of the collective over which government authority will be exercised.[23] Here the prefix 'self' simply says that the populations subjected to a political authority consider this government as their own and are justified in doing so because of democratic procedures of representation and decision-making. Self-government would thus be the broader and more generally applicable term that neither requires full sovereignty nor a right to determine or change external borders. Only this conception of self-government is compatible with multiple membership in vertically nested political communities. One can at the same time be a citizen of a federal state, of a province, and of a municipality which are all considered to be self-governing to various degrees. Of course, the smaller local or regional units are in important ways governed by federal laws. However, in a federal democracy all citizens are full and equal members of at least one collective unit at each level and in this sense they still govern themselves.

Multinational federalism offers, therefore, a solution for how a right to self-government can be made compatible with a similar right for all groups that have the requisite capacity to exercise it. It is opposed to the doctrine of indivisible sovereignty that regards only fully independent states as self-governing polities. It likewise rejects the conservative realist approach that views claims to self-government rights of national minorities as a threat to the territorial integrity of existing states. However, it does not attribute to all political communities a right to determine themselves their borders and avoids thus the non-generalizable and self-defeating principles of national self-determination or of plebiscitary choice of political boundaries.

3. Territorial Self-Government and Corporate Federalism

Liberal nationalists who do not share John Stuart Mill's preference for homogeneous nation-states may agree but still object that this approach fails to specify *which* communities seek collective autonomy and representation and *why* they seek it. For them the obvious answer is that these are national communities that need such rights in order to defend and protect the specific culture that distinguishes them from the majority population. David Copp

---

[23]   Allen Buchanan argues along similar lines that 'the right to be a distinct unit in a federation . . . does not carry the presumption that the group in question has the unlimited right to choose which forms of self-determination it will exercise' (Buchanan 1997b: 306). See also Margalit and Raz (1990), for whom self-determination is the right of a group to determine itself whether its territory shall be self-governing.

suggests an alternative answer. In his view the right of self-determination belongs to a territorial society rather than to a nation or encompassing cultural group (Copp 1997). He derives this conclusion from the observation that in plebiscitary decisions on secession all votes are counted equally and independently of cultural affiliation. While a normative theory of multinational federalism should reject such a right to secession, it still needs to answer the question who is the bearer of the right to territorial self-government within a federation.

Copp's move of replacing 'nation' with 'society' does not make sense in a multinational context. The exercise of the right to territorial self-government is clearly not neutral with regard to cultural affiliations within a regional society. It gives the largest national group a legitimate power to shape the public culture of its province or state, for example by turning its language into the dominant one in the public schools of their province. Secondly, as I have pointed out above, collective representation in multinational federalism may also provide culturally defined groups with rights that can be exercised by their dispersed members in the other 'territorial societies' of the federation, for instance by establishing their language as a second official one in public education and administration. Thirdly, if the point of territorial divisions were to make societies rather than nations self-governing, then provincial majorities could not complain when borders are revised in order to turn them into minorities. Multinational federalism must, however, prevent federal majorities from gerrymandering internal borders with the intention and effect of weakening one of the constitutive nationals groups.

It appears therefore that we may have to accept liberal nationalism as an account of territorial self-government within multinational federations after rejecting it as a theory of secession. Once the challenge of nationalism to the unity and stability of democratic states has been contained, theories about the moral value of secure membership in a national culture like the one elaborated by Will Kymlicka[24] seem much more attractive and could support a theory of multinational federalism. Nevertheless, the liberal national approach remains unsatisfactory also in this context.

One objection is that it seems to get the priorities wrong. Rather than self-government being a means to preserve cultural difference, this difference is more often preserved as a means to justify the claim to self-government. Consider the cases of Quebec, Catalonia, or Northern Ireland. In Canada it has been observed that the secessionist challenge came only after the Quiet Revolution of the 1960s which made the Francophone Quebecois much more similar to the Anglophone mainstream in terms of their ways of life (Whitaker 1995: 196). Nearly all Catalans speak the Spanish language fluently.

---

[24] See Kymlicka (1989, 1995a). Further arguments exploring the value of cultural membership have been presented by Buchanan (1991: 53), Raz (1994: 69), Parekh (1995).

They would not be deprived of individual opportunities for economic advancement or political participation if Spanish became (as it was during the Franco era) the only public language in their province. Of course, for members of minority communities a language is not merely a neutral means of communication, but transports a cultural tradition whose public recognition may be important for their self-respect (Taylor 1992). However, this is also true for immigrant minorities who do not claim that their languages be established. Catalans have an additional reason to preserve their language because it is the only difference that clearly distinguishes a Catalan polity from the Spanish state. If the language border vanished, geographic mobility would soon undermine the political significance of the province's territorial border.[25] An even more obvious case is the Irish one, where religion rather than language serves as a marker of national identities. The reason why Irish nationalists want to reunite the six counties with the Republic is not to maintain their Catholic tradition, and the reason why Protestant Unionists want to stay in the UK is not because they fear for their freedom of religion. What separates them are two different visions of the boundaries of the polity to which their province ought to belong. When dividing lines between different conceptions of membership persist over generations, they become marked by some ascriptive characteristic such as language, religion, or phenotype. The marker is, of course, not an arbitrary one, but reflects the historical origins of the conflict. But it would be wrong to interpret nationalism as being mainly about preserving a substantial cultural difference rather than a separate polity. The advantage of the federal approach outlined here over statist versions of liberalism is that it accepts the desire for self-government asserted by historic communities across generations as a basic claim that cannot be denied from a democratic perspective. Such communities can generally be identified by cultural and especially linguistic difference. Yet their right to self-government does not depend on the nature or magnitude of the differences that separate them from a majority population. And this right is also not merely instrumental for maintaining their traditional ways of life, but will more often be used to transform them into a modern national culture that provides their members with social status, political recognition, and economic opportunities.[26] The answer to the question posed at the beginning of this section is therefore that regional self-government rights are exercised by territorially concentrated historic polities, whom we may characterize as nations but which need not be primordial or encompassing cultural groups.

This is a descriptive rather than a normative observation about the desire

[25] In Dec. 1997 the Catalan parliament adopted a new law promoting the Catalan language in the electronic mass media, in the civil service, and in public schools and private business.

[26] Nationalism is therefore a homogenizing force not only within groups, but also across national boundaries. It makes the cultures it seizes much more alike than they were in their pre-national stages.

for self-government. In a liberal democracy some normative strings must be attached to granting this demand. There are important differences in this regard between the autonomy of voluntary associations or religious congregations to regulate their internal affairs, on the one hand, and the autonomy of institutions that exercise political authority within a territory, on the other. Although a provincial government formed by a regional national majority will legitimately seek to shape the public culture of its society, it must in other respects operate as a government for all citizens irrespective of their national affiliations. In all matters that do not concern specific national and cultural interests, it is indeed the territorial society that governs itself through representative democratic institutions in the same manner as it does in regional federations. More importantly for our discussion, even with regard to national cultural matters the majority cannot legitimately govern in a way that exclusively promotes its own interests. On the one hand, claiming for itself a federal privilege to establish its own regional cultural hegemony obliges it to honour similar claims by cultural minorities living in its own territory. It has no right to force established local minorities into cultural assimilation and it must provide opportunities for a public representation of minority cultures. On the other hand, because of its public hegemony the majority has a special obligation to make its own cultural traditions sufficiently open for other groups. For minorities such open access should involve general opportunities for participation in the dominant culture as well as the individual option of full assimilation. In a democratic federation of this sort, territorial self-government will therefore be rarely instrumental to preserve a regional culture in its traditional form, but it will maintain it as a marker of political identity while at the same time transforming it to reflect the multiculturalism of the regional society.

There is one major exception to this requirement of openness for self-governing territorial groups in liberal democracies: indigenous minorities often enjoy stronger powers to exclude non-members from their territory or from their public culture. I suggest tentatively that three arguments justify these special exemptions from standard requirements of liberal federalism. All refer to the entirely different significance of territory for these groups. The first reason is that some of these groups really desire what modernizing nations necessarily abandon: the preservation of a traditional way of life. The second reason is a history of forced incorporation, resettlement, and confinement in reservations that has turned their remaining territories into a last refuge. The third one is that territory itself figures as an essential cultural and religious symbol rather than merely as a space for the exercise of political power. Forcing indigenous minorities to open their territories and public cultures to the inflow of non-members would thus continue a history of colonization and would deprive them of their capability to reproduce their culture.

None of these reasons applies to other territorially concentrated national minorities marked by differences of language or religion. Far from endangering a liberal constitution by granting excessive powers to minorities, federal devolution may actually help to strengthen commitments to liberal principles among dissatisfied national minorities. The widespread rejection of multinational federalism among liberal republicans rests on the prejudice that only central state institutions are liberal and secular while national minorities will always be illiberal and abuse any power given to them in order to restrict freedom in their provinces (Kymlicka 1997: 81–2). There is little evidence for this in Canada, Belgium, Switzerland, or Spain. On the contrary, if my argument is correct, there is a reasonable expectation that, within the framework of liberal democracies, pluralistic federalism provides reasons both for enhancing the commitment of all constitutive groups towards liberal values and for maintaining the unity of multinational states.

However, multinational federalism of this sort has its limitations, too. It is not a panacea for every kind of conflict between 'identity groups'. All modern liberal societies experience a broad diversity of religious affiliations, languages, ethnic origins, sexual orientations, or ways of life. Most of these do not crystallize into regional majorities with a claim and an aspiration to self-government. Why should the federal solution of collective autonomy and representation not be extended to all these different kinds of diversity? And why should regional nationality conflicts not also be settled by granting self-government rights to membership groups rather than to autonomous provinces? This would be a membership-based 'corporate federalism' (Lijphart 1984: 183–5) instead of a territorial one.[27]

Radical multiculturalists sometimes defend this idea, which has certain attractions. From the perspective of multinational federal states a membership-based definition of constitutive nationalities would make secession much more unlikely than territorial federalism. Non-territorial units of representation cannot break away in order to form sovereign territorial nation-states. From the perspective of national minorities corporate federalism provides equal representation for their geographically dispersed members, whereas territorial federalism creates disadvantages for those living outside a province

---

[27] The Ottoman *millet* system of autonomy for religious groups is most often cited as an example for a membership-based structure of group autonomy. However, the *millet* system was a 'regime of religious toleration' (Walzer 1997) rather than a federal polity composed of constitutive self-governing units. A democratic version of membership-based federalism was first fully developed by the Austrian social democrats Karl Renner and Otto Bauer, who proposed a scheme of cultural autonomy for the nationality groups of the late Habsburg monarchy. This plan, which was never realized, combined a territorial principle of representation with a 'personality principle'. Citizens would declare their nationality and would be represented on this basis in a nationality chamber legislating in matters of culture and education (Bauer 1907).

where their group forms a regional majority.[28] From the perspective of social integration in a liberal society the advantage of membership-based federalism is that it would remove incentives to create more homogeneous national regions by promoting ethnic immigration or territorial resettlement. From an egalitarian perspective corporate arrangements could offer similar rights to all groups and abolish what appear to be arbitrary privileges of regionally concentrated nationalities.

However, there is a profound difference between these two contrasting types of federalism. In a liberal society, carving up the public sphere into separate domains for each group is not at all like dividing the territory between federal entities. Territorial federalism allows for social integration across ethnic and national boundaries and does not undermine the essential individual rights and liberties. First, it designates a regional space of cohabitation of citizens as the unit of political representation, whereas corporate federations would imply that people living in the same area belong to different constitutive units of the polity. Although we may imagine a future where public spheres no longer have any spatial correlate, this is not a particularly attractive vision. A society in which neighbourhoods are thoroughly segregated along ethnic or class lines will hardly achieve democratic integration via the Internet. And if, for example, schools, universities, and museums are generally run by religious or language groups, rather than being common institutions for all citizens living in a territory, there will be little left of what these citizens share when they enter the voting booth.

Secondly, multinational federal systems can only work if the boundaries between their constitutive units are relatively stable over time. Territorial federalism allows for a softening of group boundaries by using the geographic division as a proxy for group differences. It disconnects the unit of representation from individual group affiliation. This makes borders easier to maintain in modern societies, where group membership is essentially fluid due to geographic mobility and intermarriage. In contrast with external borders, internal ones are also open for immigration. Federal citizenship includes a right of free movement within the whole territory. Although multinational federations are created in order to represent nationalities, no federal unit may prevent an increasing diversification of origins among their population and each unit has to represent equally all its citizens independently of their origins. My initial definition of federal self-government implies, however, a

---

[28] One could, for example, discuss whether from the perspective of Francophone Canadians a non-territorial bilingualism, as promoted by Pierre Trudeau, would not have been preferable to a binational territorial federation in which French speakers outside Quebec find it more difficult to preserve their language. However, the former option would have imposed strong constraints on the political aspirations of self-government among French Canadians. My hypothesis that self-government is the defining goal for national minorities rather than merely a means for maintaining their culture accounts for the dynamic towards territorial federalism.

right of constitutive nationalities not to be outnumbered. At a point where free movement would deprive a national minority of its majority in a self-governing province it may demand either control over further immigration or a redrawing of federal boundaries which would re-establish its local majority.[29] This amounts to a *residual* and *remedial* right of self-determination to prevent the demographic preconditions for territorial self-government from being overturned. Such a residual right would also block attempts by representatives of a federal majority to undermine the status of national minorities by promoting immigration into their provinces from outside or from other parts of the federation. This safeguard would be quite different from a *primary* right to self-determination or the special rights of immigration control granted to indigenous peoples. In contrast, the units of corporate federations would only represent their respective group members. Such an arrangement would encourage all groups to seek maximum homogeneity within the constitutive unit. Political leaders and cultural élites would police their group's boundaries in order to maintain not merely their traditions, but also their political clout. Those who belong to several communities or to none and those who want to leave one community and join another one would be in a difficult position if their rights strongly depended on stable affiliations to groups (Lukes 1993: 25). Membership-based federalism could thus lead to substantial restrictions of internal liberties within groups, it would allow these groups to disregard external costs of their ways of life for non-members living in the same area, and it would destroy a common public sphere, which is essential for the integration of a democratic society.[30]

Thirdly, religious minorities, immigrant groups, other dispersed ethnic and linguistic communities, racially discriminated groups, or gays and lesbians mostly do not strive for self-government in the same comprehensive sense as national minorities (Kymlicka 1995a: 11–25). They generally understand themselves as distinct groups in society rather than as separate political communities. And their interests combine a quest for recognition of cultural difference with the demand for equal opportunities. While it is true that political and intellectual élites among these minorities sometimes use a symbolic language of self-government, radical corporate arrangements would misrepresent these interests and would create a further pretext for their segregation and discrimination in mainstream society.

For all these reasons, territorial federalism should generally be the preferred solution for disputes involving geographically concentrated national

---

[29] Quebec has, for example, limited powers to give preference to Francophone immigrants from outside Canada, but no power to regulate the internal inflow of immigrants admitted by the federal state (Carens 1994).

[30] This is why I would not endorse Yael Tamir's principle of (non-territorial) self-determination according to which 'all nations are entitled to a public sphere in which they constitute the majority' (Tamir 1993: 150).

groups. This does not rule out moderate forms of corporate federalism which can usefully supplement territorial divisions of power for national or linguistic groups that live geographically interspersed. Northern Ireland, South Tyrol–Alto Adige, and some regions in Central and Eastern Europe are obvious examples.[31] In most cases, such arrangements should, however, be seen as transitory. They may be especially appropriate as provisions for a truce after violent conflicts which have thoroughly divided groups which no longer mix socially, but are still left sharing a common territory.[32] But if such membership-based federalism becomes forever entrenched in a constitution and in the political system, it will perpetuate the conflict and block the transition towards an open liberal society.

This leaves the challenge of how to accommodate non-territorial cultural and ethnic diversity still unanswered. As with the problem of secession, liberals are divided on these questions and none of the solutions they have proposed seems entirely satisfactory. Civic republicans want to build a strong common culture of citizenship that will keep diversity at bay; libertarians plead for a cultural *laissez-faire* which reduces state intervention to maintaining public order; political liberals search for an overlapping consensus that would legitimize political institutions independently of the different beliefs and practices of various groups.[33] From a pluralist perspective, in contrast, such diversity will necessarily be reflected within the polity itself and will justify a range of group rights. There must also be some space for autonomy for groups that want to withdraw from the wider society as long as they do not restrict the liberties of their members to choose to be full citizens. However, these are cases for special exemptions.[34] The wider polity must find ways to integrate its various groups into a shared public sphere and special rights should promote rather than undermine this integration. Liberal democracies can neither build a 'wall of separation' that insulates an imagined homogeneous political community from a deeply heterogeneous civil society, nor should they build such walls within the polity between the various groups. The alternative is a pluralization of the polity that builds upon the fundamental assets of common individual citizenship and strengthens them by recognizing the impact of group membership on the citizens' social and economic opportunities, political powers, and cultural resources. What emerges from combining the federal response to national aspirations and the pluralistic integration of cultural, ethnic, and religious minorities is just the

---

[31] Non-territorial federal rights can also be useful for large and dispersed indigenous minorities such as the Maori (see Sharp 1997).

[32] Bosnia after independence could have become a test site for corporate federalism had Serb and Croat leaders in the province not supported the territorial expansion pursued by the Belgrade and Zagreb governments.

[33] See Parekh (1995) for an excellent summary of the various liberal responses to diversity.

[34] See Jeff Spinner's account of the Old Order Amish as 'partial citizens' (Spinner 1994: 87–108).

kind of structure of the polity that nationalism strives to overcome: borders of political communities and of cultural ones cutting across each other in many different lines. As in a spider's web, these lines should be seen as a texture that provides stability to the polity rather than dividing it into different compartments.

4. Conclusions

Nationalist movements for secession raise a profound challenge for liberal political theory: to define the boundaries of political communities and to explain why those of presently existing states should be defended. In reply to this challenge recent contributions have derived a right to secession from the supposedly beneficial consequences of national homogeneity, from collective choice or from serious violations of human and citizenship rights. The response I have suggested rejects the former two approaches while expanding the last one by adding violations of federal agreements and of distinctively collective rights to the list of grievances which may justify secession. A normative theory of multinational federalism must show why and when democratic states ought to devolve political power towards federal provinces and why and when groups who could potentially break away from the existing state ought to maintain its unity. My answer to the first question is that conflicts over a division of political powers involving one or more territorially concentrated groups which have asserted claims of self-government over several generations should be resolved by federal arrangements. My reply to the second question emphasizes that participating in fair arrangements of federal power-sharing creates commitments towards the common good of the larger polity. Moreover, democratic federalism allows for the emergence of multiple identities which help to integrate diverse societies.

The approach I have suggested may be broadened in two ways: by linking it, on the one hand, to a wider theory of differentiated citizenship within the democratic state and, on the other hand, to federalism in the international arena.

Multinational federalism challenges a unitary conception of citizenship. A pluralistic theory of liberal democracy argues for *differentiating* citizenship so that *substantial* equality of membership can be maintained in a complex and multilevel polity. This allows for a recognition not only of the nested structure of multiple membership in federal states[35] but also of overlapping

---

[35] As with dual citizenship emerging from migration, there are certainly 'potential conflicts about which community citizens identify with most deeply' (Kymlicka 1995a: 182). However, in both cases the escalation of such conflicts is fuelled by a unitary conception of sovereignty and citizenship much more than by reasonable demands for the recognition of multiple affiliations.

memberships which emerge from migration between independent states (Bauböck 1994b). Multinational federalism is only one chapter in a broader theory of differentiated citizenship.

With most liberal theories of justice this approach shares a preference for the internal transformation of states to bring them closer to democratic and liberal ideals. Like foreign humanitarian intervention, changing state borders should be regarded as a last remedy when other means have failed. Making governments accountable and responsive to their citizens requires a combination of collective voice through democratic representation with the liberty of individual exit through emigration (Hirschman 1970), but not an easy dissolution of political communities that would undermine their territorial stability and intergenerational continuity. This stability and continuity is not only in the interest of present rulers but also (even more) in the general interest of citizens whose opportunities and fundamental choices for their lives depend on the protection and rights provided by a democratic system of political authority. Such a presumption in favour of existing state borders does not contradict a moral internationalism which asserts that states have duties beyond borders. It neither legitimizes claims to the full value of natural resources in the state territory (Pogge 1994), nor does it in any way justify the huge global inequalities of social resources and opportunities for individuals who happen to have been born in different countries (Dummett 1992). What is excluded is only the most radical brand of cosmopolitanism which sees the solution to all these problems in a unified world-state. A pluralist approach to the problem of external borders and internal diversity within states will quite naturally advocate a similar pluralism at the level of the international political system. This allows for shifting traditional elements of sovereignty from the level of states to supra-state federations and international institutions without pursuing the goal of ultimately dismantling the state as the basic unit of the global political order.[36] Pluralistic federalism would thus take the existing states as its starting-point for moving towards recognition of lower-level polities and towards building higher-level ones. The resulting structure would retain the state as the level with the most comprehensive bundling of tasks for collectively binding decisions, but would expand in vertical and horizontal dimensions by adding other layers of political community in which citizens

[36] See Pogge (1992). Building or joining a global institution which could help to realize specific goals of international justice (such as a judicial authority, an authoritative body monitoring human rights, a scheme for burden-sharing with regard to refugee admission and assistance) is arguably a moral duty. In contrast, as I have already pointed out, forming a supranational federation from a group of independent states such as the European Union, or joining an existing federation of this sort, is generally a matter of prudence rather than of morality. However, *maintaining* such a federation and reforming it from the inside can become a duty once a state has become deeply involved in, and has benefited from, an ongoing and comprehensive co-operation.

can be simultaneously involved as multiple members. Just as federal constitutions offer the best hope for integrating internally diverse polities, so international federalism could help to reduce the danger of war and to correct gross injustices in the international system.[37]

I conclude by defending my approach against potential criticism from two opposite sides. Pluralistic federalism is hardly a novelty and it is no magical formula for beating secessionist nationalism, but rather the most common response to it in multinational democracies. The theory is 'realistic' in the sense that it accounts for many of the institutions and accommodating arrangements that have evolved in democratic states from two centuries of conflict between national groups and movements. Some readers may find this a rather disappointing proposal. What is the use of normative theorizing if it only highlights present realities, or even worse, if it merely justifies a status quo? I would like to defend this style of inquiry against the more fancy analytical approaches which derive surprising and counter-intuitive conclusions from initially plausible but over-generalized, abstract principles. I also want to defend it against the charge that it is essentially apologetic. The theory is a critical one with regard to theoretical debates as well as political institutions. While it is true that the federalist response to nationalism is in some ways accommodating by offering fair terms for self-government, it must firmly reject the nationalist interpretation of self-determination. At the same time it denies some widespread assumptions among liberal theorists about democratic citizenship as a unitary and homogeneous bundle of strictly individual rights and obligations. And while it argues for federal arrangements as a proper framework for negotiating claims to self-government, the theory also provides standards by which existing arrangements can be criticized whenever they implicitly violate the conditions for mutual trust that provide the moral glue for the federation.[38]

There is also the opposite charge of practical futility of a normative theory that appeals to moral principles that are blatantly absent in real politics. Is multinational federalism not simply an arrangement that emerges from a certain balance of powers and interests? Does the way in which theory informs our understanding of federalism in multinational democracies make any difference for the prospects of stabilizing them? I think it does. One should not underestimate the effects of public imagination on the stability of

---

[37] For the sake of simplicity I have treated nationality conflicts as internal ones. However, many involve, of course, external homelands or protecting foreign powers. Secessionist movements are often driven by demands for national union with a neighbouring state. Taking these cases into account will require combining intra-state federation with elements of inter- or supra-state federalism. The Northern Ireland Agreement of 10 Apr. 1998, with its provisions for self-government of the province and for an all-Irish dimension, has taken some significant steps in this direction.

[38] On the conditions of trust in multinational societies, see Weinstock (1999).

democratic institutions. The core questions about the nature and boundaries of political community cannot be settled simply by bargaining between representatives of interest groups. They are about what Antonio Gramsci called hegemony. As Benedict Anderson has argued, a 'nation' is a specific style of imagining a political community (Anderson 1983). There are deep structural features of modernity that make this style a pervasive one. And there are many constellations in politics that provide strong incentives for politicians to cultivate that style in their rhetoric. However, in a liberal democracy public discourses are never completely determined by structural forces, nor can they be completely manipulated by self-interested political élites. Legitimization can only be achieved by exposing candidates to competition and arguments to contestation. What critical normative theory may achieve in practical terms is to coin a few concepts and to launch a few ideas that catch public attention and will, however distorted, find their way into political discourse.

What I have presented is a rough sketch of a federalist perspective on the secession debate. There are two major issues which I have not sufficiently addressed. These are the questions of stability of pluralistic federal arrangements and of the content of fair terms of federation.[39] By examining the implications of the three questions about contract, devolution, and unity I have provided some arguments for the viability of multinational federations in liberal democratic states. When further exploring this question, one should be clear about reasonable standards of evaluation. These can only be relative. Starting from the fact that many modern societies are multinational we have to ask which solution would better satisfy stability requirements: easy secession derived from a right to national self-determination, imposed unity involving the coercive assimilation of minorities, or pluralistic federalism based on a right of territorial polities to self-government. Ultimately this is not a normative question but an empirical one. The final test is therefore in historical records. As we cannot simply wait another century to see whether Belgium, Canada, or Spain will then still exist, the task ahead is to examine in detail the sources of stability that have so far kept multinational federations of this kind together. Much the same is true for the challenge of specifying fair terms of federal arrangements. In contrast with basic individual rights, collective rights can normally only be specified in context. What is needed is the detailed examination of particular cases that can reveal which kinds of agreements have been regarded as fair by all sides concerned and which standards of fairness were used. This need not commit us to share such judgement, but a good dose of inductive generalization might be a healthy antidote to purely deductive styles of normative theorizing. General normative theory will still tell us to ask the right kind of questions, but many of the answers will only be found in the books of history.

---

[39] I am grateful to Will Kymlicka for pointing this out to me in a personal communication.

Further Reading

Editors' Note: All of the following readings have appeared since 1994. For a fairly comprehensive list of articles and books on citizenship and diversity from the late 1980s and early 1990s see the bibliography in W. Kymlicka and W. Norman (1994), 'Return of the Citizen: A Survey of Recent Work on Citizenship Theory', *Ethics*, 104/2: 352–81.

Theories of Citizenship and Civic Virtue

General

Batstone, David and Eduardo Mendieta (eds.). (1999), *The Good Citizen* (London: Routledge).

Beiner, Ronald (ed.). (1995), *Theorizing Citizenship* (Albany, NY: State University of New York Press).

Bickford, Susan (1996), *The Dissonance of Democracy: Listening, Conflict, and Citizenship*, (Ithaca, NY: Cornell University Press).

Bulmer, Martin and Anthony Rees (eds.). (1996), *Citizenship Today: The Contemporary Relevance of T. H. Marshall* (London: University College London Press).

Chambers, Simone (1996), *Reasonable Democracy: Jurgen Habermas and the Politics of Discourse* (Ithaca, NY: Cornell University Press).

Christodoulis, Emilios (ed.). (1998), *Communitarianism and Citizenship* (Ashgate: Aldershot).

Dagger, Richard (1997), *Civic Virtues: Rights, Citizenship and Republican Liberalism* (Oxford: Oxford University Press).

Hefner, Robert W. (ed.). (1998), *Democratic Civility: The History and Cross-Cultural Possibility of a Modern Political Ideal* (Piscataway, NJ: Transaction Publishers).

International Council on Human Rights Policy (1999), *Taking Duties Seriously: Individual Duties in International Human Rights Law—A Commentary* (International Council on Human Rights Policy).

Janoski, Thomas (1998), *Citizenship and Civil Society: Obligations in Liberal, Traditional and Social Democratic Regimes* (Cambridge: Cambridge University Press).

Lister, Ruth (ed.). (1998), *Citizenship: Feminist Perspectives* (New York: New York University Press).

Schnapper, Dominique (1998), *Community of Citizens: On the Modern Idea of Nationality* (Piscataway, NJ: Transaction Publishers)

Sevenhuijsen, Selma (1998), *Citizenship and the Ethics of Care: Feminist Considerations on Justice, Morality and Politics* (London: Routledge).

Shafir, Gershon (ed.). (1998), *The Citizenship Debates: A Reader* (Minneapolis: University of Minnesota Press).

Slawner, Karen and Mark Denham (eds.). (1998), *Citizenship after Liberalism* (New York: Peter Lang).

Symposium on (1996), 'Citizenship: History, Theory and Practice', *Australian Journal of Politics and History*, 42/1.

——(1997), 'Citizenship in Feminism: Identity, Action and Locale', *Hypatia*, 12/4.

——(1997), 'Citizenship: Pushing the Boundaries', *Feminist Review*, 57.

——(1997), 'Recasting Citizenship', *Theory and Society*, 26/4.

——(1997), 'Sovereignty and Citizenship', *Law and Philosophy*, 16/4.

——(1998), *Feminism and Citizenship* (London: Sage).

Tam, Henry (1998), *Communitarianism: A New Agenda for Politics and Citizenship* (New York: New York University Press).

Trend, David (ed.). (1996), *Radical Democracy: Identity, Citizenship and the State* (London: Routledge).

van Gunsteren, Herman (1998), *Organizing Plurality: Citizenship in Post-1989 Democracies* (Boulder, Colo.: Westview Press).

Almost all of the issues of the new journal *Citizenship Studies* contain articles on citizenship theory.

Citizenship Education

Bridges, David (ed.). (1997), *Education, Autonomy and Democratic Citizenship: Philosophy in a Changing World* (London: Routledge).

Callan, Eamonn (1997), *Creating Citizens: Political Education and Liberal Democracy* (Oxford: Oxford University Press).

Feinberg, Walter (1998), *Common Schools/Uncommon Identities: National Unity and Cultural Difference* (New Haven, Conn.: Yale University Press).

Fullinwider, Robert (ed.). (1995), *Public Education in a Multicultural Society* (Cambridge: Cambridge University Press).

Hahn, Carole (1998), *Becoming Political: Comparative Perspectives on Citizenship Education* (Albany, NY: State University of New York Press).

May, Stephen (1998), *Critical Multiculturalism: Rethinking Multicultural and Antiracist Education* (London: Falmer Press).

Torres, Carlos A. (1995), 'Democratic Education in a Multicultural State', *Journal of Philosophy of Education*, 29/2.

——(1995), 'Citizenship, Democracy and Education', *Ethics*, 105/3.

——(1998), *Democracy, Education and Multiculturalism: Dilemmas of Citizenship in a Global World* (Lanham, Md.: Rowman and Littlefield).

——(1999), 'Political Education', *Oxford Review of Education*, 25/1.

Cosmopolitan and Transnational Citizenship

Archibugi, Danielle and David Held (1995), *Cosmopolitan Democracy—An Agenda for a New World Order* (Cambridge, Mass.: Polity Press).

Heater, Derek B. (1996), *World Citizenship and Government: Cosmopolitanism Ideas in the History of Western Political Thought* (New York: St Martin's Press).

Held, David (1995), *Democracy and the Global Order: From the Modern State to Cosmopolitan Governance* (Cambridge, Mass.: Polity Press).

Hutchings, Kimberly and Ronald Dannreuther (eds.). (1999), *Cosmopolitan Citizenship* (New York, NY: St. Martin's Press).

Lehning, Percy and Albert Weale (eds.). (1997), *Citizenship, Democracy and Justice in the New Europe* (London: Routledge).

Linklater, Andrew (1998), *The Transformation of Political Community: Ethical Foundations of the Post-Westphalian Era* (Columbia, SC: University of South Carolina Press).

Nentwich, Michael and Albert Weale (eds.). (1998), *Political Theory and the European Union: Legitimacy, Constitutional Choice and Citizenship* (London: Routledge).

Ong, Aihwa (1999), *Flexible Citizenship: The Cultural Logics of Transnationality* (Durham, NC: Duke University Press).

Robbins, Bruce (ed.). (1998), *Cosmopolitics: Thinking and Feeling Beyond the Nation* (Minneapolis: University of Minnesota Press).

Roberts, John C. de V. (1999), *World Citizenship and Mundialism: A Guide to the Building of a World Community* (Westport, Conn.: Praeger).

Weiner, Antje (1997), *European Citizenship Practice: Building Institutions of a Non-State* (Boulder, Colo.: Westview Press).

Theories of Minority Rights and Multiculturalism

General

Baker, Judith (ed.). (1994), *Group Rights* (Toronto: University of Toronto Press).

Bennett, David (ed.). (1998), *Multicultural States: Rethinking Difference and Identity* (London: Routledge).

Bowring, Bill and D. Fottrell (eds.). (2000), *Minority and Group Rights Toward the New Millennium* (The Hague: Kluwer).

Cairns, Alan, Smith, David E., Michelmann, Hans J. *et al.* (eds.). (1999), *Citizenship, Diversity and Pluralism: Canadian and Comparative Perspectives* (Montreal: McGill-Queen's University Press).

Grillo, Ralph (1998), *Pluralism and the Politics of Difference: State, Culture and Ethnicity in Comparative Perspective* (Oxford: Oxford University Press).

Kernohan, Andrew (1998), *Liberalism, Equality and Cultural Oppression* (Cambridge: Cambridge University Press).

Kymlicka, Will (1995), *Multicultural Citizenship: A Liberal Theory of Minority Rights* (Oxford: Oxford University Press).

——(ed.). (1995), *The Rights of Minority Cultures* (Oxford: Oxford University Press).

Mahajan, Gurpreet (ed.). (1998), *Democracy, Difference and Social Justice* (Delhi: Oxford University Press).

Mahajan, Gurpreet and D. L. Sheth (1999), *Minority Identities and the Nation State* (Delhi: Oxford University Press).

Phillips, Anne (1995), *The Politics of Presence: Democracy and Group Representation* (Oxford: Oxford University Press).

Poulter, Sebastian (1998), *Ethnicity, Law and Human Rights: The English Experience* (Oxford: Oxford University Press).

Raikka, Juha (ed.). (1996), *Do We Need Minority Rights: Conceptual Issues* (The Hague: Kluwer).

Shapiro, Ian and Will Kymlicka (eds.). (1997), *Ethnicity and Group Rights: NOMOS XXXIX* (New York: New York University Press, 1997).

Spinner, Jeff (1994), *The Boundaries of Citizenship: Race, Ethnicity and Nationality in the Liberal State* (Baltimore: Johns Hopkins University Press).

Stapleton, Julia (ed.). (1995), *Group Rights: Perspectives Since 1990* (Bristol: Thoemmes Press).

Tully, James (1995), *Strange Multiplicity: Constitutionalism in an Age of Diversity* (Cambridge, Mass.: Cambridge University Press)

van Willigenburg, Theo, Heeger, Robert and Wilbren van der Burg (eds.). (1995), *Nation, State, and the Coexistence of Different Communities* (Kampen: Kok Pharos).

Walzer, Michael (1997), *On Toleration* (New Haven, Conn.: Yale University Press).

Willet, Cynthia (ed.). (1998), *Theorizing Multiculturalism: A Guide to the Current Debate* (Malden, Mass.: Blackwell).

Williams, Melissa (1998), *Voice, Trust and Memory: Marginalized Groups and the Failings of Liberal Representation* (Princeton: Princeton University Press).

Young, Crawford (ed.). (1998), *Ethnic Diversity and Public Policy: A Comparative Inquiry* (New York: St Martin's).

——'Nationalism, Multiculturalism and Liberal Democracy', *Ethical Theory and Moral Practice*, 1/2 (1998).

——'Embattled Minorities Around the Globe: Rights, Hopes, Threats', *Dissent*, Summer (1996).

Immigration and Multiculturalism

Bader, Veit-Michael (ed.). (1997), *Citizenship and Exclusion* (New York: St. Martin's Press).

Barbieri, William (1998), *Ethics of Citizenship: Immigrants and Group Rights in Germany* (Durham, NC: Duke University Press).

Bauböck, Rainer (1995), *Transnational Citizenship: Membership and Rights in International Migration* (Cheltenham: Edward Elgar).

——and John Rundell (eds.). (1998), *Blurred Boundaries: Migration, Ethnicity, Citizenship* (Aldershot: Ashgate).

Favell, Adrian (1997), *Philosophies of Integration: Immigration and the Idea of Citizenship in France and Britain* (New York: St. Martin's Press).

Jacobson, David (1996), *Rights Across Borders: Immigration and the Decline of Citizenship* (Baltimore: Johns Hopkins University Press).

Joppke, Christian (ed.). (1998), *Challenge to the Nation-State: Immigration in Western Europe and the United States* (Oxford: Oxford University Press).

Klusmeyer, Douglas (1996), *Between Consent and Descent: Conceptions of Democratic Citizenship* (Carnegie Endowment for International Peace).

Pickus, Noah (ed.). (1998), *Immigration and Citizenship in the Twenty-First Century* (Lanham, Md.: Rowman and Littlefield).

Schuck, Peter (1998), *Citizens, Strangers and In-Betweens: Essays on Immigration and Citizenship* (Boulder, Colo.: Westview Press).

Schwartz, Warren (ed.). (1995), *Justice in Immigration* (Cambridge: Cambridge University Press).

—— 'Citizenship and its Discontents: Centering the Immigrant in the Inter/national Imagination', *Oregon Law Review*, 76/2 & 3 (1997).

—— 'Citizenship and Migration', *Constellations*, 4/3 (1998).

—— 'Citizenship and Naturalization Policy', *Georgetown Immigration Law Journal*, 13/2 (1999).

—— 'European Union: Immigration, Asylum and Citizenship', *Journal of Ethnic and Migration Studies*, 24/4 (1998).

—— 'Incorporating Migrants in Multicultural Societies: Issues of Citizenship and Integration', *New Community*, 23/2 (1997).

—— 'Membership, Migration, and Identity: Dilemmas for Liberal Societies', *Stanford Electronic Humanities Review*, 5/2 (1997).

Nationalism and Self-Determination

Beiner, Ronald (ed.). (1998), *Theorizing Nationalism* (Albany, NY: State University of New York Press).

Caney, Simon, David George and Peter Jones (eds.). (1996), *National Rights, International Obligations* (Boulder, Colo.: Westview Press).

Canovan, Margaret (1996), *Nationhood and Political Theory* (Cheltenham: Edward Elgar).

Clarke, Desmond and Charles Jones (eds.). (1999), *The Rights of Nations: Nations and Nationalism in a Changing Europe* (Cork: Cork University Press).

Couture, Jocelyne, Kai Nielsen and Michel Seymour (eds.). (1998), *Rethinking Nationalism* (Calgary: University of Calgary).

Gilbert, Paul (1998), *Philosophy of Nationalism* (Boulder, Colo.: Westview Press).

Lehning, Percy (ed.). (1998), *Theories of Secession* (London: Routledge).

McKim, Robert and Jeff McMahan (eds.). (1997), *The Morality of Nationalism* (Oxford: Oxford University Press).

Miller, David (1995), *On Nationality* (Oxford: Oxford University Press).

Moore, Margaret (ed.). (1998), *National Self-Determination and Secession* (Oxford: Oxford University Press).

Musgrave, Thomas (1997), *Self-Determination and National Minorities*, (Oxford: Oxford University Press).

Spencer, Metta (1998), *Separatism: Democracy and Disintegration* (Lanham, Md.: Rowman and Littlefield).

Suksi, Markku (ed.). (1998), *Autonomy: Applications and Implications* (The Hague: Kluwer Law International).

West, Lois (ed.). (1997), *Feminist Nationalism* (London: Routledge).

Yuval-Davis, Nira (1997), *Gender and Nation* (London: Sage).

—— 'Nationalism', *Critical Review*, 10/2 (1996).

—— 'Philosophical Perspectives on National Identity', *Philosophical Forum*, 28/1 (1996).

Racial Groups

Brecher, Bob, Jo Halliday and Klara Kolinska (eds.). (1998), *Nationalism and Racism in the Liberal Order* (Aldershot: Ashgate).

Christie, Clive J. (1998), *Race and Nation: A Reader* (New York: St. Martin's Press).

Cochran, David C. (1999), The Color of Freedom: Race and Contemporary American Liberalism (Albany, NY: State University of New York Press).

Mills, Charles (1997), *The Racial Contract* (Ithaca, NY: Cornell University Press).

Indigenous Peoples

Asch, Michael (ed.). (1994) *Aboriginal and Treaty Rights in Canada: Essays on Law, Equity and Respect for Difference* (Vancouver: University of British Columbia Press).

Chesterman, John and Brian Galligan (1998), *Citizens without Rights: Aborigines and Australian Citizenship* (Cambridge: Cambridge University Press).

Cook, Curtis and Juan Lindau (eds.). (2000), *Aboriginal Rights and Self-Government: The Canadian and Mexican Experience in North American Perspective* (Montreal: McGill-Queen's University Press).

Havemann, Paul (1999), *Indigenous People's Rights in Australia, Canada and New Zealand* (Oxford: Oxford University Press).

Peterson, Nicholas and Will Sanders (eds.). (1998), *Citizenship and Indigenous Australians: Changing Conceptions and Possibilities* (Cambridge: Cambridge University Press).

References

ABDULATIPOV, R. (1995), *O federativnoi i natsional'noi politike Rossiiskogo gosudartstva* (Moscow: Slavyanski dialog).

——(1996, 18 April), 'Dva tipa natsionalnogo samosoznaniya', *Nezavisimaya gazeta*, 5.

ACTON, J. E. E. D. (1907), 'Nationality', in Acton (ed.) *The History of Freedom and Other Essays* (London: Macmillan): 270–300.

ADAMS, G. D. (1996), 'Legislative Effects of Single-Member vs. Multi-Member Districts', *American Journal of Political Science*, 40/1: 129–44.

ADDAMS, J. (1914), 'The Larger Aspects of the Woman's Movement', *Annals of the American Academy of Political and Social Science*, LVI: 1–8.

AFSHAR, H. (1987), (ed.). *Women, State, and Ideology* (Albany: SUNY Press).

AGRANOFF, R. (1997), 'Federal Evolution in Spain', *International Political Science Review*, 17/1: 385–404.

AKZIN, B. (1970), 'Who is a Jew? A Hard Case', *Israel Law Review*, 5: 259.

AL-AZMEH, A. (1993), *Islams and Modernities* (London: Verso).

ALLEN, D. (1997), (ed.). *Culture and Self: Philosophical and Religious Perspectives, East and West* (Boulder, Colo.: Westview Press).

AMINZADE, R. (forthcoming), 'Racial Formation, Citizenship and Africanization', *Social Science History*.

ANDERSON, B. (1983), *Imagined Communities: Reflections on the Origins and Spread of Nationalism* (London: Verso Editions and New Left Books).

——(1991), *Imagined Communities: Reflections on the Origins and Spread of Nationalism* (Revised ed.) (London: Verso).

ANDERSON, T. G. (1858), 'Report on the Affairs of the Indians of Canada, Section III', *Journal of the Legislative Assembly of Canada*, 6/App. 95.

ANTHIAS, F., and YUVAL-DAVIS, N. (1992), *Racialised Boundaries: Race. Gender, Colour and Class and the Anti-Racist Struggle* (London: Routledge).

APPIAH, K. A. (1996), 'Race, Culture and Identity', in K. A. Appiah and A. Gutmann (eds.) *Color Conscious: The Political Morality of Race* (Princeton: Princeton University Press).

ARCHIBUGI, D., and HELD, D. (1995), *Cosmopolitan Democracy: An Agenda for a New World Order* (London: Polity Press).

ARENDT, H. (1973), *The Origins of Totalitarianism* (New York: Harcourt Brace).

ARNESON, R., and SHAPIRO, I. (1996), 'Democratic Autonomy and Religious Freedom: A Critique if Wisconsin v. Yoder', in I. Shapiro and R. Hardin (eds.) *Political Order: Nomos 38* (New York: New York University Press): 365–411.

ASHCROFT, B., GRIFFITHS, G., and TIFFIN, H. (1996), (eds.). *The Post Colonial Studies Reader* (New York: Routledge).

AUDI, R. (1989), 'The Separation of Church and State and the Obligations of Citizenship', *Philosophy and Public Affairs*, 18/3: 259–96.

AXELROD, P. (1997), *The Promise of Schooling: Education in Canada, 1800–1914* (Toronto: University of Toronto Press).

AYUBI, N. N. (1991), *Political Islam: Religion and Politics in the Arab World* (London: Routledge).

BACHRACH, P., and BARATZ, M. (1963), 'Decisions and Non-Decisions: An Analytical Framework', *American Political Science Review*, 57/3: 632–42.

BADER, V.-M. (1997), (ed.). *Citizenship and Exclusion* (New York: St Martin's Press).

BAINHAM, A. (1996), 'Family Law in a Pluralistic Society: A View From England and Wales', in N. Lowe and G. Douglas (eds.) *Families Across Frontiers* (The Hague: Martinus Nijhoff).

BAKER, J. (1994), (ed.). *Group Rights* (Toronto: University of Toronto Press).

BAKER, K. (1988), (ed.). *A Treaty with the Aborigines?* (Melbourne: Institute for Public Affairs).

BAKHTIN, M. M. (1981), 'Discourse in the Novel', in M. Holquist (ed.) *The Dialogical Imagination: Four Essays* (Austin: University of Texas Press).

BANKS, J. A. (1992), 'Curriculum Guidelines for Multicultural Education', *Social Education*, 56/5: 274–94.

BARBER, B. R. (1984), *Strong Democracy: Participatory Politics for a New Age* (Berkeley: University of California Press).

BARRETT, M., and McINTOSH, M. (1985), 'Ethnocentrism Socialist-Feminist Theory', *Feminist Review*, 20: 23–47.

Barristers' Society. (1981), *Report on the Integration of the Two Official Languages in the Practice of Law* (Fredericton, NB: Barristers' Society).

BARRY, B. (1995), *Justice as Impartiality* (Oxford: Oxford University Press).

BARSH, R., and HENDERSON, J. Y. (1997), 'The Supreme Court Vanderpeet Trilogy: Native Imperialism and Ropes of Sand', *McGill Law Journal*, 42: 993.

BASTARACHE, M. (1987), (ed.). *Language Rights in Canada* (Montreal: Éditions Yvon Blais).

——(1987–8), 'Dualité et multiculturalisme: deux notions en conflit?', *Égalité*, 22.

BATES, S. (1993), *Battleground: One Mother's Crusade, the Religious Right, and the Struggle for Control of our Classrooms* (New York: Poseidon Press).

BAUBÖCK, R. (1994a), 'Changing the Boundaries of Citizenship', in R. Bauböck (ed.) *From Aliens to Citizens. Redefining the Status of Migrants in Europe* (Aldershot: Avebury): 199–232.

——(1994b), *Transnational Citizenship: Membership and Rights in Transnational Migration* (Aldershot: Edward Elgar).

——(1999), 'Why Secession is not Like Divorce', in K. Goldmann, U. Hannerz and C. Westin (eds.) *Nationalism and Internationalism in the Post-Cold War Era* (London: University College London Press).

BAUER, O. (1907), *Die Nationalitätenfrage und die Sozialdemokratie* (Vienna: Ignaz Brand).

BEINER, R. (1995), (ed.). *Theorizing Citizenship* (Albany: State University of New York Press).

——(1999), (ed.). *Theorizing Nationalism* (Albany: State University of New York Press).

BEITZ, C. R. (1989) *Political Equality: An Essay in Democratic Theory* (Princeton: Princeton University Press).

BENHABIB, S. (1992), 'The Generalized and the Concrete Other', in S. Benhabib (ed.) *Situating the Self* (New York: Routledge).

——(1996), 'Toward a Deliberative Model of Democratic Legitimacy', in S. Benhabib (ed.) *Democracy and Difference: Contesting the Boundaries of the Political* (Princeton: Princeton University Press): 67–94.

BEN-ISRAEL, H. (1992), 'Nationalism in Historical Perspective', *Journal of International Affairs*, 45: 367.

BERAN, H. (1984), 'A Liberal Theory of Secession', *Political Studies*, 32: 21–31.

——(1998), 'A Democratic Theory of Political Self-Determination for a New World Order', in P. Lehning (ed.) *Theories of Secession* (London: Routledge): 32–59.

BERKMAN, M. B., and O'CONNOR, R. E. (1993), 'Do Women Legislators Matter?', *American Politics Quarterly*, 21 / 1: 102–24.

BERLIN, I. (1981), *Against the Current: Essays in the History of Ideas* (Oxford: Oxford University Press).

BERNSTEIN, R. A. (1989), *Elections, Representation, and Congressional Voting Behavior* (Englewood Cliffs, NJ: Prentice-Hall).

BHABBA, H. K. (1994), *The Location of Culture* (London: Routledge).

BHATTACHARJEE, A. M. (1994), *Muslim Law and the Constitution* (2nd ed.) (Calcutta: Eastern Law House).

BIANCO, W. T. (1994), *Trust: Representatives and Constituents* (Ann Arbor: University of Michigan Press).

BICKFORD, S. (1996), *The Dissonance of Democracy: Listening, Conflict, and Citizenship* (Ithaca: Cornell University Press).

BIRCH, A. H. (1964), *Representative and Responsible Government* (London: Allen & Unwin).

——(1993), *The Concepts and Theories of Modern Democracy* (London: Routledge).

BOLDT, M., and LONG, J. A. (1985), *The Quest for Justice: Aboriginal Peoples and Aboriginal Rights* (Toronto: University of Toronto Press).

BORROWS, J. (1992), 'A Genealogy of Law: Inherent Sovereignty and First Nations Self-Government', *Osgoode Hall Law Journal*, 30: 291.

——(1997a), 'Living between Water and Rocks: First Nations, Environmental Planning and Democracy', *University of Toronto Law Journal*, 47: 417.

——(1997b), 'Wampum at Niagara', in M. Asch (ed.) *Aboriginal and Treaty Rights in Canada* (Vancouver: University of British Columbia Press).

——(1998), 'Frozen Rights in Canada: Constitutional Interpretation and the Trickster', *American Indian Law Review*, 22: 1.

BOURASSA, H. (1970), 'French Canadians and Canadian Nationalism', in J. Levitt (ed.) *Henri Bourassa on Imperialism and Bi-culturalism, 1900–1918* (Toronto: Copp Clark).

BOYD, W. L., and CIBULKA, J. G. (1989), (eds.). *Private Schools and Public Policy: International Perspectives* (London: Falmer Press).

Boyle, C. (1983), 'Home Rule for Women: Power Sharing between Men and Women', *Dalhousie Law Journal*, 7/3: 790–809.

Boyle, K., and Sheen, J. (1997), (eds.). *Freedom of Religion and Belief: A World Report* (London: Routledge).

Bradshaw, M., and Palacin, J. (1996), *An Atlas of the Economic Performance of Russia's Regions* (Birmingham: University of Birmingham).

Brah, A. (1992), 'Difference, Diversity and Differentiation', in J. Donald and A. Rattansi (eds.) *'Race', Culture and Difference* (London: Sage).

Breton, R. (1986), 'Multiculturalism and Canadian Nation-Building', in A. Cairns and C. Williams (eds.) *The Politics of Gender, Ethnicity and Language in Canada* (Toronto: University of Toronto Press) (2).

Brilmayer, L. (1991), 'Secession and Self-Determination: A Territorial Interpretation', *Yale Journal of International Law*, 16: 177–202.

Brubaker, R. (1996), *Nationalism Reframed: Nationhood and the National Question in the New Europe* (Cambridge: Cambridge University Press).

Bryk, D., Lee, V. E., and Holland, P. B. (1993), *Catholic Schools and the Common Good* (Cambridge, Mass: Harvard University Press).

Buchanan, A. (1991), *Secession: The Morality of Political Divorce from Port Sumter to Lithuania and Quebec* (Boulder, Colo.: Westview Press).

——(1997*a*), 'Self-Determination, Secession, and the Rule of Law', in R. McKim and J. McMahan (eds.) *The Morality of Nationalism* (New York: Oxford University Press): 301–232.

——(1997*b*), 'Theories of Secession', *Philosophy and Public Affairs*, 26/1: 31–61.

Bulmer, M., and Rees, A. (1996), (eds.). *Citizenship Today: The Contemporary Relevance of T. H. Marshall* (London: University College London Press).

Burke, E. (1871), 'Letter to Sir Hercules Langriche' *The Works of the Right Honorable Edmund Burke* (Boston: Little, Brown).

Burnheim, J. (1985), *Is Democracy Possible?* (Berkeley: University of California Press).

Burtt, S. (1994), 'Religious Parents, Secular Schools', *Review of Politics*, 56: 51–70.

——(1996), 'In Defense of *Yoder*: Parental Authority and The Public Schools', in I. Shapiro and R. Hardin (eds.) *Political Order: Nomos XXXVIII* (New York: New York University Press): 412–37.

Caglar, A. (1997), 'Hyphenated Identities and the Limits of "Culture"', in T. Modood and P. Werbner (eds.) *The Politics of Multiculturalism in the New Europe: Racism, Identity and Community* (London: Zed Books).

Callan, E. (1997), *Creating Citizens: Political Education and Liberal Democracy* (Oxford: Oxford University Press).

Callenbach, E., and Phillips, M. (1985), *A Citizen Legislature* (Berkeley, CA: University of California Press).

Caney, S., George, D., and Jones, P. (1996), (eds.). *National Rights, International Obligations* (Boulder, Colo.: Westview Press).

Canovan, M. (1996), *Nationhood and Political Theory* (Cheltenham: Edward Elgar).

CARDINAL, H. (1969), *The Unjust Society: The Tragedy of Canada's Indians* (Edmonton: M. Hurtig).

——(1997), *Livelihood Lands under Treaty Eight*. Unpublished LL.M., Harvard University.

CARENS, J. (1994), 'Cultural Adaptation and Integration: Is Quebec a Model for Europe?', in R. Bauböck (ed.) *From Aliens to Citizens. Redefining the Status of Migrants in Europe* (Aldershot, UK: Avebury): 149–86.

——(1996), 'Realistic and Idealistic Approaches to the Ethics of Immigration', *International Migration Review*, 30/1: 156–70.

——(1996–7), 'Dimensions of Citizenship and National Identity in Canada', *The Philosophical Forum*, XXVIII: 111–24.

CARRITHERS, M., COLLINS, S., and LUKES, S. (1985), (eds.). *The Category of the Person. Anthropology, Philosophy, History* (Cambridge: Cambridge University Press).

CASSIDY, F. (1991), (ed.). *Aboriginal Self-Determination* (Lantzville, B.C.: Oolichan Press).

CHAMBERS, S. (1996), *Reasonable Democracy: Jürgen Habermas and the Politics of Discourse* (Ithaca, NY: Cornell University Press).

——(1998), 'Critical Theory and Civil Society', in W. Kymlicka and S. Chambers (eds.) *Alternative Conceptions of Civil Society* (Princeton: Princeton University Press).

CHAPMAN, J. W., and SHAPIRO, I. (1993), (eds.). *Nomos XXXV: Democratic Community* (New York: New York University Press).

CHESTERMAN, J., and GALLIGAN, B. (1998), *Citizens without Rights: Aborigines and Australian Citizenship* (Cambridge: Cambridge University Press).

CHEVIER, M. (1997), *Des lois et des langues au Québec: Principes et moyens de la politique linguistique québécoise* (Québec: Études et documents: Ministère des relations internationales).

CHINYAEVA, E. (1996, 1 Nov.), 'A Eurasianist Model of Interethnic Relations Could Help Russia Find Harmony', *Transition*: 30–5.

CHODOROW, N. (1978), *The Reproduction of Mothering: Psychoanalysis and the Sociology of Gender* (Berkeley, CA: Regents of the University of California Press).

CHRISTIANO, T. (1996), 'Deliberative Equality and Democratic Order', in I. Shapiro and R. Hardin (eds.) *Political Order: Nomos XXXVIII* (New York: New York University Press): 251–87.

CHWASZCZA, C. (1998), 'Selbstbestimmung, Sezession und Souveräntität. Überlegungen zur normativen Bedeutung politischer Grenzen', in W. Kersting and C. Chwaszcza (eds.) *Philosophie der internationalen Beziehungen* (Frankfurt).

CLAIBORNE, W. (1999, 15 Feb.), 'Violence Hits American Indians at Highest Rate Among Ethnic Groups', *Washington Post*, A2.

CLARK, B. (1990), *Native Liberty, Crown Sovereignty: The Existing Aboriginal Right of Self-Government in Canada* (Montreal: McGill-Queen's University Press).

CLARKSON, C. M. V., and HILL, J. (1997), *Jaffey on Conflict of Laws* (London: Butterworth).

CLEVELAND, R. F. (1925), 'Status in Common Law', *Harvard Law Review*, 38: 1074.

CLYMER, A. (1993, 23 July), 'Daughter of Slavery Hushes Senate', *New York Times*.

COCHRAN, D. C. (1999), *The Color of Freedom: Race and Contemporary American Liberalism* (Albany: State University of New York Press).

COHEN, J. (1989), 'Deliberation and Democratic Legitimacy', in A. Hamlin and P. Petit (eds.) *The Good Polity: Normative Analysis of the State* (Oxford: Basil Blackwell): 17–34.

——(1996), 'Procedure and Substance in Deliberative Democracy', in S. Benhabib (ed.) *Democracy and Difference* (Princeton: Princeton University Press): 95–119.

——and ROGERS, J. (1995), *Associations and Democracy* (London: Verso).

COLE, L. A. (1976), *Blacks in Power: A Comparative Study of Black and White Officials* (Princeton: Princeton University Press).

COLLINS, P. H. (1990), *Black Feminist Thought* (London: Allen & Unwin).

Comité interministériel sur la situation de la langue française. (1996), *Le Français langue commune. Enjeu de la société québécoise* (Québec: Ministère de la Culture et des Communications).

CONNOLLY, C. (1991), 'Washing our Linen: One Year of Women against Fundamentalism', *Feminist Review*, 37: 68–7.

CONOVER, P. J. (1988), 'Group Identification and Group Sympathy', Paper presented at the Annual Meeting of the Midwest Political Science Association.

——(1988), 'The Role of Social Groups in Political Thinking', *British Journal of Political Science*, 18/1: 51–76.

COOK, R. (1991), 'Language Policy and the Glossophagic State', in D. Schneiderman (ed.) *Language and the State: The Law and Politics of Identity* (Cowansville, Que.: Éditions Yvon Blais): 73–81.

COOK, R. J. (1994), *Human Rights of Women: National and International Perspectives* (Philadelphia: University of Pennsylvania Press).

COPP, D. (1997), 'Democracy and Communal Self-Determination', in R. McKim and J. McMahan (eds.) *The Morality of Nationalism* (New York: Oxford University Press): 277–300.

COTT, N. F. (1995), 'Giving Character to our Whole Civil Polity: Marriage and Divorce in the Late Nineteenth Century', in L. K. Kerber, A. Kessler-Harris and K. K. Sklar (eds.) *US History as Women's History* (Chapel Hill: University of North Carolina Press).

——(1996), 'Justice for All? Marriage and Deprivation of Citizenship in the United States', in A. Sarat and T. R. Kearns (eds.) *Justice and Injustice in Law and Legal Theory* (Ann Arbor: The University of Michigan Press).

COULOMBE, P. A. (1995), *Language Rights in French Canada* (New York: Peter Lang Publishing).

COUSINEAU, M. (1994), *L'Utilisation du français au sein du système judiciaire de L'Ontario: un droit à parfaire* (Sudbury, Ont.: Institute franco-ontarien).

COUTURE, J., NIELSEN, K., and SEYMOUR, M. (1998), (eds.). *Rethinking Nationalism* (Calgary: University of Calgary Press).

COVER, R. M. (1983), 'The Supreme Court 1982 Term, Forward: *Nomos* and Narrative', *Harvard Law Review*, 97: 4.

——and ALEINIKOFF, T. A. (1977), 'Dialectical Federalism: Habeas Corpus and the Court', *Yale Law Journal*, 86: 1035.

CRENSHAW, K. (1991), ' "Mapping the Margins": Intersectionality, Identity Politics and Violence against Women', *Stanford Law Review*, 43/6: 1241–99.

——(1992), 'Whose Story is it Anyway? Feminist and Antiracist Appropriations of Anita Hill', in T. Morrison (ed.) *Race-ing Justice, En-Gendering Power: Essays on Anita Hill, Clarence Thomas, and the Construction of Social Reality* (New York: Pantheon).

——GOTANDA, N., PELLER, G., THOMAS, K., *et al.* (1995), (eds.). *Critical Race Theory: The Key Writings that Formed the Movement* (New York: New Press).

CROSBY, N. (1991), 'Citizen Juries as a Basic Democratic Reform', Paper presented at the Competing Theories of Post-Liberal Democracy, 8–10 Feb., University of Texas at Austin.

——(1995), 'Citizen Juries: One Solution for Difficult Environmental Problems', in R. Ortwin, T. Webler and P. M. Wiedemann (eds.) *Fairness and Competence in Citizen Participation* (Norwell, Mass.: Kluwer).

——(1996), 'Creating an Authentic Voice of the People', Paper presented at the Midwest Political Science Association, 18–20 Apr., Chicago, Ill.

DAGGER, R. (1997), *Civic Virtues: Rights, Citizenship and Republican Liberalism* (Oxford: Oxford University Press).

DAHL, R. A. (1957), 'The Concept of Power', *Behavioral Science*, 2: 201–15.

——(1970), *After the Revolution* (New Haven: Yale University Press).

——(1977), 'On Removing Certain Impediments to Democracy in the United States', *Political Science Quarterly*, 92/1: 1–20.

——(1985), *Controlling Nuclear Weapons* (Syracuse, NY: Syracuse University Press).

——(1989), *Democracy and its Critics* (New Haven: Yale University Press).

——(1992), 'The Problem of Civic Competence', *Journal of Democracy*, 3/4: 45–59.

——(1997), 'On Deliberative Democracy', *Dissent*, 44/3: 54–8.

DAHRENDORF, R. (1974), 'Citizenship and Beyond: The Social Dynamics of an Idea', *Social Research*, 41/4: 673–701.

DARCY, R., WELCH, L. S., and CLARK, J. (1987), *Women, Elections, and Representation* (New York: Longman).

DAS, V. (1994), 'Cultural Rights and the Definition of Community', in O. Mendelsohn and U. Baxi (eds.) *The Rights of Subordinated Peoples* (Oxford: Oxford University Press).

DE LA GARZA, R. O., and DESIPIO, L. (1993), 'Save the Baby, Change the Bathwater, and Scrub the Tub: Latino Electoral Participation after Seventeen Years of Voting Rights Coverage', *Texas Law Review*, 71/7: 1479–539.

DELGADO, R. (1995), (ed.). *Critical Race Theory: The Cutting Edge* (Philadelphia: Temple University Press).

DENBAR, R. (1997), 'The Legacy of Abuse in Chechnya and OSCE Intervention', *Helsinki Monitor*, 1: 59–73.

Department of Indian Affairs and Northern Development. (1969), *Statement of the Government of Canada on Indian Policy, 1969* (Ottawa: Queen's Printer).

Department of Indian and Northern Affairs. (1994), *Aboriginal Education: The Path to Empowerment* (Ottawa: Supply and Services).

Department of the Prime Minister and Cabinet (1991), *Aboriginal Reconciliation: An Historical Perspective* (Canberra: Australian Government Printing Service).

DEVINS, N. (1992), 'Fundamentalist Christian Educators v. State: An Inevitable Compromise', *George Washington Law Review*, 60: 818–40.

DIAMOND, I. (1977), *Sex Roles in the State House* (New Haven: Yale University Press).

DIMBLEBY, J. (1994), *Prince of Wales: A Biography* (London: Little, Brown).

DIRLIK, A. (1990), 'Culturalism as Hegemonic Ideology and Liberating Practice', in J. Mohamed and D. Lloyd (eds.) *The Nature and Context of Minority Discourse* (New York: Oxford University Press).

DONALD, J., and RATTANSI, A. (1992), *'Race', Culture and Difference* (London: Sage).

DORÉ, L. (1993), 'Official Languages and Multiculturalism: Choices for the Future', Paper presented at the Les droits linguistiques au Canada: collusions ou collisions? Actes du Premier Colloque, University of Ottawa.

DROBIZHEVA, L. (1994), (ed.). *Natsional'noe samosoznanie i natsionalizm v Rossiiskoi Federatsii nachala 1990-h godav* (Moscow: IEA).

DRYZEK, J. S. (1990), *Discursive Democracy* (Cambridge: Cambridge University Press).

DUMMETT, A. (1992), 'The Transnational Migration of People Seen from within the Natural Law Tradition', in B. Barry and R. Goodin (eds.) *Free Movement: Ethical Issues in the Transnational Migration of People and of Money* (Pennsylvania: Pennsylvania State University Press): 169–80.

DUMONT, L. (1965), 'The Functional Equivalent of the Individual in Caste Society', *Contributions to Indian Sociology*, 8: 85–99.

——(1980), *Homo Hierarchicus: The Caste System and its Implications* (Vol. viii) (Chicago: University of Chicago Press).

DWORKIN, R. (1981), 'What is Equality? Part II: Equality of Resources', *Philosophy and Public Affairs*, 10/4: 283–345.

EDELMAN, M. (1994), *Courts, Politics, and Culture in Israel* (Charlottesville: University Press of Virginia).

EISGRUBER, C. L. (1997), 'Birthright Citizenship and the Constitution', *New York University Law Review*, 72: 54.

ELAZAR, D. J. (1987), *Exploring Federalism* (Tuscaloosa: University of Alabama Press).

ELDERING, L., and KLOPROGGE, J. (1989), (eds.). *Different Cultures, Same School: Ethnic Minority Children in Europe* (Amsterdam: Swets & Zeitlinger).

——and VEDDER, P. (1993), 'Culture-Sensitive Home Intervention: The Dutch Hippy Experiment', in L. Eldering and P. Leseman (eds.) *Early Intervention and Culture* (Paris: Unesco): 231–52.

ELSTER, J. (1989), 'Taming Chance: Randomization in Individual and Social Decisions', in J. Elster (ed.) *Solomonic Judgements* (Cambridge: Cambridge University Press).

——(1995), 'Strategic Uses of Argument', in K. J. Arrow, R. H. Mnookin, L. Ross, A. Tversky, and R. Wilson (eds.) *Barriers to Conflict Resolution* (New York: W.W. Norton).

EVERETT, W. J. (1997), *Religion, Federalism, and the Struggle for Public Life: Cases from Germany, India, and America* (Oxford: Oxford University Press).

EWING, K. P. (1991), 'Can Psychoanalytic Theory Explain the Pakistani Woman? Intrapsychic Autonomy and Interpersonal Engagement in the Extended Family', *Ethos*, 19: 131–60.

FAVELL, A. (1997), *Philosophies of Integration: Immigration and the Idea of Citizenship in France and Britain* (New York: St. Martin's Press).

FENNO, R. F., JR. (1978), *Home Style: House Members in their Districts* (Boston: Little, Brown).

FEUCHTWANG, S. (1990), 'Racism: Territoriality and Ethnocentricity', in A. X. Cambridge and S. Feuchtwang (eds.) *Anti-Racist Strategies* (Aldershot: Avebury).

FISHKIN, J. (1991), *Democracy and Deliberation* (New Haven: Yale University Press).

——(1992), *The Dialogue of Justice: Toward a Self-Reflective Society* (New Haven: Yale University Press).

——(1995), *The Voice of the People* (New Haven: Yale University Press).

FITZMAURICE, D. (1993), 'Autonomy as a Good: Liberalism, Autonomy and Toleration', *Journal of Political Philosophy*, 1/1: 1–16.

FLERAS, A. (1995), 'Heritage Languages in Canada: A (Post) Multicultural Outlook', in S. Léger (ed.) *Les Droits linguistiques au Canada: collusions ou collisions?* (Ottawa: Centre Canadien des Droits Linguistiques).

FOSTER, D. (1994), 'Bloody Justice', *Independent Monthly*, May: 30–6.

FRASER, N. (1997a), (ed.). *Justice Interruptus: Critical Reflections on the 'Postsocialist' Condition* (New York: Routledge).

——(1997b), 'Rethinking the Public Sphere: A Contribution to the Critique of Actually Existing Democracy', in N. Fraser (ed.) *Justice Interruptus: Critical Reflections on the 'PostSocialist' Condition* (New York: Routledge).

——and GORDON, L. (1994), 'Civil Citizenship against Social Citizenship?', in Bart Van Steenburgen (ed.) *The Condition of Citizenship* (London: Sage).

FREEMAN, M. A. (1990), 'Measuring Equality: A Comparative Perspective on Women's Legal Capacity and Constitutional Rights in Five Commonwealth Countries', *Commonwealth Law Bulletin*, 16: 1418.

——(1996), 'Law, Religion and the State: The *Get* Revisited', in N. Lowe and G. Douglas (eds.) *Families across Frontiers* (The Hague: Martinus Nijhoff).

FRIDERES, J. (1993), *Native Peoples in Canada: Contemporary Conflicts* (Scarborough, Ont.: Prentice-Hall).

FULLINWIDER, R. K. (1996), (ed.). *Public Education in a Multicultural Society: Policy, Theory, Critique* (Cambridge: Cambridge University Press).

FUSS, D. (1989), *Essentially Speaking: Feminism, Nature and Difference* (New York: Routledge).

GALSTON, W. (1991), *Liberal Purposes: Goods, Virtues, and Duties in the Liberal State* (Cambridge: Cambridge University Press).

GAUTHIER, D. (1994), 'Breaking Up: An Essay on Secession', *Canadian Journal of Philosophy*, 24/3: 357–72.

GAY, C. (1996), 'The Impact of Black Congressional Representation on the Behavior of Constituents', Paper presented at the Midwest Political Science Association, 18–20 Apr, Chicago, Ill.

GEERTZ, C. (1973), *The Interpretation of Cultures* (New York: Basic Books).

GELLNER, E. (1983), *Nations and Nationalism* (Oxford: Basil Blackwell).

GHEORGHE, N. and MIRGA, A. (1997) *The Roma in the Twenty-First Century: A Policy Paper*, Project on Ethno-Relations, Princeton University (http://pw1.netcom.com/~ethnic/migra1.html).

GHERSON, G. (1997, 12 Dec.), 'Defense/Native Programs Get Least Support', *Vancouver Sun*, A1.

GHUMAN, P. A. S. (1994), *Coping with Two Cultures: British Asian and Indo-Canadian Adolescents* (Clevedon: Multilingual Matters).

GILBERT, P. (1998), *Philosophy of Nationalism* (Boulder, Colo.: Westview Press).

GILLES, S. G. (1996), 'On Educating Children: A Parentalist Manifesto', *University of Chicago Law Review*, 63/3: 937–1034.

GILLIGAN, C. (1982), *In a Different Voice* (Cambridge, Mass: Harvard University Press).

GILMORE, G. E. (1996), *Gender and Jim Crow* (Chapel Hill: University of North Carolina Press).

GILROY, P. (1987), *There ain't no Black in the Union Jack* (London: Heinemann).

——(1992), 'The End of Anti-Racism', in J. Donald and A. Rattansi (eds.) *'Race', Culture and Difference* (London: Sage).

——(1993), *The Black Atlantic* (London: Verso).

GINOSSAR, S. (1970), 'Who is a Jew: A Better Law?', *Israel Law Review*, 5: 264.

GLAZER, N. (1983), *Ethnic Dilemmas: 1964–1982* (Cambridge, Mass: Harvard University Press).

GLENDON, M.-A., and BLANKENHORN, D. (1995), (eds.). *Seedbeds of Virtue: Sources of Competence, Character, and Citizenship in American Society* (Madison Books).

GLENN, E. N. (1994), 'Social Constructions of Mothering: A Thematic Overview', in E. N. Glenn, G. Chang and L. R. Forcey (eds.) *Mothering, Ideology, Experience, and Agency* (New York: Routledge).

GLOVER, J. (1997), 'Nations, Identity, and Conflict', in R. McKim and J. McMahan (eds.) *The Morality of Nationalism* (New York: Oxford University Press): 11–30.

GOODIN, R. E. (1996), 'Designing Constitutions: The Political Constitution of a Mixed Commonwealth', in R. Bellamy and D. Castiglione (eds.) *Constitutionalism in Transformation: European and Theoretical Perspectives* (Oxford: Basil Blackwell).

GOODMAN-THAU, E. (1993), 'Challenging the Roots of Religious Patriarchy and Shaping Identity and Community', in B. Swirski and M. P. Safir (eds.) *Calling the Equality Bluff* (New York: Athene Press, Teachers College Press).

GOSNELL, H. F. (1948), *Democracy: The Threshold of Freedom* (New York: Ronald Press).

Government of Ontario. (1985), *The Report of the Commission on Private Schools* (Toronto: Bernard J. Shapiro, Commissioner).

GRANEY, K. (1997, 26 Aug.), 'Bashkortostan. A Case Study on Building National Identity', *RFE/RL*.

GRANT, C. A., and MELNICK, S. L. (1977), 'In Praise of Diversity: Some Implica-
tions', in M. J. Gold, C. A. Grant and H. N. Rivlin (eds.) *In Praise of Diversity:
A Resource Book for Multicultural Education* (Washington: Association of Teacher
Educators).

——and SLEETER, C. E. (1989), *Turning on Learning: Five Approaches for Multicultural
Teaching Plans for Race, Class, Gender and Disability* (Columbus, Ohio: Merril).

GREEN, L. (1987), 'Are Language Rights Fundamental?', *Osgoode Hall Law Journal*,
25/4: 639–69.

——(1995), 'Internal Minorities and their Rights', in W. Kymlicka (ed.) *The Rights of
Minority Cultures* (Oxford: Oxford University Press): 257–72.

——and RÉAUME, D. (1990), 'Second-Class Rights? Principle and Compromise in the
Charter', *Dalhousie Law Journal*, 13.

—— ——(1991), 'Bilingualism, Territorialism, and Linguistic Justice', *The Network on
the Constitution*, 1/3, 9–11.

GREENAWALT, K. (1995), *Private Consciences and Public Reasons* (New York: Oxford
University Press).

GREWAL, I., and KAPLAN, C. (1994), (eds.). *Scattered Hegemonies: Postmodernity and
Transnational Feminist Practices* (Minneapolis: University of Minnesota Press).

GRIFFITHS, A. P., and WOLLHEIM, R. (1960), 'How can One Person Represent
Another?', *Aristotelian Society*, suppl. vol. 34: 182–208.

GRILLO, R. (1998), *Pluralism and the Politics of Difference: State, Culture and Ethnicity in
Comparative Perspective* (Oxford: Oxford University Press).

GROFMAN, B. (1982), 'Should Representatives be Typical of their Constituents?', in
B. Grofman (ed.) *Representation and Redistricting Issues* (Lexington, Mass.: D.C.
Heath).

GUINIER, L. (1994), *The Tyranny of the Majority: Fundamental Fairness in Representative
Democracy* (New York: Free Press).

GUTMANN, A. (1989), *Democratic Education* (Princeton: Princeton University Press).

——(1992), (ed.). *Multiculturalism and 'The Politics of Recognition'* (Princeton:
Princeton University Press).

——(1993), 'The Disharmony of Democracy', in J. W. Chapman and I. Shapiro (eds.)
Nomos XXXV: Democratic Community (New York: New York University Press):
126–227.

——(1994a), 'Introduction', in A. Gutmann (ed.) *Multiculturalism: Examining the
Politics of Recognition* (Princeton: Princeton University Press): 10–2.

——(1994b), (ed.). *Multiculturalism: Examining the Politics of Recognition* (Princeton:
Princeton University Press).

——(1995), 'Civic Education and Social Diversity', *Ethics*, 105: 557–79.

——(1996), 'Challenges of Multiculturalism in Democratic Education', in R. K.
Fullinwider (ed.) *Public Education in a Multicultural Society: Policy, Theory, Critique*
(Cambridge: Cambridge University Press): 156–79.

——and THOMPSON, D. (1996), *Democracy and Disagreement* (Cambridge, Mass.:
Harvard University Press).

HABERMAS, J. (1990), 'Discourse Ethics: Notes on a Program of Philosophical Justification', *Moral Consciousness and Communicative Action* (Cambridge, Mass.: MIT Press): 43–115.

——(1996a), *Between Facts and Norms: Contributions to a Discourse Theory of Law and Democracy* (Cambridge, MA: MIT Press).

——(1996b), *Die Einbeziehung des Anderen. Studien zur politischen Theorie* (Frankfurt: Suhrkamp).

HALDANE, J. (1986), 'Religious Education in a Pluralist Society: A Philosophical Examination', *British Journal of Educational Studies*, 34: 161–81.

HALL, S. (1987), 'Minimal Selves', in L. Appiganesi (ed.) *The Real Me: The Question of Identity and Postmodernism* (London: Institute of Contemporary Arts).

——(1992a), 'New Ethnicities', in J. Donald and A. Rattansi (eds.) *'Race', Culture and Difference* (London: Sage).

——(1992b), 'The Question of Cultural Identity', in S. Hall and T. McGrew (eds.) *Modernity and Its Futures* (Cambridge: Polity Press).

——(1998), 'Aspiration and Attitude . . . Reflections on Black Britain in the Nineties', *New Formations*, Frontlines/Backyards Special Issue, 33, Spring.

HAMLIN, A., and PETTIT, P. (1989), (eds.). *The Good Polity: Normative Analysis of the State* (Oxford: Basil Blackwell).

HANAUER, L. (1996), 'Tatarstan and the Prospects for Federalism in Russia: A Commentary', *Security Dialogue*, 27/1: 81–6.

HARRIS, A. P. (1990), 'Race and Essentialism in Legal Theory', *Stanford Law Review*, 42/3: 581–616.

——(1995), 'Forward: The Unbearable Lightness of Identity', *African American Law & Policy Report*, 2: 207.

HART, H. L. A. (1994), *The Concept of Law* (2nd ed.) (Oxford: Clarendon Press).

HARTMANN, H. (1958), *Ego Psychology and the Problem of Adaptation* (New York: International Universities Press).

Haudenosaunee Confederacy. (1983), *Minutes and Proceedings and Evidence of the Special Committee on Indian Self-Government.*

HAWTHORN, H. B. (1966), (ed.). *A Survey of the Contemporary Indians of Canada: A Report on Economic, Political, Education Needs and Policies in Two Volumes* (Ottawa: Indian Affairs Branch).

HAYDON, G. (1994), 'Conceptions of the Secular in Society, Polity and Schools', *Journal of Philosophy of Education*, 28/1.

HAYNES, E. (1997), *Women and Legislative Communication* (Cambridge, Mass.

HEATER, D. B. (1990), *Citizenship: The Civic Ideal in World History, Politics and Education* (London: Longman).

——(1996), *World Citizenship and Government: Cosmopolitanism Ideas in the History of Western Political Thought* (New York: St Martin's Press).

HEILIG, P., and MUNDT, R. J. (1984), *Your Voice at City Hall: The Politics, Procedures and Policies of District Representation* (Albany: State University of New York Press).

HELD, D. (1987), *Models of Democracy* (Cambridge: Polity Press).

——(1995), *Democracy and the Global Order: From the Modern State to Cosmopolitan Governance* (London: Polity Press).

HÉLIE-LUCAS, M. A. (1994), 'The Preferential Symbol for Islamic Identity: Women in Muslim Personal Laws', in V. M. Moghadam (ed.) *Identity Politics and Women: Cultural Representations and Feminisms in International Perspective* (Boulder, Colo.: Westview Press).

HENDERSON, J. S. Y. (1994), 'Empowering Treaty Federalism', *Saskatchewan Law Review*, 58: 241.

HIRSCHMAN, A. O. (1970), *Exit, Voice, and Loyalty* (Cambridge, Mass.: Harvard University Press).

HOBBES, T. (1988), *Leviathan (1651)* (Cambridge: Cambridge University Press).

HOOKER, M. (1975), *Legal Pluralism: An Introduction to Colonial and Neo-Colonial Laws* (Oxford: Oxford University Press).

HOROWITZ, D. L. (1985), *Ethnic Groups in Conflict* (Berkeley: University of California Press).

——(1997), 'Self-Determination: Politics, Philosophy, and Law', in I. Shapiro and W. Kymlicka (eds.) *Ethnicity and Group Rights* (New York: New York University Press).

HUGHES, J. (1996), 'Moscow's Bilateral Treaties Add to Confusion', *Transition*, 2/19: 39–44.

HUGHES, J. D. (1983), *American Indian Ecology* (El Paso: Texas Western Press).

HURLEY, S. (1989), *Natural Reasons: Personality and Polity* (Oxford: Clarendon Press).

HUTCHINGS, K., and DANNREUTHER, R. (1998), (eds.). *Cosmopolitan Citizenship* (London: St Martin's Press).

HUTNIK, N. (1991), *Ethnic Minority Identity: A Social Psychological Perspective* (Oxford: Clarendon Press).

HYDE, J. S. (1990), 'Meta-Analysis and the Psychology of Gender Differences', *Signs*, 16/1: 5–73.

IGLESIAS, E. M. (1996), 'Rape, Race, and Representation: The Power of Discourse, Discourses of Power, and the Reconstruction of Heterosexuality', *Vanderbilt Law Review*, 49: 869.

International Law Association. (1998), *Preliminary Report of the Committee on Feminism and International Law: Women's Equality and Nationality in International Law.*

IVANOV, V., LADODO, I., and NARAOV, M. (1996), 'Sostoyanie mezhnatsionalnykh otnoshenii v Rossiiskoi Federatsii (po rezultatam issledovanii v regionakh RF)', *Sotsialno-politischeskii zhurnal*, 3: 33–49.

IVERS, G. (1993), *Redefining the First Freedom: The Supreme Court and the Consolidation of State Power* (New Brunswick, NJ: Transaction Books).

JACKSON, J. E., and KING, D. C. (1989), 'Public Goods, Private Interests, and Representation', *American Political Science Review*, 83/4: 1143–64.

JACOBSON, D. (1996), *Rights across Borders: Immigration and the Decline of Citizenship* (Baltimore: Johns Hopkins University Press).

JACOBSON, J. (1997), 'Perceptions of Britishness', *Nations and Nationalism*, 3/2: 181–200.

JACQUES, M. (1997, 28 Dec.), 'The Melting Pot that is Born-Again Britannia', *Observer*, 14–15.

JAMROZIK, W. (1994), 'White Law, Black Lore', *Independent Monthly*, May: 37–8.

JANOSKI, T. (1998), *Citizenship and Civil Society: Obligations in Liberal, Traditional and Social Democratic Regimes* (Cambridge: Cambridge University Press).

JOHNSON, J. (1998), 'Arguing for Deliberation: Some Skeptical Considerations', in J. Elster (ed.) *Deliberative Democracy* (Cambridge: Cambridge University Press).

JONASDOTTIR, A. G. (1988), 'On the Concept of Interest: Women's Interests and the Limitations of Interest Theory', in K. B. Jones and A. G. Jonasdottir (eds.) *The Political Interests of Gender* (Beverly Hills, Calif.: Sage).

JONES, M. H. (1976), 'Black Office-Holding and Political Development in the Rural South', *Review of Black Political Economy*, 6/4: 375–407.

KABEBERY-MACHARIA, J. (1992), 'Family Law and Gender in Kenya', *International Review of Comparative Public Policy*, 4: 193.

KAĞITÇIBAŞI, C. (1996), *Family and Human Development across Cultures: A View from the Other Side* (Mahwah, NJ: Lawrence Erlbaum Associates).

KAKAR, S. (1978), *The Inner World: A Psycho-Analytic Study of Childhood and Society in India* (Oxford: Oxford University Press).

KAMSLER, V. (1996), 'Democratic Feminism', *Unpublished paper (on file with author)*.

KANDIYOTI, D. (1991), (ed.). *Women, Islam and State* (London: Macmillan).

KANT, I. (1984), *Zum Ewigen Frieden* (Stuttgart: Reclam Universal-Bibliothek).

——(1991), 'The Metaphysical First Principles of the Doctrine of Right' *The Metaphysics of Morals* (Cambridge: Cambridge University Press).

KARNIG, A. K., and WELCH, S. (1980), *Black Representation and Urban Policy* (Chicago: University of Chicago Press).

KEYRAUCH, W. O. (1994), *Family Law: Legal Concepts and Changing Human Relationships* (St Paul: West).

KHAKIMOV, R. (1996), 'Prospects of Federalism in Russia: A View from Tatarstan', *Security Dialogue*, 27/1: 69–80.

KHALDI, T. (1992), 'Religion and Citizenship in Islam', in J. Nielsen (ed.) *Religion and Citizenship in Europe and the Arab World* (London: Grey Seal Books).

KING, P. (1993), 'Federation and Representation', in M. Burgess and A. Gagnon (eds.) *Comparing Federalism and Federation. Competing Traditions and Future Directions* (New York: Harvester): 94–101.

KINGDON, J. W. (1981), *Congressmen's Voting Decisions* (New York: Harper & Row).

KIRTON, D. (1995), *'Race', Identity and the Politics of Adoption, Working Paper No. 2*: (Centre for Adoption and Identity Studies, University of East London).

KLUG, F. (1989), "Oh to be in England': The British Case Study', in N. Yuval-Davis and F. Anthias (eds.) *Woman-Nation-State* (London: MacMillan).

KLUSMEYER, D. (1996), *Between Consent and Descent: Conceptions of Democratic Citizenship* (Washington: Carnegie Endowment for International Peace).

KOLOSOV, V., and TREIVISH. (1996), 'Etnicheskie arealy sovremennoi Rossii: sravnitelnyi analizriska nationalnykh konfliktov', *Polis*, 2/32: 47–55.

KOMMERS, D. N. (1997), *The Constitutional Jurisprudence of the Federal Republic of Germany* (2nd ed.) (Durham: Duke University Press).

'Konstitutsiya (Osnovnoi Zakon) Respubliki Sakha'. (1994)

KRAUSE, H. D. (1995), *Family Law in a Nutshell* (St Paul: West).

KUKATHAS, C. (1992a), 'Are there any Cultural Rights?', *Political Theory*, 20: 105–39.

——(1992b), 'Cultural Rights Again: A Rejoinder to Kymlicka', *Political Theory*, 20: 674–80.

——(1995), 'Are there any Cultural Rights?', in W. Kymlicka (ed.) *The Rights of Minority Cultures* (Oxford: Oxford University Press): 228–56.

——(1996), 'Liberalism, Communitarianism, and Political Community', *Social Policy and Policy*, 13: 80–104.

——(1997), 'Cultural Toleration', in W. Kymlicka and I. Shapiro (eds.) *NOMOS XXXIX: Ethnicity and Group Rights* (New York: New York University Press).

KUREISHI, H. (1986), *The Rainbow Sign* (London: Faber & Faber).

KYMLICKA, W. (1989), *Liberalism, Community, and Culture* (Oxford: Clarendon Press).

——(1992), 'Review of Buchanan', *Political Theory*, 20/3: 527–32.

——(1993), 'Group Representation in Canadian Politics', in F. L. Siedle (ed.) *Equity and Community: The Charter, Interest Advocacy, and Representation* (Montreal: Institute for Research on Public Policy).

——(1995a), *Multicultural Citizenship: A Liberal Theory of Minority Rights* (Oxford: Oxford University Press).

——(1995b), (ed.). *The Rights of Minority Cultures* (Oxford: Oxford University Press).

——(1996), 'Three Forms of Group-Differentiated Citizenship in Canada', in S. Benhabib (ed.) *Democracy and Difference* (Princeton: Princeton University Press).

——(1997), 'Do we Need a Liberal Theory of Minority Rights?', *Constellations*, 4/1: 72–87.

——(1998a), *Finding Our Way: Rethinking Ethnocultural Relations in Canada* (Toronto: Oxford University Press).

——(1998b), 'Introduction: An Emerging Consensus?', *Ethical Theory and Moral Practice*, 1/2.

——(1998c), 'Is Federalism a Viable Alternative to Secession?', in P. Lehning (ed.) *Theories of Secession* (London: Routledge): 111–50.

——and NORMAN, W. (1994), 'Return of the Citizen: A Survey of Recent Work on Citizenship Theory', *Ethics*, 104/2: 352–81.

LABELLE, M., ROCHER, F., and ROCHER, G. (1995), 'Pluriethnicité, citoyenneté et intégration: de la souveraineté pour lever les obstacles et les ambiguïtés', *Cahiers de recherche sociologique*, 25: 213–45.

LAITIN, D. (1998) *Identity Formation: The Russians in the Near Abroad* (Princeton: Princeton University Press).

LAL, B. (1990), *The Romance of Culture in an Urban Civilisation* (London: Routledge).

LAMUR, H. E. (1992), 'Was zelfmoord de enige uitweg? Antropologische dimensie van een unieke strafzaak' (Was Suicide the Only Way Out? Anthropological

Dimension of a Unique Trial)', in J. Fiselier and F. Strijbosch (eds.) *Recht der Werkelijkheid* (2): 153–60.

LAPLANCHE, J., and PONTALIS, J.-B. (1973), *The Language of Psychoanalysis* (London: The Hogard Press/The Institute of Psycho-Analysis).

LAPONCE, J. A. (1987), *Languages and their Territories* (Toronto: University of Toronto Press).

LAROQUE, E. (1997), 'Re-Examining Culturally Appropriate Models', in M. Asch (ed.) *Aboriginal and Treaty Rights in Canada* (Vancouver: University of British Columbia Press).

LASELVA, S., and VERNON, R. (1997), 'Liberty, Equality, Fraternity . . . and Federalism', in M. Westmacott and H. Mellon (eds.) *Challenges to Canadian Federalism* (Scarborough: Prentice-Hall).

LASLETT, P., and RUNCIMAN, W. G. (1969), *Philosophy, Politics and Society* (Oxford: Basil Blackwell).

LAWTON, S. B. (1989), 'Public, Private and Separate Schools in Ontario: Developing a New Social Contract for Education', in W. L. Boyd and J. G. Cibulka (eds.) *Private Schools and Public Policy: International Perspectives* (London: The Falmer Press): 171–92.

LEADER, S. (1996), 'Three Faces of Toleration in a Democracy', *Journal of Political Philosophy*, 4/1: 45–67.

LEHNING, P. (1998), (ed.). *Theories of Secession* (London: Routledge).

——and WEALE, A. (1997), (eds.). *Citizenship, Democracy and Justice in the New Europe* (London: Routledge).

LEICESTER, M., and TAYLOR, M. (1992), (eds.). *Ethics, Ethnicity and Education* (London: Kogan Page).

LEVEY, G. B. (1997), 'Rethinking Liberal Autonomy in the Light of Multiculturalism', Paper presented at the American Political Science Association Annual Meeting, Sept.

LEVINSON, S. (1990), *Constitutional Faith* (Princeton: Princeton University Press).

LEVY, J. T. (1996), 'The Multiculturalism of Fear', *Critical Review*, 10: 271–83.

——(1997), 'Classifying Cultural Rights', in W. Kymlicka and I. Shapiro (eds.) *NOMOS XXXIX: Ethnicity and Group Rights* (New York: New York University Press).

——(forthcoming), *The Multiculturalism of Fear* (Oxford: Oxford University Press).

LEYDET, D. (1995), 'Intégration et pluralisme: le concept de culture publique', in F. Blais, G. Laforest and D. Lamoureux (eds.) *Libéralismes et nationalismes* (Québec: Presses de l'Université Laval).

LI, P., and BOLARIA, S. (1988), *Racial Oppression in Canada* (Toronto: Garamond Press).

LIEBERMAN, M. (1993), *Public Education: An Autopsy* (Cambridge, Mass.: Harvard University Press).

LIJPHART, AREND (1977), *Democracy in Plural Societies: A Comparative Exploration* (New Haven: Yale University Press).

——(1984), *Democracies: Patterns of Majoritarian and Consensus Government in Twenty-One Countries* (New Haven: Yale University Press).

LINZ, J. J. (1997), 'Democracy, Multinationalism, and Federalism', Paper presented at the International Political Science Association Meeting, Aug., Seoul, South Korea.

LISTER, R. (1998), (ed.). *Citizenship: Feminist Perspectives* (New York: New York University Press).

LITTLE BEAR, L., BOLDT, M., and LONG, J. A. (1984), (eds.). *Pathways to Self-Determination: Canadian Indians and the Canadian State* (Toronto: University of Toronto Press).

LONG, J. A., and BOLDT, M. (1988), (eds.). *Governments in Conflict: Provinces and Indian Nations in Canada* (Toronto: University of Toronto Press).

LOPEZ, I. F. H. (1994), 'The Social Construction of Race: Some Observations on Illusion, Fabrication, and Choice', *Harvard Civil Rights—Civil Liberties Law Review*, 29: 2.

LUBIN, D. (1997), *The Paradox of Representation: Racial Gerrymandering and Minority Interests in Congress* (Princeton: Princeton University Press).

LUKES, S. (1993), 'Five Fables about Human Rights', in S. Shute and S. Hurley (eds.) *On Human Rights: The Oxford Amnesty Lectures* (New York: Basic Books): 19–39.

LUPUL, M. (1991), 'Comments', in D. Schneiderman (ed.) *Language and the State: The Law and Politics of Identity* (Cowansville, Que.: Éditions Yvon Blais).

LUSTICK, I. (1999), 'The Other Side of Self-Determination: State Contraction in Theory and Practice—Lessons from Britain–Ireland, France–Algeria, and Israel–West Bank/Gaza', in W. Danspeckgruber and A. Watts (eds.) *Self-Determination and Self-Administration. A Sourcebook* (Boulder, Colo.: Lynne Rienner): 101–24.

LYSENKO, V. (1996), 'Naskol'ko prochna dogovarnaya osnova federativnykh otnoshenii', *Federalizm: Teoriya, prakitika istoriya*, 3: 11–34.

McCLINTOCK, A. (1993), 'Family Feuds: Gender, Nationalism and the Family', *Feminist Review*, 44: 61.

McCONNELL, M. W. (1991), 'The Selective Funding Problem: Abortion and Religious Schools', *Harvard Law Review*, 104: 989–1050.

MacCORMICK, N. (1996), 'Liberalism, Nationalism and the Post-sovereign State', *Political Studies*, 44: 553–67.

McDONALD, M. E. (1991), 'Collective Rights, Special Issue', *Canadian Journal of Law and Jurisprudence*, 4/2: 217–419.

MACEDO, S. (1990), *Liberal Virtues: Citizenship, Virtue and Community in Liberal Constitutionalism* (Oxford: Oxford University Press).

——(1995a), 'Liberal Civic Education: The Case of God v. John Rawls?', *Ethics*, 105: 468–96.

——(1995b), 'Reply to Critics', *Georgetown Law Journal*, 84: 329–37.

McGARRY, J., and O'LEARY, B. (1993), *The Politics of Ethnic Conflict Regulation* (London: Routledge).

McKIM, R., and McMAHAN, J. (1997), (eds.). *The Morality of Nationalism* (New York: Oxford University Press).

McLAUGHLIN, T. H. (1992), 'The Ethics of Separate Schools', in M. Leicester and M. Taylor (eds.) *Ethics, Ethnicity and Education* (London: Kogan Page): 114–36.

MACLEOD, C. M. (1997), 'Conceptions of Parental Autonomy', *Politics and Society*, 25/1: 117–40.

MACMILLAN, C. M. (1982), 'Henri Bourassa on the Defence of Language Rights', *Dalhousie Review*, 62/3.

——(1983), 'Language Rights, Human Rights and Bill 101', *Queen's Quarterly*, 90.

——(1998), *The Practice of Language Rights in Canada* (Toronto: University of Toronto Press).

MCNEIL, K. (1989), *Common Law Aboriginal Title* (Oxford: Clarendon Press).

MCREAVY, (1959), 'The Power of the Church', in P. O'Mahoney (ed.) *Catholics and Divorce*.

MCROBERTS, K. (1997), *Misconceiving Canada: The Struggle for National Unity* (Toronto: Oxford University Press).

MADISON, J. (1987), 'Federalist Ten (1788)', in I. Kramnick (ed.) *The Federalist Papers* (New York: Penguin).

MAGNET, J. E. (1995), *Official Language of Canada: Perspectives from Law, Policy and the Future* (Cowansville, Que.: Éditions Yvon Blais).

MAMDANI, M. (1996), *Citizen and Subject: Contemporary Africa and the Legacy of Late Colonialism* (Princeton: Princeton University Press).

MANIN, B. (1987), 'On Legitimacy and Deliberation', *Political Theory*, 15/3: 338–68.

——(1997), *The Principles of Representative Government* (Cambridge: Cambridge University Press).

MANSBRIDGE, J. (1980), *Beyond Adversary Democracy* (New York: Basic Books).

——(1981), 'Living with Conflict: Representation in the Theory of Adversary Democracy', *Ethics*, 91/1: 466–76.

——(1983), *Beyond Adversary Democracy* (Chicago: University of Chicago Press).

——(1986), *Why we Lost the ERA* (Chicago: University of Chicago Press).

——(1993), 'Feminism and Democratic Community', in J. W. Chapman and I. Shapiro (eds.) *Democratic Community: NOMOS XXXV* (New York: New York University Press).

——(1994), 'Using Power/Fighting Power', *Constellations*, 1/1: 53–73.

——(1996), 'Fighting Power/Using Power', in S. Benhabib (ed.) *Democracy and Difference* (Princeton: Princeton University Press).

——(1998), 'The Many Faces of Representation [Working Paper]', John F. Kennedy School of Government, Harvard University.

'Many Voices, One Chant: Black Feminist Perspectives', *Feminist Review*, 17 (1984).

MARGALIT, A., and HALBERTAL, M. (1994), 'Liberalism and the Right to Culture', *Social Research*, 61/3: 491–510.

——and RAZ, J. (1990), 'National Self-Determination', *Journal of Philosophy*, 87/9: 439–61.

MARIS, C. (1995), 'Let him Wed a Female who has the Graceful Gait of an Elephant', *International Journal for the Semiotics of Law*, 8/23: 115–54.

MARKO, J. (1995), *Autonomie und Integration. Rechtsinstitute des Nationalitätenrechts im funktionalen Vergleich* (Vienna: Böhlau Verlag).

MATSON, J. N. (1993), 'The Common Law Abroad: English and Indigenous Laws in the British Commonwealth', *International and Comparative Law Quarterly*, 42: 753–79.

MENDUS, S. (1989), *Toleration and the Limits of Liberalism* (Atlantic Highlands, NY: Humanities Press).

MET (Muslim Educational Trust). (1997), *Comments on the Government White Paper, 'Excellence in Schools'* (London: MET (Muslim Educational Trust)).

MEZEY, S. G. (1994), 'Increasing the Number of Women in Office: Does it Matter?', in E. A. Cook, S. Thomas and C. Wilcox (eds.) *The Year of the Woman: Myths and Realities* (Boulder, Colo.: Westview Press).

MEZNARIC, S. (1994), 'Gender as an Ethno-Marker: Rape, War and Identity Politics in the Former Yugoslavia', in V. M. Moghadam (ed.) *Identity Politics and Women* (Boulder, Colo.: Westview Press): 76–98.

MIDDLETON, H. (1992), 'Lettre adressée aux habitants de la Province de Quebec, ci-devant le Canada, de la part du congrès américain (1774)', in A. Ferretti and G. Miron (eds.) *Les Grands Textes Indépendantistes* (Montreal: Éditions de l'Hexagone).

MIKHALEVA, N. A. (1995), 'Konstitutsionnie reformi v respublikakh—sub'etakh Russiiskoi Federatsii', *Gosudarstvo i pravo*, 4: 3–10.

MILL, J. S. (1956), *On Liberty (1859)* (Indianapolis: Bobbs-Merrill).

——(1972), *Utilitarianism, Liberty, Representative Government* (London: Everyman's Library).

——(1991), 'On Liberty (1859)', in J. Gray (ed.) *On Liberty and Other Essays* (Oxford: Oxford University Press).

MILLER, D. (1995), *On Nationality* (Oxford: Oxford University Press).

MILLS, C. (1997), *The Racial Contract* (Ithaca, NY: Cornell University Press).

MINOW, M. L. (1990), *Making all the Difference: Inclusion, Exclusion, and American Law* (Ithaca, NY: Cornell University Press).

——(1991), 'From Class Actions to Miss Saigon', *Cleveland State Law Review*, 39/3: 269–300.

MODOOD, T. (1992), *Not Easy Being British: Colour, Culture, and Citizenship* (London: Runnymede Trust and Trentham Books).

——(1993a), 'Muslims, Incitement to Hatred and the Law', in J. Horton (ed.) *Liberalism, Multiculturalism and Toleration* (London: MacMillan).

——(1993b), 'Muslim Views on Religious Identity and Racial Equality', *New Community*, 19/3: 513–19.

——(1994a), 'Establishment, Multiculturalism and British Citizenship', *Political Quarterly*, 65/1: 53–73.

——(1994b), 'Political Blackness and British Asians', *Sociology*, 28/4: 859–76.

——(1995), 'Beware of a Secular Intolerance', *Women Against Fundamentalism*, 6.

——(1996), '"Race" in Britain and the Politics of Difference', in D. Archard (ed.) *Philosophy and Pluralism* (Cambridge: Cambridge University Press).

——(1997a), (ed.). *Church, State and Religious Minorities* (Vol. Church, State and Religious Minorities) (London: Policy Studies Institute).

MODOOD, T. (1997b), 'Introduction', in T. Modood and P. Werbner (eds.) *The Politics of Multiculturalism in the New Europe* (London: Zed Books).

——(1997c), '"Difference", Cultural Racism and Anti-Racism', in P. Werbner and T. Modood (eds.) *Debating Cultural Hybridity* (London: Zed Books).

——BERTHOUD, R., LAKEY, J., NAZROO, J., SMITH, P., VIRDEE, S., and BEISHUN, S. (1997), *Ethnic Minorities in Britain: Diversity and Disadvantage—The Fourth National Survey of Ethnic Minorities* (London: Policy Studies Institute).

——and WERBNER, P. (1997), (eds.). *The Politics of Multiculturalism in the New Europe: Racism, Identity and Community* (London: Zed Books).

——BEISHON, S., and VIRDEE, S. (1994), *Changing Ethnic Identities* (London: Policy Studies Institute).

MOGHADAM, V. M. (1994a), (ed.). *Gender and National Identity* (London: Zed Books).

——(1994b), (ed.). *Identity Politics and Women: Cultural Representations and Feminisms in International Perspective* (Boulder, Colo.: Westview Press).

MONTAGU, A. (1972), *Statement on Race* (London: Oxford University Press).

MONTESQUIEU, BARON DE, CHARLES LOUIS DE SECONDAT. (1906), *Considerations sur les causes de la grandeur des romains et de leur decadence (1748)* (Paris: Librarie Hachette).

MOORE, M. (1996), 'On Reasonableness', *Journal of Applied Philosophy*, 13/2: 167–78.

——(1998), (ed.). *National Self-Determination and Secession* (Oxford: Oxford University Press).

MORONE, J. A., and MARMOR, T. R. (1981), 'Representing Consumer Institutions: The Case of American Health Planning', *Ethics*, 91: 431–50.

MOUFFE, C. (1993), *The Return of the Political* (London: Verso).

MUELLER, D., TOLLISON, R. D., and WILLETT, T. D. (1972), 'Representative Democracy via Random Selection', *Public Choice*, 12: 57–68.

MULI, K. (1995), '"Help me Balance the Load": Gender Discrimination in Kenya', in J. Peters and A. Wolper (eds.) *Women's Rights Human Rights: International Feminist Perspectives* (New York: Routledge).

MULQUEENY, K. E. (1993), 'Folk-Law or Folklore: When a Law is Not a Law. Or is it?', in M. A. Stephenson and S. Ratnapala (eds.) *Mabo: A Judicial Revolution* (Brisbane: University of Queensland Press).

MUNGRA, C. (1990), *Hindoestaanse gezinnen in Nederlan (Hindustani Families in the Netherlands)* (Leiden: R.U. Leiden/COMT).

NAGEL, J. H. (1992), 'Combining Deliberation and Fair Representation in Community Health Decisions', *University of Pennsylvania Law Review*, 140/5: 2101–21.

NASIR, J. J. (1986), *The Islamic Law of Personal Status* (London: Graham & Trotman).

NEATE, G. (1993), 'Looking after Country: Legal Recognition of Traditional Rights to and Responsibilities for Land', *University of New South Wales Law Journal*, 16/1: 161–222.

NESBITT, E. (1993), 'Gender and Religious Tradition: The Role-Learning of British Hindu Children', *Gender and Education*, 5: 81–91.

NETTHEIM, G. (1995), 'Mabo and Legal Pluralism: The Australian Aboriginal Justice

Experience', in K. Hazelhurst (ed.) *Legal Pluralism and the Colonial Legacy* (Brookfield, VT: Avebury Press).

NEUMAN, G. L. (1987), 'Back to Dred Scott', *San Diego Law Review*, 24: 485.

——(1992), 'Rhetorical Slavery, Rhetorical Citizenship', *Michigan Law Review*, 90: 1276.

NEUMANN, I. (1996), *Russia and the Idea of Europe* (London: Routledge).

NEWMAN, W. J. (1993), 'Language Difficulties Facing Tribunals and Participants: The Approach of the New Official Languages Act', in W. S. Tarnopolsky (ed.) *Discrimination in the Law and the Administration of Justice* (Montreal, Que.: Éditions Thémis).

NIELSEN, K. (1993), 'Secession: The Case of Quebec', *Journal of Applied Philosophy*, 10: 29–43.

——(1998), 'Liberal Nationalism and Secession', in M. Moore (ed.) *National Self-Determination and Secession* (Oxford: Oxford University Press): 103–33.

NIETO, S. (1992), *Affirming Diversity: The Sociopolitical Context of Multicultural Education* (New York: Longman).

NORD, W. A. (1995), *Religion and American Education: Rethinking a National Dilemma* (Chapel Hill: University of North Carolina Press).

NORMAN, W. J. (1994), 'Towards a Philosophy of Federalism', in J. Baker (ed.) *Group Rights* (Toronto: University of Toronto Press).

——(1998), 'The Ethics of Secession as the Regulation of Secessionist Politics', in M. Moore (ed.) *National Self-Determination and Secession* (Oxford: Oxford University Press).

——(1999), 'Theorizing Nationalism (Normatively): The First Steps', in R. Beiner (ed.) *Theorizing Nationalism* (Albany: State University of New York Press).

O'BRIEN, M. (1981), *The Politics of Reproduction* (Boston: Routledge & Kegal Paul).

O'BRIEN, S. (1989), *American Indian Tribal Governments* (Norman: University of Oklahoma Press).

OKIN, S. M. (1989), *Justice, Gender and the Family* (New York: Basic Books).

——(1997), 'Is Multiculturalism Bad for Women? When Minority Cultures Win Group Rights, Women Lose Out', *Boston Review*, 22: 2–28.

——(1998), 'Feminism and Multiculturalism: Some Tensions', *Ethics*, 108: 661–84.

OLDFIELD, A. (1990), *Citizenship and Community: Civic Republicanism and the Modern World* (London: Routledge).

OMAN, N. (1997), *Sharing Horizons: A Paradigm for Political Accommodation in Intercultural Settings*. Unpublished Ph.D. thesis, McGill University, Montreal.

Opinion/Editorial. (1995, 31 May), 'Memory Lapses', *Toronto Sun*, 1.

ORREN, G. (1997), 'Fall from Grace: The Public's Loss of Faith in Government', in J. S. Nye, Jr., P. D. Zelikow and D. C. King (eds.) *Why People Don't Trust Government* (Cambridge, Mass.: Harvard University Press).

PAPANEK, H. (1994), 'The Ideal Woman and the Ideal Society: Control and Autonomy in the Construction of Identity', in V. M. Moghadam (ed.) *Identity Politics and Women* (Boulder, Colo.: Westview Press): 42–75.

PAREKH, B. (1990), 'The Rushdie Affair: Research Agenda for Political Philosophy', *Political Studies*, 38: 695–709.

——(1995), 'Cultural Diversity and Liberal Democracy', in D. Beetham (ed.) *Defining and Measuring Democracy* (London: Sage): 199–221.

——(1997), 'Dilemmas of a Multicultural Theory of Citizenship', *Constellations*, 4/1: 54–62.

PARKER, A., RUSSO, M., SOMMER, D., and YAEGER, P. (1992), (eds.). *Nationalisms and Sexualities* (New York: Routledge).

PARKINSON, P. (1994), 'Taking Multiculturalism Seriously: Marriage Law and the Rights of Minorities', *Sydney Law Review*, 16: 473.

PATAI, R., and WING, J. P. (1975), *The Myth of the Jewish Race* (New York: Scribner).

PATRY, R. M. (1981), *La Législation linguistique fédérale* (Québec: Éditeur Officiel du Québec).

PATTERSON, R. H. (1992), *Not Carved in Stone: Public Schooling of Separate Schools in Ontario* (Harrow, Ont.: Friends of Public Education in Ontario).

PEARL, D. (1995), 'The Application of Islamic Law in the English Courts', *Yearbook of Islamic and Middle Eastern Law*, 2: 3.

PELIKAN, J. (1984), *The Vindication of Tradition* (New Haven: Yale University Press).

PENNOCK, J. R. (1979), *Democratic Political Theory* (Princeton: Princeton University Press).

PENTER, T. (1997), 'Die Republik Tywa (Tiuwa): Nationale und Kulturelle Wiedergeburt einer ehemaligen Sowjetkolonie', *Osteuropa*, Vol. 27, No. 7: 663–83.

PERRY, M. J. (1991), *Love and Power: The Role of Religion and Morality in American Politics* (New York: Oxford University Press).

PESHKIN, A. (1986), *God's Choice: The Total World of a Fundamentalist Christian School* (Chicago: University of Chicago Press).

PETERSON, N., and SANDERS, W. (eds.). (1998), *Citizenship and Indigenous Australians: Changing Conceptions and Possibilities* (Cambridge: Cambridge University Press).

PETERSON, R. P. (1996), 'A Re-evaluation of the Economic Consequences of Divorce', *American Sociological Review*, 61: 528.

PHILLIPS, A. (1992), 'Democracy and Difference: Some Problems for Feminist Theory', *Political Quarterly*, 63/1: 79–90.

——(1993), *Democracy and Difference* (University Park, Penn.: Pennsylvania State University Press).

——(1995), *The Politics of Presence: Issues in Democracy and Group Representation* (Oxford: Oxford University Press).

——(1997), 'In Defence of Secularism', in T. Modood (ed.) *Church, State and Religious Minorities* (London: Policy Studies Institute).

PHILPOTT, D. (1995), 'In Defense of Self-Determination', *Ethics*, 105/2: 352–85.

PICKUS, N. (1998), (ed.). *Immigration and Citizenship in the 21st Century* (Lanham, MD: Rowman & Littlefield).

PINDERHUGHES, D. (1987), *Race and Ethnicity in Chicago Politics* (Urbana: University of Illinois Press).

PISCATORI, J. (1986), *Islam in a World of Nation-States* (Cambridge: Cambridge University Press).

PITKIN, H. F. (1967), *The Concept of Representation* (Berkeley: University of California Press).

——(1981), 'Justice: On Relating Public and Private', *Political Theory*, 9: 327–52.

PLAMENATZ, J. (1960), *On Alien Rule and Self-Government* (London: Longman).

POCOCK, J. G. A. (1992), 'The Ideal of Citizenship since Classical Times', *Queen's Quarterly*, 99/1: 33–55.

POGGE, T. (1992), 'Cosmopolitanism and Sovereignty', *Ethics*, 103: 48–75.

——(1994), 'An Egalitarian Law of Peoples', *Philosophy and Public Affairs*, 23/3: 195–224.

POPKIN, S. L. (1994), *The Reasoning Voter* (Chicago: University of Chicago Press).

PORTER, J. (1987), *The Measure of Canadian Society* (Ottawa: Carleton University Press).

POSNER, R. (1982), 'Economics, Politics, and the Reading of Statutes and the Constitution', *Chicago Law Review*, 46: 263.

POULTER, S. (1987), 'Ethnic Minority Customs, English Law, and Human Rights', *International and Comparative Law Quarterly*, 36/3: 589–615.

PRESTON, M. (1978), 'Black Elected Officials and Public Policy: Symbolic and Substantive Representation', *Policy Studies Journal*, 7/2: 196–201.

PROVENZO, E. R. (1990), *Religious Fundamentalism and American Religion: The Battle for the Public School* (Albany: State University of New York Press).

PUTNAM, R. (1993), *Making Democracy Work: Civic Traditions in Modern Italy* (Princeton: Princeton University Press).

RADAY, F. (1992), 'Israel: The Incorporation of Religious Patriarchy in a Modern State', *International Review of Comparative Public Policy*, 4: 209.

RAIKKA, J. (1996), (ed.). *Do we Need Minority Rights?* (Dordrecht: Kluwer).

RAWLS, J. (1971), *A Theory of Justice* (Cambridge, Mass.: Harvard University Press).

——(1985), 'Justice as Fairness: Political not Metaphysical', *Philosophy and Public Affairs*, 14/3: 223–51.

——(1988), 'The Priority of Right and Ideas of the Good', *Philosophy and Public Affairs*, 17/4: 251–76.

——(1993), *Political Liberalism* (New York: Columbia University Press).

RAZ, J. (1986), *Morality of Freedom* (Oxford: Clarendon Press).

——(1994), 'Multiculturalism: A Liberal Perspective', *Dissent*, 41: 67–79.

RÉAUME, D. G. (1988), 'Individuals, Groups, and Rights to Public Goods', *University of Toronto Law Journal*, 38/1.

——(1991), 'The Constitutional Protection of Language: Survival or Security?', in D. Schneiderman (ed.) *Language and the State: The Law and Politics of Identity* (Cowansville, Que.: Éditions Yvon Blais).

——(1995), 'Justice between Cultures: Autonomy and the Protection of Cultural Affiliation', *University of British Columbia Law Review*, 29/1: 121.

——and GREEN, L. (1989), 'Education and Linguistic Security in the Charter', *McGill Law Journal*, 34/4: 777–816.

REESOR, B. (1992), *The Canadian Constitution in Historical Perspective* (Scarborough, Ont.: Prentice-Hall).

REITMAN, O. (1997), 'Women Unchained? English Divorce Law and the Dissolution of Jewish Marriage', Paper presented at the Political Science Department, University of Toronto, Toronto.

RENAN, E. (1939), 'What is a Nation?', in A. Zimmern (ed.) *Modern Political Doctrines, London: Oxford University Press* (Publ. Orig. in Fr. In 1882).

RENO, J. (1995), 'U.S. Department of Justice Commitment to American Indian Tribal Justice Systems', *Judicature*, 79: 113–17.

REQUEJO COLL, F. (1996), 'Pluralism, democracia y federalismo: una revisión de la ciudadaní a democrática en estados plurinacionales', *Revista Internacional de Filosofía a Política*, 7: 93–120.

RESLER, T. (1997), 'Dilemmas of Democratisation: Safeguarding Minorities in Russia, Ukraine and Lithuania', *Europe–Asia Studies*, 49/1: 89–106.

RESNICK, P. (1994), 'Toward a Multination Federalism', in L. Seidle (ed.) *Seeking A New Canadian Partnership: Asymmetric and Confederal Options* (Montreal: Institute for Research on Public Policy).

REX, J. (1983), *Race Relations in Sociological Theory* (London: Routledge & Kegan Paul).

REYNOLDS, H. (1996), *Aboriginal Sovereignty* (Sydney: Allen & Unwin).

RHEINSTEIN, M. (1953), 'Trends in Marriage and Divorce Law of Western Countries', *Law and Contemporary Problems*, 18: 3.

RICHARDS, D. A. J. (1986), *Toleration and the Constitution* (New York: Oxford University Press).

RICHARDSON, B. (1989), *Drumbeat: Anger and Renewal in Indian Country* (Toronto: The Assembly of First Nations and Summerhill Press).

RICHIE, B. (1996), *Compelled to Crime: The Gender Entrapment of Battered Black Women* (New York: Routledge).

RIKER, W. H. (1975), 'Federalism', in F. Greenstein and N. Polsby (eds.) *Handbook of Political Science* (Reading, Mass.: Addison-Wesley) (5): 93–172.

ROLAND, A. (1996), *Cultural Pluralism and Psychoanalysis: The Asian and North American Perspective* (London: Routledge).

ROSE, S. D. (1988), *Keeping them out of the Hands of Satan* (New York: Routledge).

ROSENBLUM, N. (1987), *Another Liberalism: Romanticism and the Reconstruction of Liberal Thought* (Cambridge, Mass.: Harvard University Press).

ROTAR, I. (1997, 29 Aug.), 'The Ingush-Ossetian Crisis', *Prism*.

ROUSSEAU, J.-J. (1978), *On the Social Contract (1762)*, trans. J. R. Masters (New York: St Martin's Press).

Royal Commission on Aboriginal Peoples. (1996), *For Seven Generations: An Information Legacy of the Royal Commission on Aboriginal Peoples*, i-v (Ottawa: Libraxus Inc.). [CD-ROM]

RUSHDIE, S. (1991), 'In Good Faith', in S. Rushdie (ed.) *Imaginary Homelands: Essays and Criticism, 1981–91* (London: Penguin Books).

SABETTI, F. (1996), 'Path Dependency and Civic Culture: Some Lessons from Italy about Interpreting Social Experiments', *Politics and Society*, 24/1: 19–44.

SAGHAL, G. (1992), 'Secular Spaces: The Experience of Asian Women Organizing', in G. Saghal and N. Yuval-Davis (eds.) *Refusing Holy Orders: Women and Fundamentalism in Britain* (London: Virago Press): 163–97.

——and YUVAL-DAVIS, N. (1992), (eds.). *Refusing Holy Orders: Women and Fundamentalism in Britain* (London: Virago Press).

SAID, E. (1993), *Culture and Imperialism* (New York: Vintage Books).

SAMSON, C. (1999), 'The Dispossession of the Innu and the Colonial Magic of Canadian Liberalism', *Citizenship Studies*, 3/1: 5–25.

SANDEL, M. (1996), *Democracy's Discontent: America in Search of a Public Philosophy* (Cambridge, Mass.: Harvard University Press).

SANDERS, L. M. (1997), 'Against Deliberation', *Political Theory*, 25: 347–76.

SAPIRO, V. (1981), 'When are Interests Interesting?', *American Political Science Review*, 75/3: 701–16.

——(1984), 'Women, Citizenship, and Nationality: Immigration and Naturalization Policies in the United States', *Politics and Society*, 13: 1.

SATZEWICH, V. (1990), 'The Political Economy of Race and Ethnicity in Politics', in P. Li (ed.) *Race and Ethnic Relations in Canada* (Don Mills, Ont.: Oxford University Press Canada).

SAWYER, J., and MACRAE, D. (1962), 'Game Theory and Cumulative Voting in Illinois: 1902–1954', *American Political Science Review*, 56: 936–46.

SCANLON, T. M. (1982), 'Contractualism and Utilitarianism', in A. Sen and B. Williams (eds.) *Utilitarianism and Beyond* (Cambridge: Cambridge University Press).

SCHLOZMAN, K., and MANSBRIDGE, J. (1979), 'Review of Irene Diamond, *Sex Roles in the State House*', *Harvard Educational Review*, 49: 554–6.

SCHNAPPER, D. (1994), *La Communauté des Citoyens: Sur l'idée moderne de nation* (Paris: Gallimard).

SCHUCK, P. H. (1998), *Citizens, Strangers and In-Betweens: Essays on Immigration and Citizenship* (Boulder, Colo.: Westview Press).

——and SMITH, R. M. (1985), *Citizenship without Consent: Illegal Aliens in the American Polity* (New Haven: Yale University Press).

SCHWARTZ, B. (1990), 'A Separate Aboriginal Justice System?', *Manitoba Law Journal*, 28: 77.

SCHWARTZ, W. F. (1995), (ed.). *Justice in Immigration* (New York: Cambridge University Press).

SEVENHUIJSEN, S. (1998), *Citizenship and the Ethics of Care: Feminist Considerations on Justice, Morality and Politics* (London: Routledge).

SHACHAR, A. (1998), 'Group Identity and Women's Rights in Family Law: The Perils of Multicultural Accommodation', *Journal of Political Philosophy*, 6: 285–305.

——(forthcoming *a*), 'On Citizenship and Multicultural Vulnerability', *Political Theory*.

SHACHAR, A. (forthcoming b), *Multicultural Jurisdictions: Preserving Cultural Differences and Women's Rights in a Liberal State* (Cambridge: Cambridge University Press).

——(forthcoming c), 'Against Cultural Uniformity and Cultural Fragmentation: A Critique of Okin and Kukathas', *Citizenship Studies*.

——and HIRSCHL, R. (1998), 'Looking Forward, Looking Backward, Looking Sideways: Expanding the Boundaries of Contemporary Political Analyses of Differentiated Citizenship', Paper presented at the Empires/Colonies/Legal Cultures ANZLHS, 3–5 July, Melbourne, Australia.

————(1999), 'The Troubled Marriage of Church and State', paper presented at the Legal Theory Workshop Series, University of Toronto.

SHAFIR, G. (1998), (ed.). *The Citizenship Debates: A Reader* (Minneapolis: University of Minnesota Press).

SHAPIRO, I., with ARNESON, R. (1996), *Democracy's Place* (Ithaca, NY: Cornell University Press).

——and HARDIN, R. (1996), (eds.). *Political Order: NOMOS XXXVIII* (New York: New York University Press).

——and KYMLICKA, W. (1997), (eds.). *Ethnicity and Group Rights: NOMOS XXXIX* (New York: New York University Press).

SHARP, A. (1997), *Justice and the Maori: The Philosophy and Practice of Maori Claims in New Zealand since the 1970s* (2nd ed.) (Auckland: Oxford University Press).

SHKLAR, J. (1991), *American Citizenship* (Cambridge, MA: Harvard University Press).

SINGH, K. (1994), 'Obstacles to Women's Rights in India', in R. J. Cook (ed.) *Human Rights of Women: National and International Perspective* (Philadelphia: University of Pennsylvania Press).

SKINNER, Q. (1992), 'On Justice, the Common Good and the Priority of Liberty', in C. Mouffe (ed.) *Dimensions of Radical Democracy: Pluralism, Citizenship and Community* (London: Routledge): 211–24.

SKJEIE, H. (1991), 'The Rhetoric of Difference: On Women's Inclusion into Political Elites', *Politics and Society*, 19/2: 233–63.

SLAWNER, K., and DENHAM, M. (1998), (eds.). *Citizenship after Liberalism* (New York: Peter Lang).

SMITH, A. (1995), *Nations and Nationalism in a Global Era* (Oxford: Polity Press).

SMITH, G. (1996), 'Russia, Ethnoregionalism and the Politics of Federation', *Ethnic and Racial Studies*, 19/2: 391–410.

SMITH, G. (1995), (ed.). *Federalism, The Multiethnic Challenge* (London: Longman).

SPELMAN, E. (1988), *Inessential Woman: Problems of Exclusion in Feminist Thought* (Boston: Beacon Press).

SPINNER, J. (1994), *The Boundaries of Citizenship: Race, Ethnicity and Nationality in the Liberal State* (Baltimore: Johns Hopkins University Press).

SPIVAK, G. (1987), *In Other Worlds: Essays in Cultural Politics* (London: Methuen).

STAMP, R. (1985), 'A History of Private Schools in Ontario', in Government of Ontario *The Report of the Commission on Private Schools* (Toronto: Bernard J. Shapiro, Commissioner): 193–205.

STAPLETON, J. (1995), (ed.). *Group Rights: Perspectives since 1990* (Briston: Thoemmes Press).

STARK, B. (1992), 'Forward: Rappaccini's Daughters?', in B. Stark (ed.) *International Review of Comparative Public Policy, 1992: Family Law and Gender Bias: Comparative Perspectives* (Greenwich, Conn.: JAI Press).

Statistics Canada. (1996), *Nations Series No. 5 Aboriginal Data, The Nation: 1996 Census of Population* (Ottawa: Supply and Services, 1996).

STEINER, H. (1994), *An Essay on Rights* (Oxford: Basil Blackwell).

STIMSON, J. A., MACKUEN, M., and ERIKSON, R. (1995), 'Dynamic Representation', *American Political Science Review*, 89/3: 543–65.

STONE, C. (1987), *Earth and Other Ethics: The Case for Moral Pluralism* (New York: Harper & Row).

STRATTON, L. C. (1992), 'The Right to have Rights: Gender Discrimination in Nationality Laws', *Minnesota Law Review*, 77: 195.

STRIKE, K. (1990), 'Are Secular Languages Religiously Neutral?', *Journal of Law and Politics*, 6: 469–502.

——(1994), 'On the Construction of Public Speech: Pluralism and Public Reason', *Educational Theory*, 44: 1–26.

STROEV, E. (1996), 'Rossiiskii federalizm: nuzhno idu dal'she obshchikh formul'', *Federalizm: Teoriya, praktika, istoriya*, 3: 3–10.

SUNSTEIN, C. (1988), 'Beyond the Republican Revival', *Yale Law Journal*, 97: 1539–90.

——(1993), *The Partial Constitution* (Cambridge, Mass.: Harvard University Press).

SWAIN, C. M. (1992), 'Double Standard, Double Bind: African-American Leadership after the Thomas Debacle', in T. Morrison (ed.) *Race-ing Justice, En-Gendering Power: Essays on Anita Hill, Clarence Thomas, and the Construction of Social Reality* (New York: Pantheon).

——(1993), *Black Faces, Black Interests: The Representation of African Americans in Congress* (Cambridge, Mass.: Harvard University Press).

Swann Report. (1985), *Education for All: The Report of the Committee of Inquiry into the Education of Children from Ethnic Minority Groups* (London: Her Majesty's Stationery Office).

SWEET, L. (1997), *God in the Classroom: The Controversial Issue of Religion in Canada's Schools* (Toronto: McClelland & Stewart).

Symposium on (1995), 'Citizenship, Democracy and Education', *Ethics*, 105/3.

——(1995), 'Democratic Education in a Multicultural State', *Journal of Philosophy of Education*, 29/2.

——(1996), 'Citizenship: History, Theory and Practice', *Australian Journal of Politics and History*, 42/1.

——(1996), 'Nationalism', *Critical Review*, 10/2.

——(1996), 'Philosophical Perspectives on National Identity', *Philosophical Forum*, 28/1.

——(1997), 'Citizenship in Feminism: Identity, Action and Locale', *Hypatia*, 12/4.

——(1997), 'Sovereignty and Citizenship', *Law and Philosophy*, 16/4.

Symposium on (1998), 'Nationalism, Multiculturalism and Liberal Democracy', *Ethical Theory and Moral Practice*, 1/2.

SYRTASH, J. T. (1992), *Religion and Culture in Canadian Family Law* (Toronto: Butterworth).

TAGUIEFF, P. A. (1987), *La force du prejuge: Essai sur la racismé se doubles* (Paris: Gallimard).

TAMIR, Y. (1993), *Liberal Nationalism* (Princeton: Princeton University Press).

TANNEN, D. (1994), *Gender and Discourse* (New York: Oxford University Press).

TARLTON, C. D. (1965), 'Symmetry and Asymmetry as Elements of Federalism: A Theoretical Speculation', *Journal of Politics*, 27/4.

TAYLOR, C. (1992), 'The Politics of Recognition', in A. Gutmann (ed.) *Multiculturalism and the 'Politics of Recognition'* (Princeton: Princeton University Press): 25–73.

——(1993a), *Reconciling the Solitudes: Essays on Canadian Federalism and Nationalism* (Montreal: McGill-Queen's University Press).

——(1993b), 'Why do Nations have to Become States', in G. Laforest (ed.) *Reconciling the Solitudes: Essays on Canadian Federalism and Nationalism* (Montreal & Kingston: McGill-Queen's University Press).

——(1994), 'Multiculturalism and "The Politics of Recognition"', in A. Gutmann (ed.) *Multiculturalism: Examining The Politics of Recognition* (Princeton: Princeton University Press): 10–2.

——(1997), 'Nationalism and Modernity', in R. McKim and J. McMahan (eds.) *The Morality of Nationalism* (New York: Oxford University Press).

THOMAS, S. (1994), *How Women Legislate* (New York: Oxford University Press).

TISHKOV, V. (1995), 'Chto est Rossiia?', *Voprosy filosofii*, 2: 3–17.

——(1997), *Ethnicity, Nationalism and Conflict in and after the Soviet Union: The Mind Aflame* (London: Sage).

TOMASI, J. (1995), 'Kymlicka, Liberalism, and Respect for Cultural Minorities', *Ethics*, 105/3: 580–603.

TOURAINE, M. (1997), *What is Democracy?* (Boulder, Colo.: Westview).

TREND, D. (1996), (ed.). *Radical Democracy: Identity, Citizenship and the State* (London: Routledge).

TRIESMAN, D. (1997), 'Russia's "Ethnic Revival": The Separatist Activism of Regional Leaders in a Postcommunist Order', *World Politics*, 49: 212–49.

TRONTO, J. (1993), *Moral Boundaries: A Political Argument for an Ethic of Care* (London: Routledge).

TRUDEAU, P. (1994), 'A Mess that Deserves a Big "No"', in M. Charlton and P. Barker (eds.) *Contemporary Political Issues* (Scarborough: Nelson).

TULLY, J. (1994), 'Aboriginal Property and Western Theory: Recovering a Middle Ground', *Social Philosophy and Policy*, 11: 53–180.

——(1995), *Strange Multiplicity: Constitutionalism in an Age of Diversity* (Cambridge: Cambridge University Press).

TURPEL, M. E. (1991), 'Home/Land', *Canadian Journal of Family Law*, 10: 17.

UKACIA (UK Action Committee on Islamic Affairs). (1993), *Muslims and the Law in*

Multi-Faith Britain: The Need for Reform (London: UKACIA (UK Action Committee on Islamic Affairs).

VALENTEI, S. (1996), 'Rossiiskie reformy i rossiiskii federalizm', *Federalizm: teoriya, praktika, istoriya*, 2: 23–36.

VAN DER ZWAARD, J. (1995), 'Naughty Boys and Obstinate Girls: District Nurses' Cultural and Professional Explanations of Child Rearing Practices', in I. Boer, A. Moors and T. van Teeffelen (eds.) *Orientations. Changing Stories; Postmodernism and the Arabic-Islamic World* (Amsterdam: Rodopi): 133–45.

VAN DYKE, V. (1977), 'The Individual, the State, and Ethnic Communities in Political Theory', *World Politics*, 29/3: 343–69.

——(1982), 'Collective Rights and Moral Rights: Problems in Liberal-Democratic Thought', *Journal of Politics*, 44: 21–40.

——(1985), *Human Rights, Ethnicity and Discrimination* (Westport, Conn: Greenwood Press).

——(1995), 'The Individual, the State, and Ethnic Communities in Political Theory', in W. Kymlicka (ed.) *The Rights of Minority Cultures* (Oxford: Oxford University Press).

VAN GUNSTEREN, H. (1978), 'Notes towards a Theory of Citizenship', in F. Dallmayr (ed.) *From Contract to Community* (New York: Marcel Decker).

——(1998a), *A Theory of Citizenship: Organizing Plurality in Contemporary Democracies* (Boulder, Colo.: Westview Press).

——(1998b), *Organizing Plurality: Citizenship in Post-1989 Democracies* (Boulder, Colo.: Westview Press).

VAN WILLIGENBURG, T., HEEGER, R., and VAN DEN BURG, W. (1995), (eds.). *Nation, State and the Coexistence of Different Communities* (Kampen: Kok Pharos).

Vernieuwing. Tijdschrift voor Onderwijs en Opvoeding (Renewal: Journal for Education and Pedagogy), 50/8. (1991)

——56/9. (1997)

VERTOVEC, S. (1995), 'Multiculturalism, Culturalism and Public Incorporation', *Ethnic and Racial Studies*, 19: 49–69.

VESCEY, C., and VENABLES, R. (1980), *American Indian Environments: Ecological Issues in Native American History* (Syracuse: Syracuse University Press).

VESTAL, A. D., and FOSTER, D. L. (1956), 'Implied Limitations on the Diversity Jurisdiction of Federal Courts', *Minnesota Law Review*, 41: 1.

VOET, R. (1992), 'Gender Representation and Quotas', *Acta Politica*, 4: 389–403.

WALDRON, J. (1989a), 'Moral Neutrality', in R. Goodin and A. Reeve (eds.) *Liberal Neutrality* (London: Routledge).

——(1989b, 10–16 Mar.), 'Religion and the Imagination in a Global Community: A Discussion of the Salman Rushdie Affair', *Times Literary Supplement* 248, 60.

——(1992), 'Minority Cultures and the Cosmopolitan Alternative', *University of Michigan Journal of Law Reform*, 25/3 and 4: 751–92.

——(1993a), 'Religious Contributions to Political Deliberation', *San Diego Law Review*, 30: 817–48.

WALDRON, J. (1993b), 'Rights and Minorities', in J. Waldron (ed.) *Liberal Rights: Collected Paper, 1981–1991* (Cambridge: Cambridge University Press).

——(1993c), 'When Justice Replaces Affection', in J. Waldron (ed.) *Liberal Rights: Collected Paper, 1981–1991* (Cambridge: Cambridge University Press).

——(1995), 'Minority Cultures and the Cosmopolitan Alternative', in W. Kymlicka (ed.) *The Rights of Minority Cultures* (Oxford: Oxford University Press).

——(1998), *Law and Disagreement* (Oxford: Clarendon Press).

WALFORD, G. (1995), 'Faith-Based Grant-Maintained Schools: Selective International Policy Borrowing from the Netherlands', *Journal of Education Policy*, 10: 245–57.

WALKER, A. (1981), 'Advancing Luna—and Ida B. Wells', in A. Walker (ed.) *You can't Keep a Good Woman Down* (New York: Harcourt Brace Jovanovich).

WALZER, M. (1983), *Spheres of Justice: A Defense of Pluralism and Equality* (New York: Basic Books).

——(1992), 'The New Tribalism: Notes on a Difficult Problem', *Dissent*, Spring: 164–71.

——(1995), 'The Civil Society Argument', in R. Beiner (ed.) *Theorizing Citizenship* (Albany: State University of New York Press): 153–74.

——(1997), *On Toleration* (New Haven: Yale University Press).

WARD, C. (1991), 'The Limits of "Liberal Republicanism": Why Group-Based Remedies and Republican Citizenship don't Mix', *Columbia Law Review*, 91/3: 581–607.

WASHOFSKY, M. (1981), 'The Recalcitrant Husband', *Jewish Law Annual*, 4: 144.

WEAVER, S. (1981), *Making Canadian Indian Policy: The Hidden Agenda 1968–1970* (Toronto: University of Toronto Press).

WEBER, M. (1948), *Max Weber: Essays in Sociology*, trans. H. Gerth & C. Wright-Mills (London: Routledge & Kegan Paul).

WEILER, J. (1997), 'Does Europe Need a Constitution? Reflections on Demos, Telos, and Ethos in the German Maastricht Decision', in P. Gowan and P. Anderson (eds.) *The Question of Europe* (London: Verso): 265–94.

WEINER, A. (1997), *European Citizenship Practice: Building Institutions of a Non-State* (Boulder, Colo.: Westview Press).

WEINSTOCK, D. (1995), 'Le Nationalisme civique et le concept de la culture politique commune', in F. Blais, G. Laforest and D. Lamoureux (eds.) *Libéralismes et nationalismes* (Quebec, Que.: Presses de l'Université Laval).

——(1999), 'Building Trust in Divided Societies', *Journal of Political Philosophy*, 7/3.

WEISBROD, C. (1987–8), 'Family, Church and State: An Essay on Constitutionalism and Religious Authority', *Journal of Family Law*, 26: 741.

WEISSBERG, R. (1978), 'Collective vs. Dyadic Representation in Congress', *American Political Science Review*, 72/2: 535–47.

WEITZMAN, L. (1985), *The Divorce Revolution: The Unexpected Social and Economic Consequences for Women and Children in America* (New York: Free Press).

WELLMAN, C. H. (1995), 'A Defense of Secession and Political Self-Determination', *Philosophy and Public Affairs*, 24/2: 142–71.

WERBNER, P., and MODOOD, T. (1997), (eds.). *Debating Cultural Hybridity: Multi-Cultural Identities and the Politics of Anti-Racism* (London: Zed Books).

WEST, C. (1992), 'Black Leadership and the Pitfalls of Racial Reasoning', in T. Morrison (ed.) *Race-ing Justice, En-Gendering Power: Essays on Anita Hill, Clarence Thomas, and the Construction of Social Reality* (New York: Pantheon).

WEST, L. (1997), (ed.). *Feminist Nationalism* (London: Routledge).

WEST, R. (1988), 'Jurisprudence and Gender', *University of Chicago Law Review*, 55: 1.

WEYRAUCH, W. O., KATZ, S. N., and OLSEN, F. E. (1994), (eds.). *Cases and Materials on Family Law: Legal Concepts and Changing Human Relationships* (St Paul, Minn.: West).

WHEARE, K. C. (1947), *Federal Government* (Oxford: Oxford University Press).

WHITAKER, R. (1995), 'Québec's Self-Determination and Aboriginal Self-Government: Conflict and Reconciliation?', in J. Carens (ed.) *Is Quebec Nationalism Just? Perspectives from Anglophone Canada* (Montreal: McGill-Queen's University Press): 193–220.

WHITE, P. (1991), 'Parents' Rights, Homosexuality and Education', *British Journal of Educational Studies*, 39: 398–408.

WHITE, P. G. (1992), *Understanding Canada's Cultural Reality: Accommodating Canada's Three Established Cultural-Linguistic Groups within the Canadian Federal System*, A Submission to the Special Joint Committee on a Renewed Canada, January, 6.

WILLET, C. (1998), *Theorizing Multiculturalism: A Guide to the Current Debate* (Oxford: Basil Blackwell).

WILLIAMS, B. (1969), 'The Idea of Equality', in P. Laslett and W. G. Runciman (eds.) *Philosophy, Politics and Society* (Oxford: Basil Blackwell): 110–31.

WILLIAMS, M. S. (1995), 'Justice toward Groups: Political Not Juridical', *Political Theory*, 23/1: 67–91.

——(1998), *Voice, Trust, and Memory: Marginalized Groups and the Failings of Liberal Representation* (Princeton: Princeton University Press).

WITTGENSTEIN, L. (1967) *Philosophical Investigations* (Oxford: Basil Blackwell).

——(1974), *Philosophical Investigations*, trans. G. E. M. Anscombe (Oxford: Basil Blackwell).

——(1994), *Tractatus Logico-Philosophicus* (London: Routledge).

WOLF, E. (1982), *Europe and the People Without History* (Berkeley: University of California Press).

WOO, D. (1989), 'The People v. Fumiko Kimura: But which People?', *International Sociology of Law*, 17: 403–28.

WOODMAN, G. (1988), 'How State Courts Create Customary Law in Ghana and Nigeria', in B. Morse and G. Woodman (eds.) *Indigenous Law and the State* (Providence, RI: Foris).

Women Against Fundementalism. (1990), 'Founding Statement', *Women Against Fundementalism*, 1.

YOUNG, I. M. (1989), 'Polity and Group Differences: A Critique of the Ideal of Universal Citizenship', *Ethics*, 99: 250.

——(1990), *Justice and the Politics of Difference* (Princeton: Princeton University Press).

YOUNG, I. M. (1994a), 'Gender as Seriality: Thinking about Women as a Social Collective', *Signs*, 19/3: 713–38.

——(1994b), 'Justice and Communicative Democracy', in R. Gottlieb (ed.) *Radical Philosophy: Tradition, Counter-Tradition, Politics* (Philadelphia: Temple University Press).

——(1996), 'Communication and the Other: Beyond Deliberative Democracy', in S. Benhabib (ed.) *Democracy and Difference* (Princeton: Princeton University Press): 120–35.

——(1997a), 'Deferring Group Representation', in I. Shapiro and W. Kymlicka. (eds.) *Ethnicity and Group Rights: NOMOS XXXIX* (New York: New York University Press).

——(1997b), 'Difference as a Resource for Democratic Communication', in J. Bohman and W. Rehg (eds.) *Deliberative Democracy: Essays on Reason and Politics* (Cambridge, MA: MIT Press): 383–406.

YUVAL-DAVIS, N. (1992), 'Fundamentalism, Multiculturalism and Women in Britain', in J. Donald and A. Rattansi (eds.) *'Race', Culture and Difference* (London: Sage).

——and ANTHIAS, F. (1989), (eds.). *Woman-Nation-State* (London: Macmillan).

ZARKOV, D. (1997), 'Sex as Usual: Body Politics and the Media War in Serbia', in K. Davis (ed.) *Embodied Practices. Feminist Perspectives on the Body* (London: Sage): 110–27.

ZIMMERMAN, J. F. (1992), 'Fair Representation for Women and Minorities', in W. Rule and J. F. Zimmerman (eds.) *United States Electoral Systems: Their Impact on Women and Minorities* (Westport, Conn.: Greenwood Press).

——(1994), 'Alternative Voting Systems for Representative Democracy', *Political Science and Politics*, 27/4: 674–7.

ZWAARD, JOKE VAN DER (1995), 'Naughty Boys and Obstinate Girls: District Nurses' Cultural and Professional Explanations of Child Rearing Practices', in I. Boer, A. Moors, and T. van Teffelen (eds.), *Orientations. Changing Stories: Post-Modernism and the Arabic-Islamic World* (Amsterdam/Atlanta: Rodopi Press): 133–45.

ZWEIGERT, K., and KOTZ, H. (1992), *An Introduction to Comparative Law*, trans. T. Weir (2nd ed.) (Oxford: Clarendon Press).

Table of Statutes and Cases

Adler v. *Ontario*. 140 D.L.R. (4th) 385 (1996) (Supreme Court of Canada)

Adoption of Children Law. 35 L.S.I. 360 (1981)

Andrews v. *Law Society of British Columbia*. 56 D.L.R. (4th) 3 (1986) (Supreme Court of Canada)

Baker Lake v. *Minister of Indian Affairs*, 107 DLR (3rd) 513 (1979 Canada)

Black v. *Law Society of Alberta*. 58 D.L.R. (4th) 317 (S.C.C.) (1989)

Capacity and Guardianship Law. 16 L.S.I. 106 (1962)

Coe v. *Commonwealth*, 118 ALR 193 (Australia 1993)

Connolly v. *Woolrich*. 1 RLOS 253 (1869) (Quebec)

Connolly v. *Woolrich*. 17 RJRQ 75 (1867) (Quebec)

Cormier v. *Fournier* (1986), 69 N.B.R. (2d) 155

Delgamuukw v. *British Columbia*. S.C.J. No. 108 (1997) (Canada)

Delgamuukw v. *The Queen*. 153 D.L.R. 193 (1997)

Forest v. *A.G. Manitoba* [1978] 5 W.W.R. 721 (Man.Q.B.)

Indian Child Welfare Act. 25 USC (1979)

Jacobs v. *Mohawk Council of Kahnawake*. 3 C.N.L.R. 68 (1998) (C.H.R. Trib.)

Johnson v. *M'Intosh*. 21 US 543 (1823)

Mabo v. *Queensland* (No. 2). 175 CLR 1 (1992) (Australia)

MacDonald v. *City of Montreal*. 1 S.C.R. 460 (1986)

Matter of Adoption of Halloway. 732 F. 2d 962 (1986) (Utah)

Milirrupum v. *Nabalco*. 17 FLR 141 (1971) (Australia)

Mississippi Band of Choctaw Indians v. *Holyfield*. 490 US 30 (1989)

Mozert v. *Hawkins*. 827 F.2nd 1058 (6th Cir.) (1987)

New York State's Domestic Relations Law. §253, 236 (as amended by 1992)

Official Languages Act. S.C c. 54. (1968–1969)

Oliphant v. *Suquamish Tribe*. 435 U.S. 191 (1978)

Plessy v. *Ferguson*. 163 U.S. 537 (1896)

R. v. *Berger*. 27 C.C.C. (2d) 357 (B. C. C. A.) (1975)

R. v. *Kent, Sinclair and Gode*. 40 Man R. (2d) 160 (Man. C. A.) (1986)

R. v. *Mercure*. 1 S.C.R. 234 (1988)

R. v. *Reale*. 3 O.R. 905, aff'd [1975] 2 S.C.R. 624 (S.C.C.) (1973)

Re Forest and the Court of Appeal of Manitoba (1977), 77 D.L.R. (3d) 445

Re Southern Rhodesia. AC 211 (1919) (House of Lords)

Reference re an Act to Amend the Education Act. 40 D.L.R. (4th) 18 (1986) (Supreme Court of Canada)

Reynolds v. *United States*. 98 US 145 (1878)

Santa Clara Pueblo v. *Martinez*. 436 US 49 (1978)

Settle v. *Dickson County School Board*. 53 F. 3d 152 (6th Cir.) (1995)

Société des acadiens du Nouveau-Brunswick v. *Minority Language School Board No. 50*. 1 S.C.R. 549 (1986)

Spouses (Property Relations) Law. 27 L.S.I. 313 (1973)

Succession Law. 10 L.S.I. 101 (1965)

United States v. *Wheeler*. 435 US 313 (1978)

Walker v. *NSW*, 126 ALR 321 (Australia 1994)

Wik Peoples v. *State of Queensland*, 141 ALR 129 (Australia 1996)

Wisconsin v. *Yoder*. 406 U.S. 205 (1972) (US Supreme Court)

Women's Equal Rights Law. 5 LSI 171 (1951)

Worcester v. *State of Georgia*. 6 Pet. 515 (U.S.) (1832)

Index